WOODY ALLEN

By the same author

Buñuel
Fellini
The Hollywood Exiles
Stunt: The Great Movie Stuntmen
The Cinema of Josef von Sternberg
The Gangster Film
Science Fiction in the Cinema
Hollywood in the Thirties
Hollywood in the Sixties
Sixty Years of Hollywood
Ken Russell An Appalling Talent
Steven Spielberg: The Unauthorised Biography
Stanley Kubrick: A Biography

WOODY ALLEN
A Biography

JOHN BAXTER

CARROLL & GRAF PUBLISHERS, INC.
NEW YORK

Copyright © 1998 by John Baxter

First Carroll & Graf edition 1999

Carroll & Graf Publishers, Inc.
19 West 21st Street
New York, NY 10010-6805

Library of Congress Cataloging-in-Publication Data is available.
ISBN: 0-7867-0666-X

Manufactured in the United States of America

For my parents.

'Where would I go, if I could go, who would I be, if I could be, what would I say, if I had a voice, who says this, saying it's me?'

Samuel Beckett, *Texts for Nothing*

Contents

Illustrations

Seth Green as young Allan Konigsberg in *Radio Days* (1987). (*Author's collection*)

Veteran comics and showbiz characters reminisce in *Broadway Danny Rose* (1984). (*Author's collection*)

The serious writer of humour pieces for the *New Yorker*, c. 1966, aged thirty-one. (*Bill Hamilton/Camera Press*)

The stand-up comic, c. 1964. (*Museum of Modern Art*)

Allen in October 1970, phlegmatically facing a future in Hollywood. (*Frank Herrman/Camera Press*)

Louise Lasser, Allen's unstable second wife. (*Jerry Watson/Camera Press*)

Allen directing Lasser in the 1972 *Everything You Always Wanted to Know About Sex (*But Were Afraid to Ask)*. (*Museum of Modern Art*)

'This is a film about wires.' Allen in *Sleeper* (1973). (*British Film Institute*)

Allen and Lasser in the original ending of *Bananas* (1971). (*Topham Picture Source*)

What's New Pussycat (1965) and *What's Up, Tiger Lily?* (1966) established Allen as a world-class comedy talent. (*Author's collection*)

For a publicity photo shoot for *What's New Pussycat*, Allen prowled backstage at the Crazy Horse strip club. (*Camera Press*)

Allen playing pool in the billiard room of his Manhattan apartment and showing off a painting by Gloria Vanderbilt. (*Museum of Modern Art*)

With *Play it Again, Sam* (1972), Allen transformed his image from anguished intellectual to fumbling *nebbish*. (*British Film Institute*)

Abandoned by his wife, Felix dips a toe in the singles scene. (*Museum of Modern Art*)

Saved by cinema: an imaginary Humphrey Bogart (Jerry Lacy) coaches Felix in the techniques of seduction. (*Museum of Modern Art*)

Directing Keaton in *Interiors* (1978). (*Author's collection*)

Diane Keaton, Mary Beth Hurt and Kristin Griffith as the three sisters in the Bergmanesque *Interiors*. (*British Film Institute*)

Teenage actress Stacey Nelkin tried out for a role in *Annie Hall* (1976), and shortly after became Allen's mistress. (*British Film Institute*)

Marie-Christine Barrault in *Stardust Memories* (1980). (*Author's collection*)

Mia Farrow in *Shadows and Fog* (1992). (*Author's collection*)

Allen and director Martin Ritt clown on the set of *The Front* (1976). (*Museum of Modern Art*)

'I don't eat rodent!' Allen as director Sandy Bates hassles his cook (Dorothy Leon) over his culinary requirements in *Stardust Memories*. (*Author's collection*)

Manhattan (1979), 'perhaps the best film of the seventies', in the estimation of New York critic Andrew Sarris. (*Author's collection*)

Allen directing Carlo DiPalma in *Radio Days*. (*Author's collection*)

Sven Nykvist on *Another Woman* (1988). (*Author's collection*)

Allen with Martin Landau on *Crimes and Misdemeanors* (1989). (*Author's collection*)

Allen as Sandy Bates in *Stardust Memories*. (*British Film Institute*)

'You know what turns me on? Intellectual.' Farrow as the Mafia widow in *Broadway Danny Rose*. (*British Film Institute*)

Allen and Farrow as patient and analyst, soon to become lovers, in *Zelig* (1983). (*Author's collection*)

Allen lines up a shot on *Another Woman*, watched by Mia Farrow's adopted daughter Dylan. (*Museum of Modern Art*)

Allen and Farrow with Judy Davis in their last film together, *Husbands and Wives* (1992). (*Author's collection*)

Allen with Dylan, and Farrow with their natural son Satchel, in 1987. (*Rex Features*)

On holiday in Stockholm, April 1987: Soon-Yi, Dylan, Fletcher, Allen and Farrow. (*Topham Picture Source*)

Soon-Yi with Satchel and Farrow's adopted son Moses, around 1990. (*Rex Features*)

Under police escort, Allen takes Satchel on a tour of Dublin Zoo, after a three-day court battle with Farrow to establish his rights. (*Aidan O'Keefe/Camera Press*)

Diane Keaton replaces Mia in *Manhattan Murder Mystery* (1993). (*Author's collection*)

Soon-Yi and Allen at La Scala, Milan, in 1997. (*PA News*)

Allen with Peter Falk in the 1997 TV remake of Neil Simon's *The Sunshine Boys*. (*Museum of Modern Art*)

Allen loses himself playing New Orleans jazz on the 1997 European tour with his band. (*Mark Allan/Alpha*)

Acknowledgements

Many people helped in the research of this book, including a number who preferred not to be identified. Respecting their wish for anonymity in no way diminishes by appreciation, which I hope they will take as understood.

Among those not so nervous of Woody Allen's disapproval, I particularly wish to thank Tim Carroll for generously making available a number of interviews, many of them unpublished, which he undertook for his amusing and insightful book *Woody and his Women*.

Of the people I spoke to personally, I'm grateful to Marie-Christine Barrault, Andrew Birkin, John Brosnan, Bernard Cohn, Thierry de Navacelle, Denholm Elliott, Jules Feiffer, Johnny Haymer, Ian Holm, Willy Holt, Israel Horovitz, Arvad Kompanetz, Jay Landers, Bill Moses of CBS's *60 Minutes*, Jacques Saulnier, Edith Sorel, Daniel Toscan du Plantier, Robert Parrish, Robert Rollis, Bruce Ricker and William Read Woodfield.

In making available his New York apartment for an extended period, David Thompson gave me the chance to live and work at the heart of Woody Allen's milieu. Charles Silver and Ron Magliozzi of the Museum of Modern Art and Mary Corliss of the stills archive were customarily helpful. I'm also grateful to the Museum of Radio and Television, New York, for making available early videotapes of Allen's TV work, and to Charlene Green at the Carlyle Hotel. Marjorie van Halteren, Kristi Jaas, David Stratton, David and Allison Downie, Lee Hill, Susan Owens, Mary Knight, Pat McGilligan, David Thompson and Adrian Turner helped with additional material, though to Mary Troath fell, as often before, the greatest weight of research, which she carried out with her usual energy and perspicacity. Richard Johnson remained, as ever, an unfailing source of editorial insight and professional support. Above all, my gratitude to my wife Marie-Dominique, without – as they say – whom . . .

John Baxter
Paris, August 1998

Author's Note to the 1999 Edition

Since the completion of the first edition of this book, Woody Allen has directed *Celebrity*, appeared as the voice of the leading character in the animated film *Antz*, and begun work on filming his early script, *The Jazz Baby*. These films along with recent developments in Allen's private and professional life, are dealt with in the last chapter of this revised and updated printing.

John Baxter
Paris, May 1999

Café Carlyle

The man who laughs has not yet heard the dreadful news.
Bertolt Brecht

The Carlyle Hotel fronts onto New York's Madison Avenue, but the main entrance is around the corner on East 76th Street, as if the hotel, true to its reputation for providing anonymity since 1930 to the rich and famous, from Presidents Truman and Kennedy to socialites like Brooke Astor, prefers to turn a cold shoulder to the leafy playground of Central Park only a block away.

Inside, a marble-floored lobby and a maze of carpeted anterooms offer decompression from the energy of Manhattan. One forgets the yellow cabs flooding down the avenues, the sidewalks busy with pedestrians, the more businesslike of them weaving around the gawpers clutching their copies of *New York City Starwalks* and checking out the top-floor apartment at 930 Fifth that is the home of Woody Allen.

On this warm Monday evening in June, however, Allen isn't home. For decades, Monday evening has been his night to play jazz with the New Orleans Funeral and Ragtime Orchestra, an appointment so religiously kept that he even played on Oscar night, 1978, when *Annie Hall* won Best Screenplay and Best Film. There's an element of family about the occasion. Sometimes old friends sit in, like Marshall Brickman, co-writer of *Annie Hall*, *Sleeper* and *Manhattan*, who began his showbiz career as banjo player in a folk group.

A few months earlier, Allen's long-time venue, a cavernous *faux*-British club called Michael's Pub, on the ground floor of a high rise on East 55th, closed down, so he shifted his Monday-evening date even closer to home, to the substantially more plush Café

Carlyle. Normally home to Bobby Short, the chubby interpreter of Cole Porter whom Allen featured in *Hannah and her Sisters*, the bar/restaurant on the hotel's ground floor is dark on Monday nights, when Short takes a break.

At 8.30 p.m., as the starlings twitter and swirl over Central Park, Allen makes his way through back alleys, fire doors and corridors from his apartment building to the kitchen area of the Carlyle. He could more easily have walked round the block, but it's decades since he showed himself on the streets of Manhattan when he didn't have to.

In the Café Carlyle, his audience for the night has already been gathered for more than an hour. It's an eccentric venue for a jazz band. A partner to the bar across the hall decorated by, and named for, illustrator Ludwig Bemelmans, the café boasts murals by French artist Marcel Vertés, whose work decorates a number of Paris's once-fashionable restaurants and hotels. Vertés' glosses on Picasso's blue period, all azure pierrots and harlequins dolefully strumming guitars as they contemplate white circus horses and bare-breasted ballerinas, make an incongruous background for New Orleans jazz. But Woody Allen is strictly a carriage-trade item, and the setting has been chosen accordingly.

Nobody is deluded that they are about to hear first-class music. Monday night listening to Woody Allen is an element of the New York experience, as much a part of the visit for foreigners as tossing a coin into the Fontana di Trevi in Rome or watching the Changing of the Guard in London. Few people here tonight have not seen *Manhattan*, with its self-deprecating opening – an Allen trademark – in which his character, TV writer Ike Isaacs, mocks his love of New York, running through a number of possible opening sentences for the novel he's writing – philosophical, nostalgic, reflective – before settling on 'He was as tough and romantic as the city he loved. Behind his black-rimmed glasses was the coiled sexual power of a jungle cat. New York was his town. And it always would be.' This piece of hyperbole sparks the most striking opening of any Woody Allen film, indeed one as expert as in any American film of its time, a montage of New York glimpses – night baseball at Yankee Stadium, two people kissing on a balcony, actors on the Broadway stage, Radio City Music Hall, Gucci, Sotheby Parke-Bernet, Tiffany's – culminating in the traditional New Year's Eve fireworks display over Central Park, all to Gershwin's *Rhapsody in Blue*. The crowded Café Carlyle is evidence of that sequence's popularity and continuing influence. 'I constantly run into Europeans whose only sense of New York comes from *Manhattan* and *Annie Hall*,' Allen has said. 'I'd say about 75 per cent of the people who come to see me play are Europeans enticed to the city by the images in those films. If that's what they're expecting to find, I guess they're disappointed.'

To be guaranteed a place on the banquettes that edge the room or at one of the minuscule tables that fill the floor and almost swamp the tiny bandstand, one has to book for dinner, a meal which, with $50 cover charge per head, costs more than $300 for a couple. As on most Monday nights, however, enough fans have paid to give Woody and the band a full house. Those without that kind of money can be glimpsed through a heavy glass door that leads to the marble-floored corridor. In sneakers, jeans, T-shirts and baggy jackets, they wait in the hope of an empty chair or a stool at the bar, kept from Paradise by a stone-faced *maître d'* who stands, arms folded, just inside. From time to time throughout the evening he'll expressionlessly admit people in twos and threes to squeeze in at the back of the room or sip a high-priced beer.

It takes time to serve a three-course dinner to the seventy people jammed into the café, and most are still wrestling with the crust on their Key Lime pie or waving for coffee and a cognac when, at nine sharp, a frail Allen emerges in nondescript tweed jacket and blue shirt, surrounded by the rest of the band: trombone, banjo, cornet, bass, drums. Most, like him, are amateurs: in ordinary life a stockbroker, a teacher, a clerk in a radio store, though the banjo player and band manager, Eddy Davis, is a pro whom Allen first met twenty years before. Allen carries his favourite clarinet, a battered twelve-key Rampone made in Italy about 1890, like the first one he bought for $12 when he was still a boy in Brooklyn. An Albert-system instrument with a wide bore, it's the kind played by his heroes of New Orleans jazz, like George Lewis. Now, friends like fellow clarinettist Kenny Davern keep a lookout for them; Davern found tonight's instrument in a New York pawnshop.

Ignored by the others, Allen chooses a fresh Rico Royale 5 reed from a small case and carefully inserts it into his clarinet. The 5, one of the hardest, yields strong volume but tires the lips; it has been described as 'only one step up from a roof tile'. The great clarinettist Benny Goodman once borrowed the Rampone to jam with the band, but couldn't squeeze a note out of it until he trimmed down the reed with a kitchen knife. Allen only ever plays the first set, however, so fatigue isn't a problem.

Head bent over the slip of wood, Allen looks intent and pious. He might be tying a phylactery, the leather box containing a religious text which, like all Orthodox Jews, he wore for morning devotions every day while he lived with his parents in the early forties. It's hard, indeed impossible, to associate this rabbity, rabbinical little man with the scandals of the last few years: the well-publicised rift with long-time mistress Mia Farrow, his affair with her adopted daughter Soon-Yi (and the pornographic Polaroids which revealed it), the accusations by Farrow of sexual abuse of their adopted daughter Dylan. As well to imagine one of Vertés' doleful Harlequins skinning out of his tights and groping an ethereal Columbine.

Yet would we be paying $300 a table if Allen had simply been what he was before the scandals, a successful film director and humorist? If only Soon-Yi would appear now, moon-face impassive, thin fingers closed over the stem of a Manhattan glass, our evening would be complete. But the only odd sight at the bar is four German girls sharing a single beer as they wait for the music to begin. And Soon-Yi, as we've learned from that week's *New Yorker* magazine, is working as a trainee schoolteacher at the extremely private and exclusive Spence School for Girls. Right now, she's probably marking papers two blocks away, a conjunction of primary education and adult sexuality that triggers memories of Humbert Humbert and Dolores 'Lolita' Haze.

Abruptly, the band strikes up – not a rag or blues, but the standard 'Should I?' It takes a while to separate Allen from the ensemble. His tone is reedy, with a lagging rhythm and an apologetic wavery vibrato. Like most purists, he admires and imitates New Orleans jazz as it was first heard live by collectors in the twenties and thirties, played by old men whose breath and lip were unequal to their invention.

'Should I reveal/Exactly how I feel . . . ?' It's the perennial question of Allen's films, but the piping clarinet is drowned in the raucous roar of the band. Waiters in dinner jackets deftly deliver coffee, ducking the slide of the trombone player, but Allen's eyes are closed. He's in another country where they do things very differently.

1

What did he Say?

Jane Campion, the head of the Venice jury, told me she liked Woody Allen's *Deconstructing Harry*, although for the overwhelmingly Italian audience phrases like 'world-class *meshugannah* cunt' probably lost something in translation.

Kurt Andersen, writing about the 1997 Venice Film Festival in the *New Yorker*

In 1991, a Parisian journalist was asked by a French magazine to write an article on Woody Allen and the reason for his popularity in France. Since 1986's *Hannah and her Sisters*, the editor pointed out, Allen's films had won more critical and financial success in Europe than in the US domestic market, to the extent that they now made as much money outside the country as within it. He wondered why.

'But the reason is obvious,' she replied. 'The French love smart dialogue, and Allen's films are very witty. Also the situations are adult; not at all like most American films. Not much of a story there.'

'All the same . . .' said the editor, reluctant to let his idea go.

Just to refresh her memory, she borrowed a videocassette of *Annie Hall*. The tape was one of a series issued by Allen's French distributor on which, in an attempt to satisfy both the English-speaking minority of film-goers and the francophones, the film appeared twice, first dubbed, then subtitled. She'd seen the film on its first release and, as a fluent English-speaker, had hardly noticed the subtitles; but now they became startlingly evident.

In an early scene, where Allen's character Alvy Singer revisits his old school and quizzes fellow students on their adult lives, the response of one, 'I make tallises' (Jewish prayer shawls) is translated as '*Psychologue*' (psychologist). 'I'm into leather' is translated as 'I make things from leather.' Allen's much-quoted line about Los Angeles, that he wouldn't want to live in a city where 'the only cultural advantage is you can make a right turn on a red light', is trimmed to 'a city with no cultural advantage'. At the Hollywood party where Woody and Annie are introduced to celebrities like Paul Simon, an overheard line by a young actor (Jeff Goldblum, in an early role) who says plaintively on the phone, evidently to a guru, 'I've forgotten my mantra,' is translated as '*J'ai oublié ma grande robe*' – 'I've forgotten my overcoat,' the translator evidently having misheard 'mantra' as '*manteau*'.

Worse, the subtitles rendered meaningless the first awkward conversation between Woody and Annie on the terrace of his apartment. Allen had wittily paralleled their stilted exchanges with subtitles that record their actual thoughts, but in the French version these disappear; all that remain are the banalities, carefully translated.

The dubbed version was even worse. Half the jokes weren't translatable, so the writer of the French version didn't even try. Nor was this incomprehension limited to the subtitlers. When the magazine *L'Avant-Scène du Cinema* published the full text of the screenplay in 1977, all the errors were repeated, with a few added.

Despite the evident losses in translation, *Annie Hall* had been a major hit in Paris, and still played there. The journalist proposed, then discarded, the theory that it was an example of the so-called 'Jerry Lewis Effect'. Lewis's films, especially those in which he starred as well as writing and directing, had a cult following in France, to the astonishment of American audiences, who found his frantic mugging increasingly tiresome. But the comedy of Lewis, broad and physical, needing no translation, had nothing in common with the social and cultural intricacies of Allen's work.

Aware that her editor, albeit unwittingly, had led her to a story, she began asking casual acquaintances what they thought about Allen. From delivery men to checkout girls, cab drivers to waitresses, the answer was the same. He was a *beau mec* – a great guy. They loved him.

'Do you speak English?' she asked them all. Most didn't – not enough, at least, to grasp the tortuous and fast-talking Allen humour.

'So why?' she demanded in confusion of a cab driver.

The man glanced back at her in the rear-view mirror, as if it were obvious.

'Well ... look at him, madame. He's short. He's bald. He's ugly. He can't get laid. He's just like me.'

It's not surprising that Allen should find his greatest appreciation among foreigners, since he has always presented himself since childhood as one. As his official biographer Eric Lax acknowledges, Allen's influences are 'an amalgam of old Europe and New York'. He has never hidden which of the two he preferred. Visiting his parents' Flatbush home with then-mistress Mia Farrow, he walked around marvelling out loud, 'Can you believe I came from this place?'

His earliest screen heroes were that archetypal outsider Humphrey Bogart and the Marx Brothers, whose surreal dialogue had little in common with Hollywood comedy of the time. When he discovered art cinema it was through Ingmar Bergman, who made films in a language even more alien to Americans than French was.

If, as Jean Renoir says, every artist has only one story to tell, Woody Allen's is that of the outsider unable or unwilling to understand what he's told or, if he understands, to act on it. Woody never gets the message – from lovers, who arbitrarily dump him; from fans, who demand a commitment he can't, or won't, give; from family, whose needs baffle him; from authority, with which he's hopelessly out of synchronisation. 'What do they want of me?' he wails repeatedly in his films. He looks to archetypes of omniscience – aliens, ghosts, God, Death, mediums – for enlightenment, but, like Og the alien who appears to Allen's alter ego, film director Sandy Bates, in *Stardust Memories*, they are no help.

SANDY: You guys got to tell me; why is there so much human suffering?

OG: This is unanswerable.
SANDY: Is there a God?
OG: These are the wrong questions.

What are the right questions about Woody Allen? Many of them are bound up in the conflict between the role of a writer/director and that of a star. Allen is almost alone in American cinema in playing all three roles.

There have been a few others. Charlie Chaplin is the most obvious of them, and in many respects he and Allen resemble one another. Early in his career, Allen even fancied himself as a comic in the Chaplin style. In 'Cupid's Shaft', a sketch he wrote for a 1967 TV special, he evoked *City Lights* by playing an unconvincing silent comedy routine as a park-keeper who rescues an amnesiac girl (Candice Bergen) from a thug and sets up house with her, only to see her recover her memory and run away with a rich and handsome suitor. He tried again in his first feature, *Take the Money and Run* (1968), a succession of sight gags which includes a Chaplinesque comic encounter with a shirt-folding machine in San Quentin prison. A scene in *Bananas* where, as Fielding Mellish, a professional products tester, Allen tries to demonstrate a combination desk and exerciser that goes out of control, reprises one in *Modern Times* where Charlie is the hapless guinea pig for a machine designed to feed workers without their needing to leave the production line. Nor is it hard to see *Sleeper*, with Allen re-awoken in the future, made the victim of Orgasmatron sex machines and forcibly transformed into a robot, as a Chaplin film recast.

He and Chaplin are brothers under the skin. Both came from a working-class background. Both began as stage performers. Both, as soon as they entered films, seized control of the medium from their directors and writers. Both made films of increasing cost and complexity, reshooting and recasting in search of an elusive perfection. Both were almost destroyed at the peak of their careers by sexual scandals involving younger women. And both, as their careers plateaued in America, looked for new frontiers in Europe.

Also like Chaplin, Allen has retrospectively rewritten his life, recasting himself as he often recasts his films. Through his reiteration, we've come to accept the 'Woody' of the quasi-autobiographical *Radio Days* and *Annie Hall*, the precocious son of poor, bickering but essentially affectionate parents, who won fame by wit and talent alone, who never pursued celebrity or wealth, who remained, even in adulthood, a failure with women. In reality, however, the 'Woody' of Allen's films is as remote from the real man as was 'the Little Tramp' from the millionaire autocrat, social climber and priapic fancier of nymphets who was Chaplin.

The foundation of Allen's critical success in the United States has been an enthusiastic embrace by the largely New York-based critics of his witty dialogue, little changed whatever role he plays. Outside New York, however, the audiences, considerably smaller, enjoy his ironic characterisations of Manhattan types: the anguished writer, the nervous documentary film-maker, the failed but optimistic theatrical agent, the stand-up comic. To them he's an exotic, attractive because of his strangeness.

He might as well, in fact, *be* foreign. And it is indeed startling how much sense Allen's success and failure in the United States makes if one thinks of him in that light. He has shunned the collaborative Hollywood method of film-making, after becoming convinced, like playwright David Mamet, that ' "Film is a collaborative business" only constituted half of the actual phrase. The correct rendering should be, "Film is a collaborative business: bend over." ' Instead he resurrected a system pioneered in the European theatre by producer Max Reinhardt in Vienna between the wars and perfected by French performers of the twenties and thirties like Sacha Guitry, who wrote their own work, produced it and played in it on both stage and screen. In common with another writer/director/performer, François Truffaut, Allen's films first appealed to a limited audience in a handful of American cities, built to a peak of popularity with a single widely-seen title – for Truffaut, the 1973 *La Nuit Americaine*, retitled *Day for Night* in the US; for Allen *Hannah and her Sisters* in 1986, which grossed

$59 million, $40 million of it in the United States – then fell off once more into limited art-house appreciation.

Talking to the *New York Times* in 1992, Allen refused to decline or accept the label of 'honorary European'. 'It's the question probably most asked of me [by European journalists]. They say 'We consider you a foreigner, a European film-maker. Why don't you live here? Make films here?' I'm almost so thankful for their response I don't want to probe too deeply into the reasons. The ideas and themes I'm most personally responsive to are European. Perhaps it subliminally gets into your system.'

Whether he likes it or not, Allen has been increasingly drawn to ally himself with Europe, as, since *Hannah*, his popularity base has inexorably shifted. In 1990 *Alice* grossed $8 million in France but only $6.5 million in the US. Since 1992, when *Shadows and Fog* opened in Paris before New York – a chance event, Allen says, caused by the disorder at his regular releasing company, Orion – every Allen film has premiered in the French capital. After Orion collapsed in 1992, Allen found it easier and more congenial to seek finance in Europe than in Hollywood. His current company, Sweetland, is bankrolled by the Swiss-Lebanese fortune of the Safra family and a consortium of film distributors and TV chains from Britain, Germany, Italy and France. He has toured Europe with his jazz band, talked of buying a palazzo in Venice, the city in which he married Soon-Yi Previn in 1997, and set his most successful film since *Hannah*, the 1996 *Everyone Says I Love You*, largely in Paris, where the couple spent their honeymoon. At last the *beau mec* seems to have found a spiritual home.

2

Can You Believe I Came from this Place?

I was a city child, pale, cared-for, unaware.

James Salter, *Burning the Days*

Allan Stewart Konigsberg was born on 1 December 1935, in the Bronx, that windy borough east of Manhattan to which so many immigrants had moved in search of better housing and safer living conditions than they found in the poorer areas of the island. The Bronx appealed in particular to European Jews, who, even in the ghettos of Poland and Russia, had often enjoyed a more comfortable existence than that offered by the tenements below Manhattan's 12th Street. By living in and writing about the Bronx at the turn of the century, authors like Sholom Aleichem and Sholom Asch gave it respectability, but it was also a usefully remote location for those who preferred anonymity to the limelight. When Leon Trotsky arrived in New York in 1917 as an editor for the Russian-language paper *Novy Mir*, for instance, he worked on the Lower East Side but lived in the Bronx. There was a sense, inherited by Allan Konigsberg, aka Woody Allen, that what happened in the outlying boroughs – the Bronx, Brooklyn, Queens, Staten Island – didn't really count.

Why 'Allan Stewart', two Scots names? Nobody is any longer sure. Certainly not from any Hibernian ancestors, since the Konigsbergs were 100 per cent Jewish. Allen's father, Martin Konigsberg, met his mother, Nettea Cherrie, in 1930 in the butter-and-egg market on Greenwich Street in Brooklyn. Martin's own father, Isaac, had been wealthy, owning a string of taxi cabs and a number of theatres. The Crash of 1929 made him a near-pauper, and he was reduced to running a stall in the Greenwich Street market. As a child, Nettie Cherry, as she was generally known, showed some intellectual promise, but conventional wisdom dictated that money spent educating a girl was money wasted, especially when she was the youngest of seven children. Sons received the lion's share of help, in the hope that they would become lawyers or doctors, so Nettie was stuck with the job of book-keeper for the family business, a luncheonette. It was a role often allocated to the smarter younger daughters of Jewish families. Stanley Kubrick, also born in the Bronx, in 1928, had two aunts who were book-keepers; it was his father Jack who qualified as a doctor.

Slim and redheaded, but no beauty – in middle age she developed an unfortunate resemblance to Groucho Marx – Nettie was flattered by the attentions of the good-looking, high-spending Martin, who took her to restaurants like the Tavern on the Green, on Manhattan's Central Park, where the rest of her *beaux* would have been desperately out of place. Dazzled by his stories of the lost wealth of the Konigsbergs, the fact that his father had arranged for him to be mascot of the Brooklyn Dodgers as a boy and had given him a smart Kissel car when he was stationed in Britain after World War I, she pushed to the back of her mind the fact that, despite his smooth manner, Martin, at thirty, was broke, and lacked the education or, as it turned out, the enterprise to learn a profession or support a family. They were married in 1931, and moved into a house on Argyle Road in Brooklyn.

Today's ease of access from lower Manhattan via the Brooklyn Bridge and the Brooklyn–Battery tunnel obscures the fact that, even though the subway service began in 1907, Brooklyn retained until the fifties a sense of the nineteenth-century villages – Bushwick, Flatbush, Prospect Park, Gravesend, Brownsville – from which it grew. Allen didn't visit Manhattan until he was six years old, but there was nothing surprising about that. Playwright Arthur Miller, himself raised in Prospect Park, recalled:

My mother didn't go to Manhattan more than once or twice a year. The neighbourhood was psychologically divorced from New York. There was a terrific autonomy in these neighbourhoods. It was as if they were demarcated by an iron fence. One knew when he was passing into foreign territory. My neighbour-hood was bounded by Gravesend Avenue and Ocean Parkway, a matter of six blocks, and from Avenue M over to Avenue J. Once you got out of there you might as well have been taking a voyage to Kansas.

Many Flatbush residents are Hassidic Jews, a community which in Allen's childhood had only recently begun migrating from the Lower East Side, and which congregated in the Brooklyn suburb of Brownsville. White bohemians with some money gathered in Brooklyn Heights, whose cheap houses offered spectacular views of Manhattan. W.H. Auden, Carson McCullers, Jane and Paul Bowles, and Golo, the son of Thomas Mann, once shared a house at 7 Middagh Street in Brooklyn Heights. Their cook, an ex-dancer from Harlem's Cotton Club, was sent to them by stripper Gypsy Rose Lee. On the far side of the borough, on the Atlantic coast, Rockaway and Brighton Beach, the latter home to Coney Island beach and amusement park, were resort communities, with archi-tecture that would not have looked out of place on the Venice Lido or at a Black Sea resort like Yalta. Allen retained a special affection for Coney Island, Rockaway and Brighton Beach. In *Radio Days*, his most overtly autobiographical film, he shifted Flatbush to the oceanside, setting the story in a district he had in fact only visited occasionally as a boy.

The burgling of their house shortly after they moved to Brooklyn convinced Martin that houses were intrinsically unsafe, and he relocated the family to an Ocean Avenue apartment. The move inaugurated a downward spiral in the family fortunes which would continue for a decade. Though Nettie went back to the Bronx for the birth of her son, by 1935 the family was installed in six rooms on one floor of a small wooden house at 968 East 14th Street in Brooklyn, which they shared with Nettie's sister Ciel and her husband, Abe Cohen.

Over the next seven years, the Konigsbergs moved more than a dozen times, usually sharing apartments with Nettie's sisters or with relatives who had fled Hitler. One of these was Joe Vishnetski, a tailor who emigrated from Russia and married Allen's Aunt Sadie. When Nettie's Uncle Leon arrived from Europe with his wife and children, they too moved in with the Konigsbergs. Vishnetski had friends among the fishermen who dangled their lines in Sheepshead Bay, next to Rockaway, and often returned home with burlap bags filled with their unwanted catch, which was dumped in the basement, and which the family then had to clean and eat.

Jewish culture has blurred so completely into the American-Anglo tradition that it can be difficult to visualise its original alienness. David Mamet has pointed out that anyone growing up in a *milieu* like that of the young Allen was deprived from birth of all the stimuli which normally furnish a mind with the material for art.

> None of the homemakers knew quite what a home was supposed to look like. They had no tradition of decor, the adoption of which would be anything other than arbitrary. When our grandparents left the *shtetl*, they brought nothing with them. There was, in their villages, no 'Jewish' style of decoration, or furniture; there was no ornament; the look of what domestic artefacts there were was dictated by poverty. There was no art in the Ashkenazi homes. And, as Jews, there were no religious trappings beyond, perhaps, a Kaddish cup or a menorah. Surplus income was devoted to the education of the young, to help them Get Ahead. Similarly, our second generation had no language. Our parents eschewed Yiddish as the slave language of poverty, and Hebrew as the dead language of meaningless ritual. For my generation, Jewish culture consisted of Jewish food and Jewish jokes, neither of which, probably, were very good for us.

Given this paucity of stimuli, it's not surprising that Woody Allen's first influences were oral and aural. Brought up without books, he didn't develop the reading habit until late in his teens. Ignorant of high art, he fed on its pop cultural incarnations, comic books and movies.

The first seven years of his life were a confusing succession of strange rooms and odd people talking incomprehensible lan-

guages. German was so common at home and English such a rarity
that, for a while as a child, Allen spoke that language, though he's
since lost all memory of it. At least part of the time, most of
the Konigsbergs and Cherries spoke Yiddish, the *lingua franca* of
European Jewry, created when eastern Jews who spoke only
Hebrew were forced to adopt German methods of writing, as well
as many German and French words, in order to assimilate in
western Europe. By the early twentieth century, waves of immigration had brought Yiddish to America, where it flourished, a
convenient secret language, rich in terms of irony and scepticism,
and as such central to Jewish humour. Allen was to find it crucial
in making his mark as a comic.

Since even grandmothers worked in this vigorous society,
nobody in the family had time to look after a child, so Allen and,
after her birth in 1944, his sister Letty, were entrusted to anyone,
however unqualified, who would take the job. A Mrs Wolf, who
came over from Europe with Leon Cherrie, looked after him for
a while, but he mostly remembers a series of dubious women
supplied by an agency, uneducated, often larcenous, occasionally
dangerous and usually accompanied by a 'boyfriend', who only
lasted a few weeks. According to Eric Lax, when Allen was about
three one of them wrapped him so tightly in his blankets that he
could hardly breathe, and said, 'See? I could smother you right
now and throw you out in the garbage and no one would ever
know the difference.'

The insecurity remained with Allen all his life. It wasn't helped
by his father's failure to find a job. Almost as soon as Allen was
born, Nettie went back to book-keeping. Martin continued to
work with his father and brother in the butter-and-egg market,
but Depression New York didn't offer enough business to support
all three. One of Martin's brothers made badges for the New York
Police Department, and for a while Martin worked for him. He
learned jewellery engraving, and tried to sell jewellery by mail
order; Nettie typed his solicitation letters. Later he drove a cab,
tended bar, and worked in a pool room which, when he was
offered the chance, he declined to buy, believing – erroneously, as
it turned out – that it represented a poor investment.

For a while he waited table at Sammy's Bowery Follies, a restaurant in lower Manhattan. It was here, near the notorious hangout of drunks and bums, and in a business famously connected to organised crime, that Martin Konigsberg found his level. Gangsters always had odd jobs for a personable man with a taste for the high life and not too many scruples, and Martin soon became a regular in this society. During the thirties and forties he ran bets to the racetrack in Saratoga for minor racketeers. Later he would become manager at the Bowery Follies.

From the films of Allen and others about growing up in Brooklyn, it would be easy to assume that life there, while not without its rough spots, was fairly agreeable. However, those without an artistic axe to grind often found it otherwise. Ralph Rosenblum, the editor who worked on many of Allen's early films, was also a Jew from Brooklyn.

> There was nothing comic or sensual or seductive about the Brooklyn Jewish community where I spent the first twenty years of my life. Bensonhurst was tidier, stabler, and more genteel than the commotion-prone Lower East Side where the newcomers thronged, but its lessons and ways were those of impoverished immigrants hanging on desperately to the niche they had made for themselves. Thrift, self-improvement, and a thudding practicality ruled everything, a heavy-spirited regime that was moulded into permanence by the weight of the Depression. Ten years later, when Woody Allen was growing up in the same milieu, its values and oppressive conformity would still prevail.

Though Allen has always insisted that his work isn't autobiographical, much of it, in particular *Radio Days* (1986), contains numerous reminiscences of life in Brooklyn, many of them, like the stage directions for his 1980 play *The Floating Light Bulb*, grim. The play's characters, the Pollacks, live in

> an apartment house in a poor section of Brooklyn. It is an old brown-brick building, rectangular and without any attempt at style. Cheerless, sunless, it houses an assortment of lower-income

families, some of which have devised patchwork methods of dealing with their prosaic desperation, and some not so fortunate. The apartment reeks of hopelessness and neglect. The furniture is worn out and the walls need a fresh coat of paint. It is not so much that the apartment is dirty, it is simply that it has been too difficult to keep pace with its rate of decay. [It] looks out on a bleak brick courtyard in the back and the rear of the surrounding buildings, giving the feeling of being at the bottom of a well.

If the description carries a cringing sense of remembered squalor, the Pollacks themselves – Enid, the weary wife, always dreaming of a better life; Max, her waiter husband, by turns belligerent and self-pitying; and their son Paul, obsessively practising magic tricks in his room – inevitably suggest the Konigsbergs of Allen's childhood. Max pins his hopes on winning on the Numbers, the illegal lottery that was one of organised crime's major moneymakers in New York. He carries a gun, ostensibly to protect himself in an increasingly dangerous neighbourhood, but in reality because he fears the thugs working for the Shylock from whom he's borrowed money. Enid's complaint about his poor tips triggers an argument in which her sense of having come down in the world collides with her husband's restless search for a quick buck:

MAX: I was a bookmaker, you didn't like that idea. I drove a cab, you had a stroke when I parked it in front of the house.
ENID: Is it so wonderful to drive a taxi? That's all our neighbourhood had to know.
MAX: And always lying to your sisters that I got some big propositions coming up.
ENID: I only stood up for you when they criticised.
MAX: Who the hell was your family to look down on me? You'd think your father was an Astor instead of a peddler, a glorified peddler from Delancey Street, and he don't like it 'cause I make book!
ENID: You had more in you than the rackets.
MAX: That's where I should've stayed. In those days I had the

connections. I would have moved up. Maybe we'd have some cash today. Instead of me hustling tips – and all those business schemes to please your family. Storm windows – costume jewellery – mail-order junk.

Such evocations offer an ironic counterpoint to some of Allen's statements to the press when he was accused by Mia Farrow in 1994 of molesting their children. 'I've been a model, model father with these kids,' he told Jack Kroll of *Newsweek*. 'I mean, I'm affectionate like my parents were with me, but that's it.' His films also suggest otherwise. In two of his earliest, *Take the Money and Run* and *Bananas*, the couple playing his character's parents appear masked, in the first with Groucho Marx noses, glasses and moustaches, in the second with surgical masks. 'My parents deserve to be masked,' snapped Allen when pressed on the point.

Jerry Epstein, a childhood friend, remembers the atmosphere of the houses shared by the Cherrie and Konigsberg families as anything but benign: 'In the house lived all those people he used to have arguments with, and used to provoke all the time.' On film, Allen tells a different story, especially in *Radio Days*. Despite an early attempt to create a sense of melancholy with an introductory sequence of Rockaway on a wet, windy afternoon, the suburb's resort atmosphere takes the curse off the family's life of frustration. All the same, there are numerous recollections of the Konigsberg family history. The film, like the Konigsbergs' married life, even begins with a burglary, but it's a comic one. The crooks pick up the phone in the house they are robbing, find themselves participating in a radio quiz show, successfully answer the questions, and leave their victims to receive their prizes.

The characterisations too are moved several degrees sunwards. Pop, played by Michael Tucker, is, like the father of *The Floating Light Bulb*, full of get-rich-quick ideas, including one to sell jewellery, and still drives a cab, though unlike in the play this is the subject of a running joke, with Pop refusing to reveal his job, and the Woody surrogate, Little Joe (Seth Green), only discovering it when he flags down his cab by chance. Abe (Josh Mostel) brings home burlap bags of fish, which the family has to clean, but this irritating habit now has an amusing and profitable result: the ability to distinguish between a flake and a fluke wins Aunt Bea (Dianne Wiest) a quiz-show prize. Allen even sweetens the interminable arguments that were a feature of his childhood. The parents still bicker, but about absurdities: the relative merits of the Pacific and Atlantic Oceans, for instance. The original screenplay – like most of Allen's films, *Radio Days* underwent major reconstruction during shooting – had even more parallels: Mom (Julie Kavner) types letters for Pop's jewellery business, and when she's asked what he does for a living, responds derisively, 'He's a big butter-and-egg man.'

Allen's natural melancholy manifested itself early. As young as five, he experienced an undefined but fundamental shift towards the reclusive and depressive. 'Something went sour,' said his mother. Allen doesn't remember such a change, but acknowledges that, for as long as he can remember, he was a loner, hiding out in his room from the arguments of his parents, and the readiness of his mother in particular to respond to any provocation with a slap. 'She slapped me every day of my life,' he told Farrow, an accusation he repeated in Barbara Koppel's 1997 documentary *Wild Man Blues*. Nettie acknowledged that she'd taken some of her frustrations out on Allen, responding to his precocity and nervy, demanding nature with a clip on the ear. His sister Letty received far milder treatment, a fact which further eroded Allen's sense of being valued or loved.

Allen's subsequent emotional history is typical of the neglected child. Anxious for intimacy, he views it dubiously when it's offered – where's the catch? – and keeps his partners at arm's length. 'I don't consider any girl perfect until she rejects me,' he has said. Like many lonely children, he took refuge in escapism: magic tricks, radio programmes, movies and comics. 'I like comic books,' he said later. 'I didn't read anything else until I was fifteen. All kinds. Super people, the adventures of ducks and mice.' At the age of three, in 1938, he saw his first film, Walt Disney's *Snow White*, though it wasn't until 1943, when he saw the Tyrone Power swashbuckler *The Black Swan*, that he thought, 'I could do this.'

Given the atmosphere in which he grew up, it's almost surprising that Allen didn't turn to crime. His first film as a director, *Take the Money and Run* (1968), recounts the life, in spoof TV-documentary style, of Virgil Starkwell, an inept criminal (called 'Woody Allen' in early versions of the script) who bumbles his way to a position as Public Enemy Number One. Allen, of course, plays Virgil. During promotion of the film he admitted, with tongue only half in cheek, 'There was a period when I seriously considered being a criminal. I used to read a tremendous amount about crime. I knew everything about jails and robberies. I knew the names of all the gangsters.' Some school friends became career criminals, and Allen, who claimed he was 'only on cringing acquaintance with most of them', enjoyed talking about them under their *noms de crime* – 'You mean Vinnie "The Snake" X,' or '"Two Gun" Charlie Y'.

Crime in general, even murder, often gets sympathetic treatment in Allen's films. Mia Farrow's gangster relatives in *Broadway Danny Rose* are played for laughs. A flight across New Jersey from a pair of hit men ends in a warehouse filled with inflated parade figures, and escaping helium gives everyone comically high-pitched voices. In *Radio Days*, a hit man who kidnaps Farrow after she accidentally sees him murder her boss turns out to be from her old neighbourhood, and lets her go. The murderer whom Allen and Diane Keaton uncover in the apartment next to them in *Manhattan Murder Mystery* is genial and never even remotely threatening. Certainly anything he might do to them when they break into his apartment and search it pales beside the potential embarrassment of being discovered there if he returns unexpectedly. Cheech, the gunman in *Bullets Over Broadway* sent by his boss to oversee his investment in a Broadway show as a vehicle for his chorus-girl mistress, discovers a natural genius for the stage and rewrites the play for the stunned and admiring John Cusack.

Even in his serious films, Allen gives sympathetic treatment to the worst transgressions. *Crimes and Misdemeanors* borrows *The Godfather*'s acceptance that family values must be protected, by murder if necessary. Saintly ophthalmologist Judah Rosenthal turns to his gangster brother for help when a demanding mistress threatens his happy home. The brother helps out by having her killed, but only after a speech reminiscent of the opening scene of *The Godfather*, where Don Vito Corleone chides a petitioning undertaker for keeping him at arm's length until he has a favour to ask.

Jerry Epstein traces Allen's interest in criminality to their shared adolescence. 'When we went to high school, we had lots of Italians who were organised in gangs, so we were connected. World War II was a time of great juvenile delinquency in the New York area. Most of his movies concern themselves with criminal elements and issues of criminality, so he's been very very connected to criminality and criminal things in his life.' Pressed to be more specific, Epstein said, 'You know his cousin Arnold Schuster was murdered by the Mafia, by Albert Anastasia, I think – that group – because his cousin fingered Willie Sutton, the bank robber, who escaped from prison. His cousin rode home with him from New York to Brooklyn. He recognised him as the escaped bank robber and called the police. They apprehended Sutton, and Schuster was murdered, gunned down in Brooklyn within a week. Always this side of [Allen's life] has remained secret and veiled. I don't even think he has a business connection arrangement but it follows him around and it has to do with his attitudes to it. Certain friends from childhood were marginally, peripherally connected to quasi-criminal activities. He's always got a draw on that side.'

Allen himself confirms this. Better a life of crime, he feels, than that of the urban wage-slave: 'To consign one's life to a meaningless round of subway rides, to do that hot and cold for forty years, is not being alive at all. There's no comparison between that and a life of crime.' One of the few American movies he admits to seeing and liking during the last decade is Martin Scorsese's panorama of mob life, *GoodFellas*. His own experience of crime has been benign, indeed funny. In the seventies, his apartment was broken into. But the burglars were disturbed and fled, leaving behind the loot from an apartment they had broken into earlier. Allen found himself the possessor of a new TV set.

3

My Universities

Only the dead know Brooklyn.

Thomas Wolfe

The family enrolled Allen at Flatbush's Public School 99 in 1941, when he was five. A four-storey red-brick building on East 10th Street, its grim fire-station look isn't ameliorated by the presence of a few sumacs of the type – *Ailanthus glandulosa*, the tree of Betty Smith's 1945 best-seller *A Tree Grows in Brooklyn* – that was planted in the swampier areas of Brooklyn because of an imagined ability to dispel the mists thought to cause tuberculosis and other diseases of immigrant communities.

PS 99 provided the background for the most depressing few years in Allen's life. Rote learning prevailed, and the curriculum offered little to a mind which already preferred fantasy anyway. Class projects simply encouraged him to shock. Later, he claimed in interviews that 'even when I was reading nothing but Donald Duck and Batman, I could write real prose in school compositions. There was never a week when the composition I wrote was not the one that was read in class,' but omitted to mention that his book reports, jagged with Bob Hope-like one-liners (e.g. 'She had an hourglass figure, and I wanted to play in the sand') were more often read out as horrible examples to be avoided. Asked to write at the age of twelve on 'How I Spent My Summer Vacation', he described an attractive girl as 'having a child by a future marriage,' a quip which had his parents, not for the first time, called in for a chat with the headmaster. But such anecdotes overstate the impression Allen made at grade school or high school. Almost without exception, his teachers had no memory of him.

Initially so terrified of being called to give an answer in class that he intentionally spilled his pencils on the floor, then spent long minutes picking them up, Allen graduated to indifference, daydreaming and chronic truancy. 'I never liked [school],' he said. 'I couldn't wait till I grew up. I was bad in spelling, worse in grammar, and I hated my teachers because everyone was a least common denominator. And my teachers all loathed me. I never did homework – I mean I never *ever* did homework. I'm amazed to this day that they really expected me to go home and work on those sleazy projects that they had outlined. My father and mother were called to school so often that my friends still recognise them on the street.'

He was no more impressed by his fellow students. In *Annie Hall*, his character, Alvy Singer, revisits his school and has each child stand up and recite his or her subsequent history. One says pompously, 'I run a profitable dress company.' Another confesses, 'I used to be a heroin addict. Now I'm a methadone addict.' A plain girl says impassively, 'I'm into leather.' 'I always felt my schoolmates were idiots,' Alvy says complacently.

Improbably, given his already weedy physique, Allen, known as 'Red' because of his hair, was more interested in sports than in learning. The streets afforded a physical education infinitely more tempting than the intellectual exercise offered in PS 99. Another Brooklyn boy, author and critic Alfred Kazin, wrote: 'Any wall, any stoop, any curving edge on a billboard sign made a place against which to knock a ball; any bottom rung of a fire-escape ladder a goal in basketball; any sewer cover a base; any crack in the pavement a "net" for the tense sharp tennis that we played by beating a softball back and forth with our hands between the squares.'

As he grew, Allen entertained vain fantasies of sporting fame. 'He had an aspiration to be a professional baseball player,' says Jerry Epstein, 'but in games with other teams, he didn't do very well. He was OK at baseball and flickball and very good at track. The hundred-yard dash, he was very fast. But he didn't play basketball, football or tennis. He wasn't very coordinated.' For a while, Allen even thought he might make it as a flyweight boxer, like the famous Willie Pep, and applied for admission to the Golden Gloves competition for amateur fighters. His father refused to sign the necessary release, aware from the beatings his son took in schoolyard brawls that he would end up maimed, perhaps dead. In adulthood, Allen religiously followed the New York Knicks basketball team from sideline seats, and took a meticulous interest in baseball. Playwright Israel Horovitz recalls watching a game on TV with Allen during which he pointed out the small wagon which hovers on the baseline, holding drinks for the players, and did an imitation of it, right down to the squeaky wheels: 'One of the most brilliant pieces of physical comedy I've ever seen,' says Horovitz.

School amplified Allen's sense of isolation and his tendency to avoidance. To spin out the walk of five or six blocks from home, he loitered along back lanes. The other kids noticed this inclination, and pointed it out in class as a symptom of his distaste for society. 'Amateur psychoanalysis', Allen called it derisively – not that the long professional analysis of his adulthood would discover anything very different. This juvenile skulking did have a positive side. It encouraged him to project onto his surroundings a heightened sense of his emotions. As he says of Rockaway in *Radio Days*, almost joking about his tendency to the pathetic fallacy, 'It wasn't always overcast and raining, but that's the way I remember it, because that was when it was at its most beautiful.'

When, in 1941, his father took him on his first trip to Manhattan, midtown New York conveyed an instant impression of life, colour and joy which Allen never lost. He was soon making his own illicit excursions there, playing truant with his friend Mickey Rose. His memories are a montage of the public places that make up Manhattan's glamorous shell: cinemas, restaurants, billboards, theatres, stadiums. Later, when he was able to live in Manhattan, he chose its most respectable and expensive area, the Upper East Side, where he settled down in a duplex apartment with a panoramic view of both Central Park and the East River – the kind of apartment often featured in the comedies of manners that Hollywood set in New York. His friend Dick Cavett said in amusement that it reminded him of the set for the 1932 George Arliss melodrama *The Man Who Played God*. It was also this New York that Allen would celebrate in films like *The Purple Rose of Cairo*, a penthouse society of wealthy socialites and well-bred exotics.

From the beginning, a working-class Manhattan never existed for Allen. He no more saw its bums, street-sweepers, shopgirls and cops than Ernest Hemingway imagined the forests of *Big Two-Hearted River* transformed into lumber for the building of suburban bungalows. His preoccupation with the Upper East Side has become a standing joke for New Yorkers. As Manhattan journalist Joe Klein noted, 'Woody Allen's New York City – the city of his movies – has peculiar geography. It ends at 96th Street, where Harlem begins. It extends south to SoHo, but not as far as Wall Street. It allows, grudgingly, for one outer borough, Brooklyn. In fact, there are only two *crucial* neighbourhoods in his New York: Times Square and the quiet, elegant Upper East Side, where he and the characters he plays usually live. Manhattan's two other main residential areas – the Village and the Upper West Side – exist primarily as foils for his humour. The Village (and SoHo, in *Hannah and her Sisters*) is where silly, trendy, artsy things happen; the upper West Side is where the insufferable intellectuals hang out.'

Allen's affair with the cinema was as passionate as only first love can be. In 1944, when he was eight, the family moved to 1216 East 12th Street, closer to PS 99. Just around the corner on Avenue J was the Midwood cinema, which, in a painful reminder of earlier glories, Martin Konigsberg's father had owned before the Depression. An alley ran down the back of the cinema, and the house in which the Konigsbergs occupied the first floor backed onto it. Soon after they moved there, Allen, rooting through the cinema's garbage, found a few feet of 35mm film cut from a broken print. The event can be dated precisely, since the film, *Four Jills in a Jeep*, was released on 6 April 1944. Holding the celluloid up to the light, Allen was delighted at being able to make out comic Phil Silvers and 'Brazilian Bombshell' Carmen Miranda. The strip of film was a vivid link to a movie he had enjoyed. It implanted the realisation that films had a corporeality; they didn't simply *happen*. Someone *made* them. It's significant that Silvers and

Miranda should feature so strongly in Allen's memory, since they figure well down the cast list of William Seiter's forgettable propaganda comedy about stars entertaining the troops. Kay Francis, Martha Raye, Carole Landis and Mitzi Mayfair were featured, with the Jimmy Dorsey band, Betty Grable and Alice Faye as make-weights. However, it was the brash comedy of Silvers and the febrile exoticism of Miranda that Allen admired. With the exception of *Casablanca*, which he would later exalt into an object of veneration, but which had already long finished its run when he became interested in film, Allen has nothing to say of melodrama or war films, and little of Westerns – the forms, significantly, that his father preferred. It was comedy which interested him, and a narrow area of comedy at that, one in which the comics, rather than submerging themselves in a part, essentially played themselves. Silvers, a seasoned 'top banana' from vaudeville, never stooped to change his characterisation from movie to movie. As the stage manager in *Cover Girl*, also released in 1944, he is little different to the finagling Sergeant Bilko he played in his long-running TV show a decade later.

Allen was even more enamoured of Bob Hope, a comic who, no less than Silvers, always played a version of himself, to the extent of encouraging walk-ons in his films by his regular partner in the 'Road' series, Bing Crosby, in a reminder, prescient of postmodernism, that 'It's only a movie, folks.'

The critic James Agee, in a rare ill-considered judgement, dismissed Hope as 'a good radio comedian with a pleasant presence, but not much more'. In fact Hope never mastered radio, even though it was the medium that made him famous. He inclined to a glib jabber when he read prepared scripts or tried the quickfire cross-talk demanded by 1940s broadcasting; but on stage and screen he was unequalled. Allen would later sell some gags to Hope, whom he was to celebrate in 1978, in a Carnegie Hall tribute to the seventy-five-year-old comedian, as 'vain, a womaniser, a coward's coward and always brilliant'. Allen's best comedy moments – shrinking from a live lobster in *Annie Hall*, trading cracks with Harold Gould and Olga Georges-Picot in *Love and Death*, finding himself in a bad replay of *The Godfather* when he meets Mia Farrow's relatives in *Broadway Danny Rose* – are often Bob Hope routines writ small.

The older comedian's influence on Allen extended even further. Like Allen in later life, Hope never played heroes. It was Crosby who, in the highly successful 'Road' series, made the running and, as a reward, got the songs and Dorothy Lamour. The perennial stooge, as chronically pusillanimous as he was unremittingly stupid, Hope held the bomb, carried the baby or was sold into slavery. Allen's admiration for Hope increased when he discovered he was the more professional of the duo, and by far the better comic, not to mention an adequate singer and an accomplished hoofer. Hope, who'd once taken up boxing to improve his foot-work, skilfully stumbled through his dance routines with Crosby to make his partner look good. When the nearby Kent cinema, a rerun house where you could see a double bill for twelve cents, reran Hope and Crosby's 1942 hit *The Road to Morocco*, Allen was enthralled. 'I knew from that moment exactly what I wanted to do with my life,' he said.

Hope's influence on Allen has baffled many of his admirers, like the critic Foster Hirsch, who asks, 'What do Woody and Bob have in common? Hope is the establishment Gentile, with no ethnic traces in voice or manner or appearance. Despite his famous ski nose, he is a handsome man, in a quite conventional way; there is nothing intrinsically comic about his face or physique. He looks like what he is: an arch-conservative Republican. There is nothing about Hope then that in any obvious way tags him as an outsider or as a comic figure, and so his character is a wholly manufactured product, whereas Woody's persona developed naturally from the comic possibilities of his appearance and ethnic background.' Hirsch misses the fact that what attracted Allen to Hope wasn't his real-life character – which, when he finally met the comedian, he felt to be oddly unreal and innocent, with a 'small-town quality' – but the character he created in performance. Anybody who met Hope with his comic engine turned off found him largely monosyllabic on any subject but right-wing politics and golf. Henry Fonda once had to drive him across a Pacific island to entertain some servicemen. 'How do you like it out here?' Hope asked as he got into the Jeep, and never opened his mouth for the rest of the trip. In the eighties, hosting a Miss World broadcast in London, Hope proved anything but funny when radical feminists interrupted the show. Caught without a script, he could only growl, 'They must be on drugs.'

Though it took him some time to find his own persona, Allen knew instinctively that it wasn't comics who were funny, but the characters they played. When *Saturday Night Live* producer Lorne Michaels, then a young Canadian comic, wrote gags for him in the seventies, Allen, said Michaels, 'explained something to me that I still remember vividly. He said that *he* is his premise. The premises don't have to be silly; he did the same jokes as Bob Hope.'

'People used to think that I was some poor little schnook who lived in Greenwich Village who was physically weak and so on,' said Allen, 'and I always tried to explain that this is the natural material of a comedian, whether it's Charlie Chaplin or Bob Hope. Charlie Chaplin was not inept; this was part of his art. The same with Bob Hope. He's not just a girl-chasing fool and a coward's coward. The same with me. I did a certain kind of character publicly but in real life I lived on the Upper East Side in a nice apartment. I was an athletic kid when I grew up and was not what people thought I was. I thought there was something wrong with the culture for wanting to think that. You don't want to think that John Wayne would walk around with two six-shooters. That's silly to me.'

Allen's visits to Manhattan became more frequent and far-ranging. Making their headquarters at the Automat, a self-service restaurant where you chose your meal from the dishes displayed in individual glass cases, then slipped five or ten cents into a slot to open the window, he and Rose cruised Times Square's dance halls, gambling concessions and sex shows. 'I saw a hermaphrodite at Hubert's,' Allen recalled. 'It lifted up its skirt and you could see what it had.' For Allen, Manhattan mostly meant movies. 'You'd come up out of the subway on 42nd Street,' he said, 'and there would be a whole street of movies, wonderful movies. There was the Laffmore Theater, which played only comedies. I saw Chaplin, Laurel and Hardy, W.C. Fields and the Marx Brothers there. There was the Globe Theater, which played only Westerns – Monte Hale, Lash La Rue, Hopalong Cassidy. Around the corner, on Broadway itself, you had the big theatres like the Paramount, the Capitol and the Roxy, which had movies and live shows. I saw Duke Ellington *and* a movie at the Paramount for fifty cents. I saw Jackie Gleason there, and Gypsy Rose Lee.'

Allen consummated his infatuation with Hollywood in the bedroom of his teenaged cousin Rita Wishnick, the daughter of fish-fancying Joe Vishnetski – like many émigrés, they Anglicised their name. The Wishnicks lived only a few blocks from the Konigsbergs' new home on East 12th Street. When he was too young to go to the movies alone, Rita often went with him, and young Allen spent hours with her in her bedroom, the walls of which were plastered with stills of her favourite stars. Even more than Allen, Rita was in love with Hollywood, and spent every waking minute and every spare cent either on films or on movie magazines. She was one model for Cecilia in *The Purple Rose of Cairo*, the housewife who finds a few hours' escape in the cinema, though she's more joyfully celebrated as Ruthie in *Radio Days*, a dumpy girl who only reveals her vivacity and sexuality when, with a towel for a turban and a scarf wrapped round her ample rear end, she mimes Carmen Miranda's song 'South American Way'.

Allen became even closer to Rita when the two families began to share the house on 12th Street just after he turned twelve. On and off for years, he and Rita slept in the same bedroom, a situation which Allen always claimed induced no sexual feelings on either side – an assertion that, given Allen's later priapic history, one is bound to doubt. In a sequence from the first version of *Annie Hall*, Allen invented a fantasy for his alter ego Alvy Singer, the sexual overtones of which have a special vividness. 'Little Alvy, faking a fever by holding his thermometer over a radiator, is visited by his voluptuous cousin Doris. Doris brings him comic books about Hitler, Nazi spies, German submarines, and similar subjects. As she reads them to him, he swoons over her and begins to drool. ("Alvy, you're drooling.")'

Allen's denial of any sexual feelings towards his cousin looks like part of a calculated flight from his childhood with which he, with years of professional psychiatric help, would persist for decades. Even Hollywood fell victim. The boy who in childhood had adulated the frothiest confections of the big studios would become the severest critic of the American commercial cinema, consistently bad-mouthing not only Hollywood but the entire state of California.

Despite much subsequent cosmetic reconstruction and reassessment, it is evident that Allen's childhood provided a reservoir of resentment on which he drew for decades. He emerged from his schooldays with the psychology that was to pervade his adult character already in place, a state of mind which, in the words of the critic Ivan Kalmar, 'oscillat[es] between megalomaniac paranoia, and what Edmund Bergler termed "psychic masochism"'. Such antinomies would permeate Allen's life and comedy. On screen, he exploited the lessons learned from Bob Hope, coming to appear almost heroic in the honesty with which he professed his cowardice. He seemed cute in his acceptance of incompetence, sexually attractive *because* of the ugliness and ineptitude to which he constantly drew attention. 'He's bald, he's ugly, he can't get laid – he's just like us.'

Theatre critic John Lahr wrote about this contradictory process when Allen was still a little-known Broadway playwright. Of comics like the Marx Brothers, Lahr pointed out that they 'dealt with failure. In the pratfall and the malaprop, there was humiliation, but in rebounding there was a joyous implication of power and hope. Although the characters they portrayed were often inept and daydreamy, the comedians gave them a certain nobility.' In a review of *Broadway Danny Rose* in 1984, British critic Richard Combs made a similar point about Allen: 'It has become more and more obvious that he has only one film to make. This needn't be a complaint, given that the one-subject artist is both recognised and esteemed. The trouble is that Allen's one film keeps revealing a troubling schizophrenia. This has to do with Allen's presence as a performer, the little guy with an inferiority complex as large and well-defined as the Manhattan skyline, who finally discovers that his sense of inadequacy is not a barrier to true love and/or successful sex. Alongside the romantic happy ending, there is a second, implicit one, that someone so articulate and funny about being a loser can't actually be a loser. Allen has managed to play a little man who is somehow always larger than the film.'

Few aspects of Allen's life demonstrate this more effectively than his use of his Jewishness. The Konigsbergs were Orthodox, which meant that Allen prayed each morning with phylacteries bound to his arms and forehead, attended temple in a *yarmulke*, fasted on high holidays and spent part of every Saturday for eight years in Hebrew school. All these merely accentuated his resentment of religion. He was bar mitzvahed in 1948, but mainly remembers, he says, the movie he saw on the day before – *Canon City*, the story of a Colorado jailbreak. At the party afterwards, he blacked his face and did an imitation of Al Jolson – hardly the act of a devout religionist.

From his first film, *Take the Money and Run*, all the references to his Jewishness are derisive. In jail, Allen's character, Virgil Starkwell, agrees to be guinea pig for a new drug. It turns him briefly into a rabbi, and Allen is seen sitting in his cell with rabbinical beard, hat and ringlets, discoursing on the Talmud. Later, meeting other cons in the prison chapel to plan an escape, he makes a clumsily broad sign of the cross before the altar, then kneels in a pew and, pretending to pray, falls into the bobbing movement known as 'hovelling' often adopted by older Jews at prayer. Up until *Broadway Danny Rose*, and also in oddities like *Zelig* and *Shadows and Fog*, Allen was to return for easy laughs to Yiddishisms and the use of Hassidic rabbis as joke figures. He uses the references as a means of distancing himself from these stereotypes, in the same way that his physical unattractiveness perversely turned him into a sex object. Perhaps he thought that overt Jewishness would transform him in the mind of his audience into an honorary Gentile.

The ringleted rabbis of *Annie Hall*, *Zelig* and other films, the Yiddishisms, the repeated references in many of the films to Nazis, all recall the white comic playing in blackface. Neither S.J. Perelman nor the Marx Brothers, the humourists Allen most admired, ever made an issue of their Jewishness. Chico Marx pointedly misdirected such attention, by adopting an Italian character and accent. Allen uses Jewish humour the way he uses Kierkegaard, Dostoyevsky and Flaubert in his humorous pieces for the *New Yorker*: not as a medium for humour, but as a subject of parody.

The contradictions of his philosophy caught up with Allen in middle age, and in 1982 he made *Zelig*, a fantasy about the son of a Yiddish actor who, unable to decide who he is, develops the capacity of a 'human chameleon', and can transform himself into anything: Jew, Christian, even a Nazi. Some devout Jews find Allen's comedy troubling. He has alienated many by his penchant for *shiksa* women, both in real life and in his films – almost all of the 'Woody' characters' relationships in the films are with Gentile women – his stand against Israel's anti-Palestinian policies and, of course, the scandal over Mia Farrow and their children. To many, this last seemed merely the culmination of Allen's persistent attack on the institution of the Jewish family, which he routinely depicts as riven with dissent. In *Crimes and Misdemeanors*, where Judah, revisiting his old house, relives a family *seder* of his childhood, the event is a pretext for bickering and for Judah's agonised questions about guilt and retribution. The cheerful parties of *Hannah and her Sisters* and *Everyone Says I Love You* don't mark Jewish high holidays but WASP Thanksgivings, and frequently the appearance of a Jew at such a gathering is the signal for disaster. Dining with Annie's family in *Annie Hall*, Allen's character Alvy Singer turns the event into a dramatisation of their – as he sees it – covert anti-Semitism, visualising himself as he imagines they do, as a ringleted Hassid. In *Hannah and her Sisters* and *Everyone Says I Love You*, he is, likewise, the disaffected Jewish ex-husband whose problems disturb the equilibrium of his WASP in-laws. And in *Interiors*, the wedge that drives apart the family of E.G. Marshall is Pearl, the pushy Jewish widow to whom he turns for the warmth he never received from his interior-decorating wife and emotionally constipated daughters.

The families in films like *Radio Days* and *Crimes and Misdemeanors* ring as false to most Jews as the priests and nuns of Hollywood films like *The Bells of St Mary's* do to Catholics. One doesn't have to look far for the real models. Jerry Epstein points out that he and Allen 'grew up in an essentially Jewish neighbourhood and also to a certain degree Italian. There was a demarcation line in which the Italians lived on Avenue L, and the Jews lived on I, J and K.' The first religious community Allen remembers seeing wasn't a Jewish temple but a Catholic monastery outside Washington. 'It was quiet and peaceful,' he says. 'There were very few people there. Just the thought that the monks would wake up in the morning and they would tread those paths, and they were not afraid of dying, and they didn't want anything – I loved that. It was a stoic life.'

Nostalgia for the life of the Christian culture is a common theme in Jewish art, and no less so in Allen's films. In *The Trotskys, Freuds, and Woody Allens*, Ivan Kalmar argues that Allen's families, in illustration of a long-standing example of cultural parallelism, appear less Jewish than Italian.

> The Italian is the most distinctively Christian group in the [immigrant] neighbourhood, and yet at the same time one that appears somewhat 'Jewish'. This makes the Italians the best choice for those looking for a Gentile group whose Jewish-like traits prove that the Jews are not unique. Woody has played up the ambiguity to the fullest. The 'real' Italians parodied in *Broadway Danny Rose* are resplendent with exaggerated stereotypical and definitely non-Jewish characteristics; they are superstitiously Catholic, and given to organised crime and vendettas. But under that crass veneer, they look and talk just like Jews. At a party of Italian-American crime bosses, Danny Rose, the former small-time comic, easily falls into using the same trite routines he has used with a Jewish crowd in the Catskills. There is an immediacy between Danny and Woody's Italians that is far removed from the tension we see in his other movies between himself and the WASPs, or in the desperate anxiety of his jokes about Nazis. Here he is among a related tribe, estranged cousins, long-lost relatives.

Though Allen often insists that his true cinematic hero and artistic influence is the austere Swede Ingmar Bergman, only three of his films – *Interiors*, *A Midsummer Night's Sex Comedy* and *Deconstructing Harry*, suggested by *Face to Face* and *Autumn Sonata*, *Smiles of a Summer Night* and *Wild Strawberries* respectively – show a Bergman influence. He far less readily admits the inspiration of the archetypal Italian Fellini, even though *Annie Hall* and *Stardust Memories* derive from *8½*, *Radio Days* from *Amarcord*, and *Alice* from *Juliet of the Spirits*.

4

Women and Magic

> I grew to full manhood. Actually five foot six, which is technically
> not full manhood in Russia, though you can still own property.
> Over five three you can own land. Under five three you need special
> permission from the Tsar.
>
> Allen in *Love and Death*

In 1944, when Allen was eight, his sister Letty was born. He
might, like many children, have resented the new arrival, but to
Allen it simply confirmed his conviction that whatever was given
would, sooner or later, be snatched away, and he accepted it as
he did everything else, with gloomy resignation. Far from arousing
his sibling rivalry, Letty became a fixture in his life, to the extent
that, in middle age, he often tried out his routines on her, and in
the nineties made her head of production of his first independent
company, Sweetland Films.

Letty's arrival reinforced a pattern in Allen's life. Women would
always be at its centre. 'I was the only male in a family of many,
many women,' he said. 'I had a sister, female cousins, a mother
with seven sisters. I was always surrounded by women.' It is they
and not men who would provide his benchmarks, who would
inspire him and whose advice he would seek. 'My main subject,'
he said of his philosophy of filming, 'is female psychology.' After
decades of film-making, the fascination would not have worn off.
'I rarely think in terms of male characters, except for myself only,'
he said in 1986. 'I have a tremendous attraction to movies or
plays or books that explore the psyches of women, particularly
intelligent ones. When Mary McCarthy wrote *The Group*, I
couldn't wait to get my hands on it, or the Richard Yates novel,
Easter Parade.' Some film-makers, notably Steven Spielberg, have
found a Jewish childhood in a house full of women stifling, and

reacted against it in their work. For Allen, however, the company of women, and especially those united by family ties, became indispensable.

It also made him, from early in his life, a tireless chaser of women, and whatever pose he might strike on screen, he caught plenty. The need to seduce is apparent in every film in which Allen appears. He usually presents himself as the witty, compassionate, thoughtful alternative to a more glamorous and obviously virile lover. His desperate efforts at seduction don't always succeed, but he emerges from the story as the moral hero, content to return to the surrogate sexuality of movies after having established to his satisfaction, if not that of the woman, that short red-headed intellectuals can also lead a significant emotional life.

This pattern emerged as early as *What's New Pussycat* (1965), where he bobs in the wake of Peter O'Toole as he ploughs through the women of Paris. In his first play, *Play it Again, Sam* (1969), he seduces the wife of his more handsome and richer best friend, but nobly relinquishes her at the end, with dialogue cribbed from *Casablanca*. *Love and Death* sees him as the only man who truly loves the promiscuous Diane Keaton, and whose love triumphs. And so on, through *Crimes and Misdemeanors* and *Everyone Says I Love You*, Allen remains the eunuch at the orgy of life, a pitiable figure, doomed to help more active participants out of their trousers and make sarcastic asides about their performance.

Much of this is rooted in his early sexual experience, which, given his shyness and physical oddity, was painful. Jerry Epstein recalls, 'He was a complete failure with girls. Absolutely. What held him back was his shyness. He used to get physiological symptoms in the abdomen. He would get knotted up when he had to pick up a phone and call a girl. He would get an actual physical symptom.' Allen often prevailed on friends like Jack Victor, who had a more mature voice and more of what they vaguely called 'élan', to ring girls for him. Victor had his share of dates, but his calls for Allen were usually flops; nobody wanted to date the pint-sized redhead with the squeaky voice. High school friend Jerry Cohen remembers Allen as 'a loner; always a loner. We used to hang out at Cookies on Avenue J with some of the prettier girls. It was a soda fountain used almost exclusively by us seniors. But I don't remember Woody ever being one of the gang. He was pretty much a nonentity at the time, I'd say.' Cohen's wife Barbara agreed: 'There was terrific competition between us for the guys who really mattered. Woody was definitely not one of them.'

The second major influence on Allen's early adolescence, and a related one, was magic. For his tenth birthday, a family friend gave him an E-Z Magic Set, containing a few simple illusions. When these wore out their novelty, he added new ones from Irving Tannen's Circle Magic Shop on West 57th Street, which became a regular stop on his now frequent visits to Manhattan, usually on days when he played truant from school. His interest in magic would wax and wane through adolescence, stimulated spasmodically by such things as another gift, when he was thirteen, of the book *Illustrated Magic* by Ottakar Fischer. Magic encouraged the illusion that reality could be transformed by an effort of will. When he mastered an illusion like 'the floating light bulb', in which a bulb lights up at the touch of the magician's fingers, Allen felt he had miraculously bypassed the real world. He was so convinced of this that he tried periodically to use sleight of hand in real-life situations, suggesting to a friend, Elliott Mills, that they cheat local boys with a variation on a traditional 'mentalist' act. After inviting bets on their ability to predict the outcome of a baseball game, Mills would produce a sealed envelope containing the name of the winning team – actually written by him after the event by slipping a finger into the envelope with a piece of lead under the nail. It was only with difficulty that Mills dissuaded him from what would almost certainly have been a fatally incompetent scam.

Another appeal of magic to Allen lay in the fact that, unlike music and performance, it could be perfected in privacy and silence. 'I would go in [to school] at nine and come back at three,' he said later. 'Then I'd go right into my bedroom and shut the door – immediately. Consequently, I was able to get things done. I became real adept at sleight of hand, which took me endless hours and which I can still do. My mother used to pass by the room and hear the coins dropping for eight hours; she just couldn't believe it.' In his play *The Floating Light Bulb*, Allen describes his surrogate character Paul as 'about sixteen, awkward and gawky. He is painfully shy, problematically so, always looking down, always stuttering, always keeping to his room to practise.'

Like Paul, Allen was persuaded to try his magic in public. From 1949 to 1954, NBC's fifteen-minute television programme *The Magic Clown* ran every Sunday morning. A clown named Zovella (actually magician Dick Du Bois) demonstrated tricks, and sometimes invited amateurs to perform. Allen auditioned twice, the second time with his next-door neighbour Jack Freed, but failed on both occasions because of the sophistication of his tricks, too contrived and adult for a children's show. He persisted, however, periodically trying out for people who might help him crash professional magic. *The Floating Light Bulb* evokes the humiliations of one such occasion. Auditioning for an agent, Max, whom his mother has lured to the house, Paul flops disastrously. After the débâcle his father offers the only good advice when he says, 'Poor kid. He's got an inferiority complex. Maybe the thing to do is a good personality course – how to speak slowly – use your arms to make good gestures – salesmanship.'

Allen achieved a brief moment as a stage magician in 1952, when he was sixteen. The scenic mountain areas that ring New York, like the Catskills and Poconos, were crowded with hotels and family resorts, many of them catering specifically to Jewish families. Generations of comics, singers and performers got their start in the so-called 'borscht belt', and Allen would be no exception. Weinstein's Majestic Bungalow Colony in Accord, NY, wasn't the most salubrious of the Catskill resorts, but it had an inexhaustible appetite for entertainment, and a friend from Brooklyn suggested they give Allen a chance. The owner reluctantly agreed, providing Allen pay his own way.

Allen persuaded his parents to book into a less expensive resort nearby, and did his shows at Weinstein's. He has never described the audiences' reaction, but from his later slighting references to Weinstein's we can assume he went over badly. In *The Floating Light Bulb* the loser agent, Jerry, quizzed about his client list, reveals its sleaziness by mentioning that one of his clients appears there, while in *Broadway Danny Rose*, Allen's equally second-rate vaudeville agent badgers Weinstein's owner, Chomsky, to book his blind xylophone player and one-legged tap-dancer. Chomsky refuses, pointing out that his audience – 'old Jewish people' – are mostly blind or crippled themselves. In a rueful scene in *Annie Hall*, Allen is a stand-up comic at a Borscht Belt resort, working the crowd. 'How old are you, dear?' 'Eighty.' 'You don't look a day over seventy-nine . . .'

After Weinstein's, Allen abandoned the idea of a career as a magician, though magic periodically pops up in his films. In his short film *Oedipus Wrecks* (1989) in the series *New York Stories*, a magician causes Allen's mother to disappear, after which she materialises in the sky over Manhattan, commenting to everyone on his shortcomings as a son. In *Stardust Memories*, his character, film director Sandy Bates, does tricks in a dream, after explaining 'I would always practise to be popular.' His parents are among the group watching. 'Our son's a genius,' says his mother, but his father replies, 'Well, he doesn't take after you, that's for sure.' The scene degenerates into a fight, and one of his producers, also in the crowd, enquires sourly, 'If he's such a genius, how come he can't make funny movies?'

Magic led Allen to comedy. A gag is sort of magic, the creation of something out of nothing, an intellectual sleight of hand. It was also a form of performance in which Allen's ineptitudes could be turned to advantage. While a fumbling magician is pathetic, a fumbling comedian can be hilarious, as he learned during his failed auditions for *The Magic Clown*. To cover a delay between tricks, he ad-libbed, 'Normally we have people to do this sort of thing.' Typically, his one story about his early experience of magic portrays him as a loser. One day in Tannen's magic shop he recognised the comedian Milton Berle, whose weekly TV show on NBC was then the most popular in America. Quaking in his shoes, Allen walked up, held out his hand and said, 'Henny Youngman?' – another popular stand-up comic. Going along with the gag, Berle took his hand and said, 'Red Skelton.'

They talked about magic. Handing him a deck of cards, Berle said, 'Do me a trick and I'll put you on the show.' Allen tried one he'd done thousands of times before, and muffed it – 'One of the tragedies of the little moment,' he said later.

'Sorry,' he apologised. 'I don't usually work with cards.'

Berle replied, 'That's OK. I don't usually work with kids,' then proceeded to do a faultless card trick. Had Allen succeeded in his trick, or had Berle failed, there would have been no story. But, as in many of Allen's routines and films, the interest lies in the failure. Success is seldom funny. As Mack Sennett decreed in the early days of screen comedy, 'The joke of life is the fall of dignity.'

Despite his refusal to take school seriously, or even to read anything more demanding than comic books – he barely read any books at all until his mid-teens – Allen graduated from PS 99 in June 1949, and entered Midwood High School the following year. By 1951, when he made his undistinguished debut as a professional magician at Weinstein's, it was evident that he had no future in that direction, though his skill with cards, he discovered, was useful in what became one of his favourite leisure activities: playing poker for money, at which he was an instant success. In one of the few references to Allen in Midwood's school paper, the *Argus*, the editor warned that there was 'a motto among Red's friends which throws light on some of his magician's digital dexterity. "Never play cards with Konigsberg!"' His sporting ambitions likewise led nowhere, since he was, if possible, even weedier than he'd been in public school, and his height has stabilised at five foot six inches. Asked in class what he wanted to be when he left school, Allen startled his teacher by replying, 'A sanitation worker.' Pressed, he claimed that what he had in mind was a job as a men's room attendant. The work wasn't onerous, which would give him time to think, and in his free time he could write – a career that already seemed more interesting to him than either sport or crime.

Enough of his friends found him funny for Allen to win a reputation as a comedian. He began palling around with other boys who shared his enthusiasms, in particular Mickey Rose, who would become his writing partner on his first films. The two shared an admiration for the playwright George S. Kaufman. Kaufman was everything they might aspire to be. The ultimate Jewish man of the theatre, he'd written a series of hits that included *The Royal*

Family of Broadway, You Can't Take it With You, Stage Door and *The Man who Came to Dinner*. Though he never disguised his contempt for Hollywood, Kaufman had also been persuaded to create a number of classic movies, including *A Night at the Opera* for the Marx Brothers, which he co-wrote with Morrie Ryskind, and to direct his own script of the 1947 *The Senator was Indiscreet*.

As if this were not enough to excite an adolescent's admiration, Kaufman was also a famous sexual athlete. In 1933 he'd conducted a passionate affair with the actress Mary Astor, which she'd meticulously detailed in her diary. Her husband discovered it, and when the marriage broke up in 1935 he used it to devastating effect in the proceedings over custody of their daughter. The jury heard Astor describe how Kaufman 'fucked the living daylights out of me' in both New York and California. 'Ah desert night,' she rhapsodised of one tryst in Palm Springs, 'with George's body plunging into mine, naked under the stars.' Allen adopted Kaufman's trademark two-fingered salute and offhand drawl. He even made a pilgrimage to the playwright's Manhattan home and stood reverently outside, hoping to catch a glimpse of him – a gesture somewhat neutralised when he found later he'd watched the wrong building.

In the spring of 1952, as a junior in high school, Allen sent some one-line gags to a cousin, Phil Wasserman, who worked in public relations. PR people often got their clients' names into the papers by inventing a joke they were supposed to have made and sending it to one of the columnists on New York's eight daily papers. Either the columnist or the PR man paid around $5 for such gags, and Wasserman suggested that if Allen's jokes were any good, he could work up a lucrative business, though initially he must expect no payment. Allen also began sending gags to columnists off his own bat. With each went a note: 'Enclosed are some gags for your consideration and exclusively to you.' Earl Wilson, Broadway columnist for the *New York Post*, later joked that the envelopes often arrived 'postage-due', i.e. with no stamps, but he would use the gags anyway, attributing them to the writer who by then signed himself 'Woody Allen'.

*　　*　　*

The question 'Why "Allen"?' is easily answered. 'Just why Jews in the performing arts were expected to Anglicise their names is a question worthy of a separate study,' Kenneth Tynan wrote in a profile of comic – and later Allen collaborator – Mel Brooks, *né* Melvin Kaminsky. 'To take three cases at random, is it to simplify pronunciation, to enhance euphony, or to disarm bigotry that Emanuel Goldenberg becomes Edward G. Robinson, Benny Kubelsky becomes Jack Benny, and Isadore Demsky becomes Kirk Douglas?' In Allen's case, all three applied. However much he played on his Jewishness for humour later in his career, his primary concern at the beginning was to be thought Gentile.

'Woody' is harder to explain. Allen always claimed the nickname was conferred by other boys in recognition of his skill at playing stickball with a piece of wood, but a friend offers a different story. 'He was in love with a girl from high school called Nancy Kreissman. He had this kind of attraction from afar because he was too timid and shy to approach her. He tried in some way, and I think he may have gone out with her once, but he was really enamoured of her, struck by her, and her dog was named Woody, so he took the name of the dog.' In his authorised biography of Allen, Eric Lax claims that journalists and columnists often erroneously gave him the incorrect first name of 'Elwood' or 'Heywood', and that Allen preferred to be called 'Al' in school. In fact, he did briefly use Heywood as a name. One of his early routines begins, 'Woody is short for Heywood.'

Even if the story about Nancy Kreissman's dog isn't true, the anecdote accurately reflects Allen's emotional life at the time. Growing up had not cured his shyness or made him any more attractive. 'He was one of the ugliest kids you ever saw,' said Sadie Goldstein, sister of Bryna Goldstein, one of his high school girlfriends. 'Red hair, skinny, and big glasses. That's all you saw. The red hair and the glasses.' (Actually, Allen didn't wear glasses until after he left school.)

His relationship with Bryna Goldstein was typical of his adolescent attachments. She was the one girl in Allen's group of friends, their mascot. He doted on her, turning up frequently at her home, being polite to her family, rolling out his best gags for them. He flattered her about her good points, especially her legs. When she broke one of them, he celebrated the removal of the plaster cast with the gift of a fake newspaper front page from one of the Times Square shops that printed them up to order. The headline read: 'Goldstein Cast Comes Off: Dietrich Faints'. Even when Bryna showed that her sexual interests lay with more muscular, if less intellectual, boys, Allen continued to turn up at her house and wait for hours for her to return from a date. 'Bryna said she'd be here later,' he would tell her embarrassed parents. When they did go out together, it was an event sufficiently significant for Allen to commemorate it with one of his most extravagant gestures. After one dinner at which Bryna had failed to get her dessert, rice pudding, Allen had a large box delivered to the Goldstein house. 'It was at least six feet tall,' says Bryna's sister Sadie. 'The package took us hours to unravel, one wrapping after another. And way at the bottom was a dish of rice pudding.'

After movies and magic, Allen's greatest solace in adult life has been jazz. When he can't write any more, he often takes up the clarinet and starts to practise, trying to do so for at least an hour a day. In *Wild Man Blues* he's even shown sitting alone in the back seat of a car parked on Paris's Place St Sulpice, playing scales. Partly it's for the pleasure of the music, but he acknowledges that the instrument is a surrogate friend; that he plays 'when I can't take the solitude any longer'.

It was in 1948, when Allen was twelve, that he heard his first recording of New Orleans jazz. A Saturday morning radio programme devoted itself to clarinettist and soprano saxophone player Sidney Bechet, and the effect on Allen was immediate. It was an odd taste, since New Orleans jazz was already almost a lost art. By the time records were being made in quantity, most of its better exponents, like Louis Armstrong, had moved up the Mississippi on the riverboats to Chicago, and thence to New York. Allen admired Armstrong, and nominated the opening measures of his 'Potatohead Blues' as one of the supreme musical treasures of his life, but his own tentative playing style led him to the jazz played by musicians who'd missed the diaspora to Chicago. Established in Preservation Hall, the temple of 'pure' New Orleans jazz, men like trumpeter Bunk Johnson, who was only recorded towards the end of his life, became models for hundreds of fervent 'traditional' bands across the world. British critic and jazz musician George Melly, describing one such group of the fifties, Ken Colyer's Crane River Jazz Band, disparaged them as imitating an exhausted and arid musical tradition:

> What we expected a trumpet player to aim at was the early Louis Armstrong noise. Ken didn't sound anything like that. His wavery vibrato and basic melodic approach was based on Bunk Johnson. He sounded, and intended to sound, like an old man who had never left New Orleans when they closed Storyville [the brothel quarter]. He played traditional, not revivalist jazz. There were no solos. Every number was ensemble throughout, and to my ears monotonous ensemble at that. The bass drum pounded away, the clarinet ran up and down the scales like a mouse in a wheel, the two cornets wavered and trembled, the trombone grunted spasmodically.

Allen agrees that New Orleans jazz is 'a limited art form, one you have to cultivate a taste for. What the public wants is the commercial stuff. Al Hirt, or the Dukes of Dixieland.' One of the musicians in his band has called it 'a dialect of jazz', and acknowledged that, even in New Orleans, nobody played it any more. In 1950, when he was fourteen, Allen started taking lessons on the soprano saxophone, Bechet's instrument, but he abandoned it once he heard clarinettist Gene Sedric. Sedric's career included stints with the singer and pianist Fats Waller, whose sly falsetto songs have remained an Allen enthusiasm. Envying Sedric's openness of tone, Allen rang the musician himself and asked for lessons. Sedric obliged, commuting from the Bronx to Ocean Avenue once a week for a meagre $2 a time. In between, Allen bought records by clarinettists like George Lewis and played along with them, learning to imitate their authentic style. He also mastered the clarinet's more primitive ancestor, the recorder.

With Sedric's help, and tireless practice, Allen achieved a modest mastery, though never a professional polish. Professionalism, however, wasn't his aim, any more than Hollywood slickness would be his goal in film-making. In his films he would frequently remind the audience 'It's only a movie,' by casting himself in primary roles and, in addition, stepping outside his character to deliver one-line jokes more typical of the stand-up comedian he was in real life than the TV writer, documentary film-maker or Russian *rentier* he was playing. In music, he strove for an equivalent roughness, to the extent of using only an Albert system clarinet, the type played by the New Orleans pioneers, rather than the later Boehm instrument which simplified the fingering. Albert instruments tend to play a little out of tune – exactly their attraction to Allen. 'The old bands often played sharp or flat,' he says. 'In New Orleans style, the emphasis is on how you treat the tune. You don't notice the technique.'

5

Writer

I may not have the tradition of personal conquest, Helen, but any man, if he desires something enough, can put himself in the running.

Henry James, *The Aspern Papers*

Though it would not be apparent for some time, 1952 was a turning point for Allen. It seems another America now. In November, a landslide of voters revealed the national tone by choosing Dwight Eisenhower and Richard Nixon to run the country. It would be four years before Allen Ginsberg published *Howl and Other Poems*, and five before a publisher took a chance on Jack Kerouac's *On the Road*. Greenwich Village was a cheap and obscure quarter of lower Manhattan. The beat generation and the jazz clubs and coffee shops it brought to the area still lay in the future. Rock and roll as mass-market music didn't exist. That year's hits were the theme from the film *High Noon*, sung by Frankie Laine, Rosemary Clooney crooning 'Half as Much', and Johnnie Ray's whining plaint 'Cry'. Hollywood, on the other hand, had never been better. 1952 produced *The Bad and the Beautiful*, *Pat and Mike*, *The Quiet Man* and *Singin' in the Rain*.

In 1952, while he was still in high school, Allen saw his first jokes published, by columnist Nick Kenny in the *New York Daily Mirror*, though without his name attached. In November he made the big time when Earl Wilson used a one-liner in his column: 'Woody Allen figured out what OPS prices are – Over People's Salaries'.* Allen began barraging Wilson and other columnists

---

* The Office of Price Administration had been set up during the war to control the black market by limiting the prices of everything, from car tyres to restaurant meals. It survived under Truman as the Office of Price Stabilization – OPS – but

with more gags, a percentage of which got into print, though still without payment. Wilson put some of them into the mouth of fictitious chorus girl Taffy Tuttle: 'Taffy Tuttle told Woody Allen she heard of a man who was a six-footer and said, "Gee, it must take him a long time to put his shoes on."' After a few of these had appeared, Wilson had a call from press agent Gene Shefrin, who worked for personal publicist David O. Alber. Celebrities like dance-school owner Arthur Murray and bandleader Guy Lombardo paid Alber as much as $100 each time he got their names in a column, especially that of Walter Winchell in the *Mirror*. As Wilson put it later, Alber was 'searching for a cheap gag-writer to make Oscar Wildes out of Arthur Murray and Guy Lombardo'. 'Who the hell is Woody Allen?' Shefrin asked. Wilson gave him Allen's number, and a few weeks later Allen found himself settling down behind a desk with half a dozen other men in Alber's office at 60th Street and Fifth Avenue, writing gags at seventy-five cents an hour.

'There was nothing to it,' he boasted later. 'I'd get out of school, get on the BMT subway and start listing jokes. I'd give them fifty jokes a day. Always five to a page, ten pages.' Everyone else in the Alber office was older than Allen by two decades, and while most were cordial, none had much in common with this worryingly precocious high-school kid. As a later writing partner, Larry Gelbart, said of their first meeting, 'Woody looked to be all of six years old. His previous writing credit, I assumed, must have been learning the alphabet. He seemed so fragile, a tadpole in hornrims.' (The hornrims were still in the future: though Allen was already having problems reading, he didn't get glasses until he was eighteen.)

He made friends, however, with two of the men, Mike Merrick and Don Garrett, both ex-radio comics. The three often retreated to Boyd's Chemists on Madison Avenue to drink coffee, eat doughnuts and bitch about Alber's habit of blue-pencilling their best

---

the rich found it easy to evade. Restaurants might be required by law to sell meals for $3, but a $20 tip would get you a steak. A car dealer would sell you a top-of-the-line Buick for the OPS price, if you also bought his dog for $400.

material. Merrick and Garrett would tell stories about the old days, and Allen was later to recreate these talks in the opening of *Broadway Danny Rose*, where a group of veteran comics reminisce about the characters they've known. Merrick's style in particular impressed Allen, and when he did need to get glasses, it was Merrick's thick-rimmed black ones he chose – a crucial ingredient of the evolving 'Woody' image. Merrick was also responsible for another major step in Allen's development. In the hope of meeting girls, Allen and some of his friends had taken to dropping in on a Young Israel Social Club that met in a basement under a synagogue on Ocean Avenue. Friday night was amateur night, and there was always a crowd to see other members perform. At the end of one such show, the MC, who knew about Allen's burgeoning career as a gagman, announced that next week Allan Konigsberg would tell some jokes.

When a worried Allen mentioned this to Merrick and Garrett, Merrick offered him some of the material he'd used during his own career. Helped by a supportive audience, and given confidence by the fact that the jokes had already worked for Merrick, his routines about dating and getting laid – or failing to – were warmly applauded, though Allen didn't delude himself that it would be as easy in front of a paying audience, nor with his own untried material.

Despite his job, Allen's parents were insistent he go to college, even though his high-school graduation grade average of seventy-one was barely adequate. In 1953 he entered New York University, signing up for an arts degree with a major in film production, filling out the rest of the course with English and Spanish. He'd flunked Spanish at Midwood, but NYU demanded relatively little of its freshmen. He would mock its lax academic standards in the 'What Happens During Ejaculation?' episode of *Everything You Always Wanted to Know About Sex (*But Were Afraid to Ask)*, which shows the male body in terms of Mission Control at NASA. About to have sex with a girl in the back seat of a cab, the man is briefly chilled when she mentions her college education. Once she explains that she graduated from NYU, he can relax, and the operator in charge of erections (Tony Randall) yells triumphantly, 'We're going to make it!'

Allen's attitude to NYU was casual. He ducked at least half the classes, and made up his term papers the night before they were due. The first, a study of film music that took off from the use of drums in Billy Wilder's prison-camp film *Stalag 17*, distinctly underwhelmed his teacher, critic Robert Gessner, who gave it a C. He failed Spanish entirely, and his papers in English class, many of them attempts at humour in the style of columnist Max Shulman, merely angered his teachers, who assumed – rightly in many cases – that Allen was mocking them. He got an overall D for his first semester, and the reviewing board, while cautiously holding out some hope of readmission, suggested he seek counselling for his inability to take life seriously.

With a shrug, Allen decided that if NYU could do without him, he could do without NYU, and for his second – and, as it turned out, last – semester of higher education, he enrolled in a film course at accommodating City College. With even less incentive to toe the line, he missed almost every class. His parents were deeply disappointed. A decade later, Allen would comment, 'Even now, my parents would feel much better if I had lived up to their dream and been a pharmacist. There's tremendous pressure where I come from – a middle-class Jewish neighbourhood – to be an optometrist or a dentist or a lawyer, and that's what my friends have become. They exhibited at an early age an ability to get along at summer camp.' (The comment about his friends' success wasn't entirely facetious. Jerry Epstein became a psychiatrist, Elliott Mills a professor of pharmacology.)

Also in mid-1953, Allen encountered for the first time the film-maker who was to become his first inspiration. Through the summer of 1952, Swedish director Ingmar Bergman had filmed *Sommaren med Monika*, his twelfth feature, but the one that was to launch his international reputation. It's the story of a sluttish teenager driven to frenzy by the stuffiness of provincial life. Badgered by men who sense her barely contained sensuality, she impulsively attaches herself to Harry, a naïve boy she meets casually in a café. Stealing Harry's father's boat, they flee into the wilderness of islands that, for the brief Swedish summer, becomes a prelapsarian paradise. Flight transforms them into creatures of pure appetite. They bathe naked and make love. When her ex-boyfriend finds them there and maliciously burns their clothes, Monika and Harry turn on him like savages. Food runs out, and Monika tries to steal from a holiday home. The owners catch her, and offer her a meal, but sitting down at a table again merely inflames her. She snatches the meat and races into the darkness, gnawing it like an animal.

Allen initially went to see *Summer with Monika* because of its sexy reputation, and he wasn't disappointed. Every scene containing Harriet Andersson crackled with Bergman's evident lust for his nineteen-year-old star, with whom he had become infatuated during the shooting; they found repeated pretexts to slip away back to the islands to correct 'bad sound'. One can see that Allen also found the film's plot intriguing. His own home life seemed reflected in that of Monika, crowded into a small house with her family, including a heavily drinking father, and dreaming of movie stars. Worse, a man might end up like the doleful Harry, back in town and married to Monika who, neglecting the child that's the unwanted by-product of their summer idyll, slips into her old ways and takes another lover. Stuck with his head in a book, trying to get some kind of education, Harry dully faces a life of interminable anticlimax.

Allen's films never really resembled those of Bergman more than superficially, if only because they are, almost without exception, comedies, a form at which Bergman failed as consistently as Allen succeeded. What Allen admired in Bergman was his distance from his subjects, his refusal to surrender to sentiment, but above all his preference for relationships in decline, and for stories of loss, disappointment and regret. Bergman demonstrated that films didn't need the conventional Hollywood happy ending. Even a comedy could as well end on a shrug as a clinch.

Allen started taking private lessons in writing drama from the Hungarian author Lajos Egri, whose book *The Art of Dramatic Writing* he admired. With Mickey Rose, he also auditioned for an acting teacher. Both courses carried the indelible mark of amateurism, and he abandoned them after only a few visits. He was already thinking of himself as a pro, and pros don't take courses.

Allen's parents, by now resigned to the fact that their son wouldn't make a doctor or a lawyer, began looking for ways to help his career. Nettie mentioned that he wasn't the only comedy writer in the family: her brother Paul was related by marriage to Abe Burrows. The librettist of *Guys and Dolls*, Burrows was a famous name on Broadway, in radio and TV. For a few months in 1950 he'd hosted his own talk show, *Abe Burrows' Almanac*, on CBS, and for years had been a regular on shows like CBS's *This is Show Business*, in which celebrities supposedly 'dropped in' to ask the advice of a panel on some career problem – usually the pretext to plug a new show or sing a new song. Nettie suggested Allen do just that to Burrows: drop in, and ask for his help. With a negligence he didn't feel, he dressed up and presented himself at Burrows' uptown apartment. Explaining he was part of the family and wanted to make it in show business, he thrust two pages of gags into Burrows' hands.

Burrows was immediately impressed by his cousin's talent, though less so by his ultimate ambition, to be a Hollywood screenwriter. In Hollywood, he explained, the writer was just a hired hand. Only on Broadway did he win some respect. He advised him to think about the theatre, and urged him to familiarise himself with both serious drama and comedy. On a more practical level, he also wrote letters of introduction to Sid Caesar, Phil Silvers and Peter Lind Hayes, who with his wife Mary Healy hosted *The Stork Club*, a nightly TV variety show supposedly set in the fashionable New York *boîte*, as well as a radio series. Hayes had a voracious appetite for gags, and immediately paid $50 for some of those Allen sent him.

Hoping to get an agent, Allen approached the prestigious William Morris Agency, one of whose agents, Sol Leon, liked him sufficiently to introduce him to the manager of comedian Herb Shriner. Shriner, who, playing on his Indiana roots, billed himself 'The Hoosier Humorist', had stepped in to replace the ailing Fred Allen on the popular quiz *Two for the Money*, but lacked the snappy material demanded by a nationally televised show. Allen found himself writing most of Shriner's opening monologues.

Despite this break, the William Morris Agency had no interest in an untried eighteen-year-old who thought a $50 fee was a lot of money. Instead, Allen made a deal with Harvey Meltzer, the elder brother of a school friend who had worked in the garment trade but wanted to break into show business. The quick-talking Meltzer persuaded him to sign a management deal which, in defiance of standard agent practice, paid a larger percentage the more Allen earned. Most agents took 10 per cent, but Allen's contract with Meltzer committed him to paying 35 per cent. The deal, which lasted for five years, undeniably benefited Meltzer, but it's he who is usually credited with transforming Allen from a gifted freelance gagman to a professional comedy writer. Allen, not unkindly, was to use Meltzer's Yiddishisms and relentless promotional skills in *Broadway Danny Rose*.

Allen's inattention to business was partly understandable, since he'd met the woman who was to be his first wife. Harlene Rosen had succeeded Bryna Goldstein as mascot of the group which hung out informally around the Jewish social clubs of Flatbush. Allen still carried a torch for the leggy and attractive Bryna, but a relationship that had never existed sexually became even more attenuated as she pursued her acting ambitions in Manhattan.

Harlene played piano in the impromptu jam sessions that usually included Allen on clarinet and Mickey Rose or Elliott Mills on drums. Her father, who owned a shoe store, played the trumpet, and often joined in with Harlene and Allen, but any sign of a romantic attachment was discouraged. No college dropout and part-time comic was good enough for *his* daughter. The Konigsbergs were no more enthusiastic. Nevertheless, the couple began dating, and in January 1956 they announced that they wanted to marry. Grudgingly, the Rosens and the Konigsbergs accepted the *fait accompli*.

Allen began taking a more professional interest in the comedy business. The job with Herb Shriner couldn't last forever, and with the influence of the newspaper columnists shrinking, David Alber was losing clients to companies that could get them on television. After years of serving mainly the East Coast, TV was now, via the new coast-to-coast coaxial cable, accessible all over America.

Television itself was changing faster than anyone might have expected as it extended its hold over the whole of the United States. In 1955, NBC, which had signed him to a thirty-year contract only four years earlier, dropped Milton Berle, for years the unchallenged king of TV. Essentially a borscht belt comedian, he'd appealed mainly to urban New Yorkers, but his Jewish *schtick* meant nothing to audiences in Texas or California. TV needed new comedians, and was already out looking for them. NBC, convinced that the talent-school system that had worked for Hollywood starlets would also work for writers, invited applications for a Writers' Development Program. In truth, the programme didn't offer much development. For three months, successful writers would be paid for writing one comedy piece a week. Les Colodny, an ex-agent, was retained to judge the work and make suggestions for its improvement. If, after three months, the writers hadn't come up with material that one of NBC's shows could use, they were dropped. Those who looked promising were offered to producers, after which they went on the show's budget.

Harvey Meltzer proved his usefulness by urging Allen to apply. Unconvinced that the network would accept anyone so young and with so few academic qualifications, he put together a page of gags written on a yellow legal pad in pencil, and allowed Meltzer to submit them. Ted Danielewski, director of the programme, saw past the rough execution to the originality of the humour. He convinced the programme to include Allen.

In practice, the NBC Writers' Development Program proved even less glamorous than the cynical impulse that motivated it. Most of those chosen to be part of it spent their time at home, writing, or hanging round the office, waiting for the phone to ring. Whatever ambitions the network may have had of fostering a team of innovative young gagmen, the head writers of individual shows were leery of hiring them over more seasoned, if higher-priced, colleagues.

One of the few prepared to give tyros a try was *The Colgate*

Comedy Hour. A Sunday-evening show launched in 1950, it was NBC's attempt to counter the national delirium for the New York-produced *The Ed Sullivan Show*, which dominated Sunday-evening TV. By producing in Hollywood, NBC gambled on tapping the established movie comics who lived there, and for a few seasons the heady mix of talents like Bob Hope, Dean Martin, Jerry Lewis, Donald O'Connor, Jimmy Durante and Eddie Cantor racked up good ratings. By the autumn of 1955, they were slipping. Amidst mutterings from the toothpaste-making sponsors of putting their money elsewhere, NBC hurriedly retitled the programme *The Colgate Variety Hour*, and began beefing up its comedy with all-music 'specials' like a version of *Roberta* starring Gordon Mac-Rae. This didn't work, and from the end of 1955 Colgate definitively cut their sponsorship. Stuck for underwriting, NBC renamed the show *The NBC Comedy Hour*, installed ex-Hollywood Western actress and TV star Gale Storm as compere, and began looking around for other ways of cutting costs. Suddenly, the low-priced newcomers of the Development Program looked more attractive, and head writer Danny Simon, brother of the more famous Neil, agreed to take Allen on trial. When David Alber called Allen into his office late in 1955 and told him he wouldn't be needed any more, Allen took some satisfaction in announcing that he was leaving for California and a steady NBC salary of $169 a week.

6

Render Unto Caesar ...

Never look back. Someone may be gaining on you.

Baseball player Leroy 'Satchel' Paige

Life on the *Comedy Hour* echoed that in the Alber office. Lacking space in their ancient building, ironically situated at the legendary corner of Hollywood Boulevard and Vine Street, Danny Simon installed his writers at the nearby Hollywood Hawaiian Motel at Yucca and Grace, where a one-bedroomed 'suite' cost $290 a month. Some writers supporting families back in New York couldn't manage on their $300-a-week salaries, so when Simon asked one of them, Milt Rosen, to share with Allen in return for part of his rent, he was delighted to accept.

Rosen and Danny Simon crucially influenced Allen. Later he would acknowledge, 'Everything I learned about comedy writing, I learned from Danny Simon' – a gracious compliment. Creating sketches for the procession of movie comics that passed through in *The NBC Comedy Hour*'s brief life – the show was axed in June 1956 – gave him his first experience of writing for comedians who'd had the benefit of the best material Hollywood could offer, but it was Simon and Rosen who taught him to transform his talent for one-liners into the ability to build sequences, sketches, and eventually screenplays.

Asked what he wanted from life when he arrived as a twenty-year-old in Los Angeles in 1956, Allen answered, 'To host the Oscars and write for Bob Hope.' During his early days with Alber, he'd created some material with Hope in mind, and Alber arranged to get it to Hope's manager, James Saphier, at the comedian's headquarters in Palm Springs. Hope liked the gags, Saphier said, and wanted to meet Allen next time they were both in New York.

As it turned out, Allen got to Los Angeles before Hope made it to the east coast, and one of his first acts was to ring Saphier for an appointment with Hope. Allen found Hope cordial, with a small-town manner that contrasted oddly with his evident wealth and the snappy banter of his material. Hope offered a vague promise of work, and Allen did some gags 'on spec', writing to Harlene back in New York that he was 'working for Bob Hope on assignment', but none of his material was ever used. This was perhaps just as well, since Hope habitually hired writers for life, locking them into long-term contracts that made alternative careers impossible.

Allen also hoped to lose his virginity in Los Angeles. The city deserved its reputation for beautiful girls on every corner, but Allen, spike-haired, goggle-eyed and limping in cheap new shoes, didn't look like the film producer or casting director most of them were there to meet. His sexual naïveté was all too obvious to Simon and Rosen, who couldn't resist making fun of it, and suggested he patronise a prostitute who regularly serviced guests of the Hawaiian Motel. Allen was immediately intrigued. In the guise of assuring themselves that he would enjoy the experience to the full, Simon and Rosen quizzed him about female anatomy. He did know, for instance, that women had four vaginal compartments, each with a different function? 'Don't worry. I know, I know,' Allen said dismissively.

Whether he ever visited the hooker isn't known, but an attraction to the idea of paid sex persisted. Asked why he put prostitutes in so many of his films, Allen explains, 'Quite simply because they are tremendous people, very strong symbols of our society, a little like the Mafiosi and gangsters of Coppola or Spielberg. Dostoyevsky depicted them in his novels, Fellini in his films. They are the women who add colour to life but who are always considered, here, as less than nothing, destined to be punished by humiliation or death.'

One of his best comic 'casuals' for the *New Yorker* was 'The Whore of Mensa', a Raymond Chandler pastiche about private eye Kaiser Lupowitz nosing out a network of educated prostitutes who offer something more exotic than sex: intellect. 'For a hundred, a girl would lend you her Bartok records, have dinner, then let you watch while she had an anxiety attack. For one-fifty, you could listen to FM radio with twins. For three bills, you got the works: a thin Jewish brunette would pretend to pick you up at the Museum of Modern Art, let you read her master's, get you involved in a screaming quarrel at Elaine's over Freud's conception of women, and then fake a suicide of your choosing – the perfect evening, for some guys.'

In a shot cut from *Sleeper*, Allen looks down at a recumbent female robot and enquires, 'Did a bellhop ever send you to my room in the Dixie Hotel?' *The Purple Rose of Cairo* and *Shadows and Fog* both contain sequences set in brothels. In *Husbands and Wives*, Sidney Pollack finds relief from his sexless marriage to Judy Davis in the bed of a hooker 'with a mouth like velvet'. Allen's sportswriter in *Mighty Aphrodite* tracks down the mother of the child he and his wife have adopted to find she's an airhead whore and porn star. In 1991, asked to submit ideas for a commercial for Campari, he proposed one set in a brothel, which the company rejected as 'too sexy'.

It is in Allen's searchingly self-critical *Deconstructing Harry* that prostitutes occupy the most important position. The Allen character, a middle-aged writer, 'blocked' both in his work and his life – and called, with heavy irony, 'Harry Block' – routinely relies for sexual gratification on prostitutes. 'Tie me up, hit me, give me a blow job,' he orders, confident that he will be obeyed without question. No hooker would undergo a religious conversion in the middle of a relationship, like his psychiatrist ex-wife, or run off with a more suave rival, like his much younger mistress. They offer sex without guilt, without remorse, without strings. Desperate for someone to hold his hand while he gets an honorary doctorate from his old college, Harry persuades Cookie (Hazelle Goodman), the black hooker he'd hired for a quickie, to stay the night and drive upstate with him next day. As the disastrous day unrolls, culminating in the death of another companion and Harry's arrest for kidnapping his son, Cookie alone keeps her cool, calmly organising the trip, counselling Allen on his social errors, talking him down from a panic attack.

Before his first week was out, Allen's antipathy to California was firmly entrenched. He would never forgive the state for not being the land of opportunity he had envisaged, and for the rest of his life he shunned Los Angeles. In March he abruptly suggested to Harlene that they get married. Despite her parents' reservations, she immediately flew to California, and a rabbi carried out the ceremony at the motel on 15 March. Allen was twenty, Harlene seventeen. Acknowledging his sexual ignorance, which Harlene shared, they asked the rabbi for counselling. 'All you do is mount her like a young bull,' he told the startled couple – bad advice which put the marriage under a cloud from the start. Within a few weeks of their wedding, Allen was 'seized with a selfish horror' at what he'd done.

Hollywood soured Allen not only on Los Angeles, but on the craft of writing comedy for TV. The team working on the *Colgate Comedy Hour* offered a grim example of what awaited him. 'There is no future in being a TV writer,' he told agent Danny Wilde. 'You hack around from show to show and you're always worried – is the comedian you're writing for going to be dropped because of bad ratings? And if he is dropped you may find yourself moving three thousand miles to the other coast to write for a new comedian. It's a rough business.' When the show folded in June, he and Harlene returned to New York via Las Vegas, where Allen tried his luck at the tables and, as usual, won. In New York they lived briefly with her parents before finding an apartment at 110 East 61st Street. Harlene went back to school, enrolling at Hunter College to study philosophy, and Allen looked for work.

Now that Allen had a track record and some useful friends, like Danny Simon, also back in Manhattan, jobs were forthcoming. He supplied gags for most of the shows written by Simon, who also recommended him for a job at Tamiment, a resort near Stroudsberg, Pennsylvania. Set up as a summer retreat for young Jewish socialists, it boasted excellent accommodation, a first-class golf course, boating lake, dance hall, a 1200-seat theatre and, more to the point, a clientele mostly young, Jewish, middle-class, and on the lookout for a summer romance. 'You couldn't walk across the golf course at night,' recalled Christopher Hewett, one of the directors there, 'without tripping over them.'

Tamiment prided itself on its shows, which were assembled by a full-time professional producer with a musical staff, orchestra, arranger and composer at his disposal. Under producer Max Liebman, who had run them until two years before, Tamiment's Saturday and Sunday night revues had become a hothouse of comedy talent. Sid Caesar, Danny Kaye, Imogene Coca, Carl Reiner and Mel Brooks all made a start there before going on to Broadway or, increasingly, TV.

In 1949, Liebman made exactly the same switch, launching *The Admiral Broadway Revue* for NBC and Dumont – the only programme ever shown on two networks at once – and NBC's ninety-minute *Your Show of Shows* in 1950. Exploiting the formula of sketches, parodies and big musical numbers that had worked at Tamiment, *Your Show of Shows* made stars of Caesar and Coca, who performed material written for them by Mel Brooks, Carl Reiner, Mel Tolkin and other Tamiment veterans. Anyone who proved themselves at Tamiment stood a good chance of finding a spot in Liebman's TV empire. Allen spent the summers of 1956 and 1957 there, turning out material for the resident comics. Liebman had been replaced by the less distinguished Moe Hack, and the shows boasted no big names, but Allen became friends with Len Maxwell, Johnny Haymer, Bob Dishy and a number of second bananas who were to figure in his later career.

Hack wasted no money on the lesser help. Hired writers, of whom Allen was one, got $150 a week, and were boarded three or four to a room in cabins too squalid for paying customers. No arrangements had been made for Harlene. The couple lived in a nearby boarding house until Moe Hack hired Harlene as part-time secretary/typist, and gave the Allens a room with bath in the building where he had his office. Allen and Harlene had brought recorders, on which they would play duets in the evenings on the verandah, an oddly antique vision to couples en route to the woods.

Behind this façade, Allen was seething with frustration. As soon as he could get away, he took to spending time with the off-duty musicians and writers. The atmosphere in their cabins, evoked in Emile Ardolino's 1987 film *Dirty Dancing*, set in a resort like

Tamiment in 1963, was a good deal more unbuttoned than recorder duets with Harlene. Musician Dick Davy recalled: 'They lay around on these chaise longues with their music and their gin and the watermelon, and making out. And Woody looks at it like it's a scene from a strange movie. And he got all excited. "Is this what goes on here all day, all those naked women? Wow, you must have a ball. Wow!" And he's looking at all these girls. And he was like very uncomfortable, a fish out of water, looking around. 'Cause he was always writing. He had sticks of spearmint gum. You know, for the nervousness and writing.'

In between summers at Tamiment, Allen continued to turn out work on demand. In *Annie Hall*, he parodied this period in his life. The young Alvy Singer sits in the office of a sleazy agent, watching a tenth-rate comic, played by Johnny Haymer, run through his act, for which Alvy is supposed to write new material. 'Look at him mincing around,' Singer thinks, 'like he thinks he's real cute. You wanna throw up. If only I had the nerve to do my own jokes. I don't know how much longer I can keep this smile frozen on my face. I'm in the wrong business. I know it.'

Allen continued to think of himself as single, and still part of the old Brooklyn gang. He kept up with friends from the neighbourhood like Jack Victor and Jerry Epstein, who were themselves married now, and making careers. All basked to some extent in Allen's reflected glory, an admiration to which he played up with stories of the stars he'd met and written for.

The marriage to Harlene remained tentative. She had none of his interest in movies, jazz, gambling or comedy. Nor was the relationship successful sexually, once the novelty had worn off. At Tamiment he would tear himself away from his new friends with a resigned, 'Well, I got to go back to the cabins and do the husband bit.' Harlene, universally referred to as 'Mrs Woody', was already a comic creation to Allen, who retailed stories of his sexual initiation to the gang lounging around in their underwear. Some of these gags, worked up into routines, would find their way into his stand-up act a decade later. The first wife, always called 'Mrs Allen', 'the first Mrs Allen' or, occasionally, 'the notorious first Mrs Allen', was often charged with sexual unresponsiveness ('My first wife got a traffic ticket. Knowing her, it couldn't have been a moving violation'), and the theme of a husband who finds his wife unsatisfying runs through *Play it Again, Sam* and his films from *Annie Hall* onwards. Allen's sexual tastes would always be less like those of a married man than those of a single 'swinger', as his behaviour towards Harlene foreshadowed. Jack Victor and other friends were taken aback when he casually passed around some nude pictures he'd taken of her – and even more so when she walked in while they were examining them.

Allen also struck up an odd three-cornered relationship with Jerry Epstein and his wife Pearl. Epstein was qualifying as a psychiatrist, and was intrigued by evidence of extra-sensory perception and other 'wild talents' emerging from tests conducted by Dr J.B. Rhine at Duke University. The three often experimented with ESP, and Epstein became convinced that Allen had heightened psychic ability. Some friends implied that the plot of *Play it Again, Sam*, in which Allen's character, increasingly alienated from his wife, drifts into a romance with the wife of his best friend, owed something to Allen's relationships with old schoolmates.

Allen's first major job as a comedy writer came through Max Liebman, who had become an independent producer after Sid Caesar left *Your Show of Shows* to launch his own *Caesar's Hour*. Ambitious to go beyond his highly successful variety shows, Liebman conceived a half-hour situation comedy series for pudgy comic Buddy Hackett, to be broadcast live, in order to highlight Hackett's supposed ad-libbing talent. *Stanley*, which debuted in September 1956, starred Hackett as a simple soul who managed a news-stand in the lobby of a New York hotel. Liebman both directed and produced the show, which also starred Carol Burnett as Hackett's girlfriend. Neil Simon wrote the first episode with Billy Friedberg, but the chore of finding routines suited to the limited talents of Hackett soon palled. Simon, nicknamed 'Doc' and commonly regarded as the most brilliant talent in American comedy, handed over to his brother Danny, who, not for the first time, brought in Allen.

Liebman found Allen an enigma. In a society where horseplay and exaggerated reactions were common, he offered no more than 'Good morning' and 'Good night'. 'We didn't converse at all,' says Liebman. 'I began to wonder if he was dumb.' It quickly became apparent that neither Simon nor Allen could write routines which the inept Hackett couldn't mangle. Liebman became more demanding. 'Woody would listen, nod, then go away that night and come in next day with reams of paper. I got the impression he'd been working half the night. But it wasn't right! It wasn't what I wanted for the show.' Liebman replaced Allen, but no other writer proved capable of providing material for Hackett, and *Stanley* folded in March 1957, at the end of its first season.

In the few weeks he'd written for Buddy Hackett, Allen got a dizzying $1000 a week. For a brief moment after the show closed, he thought he might be able to carry on earning such exalted sums when Milt Kamen, who'd worked with him at Tamiment the previous summer, recommended him to Sid Caesar for *Caesar's Hour*. But the show was winding down to its last few episodes, and there was no money for new writers. Allen signed up for another summer at Tamiment, but not without the satisfaction of knowing that he had almost worked for the hottest comic in the country.

Whenever novelists or film-makers of the fifties and sixties conceived a megalomaniac comic, heavy-drinking, cigar-chewing, tyrannical, it was usually Sid Caesar they had in mind. Caesar's ego was gigantic, his self-doubt even larger. Faced with a routine he didn't like, he would storm into the writers' room, fling the pages at them, then grab a heavy metal desk and heave it at the wall. During such attacks, Mel Brooks, one of his most durable and devoted writers, would climb onto a filing cabinet and leap on the back of the lanky Caesar, shouting 'Down, boy!' until he became calm.

On stage and screen, Caesar and Imogene Coca, a working team for years, had blended perfectly, but in 1954 Caesar abruptly called a press conference and, without having warned Coca, announced that he was ditching the ailing *Your Show of Shows* to launch his own solo series. In front of everyone, Caesar asked Coca if she didn't agree that everyone should have the right to star in their own show. 'Oh, I suppose that's quite true,' she said falteringly, before bursting into tears.

For the new show, Caesar creamed off the best writers from *Your Show of Shows*. Chief among them was Mel Brooks, already a master of the Hollywood parody on which he would build his career as director and performer. His later send-ups of westerns (*Blazing Saddles*), Hitchcock thrillers (*High Anxiety*), silent cinema (*Silent Movie*) and horror films (*Young Frankenstein*) all began as sketches for Caesar. After three seasons, however, and despite five 1957 Emmys, it was evident that *Caesar's Hour* could not outdraw the rival *Lawrence Welk Show* fronted by the soupy bandleader. NBC asked Caesar to economise on the weekly $110,000 budget, and Caesar walked out. After a summer of inactivity, he swallowed his pride and begged Imogene Coca to re-form their old team. Having done poorly as a single, she agreed. For six months in early 1958 they appeared together in *Sid Caesar Invites You*, but without success. More desperate than ever, Caesar looked around for new opportunities, and found them in two variety specials for Chevrolet cars, the first of which, broadcast on 2 November 1958, celebrated his ten years on TV.

Turnover on his writing team was understandably high, with the most junior member usually the first to crack. For the Chevrolet shows, Caesar assembled a new group. Michael Stewart, youngest of the old crew, had left to live in France, from where he would write the 'books' of the hit Broadway shows *Bye Bye Birdie*, *Carnival* and *Hello, Dolly!* To replace him, Caesar brought in the even younger Larry Gelbart, later the architect of *M.A.S.H.* and other hits. 'My one condition,' recalled Gelbart, 'was that I be allowed to write [the shows] alone with him and not in a roomful of cigars attached to a platoon of writers.' But undiluted Caesar soon proved too much for Gelbart, and he was secretly pleased when Milt Kamen proposed Allen, whom he described as 'the young Larry Gelbart'. Gelbart bridled. 'The young Larry Gelbart is *here*,' he said, pointing to himself. But he was mollified by Allen's youth. The newcomer looked, he said, 'fragile, unformed, a tadpole in horn-rims'. Mel Brooks was less complimentary, calling Allen 'a little red-haired rat'.

Gelbart and Caesar kept working for the rest of the afternoon, with Allen making the odd *sotto voce* interjection. His self-effacement recalled that of 'Doc' Simon who, as part of an earlier Caesar team, had whispered his contributions into the ear of noisier collaborators like Mel Brooks rather than speak up himself. Caesar acknowledged none of Allen's ideas, but when he rose at 5 p.m. to go home, he told him tersely, 'You're hired.'

Allen found writing for Caesar a debilitating experience. 'You'll see people on a comedy with long faces,' he said later, 'wondering where the laughs'll come, how to get them, how to get the rhythm right. It can make for a terrible atmosphere. When I was writing for the Sid Caesar shows, they were a mass of hostilities and jealousies.' He never could adjust to Caesar's rages, and quailed when the comic began throwing furniture about.

One afternoon, Caesar summoned Allen and Gelbart to join him in the steam room. Gelbart was game, but Allen refused. He couldn't, he said, be funny naked. The refusal may also have been due in part to Allen's nervous reservations about hygiene. He never takes baths, and confines his showers to every third day, believing that 'bathing washes off the natural juices that keep you young'. Convinced of the mystical importance of never 'breaking a sweat', Allen, whenever he took exercise, preferred to stay unwashed until his body had cooled. During the location shooting of *A Midsummer Night's Sex Comedy* in 1981, Allen's companion Mia Farrow had a shower built for him in the house they rented on Martha's Vineyard. She recalled, 'There was no doubt in my mind that the gleaming shower would please him; on the evening of his second visit I watched him take a white rubber shower mat (for germs) out of his bag and carry it into the bathroom. But seconds later he emerged with the mat still rolled under his arm.

' "What happened?" I asked. "What's wrong?"

' "The drain is in the middle," he said, shaking his head dismissively, as if I should have known. No further explanation ever came.'

In Barbara Koppel's 1997 documentary *Wild Man Blues*, Allen went to the trouble of giving a prosaic explanation: the rubber mat was to insulate his feet from cold tiles, but it blocked the central drain. In hotels, even accompanied, Allen demanded a separate bathroom. Farrow was convinced that Allen's foibles were part of his general disquiet about his body. In particular, she believed he used the superstition about 'breaking a sweat' to avoid spending any more time in her company and that of her children than was absolutely necessary.

Allen and Gelbart turned out to be an ideal team for Caesar. Too nervous and junior to represent a threat, they could be bossed around in a way that Brooks, Reiner and the Simon brothers increasingly refused to stand for. For their part, the old timers looked on Allen dubiously. He was too quiet, too private, and he took no part in the horseplay of the writing room.

The sketches Allen and Gelbart wrote for the first Chevrolet show, including parodies of the portentous live drama series *Playhouse 90*, provided perfect material for Caesar, and ratings were gratifyingly high. They continued to work together, though not with Caesar, who never made the second Chevrolet special. Harvey Meltzer, still representing Allen and taking a larger slice than ever of his salary, persuaded Chevrolet to hire his client and Gelbart to write their next show, which starred the wholesome singer Pat Boone. Boone recalls cracking up when Allen pitched a possible routine to him, then reluctantly rejecting it as inconsistent with his white-bread/Christian/moral image.

In the hope that it would inspire them to come up with ideas less sophisticated and Manhattan-oriented, Gelbart suggested they work at his farm in upstate New York, a prospect that filled Allen with trepidation. At Tamiment, musician Dick Davy had proposed that Allen meet him by the resort's lake one afternoon, where he would be playing the guitar. It turned out that Allen had never stirred outside the cabins all summer.

He was no more enthusiastic now about the great outdoors, as Gelbart recalls. 'I remember picking up Woody and his then-wife Harlene at the train station the first time they came to visit for a working weekend. In his three-piece suit (at least), button-down shirt and black tie, Woody got off the train looking like a rabbi in mid-elopement. Harlene, resembling his bride and widow all in one, wore a black dress, a veiled hat and elbow-length gloves. I very quickly learned what a totally urban creature Woody is. For example, he hated flies; feared them, really, not so much that one might bite him but rather possibly carry him off. He never went near, let alone into, the swimming pool. There were "things" in these, he said. To him, the sparkling blue water was a black lagoon. A hundred and twenty five miles north of Manhattan, Woody gave the impression of someone lost in the Amazon.'

In 1958 Gelbart and Allen won a prestigious Sylvania Award for the Caesar special, and were nominated for Emmys. Success, however, made Allen, if possible, even less able to relate to people. 'There was a dinner given at Toots Shor's club by the Writers' Guild [to present the Sylvania Awards],' he recalled in 1981. 'And at that age – nineteen [he was actually twenty-two] – it was a big honour for me. And I went up to the door at Toots Shor's and I couldn't go in, and I never did go in. I went home, and I felt so relieved when I got home. And I've repeated that problem or syndrome or symptom many times.'

7

Stand-Up

Woody Allen was a slight man with a startled look about him, as if just caught in an unspeakable act.

Phil Berger, *The Last Laugh: The World of Stand-Up Comics*

The Pat Boone Show again won Allen and Gelbart Emmy nominations, but no awards. Now established as a top comedy writer, Allen had plenty of invitations to work. The one he took, in the autumn of 1958, was from CBS, which needed writers to revamp *The Garry Moore Show*. The laid-back Moore had been a TV star since 1950, sometimes in a half-hour sitcom in which he entertained visiting comedians, at others in a nightly talk and variety show with some improbable guests, ranging from unusual zoo animals to architect Frank Lloyd Wright. Moore also hosted the popular *I've Got a Secret*, in which a panel of celebrities tried to guess the secrets of their guests – a show Allen would later parody as *What's My Perversion?* in *Everything You Always Wanted to Know About Sex (*But Were Afraid to Ask)*.

Pleading overwork, Moore 'retired' in 1958, but returned in the autumn with a new prime-time variety show. Allen became one of its top writers, earning as much as $1700 a week. But he could barely conceal his distaste for the nine-to-five routine of the cigar-smoke-filled writers' room. He began to make his contempt visible, wisecracking about the show with *bons mots* in the style of his hero, George S. Kaufman. Also, again in the Kaufman style, he was working on a play, and thinking of how he might escape from the treadmill of TV comedy. He spent so little time in the writers' room that, according to Moore, his colleagues, noticing him trying to sneak out one afternoon, tried to tie him to his chair to make sure he'd be present for the next morning's meeting. 'Both his contributions and personal appearances were – well, random,' says Moore. 'As I recall, we fired him eventually for nonfeasance, which resulted in some kind of brouhaha with the writers' union. Our viewpoint was upheld.'

In 1960, Allen and Gelbart did a show for comedy veteran Art Carney, who had achieved belated fame as Jackie Gleason's sidekick on *The Honeymooners*. For the Carney show, *Hooray for Love*, Allen wrote an elaborate parody of Ingmar Bergman's *Wild Strawberries* which he liked well enough to have reproduced in Eric Lax's *On Being Funny: Woody Allen and Comedy*. While laboured in its sarcasm about art-house movie subtitles, the sketch does show Allen heading in a new direction. Gelbart called the sketch 'cerebral, somewhat cool'. But cerebral and cool wasn't what TV wanted, and after *Hooray for Love* Allen never again worked as a hired comedy writer for TV, except to write material he delivered himself.

By 1960 it was already apparent to Allen, and to most comedians, that their business was about to become infinitely more lucrative and popular. TV had so commodified comedy that stars like Sid Caesar and Red Skelton couldn't hope to satisfy the demand. With TV and radio now national media and record albums a major source of income, it seemed that almost anyone could be a comedy star. All around Allen, reputations were being made. Neil Simon was establishing himself as a playwright. At a party thrown by talk-show host Steve Allen (or, in some versions of the story, producer Joe Fields), Mel Brooks and Carl Reiner improvised a surreal dialogue in which Brooks played a two-thousand-year-old man being interviewed by Reiner about famous people he'd met, like Jesus ('I knew him well. Thin. Beard. Came in the store. We gave him water'). Afterwards, George Burns told them, 'Listen, you better put that on record, because if you don't, I'll steal it.' Their album on World Pacific Records, released in 1961, sold more than a million copies, and helped launch both the boom in comedy LPs and the careers of Brooks and Reiner as stand-up comedians. Even Allan Sherman, who had helped conceive Garry Moore's *I've Got a Secret* and who made up most of its weekly 'secrets', recorded an album of song parodies like 'Hello Mother, Hello Father', which became worldwide hits.

Most significantly, the Compass Players, a Chicago improvisational group that also produced Alan Arkin and Severn Darden, brought together writer Elaine May and aspiring director Mike Nichols. They became a popular and influential dialogue duo, specialising in improvised conversations redolent of Manhattan angst: lovers' tiffs between surgeon and nurse hissed over the anaesthetised patient; female analyst driven from emollient calm to shrieking jealousy by her delinquent patient/lover. Allen admired Nichols and May hugely, and, once he became a comic himself, drew on them for inspiration more than on any other single writer or performer.

The proliferation of jazz clubs, especially in California, fanned the market for live stand-up comedy. It was fostered in New York's Greenwich Village, a traditional hangout for students, artists and bohemians since the turn of the century. Revived in the fifties as returned soldiers from Korea studying under the GI Bill joined New York's floating population of semi-professional artists and writers, its coffee-shop culture incubated most of the major elements of sixties American style.

The tendency of jazz musicians to chat with the audience while setting up their instruments developed into a tradition of warm-up acts and, in the mid-fifties, stand-up comedians. Their doyen was Mort Sahl. Sahl had been a Californian college dropout with a fascination for jazz when, in 1953, a girlfriend suggested he put his wisecracking talent to work.

'Why don't you try out in this club in San Francisco?' she suggested. 'It's in North Beach, which is the bohemian area – which means a lot of Jewish people acting like Italians. Why don't you go to the hungry i?'

Sahl auditioned for the club's manager, Enrico Banducci, who, in imitation of the black bop musicians who played there, affected their trademark black beret. Banducci let Sahl work one night when their regular singer was ill. Sahl borrowed a suit from a member of the Stan Kenton band. The second night, the musician needed it, so Sahl went on in a sweater over an open-necked shirt. Nervous that he might forget his material, he carried a folded newspaper with the jokes inside. The paper and the sweater were to become his best-known props, as distinctive as Jack Benny's violin or Will Rogers' lasso and ten-gallon hat.

From the start, Sahl's work was as uncompromising as the bare brick wall and raw concrete of the hungry i. At the height of Senator Joe McCarthy's Communist witch-hunt, he joked that Washingtonians were wearing 'McCarthy jackets' – just the same as the military-style Eisenhower jacket with its flap pockets, except that the flap was over the mouth. 'Every time the Russians throw an American in jail,' he said, 'the UnAmerican Activities Committee retaliates by throwing an American in jail.' Sahl didn't mind scoring off personalities either. Anodyne talk-show host Johnny Carson never escaped the tag 'Prince Valium', which Sahl coined.

At Tamiment, Allen had written a sketch in which Milt Kamen played Marlon Brando advising a starlet on how to become famous (he shoots her, guaranteeing a spot on the front page). Sahl pushed past such obvious material to target the essence of Brando's self-serving public persona and that of other Hollywood stars. A number of actors, he joked, had been offered the role played by Tony Curtis in Stanley Kramer's 1958 film *The Defiant Ones*, in which racist Curtis escapes from a chain gang while manacled to black actor Sidney Poitier. One refused to work with a black; Kirk Douglas said he'd do it if he could play the black, and Brando said he'd do it if he could play both roles.

Seeing Sahl for the first time in person at New York's Blue Angel in 1954 confirmed Allen even more in his conviction that his own future lay in live performance. In Sahl's offhand manner, downbeat style and topical material, subsumed under the all-purpose adjective 'hip', one of the New Comedy's many borrowings from jazz, Allen thought he saw the answer to his image problem. Sahl demonstrated that educated audiences would respond to jokes that flattered their intelligence. As a girlfriend had counselled him, 'The audiences [in North Beach] are all intellectuals, which means if they understand you, great, and if they don't, they will never admit it because they will think it is whimsical humour.'

'Seeing Sahl,' said Allen, 'I felt I had two options, to kill myself or quit the business. There was nowhere to go after that. He cut a great figure in those days. He had a canine intelligence, he was witty and attractive. He wasn't a comedian in the old mode – some cuff-shooting tuxedoed guy who'd come out and lapse into comfy purchased material.'

Imitation being the sincerest form of flattery, Allen borrowed some of Sahl's material, notably a routine about a bank robber who slides a note across the cashier's desk: 'Give us all the money in the bank. Act normal.' The cashier returns it with the notation, 'Define "Normal".' This would blossom into an entire sequence in Allen's first film, *Take the Money and Run*, where Virgil Starkwell's attempt at a bank robbery founders when he starts arguing with the staff over his illegible writing.

Knowing that he wanted to be like Sahl and achieving this ambition were, however, two different things. At Tamiment, Allen had pushed his parody-driven comic invention to its limit, sometimes achieving a surrealistic frenzy that filled the stage with people wearing Groucho Marx glasses and moustaches, or depicted a convict stage show in which thugs present their annual awards for Best Murder, Best Robbery, Best Assault with a Deadly Weapon. Given the ease with which colleagues like Allan Sherman made the switch from writing to performing, Allen had no reason to believe that his ease in spinning jokes in the writers' room of a TV show or over coffee with friends couldn't be transformed into a successful stand-up act. But cutting back his invention to a single attenuated comic strand, delivered to a demanding audience in person, without props, supporting cast, even a setting, would prove to demand a discipline and confidence he lacked.

Len Maxwell, his friend from Tamiment, finally forced the transition. Harlene's philosophy course at Hunter had accelerated her intellectual development, and Allen, piqued, embarked on his own course of self-improvement. With Maxwell he'd spend one hour every day at a new art show, which they discussed as they walked home. During these walks Maxwell badgered him to drop Harvey Meltzer and to talk to his agents, Jack Rollins and Charles Joffe, who, among other talents, handled Mike Nichols and Elaine May.

Rollins and Joffe made an odd pairing. Rollins, born Jack Rabinowitz in 1914, was a Brooklyn boy like Allen, though old enough to be his father. He had little formal education, and relied on his nose for talent and a prodigious enthusiasm to get work for his clients. After working as assistant to theatre producer Max Gordon, he moved into personal management in 1951 when his wife, a singer herself, suggested he help an unsuccessful black crooner named Harry Belafonte, then running a tiny hamburger joint in Greenwich Village.

Joffe, sixteen years younger than his partner and a college graduate, had gone into the giant agency MCA after a brief career as a singer, but had been fired. After an equally unsuccessful attempt to be a band booker, he drifted into partnership with Rollins. The team handled a heterogeneous range of talents, most of them solo singers and comics bookable into the small clubs then mushrooming all over the country. They were the first New York management to handle Lenny Bruce, the comic who'd erupted from the jazz clubs of California with a line in savage improvised humour, blasphemous, drug-driven and often obscene – his autobiography was called *How to Talk Dirty and Influence People* – that created a sub-genre of stand-up, so-called 'sick comedy'.

In the spring of 1960, Maxwell's importuning of Allen began to have an effect. Rollins and Joffe ran a small café in Greenwich Village which used their clients as entertainment, and Allen went to see Rollins there. 'He asked if we could conceivably be interested in him as a writer of material for our artistes,' says Rollins. In particular, Allen thought he could write routines for Nichols and May. 'The answer was no. Because there was no need for any of the artistes we represented to use his or anyone else's material. They didn't need it.'

Discouraged, Allen tried Broadway. A manager had included two of his sketches in a revue called *From A to Z* with British comedienne Hermione Gingold, which opened at the Plymouth Theater on 20 April 1960. Allen hoped this might lead to his getting a full-length play staged, but the revue closed after fourteen performances. The failure chilled his Broadway ambitions. Sensing his moment, Maxwell said simply, 'We're going,' and led him to 200 West 57th Street, where, the café having closed, Rollins and Joffe now had their office.

This time, Allen made an entirely different impression on

Rollins. 'Woody wanted merely for us to manage his affairs in a conventional fashion, to better his career as a TV writer. But in talking to him, we felt for sure he displayed the talents of a director. He'd see things and say why something was handled right or wrong. Well, we just thought he had the potential to be a triple threat, like Orson Welles – writer, director, actor.' Allen diffidently suggested he might even try doing his own material on stage as a stand-up comedian. Both Rollins and Joffe were sceptical, but the moment he took out a new routine and began reading it, their opinion changed. 'He'd be dead serious when he read a sketch of his, but it hit us funny. He didn't know why we were laughing. He'd give a what's-so-funny? look. Very removed, he was. Quiet and shy. And the whole thing struck us as funny. He undersold everything.'

Not yet entirely sure of their belief in Allen, Rollins and Joffe suggested a six-month trial period. If for nothing else, they thought, he could be useful as a sort of resident writer, creating topical gags for non-showbiz clients. They shook hands – the only agreement they were to have in a relationship with Allen which continued for decades.

With Broadway apparently closed to him and TV writing increasingly unattractive, Allen found performance an interesting option. A few days after his meeting with Rollins and Joffe, he returned with a sheaf of new material, and requested that they find him a spot to try it out in front of an audience.

'The only thing you need is a showcase,' said Rollins. 'You need the Blue Angel.'

The Angel, at 152 East 55th Street, had a reputation as an elite venue. Jack Kennedy frequented it in his days as a senator. Belafonte and Pearl Bailey both made their reputations there. More recently, it had launched Nichols and May. Barbra Streisand had just made a hit there. (She and Allen knew one another, since in those days the future star of *Funny Girl* and *Hello Dolly!* lived in a cramped apartment over Oscar's Fish Restaurant on Third Avenue, where Allen would go for an easily digestible meal before his evening's stint on stage.) When Rollins brought in Allen,

Shelley Berman, a suave, nervous Jewish comedian with an *en brosse* haircut, sharp suits and a line of comedy phone-calls that had made him a national stand-up celebrity, was doing turnaway business.

The Angel was notoriously difficult to play. A red carpet laid across the footpath led clients into a front room decorated entirely in black, down to black patent leather walls. This room held the bar, and generated most of the club's income. The narrow back room, painted and carpeted in pink, might have been planned to resemble an open mouth, with the tiny stage, lit by a single motionless spot, stuck in the back of its throat.

Rollins took Allen to see veteran club manager Max Gordon – not to be confused with the theatrical impresario – who managed the Blue Angel with his partner, Herb Jacobi. Gordon recalled, 'We saw a kid with glasses and uncombed hair sitting at a table. The kid got up as Jack introduced us. He was a short, frightened kid with a weak handshake.

'"Meet Woody Allen," said Jack. "The kid is a writer. He writes the most brilliant comedy material in New York. But what does he do with it? Gives it away. That is, he sells it for peanuts to other comedians who are making a fortune out of it – Sid Caesar, for instance, Garry Moore, Peter Lind Hayes."

'Rollins warmed to his subject. "So he goes around with his toes sticking out of his shoes while others get rich on his material. So I said to him, 'Woody, why don't you get up and do this material yourself? Then you'd be rich and not the *shlep* you are.'"'

Woody lifted his eyes gravely at this build-up. Still unconvinced, but ready to do a favour for an old friend, Gordon agreed to give Allen a try-out.

In October 1960, Allen did his first formal stand-up date at the Blue Angel, following Shelley Berman – a daunting debut. By day, he was writing *The Pat Boone Show* with Larry Gelbart, who was in the audience that first night, and wasn't impressed. His partner came over, he thought, 'like Elaine May in drag. Out of nervousness, Allen squandered the initial goodwill of the audience, perversely recoiling into his shell at their early laughter. His delivery became monotonous as he relied on the intelligence of the audience to get the joke.'

The hostility of the crowd took Allen aback. 'I thought, gee, I write funny material, I bet I could get up and just read this to people and they would laugh,' he said later. 'I tried that. I took the sheets of paper out in the nightclub and it meant nothing to the audience. They wanted something else entirely. What [audiences] want is an intimacy with the person. They want to like the person and find the person funny as a human being. The biggest trap comedians fall into is trying to get by on the basis of their material. That's just hiding behind jokes.'

Nothing if not persistent, Allen told Rollins and Joffe he wanted to continue. He wrote some new material, and took it round to Rollins' house to read it for him and his wife Jane. As he sat on the couch and ran though a routine about the type of comic strips which the *New York Times* might run after it rescinded its ban on such triviality, the Rollins' baby daughter, only a few months old and fascinated by this newcomer, crawled over to him. Allen, never warm towards children, responded much as one might expect. 'She pulled herself up,' recalls Jane Rollins, 'and he looked at her and pushed her down. She toppled over, but she got up and he pushed her down, and she got up and he pushed her down again.'

After his disastrous audition, the Blue Angel had no further use for Allen, so Rollins approached a much smaller and less distinguished club on Grove Street, the Duplex, which, as its name implied, had two levels. The manager agreed to book Allen into the smaller of them, Upstairs at the Duplex, for two shows a night, six days a week. There was no raised stage, and not much of an audience either; sometimes he played to two or three people.

He later called his early time as a stand-up act 'the worst year of my life. I'd feel this fear in my stomach every morning, the minute I woke up, and it would be there until I went on at eleven o'clock at night.' It took all of Rollins and Joffe's confidence to reassure him that he hadn't made a dreadful mistake.

He wasn't paid, though a waitress would circulate with a hat which yielded a few dollars. Allen was attracted to one of these girls, a sensuous blonde named Vicki Tiel, who had ambitions to live in Paris. He christened her 'Peaches LaTour', and they flirtatiously planned the lost weekend in the French capital which neither imagined would ever take place. Otherwise, between shows, Allen cruised the Village. 'I'd just walk through book and record shops,' he reminisces, 'and try to pick up girls.' He was heartened to find that, whatever the reaction of women in Flatbush and Los Angeles, those in downtown New York didn't find his nervy charm entirely repellent.

Gradually, Allen won a following. Part of his appeal was the way he looked on stage – naked, helpless to defend himself against indifference or hostility. A puzzled psychoanalyst who saw him perform at this time recalled him in terms more appropriate to a patient than a performer: 'He was in a state of acute anxiety as he recited examples of his writings.' Rollins remembers, 'He was heckled once in a while, and he didn't answer them. He would stoically go through with his lines and do his twenty-five minutes like they weren't there, kind of look at them out of the corner of his eye. He would get up there and wrap that cord around his neck. You thought he was going to choke himself. Oh, and filled with nervous tics. Nervous, nervous. It was a sight. I mean, you just had to see him. It's hard to describe.'

Either Rollins or Joffe would drive Allen to the Duplex every night. Between the early and late shows they reassured him, like a trainer keeping up his fighter's spirit between rounds. Afterwards they'd take him out to the Stage or Carnegie delis, where they rehashed his routines and discussed audience reactions well into the early hours. 'Woody was just awful,' Joffe admits cheerfully. 'Of course, he had good lines. But he was so scared and embarrassed and – rabbity. If you gave him an excuse not to go on, he'd take it. Woody quit five or six times. We'd sit up all night talking him out of it.' Allen would fret, 'They're fighting me, they're fighting me.' Rollins told him, 'They have to know about you and care about you first. It'd be nice if you'd come out and say, "Good evening, how are you?" *Talk* to them rather than act.' Allen just stared at him.

He never made that sort of concession, but his delivery did

become more confident, and he learned to coax the audience out of its indifference before launching into his routines. Many who came to see him were college kids, the backbone of stand-up audiences. Allen would treat them like a class, explaining that a number of interesting things had happened to him since they last met, and that he was going to go over them for their benefit.

In 1961 Rollins took Allen back to the Blue Angel, and persuaded Jacobi and Gordon to book him for a long run. 'The salary isn't important,' Rollins told them. 'Pay him what you want. I want a place where he can stay awhile. I'll give you all the options you want. If he loses you any money, I'll pay his salary myself.' ('I took this as a metaphor', says Gordon wryly.)

Rollins was there every night to nurse Allen through his pre-performance agonies. 'He would walk like a small caged lion, up and back, up and back. He'd wear out a path. He worked the energy off by walking up and back.' Occasionally, when doubts assailed Allen between shows, Rollins called in Max Gordon to add his voice. 'Tell him, tell Woody he's doing OK,' he cajoled. 'He thinks he's terrible. He's ready to quit. You're doing terrific, you hear? Terrific! Tell him.'

Gordon did as he was asked, but privately he didn't believe it. 'Woody wasn't doing *that* terrific, a fact I didn't think it right to bring up at that particular moment. Woody hadn't yet learned how to deliver. Only sophisticates who were tired of being assaulted by nightclub comics welcomed his low-key *schlemiel* delivery. But he was learning. We kept him three months. We weren't paying him the kind of money that hurt.' Technically, Allen was still writing for Garry Moore, *The Pat Boone Show* having folded in June 1960, but the talk-show host fired him shortly after he began his stand-up career. 'I didn't blame them,' Allen said later, 'but after that I wasn't making a cent.'

In 1959 Allen had begun Freudian psychoanalysis, which he would continue until the nineties, and which he was to urge on his lovers and friends. It became the motif of his relationships and a source of material for his films and comic pieces. In many ways, it resembled religious conversion more than medical treatment. Far from, in

Freud's words, helping exchange unbearable psychosis for simple unhappiness, Allen's analysis acted as a hothouse for his chronic melancholy, coaxing it into, if not psychosis, then an artistically fruitful self-absorption. When, during the scandal of his relationship with Soon-Yi Previn, puzzled writers asked how someone who'd spent more than thirty years on the couch, sometimes as often as three times a week, could behave with so little insight into his own motives or the effect of his behaviour on others, psychiatrists were quick to explain that Allen wasn't in therapy, which aimed to correct a problem, but analysis, which merely helped one to live with it.

Like Catholic confession, Allen's form of analysis let the penitent go free to sin again – another sign of his affinities with an Italian-style emotional life rather than the stricter Jewish model. Allen obviously found analysis stimulating, even exciting. In many films he betrays a lubricious and voyeuristic interest in the analysis of others, similar to that which some Catholics harbour for the secrets of the confessional. There are few Allen films that don't contain an analysis scene. In *Another Woman*, *Alice*, *Zelig* and *Everyone Says I Love You*, characters overhear conversations between analysts and patients, while in *Annie Hall* we're treated to a split-screen comparison between Annie and Alvy's conversations with their doctors. In *Alice* and *Everyone Says I Love You*, the eavesdropping has specifically erotic overtones. In the former, Joe Mantegna, rendered invisible, sits in on the sessions of his ex-wife (Judy Davis) after sharing a changing room with statuesque model Elle Macpherson, while in *Everyone Says I Love You*, Allen's daughter, after overhearing Julia Roberts outline her ideals to her analyst, is able to coach her father in how to seduce her. In *Deconstructing Harry*, Allen's character Harry Block entertains erotic fantasies about his analyst – in real life, Allen's third analyst was a woman – and is elated when she suggests they break off treatment and resume contact as lovers. An analyst, after all, knows all one's secret sexual desires and, by implication, not only forgives them but is prepared to co-operate in satisfying them. 'You know all my secrets,' gloats Block. 'Every nuance of my psychic life. There isn't a feeling or desire that I haven't admitted to you during therapy. All my perversions – you accept them. My need to be tied up, to watch you with other women, to feel your spike heels in my mouth.'

At the root of Allen's entry into analysis was the failure of his marriage. Alienation from Harlene had developed into outright hostility, exacerbated by the new friends Allen was making in Greenwich Village. He was not the first ambitious man to find that a wife could only stifle his ability to exploit a newfound freedom and prosperity. 'He was leading a very schizophrenic lifestyle when they were together,' says his childhood friend Bryna Goldstein. 'In one year he would be making lots of bucks working for Garry Moore or Bob Hope, and the next year he'd be out of work and she'd be supporting him. She put up with a lot of very hairy creative insecurities and neurotic *schtick* and then didn't get around to any of the gravy. She was the one who got him where he is, and she was with him until months before his ship came in.'

Once Harlene had graduated from college, Allen's lack of interest in their marriage became more obvious. For her part, she opposed Allen's switch to stand-up. After seeing one of his early club appearances, she railed against Jack Rollins for taking a productive and lucrative writing talent and launching it into the choppy waters of performance.

Rollins, though, convinced that in Allen he had a major talent, likely to be as influential and popular as his other protégé Harry Belafonte, encouraged Allen by insisting on his superiority to other stand-up stars. Shelley Berman and Jonathan Winters, he said, were flashes in the pan, one-note talents who wouldn't last. Even Mort Sahl lacked the resources to grow and develop beyond the narrow confines of satire. Sahl, painfully aware of this, later dismissed Allen, who represented, he said, 'the degeneration of the Jew as a social force. To go from John Garfield to Woody Allen is putting in a lot of Clorox' – a well-known brand of bleach.

Stand-up did more than accustom Allen to working with live audiences and help him define his comic persona. On a more practical level, it introduced him to people who would become his future friends and collaborators. One was a nervy, finely-drawn young man named Dick Cavett, a one-time stand-up from

Nebraska who had been hired as a writer for TV talk-show host Jack Paar. Paar sent him along to check out this new kid.

Cavett saw Allen at the Blue Angel, and was as impressed by his material as he was appalled by the indifference of the crowd. 'About a third of the way through, the audience began to murmur and talk. Woody ploughed on, his face largely concealed by the mike, and ended, more by excusing himself than finishing, and left the stage to polite applause. They were mildly appreciative, but they would have preferred a folk singer, which they soon got. Woody had been casting pearls over the heads of swine.'

During the folk singer's set, Cavett found Allen and conveyed his congratulations. They sat in one of the club's sinister booths and talked. The two became close friends. Cavett, later a successful talk-show host himself, shared many of Allen's hang-ups. He had even, as an unhappy adolescent, mastered magic tricks.

Rollins and Joffe also managed a folk quartet called The Tarriers. Its banjo player was Marshall Brickman, who, as the fastest-talking of the group, did some impromptu warm-up gags while the others tuned their instruments. Early in the sixties, Brickman had what he called 'an epiphany on West 57th Street. I saw myself one day in a slightly warped mirror, carrying a guitar. There I was, a Jewish boy from Brooklyn, singing "Take this Hammer".' He got out of folk singing and found jobs as a gagman in TV. On the principle of 'putting his clients into bed together', Rollins introduced Allen to Brickman, who became a long-time friend, advisor and collaborator. Among the films they would write together was *Annie Hall.*

Allen also, as Rollins and Joffe had hoped, proved useful in writing material for other clients. After a Madison Square Garden anti-nuclear rally at which actor Tom Poston made a witty and effective speech, cartoonist Jules Feiffer, whose mordant comic strips for the *Village Voice* were earning him an international reputation, complimented him. 'Well, meet the guy who wrote it,' said Poston, introducing Allen. Allen and Feiffer continued to see one another socially. Feiffer followed Allen's rise in stand-up, attending his opening night at the Bitter End in 1961, and often catching his show thereafter. Less publicly, Allen was checking out Feiffer's strips for material.

Almost as important as the social and professional opportunities of the club scene, however, were the sexual ones. Particularly in Greenwich Village, casual sex was not only commonplace but nearly obligatory. Famously, Lenny Bruce's wife, ex-stripper 'Hot Honey' Harlow, had once posed herself naked, blindfolded, on her knees with her hands tied behind her back, just inside his dressing room, and fellated the first man to open the door. Allen didn't move in such circles, but, from his days on the *Colgate Comedy Hour* and at Tamiment, he was more than aware of what went on in them.

Allen was introduced to Louise Lasser by her boyfriend of the time, who'd decided they shared the same eccentric humour. To Allen, the voluptuous brunette, the daughter of a wealthy accountant from the Upper East Side, might have been invented with him in mind. She was even Jewish, though the Lassers lived like the most solid of WASP families and eschewed any sort of religious observance. She'd graduated from private school and started a university course in political theory before dropping out to join the restless youth culture eddying around Manhattan. Brought up by her father, who'd freely discussed sex with her and, when she fell for an older man in college, suggested she set up house with him, Lasser epitomised sophisticated sexuality to Allen. The talented but essentially shallow Rain in *Husbands and Wives*, casually seducing her professors with the complaisance of her parents, owes something to Lasser as Allen first knew her, though Lasser's adult persona is closer to that of Dorrie in *Stardust Memories*, neurasthenic, febrile, racked with incestuous guilt over her love for her father.

What Allen did not know was that mental disturbance ran in Lasser's family. Her mother had been hospitalised as 'incurably insane' as a result of her repeated suicide attempts. Lasser had saved her following one of these, but after three days in coma she woke to attack her daughter for having done so. 'I'll never forgive her,' she said. Lasser herself had dropped out of college because of clinical depression, a condition, exacerbated by drug abuse, that would trouble her for the rest of her life.

In 1961, however, Lasser, witty, sexy, available, was the partner

Allen had dreamed of. He began courting her intensively, even, in a perhaps conscious recollection of George S. Kaufman's idyll with Mary Astor under the same circumstances, trying to seduce her in a horse-drawn cab in Central Park. She resisted, but was soon a familiar friend of the family, often dining with Harlene and cronies like Jack Victor. One night Lasser rang the Allens to ask if she could borrow some bed linen. Allen wasn't home, but Harlene told her to come round and collect it. Later she told Lasser, 'I knew you had your eyes on my husband from the moment you came round to my house for those sheets.' Shortly after, Allen moved out, and started living with Lasser.

Allen embarked on a round of the national club circuit designed to establish him as a single act. Among the cities he played was St Louis, where transplanted New York entrepreneur Jay Landesman had opened a nightclub, bar and little theatre called the Crystal Palace. Situated in Gaslight Square, a self-consciously *fin-de-siècle* quarter, the club was dedicated to importing into deepest Missouri some of the sophistication of the east. Landesman made it a centre for jazz and alternative comedy, presenting Beckett's *Waiting for Godot* and hosting the Compass Players. Lenny Bruce did a brief season, commenting, as he stared at the *faux*-Edwardian stained-glass windows, that he'd never played a church before.

Landesman also booked Allen. Still unhappy on the road, he found St Louis alien, and the Crystal Palace daunting. In a letter to Joffe, Rollins and their secretary that strained, mostly without success, for the effect of Perelman's word-play ('I have managed to befriend a local artist who is doing enormous things with Silly Putty. He has some interesting abstract, non-objective items that the museum is quite agog about. He says that he will let them go for a song and while I feel he displays great skill and depth, I frankly can't sing that well'), he described the theatre as 'a study in anti-matter [which] turns in on itself. Rococo balconies abound in every drawer, and magnificent stained glass windows give one the feeling of being in the actual Crystal Palace.'

Cracking wise, as usual with Allen, disguised deep disquiet. Without Rollins to encourage him during the intervals, he fretted.

Landesman says, 'Woody was terrified of an audience. He used to pace the dressing-room floor muttering, "I hope they like me. I hope they like me." They didn't. At the end of each performance he'd make a long-distance call to his psychiatrist to get him out of his desperate situation. By the end of the first week his phone bill was larger than his salary. He felt so bad about his reception that he told us to give his cheque to the musicians "who at least earned it". By the close of his engagement we gave him a gold watch for bravery beyond the call of duty.'

Back in New York, Allen was calmer. His relationship with Lasser offered the first tangible proof of the rightness of his change in lifestyle. She was everything Harlene had not been. She could work with him and understand his professional problems, accommodate his moods and keep out of his way while he was writing, but be there when he needed companionship, consolation and cuddling. Above all, she was sexy, gratifying his taste for an exhibitionist partner. 'He was the first person I wasn't embarrassed with physically,' Lasser says. 'I would wander around the apartment naked and he would accuse me of flaunting myself, but really I was just enjoying that liberated feeling.' Allen was delighted to have his own private *Playboy* centrefold waiting when he returned from some distant stand-up date. He was less enamoured of Lasser's personal sloppiness, her vagueness about her possible career as an actress, and the periods of depression during which she would sleep around the clock, but he closed his eyes to all of them.

In 1961 he and Harlene were quietly divorced. The separation proved almost as liberating for her as for Allen. She moved to Italy, where she had an affair with a Florentine sculptor, then returned to America to flirt throughout the sixties with its alternative culture, living for a time in a Canadian commune and at Woodstock before settling down on the edge of Greenwich Village as an artist and, eventually, teacher. Anyone who tried to draw her on life with Woody was met by thin-lipped silence.

Gradually, Allen worked his way into his new life as a performer. In Dick Cavett he had a friend who shared not only his enthusiasms for jazz, magic and the great movie comedians, but some of his hang-ups as well: Cavett's career would be blighted

by periods of clinical depression. Playing Los Angeles, Allen found
Cavett writing for Jerry Lewis, and the two palled around the city,
hiring a large Cadillac and touring the stars' homes in Beverly
Hills, though in their case the stars were comics like Jack Benny,
Groucho Marx and Bob Hope. Through Cavett, Allen began writing material for Jack Paar, and became a familiar guest on TV's
proliferating night-time chat and variety shows.

Early in 1962 he appeared on *The Ed Sullivan Show* and *The
Tonight Show*, hosted by Jack Paar. Now, at last, Allen's parents
had tangible evidence that their son was a success. For his appearance with Paar, they invited the neighbours around to watch. One
of them recalled, 'I think the whole neighbourhood in Flatbush
must have been watching that night. Mrs Konigsberg had let it be
known that Woody was on. We were invited along to see it at their
house. We sat around and watched Woody do his act, which was
really very funny. Then I looked over at Mrs Konigsberg and it
seemed to me she didn't know whether to be pleased or not. She
wasn't laughing, and I remember wondering why.' Allen's mother
didn't like Allen's routines, including one which posited a society
where sex is accepted but eating is taboo. Paar hadn't heard the
material, was furious, and barred Allen from the show for years.

Allen's comic technique quickly hardened, becoming more nervy
and slick. It's hard to discern in those early appearances the
crumpled, diffident 'Woody' character of his films. This Woody
Allen is close to his real-life character, a cynical, upwardly mobile
Jewish intellectual. Realising he couldn't match Sahl's offhand
polish on stage, Allen made a virtue of necessity by working up routines which exploited the areas where he felt most vulnerable, in
particular his psychoanalysis. As part of group analysis, he joked,
he'd been a captain in the Saturday-morning softball games – Nail-
biters v. Bed-wetters. He traded too on his lack of education: he'd
enrolled in college courses like 'Advanced Truth and Beauty' and
'Death 101', he said, but cheated in the exams by looking within the
soul of the boy next to him. This wiry hipster in collar and tie, tweed
jacket and dark slacks, hair brushed forward in a style he later called
'silly', and which some people thought looked like a toupee, swoops
and dodges, primate-like, through his gags, hitting words hard,

over-emphasising some syllables, biting off others. Throughout, his right hand clutches a detachable microphone while his left grips the top of the microphone stand as if glued there. Here is a man living on his nerves, feeding off his fear, finding laughs in the face of disaster.

From 1962 to 1964, Allen was seldom off the road or out of the public eye. He routinely worked the club circuit of San Francisco's hungry i, New York's Bitter End, Mr Kelly's in Chicago, the Crystal Palace in St Louis, the Shadows in Washington DC, the Crescendo and the Troubador in Los Angeles. Often he followed or shared the bill with the same people as in New York. In 1963 he played the hungry i with Barbra Streisand, famous for having burst into the Associated Booking Office in New York, which provided talent for most of the jazz and comedy clubs. Finding Enrico Banducci, the hungry i's owner, there, she addressed him as 'that moron in the beret'. 'You're going to be down on your scabby knees,' she told him, '*begging* me for a contract before the year is out, you *idiot*!'

Allen grew accustomed to the perils of the club circuit: the fatigue, the insomnia, the sore throats as his untrained voice strained with performing in rooms filled with cigarette smoke. The much-remarked-on jars of honey and portable apparatus for making chocolate malteds in his dressing room had less to do with his sweet tooth than with his need for emollient drinks to soothe his throat.

'The simple fundamentals of working in clubs can be unequivocally learned in a month,' he said. 'I learned about the controllable externals in a couple of weeks, and I think these instincts are either inborn or give up – it's hopeless. This business about needing "ten years of experience" has no meaning to me.' Among the 'controllable externals' were the graft and kickbacks demanded by some owners and staff. 'I noticed,' he said, 'that in one club I played, nobody would be seated at the front tables unless they slipped the head waiter a five-dollar bill. Sometimes the whole club would be filled except for the tables right in front of me, and then in the middle of the act a group of four or five people would shuffle down front. Once, I followed Shelley Berman into a club, and he had all these signs up. "No waiters are allowed to serve while Shelley Berman is on." "This telephone receiver is to be taken off the hook while Mr Berman is performing."'

Owners were the bane of the comic's life. Some treated the performers as they treated their waiters. Others – which was almost worse for the reclusive Allen – liked to feel the comics were their friends, united with them in their view of the audience as 'patsies' and 'marks'. Dick Cavett recalled, 'I had one owner once told me in a place in Massachusetts to *mix*. And I said, "What?" He said, "I want you to mix. Come on, have some customers buy you a drink." I said, "Wait a minute, man. I'm not a broad." And the guy said, "C'mon, c'mon, I'll give the agency a bad report on you." I mixed.'

The club scene was a seething stock market of talent, some heading up, some down. The barman at the Gaslight in Greenwich Village and later the Wha? was so good at cracking jokes that the owner raised his salary to $7.50 a night. His name was Bill Cosby. At the hungry i, the stage manager was novelist, playwright and ex-Hollywood screenwriter Alvah Bessie. Jailed in 1947 as one of the 'Hollywood Ten' and subsequently blacklisted, Bessie was befriended by stand-up comic 'Doctor' Irwin Corey, who persuaded Banducci to let him run the lights. Bessie spent seven and a half years there, working up his salary to $105 a week – a far cry from the fortune he'd earned in Hollywood. He and Allen became friendly. 'Once we were coming out of a restaurant,' Allen recalled, 'and a man getting out of a car gave Alvah a cheerful hello. Alvah said, "How can you say hello to me, after the things you said about me?" And then he punched the man.' It was a lesson on the persistence of hate that Allen was to recycle in *The Front*.

When Allen played Mr Kelly's in Chicago, Jack Rollins asked an old friend, John Doumanian, a talent booker for Capitol records, to keep an eye on his protégé. Doumanian and his wife Jean took Allen under their wing, and Jean in particular, a tall, dark ex-model with ambitions in management, became his confidante. Even after they divorced, the Doumanians remained close to Allen, Jean finally becoming his business partner in the eighties. On the same date at Mr Kelly's, Allen asked if he could sit in with the band, on clarinet. Its members included Eddy Davis, who became a lifelong friend and playing partner.

Rediscovering his old enthusiasm for cards, Allen became a skilful high-stakes poker player, often returning to New York with his salary doubled at the card table. There were few jobs Allen would turn down – on *The Garry Moore Show*, for which he had once worked as a writer, he sang a duet with a dog. A film-maker hired him to crash New York's exclusive Four Seasons restaurant dressed in Confederate uniform. The manager firmly stopped him at the door. Marshall Brickman was working for Allen Funt's TV show *Candid Camera*, inventing gags to inflict on hapless members of the public, who were filmed with a hidden camera. 'It was our job to come up with all the humiliating vignettes that appealed to the voyeuristic psyche,' Brickman recalled. His main source of inspiration was the Manhattan Yellow Pages. 'If the directory opened at Roofing, we'd interview people for steeplejacks. If it opened at Home Nursing, we had to think again. It taught me how productive you can be if you have to. It certainly absolved me of any notion of creativity or inspiration. The train left each day and something had to be on it.' The 'something' was often Allen, who Funt used as an on-camera shill, giving him his first experience doing humour under film-making conditions. Much of his work on screen in his early films reflects the sight-gag model of *Candid Camera*.

In August 1962 *Newsweek* devoted an article to Allen as the most innovative of the young comedians coming up in the wake of Berman, Sahl and Lenny Bruce. In March 1963 the *New York Times* reviewed his appearances at the Blue Angel and the Bitter End as a fresh new departure in stand-up:

> Allen does not have Mort Sahl's brassy expansiveness or Shelley Berman's ferrety persuasiveness; nor does he indulge in the shock-for-shock's-sake approach practised by Lenny Bruce. What Allen projects – and his work has been called 'fresh', 'bright', 'individual' – is wistful futility. He is a waif in schnook's clothing – bedevilled always by the world and society.

By this time Allen could command $5000 an appearance. This was augmented by Rollins and Joffe's skilful exploitation. They insinuated him into magazine ads for products like whiskey – which he never drank – and encouraged Earl Wilson to let him, in effect, guest-edit his column during vacations.

Early in 1964, Colpix recorded Allen's appearance at Mr Kelly's for his first album, on the spine of which, he was chagrined to note, the company mis-spelled his name as 'Woddy'. The record was released in July, and sold moderately well, boosted by Allen taking over for a week as summer replacement for Johnny Carson on his popular *Tonight Show*. While he was still somewhat lower on the scale than Berman, and well below the hit-parade standing of Allan Sherman, Woody Allen was very far from the myth of a struggling and impoverished humorist. As one of the hottest comics on the stand-up circuit, he was earning $10,000 a week.

All the time he was working as a stand-up comedian, Allen was planning his next move. After the failure of *From A to Z*, producer Max Gordon had urged him to write something more ambitious than sketches, and he already had a few plots well advanced. He could also see himself as a film writer and, perhaps, director. In Los Angeles he confided his ambitions to Dick Cavett, who was impressed. By comparison, Cavett felt rudderless and undirected. In 1969 he would find his niche as a talk-show host, and would prove a valuable ally for Allen. One of his writers would be Marshall Brickman, and it was with Brickman that Allen made his first try at a feature screenplay in the early sixties. 'The Film-Maker' didn't inspire anyone, however, and it went on the shelf. Allen's ambition remained, though the chance to realise it didn't come, as he expected, from New York and the new world of stand-up comedy, but from the humour of his childhood enthusiasms, and from Hollywood.

8

What's New Pussycat

'Oh, son, I wish you hadn't become a scenario writer!'
'Ah, now, Moms,' I comforted her, 'it's no worse than playing the piano in a call house.'

S.J. Perelman, 'Strictly from Hunger'

The comedy and satire boom of the 1960s wasn't an exclusively American phenomenon. In Britain in particular, university students of the late fifties had developed a school of surrealist/absurdist comedy that was to dominate British humour for decades.

American movie comedy, derived from stage farce, was driven by situation: the perennial 'what if?' – What if John Barrymore's bankrupt theatrical producer and Carole Lombard as his ex-star and -lover met on the Twentieth Century Express? What if Bud Abbott and Lou Costello were stranded in a haunted house? Even revue artists like the Marx Brothers were shoehorned into 'vehicles' which demanded at least lip-service to a plot: what if Groucho became president of a university, or even of a country?

By contrast, British comedy retained the more fragmentary structure of vaudeville and revue, and those forms' amusement with word-play and satire. Its traditions were nourished by talents as miscellaneous as the Crazy Gang, Noël Coward and particularly Peter Sellers, projected to fame by radio's *The Goon Show*, who impressed Hollywood with his ability as a mimic and quick-change performer. In 1961 four graduates from the Cambridge Footlights, a noted hothouse of theatrical talent, arrived in London, via the Edinburgh Festival's experimental 'fringe', with a revue called *Beyond the Fringe*. Almost overnight, Alan Bennett, Jonathan Miller, Dudley Moore and Peter Cook became household names, and their offhand style of slim-cut black suits, drawling voice and cool, camp manner – an American would have said 'hip' – was much imitated. Their comedy, aimed, like that of Sahl and Allen, at topical social, religious and political targets rather than archetypes, spun off into television with shows like David Frost's *That Was The Week That Was*, which became obligatory viewing for Britain's chattering classes.

While this revolution was taking place, the European film industry was also flourishing, fanned by a low pound, a high US dollar, cheap technicians and facilities compared with the highly unionised American industry, and the readiness of governments like Britain's to subsidise local productions via its Eady levy on cinema seats, which kicked back a few pence on every seat sold to the film's producers. 'Runaway' productions flooded into Europe, and though most of these films were epics, comedy also benefited. Peter Sellers starred in *Lolita* and *Dr Strangelove, or How I Learned to Stop Worrying and Love the Bomb* for transplanted American director Stanley Kubrick, and for almost a decade did half a dozen films a year. Young directors like Clive Donner or the Canadian-born but London-based Richard Lester found it relatively easy to raise money: Lester for his films with the Beatles, who started their groundbreaking American tour in February 1964, or his adaptation of the play *The Knack*; and Donner for 'swinging London' comedies like *Here we go Round the Mulberry Bush* and particularly *Nothing but the Best*, also released in February 1964.

To make an episodic comedy in Europe, directed by Donner and starring an American, backed up by Sellers and some of European cinema's brightest young comics, in a script by an equally brilliant American comedy writer, was the idea of producer Charles K. Feldman. Described half-admiringly by Warner Brothers producer Robert Lord as 'the arch bullshitter of all time', Feldman, as president of the Famous Artists agency in the thirties, had been instrumental in launching the American careers of émigré directors like Anatole Litvak. By inflating their Continental achievements and surrounding them with an aura of intellectual exclusivity, he soon had studios clamouring to sign artists who were unemployable in

Europe. After the war, Feldman represented Hollywood's biggest names – Monroe, Garbo, Dietrich, Cooper, Wayne – and followed many other agents into talent packaging and production, assembling a string of hits built around his clients: *Red River*, *The Glass Menagerie*, *A Streetcar Named Desire*, *The Seven-Year Itch*. Such was Feldman's clout that, uniquely, Darryl Zanuck of Twentieth Century-Fox would deal with him personally, while others had to be content with underlings. In the trade he was nicknamed 'The Caliph' and 'King Midas'.

Following *The Seven-Year Itch*, Feldman fell victim to the US government's insistence that talent agencies separate themselves from production. Lew Wasserman, one of his main competitors, closed his agency, MCA, bought Universal studios and became a full-time producer. Feldman remained an agent, but switched his focus to less well-established artists, and to projects that would let him spend more time in Europe, where he maintained houses in Paris, London, Rome and on the French Riviera. He shared Darryl Zanuck's taste for svelte, elegantly turned-out European ladies, and maintained a string of them, both for his own entertainment and for the diversion of friends like actor Warren Beatty, whom Feldman regarded as a surrogate son and who was more or less permanently resident in his Beverly Hills home.

Feldman's European mistress in the mid-sixties was Germaine Lefebvre, a willowy French model with a mannish Nefertiti profile and a taste for Saint Laurent couture. At Feldman's insistence she abandoned the catwalk for movies, and changed her name to 'Capucine'. In 1964 she co-starred with Peter Sellers in the comedy hit of the decade, *The Pink Panther*, directed and written by American expatriate Blake Edwards from a play by the unknown Maurice Richlin.

The plot of *The Pink Panther*, in an S.J. Perelman phrase, was 'woven of summer-weight thistledown'. The cast of David Niven, Robert Wagner, Claudia Cardinale and Capucine found themselves, much to the irritation in particular of Niven, who was technically the lead, reduced to stooges for Peter Sellers. Taking over a supporting role originally written for Peter Ustinov, Sellers bumbled through the story as the incompetent Inspector Clouseau, chasing Niven's jewel thief whose confederate is actually Clouseau's own wife. Not for the first time in his career, Sellers stole the film. The action of *The Pink Panther* was familiar from French farce, and Feldman was not slow to see how, notwithstanding the fact that Edwards already had a sequel in the works, he could repeat it for himself, especially with Capucine and Warren Beatty in his pocket. He was even more confident when he persuaded Peter Sellers to take part.

Feldman grasped before his competitors that British comedy caught the *zeitgeist* in a way that Hollywood had so far failed to do. Not until Mel Brooks' *The Producers* four years later would it start to catch up. Once the British style became fashionable, Renata Adler, the *New York Times* film critic in the late sixties, deprecated its 'episodic, revue quality – not building laughter, but stringing it together skit after skit, some vile, some boffo'. But young audiences liked the new style, whether in TV series like *Rowan and Martin's Laugh-In* or movies like *The Pink Panther*.

Most of these movies were about sex – but less about its pleasures than its problems. As Roger Lewis remarks in his biography of Sellers, *The Pink Panther* was 'a sex comedy in which the characters don't get to have any. Claudia Cardinale's whorish princess gets drunk on champagne and passes out on Niven's Sir Charles; Capucine fends off Robert Wagner; Niven is always called away or otherwise distracted if Capucine comes close . . .' Clouseau in particular is cursed with a sexual itch that he can't scratch. Capucine invents pretext after pretext for not making love to him, including keeping him trudging from bed to bathroom in search of aspirin and glasses of water, or demanding a hot bath, leaving her erstwhile lover Wagner, equally frustrated, cowering, sodden, in the shower.

Feldman decided to repeat the *Pink Panther* formula, but with a healthier salting of sex. He'd chosen his time well. *Playboy*, launching its second decade, had become a national institution in America. 1964 was the year of Californian designer Rudi Gernreich's topless dress, the body stocking and, in London, Mary Quant's miniskirt. The phrase '*au pair*' entered the language, along with the potent fantasy, well-cultivated by the media, of foreign girls far from home and eager for experience. The American public hungered for more explicit sexual material on the screen, particularly if, like *The Pink Panther*, it came in a glossy European package.

Even though much of its nudity and many of its more provocative situations were cut before it reached the screen, *What's New Pussycat*, which *Time* magazine would dismiss as a 'bathroom farce', reflects this fusion of rampant sexuality and covert desire. British critic Raymond Durgnat would write:

> It's about a world of shamelessness, and not simply about sex. Where most people, however free in their thoughts, are, in fact, scared stiff of letting other people know about their immoral desires, their irresponsibilities, their spats, kinks and phobias, what's new about *What's New* is that it's about people who, instead of hiding them, display them as proudly as peacocks, and instead of ridiculing or resenting them in others, tolerate and enjoy them, so becoming as good-natured and obliging as they are colourful. The cavaliers ride again. It's interesting not just because it's the Kinsey Report as it might have been filmed by Mack Sennett, but because it's a festive escape from the general anxiety to be, or at least to appear to be, 'normal' and well-adjusted.

Feldman already had the ideal story for this film. *Mittel*-European playwrights of the thirties like Ferenc Molnar had refined the sex comedy to near-perfection. Feldman owned the rights to many such plays, including one called *Lot's Wife* by Molnar acolyte Ladislau Bus-Fekete, who specialised in the more domestic end of this market. His biggest success, winning an Oscar for director Ernst Lubitsch, had been the 1943 *Heaven can Wait*, in which philandering Edwardian husband Don Ameche always finds his way back to long-suffering wife Gene Tierney. Ameche recounts his adventures to Laird Cregar's Mephistopheles in the ante-room of Hell. The plot of *Lot's Wife* isn't much different, except that the interlocutor is a psychiatrist. Feldman had bought the play as a possible Cary Grant vehicle, and commissioned several scripts over the years, including one from Billy Wilder's writing partner, I.A.L. 'Izzy' Diamond. Raymond Durgnat, subliminally sensing the film's Viennese sources, would describe *What's New Pussycat* as 'Lubitsch on rollerskates'.

To turn *Lot's Wife* into a film that was half Sennett slapstick and half Kinsey Report, Feldman needed someone adept at what he called 'way-out swingers' comedy'; somehow who could mix American screwball farce with a wisecracking modern sensibility; someone, moreover, who regarded sex with guilt and pleasure in almost equal quantities. He thought he'd found him when, one Friday evening in the summer of 1964, he caught Woody Allen's stand-up act at the Blue Angel.

Allen had been spotted by Sam Shaw, a shambling, untidy photographer who acted as Feldman's Broadway legman. It was Shaw who wandered into the Rollins and Joffe office early in 1964 with an enquiry about their client. Rollins was in Los Angeles, but when he called that evening, Joffe told him, 'We had a strange character in today who works for Charles K. Feldman. What do you know? He likes Woody Allen.'

Rollins takes up the story. 'He came in to see Charley, wearing a sweater and sneakers. And in those days people didn't wear them on business visits. He also had a dirty old copy of the *New York Times* under his arm. If he was Woody's Good Fairy, he was the most unlikely-looking one Charley had ever seen.'

Shaw told Joffe that Feldman needed a young comic who'd never written for the movies. So convinced was he that Allen was the man that he'd persuaded Feldman to catch the show that night. Joffe immediately rang Allen with the news, inducing a case of nerves that wouldn't pass for days. The agent had been smarting from Allen's criticism that he and Rollins had done too little to find him film jobs after their failure to sell 'The Film-Maker'. The best they could manage was a vague proposal of a part with Marcello Mastroianni and Sophia Loren in *Ieri, Oggi, Domani* (*Yesterday, Today, Tomorrow*), a universally panned anthology of three mildly salacious stories which nevertheless was to win the Best Foreign Film Oscar in April 1965. He was also offered a small dramatic role as an ineffectual sailor in *The Bedford Incident*, a

Richard Widmark film about a nuclear stand-off which Stanley Kubrick's late partner James B. Harris was about to direct. (Taking on *What's New Pussycat* allowed Allen to turn down the role, which went to Wally Cox.)

Warren Beatty often claimed to have accompanied Feldman to the Blue Angel that night, but his companion was actually Beatty's sister, Shirley MacLaine, whom Feldman was trying to woo away from a long-term deal with Universal by tempting her with *Lot's Wife*. In 1964 the producer was sixty, suave, soft-spoken, with what journalist Sheilah Graham called 'a deceptive air of vagueness', and bearing more than a passing resemblance to Clark Gable. In a period of tight black suits, button-down collars and black ties, Feldman's casual European elegance impressed even as tough an observer of power dressing as Jack Rollins' wife Jane: 'The white polo coat,' she recalled respectfully, 'the silk scarf.'

What Feldman heard that night was much the same sort of material as on Allen's just-released album – routines rooted in his New York experience, most of it personal to him: growing up Jewish in Brooklyn, his recent move to an apartment on Central Park East opposite the Metropolitan Museum, and his attempts to pick up women there – a scrap of personal experience that inspired his *New Yorker* piece 'The Whore of Mensa'. There were bitter references to Harlene, 'the dread Mrs Allen', including one of his favourite slurs: 'The Museum of Natural History took her shoe and, based on her measurement, they reconstructed a dinosaur.' As usual, however, Allen's routines dwelt mostly on those areas where he felt even more sensitive, in particular his psychoanalysis.

Allen's friend and fellow comedian Bob Dishy was in the audience, and kept one eye on Feldman. 'I could see that Feldman really liked the show,' Dishy recalled, 'but Woody was nervous as a kitten. That Saturday we went to a movie, and he couldn't sit still. He was waiting for a call which hadn't come and he was beginning to get the jitters.' The call didn't come until the following week. Feldman sent Sam Shaw around to Rollins and Joffe with a proposition: $30,000 for Allen to write the screenplay for *Lot's Wife*. Neither Rollins nor Joffe had liked the screenplay for

'The Film-Maker', which may have made them too anxious to grasp this Hollywood deal. They accepted the $30,000, though it emerged later that Shaw had been authorised to offer up to $60,000. Allen, at the time as eager as Rollins and Joffe for the job, was bitter when the film grossed $14 million. In a line Perelman might have written, he joked sourly that Shaw 'offered [Rollins and Joffe] six figures for my services. After much haggling they picked one and a deal was made.'

Allen quickly realised he'd short-changed himself, and suggested also acting in the film in order to be paid more. Feldman agreed on $35,000 for both writing and performing. Given that Allen's fee for a single stand-up spot had risen from $5000 at mid-year to $10,000 by December 1963, the sum was still derisory. Joffe, however, pointed out how desirable it was for Allen to get into the movies. And Feldman insisted that the film would be an intimate low-budget comedy, shot in the style of the *nouvelle vague* and Richard Lester, probably in black and white, and demanding little of Allen's time. The deal also included an option on two more films, at an escalating pay scale, which considerably sweetened the pot.

Feldman continued assembling his ideal cast and crew by approaching Clive Donner to direct. Donner's reputation rested largely on *Nothing but the Best*, a 1963 comedy of manners about urban professionals on the make in the new London, with Alan Bates as an amoral young estate agent who gives room and board to seedy remittance man Denholm Elliott in return for the use of his Savile Row tailoring and upper-class *savoir-faire*. The film benefited, to a greater extent than anyone was prepared to credit, from Frederic Raphael's wittily sarcastic screenplay. Convinced, however, that Donner was its true *auteur*, Feldman offered him the choice of four feature subjects, including a script for Ian Fleming's first James Bond novel, *Casino Royale*, by veteran Ben Hecht, who had just died with the screenplay unfinished. Donner, the brashness of whose work disguised a diffident manner and nervous temperament, accepted the satirical comedy by the new and unknown Allen, the least daunting option.

Through the spring of 1964, Allen wrote the first draft of *Lot's*

Wife. Feldman offered him a copy of Izzy Diamond's version, but, fearful of being influenced, he refused to read it. Feldman didn't push him. 'Just write something where we can all go to Paris and chase girls,' he said vaguely before himself jetting off for Europe. It was puzzling advice from someone who hadn't needed to chase girls for some time, and was probably intended more as a personal temptation to Allen than as critical counsel. Still, Allen took it as a hint of the approach Feldman wanted, and wrote a story about, as he put it later, 'two Americans and their romantic adventures in Paris' – one of them his character, an unsuccessful painter whom he named, with the heavy innuendo that was to characterise the film, 'Victor Shakapopolis'.

As yet, Allen had no sense of structure. He still saw feature films as extensions of his stand-up routines: assemblages of sketches, parodies and pastiches, the construction that would typify *Take the Money and Run*, *Bananas*, *Everything You Always Wanted to Know About Sex* and *Sleeper*. Worse, he lacked the compassion necessary for high comedy, the interest in character that goes beyond the pleasure in autopsy that underpins satire. His stand-up routines depicted everyone, including himself, as absurd, pathetic or grotesque, and *What's New Pussycat* would bear their mark. One-liners fell thick and fast, but the pace of invention failed to disguise the coldness of conception, the emptiness of the life depicted. Feldman had hoped to see Allen's firecracker humour integrated into a coherent romantic story, like *The Pink Panther*. By refusing to read the Diamond script, however, Allen cut himself loose from narrative. So complete was the separation that the film's final credits bore no reference to either *Lot's Wife* or Bus-Fekete, and his widow announced her intention to sue, 'for either some financial or credit recompense', according to *Variety*.

Although the film's eventual star, Peter O'Toole, would describe it as 'brilliant, sketchy [and] Perelmanesque', the first draft of *Lot's Wife* wasn't what either Feldman or Beatty wanted. It relied too heavily, for one thing, on parody, mostly of Allen's favourite films. When the hero and his fiancée split up and he asks how she lives, she replies with Paul Muni's famous last line from *I am a Fugitive from a Chain Gang*, 'I steal.' The pastiche of Michelangelo

Antonioni which Allen later inserted into *Everything You Always Wanted to Know About Sex* is left over from this film. Allen also proposed Groucho Marx for the psychiatrist's role taken by Peter Sellers.

Feldman summoned Clive Donner to New York to work with Allen. The two collaborated for six weeks, 'revis[ing], reconsidering and polish[ing]', says Donner, 'nevertheless still keeping the very free-form farce/light comedy structure which we thought would find a reasonable audience who were open to something fresh'. He persuaded Allen to delete many of the film-buff references, including the ending, where Victor, trying to rob a bank, dies in a hail of police bullets like Cagney or Bogart in a thirties crime movie – and as Beatty would die in *Bonnie and Clyde* in 1967. Allen clung to it, and later tried to use it for *Take the Money and Run*. Of the rest, a vague *hommage* to *8½* survived, complete with an appearance by American opera student Edra Gale, who played the mountainous 'La Saraghina' in Fellini's film. Ursula Andress, who appeared as Honeychile Rider in *Dr No*, is introduced as 'a friend of James Bond', and there are nods to *Lust for Life* and *Moulin Rouge* with a walk-on by Toulouse-Lautrec, who joins Van Gogh at a table at the Closerie des Lilas, as well as a reminder of a popular CBS TV show of the fifties when O'Toole turns to the camera and says, 'A man's life goes down the drain – and You Are There.'

Allen found collaborative film-making dispiriting but educational. 'I had written what I felt was a very offbeat, uncommercial film,' he later told Swedish critic and film-maker Stig Bjorkman. 'It was not a factory-made kind of film. And the producers I turned it over to were the quintessential Hollywood machine. They undertook to execute this project with everything that everyone hates about Hollywood films. People that had no sense of humour deciding what's funny and what's not. People putting their girlfriends in roles. People writing special roles just to accommodate stars, whether those roles worked or not. The worst nightmare one could think of.' To *Time* magazine he admitted, 'I learned something about picture-making. When you're making a big picture for $4 million, there are a lot of people around, and they tell you they are Protecting The Investment. They wanted a girl-girl sex-sex picture to make a fortune. I had something else in mind. They got a girl-girl sex-sex picture which made a fortune.'

The main character of the new script remained Michael James, features editor of *Chic*, a Paris fashion magazine. Unable to resist the women who besiege him, James, also eager to settle down with his innocent and unpredatory fiancée Becky, consults a psychiatrist, Fritz Fassbender, who, though married to a mountainous and jealous opera singer, is even more badly afflicted with satyriasis than him. Fifteen minutes of James's confessions, he complains, is all he can take. The situation comes to a head when Becky's parents plan to visit Paris, and she demands that James either marry her or break off their engagement.

Though Michael is the romantic hero of the story, his friend Victor, an unsuccessful painter, is just as important a character, and has many of the best scenes, some of which recall the relationship between Crosby and Hope in the *Road* films. One of them at least made it to the final version. Victor works at the Crazy Horse strip club – 'I help the girls dress and undress,' he tells Michael, in one of the few exchanges in the script redolent of the Allen sense of humour.

'Nice job!'

'It's twenty francs a week.'

'Not much.'

'It's all I can afford.'

As if this were not frustration enough, Victor in the original script is also hopelessly in love with Becky, who shows no interest in him. Once Michael refuses to marry her, Victor, hoping to catch her on the rebound, courts her vigorously in the Bois de Boulogne, the Paris sewers and at a carnival. When she turns him down with, 'No Victor, not here,' even in the tunnel of love – a gag cut from this film but later used in *Love and Death*, where Diane Keaton fends off Allen even though they're married and sharing a bed – Victor decides his only chance is to murder James, which he attempts, ineptly, by turning up the steam at his health club. This merely drives everyone out into the street.

The plot sweeps Victor up with the rest of the characters and carries him to the Château Chantelle, a remote country hotel, for what the press release would insist was 'a hilarious chase in and out of bedrooms, resulting in utter confusion and chaos', but is in fact the millionth rerun of the farce form made classic by Feydeau, with rooms named after sexual legends – one guest sends down for a dozen loaves of bread and a Boy Scout uniform to be delivered to the Marquis de Sade Room – and people hiding in wardrobes, laundry baskets and under beds. The script ends in typical Allen wish-fulfilment, with Victor marrying Carol while Michael continues on his feckless way, Don Juan to the end.

Despite the script's deficiencies, Feldman remained confident about the film, which, on paper, had everything that *The Pink Panther* had, and Warren Beatty and Shirley MacLaine besides. As production loomed, however, people began having second thoughts. First to drop out was MacLaine. Her friendship with Dean Martin and Frank Sinatra's 'Rat Pack' had attracted the attention of their friends in organised crime, and MacLaine was warned of a plot to kidnap her daughter Sachi. She and her TV producer husband Steve Parker, who worked most of the time in Japan, decided they should begin spending more time out of the United States.

Next, Warren Beatty began to express doubts. Despite having starred in only two films, he already felt trapped by the Hollywood machine. In 1962 he made John Frankenheimer's *All Fall Down* at the behest of MGM, to whom he was under contract, but left the studio immediately after and, in an even more obvious gesture of independence, exchanged Feldman's guest house for a new pink stucco home on Sunset Strip. From there he announced that he was available for dramatic roles. He considered Herman Wouk's *Youngblood Hawke* and the John Kennedy part in *PT 109*, but eventually took the role of a male nurse in a mental hospital opposite Jean Seberg in Robert Rossen's *Lilith*. This tone of high seriousness would continue for the next few years. On a promotional tour of the Far East and Australia in 1967, Beatty announced that he would make press appearances only at institutes of high learning, and then solely with university professors. He never completed the tour, however, since, passing through London as part of the trip he encountered Julie Christie, with whom he immediately shacked up at one of the capital's best hotels.

Allen found writing for Beatty an unscalable barrier. Tall and classically good-looking, the actor already enjoyed a reputation as a serial seducer and marriage-breaker: his lovers included Joan Collins, Vanessa Redgrave, Natalie Wood and, most recently, Leslie Caron, in whose divorce case, as well as that of Wood, he was cited. His easy way with women supplied the film's title. Listening to Beatty working the phones day and night, Feldman got used to his conventional greeting, 'What's new, pussycat?' and attached it to the script.

Allen's hostility towards Beatty was predictable, a mixture of envy and dislike. For some years a quip circulated, attributed to Allen, that if he were to be reincarnated he'd like it to be as Warren Beatty's fingertips, but he later denied this. 'I *could* have said it,' he told Michael Blakemore, 'but I didn't.' Instead, Allen, who had always had to work hard for his women, and for whom sex without effort and guilt was inconceivable, found such people inexplicable. For most of his career, on the few occasions he showed sexually successful men in his films, Allen would do so with sarcasm and bitterness. Tony Roberts in *Annie Hall*, the old friend who has 'gone Hollywood', smacking his lips over 'twins, sixteen-year-olds. Can you imagine the mathematical possibilities there?' or Paul Simon's rock star Tony Lacey in the same film, who steals Diane Keaton from him (as Beatty was to do in real life), are both shown as preening narcissists. In *Manhattan*, Allen casts as Keaton's ex-husband and sexual dynamo the least probable actor in the world, dumpy, bald, squeaky-voiced Wallace Shawn, while in *Crimes and Misdemeanors* he lavishes all his bile on Alan Alda's womanising TV producer brother-in-law, about whom Allen's character is forced to make a documentary.

When success brought him more and better sexual partners, Allen came to realise that he and Beatty had much in common. Vicky Tiel, the costume designer with whom Allen was to have a flirtation during the filming of *What's New Pussycat*, remarked, 'The girls that would go with Woody are the same that would go with Warren because they were interested in being with men that are successful. But with Warren they would fall in love with him because he would dominate them sexually and Woody couldn't.'

Allen would sum up his ambivalence about, but final grudging acceptance of, the sexual advantages of celebrity in *Stardust Memories*. Returning to his hotel, where a group of grotesque fans are fêting him, his character, film director Sandy Bates, finds Shelly, a spotty-looking girl, in his bed. She announces she's there to have sex with him, and that her husband, sleeping downstairs in their van, will be 'honoured' by the fact.

Sandy acts scandalised and exasperated. 'Hey, look, I don't feel that well. I'm tired. I don't want to go through an empty experience.'

But Shelly brushes aside his protests as what they clearly are – gestures towards conventional guilt. 'Listen, empty sex is better than no sex, right?' she says briskly – repeating a line Allen first used in *Love and Death*, his 1975 satire on *War and Peace*, where he added, 'But as empty experiences go, it's one of the best.'

'Come on, don't be angry,' Shelly continues. As she makes room for him in the bed and turns out the light, it's evident from the immediate fade that Sandy's scruples haven't withstood the test.

In 1964, however, Allen's confidence was less robust and his guilts more galling. Beatty brought out all his instinctive rivalry.

Donner and Allen's rewrite made Michael's role not only shorter, but less sympathetic – something like the arrogant, seductive Alan Alda in *Crimes and Misdemeanors*. Once he had read it, Beatty became even less attracted to the project. 'Woody couldn't quite grasp what was funny about a compulsive, successful Don Juan,' Beatty complained. Though he diplomatically described the Allen/Donner rewrite as 'the funniest script I've ever read', Beatty had been hoping for a romantic comedy that showed Michael as poignant but not ridiculous; a Don Juan in the heroic mould, a victim of his need to love and be loved. In short, he wanted a character just like the one he and Robert Towne would write for the 1975 *Shampoo*, in which he would score a huge success as a sensitive but ambitious Hollywood celebrity hairdresser whose philandering ruins his relationship with his fiancée.

Beatty was further angered by Feldman's refusal to cast him opposite Leslie Caron, who had just abandoned her husband, British theatre director Peter Hall, to live with him. Feldman suspected, rightly, that this would put control of the film in the couple's hands. He also feared, again correctly, that they could soon become front-page news, and indeed Hall did sue for divorce, naming Beatty as co-respondent. In any event, Feldman, who after *The Pink Panther* believed he knew what sort of European women American audiences wanted, had already forced Allen and Donner to change the name of the main character from Becky – too Jewish, he thought – to Carol, and pencilled in some of European cinema's most seductive actresses, including Romy Schneider and Ursula Andress.

Instead of Caron, he cast his mistress, Capucine (who plays a character named Renée Lefevbre, not far from her real name), and Paula Prentiss, a leggy comedienne with a flat Texas drawl and poker face. Prentiss had had a patchy career in the US, seldom making more than one film a year. A serious drinking problem exacerbated her tendency to hysteria. 'The furies are all around us waiting to swoop,' she told a puzzled journalist on the set of *Pussycat*. But she had worked with Peter Sellers in George Roy Hill's 1964 *The World of Henry Orient*, and so knew the actor's oddities.

Sellers was proving the film's major problem. By the mid-sixties his prodigies of disguise in *I'm All Right, Jack*, *The Battle of the Sexes*, *The Mouse that Roared*, and in particular Stanley Kubrick's *Lolita* and *Dr Strangelove*, had made him the sole bankable British comedy performer. By playing one character, or a dozen, Sellers could, it was thought, carry any film, never mind the plot or lack of one. On his first visit to America in 1960 he'd been offered twenty-five roles by Hollywood producers, and in the next five years the flood didn't decrease. After his success playing three characters in *Lolita*, Columbia demanded he also play multiple roles in *Strangelove* as their price for investing in Kubrick's film.

Sprinting from film to film, restoring himself with heart-straining amyl nitrate 'poppers' that also fuelled his vigorous sex life, Sellers could not long escape a physical breakdown. It came in Hollywood in 1964. After having married the voracious young Britt Ekland in February, he was preparing *Kiss Me Stupid* for Billy Wilder when he had the first of a series of heart attacks. He made a quick recovery and was eager to get back to work, but the production guarantors on *What's New Pussycat*, aware that Wilder had to close down *Kiss Me Stupid* and recast Sellers' role with Ray Walston, demanded a £350,000 insurance premium. They also urged that Sellers' duties be kept as light as possible. So determined was Feldman to have the comedian in the film that he put up the premium from his own pocket.

In the summer of 1964, Feldman set up his production office in London. Allen and Joffe were flown in and put up at luxurious West End hotels. Feldman was angling for British government underwriting for the film. However, with Warren Beatty as its star, it had no chance of Eady funding. Allen complained that he was 'the fiftieth to get the news' that Beatty had finally bowed out and that Feldman had offered his role as Michael to Peter O'Toole, whose casting would guarantee British government support.

O'Toole had never done comedy on film, but after four years playing Lawrence of Arabia for David Lean, he hungered for a change. After trying to set up a low-budget production of Samuel Beckett's *Waiting for Godot*, he'd played Henry II in the film of Jean Anouilh's *Becket* opposite Richard Burton, who would obligingly do an unbilled walk-on in *Pussycat, and* Conrad's guilt-ridden hero in *Lord Jim*, then returned to the stage with Brecht's *Baal* and, in October 1963, an average *Hamlet*, directed by Laurence Olivier, in the National Theatre's temporary quarters at the Old Vic. With a major drinking problem and a sense that his career had lost its way, O'Toole embarked on a series of ill-advised Continental film roles, beginning with *What's New Pussycat*.

Allen sensed, like everyone else, that O'Toole was a calamitous choice. When someone commented on his commanding presence and piercing blue eyes, he said contemptuously, 'They put drops in them before every shot. And then they shine a baby spot on them from on top of the camera. Sam Spiegel had him fix his nose for *Lawrence of Arabia*. Never trust a man who's had his nose fixed.'

Where *What's New Pussycat* would be shot continued to be an open question, but the front-runner was Rome. Following the success of *Three Coins in the Fountain* in 1954, American film companies had flocked there, drawn by fine weather, cheap facilities and an almost total absence of unions. The Rome section of Feldman's little black book overflowed with useful numbers. Allen argued that the script was set in Paris, and that many of the gags hinged on locations there, but Feldman brushed aside his objections. 'Rome's the place,' he told Allen and Joffe, ordering them to the Italian capital in September 1964.

Allen would later become an enthusiast for Italy, but its charm escaped him on this visit. He was particularly nervous about the food. In what was to become his habitual culinary response to European cooking, he ate only grilled fish, or steak flown in from New York, and boiled vegetables, which he consumed with his usual absorption. If anyone joined him at dinner he'd hardly speak to them, not solely out of reticence but from an acute shyness about the act of eating. Film editor Ralph Rosenblum remembered that the first time they ate lunch together, he understood almost nothing Allen said, as if he had to speak while eating he always raised a hand to cover his mouth.

Feldman announced that shooting would begin on 1 October, but after six weeks in Rome he informed Donner and Allen that the production would be moving to Paris, at the behest of Peter O'Toole. Years before, O'Toole had been so harried by Roman *paparazzi* that he took a swing at some of them, following which the photographers put him 'on trial' and condemned him – though what penalty could be worse than their intrusive attentions wasn't clear. The thought of working in Rome again unnerved him, and to Allen's relief they moved to the Billancourt studios outside Paris.

Allen was installed with the other key personnel at the sumptuous George V Hotel, just off the Champs-Élysées, and in the same street as the Crazy Horse nightclub, where Victor works in the film. He felt a lot happier in Paris, if only because it was Europe's jazz capital. For years he'd wanted to hear soprano saxophonist Sidney Bechet, who'd lived and played there, but Bechet had died in 1959. Another hero, Bop pianist Bud Powell, later to become the inspiration of Bertrand Tavernier's 1986 film *Round Midnight*, had also just ended a long stay in Paris, and left for New York, where he died the following year. Allen had to console himself by visiting all Paris's cellar jazz clubs and becoming friendly with Claude Luter, a white clarinettist who fostered the black New Orleans tradition from the bandstand of the Slow Club, just off the rue de Rivoli.

He was no happier about the food, however, and after some unhappy experiences at pricy tourist traps like Maxim's (where he was ordered to put on a tie), he ate every night for six months at the same local restaurant, on an unrelieved diet of soup, grilled sole and crème caramel. Some nights he joined the high-stakes poker games which Feldman, a keen gambler, hosted. As usual, he won – enough to dwarf his meagre fee for the film. Otherwise he stayed in his hotel room, practising on the clarinet which, in a burst of generosity, the production had bought for him, nibbling Hershey Bars, another Feldman gift, writing, and reading the English-language papers, particularly the *International Herald Tribune*, which could still be bought from T-shirted girls in the Champs-Élysées, as Jean-Paul Belmondo buys his from Jean Seberg in *À Bout de Souffle*.

Though the conflict in Vietnam was rushing towards full-scale war and the ghettos of America's inner cities were aflame, papers like the *Tribune* remained preoccupied with the Soviet threat. In May the US Embassy in Moscow, acting on a defector's tip, had discovered forty microphones buried in its walls. Since 1949, the State Department announced, it had found 130 listening devices in American embassies around the world. The US government cut off aid to Indonesia following continued harassment of the embassy there. America's diplomatic outposts increasingly appeared as embattled havens of democracy in a hostile world. Since 1956 Cardinal Josef Mindszenty had lived in the US Embassy in Budapest, diplomatically untouchable in the midst of a Communist state.

Back home, Lyndon Johnson was running for the office of President he'd inherited on the death of John Kennedy. Officially, Allen supported Johnson – not a particularly difficult choice, since the Republican candidate was rabid right-winger Barry Goldwater, a lightning rod for satiric comedians and the growing support industry of magazines, T-shirts and bumper stickers, which turned his campaign slogan, 'In Your Heart You Know He's Right' to 'In Your Guts You Know He's Nuts'. Allen performed at an election rally held by a Democratic pressure group, Americans Abroad, at the Eiffel Tower; 'This is my first tower,' he told the crowd. Americans Abroad gave Allen a closer look at Paris's expatriate community, and reinforced his sense of being a foreigner in a hostile culture. The experience nudged him into starting work on the full-length play Max Gordon had asked for. For structure he studied John Patrick's Broadway hit *The Teahouse of the August Moon*, about Americans stationed on Okinawa after World War II. For content his inspiration was Kaufman and Hart's *You Can't Take it with You*, the story of a family constantly but comically bickering with itself. Allen invented Walter Hollander, a Jewish caterer from Newark visiting the Iron Curtain country of Vulgaria in 1961 who, unjustly accused of spying, takes refuge with his wife and daughter in the US Embassy, where a dissident priest is also in residence, and the oil-rich Sultan of Bashir is about to arrive on a state visit. His original title was 'Yankee Go Home!', but in an explicit reference to his fears about European plumbing, it became *Don't Drink the Water*.

At every turn, *Don't Drink the Water* betrays its roots, both artistic and personal. *Teahouse of the August Moon* is narrated by an Okinawan local, *Don't Drink the Water* by Father Drobney, the priest marooned in the embassy for six years who keeps himself sane but drives everyone else crazy with inept magic tricks – another Allen motif. *Teahouse* bypasses individuality to allocate each character a specific problem which the plot miraculously resolves; *Don't Drink the Water* is also plot-driven. It begins with a situation of chaos: the Hollanders and their daughter fleeing to the embassy, pursued by the secret police. In the absence of the Ambassador, the embassy is in the charge of his inept son, Axel Magee. The Sultan arrives with his wives, and a riot erupts as the chief of the secret police tries to force America to exchange the Hollanders for their own ace spy, just captured. The one efficient person in the embassy, the xenophobic First Secretary Kilroy, is struck on the head with a brick during a riot and becomes convinced that he's both Wilbur *and* Orville Wright.

Responsibility for the Hollanders and American prestige in general falls on the narrow shoulders of Magee, so maladroit that he was once declared *persona non grata* not simply by one African nation but by the whole continent (Allen saw himself in the role, and briefly considered playing it). The Hollanders bicker, the accident-prone Walter, given a gun to aid his escape, accidentally shoots Kilroy, their daughter Susan breaks off her engagement with her lawyer fiancé, Father Drobney is suffering from terminal cabin fever and the cook becomes hysterical at Walter's culinary demands. Things could not be more disorganised if the Marx Brothers were in charge.

Food and its risks pervade the play, with an emphasis on the shortcomings of European cuisine. Walter is proud of having pioneered the use of potato salad to sculpt the happy couple at the wedding banquets he caters for. He's on the phone constantly to Newark, raging about a food poisoning scare caused by his partner, while in the embassy he's nauseated by the dishes the chef serves up: oysters, eel, hare.

Most of *Pussycat's* stars were also staying at the George V, but Allen seldom met them, except under the artificial conditions of publicity shoots like one at the Crazy Horse, where he posed with the strippers to whom club owner Alain Bernardin had given fanciful pseudonyms like 'Rita Cadillac', 'Vodka Samovar', 'Akky Masterpiece', 'Vanity Obelisk' and 'Polly Underground' – a practice which inspired Allen to christen Paula Prentiss, who plays a Crazy Horse girl in the movie, 'Liz Bien'. 'I spent quite an hour and a half in there chatting with them,' Allen wrote to his New York press agent, Richard O'Brien. 'The fact that I didn't understand a word of it didn't matter. I just nodded my head, smiled, and kept looking.' He didn't mention that the publicist had had him photographed repeatedly as a nervous voyeur peeking round the scenery at half-naked girls, and had dreamed up a stunt in which some of them, stripped to the waist, play football with a likewise bare-chested Allen. Once the film had been successfully released the football pictures appeared, with a facetious commentary by Allen, in the August 1965 issue of *Playboy* under the heading 'What's Nude, Pussycat?'

Considering that Feldman had sold him on the idea of *What's New Pussycat* as a pretext to go to Europe and chase girls, Allen had little time for sex, though, in the tradition of 'It doesn't count on location,' it flourished all around him. When he was presented with opportunities, he fudged them. Staying with Feldman in Antibes, he was casually allocated one of his tame women for the evening. He shrank away from her, claiming later that she reminded him of his aunt, but it's more likely he couldn't handle this degree of sexual insouciance. To cap his grim experience of the Riviera, he made one of his rare attempts at outdoor sport by swimming from Feldman's private beach, and cut both his knees.

In Paris he went round town with Paula Prentiss and Capucine, but the only woman he ever looked like sleeping with was the girl assisting New York designer Mia Fonssagrives, hired to do Paula Prentiss's costumes. Allen recognised her as Vicky Tiel, who'd introduced his act at the Duplex in Greenwich Village and collected the money afterwards. Delighted to see a friendly face, Allen began dating 'Peaches LaTour', as he'd christened her in the Village. But he remained, in the words of Len Maxwell, the 'scared rabbit', frightened to take it further.

Tiel was also dating Clive Donner, and the crew, sensing the competition between the two men, planned a typical movie-location celebration for her birthday on 21 October. She recalled, 'The crew told us, "Look, this is the movie business! Everyone sleeps with everyone else in this business, so you two had better start joining in." That's when they devised the competition between Clive and Woody, both of whom had dated me, but neither of whom had gotten as far as first base.' Both men were challenged to present her with a lavish gift, the most generous and inventive winning the right to sleep with her. Donner offered Godiva's largest box of chocolates, but Allen scoured Paris for a pinball machine which, by acclamation, took the prize.

Nervously, Allen coached Tiel in the choreography of their big night. She was to come to his room, undress in the bathroom and, without conversation, join him in bed. There would be no troublesome 'date' beforehand, none of the rituals of drinks and dinner which, so often in Allen's early films and in his life, went disastrously wrong. If guilt-free sex existed, this was it. True, he had no strong emotional tie to Tiel – but empty sex . . .

The fabulous night with Peaches LaTour, however, never took place. In a scene that, once again, belonged in an Allen movie, Tiel, whether from cold feet or in a genuine *coup de foudre*, spent the night with neither Allen nor Donner but with a man she met at lunch that day, Ron Berkeley, Richard Burton and Elizabeth Taylor's private make-up artist, on hand for Burton's cameo appearance in *Pussycat*.

'I fell in love with Ron on the spot,' she says, 'and went to bed with him straight away. It was only in the morning that I realised I'd been supposed to spend the night with Woody. The next time I saw him was the following morning on the set, and I just didn't know how to apologise to him. He was absolutely devastated. He'd spent the evening getting himself ready and planning what we were going to do. I tried to explain. "I've just met the man of my dreams. I've fallen in love with him and I'm going to marry him." He said, "Where?" I said, "Over lunch." He was incredulous. He said, "Over *lunch!*"' He reproduced that moment in *Manhattan*. His character, Ike, warns his teenage lover that if she studies theatre in London, 'You'll be with actors and directors. You know, you go to rehearsal and you hang out with these people. You have a lot of lunches. And . . . attachments will form.'

Before Allen had a chance for any more sexual adventures, Louise Lasser rang from California with the news that her mentally ill mother, after a number of attempts, had committed suicide. Allen told her to fly to Paris, and she remained there for the remainder of the shooting.

Lasser's presence placed another pressure on Allen, who was already near to caving in under the problems of the film. For financing, Feldman had gone to United Artists, who also funded *The Pink Panther*. Originally set up by Charlie Chaplin, Douglas Fairbanks, Mary Pickford and D.W. Griffith to oppose the monopoly of the big studios and the commodification of star talent, UA had no studios and filmed nothing itself, but bought or financed independent films. It existed solely as a funding and distribution organisation, as which, under the administration of Arthur Krim and Robert Benjamin, it was highly successful. It had done well from the 'runaway' Hollywood production of the sixties, backing the independent companies of stars like Kirk Douglas and John Wayne as they made films in Rome, Paris, Madrid and Belgrade.

By going with United Artists, Feldman retained most of the autonomy he would have been forced to relinquish by a major studio, which would have put one of its own men in charge, but in return UA demanded strict accounting and took a hard line on creative excesses. 'A typical UA contract,' says Hollywood historian and ex-United Artists executive Steven Bach, 'reserved to itself standard approvals of script, director, cast, production manager, cameraman, budget, playing time, rating, composer, technical personnel, locations, raw stock, aspect ratio, processing laboratory, number of release prints, advertising campaign and budget, and so on.' By remaining as producer, however, Feldman guaranteed that he would take the maximum profit from the film should it be a success. It grossed $17.2 million, of which his share was a reputed $2 million.

A French crew was hired and supplied with copies of Allen's second script, rewritten with Donner. From what they could see, it was a pleasant little farce; so little, in fact, that Jacques Douy, one of France's best-known designers, turned it down, and suggested Feldman find some young *nouvelle vague* graduate accustomed to limited budgets. He recommended Jacques Saulnier, who had designed *Last Year in Marienbad* and *Muriel* for Alain Resnais, and the intensely coloured *Landru* for Claude Chabrol.

Saulnier's trademarks were tight, low-ceilinged spaces and walls painted in deep purples, greens and reds; all of which irritated his directors of photography, who had to pour enormous quantities of light into his sets. But Feldman already visualised the film as the embodiment of the way every American saw Paris: a cultural Disneyland of art nouveau nightclubs painted in the hot, dark shades of Toulouse-Lautrec, and sidewalk cafés where famous painters rubbed shoulders with whores with hearts of gold; a vision for which Saulnier was the perfect choice. 'When I was first approached,' Saulnier recalls, 'the film was very low budget. The script was entirely credited to Woody, and was very intimate and charming. All they wanted from me was two or three sets, very small; Michael's apartment and a few other things; a psychiatrist's office. Only about six or eight weeks' work, they said. It wasn't much, but I was young, and anxious to make my name, so I took the job.'

Serious trouble began when Peter Sellers checked into the George V with Britt Ekland. He and Allen met briefly in the hotel lobby. As usual in the company of other comedians, Sellers was alternately defensive and exhibitionist. In New York a few years before, he'd embarrassed his host Kenneth Tynan and everyone else at a party in the apartment of *Paris Review* editor George Plimpton by trying to trade gags with Mike Nichols. 'Nothing that Peter said amused Mike,' Tynan recalled, 'nothing that Mike said amused Peter; and the giggly facetious whimsical fantastic Goon-jokes of Sellers seemed merely embarrassing to Mike. I've never been more conscious of the abyss that separates British humour from the specialised world of Jewish Manhattan.'

The rivalry was exacerbated by the resemblance the newly slimmed-down Sellers bore to Allen. Occasionally, people even took him for Allen, as was to happen – disastrously for the production – on *Casino Royale* the following year. The resemblance made Sellers even more hostile towards Allen's script. All the meat was parcelled out between Michael and Allen's character, Victor, who had roughly equal shares of the story, and of its gags. His character, Dr Fassbender, was reduced to a few scenes set in his consulting room, a psychoanalytic version of Laird Cregar in *Heaven can Wait*.

'There were fewer scenes in it for him when he accepted the

part,' Clive Donner acknowledges. 'That was one of the reasons he had decided to do it – it wouldn't overstrain him. But something curious happened.' The 'something curious' was a campaign by Sellers, his heart condition forgotten, to win back at least half the film from whoever would surrender it, a repeat of his performance on *The Pink Panther*. O'Toole, given to violent mood changes, especially when drunk, was easily convinced by Sellers to make common cause against the diffident Allen, and even took to claiming that his character was based 'very much on me, in my scampish days'. Between them, the two men began improvising new sequences, and taking over those Allen had written for Victor.

'I felt that nobody seemed to understand what to do with the film,' complained Allen. 'Clive Donner had no power, because all the studio people were sitting on him and the stars were badgering him and forcing him to do things.' Allen watched, helpless, as Fassbender's consultation scenes with Michael became longer and longer. Sellers fell into his stock wartime concert-party imitations, while O'Toole played up (literally) to his repressed Lawrence of Arabia persona by telling Fassbender that his skill at cricket attests to his ability to control his carnal urges, and demonstrating his bowling action in Fassbender's consulting room. 'Is there any sex in it?' asks Fassbender. 'Cricket is a game played by gentlemen for gentlemen,' O'Toole tells him. 'Then it is sick, sick . . .' shudders Sellers – though not as much as Allen shuddered at these interpolations into his script. 'We did improvise a lot,' agrees Donner, 'and Woody was petrified,' though he insists he never changed a line without Allen's consent, which, he claims, was never withheld. With UA's accountants looking over his shoulder, Feldman wouldn't intervene. 'I didn't complain about Peter then and I won't now,' he said the following year, after having gone through a similar travail on his second film with Sellers and Allen, *Casino Royale*, 'even though he rewrote the script fifteen times. The only way to make a film with him is to let him direct, write and produce, as well as star it it.'

'It was an entire shambles,' says Jacques Saulnier, 'mainly I think because of financial problems. Every few days, someone from the production would come in with a new idea. I got the impression that each new actor demanded something different. I'd be working on a set and they'd say, "No, no, that's all been changed." They decided that the doctor's office should be in some sort of strange house, and I remembered one I'd seen in the suburb of St Cloud.' New scenes were written for the exterior of this bizarre building, a narrow villa in grey stone festooned with art nouveau metalwork, in which Fassbender's soprano wife pursues him up and down its staircases in her costume for *Die Walküre*, including spear.

For Victor, Saulnier designed an artist's studio, which Allen particularly liked. It was exactly, he told the designer, like the equivalent space in New York. But it too was dropped. Allen had also written an elaborate scene in which, as a despondent Fassbender tries to commit a Viking suicide by wrapping himself in the Danish flag and pushing himself out on the Seine in a burning rowing boat, Victor arrives with a collapsible table, a bottle of champagne and a chicken, and tries to celebrate his birthday. Saulnier built a set for the bank of the Seine and part of a bridge, only to have the production manager order it torn down. Later the scene was restored, with Donner using the real banks of the Seine, shooting Allen's dinner on the icy night of 1 December – Allen's twenty-ninth birthday.

Paula Prentiss, whose character Liz Bien emerged on film not as a lesbian but as alternately frigid and a nymphomaniac, with pretensions to intellect, became increasingly distraught by the combination of being far from home and being tied to a production in constant flux. For Romy Schneider's apartment, Jacques Saulnier had designed a bathroom with lots of mirrors. When Clive Donner saw it, he said, 'For God's sake, take down the mirrors, or Paula will freak.' Prentiss did hate the bathroom, claiming it reminded her of one back in the United States that had unhappy memories. Saulnier rebuilt it, while elsewhere Sellers and O'Toole improvised, and then improvised some more.

With a distracted Lasser to deal with at the hotel and the rival egos of his co-stars on the set, Allen quickly descended into depression. It's ironic that he should later criticise *Pussycat*'s producers for putting their girlfriends into the film, since this is exactly what he did. To divert Lasser, he persuaded Donner to give her a small role; she's the girl in an improbably long brown wig who massages Sellers' back during a group analysis sequence. Lasser had no ambitions to play comedy, didn't enjoy the experience, and later came to resent Allen for, as she thought, forcing her into it. Allen also tried to get a part for Vicky Tiel. 'It was ridiculous,' says Tiel. 'I was a dress designer, not an actress. In any case, Woody was a nobody on the set. He was totally eclipsed by Sellers and O'Toole. Nobody was listening to a word he said.'

So little notice did the producers take of him that Robert Rollis, who played a small role as a gas station attendant, was astonished to find out later that he'd worked with Woody Allen. 'This little man eating one banana after another on the edge of the set? I had no idea who he was, and since nobody paid him any attention, neither did I.' Rollis remembers the production with nostalgia, but not for its creative vitality. 'The production manager told me, "We'll need you for three or four days; maybe five." I eventually worked for fourteen days. The stars seemed to spend most of their nights at some cabaret, and didn't feel like working in the morning. There were lots of late arrivals. Peter O'Toole loved champagne, so most mornings the assistant director would tell us, "We're starting a little late. Mr O'Toole is a bit upset." "Upset" meant hungover, obviously. Once we did start, though, the atmosphere on the set was like a party.'

In this atmosphere, finishing *Pussycat* became increasingly troublesome. The ending in particular went through half a dozen versions. Allen had closed the story after the shenanigans at Château Chantelle, but Feldman demanded a conclusion more like that of *The Pink Panther*, which tops its country-house party sequence with a car chase ending in a multiple pile-up. Accordingly a new climax was written, in which Michael, Carol and many of the other characters, driven out of Château Chantelle by the police, pursue one another through a nearby village in go-karts.

The ending changed yet again when, in a final blow to Allen's self-esteem, Romy Schneider announced that she wouldn't be seen marrying a weed like him, and insisted on this being provided for in her contract. Sellers too was furious at an ending which featured

Allen and not him. After one particularly disastrous screening of rushes during which some of the film's hangers-on were outspoken in their criticism, Allen and Joffe lost their tempers. 'I told Feldman to fuck off,' Allen recalled.

Joffe agreed that Feldman was 'crucifying' Allen, who threatened to take his name off the film if the liberties being taken with his script continued. Feldman swore they would stop, then simply stopped telling him about them. Retreating with Donner to Sellers' house in England, O'Toole and Sellers spent a weekend composing a wedding scene for Michael and Carol, carried out by the local mayor, with Fassbender as best man, and Michael chatting up the mayor's secretary, played by pop star Françoise Hardy. The film ended arbitrarily, although it could seemingly have gone on forever, a sexual daisy chain endlessly adding new links in a haze of sex and booze.

For the rest of his career, Allen and his champions would dismiss *Pussycat* as unworthy of the later mature artist. They ignore the fact that, in its essentials, Allen's comedy didn't change. The plot, with its linked series of stories about unrequited love, reminiscent of Max Ophuls' film of Schnitzler's *La Ronde* and Renoir's *La Règle du Jeu* – both of which Allen much admires – would, with only minor changes, underlie later films like *Hannah and her Sisters* and *Interiors*, though Jessica Harper spells it out most wittily in a speech from *Love and Death*:

> It's a complicated situation. I'm in love with Alexei. He loves Alicia. Alicia's having an affair with Lev. Lev loves Tatiana. Tatiana loves Simpkin. Simpkin loves me. I love Simpkin but in a different way than Alexei. Alexei loves Tatiana like a sister. Tatiana's sister loves Trigorin like a brother. Trigorin's brother is having an affair with my sister, whom he likes physically but not spiritually . . .

As Foster Hirsch writes in one of the first books about Allen, 'The preoccupation with sexual image, the stereotyped sexual labelling of both male and female characters, the obvious envy with which the slick stud hero is regarded – these are to be staples of Woody's later work. When he had the freedom to make the kind of comedy he wanted, he turned out movies that are thematically similar to *Pussycat*. Woody's comedies are better, but they're not fundamentally different.'

9

Casino Royale and *What's up, Tiger Lily?*

INTERVIEWER: 'You're often portrayed as a loser in your films, Woody. Are you?'
ALLEN: 'I was. Now I'm a winner.'

British *Rolling Stone*, 30 September 1971

Allen arrived back in New York in the wake of Lyndon Johnson's re-election. The inauguration for his first full term as President on 18 January 1965 was accompanied by the usual celebration balls, and Allen, along with Johnny Carson, Rudolph Nureyev, Barbra Streisand and Carol Channing, was invited to play one of them. Later in the year he went to Washington again, this time to the White House for a banquet celebrating the artistic component of Johnson's Great Society.

The invitation flattered him. He mentioned it in newspaper interviews, joking that he supposed, like any good Jewish guest, he should take a cake as a gift to his hostess. At the reception, one of Johnson's daughters referred to this joke in conversation, which pleased him even more. Little Allan Konigsberg in the White House! 'God, if only our grandparents could see us now!' composer Richard Rodgers whispered to him. 'And I was thinking the same thing,' said Allen. After dinner with the First Family, he tried to phone Louise Lasser, thinking it would impress her to say, 'Hi, I'm calling from the White House.' But she wasn't in. 'It was so annoying,' he said, with a pique worthy of Andy Warhol.

Celebrity also had its downside. Allen found himself in court when a woman claimed he was the husband who had deserted her. He'd been a garage mechanic when they were married, she said, but also a great joker. When she saw Allen on television, she recognised him and his jokes immediately. Despite his protests that had he been married to this woman when she claimed, he would have been only thirteen, Allen was forced into two court appearances before the case was thrown out.

What's New Pussycat, not due to open until June, was in post-production in London. After Allen left, it suffered further indignities. Taking his tone from Jacques Saulnier's sets, British animator Richard Williams, whose visual style mixed *art nouveau* and psychedelia, the drug-inspired style being pioneered in San Francisco by designers like Peter Max, created a gaudy credit sequence and some special design features within the film, one of which particularly angered Allen. As part of his subversion of Michael's romantic image, Allen had him proclaim primly, 'Human fulfilment does not come from short physical random adventures, but from a deep relationship which is quite often right under one's very nose.' As he spoke these lines, a subtitle was supposed to wink discreetly, 'Author's Message'. Instead, Williams animated the words and added a rococo frame so that they occupied a quarter of the screen.

A score was commissioned from Burt Bacharach and Hal David. It included a theme song in waltz time, scored for a band heavy on the brass, and with lyrics that mostly reiterated the film's title. Guesting on *The Tonight Show* after the film's release, Allen would offer his own version of the words, bellowing them to a tune of even greater banality, but the original earned Welsh baritone Tom Jones a Grammy as 1965's Best New Artist, and the song reached the top ten.

Convinced that the film would flop, Allen returned to the stand-up circuit. In April he played the Shadows in Washington DC, a performance taped by Colpix for his second album, *Woody Allen Volume 2*. A lengthy segment was devoted to his adventures on *Pussycat*, which he describes as 'an autobiographical movie, based on the life of a great ladies' man'. As usual, however, his routine devolved into a recital of sexual failures and disappointments, one of them based on the failed assignation with Vicky Tiel. Getting ready to spend the night with a girl he's met at his analyst's, he tries to heat his hotel room by turning on the shower and leaving the bathroom door open. Hot, moist air meeting the icy draught from the window causes it to start raining over the bed.

1965 was a crossroads year for Allen. Even in the few months he'd been away, the comedy business had changed fundamentally. The satire boom was running out of steam. Comedy on record had proliferated, but most of it was simple-minded. The more successful comedians had priced themselves out of business, and were now looking to movies for a career; even Mort Sahl made a couple of lacklustre film appearances.

Fewer people were prepared to dress up, go out and pay at least $25 to see Bob Newhart, Shelley Berman or Woody Allen when television offered *Get Smart*, *F Troop*, *Green Acres* and *I Dream of Jeannie*, all of which first appeared in 1965, or that year's Emmy winner *The Dick Van Dyke Show* – ironically about the life of a TV comedy writer, with its producer, Carl Reiner, making occasional appearances as Van Dyke's employer, a tyrannical comic patterned on Sid Caesar. Clubs were going the way of the borscht belt hotels, whose family clientele had been melting away for a decade. Just before the country returned Johnson to the White House, Grossinger's in the Catskills held its first singles-only weekend. Singles bars and singles-only apartment blocks were springing up everywhere.

On 23 June, *Pussycat* went on US release. What path would Allen's career have taken had it flopped? Instead, despite almost entirely negative reviews from the major daily newspaper critics, and even from Allen's own mother, who thought it, according to Mickey Rose, 'a bunch of nonsense', it became the year's fifth biggest money-maker. Unexpectedly, the film even won some intellectual credentials when Andrew Sarris in the *Village Voice* confessed he'd seen it four times, and found 'each time nuances in the direction, the writing, the playing and, above all, the music. This is one film that is not what it seems at first glance. None of the characters are ever reduced to villains and stooges. Sex in this instance is a game that everyone plays with the same rules, and

Allen and Donner manage never to humiliate any of the characters.'

Since Allen had sole script credit, Feldman urged him to become the film's spokesman in the United States, and Joffe agreed; as long as the film was a success, he'd be a fool to pass up the opportunity. Allen found himself in the odd position of spieling a hit he despised. As he told Eric Lax, 'I was not in the position to tell the public, "It's not my fault, this is not what I would make as a picture." It was the whole approach to film-making that I hate and I've since demonstrated that it isn't my kind of film. But I've never had anything as profitable. *Pussycat* was just born to work. There was no way they could screw it up, try as they might, they couldn't. It was one of those things where the chemicals accidentally flow right.' Had they made his version, it would, he agreed, have been twice as funny and half as profitable.

Pussycat launched Allen as an international comedy star. *Woody Allen Volume 2* was released in the autumn of 1965, but he did less and less club work, especially out of town. He didn't need it, since offers poured in. He appeared on the television shows of Andy Williams and George Plimpton, and even on the rock programme *Hullabaloo*. Publishers and producers approached him to write or edit books, front TV shows, direct and/or star in movies and plays. He turned down most offers, but their proliferation showed him a path away from stand-up comedy.

Having money to spare meant that Allen could afford to be generous, and he bought his parents the first apartment they had ever owned. He also set up his father in a small jewellery engraving business in Manhattan. Now that their son was a national figure, the Konigsbergs let up on him. 'They pay him $10,000 for eight minutes on TV,' Martin said proudly, 'and little fortunes for plays and movies.'

After he returned from Paris and the *Pussycat* shoot, Allen had sent *Don't Drink the Water* to Max Gordon (the Broadway producer, not the club owner), who assigned a director, Bob Sinclair, to work with him on rewrites, only for Gordon to decide that it wasn't the play to bring him out of retirement. Stage success, however, was just a matter of time. Allen was *the* comic for the sixties. As critic John Lahr commented, his humour, being 'about emotional paralysis, was the right subject for uneasy times. A conventional society wanted the titillation of the unconventional. Lenny Bruce found vulgarity; Mort Sahl found politics; and Allen – best exemplifying his narcissistic era – found himself.'

The mirror in which the new Woody Allen could best see himself was the *New Yorker*. In common with James Thurber, Robert Benchley and S.J. Perelman, his acknowledged models or inspirations, Allen was a child of the magazine. When Harold Ross founded it in 1925, his manifesto announced that it wouldn't be edited for 'the old lady in Dubuque' – a town counted as an ornament of Iowa's corn belt, but not famed for its sophistication. 'The *New Yorker*,' said Ross firmly, 'is a magazine avowedly published for a metropolitan audience.' If Allen had been among the writers gathered at Manhattan's Algonquin Hotel when Ross tabled this document, he'd surely have put his name to it, and all the more readily for the fact that Ross was a man after his own heart, a perfectionist with a history of mental illness who shunned intimacy. In his memoir *The Years with Ross*, James Thurber recalls him unbending only once. 'God bless you, Thurber,' growled Ross. 'Goddammit.'

Increasingly testy as his sight failed – he was effectively blind by 1947 – Thurber had moped around the *New Yorker* offices – 'an aged, grey-eyed respected ghost', he told his friend Wolcott Gibbs. Colleagues got used to his favoured graffito, which he meticulously lettered in the most disturbing places: at a turn in the corridor, for instance, one word on one wall, the next around the corner; or on the inside of a lavatory door, to be glimpsed with sinking heart as they lowered themselves to the seat. The message was always the same: 'Too late'.

'Too late' is likewise an Allen refrain. The antinomies of his childhood, between hope and despair, fame and obscurity, love and death, the need both for company and to be alone, continued to drive his talent more relentlessly than ambition. In his spoken epigraph to *Annie Hall*, which he originally wanted to title 'Anhedonia' – the inability to experience pleasure – he tells a joke about two elderly women at a Catskills resort.

'Boy, the food at this place is really terrible,' says one.

'Yeah, I know,' replies her friend. 'And such small portions.'

Allen adds, 'That's essentially how I feel about life. Full of loneliness and misery and suffering and unhappiness – and it's all over much too quickly.'

From Dorothy Parker's jaded book reviews as 'Constant Reader', notably her dismissal of the baby talk of A.A. Milne's *The House at Pooh Corner* with 'Tonstant Weader fwowed up,' to the anguished cry of the Thurber husband, 'With you I have known peace, Lida, and now you say you're going crazy,' and Peter Arno's barman grabbing a garrulous drunk around the neck to snarl, 'Now let *me* tell *you* about *my* troubles!' *New Yorker* humour thrived on anhedonia. 'The humorist has to find himself in conflict with his environment,' said Perelman. 'He has to pretend he's sublimely unhappy in most places.' It's an insight that Allen was born to embody. His Upper East Side sensibility was tailor-made for the *New Yorker*. Who else but its readers would understand his jokes about New York garment manufacturers who had affairs with Emma Bovary, his parodies of Karl Barth and Søren Kierkegaard in the form of restaurant reviews that echoed the style of the slim books of philosophy and apologetics that were emblems of intellectual rectitude in sixties coffee-house Manhattan? For their benefit he peppered his work with references to Van Gogh, Ibsen and T.S. Eliot, and to his own Jewish background.

There was no market Allen was more eager to crack than the *New Yorker*, and in January 1966, after several rejections, it published his first piece, known in-house as a 'casual'. 'The Gossage–Varbedian Papers' was a comic exchange of letters, a form which the *New Yorker* had made peculiarly its own, and which both Perelman and Thurber used often. Chess had lately come to interest Allen, and he'd begun to take lessons, so he made his correspondents two intellectuals trying to play a game of chess by mail, but becoming increasingly confused and irascible. He was elated when his submission was accepted; so much so that he didn't quibble when the magazine's notoriously fastidious editors requested a new ending. 'I would have been willing,' he told Eric Lax, 'to turn the ending into an aquafoil.' In May they published another piece,

'A Little Louder, Please', Allen's satirical take on the fashion for mime. Thereafter he would publish two or three pieces a year in the *New Yorker*, with occasional excursions into magazines like *Playboy*, which paid more generously than the $1000 a piece offered by the *New Yorker*. It was the latter, however, to which his heart truly belonged.

Allen's early humorous pieces were frankly imitative of S.J. Perelman, often employing his technique of the ironic observation of popular culture in terms of high culture, though lacking his genuinely inventive literary style, nourished through the same Surrealist roots that fed the work of his brother-in-law Nathanael West. As Adam Gopnik remarked in a *New Yorker* profile of Allen, 'Perelman made Joycean jokes. Allen made jokes about Joyce.' Perelman's speculation in 'Genuflection in the Sun' that the overheated description of an egg cream in a soda fountain menu was written by a Theosophist poet, or his version of a scene in Santa's workshop in the proletarian theatre style of Clifford Odets' *Waiting for Lefty* were undoubtedly mirrored in Allen casuals like 'Notes for the Overfed', a meditation on a weight watchers' magazine in the style of Dostoyevsky. When editor Roger Angell told Allen pointedly, 'We already have one Perelman. We don't need another,' he dutifully changed direction, away from literary parody and word play, and towards a more ironic search for significance in the quotidian. His new model became Robert Benchley, troubled, muddled, querulously following the wrong track into a landscape of bumbling illogic.

The *New Yorker* set its mark on Allen's humour. Intellectual élitism was a key factor in the magazine's appeal to him, and vice versa. In contradistinction to Hollywood, being instantly understandable had never been its preoccupation. On the contrary, a certain obscurity was preferred, not to mention a sly affirmation of New York's superiority over the City of the Angels and pretty well everywhere else except Paris and London. It was, after all, the *New Yorker* that first published on its cover Saul Steinberg's illustration, since much imitated, showing a New Yorker's vision of the United States: the towers of Manhattan bulking huge, the rest of the country wandering off in an insignificant and featureless landscape, with Los Angeles a village on the horizon. Perelman, who served his time in Hollywood with his wife Laura confecting dialogue for the Marx Brothers and vehicles for Joan Crawford, described his experience there in terms Allen would have appreciated: 'We ourselves are still flailing away at this picture and are about halfway through a treatment which is purest cat-vomit. There is no rhyme or reason to anything in it, the characters behave as in a dream. From where we stand now, all we can see is a vast expanse of shit stretching away to the horizon.'

Despite the scorn for Hollywood that he shared with Perelman, Thurber, Dorothy Parker, Robert Benchley and the rest of the *New Yorker* community, the money remained in Allen's case, as in theirs, too seductive to refuse. Early in 1966 MGM invited him and Mickey Rose to adapt *Don Quixote USA*, a novel by Richard Powell about a bumbling Peace Corpsman trying to survive in the Central American dictatorship of San Marco. The studio planned it as a vehicle for diminutive comic Robert Morse, who hadn't found a niche in show business since his Emmy-winning Broadway performance in the 1961 musical *How to Succeed in Business Without Really Trying*.

Powell's unfunny book, closer in spirit to *Candide* than to Cervantes, turns on the single joke that the hero, Arthur Peabody Goodpasture, an expert on bananas mistaken for a CIA man, is blind to the dishonesty of the locals and the corruption of San Marco's administration. Set up to be shot in a staged skirmish with the rebels which the dictator hopes will attract American sympathy and support, he's instead captured by them. Winning their sympathy by improving their diet, he befriends the Castro-like leader, El Gavilan, and takes a lover from among the group. His stuffy WASP girlfriend, a news photographer, visits the camp and, not recognising him in his beard, has better sex with him than they ever had when he was a *nebbish*. Eventually, Goodpasture, assumed dead, takes over as President of San Marco, newly prosperous on its cash crop of bananas.

Rose and Allen worked up a forty-page treatment which they retitled 'El Weirdo'. Morse and his producer weren't impressed, however, so they shelved it and started work on the script for what would become *Take the Money and Run*, which they hoped Charles Feldman would agree to produce with Allen as director and star. Allen, in Hollywood during July 1965 for a stand-up performance at the Greek Theater and a guest appearance at the launch of Blake Edwards' comedy *The Great Race*, told *Variety* that the film would start shooting in September, with himself directing but Peter Ustinov as the star. The trade paper, in a further improbability, also claimed he 'planned a fall vidventure', i.e. television production, of *Pinocchio*. Both of these might have been examples of Allen misinformation, since he went on to say he'd written the Fassbender role in *Pussycat* hoping bullying *Lawrence of Arabia* producer Sam Spiegel would play it. 'He has hopes Spiegel yet will act in one of his screenplays,' the report continued. 'And, after meeting Jack Warner, Allen is equally anxious to cast the studio topper in a pic. Otto Preminger is another the youngster has mentally pencilled in for thesping.'

Take the Money and Run caught Hollywood's attention. The subject, a life of crime, was topical. Murder was in the air. In the summer of 1966, Richard Speck murdered eight student nurses in Chicago. Two weeks later, Marine-trained rifleman Charles Whitman opened fire on passers-by from the top of a twenty-seven-storey water tower in Austin, Texas, killing fourteen and wounding thirty. Documentaries on the lives of such killers jammed the airwaves. Allen and Rose parodied them in their script for *Take the Money and Run*, using a portentous narration as the skeleton on which to hang a series of gags built around the supposed career of one Woody Allen, bank robber and jail-breaker. Parody like this was more to their taste than 'El Weirdo', and they finished the first draft screenplay in a few weeks. The work on Powell's book wasn't wasted, however. Allen used its idea for 'Viva Vargas!', subtitled 'Excerpts From the Diary of a Revolutionary', which *Evergreen Review* published in August 1969, and the treatment was to become the basis of his 1971 hit *Bananas*.

Since *What's New Pussycat*, Feldman had been cruising Europe, trying to set up a new production. His first thought was a film as far as possible from comedy, but still using the most bankable performer he knew, Peter Sellers. In 1961, British-based producers Harry Saltzman and Albert 'Cubby' Broccoli purchased the rights to most of the James Bond novels of Ian Fleming, and began to create the films, starting with *Dr No* (1962) and *From Russia with Love* (1963), that would make Sean Connery an international star. They didn't, however, acquire the first book, *Casino Royale*, the rights to which Feldman had bought in 1960 from the estate of chubby actor/director Gregory Ratoff, who grabbed them as a speculation long before the Bond novels became famous as John Kennedy's favourite reading. Knowing Sellers fancied himself as a serious actor, Feldman suggested an adaptation of *Casino Royale* with him as Bond. Even Sellers' vanity was not equal to such a radical leap – despite the $1 million Feldman offered.

'You must be out of your bloody mind,' Sellers told him. 'Because what about Sean Connery, Harry Saltzman and all that kind of thing?'

'Yes, I know,' said Feldman, 'but I have this book and I am going to make it.'

'I certainly can't play James Bond,' Sellers said. 'It's not my scene at all.' Nor, as the Bond films continued to make money, were Saltzman and Broccoli prepared to lend Connery to Feldman, or to tamper with a successful formula by switching to Sellers. Ian Fleming himself was even less enthusiastic, not only because he'd sold the rights to *Casino Royale* for a mere $1000; no humorist at the best of times, he saw nothing comic about James Bond.

In the novel, Bond is directed to bankrupt 'Le Chiffre', Russia's spy paymaster in Europe, by playing him at baccarat in the casino at the fictitious town of Royale, in the south of France. Such a casino sequence would make an ideal climax for Feldman's film, but Saltzman and Broccoli had already featured casinos in *Dr No* and *Thunderball* (1965). The only other set-piece was a scene of Bond being tortured with a cane carpet-beater applied to his testicles – not, Feldman decided, ideal for family cinema.

Undeterred, he cast around for a new approach. As *Pussycat* began to rack up its eventual $17 million, he thought of filming *Casino Royale* against type, as a comedy – still featuring Sellers, but now in a comic role, and supported by some of the people who'd turned *The Pink Panther* and *Pussycat* into hits. Sending the novel to the best scriptwriters he knew, he invited them to come up with ideas of how it might be played for laughs. Meanwhile, Shirley MacLaine's negotiations with Universal for an extension of her contract had hit a snag, and the actress told Feldman she would appear in *Casino Royale* – almost certainly a bargaining device, though Feldman was a shrewd enough campaigner to leak the news immediately to the press, despite no contract having been signed. 'I signed contracts for all the actors on *Pussycat* after the picture had finished shooting,' he confessed casually to *Variety* when *Casino Royale* – *sans* MacLaine – was about to start pre-production.

Allen meanwhile had accepted what looked like an easy-money job. American International Pictures, a Hollywood company which by the mid-sixties had graduated from making starvation-budget horror movies to modestly funded Edgar Allen Poe adaptations and biker films like *The Wild Angels*, all directed by Roger Corman, ran a useful sideline in purchasing foreign films and giving them new titles and/or new footage with American actors. In 1963 they turned the inspirational Russian science fiction movie *Nebo Zovet* (The Heavens Call) into a monster picture called *Battle Beyond the Sun*. The UCLA film student disguised in the credits as 'Robert Colchart' whom Corman paid $250 to do the adaptation was Francis Ford Coppola. Joe Dante (*Gremlins*) would later transform *The Submersion of Japan* into *Tidal Wave* under similar conditions, and for only marginally more money.

Harry G. Saperstein, a Chicago theatre owner, had broken into TV in the fifties, producing *All-Star Golf* and *Championship Bowling*. Acquiring the inventive UPA animation company from its founder, Steven Bosustow, he merchandised its most successful character, short-sighted Mr Magoo, and produced *Gay Purree*, an animated feature by Chuck Jones. Renovating cheap Japanese features for the American market seemed a logical extension of his business, but the Toho company's *Kagi no Kagi*, an imitation James Bond thriller, was a poor choice to start with. Toho's own foreign version, dubbed by Japanese actors speaking execrable English and retitled *Keg of Powder*, was so bad that a preview audience began shouting comic rejoinders to the dubbed dialogue.

Seeing his profit slipping away, Saperstein decided to try to save his investment by adapting the profitable sideline of a rival animation entrepreneur, Jay Ward (*Rocky and Bullwinkle*). Acquiring silent movies from notorious movie pirate Raymond Rohauer, Ward added a facetious commentary in a comic accent by Hans Conreid and, to the horror of film scholars everywhere, released them in half-hour packages for TV as *Fractured Flickers*. Allen, the hottest new comic in the country, was an obvious choice to do something similar for *Kagi no Kagi*, and despite having signed up to play the Royal Box in New York's Americana Hotel throughout February, he accepted what looked like an easy $66,000 for turning the film into a sixty-minute TV special. Not blind to the value of exploiting Allen's last success, Saperstein – despite his protests, Allen claims – called the film *What's up, Tiger Lily?*

Using his animation connections, Saperstein shot new credits designed by Jimmy Murakami. At the beginning, an animated Allen crawls, rolls and leers over a series of pin-up pictures, extracting names from cleavages and navels. At the end, a live-action Allen lies on a couch eating an apple and, with evident boredom, watching China Lee, a *Playboy* regular (and Mort Sahl's wife), stripping to black underwear. She's doing her best to interest him, but the moment he shows signs of arousal, she cools off. These closing credits incorporate an eye-test chart, for people who've been reading them rather than looking at the girl.

Other animated elements and superimpositions crop up throughout the film. In one, Allen and Louise Lasser in silhouette play the projectionist and his girlfriend having an assignation in the bio box. In a nightclub striptease, red crosses and the caption 'Foreign Version' obscure a girl's naked breasts – a confusing gag to people who don't realise that nipples and pubic hair are routinely blotted out in Japanese films, even in preview prints intended for export. Allen also appears in an opening live-action sequence, sitting in a book-lined study and describing to an unseen interviewer his reasons for making the 'definitive spy picture'. 'Death is my bread and danger my butter,' he explains, then changes this to 'Danger is my bread and death is my butter,' before settling on 'Death and danger are my various breads and butters' – a preview of the first reel of *Manhattan*, where Ike, the failed novelist, rehearses openings for his autobiographical novel.

To fill the remaining forty minutes, Allen sequestered himself in a suite at the Stanhope Hotel in Manhattan with half a dozen friends, including Lenny Maxwell and Frank Buxton, ran the movie repeatedly, and kibitzed on it as he'd done in the old days at Brooklyn. Improvised jibes at the bad dialogue coalesced into a narrative in which the Bondian hero of *Kagi no Kagi* becomes 'lovable rogue' Phil Moskowitz, who's seeking the ultimate recipe for egg salad. Love interest is provided by two sisters, christened Terry Yaki and Suki Yaki.

The culinary reference is one of many Allen trademarks on the film; as he told Mel Gussow, 'Food and sex are always good for a laugh.' Sex appears in its usual Allen guise, draped in guilt and a sense of rejection: in a gag cut from *Pussycat*, Terry tells Phil, 'I'd like to tear your clothes off and make violent love to you right now,' but when he responds, complains, 'Oh, Phil, all you ever think about is sex.' Allen also incorporates the theme of a person with no roots and no home. With the egg salad recipe, Moskowitz hopes to win recognition for his nation, still country-less: 'People are still locked in crates . . . They're hoping for somewhere warm, between Greece and Spain' – in short, like Israel, another Allen theme. Yiddish words are scattered about. Wing Fat, the villain, talks about an egg salad 'so delicious you could *plotz*', and the search is commissioned by a 'high *macher*'. There's an archetypal Jewish mother ('You never write, so I decided to take a cruise'), and a dying Asian yells, 'Call my rabbi!'

Through January 1966, Allen played the Royal Box until 3 a.m., for a salary of $9000 a week plus a percentage of the gross, but would be in the Teachers' Sound Studio on Broadway by 7 a.m. to record the dialogue for *What's up, Tiger Lily?* He lived at the Plaza, whose views of Central Park always seemed to him among the most evocative in the city; he would feature them as the climax of the opening scene of *Manhattan*.

Since the suicide of her mother, he and Louise Lasser had seldom been apart, and the ease of the relationship thawed Allen's nervousness about marriage, although both still had qualms about such a step. 'He was reluctant because so many times before I'd backed away from the commitment,' she says. 'It wasn't that I was being mean – although he might say so – but I was troubled by a whole lot of stuff and I kept asking myself, "Should I or shouldn't I?"' The deciding factor turned out to be a prosaic one. Lasser's father and stepmother, whom she was insistent should be at the wedding, were about to leave on a world trip, so Allen quietly applied for a marriage licence and took the obligatory blood test for venereal disease – at which he fainted.

The day they chose, 2 February, happened to be Groundhog Day, traditionally the moment at which winter begins to turn to spring, signified by a groundhog in Punxatawney, Pennsylvania, emerging from his burrow and seeing his shadow for the first time since November. (The omens were dire, in fact; that day a massive snowstorm enveloped New York.) There were only five guests at the wedding in the Lasser home at 155 East 50th Street: Lasser's father and stepmother, Mickey Rose and his wife Judy, and Allen's friend from Chicago, Jean Doumanian. Allen invited his parents, but they refused to attend their son's marriage to a girl who, though actually Jewish, came on like a *shiksa*. The officiating judge, George Postel, a justice of the New York Supreme Court and friend of the Lassers, knew Allen so little that he called him 'Woody Herman'. Asked if she took the well-known bandleader as her lawful wedded husband, Lasser said 'No,' but Postel ploughed on. 'I always thought that would be my get-out clause later on,' she joked. 'I never agreed to marry *him*, technically.'

Loath to make too big an event of it, Allen held the reception quietly at the Americana, where he was then appearing. His old friend Jack Victor, who'd asked some weeks before to meet Lasser, was invited to the show that night. As he and his girlfriend finished their expensive meal and wondered how they would pay for it, the waiter told them they were Allen's guests, and asked them to join him upstairs. They found a wedding party in full swing, the first they knew of the marriage. Most of Allen's friends, even Len

Maxwell, who worked with him every day, had to read about it in the *New York Times*. When Allen turned up at the recording studio on the day following the wedding, Maxwell asked where Lasser was. 'Probably on the way to my bank with a fucking wheelbarrow,' said Allen dourly. His misgivings were an ill omen for a second marriage that would last even less time than his first.

Allen meanwhile was approaching another ominous crossroads in his career. In May 1966, Feldman optioned *Take the Money and Run* as the second film in his three-film contract. Any elation Allen might have felt was eradicated by Feldman's remark that it would take some time to raise money for a film with a newcomer like him as director, especially one shot, as Allen wished, in black and white. While he was doing so, would Allen give him a hand with *Casino Royale*, by helping to write the script, and also by playing a role?

Over the previous year, Feldman had invested all his energy in *Casino Royale*, accumulating half a dozen screenplays or treatments. Despite having been warned by Wolf Mankowitz that Peter Sellers was 'a treacherous lunatic' with whom he should on no account become involved again, Feldman persuaded him to appear by claiming that the story, like *What's New Pussycat*, offered two male starring roles of equal value, and that the other would be played by David Niven. Seeing the promise of another *Pink Panther*, Sellers agreed to play Nigel Force, an expert on card games who's roped in to play against Le Chiffre. Feldman then approached Niven and, using Sellers' acceptance as a lever, prevailed on him to play the super-spy. An old friend of Fleming – the writer had once nominated Niven as the actor he'd most like to see as Bond – he accepted. Privately, however, he commented, '*Casino Royale* is either going to be a classic bit of fun or the biggest fuck-up since the Flood. I think perhaps the latter.'

Stars in place, Feldman began looking for a director. Sellers demanded Joe McGrath, who had directed Dudley Moore in *Thirty is a Dangerous Age, Cynthia*, one of the films that helped launch the school of comedy *Casino Royale* was supposed to exemplify. Feldman, though, nervous about handing a $4 million project to someone so inexperienced, tried to recruit Clive Donner, but after *Pussycat* the director wanted nothing more to do with Sellers. British writer/director Val Guest eventually got the job. He'd been making low-budget comedies since 1942, and had just done a spy spoof, *Where the Spies Are*, written by Mankowitz and starring Niven.

'Look,' Feldman told Guest, 'I'm going to give you six scripts of *Casino Royale*, and I want you to try and get one out of them all.'

Among the writers who'd responded to Feldman's call were Terry Southern, co-writer of Kubrick's *Dr Strangelove*, and Joseph Heller, author of *Catch-22*, who in his own words 'worked for two weeks and wrote scenes nobody ever used'. Other contributions of varying length and relevance were made by Ben Hecht, Billy Wilder, Orson Welles and Dore Schary, ex-head of MGM. (Allen, when he came onto the film, was to join a swelling list of writers that included his friend and collaborator Mickey Rose, Frank Buxton, Joe McGrath, John Huston and Guest himself. Huston later asked Robert Bolt to do a quick rewrite of his episode, but the scenarist of *Lawrence of Arabia* dismissed the material as garbage.) Quizzed by *Variety* about the disposition of credits, Mankowitz suggested they should read 'Wolf Mankowitz and Friends'.

Guest did his best to rationalise this gallimaufry of parody, slapstick and dream sequence, but soon had to tell Feldman that making sense of the rival screenplays was impossible. Feldman declined his resignation. Sellers would arrive in Britain in April, and if they weren't ready to shoot, he'd lose not only the actor but most of the $1 million he was paying him. Guest agreed to work for seven weeks to launch the production, possibly handing over after that to another director. Though the credits would list Mankowitz, the unknown Michael Sayers and John Law as screenwriters, *Casino Royale* never had much more of a screenplay than the rough draft Guest cobbled together to start filming.

This puzzling document began with the leaders of the European secret services, including John Huston as M, head of British intelligence, and William Holden as the chief of the CIA, calling on Sir James Bond (Niven), now retired. Living in the highlands of Scotland, he spends his time in meditation and 'playing Debussy every night', explains M in one of the film's few good lines, 'from sunset until it's too dark to read the music'. They tell Bond that the world is being menaced by a mysterious mastermind, Dr Noah, who is threatening to unleash a deadly bacillus which will render all women beautiful and kill all men over the height of four feet six. Bond agrees to come out of retirement, and after an interlude in Scotland consoling the widow (Deborah Kerr) of another agent, joins a number of fake Bonds created by M in the hope of confusing Dr Noah, who is revealed as Bond's ineffectual but lecherous nephew, little Jimmy Bond (Allen).

This was to be a framing story for a parody of the original Fleming novel, with Sellers' character, now renamed Evelyn Tremble, taking centre stage. He would be sent to Paris, put in touch with the local head of British intelligence, be seduced by the beautiful Vesper Lynd and, through her, reach Le Chiffre for the big showdown. The script wasn't much, but it was enough for Feldman, who commissioned sets and started rounding up talent – at which point, according to Guest, the project started tottering dangerously.

'It just became a sort of psychedelic nightmare,' said Guest, 'because Charlie would ring me in the middle of the night and say, "Look, I can get Bardot next Wednesday. What set are we on? Well, write her in." I used to sit in his place while he conned people on the telephone.' William Holden and Charles Boyer agreed to play cameos out of loyalty to Feldman, who had been their agent before he got into production. Bardot reneged, but Peter O'Toole volunteered to do a bit in a bar. Feldman even had Ursula Andress, cast as Vesper, badger her ex-lover Jean-Paul Belmondo to appear. 'OK, I'll do anything,' Belmondo told Feldman at last. 'Just get her out of my hair!'

To play Le Chiffre, Feldman hired Orson Welles. At Cannes for the presentation of his Shakespeare adaptation *Chimes at Midnight*, Welles was asked by a journalist what criteria he used to select acting roles. 'Money,' he rumbled. Playing Le Chiffre was better than prostituting his bass tones on commercials for frozen peas and beefburgers, and he installed himself in a disordered apartment in London above the Mirabella restaurant, where amid emptied caviare pots and bottles of Dom Perignon he held jovial court.

It was at this point that Feldman approached Allen for his help. Given his famous proclivity for manipulation, it's entirely possible that he optioned *Take the Money and Run* just to hook Allen for the vastly more promising Bond movie. 'He was a big-time charming con man,' Allen says of Feldman, 'and I never trusted him on anything for a second. He was just an out-and-out, hundred-times-over proven liar to me. I worked with him knowing that.' He agreed to work for six weeks on *Casino Royale*, but as an actor, not a writer, a provision he insisted on being included in the contract; accordingly, he's not credited as a writer, though Feldman was able to coax him into doing a treatment for the last part of the film which contained his scenes as Jimmy Bond.

London was a magnet that year. Everyone seemed to be passing through. In March, Michelangelo Antonioni came to a party at Kenneth Tynan's, lurked around in a dark suit looking, wrote Tynan, 'grave and stricken', and later used the experience as the basis of his film *Blow-Up*. Welles was courted by admirers, including Tynan, who profiled him for the *New Yorker*, and Princess Margaret – the Royals were In, the queen having just given OBEs to the Beatles.

Feldman angled an invitation for Allen to the Royal Command Performance film, at which, unrecognisable in white tie and tails, and flanked by Raquel Welch and Ursula Andress – 'The girls look great,' he said later, 'but I look like a magician' – he was introduced to the Queen: protocol relegated Lasser to the second rank. Allen claimed to have asked the Queen conversationally, 'How are you enjoying your power?' but Lasser insists he was 'too nervous to say anything clever'. After the presentations, Allen and Lasser ducked into a convenient elevator, left the cinema, went back to their hotel and changed into comfortable clothes – 'very high,' said Lasser, 'just to be free.'

Though Welles was content with a flat, Sellers, as usual, demanded a suite at the Dorchester, his non-negotiable requirement on any film, even though he owned a large apartment in Hampstead. Allen and Joffe were also installed there, with most of the other writers and actors. Even so, they were supposed to be ignorant of one another's presence, Feldman fearing that any contact would dilute their ideas. But chance meetings in the lift led to a tradition of lunch together most days, and poker games in the evenings at which Allen was, as usual, often a big winner. Outside, however, the illusion of ignorance was continued for Feldman's benefit. Periodically, according to Welles, the writers would 'arrive at various hours at Charlie's house with our secret scripts, which he would take and put in his safe on the theory that our ideas were so brilliant that people would try to steal them'.

While Guest and Feldman played cat-and-mouse with the script-writers, *Casino Royale* metastasised through London's film facilities. In addition to the main set at Shepperton, others were built at Pinewood and MGM's Borehamwood. Dr Noah's plots demanded futuristic headquarters, while one of the fake Bonds, supposedly Bond's daughter by Mata Hari, was introduced in a German expressionist set inhabited by twitchy British comic Ronnie Corbett and an imperious Anna Quayle. Joanna Pettet plays Mata Hari, in a role at one time intended for the drag performer Danny La Rue. Hollywood stunt arranger Richard Talmadge was offered co-directing status to handle the fights and chases. Robert Parrish and Ken Hughes did the dialogue scenes not handled by Joe McGrath, who directed all Sellers' appearances. John Huston took charge of the Scottish sequence, and promptly escaped with Niven, Kerr and a large crew to Ireland, where he owned a castle and could ride to hounds. Later Feldman quantified the contributions of the five credited directors to the 129-minute running time as Huston thirty-eight minutes, Hughes twenty-five minutes, McGrath twenty minutes, Parrish twenty minutes and Guest twenty-six minutes; but by then everyone involved had lost count.

At Shepperton, on a 'closed set' which publicists hoped would induce curiosity about who was playing Bond, McGrath began work with Sellers, who was at his mercurial best and worst. Feldman's gift of a white Rolls-Royce on the first day of shooting hadn't improved his behaviour. Showing it off, Sellers drove to the premises of fashionable tailor Douglas Heyward and ordered forty-five suits, charging them to the production. Feldman refused the bill, saying he'd already provided Sellers' wardrobe. When Heyward complained, Sellers paid for the suits himself, but with ill grace, chiding him, 'That'll teach you never to make anything without a contract.'

Some of Sellers' scenes were dreadful, in particular a series of impersonations – Toulouse-Lautrec, Hitler, Napoleon – put on to amuse Andress. Others show his brilliant timing, including a meeting with Duncan Macrae as the Paris spymaster in a Paris *pissoir* ('Here are my credentials.' A glance down by Macrae: 'They appear to be in order.') Sellers and Andress also played an effective slow-motion love scene, mostly shot through an aquarium, to the accompaniment of Dusty Springfield singing the film's Bacharach and David theme, 'The Look of Love'.

Everyone was desperate to finish shooting before Sellers' health failed or his tantrums led to an open break with Feldman or the financing studio, Columbia. Allen's presence on the film angered Sellers, but according to Wolf Mankowitz, 'He was *terrified* of playing with Orson, and converted this into an aversion for Orson before he even met Orson.' Shortly before their first scene together, Sellers and Welles found themselves in a lift at the Dorchester. Sellers wisecracked about whether it could stand the weight. Welles regarded his insolent buzzing as a bull might a bee, which only increased his anger, already honed by Welles' magisterial manner on the set, and his habit of showing off his considerable skills as a stage magician; skills eventually incorporated into his performance.

Matters came to a head when Sellers invited Princess Margaret to lunch on the set, having given everyone the impression he was having an affair with her. He was unaware that the woman he called cosily 'Ma'am, darling' had known Welles since he did *Othello* on stage in London in 1949. 'She walked on the set,' recalled Welles, 'and passed [Sellers] by and said, "Hello, Orson, I haven't seen you for days!"' He went white as a sheet because *he* was going to get to present *me*.'

Sellers began a war of nerves. For a start, he told McGrath that he wouldn't appear in any shot with Welles. 'We were shooting

Panvision,' recalls McGrath, 'and the shots were very wide, so that caused a lot of problems.' Each actor played to a stand-in, and on alternate days. As a result, their scenes took two months to shoot. With dialogue often rewritten between takes, Sellers and Welles quickly slipped out of synch. 'When he asked me a question, my answer didn't make any sense at all,' chuckled Welles, relishing the 'marvellous surreal quality' of the result, but McGrath wasn't so amused. Sellers and the director came to blows, and Sellers, leaving the set on the pretext of making a phone call, returned to the Dorchester. In the lobby he was accosted by Leo Jaffe, the Executive Vice President of Columbia, which was backing the film. Mistaking Sellers for Allen, Jaffe told him, 'Don't worry about that guy Sellers. We'll take care of him. I'm sorry we ever hired him. But you're a gentleman, Woody.' Sellers, straight-faced, pretended to be Allen. The next day, he didn't show up at the studio.

For three weeks, Sellers' whereabouts were a mystery; in fact he was hiding with Britt Ekland's mother in Sweden. The casino scenes were stalled with, by Feldman's estimate, two thousand people waiting around on full pay for Sellers to reappear. Desperately, he promoted Val Guest to the dubious position of 'supervising director'. 'Look through everything we've got,' he told him, 'and see if we've got enough of him on film to make sense of his part.' When Sellers did come back, Feldman had no alternative but to fire him and close the production down. Feldman told Guest, 'You've got to write some links.' Guest, who had initially been hired for seven weeks, but who had already been on the film for six months, and would eventually work for nine, resignedly called back Niven and Andress, and shot some new sequences.

The stars went home, as did Joffe and Allen, loaded with loot acquired with his salary and his poker winnings, including an Emil Nolde watercolour as a gift for Louise. He also carried the fully revised script of his play *Don't Drink the Water*.

In June Allen's old employer, the columnist Earl Wilson, had asked if he was one of the writers on *Casino Royale*, which Feldman was desperately trying to salvage in London. Allen insisted that he was one of the few writers *not* working on it. The film, he said, was $5 million over budget. 'There's not a tiny role that isn't played by a big star. Charlie Feldman has spared no expense to make it an opulent production.' Seeing the piece may have nudged Feldman's memory about Allen, because he rang soon after and asked if he still had a carbon of the ending he'd written months before; the original had been lost. Allen mailed it off, and a few days later was on his way back to London, this time not only to play Little Jimmy Bond but to rewrite a film that, lacking Sellers, looked uncompletable.

Guest and Allen huddled in Guest's house in St John's Wood, a leafy suburb of north London, and an improbable milieu for Allen. 'He would do a scene and I would do a scene,' said Guest, 'and Woody would work over mine and I would work over his. And sometimes the scenes would come through the office, which Charles Feldman had suggested, and it was all perfectly smooth. I found Woody *completely* smooth, no problems at all. I mean, he was a very pleasant young man, but he seemed to live in a world of his own. Feldman was the one person Woody hated, because he had a terrible habit of making changes. We had a hell of a time trying to keep the script away from him and prevent him cutting our laugh lines. He'd go through all our stuff we'd beaten out, cut out all the gags but leave in the build-up! He had no *idea*. So Woody spent his time moaning to me, "This murderer! This murderer!" So I said, "Don't worry about it, we'll put it back, on the floor." And we did.'

Allen found time for freelance work. He appeared at the opening of the London Playboy Club, guested on local comic Bob Monkhouse's television show *Chelsea at Nine* and for Eamonn Andrews on his programme, and acted as one of the hosts for a TV circus and variety show called *Hippodrome* which required him, among other things, to step into the ring with a boxing kangaroo. In September Dusty Springfield invited him on her TV show *Dusty*. He also made a forty-minute comedy special, most of the material for which came from his 1964 club routines. Much of it was on the second Colpix album, which, to Allen's disappointment, wasn't selling as well as he'd hoped. It outsold the new albums of Shelley Berman and Bob Newhart, but never got higher on the

charts than number five. The most successful comedy album of
1966 was the lumbering musical parodies of Allan Sherman.

Writing to Rollins and Joffe publicist Richard O'Brien, Allen
reported optimistically that he'd been interviewed by some London
papers about the album, and that Kenneth Tynan was said to love
it, but there was an unaccustomed sense of the travelling salesman
in the way he displayed it in his comedy special, holding the cover
up to the camera.

Having written his part, Allen started work as an actor on
Casino Royale. Val Guest directed all of his scenes. Art director
Norman Dorme had built a giant futuristic set at MGM's Borehamwood studios, where Stanley Kubrick had shot *2001: A Space
Odyssey*. Wearing a uniform patterned on Joseph Wiseman's in
Dr No, Allen as Dr Noah runs through all the trademarks of the
villainous Fleming mastermind, showing off his culture by playing
the grand piano, lording it over a gang of underlings and doing
his incompetent best to torture a rival agent, in this case 'The
Detainer', played by Daliah Lavi. Unmasked by his uncle, he's
reduced to stammering recrimination, after which he commits suicide by swallowing the 'tiny time pills' advertised as the major
ingredient of a cough medicine.

As in *What's New Pussycat*, Feldman elected to finish the film
with an action spectacular, a brawl, directed by Richard Talmadge,
which demolishes the set with the help of every stunt man in
London, aided by more guest stars, including a group of girls in
gold paint (a reference to the demise of Shirley Eaton in *Gold-
finger*), the Keystone Kops, monkeys, seals, mounted cowboys,
masses of soap bubbles and Jean-Paul Belmondo as a French
Foreign Legionnaire. Before then, however, Allen was back in New
York, convinced that *Casino Royale* would be a 100 per cent flop.

10

Don't Drink the Water

The trouble with washing garbage is that when you're done, it's still garbage.

Composer Sheldon Harnick on rewriting plays for Broadway

While Allen was working on *Casino Royale*, he was also trying to find another Broadway producer to take on *Don't Drink the Water* after Max Gordon's decision to relinquish it. Racked with incompetence, corruption, superstition and stupidity, Broadway nevertheless retained much of its glamour, especially for native New Yorkers, and though the chances were enormously against comedies by even the most gifted writers – Carl Reiner's *Something Different*, for instance, would close in November 1967 after only a handful of performances – producers were besieged with plays. Even had he known the problems that would attend the production of *Don't Drink the Water*, Allen would have persisted. Ambition was by now the driving force in his character, outstripping even his innate sense of guilt and incompetence. Once the script fell into the hands of David Merrick, however, these would return, and in spades.

Some years later, during the post-production in London of his 1974 *The Great Gatsby*, director Jack Clayton was invited to the first screening of the credit sequence, made by a small independent company. As the camera panned and tracked over a bedroom strewn with discarded clothing and food scraps, the film-makers noticed something they'd missed in the panic of editing: a large blowfly droned into shot and settled just as the name of the film's producer, David Merrick, appeared on screen.

'We'll change that, of course,' a partner in the firm muttered embarrassedly in the dark.

After a long pause, Clayton murmured, 'No, don't bother.'

Merrick, who with Hal Prince was Broadway's most successful and prestigious producer of the sixties, invited such reactions. Dubbed 'Typhoid David' and 'The Abominable Showman', he was one of the few theatre entrepreneurs to bear comparison with pre-war leviathans like Jed Harris. His films were a sideline. He distinguished himself mostly with prestigious American stage premieres like John Osborne's *Look Back in Anger*, *Epitaph for George Dillon* and *Luther*, and Jean Anouilh's *Becket*.

But in 1964 his flair for publicity transformed *Hello Dolly!* from a minor musical into a showcase for a succession of ageing *monstres sacrées*, and he won notoriety for some of Broadway's most outrageous publicity stunts. When New York critics panned one of his shows, he found ordinary citizens with the same names as the critics and published their raves in splashy newspaper ads. For the opening of *Fanny*, he smuggled a nude statue of a belly dancer onto a plinth in the Poets' Corner of Central Park, and when his *The World of Suzie Wong* was running he hired pickets to parade outside the rival *Flower Drum Song* with signs that read 'The World of Suzie Wong* is New York's Only Authentic Oriental Show'. As ticket sales for *Look Back in Anger* flagged, he paid an unemployed actor $50 to climb on stage and punch Kenneth Haigh, who was playing Osborne's grating hero Jimmy Porter. Pictures by the press photographer who just happened to be in the audience that night made *Time* magazine.

The soft-spoken Merrick, born Margoles, always sported a dark suit – 'and,' remarked John Osborne, 'a mournful moustache and eyes to match'. He claimed to have left the law for Broadway because he thought he'd meet more girls as a producer, but if he exercised the *droit du seigneur* of the casting couch, he did so only in passing. 'Merrick,' observed Osborne, 'had an almost sinister obsession with the theatre which made his conversation quickly pall. He had scarcely any smalltalk except occasional satisfaction at someone else's out-of-town disaster, when the sad-dog eyes would brighten slightly.'

To Osborne, Merrick confided, 'I *hate* actors. I *love* writers.' But, growled Osborne, 'he liked writers in the way that a snake likes live rabbits. Unfortunately they were more difficult to dis-patch than actors. They could take their plays with them. It could be said that firing actors was his profession, producing plays his hobby. When he sat beside me at a rehearsal, if I made a note or said something to the director, he would turn hopefully. "What's the matter? You want me to fire him?" Fortunately, rehearsals seemed to bore, even mystify him. He preferred the out-of-town previews with the backers to appease.'

It was to this 'Rasputin', as New York journalist Tom Burke christened him, that Allen showed *Don't Drink the Water*. To his delight, Merrick agreed within forty-eight hours to produce it. He undertook to cast it with the best people, and to get the best designer to create the set; eventually it was done by Jo Mielziner, whose Broadway premieres included Eugene O'Neill's *Strange Interlude* and Tennessee Williams' *The Glass Menagerie* and *A Streetcar Named Desire*. Merrick probably never read the play, but relied on the opinions of people in his office. When he claimed to have accepted Tom Stoppard's *Rosencrantz and Guildenstern are Dead* from 'a single reading of the text', a colleague commented, 'That is the single most inconceivable event in the history of the world, since David doesn't read anything.' Another said in evident disbelief. 'I saw him reading a script once. It was open and so were his eyes. My conclusion can only be that he was reading.'

Merrick didn't need to read *Don't Drink the Water*. The ingredients were enough. Allen was a fashionable young comic, the subject was topical, and even with a cast of sixteen it wouldn't cost much more than the $100,000 of the average Broadway comedy. He scheduled *Water* to open at the Morosco in New York on 17 November 1966, after try-outs in Philadelphia and Boston.

Almost immediately, however, Merrick began behaving in compliance with his image. While Allen was in London working on *Casino Royale*, he'd cabled that he'd retained Vivian Vance for the part of Marion Hollander. Vance had been a staple of Lucille Ball's sitcoms *I Love Lucy* and *The Lucy Show*, playing her dumpy neighbour and best friend, a role for which she was required by contract to remain twenty pounds overweight, but in the autumn of 1965 Ball shed all her supporting players, leaving Vance looking for work. Allen protested that he'd based the Hollanders on his own parents, and wanted someone more Jewish in the role, but Merrick was adamant that a sitcom star would be good box office, and Vance was hired.

Max Gordon's director Bob Sinclair was still attached to the project, and Merrick began undermining his control, though it wasn't until try-outs that he was fired. As Merrick was too busy with other projects to find a replacement, Allen took over, but as later directors of his stage work like Michael Blakemore were to comment, he was too single-mindedly respectful of his text and too abrasive with his cast to be effective. His aggressive 'notes' reduced actors to depression or to tears.

Merrick installed Stanley Prager in time for the Boston preview, which brought about an immediate improvement to the production. At Prager's insistence, Kay Medford replaced a floundering Vivian Vance. The purge continued, House Jameson becoming Ambassador Magee and Tony Roberts his son Axel. Most important, Allen's first choice, Lou Jacobi, tall, fat and Jewish, with an absurd Hitler moustache, a fretful, scurrying style and querulous voice, was cast as Walter Hollander. Later, Allen said almost proudly, 'We made twelve cast changes – the most in history for a straight play out of town.'

Racked with a bronchial infection that drove his temperature to 102 degrees, Allen nevertheless rewrote large parts of the play on the road. Merrick, increasingly sceptical of success, suggested closing it down then reopening in Florida, where he had an interest in a theatre. Allen came to regard him, as had so many other playwrights, as 'like the angel of death. He'd come to the show and say, "Oh, they're going to back the scenery truck up to the theatre on Monday."' Certain jokes attracted Merrick's arbitrary dislike. When Allen tried to add a new line on opening night, having the Sultan ask Axel of the Hollanders, 'Are those people Jewish?' Merrick wanted it removed. Allen, backed by Prager, dug in his heels, and Merrick said, 'OK, but if that line plays, I'm firing the director.' It did get a laugh, but so good were the reviews that he let it – and Prager – stay.

On the play's first night in New York, Allen and Mickey Rose slipped away just after the curtain went up; the thought of enduring the first-night tradition of going onstage to acknowledge the applause brought Allen out in a cold sweat. Walking up Eighth Avenue, they shot some pool in McGirr's Billiard Academy, and, in a nostalgic reminder of their truant days from PS 99, dined at the automat on a typically bland Allen dinner of macaroni and pumpkin pie.

'Some nice people who looked like bookies came over and wished me good luck,' Allen recalled. He didn't need it. Though the play's structure remained ramshackle, he'd piled in enough one-liners and sight gags to satisfy the uncritical audience, if not the reviewers, who complained about the play's lack of coherence and its clichéd characters. The new cast played with vigour – almost too much in the case of Jacobi, who made such broad gestures on opening night that a cufflink flew into the audience. When they met next day at the Russian Tea Room, Allen joked that they should get Jacobi's wrists pierced.

Despite having ducked the opening night, Allen returned religiously throughout the run, seeing the play at least a hundred times, and giving notes to the cast afterwards every time – a practice that would wear down the performers in every one of his stage pieces. But part of him had already put *Don't Drink the Water* behind him. When he woke on the morning after the first night, he sat down and continued work on the project that was to follow it.

Harry Saperstein scheduled *What's up, Tiger Lily?* to open the day after the play's first night. Without Allen's agreement, he'd brought the film up to seventy-nine minutes by adding scenes from other Japanese movies, with an actor imitating Allen's voice (the *New York Times* index listed Allen's contribution to the film as 'Miscellaneous'). Another director filmed nightclub sequences featuring frug and twist numbers by John Sebastian's imitation Liverpool pop group the Lovin' Spoonful. Allen filed an injunction to stop this version being released, but while his irritation is understandable, it's hard to believe he was surprised that Saperstein acted as he did. Having paid $75,000 for the rights to *Kagi no Kagi* and $66,000 for Allen's rewrite, plus the cost of recording, new shooting and animated titles, he was rightly doubtful that television alone would repay his investment. Allen was confounded when the film did well – a success due in no small part to the Lovin' Spoonful, who had just had a hit with 'Summer in the City' (a subsequent *Tiger Lily* soundtrack album was, however, a dud). Reviews of the film were almost unanimously favourable. *Variety* predicted that, 'with Allen's name prominent in the sell, [it] will appeal to youthful camp followers, particularly ozoner [i.e. drive-in cinema] types, with OK or better b.o. likely on general deals.' Allen dropped his lawsuit. He seemed doomed to be popular for all the wrong reasons.

Anticipating the highly popular TV series *Rowan and Martin's Laugh-In*, which opened in 1968, and a school of comic paperbacks and magazines like *Help* which featured movie stills with added dialogue, and comedy sketches in the style of the Italian photo-romances called *fumetti*, *Tiger Lily* foreshadowed the demise of satirical comedy. In one aspect, however, the production conformed to its oldest and most revered traditions: despite worldwide distribution, none of the artists, Allen claimed, ever saw any money.

All the same, 1966 ended with him $250,000 richer, and looking forward to a 1967 in which he would earn twice that. In a season during which only a handful of plays ran longer than a week, *Don't Drink the Water* racked up 598 performances on Broadway, and might have continued had Merrick not periodically moved it around to clear the Morosco for other productions. Allen always retained a sentimental affection for the theatre. He was to shoot scenes in front of it in a number of his films, featured it in *Radio Days* and used it as the site of John Cusack's play in *Bullets Over Broadway*. Many people, watching that film thirty years later, tried to equate Cusack's problems with Allen's trials on *Don't Drink the Water*, but he denied the connection, instead insisting that he was 'protected' by Merrick. At the time, however, he was anything but complimentary. 'To me, he's Santa Claus,' he said of his producer, 'but with a Luger.'

The fact that their son had a play on Broadway mightily impressed Allen's parents. Martin Konigsberg proudly displayed posters for the play in the window of the shop Allen leased for him on Eldridge Street in Manhattan, and took the subway to the Morosco every day to pick up tickets which he sold to clients. He wasn't the only one to profit from Allen's new prosperity. Harlene, not heard from in years, filed a $1 million lawsuit against him and NBC, charging that his routines featuring 'the dread Mrs Allen' constituted 'holding her up to scorn and ridicule'. Allen believes a lawyer talked her into the suit as a means of skimming off some of his newfound wealth, and shrugged off the charge. 'Wouldn't it be funny if I lost,' he told columnist Leonard Lyons. 'It would take me at least six weeks to pay it off.' Harlene and Allen settled out of court in mid-1967, and haven't spoken since.

Allen and Lasser moved into a newly renovated six-room duplex occupying the top two floors of a brownstone townhouse on East 79th Street, just off Sixth Avenue. The rent was $900 a month: high for the time, and the area. Appropriately for someone who was to take a meticulous interest in the décor of his films, dictating interiors that hint at the preoccupations and social aspirations of his characters, Allen's homes, with their worn but comfortable furniture, open fireplaces, baskets of logs, kerosene lamps and walls decorated with Early American folk art and photographs of his heroes – Cole Porter, Sidney Bechet, Dostoyevksky, Houdini – would always reflect his character.

But sharing an apartment with Lasser brought his essential neatness and respect for hallowed objects into conflict with someone whom a valet described as 'the sloppiest lady I ever saw'. There was a sense of rival lifestyles crammed into too little room. A Matisse drawing leaned against the wall, unhung, sharing space with the Lasser family's wedding present, a film projector, as well as the jukebox Allen had bought her for her birthday and a pile of magic equipment. A full-sized pool table bought by Allen from McGirr's filled the 'library', a room so small that when a player reached back for a long shot, the butt of the cue thumped the wall. Not that the table got much use, any more than did the jukebox or the magic equipment. 'We had a beautiful bedroom which was decorated with antique French furniture, but in a cosy way,' said Lasser, 'but none of the rooms were really finished or anything.' It remained that way as long as they were married.

Through the end of 1966 and into 1967, Allen became one of the most widely profiled showbiz personalities, with articles in scores of papers and magazines. A long feature in *Life* showed him playing pool in his apartment, the shot carefully framed to disguise the room's smallness, mixing his favourite malteds with Lasser, practising on the clarinet and dealing blackjack at Caesar's Palace in Las Vegas, where, at the end of the year, he played two shows a night for two weeks for $50,000.

Initially, the idea of playing Vegas excited him. It showed that he had graduated. 'When I was breaking in down in Greenwich Village,' he said, 'I was told, "They like you down there, but we don't know about uptown. Your humour is very special." When I worked uptown, they said, "Well, it's New York. We don't know how they'll take you in other places." I wanted to go to Las Vegas and play the big hotels with the best jokes I could manage, not those terrible drunk jokes and the wife jokes.'

Las Vegas, however, confronted Allen for the first time with the juggernaut of fame. The man who identified with self-effacing humorists like Perelman and Thurber found himself a 'lounge act', equated with fellow performers on The Strip like Eddie Fisher. A thousand people jammed the Palace's club twice a night to hear such stars, sandwiched between massive floor shows in which showgirls paced regally in towering head-dresses, stiletto heels and not much else.

Even trying to get breakfast was a trial. Waiting in line at the hotel coffee shop, Allen cringed as other guests, flooding past en route to the slots that jingled and clattered day and night, pointed him out. When a glamorous 'hostess', dressed like everyone else at Caesar's Palace in mock Roman gear, spotted him in line and, calling his name, waved him to a table, Allen fled in panic, confiding to a friend, 'I guess I might have made it all right, if I'd gotten to a table. But I felt fear. I don't have the standard performer's personality.' Thereafter he ordered room service, and spent his time hiding in his room, practising his clarinet and working on screenplays.

He was, he said, 'a compulsive writer. I write every day. I feel this enormous guilt if I don't.' Even Allen's prodigious invention wasn't equal to the task of servicing the one-man industry he'd become, however, and Jack Rollins began quietly auditioning promising comic writers and performers, often from out of town, with a view to using their material. Among the young comics who did supply Allen with gags were two from Toronto, Hart Pomerantz and his partner Lorne Michaels, later producer of the hit TV show *Saturday Night Live*, which would nurture the careers of John Belushi, Dan Aykroyd, Chevy Chase and Bill Murray.

At the end of 1966, Allen and Lasser threw a combination New Year's Eve party and housewarming. Like his magazine feature articles, his guest shots on talk shows and on *Candid Camera*, his TV commercials and *Playboy* appearances, the references to his career in the columns of Earl Wilson and others, the party was designed to promote him as a major talent on the rise. With *Don't Drink the Water* and a hit Hollywood film to his credit, and all the stand-up dates he could want, he seemed to have reached the peak of professional achievement. His wife was beautiful, sexy and accommodating, falling in with his dislike of social life and a need to work that kept him locked in his room for fifteen hours at a stretch.

For the party, Allen bought an expensive video outfit and hired, in his phrase, 'an Oriental from Sony' to tape the guests as they arrived, encouraging them to say something for the camera. Twenty-five people were employed to help, including a chef. He planted numerous references to the party in the press, including an item in Earl Wilson's column: 'Woody Allen contributed to New Year's by planning a party where he'll turn his apartment into a discotheque with topless waitresses. *Flash Correction!* He was *going* to have topless waitresses. "I discussed it with my wife Louise, whom I married on Groundhog's Day. She said either they went or I went," said Allen. "*We* decided *Not* to have topless waitresses."' He did, however, retain the discotheque theme.

They invited 150 people, but between five hundred (Allen's estimate) and seven hundred (Lasser's) turned up, engulfing the apartment, draining the supply of liquor and carrying off some of the couple's possessions; they would find their Matisse on the staircase the following day. Appalled, Allen and Lasser sneaked away from the riotous scene, just as they'd ducked out of the Royal Command Performance in London. While the party raged they sat on the kerb in front of the house and cried, then shared sandwiches and sodas at a nearby deli. The moment was a turning point in Allen's life, as unexpected and inexplicable as the infantile transformation that turned young Allan sour and negative. 'The next day,' recalled Lasser, 'Woody was truly nauseous at the thought of fame.' By the first months of 1967, he was in full retreat from celebrity.

11

Take the Money and Run

Q: 'Why do you rob banks?'
A: 'Because that's where the money is.'

Bank robber Willie Sutton

Casino Royale, trimmed from a first cut of three hours to one hundred minutes, was released on 29 April 1967. Allen never saw it. 'I knew it would be a horrible film,' he said. 'The set was a chaotic madhouse. I knew then that the only way to make a film is to control it completely.' Nevertheless, with its Bacharach/David score, Richard Williams credits and a publicity campaign built around the image of a nude woman painted in Op Art colours, the film, despite its incomprehensible plot, broke records for the first three days of any Columbia release, and went on to become the year's third biggest money-maker. There was little hope, however, that it would ever earn back its cost, estimated by Wolf Mankowitz as $28 million. Feldman too paid a heavy price. Journalist Sheilah Graham was horrified at his appearance when he returned to Hollywood. In the nine months it took to make the film he'd aged ten years, she said. Like most people, she put his appearance down to exhaustion, unaware that he'd been diagnosed with pancreatic cancer.

Anxious to keep up the momentum of his relationship with Allen, Feldman pressed him to think about a new film. *Take the Money and Run* came back into play. Since Allen agreed to star only if he could also direct, and in black and white, United Artists grudgingly offered $750,000, which might have been enough to shoot the film in Britain. Allen and Feldman flew to London, where they tried to persuade Val Guest to repeat his *Casino Royale* role as co-ordinating producer and informal artistic guarantor of Allen's ability to finish the film. But Guest was too canny to accept this poisoned chalice. Then, in May 1968, Feldman died unexpectedly of complications following cancer surgery, and the film went on the shelf again.

Lasser won a Broadway role in *Henry, Sweet Henry*, a musical based on *The World of Henry Orient*, a novel, then film, about an egomaniac concert pianist victimised by two girls who, infatuated with him, follow him about, ruining his sex life by making nuisance phone calls, whispering, 'I know who you are, and I saw what you did.' Don Ameche played the role taken by Peter Sellers in the film, and George Roy Hill, who had also made the movie, directed.

Lasser, playing a married woman with whom Ameche is having an affair, went on the road with *Henry, Sweet Henry* in September 1967. Allen wired her from Las Vegas, 'Don't cause mischief on stage, don't be a pest and a jerk, and wash.' Before the Broadway premiere on 25 October, touted as the biggest event of a lacklustre theatrical year, he cabled, 'I'm bringing five hundred mice to your opening. Please be grand.' In the event, Lasser didn't have a chance. The show limped through a ten-week run and closed with a loss of $400,000.

Such failures were symptomatic of a city bored with itself, and with the world. The year's biggest movie was *The Graduate*, a version of Charles Webb's novel about an affectless nerd who solaces himself with loveless sex with an older woman. A film which reflected Hollywood's brief flirtation with Jewish angst during the mid-sixties, its director was Mike Nichols, reborn in a new career after the dissolution of his partnership with Elaine May, who had herself graduated to a new role as occasional actress and director, but mainly as Hollywood's most sought-after script doctor and comedy rewrite artist. Broadway itself offered hymns to elegant despair and alienation: the revue *Jacques Brel is Alive and Well and Living in Paris*, the first look at upmarket gay culture in *The Boys in the Band*, and *Promises, Promises*, a musical based on Billy Wilder's most jaded comedy, *The Apartment*.

· It was into this dismal milieu that Allen was invited to inject laughs when NBC asked him to write and present *The Year 1967 in*

Review as part of its occasional *Kraft Music Hall* series. The project represented everything he affected to dislike: topical humour, his least favourite kind; the certainty of network censorship, which he'd already experienced on the *Ed Sullivan* and *Tonight* shows; and the demand by the sponsors for some right-wing guest to balance Allen's supposedly liberal stance.

Allen wasn't as left wing as Kraft or NBC feared, however. His politics, always vague, moved substantially to the right as he became richer and more famous. Far from sharing the radical views of friends like Jules Feiffer, he was now largely indifferent to all shades of opinion. Against this background, his agreement to host *The Year in Review* becomes more consistent with his real attitudes, as does his choice of a conservative guest for the show. Journalist, editor and, eventually, novelist William F. Buckley Jr was the son of an oil millionaire. Educated internationally, he became America's most persuasive spokesman for the far right. In 1954 he'd defended Senator Joe McCarthy and the blacklist in his book *McCarthy and his Enemies*, and he continued to savage the left as editor of the conservative weekly *National Review* and in his television show *Firing Line*, which made his toothy smile and plum-in-mouth accent nationally famous. 'I think he'll offer a good contrast to me,' Allen said of this improbable debating partner.

Behind the invitation, however, lay the envy Allen felt for Buckley's aristocracy and air of effortless supremacy. 'On one early tour of the East Side,' recalled Mia Farrow, 'Woody pointed out William Buckley's house. This was a point of interest for him since the Buckleys, their family, and their friends are in essence what drew him to the East Side. But the precise location of the Buckley house failed to lodge in my mind, and some months later, when again we were walking in that vicinity, I asked in passing whether a familiar-looking house might be William Buckley's. To this day I don't know what prompted the attack that followed, which was more stunningly awful than I had ever weathered in my life, and it did not cease until I was sobbing on the sidewalk, vaporised in front of a house that presumably was not William Buckley's.'

Superficially, the NBC show seems meticulous in its determination to avoid accusations of bias on the grounds of colour, religion, age or politics. Black soul singer Aretha Franklin contributes two numbers – ironically 'Respect' and 'Chains'. Both, however, were pre-recorded, so that Franklin never interacts with Allen, unlike a mini-skirted Liza Minnelli who, after warbling the anodyne 'Feelin' Groovy' and 'Up, Up and Away (in my Beautiful Balloon)', plays in two sketches. In one, she's Bonnie Parker to his Clyde Barrow, with Allen parodying the stammering inarticulateness of Warren Beatty in Arthur Penn's film. In the other, Allen plays a Little Lord Fauntleroy-type film star who tries to enter politics as an adult, only to descend into infantile recriminations when he's not elected. The effect is to make the entire political process seem absurd.

Allen's opening stand-up routine, though ostensibly political, mocks both sides of the argument. Denying all political allegiance, he says he only knows one joke about Johnson: that the President is most popular in February, because it's the shortest month. He tried to enlist in the army, he says, but the draft board burned his draft card. It's the appearance of William F. Buckley, however, which most clearly conveys Allen's indifference to politics. Fulsomely introduced by Allen as 'one of the most controversial and challenging men on TV', Buckley effortlessly takes charge. After he and Allen banter amiably, the floor is opened to questions from a series of expensively dressed young people, professionally made-up and flatteringly shot. Should the Israelis give back the Arab land seized in the Six-Day War, asks one. '*Sell* it back,' cracks Buckley. Allen laughs along with the implicitly anti-Semitic joke. The non-political political satirist is also the non-Jewish Jew.

With his TV chore out of the way and any hope of making *Take the Money and Run* blighted by Feldman's death, Allen had begun thinking about a new play. His model this time was George Axelrod's hit comedy *The Seven-Year Itch*, about a Manhattanite's yearning for sexual variety after seven years of marriage. With his family away on holiday, the publisher hero of Axelrod's play is charmed by the girl who moves in upstairs, and after a series of fantasies about taking her to bed, does so, only to be tormented next day by guilt. A psychiatrist whose book the hero is editing offers some insight into his anguish, and in the second act the man deludes himself into believing that his wife is also having affairs at her resort, and storms off to reaffirm the marriage. In 1955 Billy Wilder filmed *The Seven-Year Itch* (in a production by Charles Feldman), salting the story with parodies of famous movie romances like *From Here to Eternity* and replacing Axelrod's romantic youngsters with Marilyn Monroe at her most voluptuous and the dour, middle-aged, embittered Tom Ewell, in private a chronic alcoholic. Hollywood morality dictated that Ewell and Monroe couldn't have sex, a fundamental change which recast the story into a cynical Wilder depiction of lust, cowardice and cupidity laying waste to middle-class morality.

It was Wilder's film, not Axelrod's play, which really inspired Allen, who didn't have to look far to find parallels in his own domestic life. By late 1967, his marriage had begun to teeter. Volatile and addictive, Lasser oscillated between periods of intense sexual activity and spells of chronic laryngitis or depression. Her emotional metabolism was out of synch with that of Allen, who became frustrated by her unwillingness to spend time at galleries and the movies, his favourite leisure activities. They compromised by eating out, and playing poker together at home.

Their lives became increasingly eccentric. Like many unhappy couples, they embraced dysfunction, as if the best way to prove the relationship didn't work was by making sure it didn't. Though Allen was earning a fortune, they seldom had money in the house, and would sometimes find themselves in a restaurant without the cash to pay their bill. On such occasions Allen would ring up his father, who was now moonlighting at nights as manager of Sammy's Bowery Follies. Martin would send the nearest available layabout to the restaurant with some cash. Diners at the Chambourd, one of the city's most fashionable eateries, were startled when a furtive character arrived at Allen's table and handed him a wad of banknotes from his father. It strains belief that such episodes were caused entirely by Allen's absent-mindedness about money. He relished emphasising how far he had come from his roots, and still returned to his old neighbourhood, not driving but driven, and cruised the Brooklyn from which he escaped. The

1997 documentary *Wild Man Blues* records such a visit to his parents' apartment, Allen presenting them with the latest prize statuettes and awards, his father rambling about the quality of the engraving on them, his mother still, in her late eighties, lamenting that her boy didn't become a dentist and marry a nice Jewish girl. 'This is the lunch from hell,' says Allen morosely. In a press release for *What's New Pussycat*, Allen joked of his parents, 'When I was a child they'd give me a quarter to leave them alone. Now, I give them money to leave me alone.' During the seventies, Martin Konigsberg gave up his shop and became Rollins and Joffe's office messenger, running errands around Manhattan. Most people considered this less humiliating for him than for his son. Allen, however, showed no inclination to dissuade him from doing the job; to show how far you'd come, someone had to illustrate where you'd come from.

Allen and Lasser were obviously heading for divorce. As the marriage deteriorated, friends rallied round, trying to 'fix him up', though how much he needed or desired any help in this department is debatable. Plenty of women would have slept with him, given the chance, but Allen seldom offered it. When he did, the liaisons never lasted long. It was in maintaining relationships that Allen failed, and this, as would become apparent over the next decade, was what his analyst would call 'a life decision'.

In Chicago in 1968, while playing at Mr Kelly's, he started serious work on the new play, which plainly reflected his despondency, resignation and relief at the end of his second marriage. Like many later Allen stories – and *The Seven-Year Itch* – it's another story of a man who snatches failure from the jaws of success. Allen Felix, an archetypal New York intellectual, is married to a lively and energetic woman whom he can't satisfy sexually, any more than she can gratify him intellectually. At the opening of the play she's left him, and Felix mopes around his cluttered apartment, the most striking visual element of which are posters for films by his hero, Humphrey Bogart.

His friends Dick and Linda Christie try to console him. Dick, a workaholic entrepreneur, is always on the phone or disappearing for meetings. Linda, in reaction to the lack of attention, obsessively takes tranquillisers. She and Felix are obviously in tune, and in the course of the play, during which she and Dick introduce him to various unsuitable women, he falls in love with her. His fantasy impulse to seduce her would fail, but for the magical manifestation of Bogart himself, who emerges from the shadows to coach him in seduction technique. With Bogart's help Felix gets Linda into bed, but the next morning, ostensibly out of friendship for Dick, he renounces her with the lines Bogart uses to kiss off Ingrid Bergman in *Casablanca*. To find at last a correlation between his fantasy life and reality is all the satisfaction Felix desires. As the journalist decrees in John Ford's *The Man who Shot Liberty Valance*, 'When the legend becomes the fact, print the legend.'

Allen saw more than casual parallels between himself and Bogart, who was the son of a wealthy Manhattan doctor and grew up on the Upper East Side. Despite his reputation as a Hollywood cynic and bar-room brawler, Bogart was as thoughtful, unsure, nervous and reclusive as Allen, preferring the solitude of a bar or of his boat *Santana*. No more successful in his relationships than Allen, he would have five marriages, all more or less failures. Allen joked that when he saw his first Bogart film, *The Maltese Falcon*, he identified not with the hero but with Peter Lorre, who played the effete Joel Cairo. The remark was made to get an easy laugh, but it does underline the improbability of Bogart as a role model for Allen: a posed photo of him in Bogart trenchcoat and felt hat used to promote Herbert Ross's film of the play is simply embarrassing.

Not for the last time, Allen was working on similar material to Stephen Sondheim, the other archetypal Manhattanite of his generation, and a man whose parallels with Allen are striking. 'I like neurotic people,' says Sondheim. 'I like troubled people.' *New York Times* journalist Samuel Freedman also evoked Allen when he called Sondheim 'a New York sophisticate [who] has lived most of his life in a ten-by-thirty-block morsel of Manhattan, someone who subscribes to *Verbatim: The Language Quarterly*. In his lyrics one hears words like "acquiesce" and "ameliorate", references to Proust and Pound.'

In 1970 Sondheim would launch his independent career as a songwriter/lyricist with *Company*, the story of a philanderer who yearns for the security of a stable relationship, for 'company', while just as strenuously resisting commitment. His friends both envy his independence and do all they can to induct him into the grey legions of the married. Particularly in the song 'Have I Got a Girl for You', male friends try to match him with the sexually voracious women they themselves don't dare approach.

For the next decade, before he stabilised his emotional life with Mia Farrow, Allen's relationships obeyed the same cycle. Courtship, seduction and honeymoon were followed by a 'get away' phase when, the novelty of the sex having worn off, he needed to concentrate on work. The woman would become increasingly marginalised, until the relationship ended. In this sense, *Company* is a Woody Allen movie set to music. In its finished form, the show ends with the optimistic 'Being Alive', in which the hero, Bobby, embraces his need for a permanent and loving relationship. But, as Samuel Freedman explains, Sondheim meant *Company* to close with Bobby, far from surrendering to his emotional needs, 'denounc[ing] wedlock as akin to hell in a song sardonically entitled "Happily Ever After" [which is] musical theatre's equivalent of the "We need the eggs" speech with which Woody Allen ended *Annie Hall*.'

Sondheim too would continue to worry at the problem of the artist's need for both 'company' and the freedom to work, embodying it finally in his 1984 musical *Sunday in the Park with George*, particularly in the song 'Finishing the Hat', in which the impressionist painter Georges Seurat reflects that the woman whom an artist hoped to find waiting for him when he'd finished work was not generally the sort of woman prepared to wait. His mistress and model runs off to America with a pastrycook, and Seurat is left with his masterpiece *Sunday on the Island of la Grande Jatte* – more important, he reasons, than any woman could possibly be. Allen would have approved.

Though Allen returned to David Merrick for the production of *Play it Again, Sam*, he did so warily, determined not to make the same mistakes as he had with *Don't Drink the Water*. For one thing, he would play Allan Felix himself. Rollins and Joffe would share the production, which Allen hoped would forestall Merrick's worst excesses. Rather than risk more of the bizarre casting that had almost ruined *Don't Drink the Water*, he sat in on all auditions, and insisted early on that his friend Tony Roberts play Dick. He also had a girl in mind for Linda, an actress with whom he was enjoying a brief relationship, but in deference to Merrick he agreed to see other possible leads. One of them was Diane Keaton.

At a period when young performers from the East Coast gravitated automatically towards the West, and Hollywood, Keaton made the pilgrimage in the opposite direction. Born Diane Hall in the Los Angeles suburb of Highland Park, the daughter of an ex-Miss Los Angeles, and educated in Orange County, she showed every sign of developing into the conventional LA 'airhead'. 'I went to school as a social occasion,' she admitted. 'I was more interested than anything to be in the choir and the talent show. I was always motivated in performing.' She might have been expected to satisfy her theatrical ambitions in California. Instead, with an eccentricity that became the ruling aspect of her character, she migrated to New York and started taking classes with veteran teacher Sanford Meisner and studying dance with Martha Graham. Equity refused to admit her under her own name, since they already listed another Diane Hall, so she adopted her sister's first name and her mother's maiden name. As Dorrie Keaton, she worked in summer stock and pursued an unpromising singing career with a semi-amateur band called the Road Runners; when she wasn't singing, her instrument was the tambourine.

Her break came when she was cast in the musical *Hair*. It opened at the Biltmore on West 47th Street on 29 April 1968, and immediately became *the* hot ticket, partly for its rock/folk score, but mainly because of the famous finale where many of the cast threw off their clothes and invited members of the audience to climb on stage and join in. Actors who agreed to go naked received an extra $50 a week, but Keaton refused to reveal her unremarkable body, even when, as Lynn Kellogg's understudy, she stepped into the lead role of Sheila. The producer offered her the role permanently, but Keaton only stayed for a few weeks. Fellow actors like Al Pacino, with whom she was having a tentative affair, were urging her to widen her horizons. Accordingly, in the autumn of 1968 she auditioned for Allen's new comedy, which was to be directed by Joe Hardy, another ex-student of Lucian Scott, her drama teacher at Orange Coast Junior College.

Watching from the dark at the back of the theatre, Allen wasn't sure what to think about the diffident, awkward and eccentrically dressed girl onstage. But Sanford Meisner had told Merrick she was 'the best young actress around'. Allen was frankly awed. 'She was a Broadway star,' he said, 'and who was I? A cabaret comedian who had never even been on the stage before.' Even so, he needed to establish at least one important thing before he acquiesced to her casting, and he climbed onstage to do it. Fortunately, Keaton in bare feet was five foot seven inches, compared to his five foot six. If she was a little taller than him in the role of Linda Christie, at least she wouldn't tower over him by so much as to make him appear ridiculous.

The first audition went well, and while Allen tried other actresses, Keaton remained in his mind. Thinking of her as Linda changed the balance of the play. Opposite her, his own role dwindled, if not in size then in significance. Felix began to look less like the real Allen and more like a *schlemiel*. Mentally, Allen shrank his own cluttered but relatively luxurious apartment into the boxy dump where Felix lives. Like Allen, Felix surrounds himself with the debris of his calling, as a film critic, but instead of providing an attractive background, the film projector and posters intrude and dominate. In particular, a giant poster for Humphrey Bogart's *Across the Pacific* towers over his bed. With a wolfish Bogart sneering down on one's performance, who wouldn't be impotent?

During the writing and casting of *Play it Again, Sam, Take the Money and Run* came to life again. *Pussycat* had made enough money for United Artists to be interested in backing it, subject to an acceptable script and director. Watching Charles Feldman's experience on *Casino Royale* confirmed Allen even more in his conviction that he didn't want to make movies unless he could be insulated against the demands of collaborators like Sellers. He cajoled Rollins and Joffe into embarking on a new career as film producers. Val Guest was approached again to co-produce, but again declined. After this, the project was floated as a possible film for Jerry Lewis, who had launched himself as a director a few years before, and was looking for scripts that could be filmed in Britain. Allen and Lewis discussed the possibility amicably enough, but it soon became evident that working with Lewis threatened the same ego problems that Allen had experienced with Sellers.

In particular they fell out over a difficulty that was to dog Allen's films: his preference for parodies or collections of sketches rather than sequential narratives. As he and Mickey Rose had conceived it a few years before, *Take the Money and Run* was a feature-length parody of the documentary-style crime stories pioneered by films like *Naked City* in the late forties and carried on by TV series such as *The Untouchables*. The main character then had been called 'Woody Allen', but though Allen rechristened him 'Virgil Starkwell', the inept criminal whose bumbling career concludes in a dramatic shootout was, he later admitted, a reflection of how he might have ended up had he, as he sometimes half-jokingly imagined, followed a life of crime. Numerous personal references buttress this impression. Virgil's parents appear periodically to bicker about their son, the father to disparage, the mother to defend. Both, in the interests of anonymity, wear Groucho Marx masks. A psychiatrist, Dr Julius Epstein, obviously based on Allen's boyhood friend Jerry Epstein, speculates about the youthful traumas that led to Virgil's life of crime. Louise Lasser even has a cameo, as one of the neighbours who comment on him when he's become notorious. Improvising, Lasser says, 'Everyone thought he was such a *schlemiel* and it turned out he's a criminal! You have never met anything like this in all your life, such a nothing.' Allen laughed ruefully at the accuracy of her tone. She'd caught exactly the jeering quality of the schoolyard ribbings at PS 99 that drove him to escape from Flatbush.

Virgil also reflects Allen in many other respects. Physically inept, with poor eyesight – throughout the film, authority figures are forever snatching off his glasses and crushing them underfoot – he joins a gang, but is always the member who gets caught. He inaugurates his criminal career by robbing local stores, disastrously. Trying to knock over a pet shop, he is pursued by a gorilla. A butcher is next, but Virgil escapes not with money but with veal chops. Equally clumsy with women, he tries to bluff a pretty laundress (Janet Margolin) by claiming to play the cello in the New York Philharmonic, a subterfuge which fails when she mentions Mozart and he can't place the name. Taking her to dinner, he robs a gum machine to fund the evening, paying the bill with double handfuls of small change; a gag that would recur in *The Purple Rose of Cairo*, where Jeff Daniels, having stepped out of a movie to be with Mia Farrow, tries to pay for a meal with fake movie money.

Virgil and his girl find brief happiness together, and she remains faithful while he's in jail, where he agrees to act as guinea pig for an experimental drug which, in an unexpected side effect, turns him for some hours into a rabbi. She protects him when he escapes from a road gang chained to half a dozen other prisoners, but Virgil, as enamoured of his myth as was Allen himself, has no need for women.

Take the Money and Run tests the legend of Woody Allen's comic invention, since, like all his early parody-driven work, it's intensely derivative. Interviewed in San Francisco by journalist Judy Stone, with Janet Margolin looking on, Allen told her self-importantly, 'I do not want this film to be eclectic. I don't want people to say I've borrowed a little bit from this director and a little bit from that director.' At this, Margolin, who had become close to Allen during the film, protested, 'But Wooood, that's exactly what you've been doing.' She then excitedly detailed all the films Allen had screened in the run-up to production: Antonioni's *Blow-Up*, Godard's *Vivre sa Vie*, Bo Widerberg's *Elvira Madigan*, the classic *I am a Fugitive from a Chain Gang*, and a documentary about Eleanor Roosevelt, to check details of newsreel shooting. He also wired Carlo DiPalma, who lit *Blow-Up*, in the hope that he would shoot the film, and also one of the great Japanese director

Akira Kurosawa's lighting cameramen, but neither was available.

The chaingang gag is traceable to Stanley Kramer's *The Defiant Ones* (1958), which had also attracted the attention of Mort Sahl. Sahl too inspired the film's most famous scene, where Virgil tries to rob a bank by pushing a note across the counter warning that he has a gun. He's helpless, however, against the bank's bureaucracy. First he's told to get the note countersigned by a manager. Then the tellers and other customers begin to bicker over his handwriting: is it 'gun', or 'gub'? Other routines are taken from real life. Virgil tries to imitate one of John Dillinger's most famous escapes by whittling a gun from a bar of soap, only to fail when it rains and the gun turns to suds. To end the film, Allen was to have used Victor's death in *What's New Pussycat*, which Donner cut. In a *hommage* to *Bonnie and Clyde*, Virgil died riddled with bullets and was last seen as a bloody corpse being carried away on a stretcher. As Margolin mourned at his grave, however, a voice hissed from the coffin, 'Psst! It's me. Get me out.'

Palomar, the short-lived feature subsidiary of ABC television, grudgingly offered a $2 million budget for *Take the Money and Run*, providing Allen dropped the idea of filming in black and white. At this price, they would even let him direct, though only if he worked in Hollywood: the East and West Coast branches of the main movie unions were locked in one of their periodic disputes. Allen agreed, and filming started on 17 June 1968 in San Francisco, where the authorities at San Quentin had agreed to let him shoot the prison scenes.

Allen was casual about the demands of film-making. He'd talked to other directors, like Arthur Penn, before he started, but that was mainly to pick Penn's brains about how to wire himself with bullet 'hits' for the final shootout. The rest, he assumed, was just common sense. And so it largely proved during the main filming. Despite ominous warnings from the San Quentin authorities that, should the crew or Allen be taken hostage, they would on no account open the gates, everything went well. 'There are hundreds of prisoners,' Allen recalled, 'and I had to get them to riot. I thought it was going to be very, very difficult starting with that kind of scene. I said, "OK, now, riot, you guys," and they just pitched in and rioted. It was so easy, we should have filmed the rehearsal, because it was sensational.'

As director, writer and sole major cast member, Allen was free to concentrate on the gags to the exclusion of everything else. An old hand would have warned him that such focusing of talent encourages a tendency to tunnel vision, but few people cared to give advice to the writer and star of the year's most successful comedy. For their part, Palomar had no complaints, since Allen was shooting with exemplary confidence and restraint. He even brought in the film with a quarter of the budget unspent.

Partway through shooting, Allen had a panic call from Caesar's Palace in Las Vegas. Milton Berle had broken his leg, and they desperately needed a replacement. Would Allen stand by in case Berle couldn't go on? Allen flew to Vegas and waited unnoticed at the back of the nine-hundred-seat Circus Maximus until Berle rolled out in a wheelchair, his leg in a cast, and announced he would go ahead with his act. He then pointed out Allen and thanked him for standing by. Weakly, Allen stood up in the spotlight and waved, muttering to his companion, 'This is the most embarrassing moment of my life.'

In August Allen also appeared at a San Francisco fund-raiser for Democratic presidential hopeful Eugene McCarthy. (Aware that they might not have another chance, Colpix recorded the set for his third and, as it turned out, last album.) A liberal senator from Minnesota with many friends in literature and the arts, McCarthy had chosen to run when Lyndon Johnson announced he did not intend to stand for re-election. An electorate traumatised by the losses in that January's Tet offensive in Vietnam welcomed McCarthy's peace platform, as did young voters, and he polled surprisingly well in the New Hampshire primary, regarded as an important indication of the national mood.

To exploit his liberal image and showbiz supporters, McCarthy's campaign managers conceived 'Eugene's', a movable cabaret presented at locations around the country where performers like Allen shared the platform with the candidate. But both McCarthy's artistic and political backing proved too weak to resist Republican candidate Richard Nixon, who rallied stodgy but overwhelmingly popular stars like Lawrence Welk, Pat Boone and Connie Francis to his cause. At the Democratic convention in Chicago in August, McCarthy and fellow liberal George McGovern were decisively defeated by Hubert Humphrey, who received the party's endorsement on the first vote. Furious, his more radical supporters, including the Youth International Party or 'Yippies', the Black Panthers, and Students for a Democratic Society demonstrated in the streets. Heavy-handed police intervention turned the protests into riots that injured more than a thousand people. Film of the disturbances carried on TV sets all over the world did much to discredit the Democrats and ensure Nixon's narrow victory in November.

Allen returned to the post-production of *Take the Money and Run*. To speak the commentary he hired Jackson Beck. As well as being the original voice of the Paramount newsreels of the forties and of countless commercials and documentaries, Beck had boomed some of the most famous words in the history of radio: 'Is it a bird? Is it a plane? No, it's Superman!' He was offended therefore when Allen, though they worked for several days on the recording, refused to speak to him directly, instead audibly relaying orders via the engineer: 'Tell him to talk more softly,' 'Can't he do that slower?' A few weeks later, Beck, who also lived on the Upper East Side, was walking his dog one evening when he saw Allen approaching. As they noticed one another, Allen paused and hovered, obviously wondering if he should greet the actor. He never had the chance. 'I cut him dead!' said Beck with glee.

Once the musical score had been laid, Allen previewed the film for a group of off-duty servicemen recruited from a USO club, as close as he could get to a typical national audience. Their response was deadly. They found nothing whatever to laugh at, a reaction shared by everyone who saw the film.

Movie wisdom decreed that, when all else failed, a dud might be rescued in the cutting room. In panic, Rollins and Joffe turned to Jack Grossberg, the film's production manager and an old hand.

He put them in touch with a friend, Ralph Rosenblum, who had trained in the hard school of documentary and was an industry legend for having saved William Friedkin's 1967 comedy *The Night they Raided Minsky's* with his brilliant reconstruction. In January 1969 Rollins and Joffe screened the film for him, and asked nervously if he could he save it.

Rosenblum discussed the project with Grossberg. They agreed that the shooting was, in Rosenblum's word, 'primitive', but that that wasn't the problem. More difficult to repair was the fragmentary nature of the material. But Grossberg surprised Rosenblum by telling him that much more footage had been discarded in the editing.

Rosenblum suggested to Rollins and Joffe that they get together with Allen, and the four met for a working lunch at a New York seafood restaurant. The solicitude of Rollins and Joffe towards their client surprised Rosenblum, who was used to more robust exchanges. What was it about this young comic that inspired such careful attention to his feelings? Perhaps that was the problem with *Take the Money and Run*: nobody had been brave enough to tell Allen he was on the wrong track. But Rosenblum was surprised at Allen's calm when he explained to him that in his opinion only radical surgery would render the film releasable. The ending would need to go, as would much of the music, and he proposed to restructure the rest. Allen didn't protest. He was going on tour to preview *Play it Again, Sam*, so Rosenblum would have a free hand to come up with a better version. The next day, two hundred boxes of film were delivered to his cutting room, and Rosenblum got down to saving *Money*.

12

Play it Again, Sam

His one regret in life is that he is not someone else.

Biographical copy for Allen's first humour collection, *Getting Even*, 1971

Play it Again, Sam required little tinkering to bring it up to Broadway standard. At the Boston preview, David Merrick, impeccably turned out as ever, suggested that Allen change a line. Allen snapped back with unexpected arrogance, 'I've made over a million dollars in my life by not listening to men in blue suits.' Thereafter, Allen became increasingly acerbic about Merrick. Asked what he thought about him during a press conference, he said, 'He reminds me of a camel. Does that convey anything to you?'

The play opened at the Broadhurst on 12 February 1969, to mostly excellent reviews. Behind its apparently off-handed writing and visual style lay an enormous effort on Allen's part. No star was more insistent on his work being played as he wrote it, nor on the audience disgorging every laugh of which it was capable. Journalist Alfred Bester was struck by Allen's physical preparation. Before each performance, he skipped an imaginary rope and shot fantasy basketballs.

'OK, we're going to kill 'em tonight,' he would tell the cast. 'We killed 'em at the matinee and we're going to kill 'em tonight.'

Jogging offstage in the interval, he said to Bester, 'We should do research on how often a laugh should come. Every minute? Every half minute? I don't know. Did you check our laughs the other night?'

'Yes.'

'How many?'

'Sixty-nine in the first act, sixty in the second . . .'

'That runs five minutes shorter,' Allen interposed quickly.

'Twenty-six in the last act. Total: 155.'

'Not bad. Not bad at all.'

Even before the play opened, producer Arthur P. Jacobs, unpromisingly best known for *Planet of the Apes*, had bought the film rights, and within its first few weeks it was snapped up for London, where Allan Felix, at the suggestion of Val Guest, was played by Dudley Moore from *Beyond the Fringe*. All Moore's previous work had been in revue and small roles, but his success as Felix paved the way for his emergence as an improbable romantic leading man in Hollywood films like *10*. The play was similarly lucky in all its versions, both professional and amateur. For years it was the eleventh most popular play on the American amateur stage – *Don't Drink the Water* rating fifth.

1968 saw the birth of the character soon to become internationally known as 'Woody Allen'. The background against which it took place was *Play it Again, Sam*.

Allen began the year as the very model of the modern wised-up Manhattanite. In his television appearances, as on stage and record, he was snappy, confident, well-dressed, urbane. His supposed failures with women were balanced with a witty insouciance; the audience never believed he slept alone for long. Likewise, his psychoanalysis seemed as much an excuse to air his amusing hang-ups as a genuine cry for help.

The motives behind Allen's transformation from playboy to recluse have been much commented on. Some friends insist that the 1966–67 New Year's Eve party, with its battalions of gate-crashers, soured him forever on the pleasures of fame. Others suspect that, having realised he'd extracted as much value as he could from conventional self-advertisement, he calculatedly embarked on a long-term strategy to build a new persona, and with it a more marketable character. Whatever his motives, he soon became enamoured of his new role as New York's most famous recluse. 'I was telling my analyst just a while ago,' he said in an interview, 'that I had a certain admiration for Howard Hughes. He was living out a certain reclusive quality that I liked. My idea of a good time is to take a walk from my house to the office and not for the entire walk have to worry about hearing my name being called from a passing car or being spoken to at all. That would be perfect.'

Such statements, repeated over the next three decades, became the cornerstone of Allen's celebrated dislike of being recognised. Yet, as writers like J.D. Salinger and Thomas Pynchon had proved, it was no problem to lose oneself as an individual while continuing to work as a creative artist. Had he truly wanted anonymity, Allen could have simply left Manhattan. Even while remaining in the city he could easily, like Greta Garbo, have retained a good deal of his privacy. In truth, Allen wanted both fame *and* obscurity. Broadway habitués joked about his habit of eating in popular restaurants with his hat on, as if to avoid identification. His home on East 79th Street became one of the best-known celebrity sites in New York. Fans sat on the front steps day and night, and even tossed pebbles at the windows to attract his attention.

Allen's insecure aspect, the cringing schoolboy addicted to analysis, might have preferred to remain in the shadows. But most of his life had been dedicated to transcending this element of his character: becoming a performer, a seducer, a wealthy and important man. And Allen the swinger, gambler, businessman, talk-show host, shrank from the loss of everything he had attained. He also, more importantly, realised that Manhattan, both as a stage for his creations and as a source of characters, was crucial to his work.

Allen found himself in a quandary. He shrank from a future in which, like Danny Kaye or Jerry Lewis, he switched persona from film to film. Nobody would believe him as the bellboys and bumpkins, nervous nellies and frenetic victims of scientific experiments out of which those two fashioned their stardom. Nor could he hope to take the line of high satire of Mike Nichols and Elaine May, with their rueful meditations on the plight of twentieth-century man. Allen, wrote critic Andrew Sarris in the *Village Voice*, 'seems never to have had such lofty ambitions. He simply wanted power and glory for himself, and a pox on the world with its cosmic distractions.' Sarris didn't see Allen going anywhere: 'He was a real-life celebrity before he had assumed the slightest vestige of a fictional persona, and thus he is compelled by his status to undermine the very notion of a fictional persona in his films.'

Allen did find a way, though it was a radical one. His decision, in which his 'I want to be alone' protestations played a part, was, in effect, to become two people, continuing the process begun in 1952 when Allan Konigsberg transformed himself into Woody Allen. In an audacious act of self-abnegation, he abandoned the reality Sarris described, of the well-heeled, intellectual comedy writer successful with women. Replacing it was the image of a *nebbish*; in Leo Rosten's definition 'an innocuous, ineffectual, weak, helpless or hapless unfortunate, a loser'. On screen, 'Woody' was a hangdog, whining victim, pill-popping, indecisive, impotent, unattractive, physically and socially maladroit, occupying himself with the most trivial of tasks. His hair, once neatly clipped, became lank and disordered. His rounded shoulders slumped even further.

Smart casual clothes were replaced by the baggy corduroy trousers, soft shirts and crumpled sweaters *Life* writer Paul O'Neil called 'Greenwich Village fatigues', augmented by a wrinkled car coat and a shapeless hat in canvas or tweed. The wardrobe was brilliantly chosen by a man who, for all his self-effacement, was more than a little of a dandy. Allen had often gone out of his way to disclaim any interest in what he wore. 'I have very low aesthetic ideals,' he said in the mid-sixties. 'Clothes are not the things that motivate me. That's why I loved doing *Play it Again, Sam* on Broadway. I didn't have to dress at all. I could leave home dressed in my normal clothes and walk right out on stage just as I was. All I had to worry about was being neat. I was funnier because of it.'

Far from being cheap K-Mart products, however, snatched up from the floor by the bed each morning, these clothes were expensive, and artfully chosen to sustain the 'Woody' image. 'I never knew anybody, man or woman,' wrote Mia Farrow, 'who cares so much about clothes as Woody Allen. He pored over *Vogue* magazine each month. His own "casual, crumpled look" was in fact carefully assembled; the linen suits and tweed jackets were tailor-made, his shirts were the finest Sea Island cotton, his sweaters were cashmere.' When she began her relationship with Allen in 1980, Farrow quickly became aware of the gap between the 'Woody' persona and the hard-thinking, self-interested business-man underneath. 'Woody the actor had long ago invented his screen persona: a loveable *nebbish*, endlessly and hilariously whin-ing and quacking, questioning moral and philosophical issues great and small. He was a guy with his heart and his conscience on his sleeve, whose talk was peppered with quotes of Kierkegaard and Kant; an insightful and unthreatening mascot of the intelligentsia. A guy who is nothing like the real Woody Allen.'

In his limp 1992 biopic of Chaplin, Richard Attenborough drama-tised the comedian's creation of the Little Tramp character with comic-book simplicity. Desperate for a new outfit, Chaplin looks around the changing room at the Mack Sennett studio. A cane glows magically, and leaps into his hand. Likewise a pair of boots, baggy pants, a too-tight jacket, a battered bowler. A quick smear of a greasepaint moustache, and *voilà*! the Little Tramp is born. Attenborough ignores the calculated borrowing of the tramp character from Fred Kitchen, a little-known British vaudeville star, and the selective looting of tricks from French comic Max Linder – but then, Chaplin himself was never generous in crediting others.

When it comes to explaining his own transformation in 1968, Allen is similarly reticent about his influences. 'Woody' is a skil-fully assembled anthology of attitudes, poses and character traits fashionable in the mid-sixties, a pastiche as ably crafted as Allen's parodies of literary style. On one level, 'Woody' and his first incarnation in Allen's work, Allan Felix in *Play it Again, Sam*, is a downmarket Benjamin Braddock from *The Graduate*, so sex-hungry that he'll do almost anything to get it, but tormented with guilt when he does. There's also more than a little of Charles Schulz's character Charlie Brown from *Peanuts*, which in 1967 was the most popular comic strip in the world. Like 'Woody', Charlie is racked by insecurity and bullied by women, and takes solace in psychoanalysis.

Far more fundamental, however, is Allen's debt to Jules Feiffer, whose *Village Voice* work throughout the late fifties and the sixties traded on the insecurities of Greenwich Village life. Many situations and characters in Allen's early plays and *New Yorker* pieces recall Feiffer panels of a decade before. In Feiffer's first collection, *Sick Sick Sick*, published in 1959, a Godlike figure in robe and sandals gives a literary review of the Bible, an idea redolent of Allen. Elsewhere in the book, overbearing women and arrogant men terrorise his archetypal nervous wimp, Bernard Mergendeiler: girls at parties give off provocative signals, rebuff him when he approaches them, accusing him of 'only being interested in one thing', then stroll off with the first hunk who crooks a little finger.

In all his work, Allen refers only once to Feiffer. In the stage directions to *Play it Again, Sam*, Felix is described as:

a slight, bespectacled young man of about twenty-eight or nine who looks as if he just stepped out of a Jules Feiffer cartoon. He earns a decent living as a writer of articles and reviews, some literary, but mostly cinematic, as he is a film buff, for a little intellectual film magazine. He daydreams of someday doing something important in either literature or film. Allan daydreams a lot – in fact, his mind is a hyperactive mass of preposterously neurotic contradictions that make the world a little too much for him. He is nervous, shy, insecure, and has been in and out of psychotherapy for years.

Asked if he influenced Allen, Feiffer says, 'Well, *I* think so, but I'm not sure *he* would. Like everyone, he picked up stuff from the people around him. It's just that, in this case, Woody is loath to acknowledge it.' The two had often socialised during Allen's stand-up days, but by the mid-sixties the relationship had cooled. 'Before he became Woody, he was extremely friendly towards me,' says Feiffer, 'but when he became who he came to be, he became quite distant.' By the time of Allen's break with Mia Farrow and the relationship with Soon-Yi in 1992, the two men had not spoken for years, and Feiffer created two of the most mordant commentaries on the events in panels for the *Village Voice*, where Allen reverts to his stand-up persona to deliver a jokey commentary on his plight, and, ironically, in the *New Yorker*, which devoted three pages in colour to Feiffer's fairytale satire on Manhattan's well-bred outrage at Allen's behaviour.

Having created his new character and its costume, Allen also marked out his territory. He gave up the East 79th Street apartment, which had remained in its half-furnished state throughout the time he and Lasser shared it, the symbol of an awkward marriage. In 1969 he acknowledged to Alfred Bester that he'd never intended to finish it: 'I stopped decorating when I was only half-finished. I've decided it's too much rent and I want to get more for the money, so I'm looking to buy a co-op apartment or a town house.'

'You can get some wonderful places on Central Park West,' Bester suggested.

'No, I couldn't live on the West Side,' Allen said firmly. 'I have to be on the East Side, in the mid-Seventies, just about ten blocks away from the mainstream.'

The choice of location precisely defined the character Allen had chosen for 'Woody'. Manhattan, and particularly its Upper East Side, mainly white Anglo-Saxon Protestant, prosperous, educated, apartment-living, preoccupied with money, intellect and sex, was, as it had been for Harold Ross, as wide a world as he wished to deal with. *Annie Hall*, *Hannah and her Sisters*, *Alice*, *Crimes and Misdemeanors*, *Manhattan*, *Everyone Says I Love You*, *Deconstructing Harry* and *Celebrity* offer characters and situations that could have sprung from the pages of the *New Yorker* itself. Allen's people – academics, TV documentarists, surgeons, rabbis, architects and journalists for the intellectual monthlies – meet for lunch at the Carnegie Deli or the Russian Tea Room or run into one another at the Metropolitan or the Museum of Modern Art, all the while fretting about their health – physical, mental, social and professional – and the meaningfulness or otherwise of their lives and relationships. In 1968 Allen made what was to be his definitive relocation on the Upper East Side. He bought an eleven-room top-floor duplex in a building at Fifth Avenue and 79th Street, overlooking Central Park, and immediately began renovating it into the spacious and private hideout where he still lives today.

*   *   *

Over the next three decades, Allen would skilfully use the 'Woody' character in an elaborate game with his audience and the public until, as had been the case with Bogart, it became difficult to separate the two, even for Allen himself. Men in bars would challenge Bogart to fights, and Bogart, no more a man of action than Peter Lorre – or Woody Allen – would feel impelled to take them up on it. Likewise, Allen the swinger/millionaire, accosted on the street by someone who confused him with his screen character, would play up to his fans' vision of the fumbling, self-effacing Woody.

Shrewdly, Allen exploited his schizoid nature in his screen roles in a way that no other performer, with the exception of Bob Hope in the *Road* movies, had been able to do. Not content to let the awareness of his dual nature sizzle at the back of our minds, he would periodically remind us of it by slipping out of character to interject an intellectual aside. In the early films and plays, 'Allen' supplies an ironic commentary, through a disembodied voice (*Take the Money and Run*), an onstage narrator (*Don't Drink the Water*) or, most sophisticated of all, in *Play it Again, Sam*, a series of onstage conversations addressed directly to the audience by Allan Felix or to the imaginary figure of Bogart. In time he discarded these theatrical devices for the out-of-character wisecrack, a one-liner of which his character would not have thought, least of all at that moment, but which the audience might expect from the writer/director/star.

'I was just sitting here, looking through the magazine section. No, I didn't read the article on China's starving masses. I was checking out the lingerie ads.' (On the phone with Diane Keaton in *Manhattan*)

'That's eight and a half bucks. For that kind of dough I could get the waitress to sleep with me.' (Leaving a greasy spoon in *Broadway Danny Rose*)

When Mia Farrow suggests his infertility may be the result of excessive masturbation: 'Don't go knocking my hobbies.' (*Hannah and her Sisters*)

'The last time I was inside a woman was when I visited the
Statue of Liberty.' (*Crimes and Misdemeanors*)

Triviality, cheapness or concupiscence are established but, at
the next moment, neutralised with a quip that could have come
from someone else – as indeed it did: from Woody's *alter ego*, his
smarter, shrewder self. This sense of having it both ways, of
making a sarcastic comment then turning hurriedly to look over his
shoulder and demand, 'Who said that?' was to become increasingly
typical of both Allen's work and life, and to subtly undermine
them, with disastrous results.

Nothing better dramatised the gap between the real Allen and his
new character than his interaction with Diane Keaton, both
onstage in *Play it Again, Sam* and in person. In the play, Felix
agonises over his attraction to her, they sleep together once, following which he renounces her for his old friend, a conclusion
exactly in line with the jaded philosophy of Feiffer and Billy
Wilder. In real life as well the two stars felt a growing attraction
which, as in the play, both tried to ignore. 'Outside of rehearsal,'
reminisced Allen, 'I was frightened to talk to her, and she was
frightened to talk to me, and we'd go home separately every night,
and nothing ever happened.' This situation continued well into
the play's previews on the road. However, in Washington DC they
went out together, and by the time the play opened on Broadway
they were lovers.

With sexual interest came an increasing admiration on Allen's
part of Keaton as an actress, particularly after Jack Benny came
backstage after a performance and told him, 'That girl is going to
be gigantic.' Four months into the 453-performance run, Lasser
left the marital apartment and Keaton moved in, remaining with
Allen through 1969 and early 1970.

In *Love, Sex and the Meaning of Life*, Foster Hirsch perceptively
analyses the appeal which Keaton represented to Allen:

Like Alexander Portnoy, Woody stands before the otherness of
the *goyim* with a mixture of awe and condescension, and like

many Jewish romantics he is drawn to *shiksas* whose pretty blonde blandness represents both forbidden fruit and the incarnation of the American dream. The ideal totem for the jittery Jewish playboy varies of course from man to man; for Portnoy, it is [his mistress] The Monkey, dumb, pliant, hot to trot. For Woody, it is Diane Keaton. Now Keaton is as deeply and intensely *goyische* as Woody is Jewish. Tall, lanky, with even features and a bland voice, Keaton is the real thing, a dyed-in-the-wool Californian Gentile. There isn't a trace of ethnic colouring in her voice or demeanour or in the way she carries herself.

These were more than usually hectic days for Allen. In the evenings and twice a week at matinees he acted in *Play it Again, Sam.* By day he and Ralph Rosenblum worked on restructuring *Take the Money and Run.* Music proved to be a crucial element in the new version. Allen's choice had been heavily programmatic – either portentous, for the prison segment, or poignant, for scenes like that in which Virgil bumbled, Chaplinesque, around his hovel of an apartment preparing for his first date with Margolin.

For the latter, Rosenblum persuaded him to use instead some sprightly New Orleans jazz, which lifted the scene and gave it a sense of careless comedy. Chaplin was transformed into Mack Sennett. Other music was composed by a young songwriter named Marvin Hamlisch, so anxious to please that he badgered and pestered Allen and Rosenblum, even playing new compositions over the phone to them. There's little in his contribution, however, to point to the later composer of *A Chorus Line* and hits like 'They're Playing Our Song'.

New Orleans jazz proved the ideal accompaniment to Allen's style of physical comedy, playing the same role as the pit band in silent movies, and it became standard in his later films. For more reflective themes he used popular songs of the twenties and thirties, complete with antique acoustics and, occasionally, the hiss of a steel needle. This idea, popularised in 1967 by Arthur Penn for *Bonnie and Clyde*, in which Rudy Vallee's version of 'Deep Night', crooned over the credits, establishes the tone of ominous nostalgia

Seth Green as young Allan Konigsberg in Allen's affectionate fable of his Brooklyn childhood, *Radio Days* (1987). Like Fellini's *Amarcord*, its model, the film softened and sweetened both family and community.

Schmoozing with the guys: veteran comics and showbiz characters including Allen's long-time agent/producer Jack Rollins (far right) reminisce about an imaginary Broadway character, Danny Rose, in *Broadway Danny Rose* (1984). Sessions like this during the fifties educated young Allen in the traditions of comedy.

The serious writer of humour pieces for the *New Yorker*, c. 1966, aged thirty-one. (The caption identifies him as Heywood 'Woody' Allen, and gives his age as twenty-eight.)

The stand-up comic, c. 1964. Audiences feared he would strangle himself with the microphone cable as he paraded his neuroses on stage.

Louise Lasser, Allen's unstable second wife.

Allen in October 1970, phlegmatically facing a future in Hollywood.

Allen directing Lasser in the 1972 *Everything You Always Wanted to Know About Sex (*But Were Afraid to Ask)*.

'This is a film about wires.' Allen dangling between Hollywood stunt comedy and his own kind of humour in the science fiction parody *Sleeper* (1973).

Allen and Lasser in the original ending of *Bananas* (1971), where he escapes a bomb, only to be greeted as an honorary black by his failed assassins.

What's New Pussycat (1965) and *What's Up, Tiger Lily?* (1966) established Allen as a world-class comedy talent.

The producer of *What's New Pussycat* told Allen to write a film set in Paris so they could go there and chase girls. For a publicity photo shoot, Allen prowled backstage at the Crazy Horse strip club. Later he gave his character in the film a job helping the girls in and out of their costumes.

Living up to the image: Allen playing pool in the too-small billiard room of his Manhattan apartment (the butt of the cue routinely collided with the wall), and showing off a painting by Gloria Vanderbilt. Louise Lasser thought they should have original art; Allen preferred movie posters.

With *Play it Again, Sam* (1972), Allen transformed his image from anguished intellectual to fumbling *nebbish*. 'Woody' arrived, in the person of film critic Allan Felix, who aspires to life as a *Casablanca* rerun.

Abandoned by his wife, Felix dips a toe in the singles scene, but is out of his depth with a sexy blonde (Suzanne Zenor) in *Play it Again, Sam*.

Saved by cinema: an imaginary Humphrey Bogart (Jerry Lacy) coaches Felix in the techniques of seduction in *Play it Again, Sam*.

and melancholy, also became part of Allen's repertoire, and an indelible trademark of his film style.

The revised version of *Take the Money and Run* opened on 19 August 1969. Palomar, gloomy about its prospects – at a preview, one executive turned to Rollins and Joffe after the first ten minutes and enquired sharply, 'Are all the reels like this?' – only made two prints, and initially screened it only at New York's tiny 68th Street Playhouse. Nevertheless, the following Sunday Vincent Canby in the *New York Times*, soon to become Allen's staunchest champion among critics, hailed it as a film that 'illustrated in fine, absurd detail the world that Allen has been talking about all these years'. In the way of enthusiastic reviewers, Canby found merit in the very deficiencies Allen and Rosenblum had laboured to disguise. The episodic structure, to him, recalled Allen's stand-up routines. What he called 'loose-leaf' form made the film look 'effortless'.

In films as on Broadway, a *Times* review could make or break a production, and this was a money-maker. *Take the Money and Run* broke box-office records at the Playhouse, but lacking mass exposure, lost $610,000 on its initial release, during which it only played on eighteen screens in fifteen US cities. It would take seven years for Palomar to see a profit on its modest $1.53 million investment.

The need to concentrate on *Take the Money and Run* and *Play it Again, Sam* meant that Allen didn't have time to supervise another project, the filming of *Don't Drink the Water*, which had been bought by the independent Avco-Embassy, founded by arch-promoter Joseph E. Levine. As devout a believer in hype as David Merrick, Levine made his fortune repackaging Italian muscle-man epics with Steve Reeves for the American market, and hustling Fellini's 8½ into a box-office hit by deluging New York opinion-makers with preview screenings, even though he privately considered the film a load of garbage and Fellini 'as phoney as a glass eye'.

Rollins and Joffe remained co-producers of the film, but they could do little as Avco-Embassy cast portly, Gentile television comic Jackie Gleason as the Jewish Hollander, and Estelle Parsons, briefly 'hot' since her role in *Bonnie and Clyde*, as his wife. Such was Gleason's clout on the back of his hit TV show *The Honey-mooners* that shooting was summarily relocated to Miami, where he lived, although the Vulgarian exteriors were shot in Quebec. To direct, Gleason chose Howard Morris, Sid Caesar's short and sassy sidekick on *Your Show of Shows*. Morris had descended to doing voice-overs for cartoons until R.S. Allen and Harvey Bullock, two writers from the Hanna-Barbera cartoon stable who created *Top Cat*, let him direct their highly successful screenplay *Who's Minding the Mint?* in 1967.

Rollins and Joffe, trying to keep at least part of the project 'in house', assigned Marshall Brickman, Allen's writing partner on the unproduced 'The Film-Maker', to write the script. Since 'The Film-Maker', Brickman had had a variety of television writing jobs. After working on *Candid Camera* he sold single gags to comics, then landed a job as writer on Johnny Carson's popular *Tonight Show*, and with Allen's friend Dick Cavett, now a successful talk-show host, who worked the higher end of the guest list, interviewing Laurence Olivier and artist/designer Edward Gorey rather than Phyllis Diller and Andy Warhol. Brickman was eager to work on *Don't Drink the Water* as a route out of TV, but Howard Morris persuaded Avco that the *Who's Minding the Mint?* team of R.S. Allen and Bullock would be a better choice. Woody and Brickman couldn't prevail against such box-office logic.

The decision proved disastrous. Comfortable with farce, Morris was at sea in the deeper waters of Broadway comedy, even one as broad as *Don't Drink the Water*. Alarmed that the first cut was utterly bereft of laughs, Rollins and Joffe turned to Ralph Rosenblum, who wasn't surprised to receive a call from Morris in Florida which began, 'Hi, Ralph. I understand you're the guy who saves directors.' Rosenblum flew to Florida, but found Morris infinitely less malleable than Allen had been on *Take the Money and Run*. 'Regardless of how small the issue,' he said, 'he insisted on having his way, and always in a style that was calculated to remind every one of his co-workers that he was his subordinate.' Morris insisted on retaining his original cut despite all Rosenblum's suggestions, and it was cold comfort that when Avco-Embassy saw the result they called Rosenblum in to re-edit the film anyway. By then there was little he could do to save it, and its 10 March 1969 release was greeted with universal indifference. The failure rankled with Allen, who felt that his preoccupation with other projects had blighted *Don't Drink the Water*'s chances of success. Unusually for him, he would agree to a television remake almost thirty years later, taking the lead role himself.

In a further distraction, Allen agreed to write and present another Kraft TV special, to be aired in September 1969. Joffe produced, and Marvin Hamlisch provided the music. The contrast with his earlier special is marked. Allen, though still neatly turned out in green corduroy suit and striped tie, is noticeably more rumpled. His hair, no longer neatly brushed forward, is untidy. He doesn't use a mike, and from his opening monologue he follows a more rueful, self-deprecatory line. He jokes about sex and death – 'the two subjects that interest me most. Both come only once in a lifetime.' With Candice Bergen he does a limp parody of rehearsing for an off-Broadway play, and *Cupid's Shaft*, a mock silent movie in which a white-faced Allen looks more like minor silent comic Larry Semon than Buster Keaton or Chaplin, at whom he aimed.

He had yet another conservative guest, in the preacher Billy Graham. Instead of the studio setting of the Buckley confrontation, however, the two chat over coffee in a set imitating a panelled study. After a snappy opening, in which he demands to know what is Graham's favourite commandment, Allen settles down to trading amiable sallies with the grinning evangelist. Pre-marital sex? Graham is against it, but Allen thinks that marriage without it is 'like getting a driver's licence without a learner's permit'. They part with mutual assurances of esteem. Allen even promises to attend a Graham rally – if the preacher will see one of his films.

13

Bananas

I learned three things in Zurich during the war. I wrote them down. Firstly, you're either a revolutionary or you're not, and if you're not you might as well be an artist as anything else. Secondly, if you can't be an artist, you might as well be a revolutionary . . .
   I forget the third thing.

Henry Carr, in *Travesties* by Tom Stoppard

In 1969 Charles Joffe attended a rally for New York mayoral candidate John Lindsay at Madison Square Garden. The visit was semi-professional: Lindsay was one of the clients for whose speeches Woody Allen supplied jokes. At the rally Joffe ran into David Picker, president of United Artists. Joffe thought UA might be more congenial to Allen than larger studios that would expect him to work in Hollywood and follow their methods, and Picker regretted that UA had failed to grab *Take the Money and Run* by making too low a bid. He asked Joffe what Allen would demand to make films for UA. '$2 million budget,' said Joffe, 'total control after you approve the story, and a three-film contract.' Picker said, 'Get your lawyers on it.'

Eighteen months later, when the deal had finally made it through the thicket of legalese, much more was spelled out than the basic terms proposed by Joffe. UA guaranteed Allen a ten-to-twelve week shoot on each film, and a salary of $350,000, with a further $200,000 once the film had earned 2.7 times its budget. Joffe and Rollins got $125,000 per film as producers, with a further $50,000 deferred until the film went into profit. Once it did, UA took the first 30 per cent of the gross and 50 per cent of the rest. Allen got the remaining 50 per cent, which he split with Rollins, Joffe and others. The studio's share was substantial, but so was the degree of independence ceded to Allen. If a film went over budget, he and his producers would pay, though UA would reimburse them once it began making money. UA executive and historian of the studio Steven Bach hailed Picker's foresight and instinct: '[Allen's] career that seemed at the beginning a fluky and limited one, full of New York angst and *schtick*, which didn't travel well into middle America and had almost no foreign passport, turned into a prodigiously likeable series of pictures, original not only in subject but in their angle of vision and style. Taking a flyer on Allen had proved to be one of the happiest and smartest gambles in recent movie history.'

Pressed to describe the films he would make under the contract, Allen composed a jokey press release, issued deadpan by UA:

Mr Allen describes his first picture as a pro-Catholic pornographic musical about outer space in which he plays a reformed homosexual. His second work, entitled 'So Loud, So Vapid', is based on the life of Spiro Agnew [Nixon's Vice-President, who would resign in disgrace in 1973]. United Artists is not thrilled with the acquisition, but Mr Allen is one of the few young film-makers around who will work for expenses and a little money for the track. Mr Allen will be required to fix lunch for the crew by contract, which also states he will have final cut of every third frame. Executives of UA responsible for the signing have either left the country or taken their own lives.

Having bought Allen's comic expertise, UA were taken aback when, for his first project, he submitted a drama. While shooting *Take the Money and Run* in San Francisco, he'd been invited to sit in with Turk Murphy's band at the club called Earthquake McGoon's. Later he played with Pops Foster, Wild Bill Davison and other heroes. The experience revived his interest in jazz, and he was now practising more religiously than ever. Inspired, he wrote 'The Jazz Baby', a script based on the early days of jazz, but UA were horrified by such a dour theme. They strenuously urged him to think of a comedy, as much like *Take the Money and Run* as possible.

Allen resurrected 'El Weirdo', the forty-page treatment of *Don*

Quixote USA he'd written with Mickey Rose, and with Rose he fleshed it out into the screenplay that became *Bananas*. Richard Powell, author of the original novel, receives no credit, even though the plots of the book and the film are almost identical. But plot isn't what makes *Bananas* worth watching. A century of immigration had created a Cuban-American social stereotype that amused Allen, much as he was amused by the ingredients of Allison Portchnik's upper-middle-class liberal Jewish persona in *Annie Hall*. Americans accustomed to seeing Hispanics as busboys or band leaders found it hard to accept them as revolutionaries and/ or heads of state, a fact on which Allen and Rose played at every turn.

A visit to Mexico with Louise Lasser to get a quickie divorce in 1969 refreshed Allen's imagination. 'We had a good time,' Lasser recalled. 'We stayed together that night in the same hotel room. We had a lot of what now appear contradictions like that. Because at the time we were still drawn together.' The divorce itself took place with almost indecent haste – such haste that neither really felt the separation. Later, Allen's American lawyers warned that US courts sometimes ruled Mexican divorces invalid. For this reason, and out of a vestigial loyalty to Lasser, Allen preferred to describe their marriage as 'dissolved' rather than definitively terminated, a word which infuriated Lasser. 'Dissolved?' she says. 'Dissolved! I like that. A divorce is a cut-off, whereas "dissolved" means it gradually goes into something different.' She continued to sign herself 'Louise Jane Allen'. Shortly after the divorce she had a nervous breakdown. Once she recovered, Allen, perhaps motivated by guilt, asked her to star opposite him in *Bananas* when it began shooting in Puerto Rico in May 1970.

Allen took UA at their word and gave them a film that is, in most respects, a revamp of *Take the Money and Run*. Once again the form is semi-documentary, telling the story of *nebbish* Fielding Mellish, played by Allen in his new incarnation as 'Woody', who's lured into politics by his attempts to impress a woman, in this case the naïve student political activist Nancy, whom he meets when she comes canvassing to his door. (In another gibe at an institution that rejected him, Allen makes her a City College student.) To impress her, Mellish, actually a tester of gadgets like an office desk *cum* exercise machine and a coffin with stereo sound, joins the rebels of the South American country of San Marcos in their attempt to overthrow the dictator Emilio Vargas. When the insurgents unexpectedly win power, Mellish, in a Castro-like beard (but red), visits New York to negotiate an aid package. Nancy, as enamoured as ever with revolutionaries, sleeps with him, unaware that he's Fielding, but the FBI penetrate his disguise and indict him as a 'subversive impostor', only to release him after a comic trial that recalls the Marx Brothers at their most frenetic. He marries Nancy, and the film ends with sportscaster Howard Cosell giving a blow-by-blow description of the wedding night live on television. The logorrhoeac Cosell also opens *Bananas*, describing the assassination of the President of San Marcos as if it were a sports event.

Allen had as little sympathy with the brushfire revolutions then endemic in Central and South America as he did with the US's attempts to back up its business interests by subverting local governments. In that sense, '*Bananas*' is a well-chosen title. Not only does it mean insane, but also rubbish, as in the verse to Gershwin's 'They All Laughed', which dismisses the popular scepticism about historical events as 'all bananas'. It also evokes the hegemony of the United Fruit Company, and the derisive term 'banana republic'.

A less politically correct society than today's was indifferent to the film's racial stereotyping of comic Hispanics. Blacks too fare poorly, as they often do in Allen's films. At Fielding's trial, a large black woman testifies against him, claiming to be J. Edgar Hoover in an impenetrable disguise. And Allen could not resist introducing a parade of hassidim and rabbis who stroll through the gunfire of the San Marcos insurgence, bickering among themselves. This shot is all that remains of a long sequence in which Vargas, in New York to solicit help to prop up his administration, misses the office of the CIA and stumbles into that of the UJA – the United Jewish Appeal, who send in their own shock troops. In Allen's first cut, jokes like this padded out the revolution sequence to almost an hour. In the release print it lasts thirty seconds.

In his first film partly set in his home town, Allen shows New York as a city of elevated ambitions and lowered expectations. Humiliation comes with the territory. Fielding, turned down for a date even by the office nymphomaniac, decides to buy a porn magazine, disguising it in an armful of intellectual weeklies. The shopkeeper bawls to his assistant, 'What's the price on this *Orgasm*?' In the subway he buries his head in *Commentary* while two juvenile delinquents (one of them the young Sylvester Stallone) terrorise the other passengers, including a woman on crutches. Mellish eventually succeeds in shoving them out the door, only to be menaced himself when they break back in. The scene ends with him fleeing down the carriage while the handicapped woman reads his copy of *Orgasm*.

Like Virgil in *Take the Money and Run*, Fielding fakes an intimacy with the work of heavy-duty intellectuals, in this case Kierkegaard, but to his friends at work he laments the fact that he never went to college. Had he entered a Black Studies programme, he tells them, he would be black by now. He is also, inevitably, in analysis, though his doctor, a matronly woman, seems uninterested in his ramblings. The analysis sequence triggers Allen's first movie dream, and a memorable one: he imagines himself nailed to a cross and being carried by flagellating monks through New York's downtown business district. They try to 'park' him, only to get into an argument about the space with another group of monks and another crucifee – an early role for comic Allen Garfield.

Louise Lasser, though not included in the Puerto Rican scenes, flew to San Juan to spend a weekend with Allen, 'determined,' she later said, 'to do anything he wanted. I went down fully prepared for *anything*.' At the back of her mind may have been hope of a reconciliation, or at least some sort of *rapprochement*. 'That little inner person in me wanted to be taken care of like a child,' she said. She was mortified to find Allen installed with Diane Keaton in a hotel suite. 'He was awful to me, and flaunted Keaton,' said Lasser. 'As soon as I walked into his room he pointed to a chest and said reverentially, "That's Diane's drawer." He spent the rest of the weekend telling me what an unbelievable actress Diane was. He told me, "Diane is America's greatest actress," and "Diane is the greatest companion I ever had."' A hysterical Lasser phoned her father, who urged her to come home.

When shooting returned to New York she carried on her role in the film, her hopes of a reconciliation kept alive by Allen's tantalising insistence that she remained the only woman with whom he enjoyed sex. She says today, 'Obviously [he and Keaton] had sex, but he led her to believe he wasn't interested. He was not attracted to her. He said he just didn't feel for her sexually. He'd feel for her, but she had a great sexual appetite. Not that he wouldn't do stuff with her, but it wasn't like with me or some hooker. He carried on insisting that he was really attracted to me and that I was the one he wanted to have sex with. He was keeping me dangling, but I'm happy he did because otherwise I would have flipped.'

In December Keaton went home to California for Christmas, and Allen invited Lasser to stay with him. They spent the month together, though the experience effectively ended their emotional involvement. Separation had given her a new perspective. 'I related more to him as a father than a lover,' she decided.

On Keaton's return from Los Angeles, her relationship with Allen continued as before. They collaborated on furnishing the 79th Street apartment, which had remained largely bare while Allen was shooting, but he was in no mood for any more lasting commitment. For him, as for Allan Felix in *Play it Again, Sam*, dreams offered more reliable gratification than reality. He had enjoyed the pursuit of the apparently unattainable Keaton, and relished the pleasure of victory, but like the sportsman who throws back the fish he's battled to catch, he no longer wanted her around. As he had with Harlene and Lasser soon after they submitted to him, he became dismissive, often contemptuous, towards her, as a prelude to severance. 'When I first met her,' he said of Keaton in an interview, 'she was a real hayseed, the kind who would chew eight sticks of gum at a time. I talked to her on the phone once when she was in California and she was about to drive to the supermarket – which was across the street. Literally.' Anyone who knew Allen would have got the message instantly. The relationship had entered what his friends had come to know as his 'Get Away' phase.

An incident towards the end of 1969 made the situation plain. During the run of *Play it Again, Sam*, seventeen-year-old Linda Hersch, an attractive high school senior from Queens, formed a Woody Allen fan club with a few of her friends. Allen encouraged them by giving them access to free 'house seats' and letting them visit him in his dressing room. On 1 December Hersch arranged a birthday celebration for him at the theatre. She had been struck on earlier visits by the obvious affection between Allen and Keaton, who would hold hands backstage like young lovers. On this occasion, though, all of them sensed a tension, not helped when Hersch unveiled her surprise birthday present, a tape of the music from *What's New Pussycat*. Allen clamped his hands over his ears. 'I never want to hear that music again!' he moaned.

After the cake had been cut, Allen softened, and impulsively offered Hersch a gift in return: an anthology of poems published in 1911 called *For Auld Lang Syne: A Gift from a Friend*. When Hersch opened it, she found a small piece of plastic fern pressed between the pages, and an inscription from Keaton to Allen on the flyleaf: 'I guess I want to thank you for all the good times.' 'All' was heavily underlined. On another page, before the introduction, a page and a half of pious sentiment about friendship, Keaton had written, under a star of David, 'To Woody – Well, you know, you just don't find beautiful books like this any more. I find the introduction especially meaningful.'

'Diane was right there in the room with us,' said Hersch. 'It seemed incredible to me that he could be giving away something so very personal and intimate to them both. I asked him, "Do you really mean me to have this, Woody?" He didn't answer right away, but I burbled something like, "I mean, didn't Diane give it to you specially?" But Woody reassured me. "No, that's OK," he told me. "You take it."' When she read the introduction, Hersch 'tried to imagine how [Allen's gift] would have seemed to any girl in love with the man she was giving it to, [and] it seemed all the more astonishing that Woody had given me the book.'

Around the same time, Stephen Sondheim was musing again – it had also been the subject of *Company* – on this need among his contemporaries first to find a relationship, then to wriggle out of it. He summarised it in 'Buddy's Blues', which appeared in *Follies* the following April, as:

> Those God-why-don't-you-love-me-oh-you-do-I'll-see-you-later Blues.
> That Long-as-you-ignore-me-you're-the-only-thing-that-matters Feeling . . .

Allen wrote his own version in 'Retribution', a lengthy story which would appear in the magazine *Kenyon Review* in the summer of 1980 and which he would choose to conclude the collection of his writings, *Side Effects*, also published that year. In a preview of *Annie Hall*, he describes Harold Cohen, a twenty-four-year-old Jewish writer who's bowled over by Connie Chasen, a beautiful *goyische* blonde he meets at a party on Central Park West. Their affair prospers, only to founder on Howard's disbelief that anyone so beautiful, sexually inventive and – Allen invents here – intimate with both the *Rig-Veda* and the lyrics of Cole Porter, could find him attractive. Displacing his affection for Connie, he begins an affair with, then marries, her mother, only to find Connie turned on all over again by the prospect of sex with her stepfather.

For Keaton, life with Allen had been more like college than cohabitation. 'Woody's life is his work,' she said. 'He is just not a relaxer.' Allen agreed. 'I have to work every day, otherwise I hear voices nagging me on and on.' And while he worked, Keaton had to work too. At his urging, she began seeing an analyst several days a week. He'd also introduced her to his roots, taking her to the Catskills to see Jerry Lewis perform at one of the last of the big hotels to stay in business. In return, he expected her to share his other obsessions, including old movies. Allen's idea of a dinner party was to invite friends like Tony Roberts over to watch baseball on TV or a screening of a good/bad film like *The Oscar*,

Russell Rouse's 1966 melodrama about the efforts of ruthless actor Stephen Boyd to win the statuette, trampling everyone in his path. The film, with its rich cast of celebs like Milton Berle, Bob Hope and Merle Oberon in self-conscious walk-ons, never failed to amuse Allen. He called it 'conceivably the worst movie ever made. It's so rich in aesthetic incorrectness. There is an unself-conscious badness about it.'

He and Keaton also followed the New York Knickerbockers basketball team, whose games he endowed with an almost mystical significance. Allen had followed the Knicks since the sixties, initially buying tickets from scalpers outside Madison Square Garden, but once the team and its stars Walt Frazier and Earl 'The Pearl' Monroe caught his imagination in the seventies, he asked Howard Cosell to use his influence to get him four season tickets. Initially they were high in the bleachers, but each year he moved closer to courtside, where seats sold for $12,900 per season in the nineties, and much more on the black market. Such was the value of sideline tickets to Knicks games that Allen joked about them in *Mighty Aphrodite*. When Mira Sorvino's murderous pimp threatens to kill the Woody character for luring her away from prostitution, he placates him by offering him seats at the Knicks. At the end of the film the pimp and his bar-owner friend are seen jumping for joy like schoolkids and embracing in their new courtside places. Ironically, Allen's presence on the sidelines, like Jack Nicholson's at Lakers games in Los Angeles, became as much a part of the Knicks' appeal as the players themselves. 'Sports to me is like music,' he said. 'It's completely aesthetically satisfying. There were times I would sit at a game with the old Knicks and think to myself in the fourth quarter, "This is everything the theatre should be and isn't. There's an outcome that's unpredictable. The audience is not ahead of the dramatist. The drama is ahead of the audience, and you don't know exactly where it's going." You're personally involved with the players – they had heroic dimensions, some of those players.'

To Allen, the team of the seventies was 'like a movie with a group of stars in it'. He enthused, 'When the Knicks were hot and everyone would go to the Garden to watch them play, every game was an event. You'd see everyone you knew, and then we'd all go out to dinner at Frankie and Johnnie's or 21. That was something really exciting for the city – nineteen thousand people exiting the Garden together, into the night. That's a great feeling.' In a letter to a fan in Florida, he wrote, 'I'm blue because the Knicks lost and basketball season is virtually over.' On location in Colorado for *Sleeper* in 1973, he wrapped the production at 6 p.m. in order to be back in his hotel in time to watch the Knicks play the LA Lakers on TV.

As eager as any fan to be involved with his heroes, Allen wrote a scene for *Annie Hall* in which his character Alvy Singer, as part of a pick-up team with Franz Kafka and Friedrich Nietzsche, stands on the court in evening dress (minus trousers) and with a thermometer in his mouth, and sinks basket after basket while the Knicks, including Earl Monroe, look on and cheer. He hired the team and Madison Square Garden for days to shoot the scene, but, perhaps fortunately, it was never used.

For the Knicks, Allen would endure much. In 1979 he agreed to write a feature for *Sport* magazine about Earl Monroe. An appointment was arranged, but Monroe didn't turn up, leaving Allen to cool his heels and chat with the player's girlfriend. Gritting his teeth, Allen turned the snub into humour, as he often did in his films. 'This great athlete is unconcerned about the usual nonsense of social protocol,' he wrote. 'Unimpressed by me, a cover interview and all the attendant fuss and adulation that so many people strive for, he simply fails to show up! Probably off playing tennis or fooling with his Mercedes. Whatever he was doing, I admired him for his total unconcern.'

Returning from a Knicks game late in 1969, Allen and Keaton automatically turned on Johnny Carson's *Tonight Show*. One of Carson's guests, making a highly successful fourth appearance, was author Dr David Reuben. A personable psychiatrist of thirty-four with a practice near San Diego in California, Reuben had been on holiday in Acapulco two years before with his wife Barbara at a hotel popular with honeymoon couples. 'They'd be laughing, dancing and sitting so close together that they'd only be using one chair,' recalled Reuben. 'The next morning we'd see them at breakfast – angry, discouraged. In the middle of breakfast, the wife would get up and walk away.'

Reuben diagnosed simple sexual ignorance. Back home, he bought himself a typewriter and a one-dollar manual on how to use it, and tapped out a book he called *Beyond the Birds and the Bees*. Having spent three years at Cook County Hospital in Chicago and two more as chief of neuropsychiatry at Walker Air Force Base, he had a firm grasp of the sexual fears and eccentricities of *Homo Americanus*. He constructed his book as a series of answers to questions he'd been asked a thousand times, beginning with one of the most common: 'How big is the normal penis?' No response was longer than three paragraphs; if an answer needed more space, he inserted a supplementary question, e.g. 'Do peepers and exhibitionists ever get together?' Potted case-histories, supposedly from his own experience, enlivened the material. Venereal disease, trans-sexual surgery, prostitution, frigidity and homosexuality were dealt with matter-of-factly. The book fulfilled perfectly the recipe for the later success of *People* magazine, as articulated by Jeff Goldblum in Lawrence Kasdan's 1983 *The Big Chill*: nothing in it took longer to read than the average crap.

In 1969, obscure New York publishers David McKay paid Reuben a $3000 advance for the book, but wanted a new title. Reuben was stumped. What, he asked rhetorically, could you call a book that simply explained everything you always wanted to know about sex but were afraid to ask? It was under this title that the book was issued at the end of 1969, though the publishers couldn't resist tinkering with it. The true title was *Everything You Always Wanted to Know About Sex**, with 'sex' in red. The asterisk led readers to the second half of the title, '*but were afraid to ask*', printed in lower-case letters lower down the page. To suggest that the book was more consultation than publication, the contents were credited as 'Explained by David Reuben, M.D.'

Initially the book flopped. The few papers that reviewed it, including the *New York Times*, dismissed it in a paragraph. Those critics who did notice it often accused Reuben of oversimplifying or, as in a vigorous attack by Gore Vidal, reprinted as 'Doc Reuben', of homophobia and ignorance of homosexual practice. But the publishers managed to get Reuben on Dick Cavett's new talk show, launched in May 1969. As another guest, Betty Furness, inveighed boringly against the increasing ubiquity of credit cards and Cavett sensed viewers switching to other stations, Reuben volunteered that many call girls took plastic. This startling fact instantly revived audience interest. The show took off, as did Reuben's book. It would spend thirty weeks on the *New York Times* bestseller list, be translated into twenty-two languages and spawn a crowd of sequels. In 1971 *The Chronicle of Higher Education* listed it number one among campus bestsellers, ahead of *Love Story*, *Future Shock*, *The Prophet* and *The Godfather*.

On the *Tonight Show* Keaton and Allen saw, Carson asked Reuben provocatively, 'Is sex dirty?' To Allen's surprise and pleasure, the doctor responded with a line from *Take the Money and Run*: 'Only if you're doing it right.' Reuben then proceeded, in a manner which Vidal characterises as shifting 'from nightclub comedian to reform rabbi', to expound his theories about the widespread American repression of the sexual instinct. As Vidal remarked, much of Reuben's theory didn't hold good for America as a whole, but rather reflected his own religious and cultural background, and particularly his Jewishness. 'Essentially he is a moralist,' Vidal wrote, 'expressing the hang-ups of today's middle-aged, middle-class urban American Jews, hang-ups which are not necessarily those of the Gentile population or, for that matter, of the rising generation of American Jews.'

Discussing the exchange, Keaton and Allen had the same idea – that Reuben's book, though neither had read it, might provide a useful departure point for his next film. Sex and its frustrations were, after all, Allen's primary subject, and Reuben's added shot of Jewish guilt made a potent cocktail. Allen may also have recalled the inadequate sexual advice dispensed by the Los Angeles rabbi who married him and Harlene. The next day he rang Joffe and suggested they find out who owned the rights.

* * *

Allen credits Diane Keaton with widening his horizons, though they were never to expand much beyond the Upper East Side. 'She has an utterly spectacular visual sense,' he enthused. 'I see many things today through her eyes; textures and forms I would never have seen without her. She showed me the beauty of the faces of old people. I'd never been sensitive to that before. And there's a certain warmth and poignance associated with young women I would never have seen without her. She's increased my affection for women in general.'

For all their shared enthusiasms, the relationship between Allen and Keaton remained, like all his romances, constricted by his nervous avoidance of commitment. Keaton acted in many of his later films, but always as a woman whose independence irritates or angers the Woody character. Though *Annie Hall* charts the decline more directly, *Manhattan*, with its admiring view of life among New York's chattering classes, reflects the banteringly hostile nature of their relationship. The didactic Ike is utterly convinced of his enthusiasms, while the equally determined Mary thinks Ingmar Bergman overrated, disparages Ike's interest in younger women, and in general has more than enough internal strength to resist his influence.

Not surprisingly, Allen and Keaton only lived together until *Play it Again, Sam* closed its Broadway run on 14 March 1970, by which time Bob Denver had taken over the Allan Felix role. Allen began shooting *Bananas* on 4 May, and though Keaton spent some time with him on location in Puerto Rico, the relationship effectively ended after that. 'We talked about the idea that we had been living so closely for years,' Allen said, 'and it might be nice, we thought, to try with her *not* living here. That was a mutual decision. And if we didn't like that, we'd move back in together.' Keaton took a two-bedroom apartment on East 68th Street. 'We were still lovers intermittently after that for a while,' said Allen. 'Gradually we sort of cooled down and drifted apart more.' When Mia Farrow began seeing Allen in 1980, she was surprised to find one shelf in his bathroom cabinet still filled with Keaton's pills and personal items – a shelf she touched at her peril. Keaton also befriended Soon-Yi Previn after the revelation of her affair with

Allen in 1992, and became one of her closest confidantes.

Professionally, Keaton could ill-afford the break with Allen. She'd won a role in David Susskind's film *Lovers and Other Strangers*, but wouldn't get another movie for two years. She survived by doing TV commercials for products like Hour After Hour deodorant, in which she's shown jogging all day, cooking her husband's dinner but still able to cuddle up to him afterwards without, apparently, having showered. Her manager Arlyne Rothberg succeeded in pushing her fee to $25,000 for each commercial, but Keaton knew she was going nowhere. When Francis Ford Coppola offered her a small role as Al Pacino's wife Kay in his film of *The Godfather* she jumped at it, even though the fee was a derisory $6000 – as against the $21,000 she would receive for recreating her stage role in the film of *Play it Again, Sam*. The task of promoting Hour After Hour passed to another up-and-coming actress, Susan Sarandon.

During the break-up, Allen concentrated on editing *Bananas* with Ralph Rosenblum, who requested, and got, associate producer credit – his old friend Jack Grossberg, who'd recommended him to Allen in the first place, was the film's line producer. Rosenblum even spent some time on location in Puerto Rico, a uniquely disquieting experience which convinced him he functioned better in the gloom of a cutting room. There, he and Allen were now comfortable enough with one another to wrangle over larger questions of form and content.

The problem with *Bananas*, Rosenblum contended, was the same as that of *Take the Money and Run*. Determined to make a film that, from the start, concentrated on laughs above all, Allen piled in every gag he and Rose could invent, and emptied his notebooks of many more. 'Because Woody's comedies are based on a continuous stream of jokes and skits,' said Rosenblum, 'a larger than usual portion of our editing work entails a search for the moments that work and a careful weeding out of the ones that do not.' Among the scenes that didn't work was an attack on the rebel camp by Vargas' soldiers disguised as a rumba band. Some of the starch was taken out of the scene when a downpour interrupted filming, soaking the flounces of the maracas-rattling bandsmen, and Allen needed little persuasion to ditch the whole thing. Also discarded was a parody of Bob Hope, an indefatigable performer in war zones. Allen shot a scene where Hope apparently arrives to entertain the rebels, but turns out to be a fake, diverting their attention from yet another Vargas attack.

More successful was Allen's expansion of his 1965 quip about bringing a cake to Lyndon Johnson's White House. Fielding calls on President Vargas with a cake, evoking a complaint from the dictator that he prefers cherry to prune, and a tirade from an aide because he hasn't brought an assortment. The sequence originally continued with an elaborate argument about cake, with Fielding holding out for corn muffins and being abused by Vargas, but preview audiences reacted so well to Allen climbing out of the limo with his cake-box tied up with string that he dropped the rest of the scene. Retained were a knowing reference to *Battleship Potemkin*, with a pram rattling down a staircase in the midst of a battle, and a fake TV commercial for New Testament cigarettes, delivered by a suave priest and ending, 'I smoke them . . .' A glance to heaven. '*He* smokes them.'

Rosenblum persuaded Allen that even a farce like *Bananas* needed some kind of story to capture its audience, which would feel more comfortable if gags that appeared earlier in the film returned at the end, amplified or reinvented. He thought up Howard Cosell's coverage of the wedding night. It replaced the original ending, in which Fielding survives an assassination attempt by Black Power activists while making a speech at Columbia University. The explosion blackens his face, and his three putative assassins immediately greet him as a brother. As well as being somewhat limp, the sequence might have seemed, in retrospect, to add more weight to the film's overall xenophobic and racist tone.

Though Marvin Hamlisch supplied the music, *Bananas* used New Orleans jazz in a few scenes, a practice that was to continue throughout Allen's career. While he was shooting in Puerto Rico he took a few days off to fly to New Orleans for the Jazz and

Heritage Festival. He took his clarinet, and was gratified when trumpeter Punch Miller invited him to sit in at an afternoon concert on Beauregard Square. He went back in 1971 with a group of amateur musicians from New York who called themselves the Galvanized Washboard Band. Supposedly promoting *Bananas*, they managed to play in Economy Hall, a jazz club in the basement of the Royal Sonesta Hotel.

Emboldened by such experiences, Allen formed his own pick-up group in New York, the New Orleans Funeral and Ragtime Orchestra. All the players were amateurs: Dick Dreiwitz, a teacher, on trombone; his wife Barbara on tuba; stockbroker John Bucher cornet; college professor Dick Miller piano; Jay Duke, who worked in a New Jersey radio store, drums; while Allen played clarinet and Marshall Brickman banjo. From October 1970 they started playing on Wednesday nights at Barney Google's on East 68th Street. Their performances were politely reviewed in the *New York Times*, which described Allen as 'a confident, surprisingly adept performer who holds his own with a band that rolls through tightly-knit, lusty ensemble passages'. On the strength of such notices the band moved to Michael's Pub, a bigger, if characterless, bar/restaurant on the ground floor of a large building at 211 East 55th Street. With many changes of personnel, the group would support Allen through two sets every Monday night for more than two decades.

Bananas, trimmed to a lively eighty-three minutes from a first cut of two hours, opened in May 1971, exactly a year after Allen started principal photography. It only cost $2 million, but grossed $3.5 million domestically on its first run. By the time it arrived in Europe, Allen was close to earning his first million from the film. Most critics reviewed *Bananas* tolerantly, as an amiable experiment in new directions by an artist more likely to succeed elsewhere. In *Time*, Jay Cocks commented: 'Allen is an expert practitioner of the scattershot technique, in which anything is attempted for the sake of a gag. Continuity and coherence are early victims of such an approach, but Allen keeps you laughing so steadily that you notice only later that nothing really hangs together or makes much sense at all.' It was left to the *New Yorker*'s Pauline Kael to acknowledge the film's 'wild highs that suggested an erratic comic genius'.

Now a major name, Allen had no trouble persuading the prestigious Random House to publish a collection of his humour pieces under the title *Getting Even*. In *Bananas*, audiences were seeing 'Woody Allen', a *nebbish* with uncombed collar-length red hair and an obvious bald spot, dressed mostly in shapeless military fatigues. *Getting Even* represents Allen the humorist and writer. Both back and front covers feature an Allen very different from his film persona. Impassive, large-eyed, slightly pained, he stares out from a thoughtful gloom, every man's model and every woman's ideal intellectual lover.

'Viva Vargas!', which inspired *Bananas* and appeared in the liberal *Evergreen Review*, owned by Barney Rosset's *avant-garde* Grove Press, was one of the few pieces in *Getting Even* not to have been first published in the *New Yorker*. Most reflect Allen's debt to Perelman. 'Mr Big', in which Allen's private eye Kaiser Lupowitz is asked to find God, recalls Perelman's hard-boiled crime pulp parodies, while the fake history of the sandwich in 'Yes, But Can the Steam Engine Do This?' is Perelmanesque from the first lines of the introduction, in which the writer reads a magazine in the office of the dog analyst who's trying make his beagle less self-conscious about his jowls.

The most characteristically 'Woody Allen' piece in the collection is *Death Knocks*, a short play first published in the *New Yorker* in July 1968. Allen's imagination had been seized by the image of Death in Bergman's *The Seventh Seal* as a chess-playing figure in a cowled black robe and carrying a scythe, and he would incorporate him into half a dozen of his films. In *Death Knocks*, this apparition appears in the Manhattan apartment of garment manufacturer Nat Ackerman, who cunningly challenges him to a game of gin. Bickering and gossiping, the two play until Death is cleaned out and Ackerman has won another day. As Death fumbles down the stairs, Ackerman rings a friend to crow: Death is 'such a *schlep*!' Once again, Allan elects to work both sides of the street at the same time. Smart Jew defeats stupid Christian Death. But

Death will win in the end, a fact that Allen realises more than most.

In October 1971 shooting started on the film version of *Play it Again, Sam*, a project that had kicked around Hollywood since Arthur Jacobs optioned it early in 1969. Allen adapted the play, and pocketed $400,000 for the rights. Dustin Hoffman was suggested to play Felix, but Allen responded by proposing the tall and good-looking Richard Benjamin, with whom he identified sufficiently to cast him as his *alter ego* in the autobiographical *Deconstructing Harry* more than twenty-five years later, and Benjamin's real-life wife Paula Prentiss as the febrile, pill-popping Linda. Despite later protestations to the contrary, Allen would much rather have repeated his stage role on film, but nobody in Hollywood believed his name would draw crowds. 'They didn't want me in it until *Bananas* started doing well,' he says.

In the end, *Bananas* proved such a success that Paramount, to whom Jacobs had taken the project, agreed to all the principals from the stage production playing in the film, though there was never any thought that Allen would direct. 'This is a story with plot and character,' he told eventual director Herbert Ross during rehearsals, 'and I couldn't do that.' He remained for the moment, in his own mind at least, a glorified stand-up comedian skilled primarily in inventing gags and stringing them together.

The technicians' strikes which plagued Hollywood in the seventies intervened again just as the production was getting underway, and Paramount decreed that the film be shot on the West Coast, away from dissident East Coast union members. Allen reluctantly agreed to San Francisco, more congenial to him than Los Angeles, and the film was shot there in relative calm and efficiency through the winter of 1971–72. Allen's rewrites modestly opened out the play, incorporating some party and disco scenes and a few fantasies in which Felix imagines his runaway wife (Susan Anspach) exploring her sexuality with other partners, including a handsome Gentile biker whom he immediately condemns as 'a Nazi'. On screen, Allen was more able to pursue the play's theme, that dreams can be a satisfactory substitute for an emotional life –

particularly if they're all you have. The film opens with an enthralled Felix sitting in a movie theatre watching *Casablanca* for the millionth time and mouthing its famous dialogue, a motif he pursues to the end, where, renouncing Linda after their one night together, he doesn't simply, as in the play, quote from *Casablanca*, but reproduces the entire last scene of Michael Curtiz's classic. The film of *Play it Again, Sam* is much more of a paean to escapist cinema than is the play, and contributed substantially to the continuing popularity of *Casablanca* and Humphrey Bogart. It opened in May 1972 at New York's famous Radio City Music Hall, gratifying a childhood fantasy of Allen's, and grossed $11 million in US domestic rentals on an investment of $1.3 million.

After *Bananas*, politics would continue to figure occasionally in Allen's films, but always as an amusing oddity rather than a serious subject. When in October 1969 activists demanded that, as part of a 'Vietnam Moratorium', everyone opposed to the war stop work for the day, Allen agreed not to perform in the matinee of the stage version of *Play it Again, Sam*, and urged other actors to do the same. He also wrote a clause into his later contracts that his films could not play in South Africa under apartheid, though the stand wasn't one he took particularly seriously. 'This unfortunately failed to topple the regime,' he joked, 'and apartheid continued, though I have received a number of grateful letters from Afrikaners who say that while they avoided my films before, now they are prevented from even wandering into one of them accidentally, and for this they thank me with all their hearts.'

His general attitude to politics remained 'a plague on both your houses'. 'I hate politics,' he said in the sixties. 'Political thinking throughout history has never worked. As long as it's a question of is it going to be Democrat or Republican, Communist or whatever, as long as people delude themselves into thinking if they can solve those issues they'd be happy, nothing's going to happen. I think that if there were only two people in the world and they were identical twins, one would find something wrong with the other somehow.'

In 1972 he dismissed American party politics as just 'an aimless shuffling of group leaders'. Despite his having appeared at Johnson rallies in Paris and London, by the time of *Annie Hall* he would have his character Alvy Singer, earlier shown campaigning for liberal Democrat Adlai Stevenson against Dwight Eisenhower, rail, 'Lyndon Johnson is a *politician*. You know the ethics those guys have. It's like – uh, a notch underneath child molester.' After having boasted of his conversations with Lyndon Johnson's daughters at the White House reception, he later dismissed them as 'two of the ugliest sisters I've ever seen'.

Manhattan was meant to include a sequence suggested by a march of neo-Nazis through Skokie, Illinois. When a Nazi group decides to parade in New Jersey, Ike Davis suggests to his friends that they 'get some guys together, you know, get some bricks and baseball bats and really explain things to 'em'. Who among Davis' circle of academics and arts journalists would join such a group is never made clear, and they unanimously decide that a 'devastating satirical piece' on the op-ed page of the *New York Times* will satisfy their need for protest. United Artists, the backers of *Manhattan*, found the scene 'strident and depressive', and Allen dropped it, leaving as the film's only political element a fund-raiser for the Equal Rights Amendment held in the sculpture garden of the Museum of Modern Art, with the radical former Congresswoman Bella Abzug playing herself. Thereafter, any comments by Allen on anti-Semitism would be confined to his 'casuals' for the *New Yorker*.

Allen's description of the 1965 White House reception hints at what he finds truly interesting in the political process. The resonances with the Texas prodigality of films like *Giant*, the warm night, lanterns on the terrace, dancing, the flattering attention of Johnson's daughter – he makes almost no reference to LBJ or Lady Bird – have a playful, even erotic subtext. 'Power,' said Henry Kissinger, 'is the great aphrodisiac.' Politically committed women both excite and frighten Allen's men. Political events are almost exclusively an opportunity to get laid. In *Bananas*, Fielding Mellish joins a Central American revolution to impress airheaded Louise Lasser. In the 'Do Aphrodisiacs Work?' episode of *Everything You Always Wanted to Know About Sex*, Allen plays the court jester who is executed for trying to sleep with queen Lynn Redgrave –

not out of passion but because his father, appearing as a ghost, has urged him to do it for every *schlemiel* who's ever wanted to *stumpf* a *shiksa*.

Doing a stand-up at the Stevenson fund-raiser in *Annie Hall*, an incident based on Allen's appearance at an August 1968 rally for Eugene McCarthy, Alvy Singer jokes that he dated someone during Eisenhower's administration and 'was trying to do to her what Eisenhower has been doing to the country for the last eight years'. Stage-manager for the event is Allison Portchnik (Carol Kane), who's writing a thesis on 'Political Commitment in Twentieth-Century Literature', a theme Alvy scorns. 'You're, like, New York Jewish left-wing liberal intellectual Central Park West Brandeis University . . . uh, the socialist summer camps and the . . . the father with the Ben Shahn drawings, right? And you're, really, you know, strike-oriented . . .' When Allison protests at this cultural stereotyping, Alvy justifies himself by saying, 'I'm a bigot, you know, but for the left,' and seduces her. The relationship expires during an argument about the Warren Report on the Kennedy assassination, which Alvy uses as a pretext to avoid having sex with her. Politics, a means of getting into her bed, serves also to get him out of it.

Allen's one attempt at political satire foundered on just such a blurring of sex and power politics. In December 1971 he wrote, directed and appeared in *The Politics and Humor of Woody Allen*, an hour-long TV special commissioned from producer Jack Kuney by Jim Day, president of WNET Channel 13, New York's innovative Public Broadcasting System station. Allen accepted Equity scale for an actor of $135, though with the promise of more once the programme was aired by WNET and a possible 219 other PBS stations across the country.

As well as a stand-up routine and an interview in which Allen said he 'loathed' Nixon's administration, *The Politics and Humor of Woody Allen* contained a thirty-minute fake documentary, supposedly one in a series called *Men of Crisis*, titled 'The Harvey Wallinger Story'. In this forerunner of *Zelig*, Allen parodied not only Nixon but the candidates running against him, both from the left (Hubert Humphrey) and the right (George Wallace). His

real target is Henry Kissinger, the guttural-voiced ex-Harvard professor who in 1973 would become Nixon's Secretary of State,
and in particular the attraction he exercised for attractive young
women.

Allen plays Wallinger, whose life is fraught with cross-
connections between sex and power. His mother, a journalist,
briefly married Mussolini 'until she discovered he was Italian'.
Wallinger himself marries Renata Baldwin (Diane Keaton), daughter of a newspaper magnate, but they divorce when she finds
he's slept with a Democrat. 'I would not have minded if he had
committed adultery with a member of his own party,' she says
piously, but Wallinger explains, 'Sex is a capricious thing. Sometimes I feel like making love to a Republican. Generally I like to
wait and see what the Russians do first.'

Wallinger is the power behind Nixon's throne. 'Nobody goes
in to see the President without going through Harvey Wallinger,'
explains one politician. 'If you want something done, you've got
to be in good with Harvey. If Mrs Nixon wants to kiss her husband, she has to kiss Harvey first.' Wallinger confirms that even
the First Lady is not immune to his charm. 'Dick is out of the
country a lot and sometimes Pat calls up and asks me to come
over, but I say no.' He is often seen 'escorting some of the capital's
most exciting women', says the commentary. One of them, a nun,
Sister Mary Elizabeth Smith, confesses, 'He's an unbelievable swinger, a freak.' Wallinger says, 'My social life has been greatly exaggerated. I like pretty women – who doesn't? I like sex, but not
un-American sex. I think sex without guilt, without shame, it's
not good; it becomes almost pleasurable.'

Jim Day cut a few of the more outrageous lines, but basically
approved the programme. Some scripts found their way to Washington, where Nixon's re-election committee (the Campaign to
Re-Elect the President, immortalised by the acronym CREEP), had
become notorious for its dirty tricks campaign and ruthless misuse
of presidential power. Nixon felt that PBS's programmes were
biased against him, and Clay T. Whitehead, head of the White
House Office of Telecommunications Policy, told PBS general
manager Gerald Slater that any further criticism of the adminis-

tration might result in funding cuts to the entire network. When news of Allen's project reached the White House, Whitehead told a House Subcommittee that, in his opinion, PBS had moved 'too far' towards the left, and that 'at this time' the administration would not support any long-term financing.

'The question I had to ask myself,' said Day, 'was: had I the right to jeopardise the whole financial future of PBS by showing [Allen's film]?' The station's attorneys viewed the programme, and advised Day to remove all the Pat Nixon references, plus a news clip in which Hubert Humphrey, stumbling on his way to receive a doctorate, accidentally gives his audience the finger.

Day stalled, insisting that only the station president, Ethan Hitchcock, could decide such matters. 'By the time I got to my office on Monday morning,' says Day, 'Ethan was already in the theatre seeing a screening. When he came out his face was a picture. He said nothing to me. He went straight back to his office in Rockefeller Plaza and within an hour I received a typed memorandum from him saying that *on no account* must the programme be shown.'

By mid-February 1972, press reports had piqued the interest of many PBS affiliates. WNET promised to screen *The Politics and Humor of Woody Allen* on closed circuit, then reneged, claiming it couldn't find a finished tape. This was probably true, since by then the show had been cut and cut again until it ran only thirty minutes. 'Woody himself had been brought back time and time again to try to make it work,' says Day. 'In the finish, I even tried once again to salvage at least some of the material in another show entirely, one we were planning to do on political satire. Unfortunately Woody was by then so outraged by what he was being told was our reluctance to show his work that he refused to make any more cuts.'

Though it wouldn't be running the programme, which it was now publicly calling 'a scathing and personal attack' on Nixon, WNET told other stations that they were free to buy it, but should be aware of the risk of libel suits from Pat Nixon and Kissinger. Also, other political parties might argue that the show represented campaign programming for the Democrats, and demand equal time to put their own point of view, a nightmare for small local stations, who visualised themselves besieged. After that, nobody dared air *The Politics and Humor of Woody Allen* even in its truncated form, and it was shelved.

Such experiences didn't enamour Allen of politics, but simply reinforced his antipathy. In 1988, weighing in about the Israel–Palestine controversy – inevitably on the op-ed pages of the *New York Times* – he began his criticism of Israeli excesses with a few paragraphs of self-introduction that comprise a political credo of sorts.

I'm not a political activist. If anything, I'm an uninformed coward, totally convinced that a stand on any issue from subway fares to the length of women's skirts will ultimately lead me before a firing squad. I prefer instead to sit around in coffee houses and grouse to loved ones privately about social conditions, invariably muttering imprecations on the heads of politicians, most of whom I put in a class with blackjack dealers. Take a look, for instance, at the Reagan administration. Or just at the President himself. Or the men hoping to become President. Or the last cluster of Presidents. These characters would hardly inspire confidence in the average bail bondsman. Another reason I'm apathetic to political cross-currents is that I've never felt man's problems could be solved through political solutions. The sporadic reshuffling of pompous-sounding world leaders with their fibs and nostrums has proved meaningless. Not that one is always just as bad as the next – but almost. The truth is that whenever the subject turns to ameliorating mankind's condition, my mind turns to more profound matters: man's lack of a spiritual centre, for example – or his existential terror. The empty universe is another item that scares me, along with eternal annihilation, ageing, terminal illness and the absence of God in a hostile, raging void. I always feel that as long as man is finite he will never be truly relaxed.

14

Everything You Always Wanted to Know About Sex (*But were Afraid to Ask) and Sleeper

TOKLAS: 'What is the answer, Gertrude? What is the answer?'
STEIN: 'What's the question?'

Reputed deathbed conversation between Gertrude Stein and long-time companion Alice B. Toklas

During the preparations for filming *Play it Again, Sam*, Allen and Marshall Brickman had been working on an adaptation of *Everything You Always Wanted to Know About Sex*, and finding it difficult. Actor Elliott Gould and his partner, producer Jack Brodsky, who optioned the book as soon as it hit the bestseller list, had since split, and happily sold the property to UA, having realised, as Allen and Brickman were now doing, that there was not much to it beyond the title. Not that this was an insurmountable problem. A catchy title was half the battle in winning an audience. At various times *The Origin of Species* and *The Decline of the West* had both been optioned by Hollywood, while S.J. Perelman had been hired in the thirties – vainly, as it turned out – to find a film in Dale Carnegie's bestseller *How to Win Friends and Influence People*. More recently, *Sex and the Single Girl*, a factual primer by magazine editor Helen Gurley Brown not dissimilar to Reuben's book, had been successfully translated into a movie in 1964, followed by *A Guide for the Married Man* in 1967.

With the benefit of their intimacy with European cinema, Allen and Bridgeman saw that Reuben's book could be an effective pretext for what the French called a *film à sketches*, an anthology of short films hung on nothing more than a promising title. 'The Seven Deadly Sins', 'Love and the Frenchwoman' and 'Love at

Twenty' had all inspired successful films in the sixties. Even more attractive to Allen were the opportunities to satirise not only the sexual oddities reflected in Reuben's answers to the questions he posed, but the assumption implicit in those questions that most Americans knew nothing whatsoever about sex. Long acquaintance with the subject had satisfied Allen that the reverse was true.

The production of *Everything You Always Wanted to Know* represented a departure from the casual methods of his earlier films. Confident that this could be Allen's 'breakthrough' movie, catapulting him out of the East Coast stand-up ghetto and into middle America, UA allocated it a $2 million budget, but insisted he film in Hollywood, which could provide the production values they felt it needed. Allen found Los Angeles no more congenial in January 1972 than he had in 1956. Career Hollywood film-makers knew nothing of his work, and cared less. Cameraman David M. Walsh initially didn't want to light it, regarding Allen's earlier efforts as murky and amateurish. Also, Ralph Rosenblum would be occupied directing the documentary *Turner*, and couldn't cut the film. There was one plus: Dale Hennesy, who did the sets for *Fantastic Voyage*, in which a miniaturised submarine under the dubious command of Raquel Welch, Stephen Boyd and Donald Pleasence voyages through the bloodstream of a stricken diplomat to mend a brain lesion, signed on to design the futuristic final episode 'What Happens During Ejaculation?', where Allen plays a sperm about to go 'over the top'.

Big-name performers were also leery of appearing in something that looked like sexploitation. The sportscaster Howard Cosell, whom Allen described deadpan as looking like 'a young Bela Lugosi', declined to be cast as mad scientist Dr Barnardo, as he was worried that it would damage his image. For an episode called 'Why do Some Women have Trouble Reaching an Orgasm?', a parody of Italian cinema in which a wife finds that she can only achieve satisfaction if she has sex in a public place, Richard Benjamin and Paula Prentiss refused the roles, as did John Cassavetes and Raquel Welch, so Allen played the man himself, opposite Louise Lasser.

A few stars did agree to do cameos, including Tony Randall and Burt Reynolds, who volunteered to appear as technicians in 'Ejaculation'. In April 1972 Reynolds' notorious nude centrefold had appeared in *Cosmopolitan* magazine, giving his inclusion in the film an additional topicality. Talk-show veterans Regis Philbin, Pamela Mason and Dan Barry (disgraced host of the 'fixed' TV programme *Twenty-One*, subject of Robert Redford's 1994 film *Quiz Show*) played in 'What are Sex Perverts?', a parody of *I've Got a Secret* in which the panel tries to guess the perversion of the guest who, if he stumps them, gets to enact his fantasy on TV. In this case, a rabbi asks to be tied up and beaten by a beautiful *goyische* girl while his wife sits at his feet and eats pork chops.

As Allen shops among the fashionable themes of 1972 for inspiration, *Everything You Always Wanted to Know* veers as jarringly in style as it does in content. New York critic Andrew Sarris would rate the sketches as 'one brilliant, one just bearable, and five in the dismal range between tasteless and tedious', and would point out their debts – to Terry Southern's novel *Flash and Filigree*, which contained a game-show called *What's My Disease?*, not unlike *What's My Perversion?*, and to Jules Feiffer's screenplay for Mike Nichols' 1971 *Carnal Knowledge*, which reflects many of Allen's preoccupations. Allen admitted that he used the film to try out different ways of shooting. 'It was experimental for me to do all those short pieces – but it helped me to improve a little technically.' The elaborately designed 'What Happens During Ejaculation?', with its futuristic white interiors, contrasts with 'What are Sex Perverts?', which recreates not only the boxy sets of early television but the murky and jittering image of the crude kinescope film copies in which such programmes survive.

'Why do Some Women have Trouble Reaching an Orgasm?' should have been shot in the style of fifties neo-realist Italian comedies, but UA feared that a black-and-white segment would alienate the audience. Allen switched to what he claimed was the style of Michelangelo Antonioni, whose first colour film, *The Red Desert*, had come out in 1964, but the resemblance is perfunctory, as is the episode's rote-learned Italian dialogue. But Allen's idea of working in black and white persisted, eventually to surface in the magnificently atmospheric *Manhattan*.

Two or three of the film's episodes are relentlessly facetious shaggy-dog stories. They include 'Are Transvestites Homosexual?' featuring Lou Jacobi as a cross-dresser caught out when he indulges his penchant at the home of a couple he and his wife are visiting. 'Are the Findings of Doctors and Clinics who do Sexual Research Accurate?' (a question Reuben's book never posed) parodies sf/horror films like *Attack of the Fifty-Foot Woman*. Allen, playing his *What's New Pussycat* role of Victor Shakapopolis, visits the remote house of mad Dr Barnardo (John Carradine), only to be pursued by his greatest creation, a giant breast. 'What is Sodomy?', the subject of which isn't sodomy but rather bestiality, is saved by a performance of inspired mortification and misty-eyed fascination from Gene Wilder as a doctor who falls in love with a sheep.

Allen still fancied himself a parodist, but the Barnardo sequence and 'Do Aphrodisiacs Work?', which opens the film, show his growing impatience with the form. In the best parody, the author immerses himself in the style he means to satirise. But Allen was simply too interested in words, and in getting a laugh, to make the sacrifice. His quips have the wiseacre tone of the guy in the front-row stalls muttering comments to his friends during a bad movie. Just as an imitation begins to amuse, he pops out from behind the decor with a one-liner, as if scared that he's lost his audience.

'Do Aphrodisiacs Work?' begins with Allen as the unfunny jester at the medieval court of Anthony Quayle and his queen, Lynn Redgrave, only for him to become Hamlet when he encounters the ghost of his father – played in an anonymous cameo by writer Alan Caillou – on the battlements, and decides he must make love to the queen or die trying. Obtaining an aphrodisiac from the palace magician, he administers it successfully, but is caught with his hand trapped in her chastity belt, and beheaded. The comedy is just as eclectic as the story, switching from straight twentieth-century stand-up as the fool tries to divert the court ('How about that plague? Looks black, doesn't it?') to heavy-handed 'doth-ing' and 'prithee-ing' with the queen ('Do I senseth that thou hath copped a feel . . . ?' etc.), interspersed with Allen musing to the camera in the style of his more mature nightclub act. Nothing works, however, and Quayle's repeated assertions that 'He just isn't *funny!*' find an echo in us. The gags have a whiff of mothballs, and, as Andrew Sarris remarked, 'His locution "cops a feel" is strictly Flatbush fifties.'

Some episodes were dropped from the script early, mostly in deference to UA, though Louise Lasser claims credit for talking Allen out of a Biblical sequence based on the Old Testament's famous masturbator, Onan, to have been played by Allen, and substituting the Italian parody 'Why do Some Women have Trouble Reaching an Orgasm?' One eventual reject survived long enough to be filmed. 'What Makes a Man a Homosexual?' featured Allen and Lasser as black-widow spiders named Sheldon and Lisa. They go through a conventional sexual chat-up and make love, after which Lisa devours him. The sequence ends with Allen, now playing an entomologist, watching the scene through a microscope. His secretary (Lasser) comes in, and Allen, in a voice heavy with homosexual emphasis, wishes her goodnight. Allen agonised over this sketch, aware that it encapsulated a truth about the essential menace women represented to him, and his view of the destructive nature of sex in general, but was unable to make it work. It was deleted from American prints of the film, but survived in some European versions.

A similar disquiet underlies most other episodes of the film, even 'What Happens During Ejaculation?' which, critic Maurice Yacowar theorised, illustrates a theme in Ernst Becker's classic text *The Denial of Death*, an Allen favourite which Alvy recommends to Annie in *Annie Hall*, and of which Allen has said 'I firmly believe [its] ideas.' Becker posits that the terror of sex is a disguised terror of death, since sex draws attention to the nature of the body and its unavoidable dissolution. 'The entire film,' says Yacowar, 'demonstrates Becker's thesis that sexuality is a primary means by which man attempts to evade his mortality.' Gene Wilder confirms that the shoot, in line with such preoccupations, was a dour experience. 'It was like walking on a Bergman set: people talking in whispers, serious looks on Woody's face. He communicates through silence.' Dr Reuben accurately saw the film as 'a sexual tragedy. Every episode in the picture was a chronicle of failure, which was the converse of everything in the book.'

Allen continued to tinker with *Everything You Always Wanted to Know* right up to its release in August 1972. The version shown at critics' previews began with 'What Happens During Ejaculation?' and ended with the horror-film parody 'Are the Findings of Doctors and Clinics who do Sexual Research Accurate?', but once it became clear that 'Ejaculation' was the most successful and popular episode, Allen switched it to the end. Whatever the critics' reservations, audiences loved the film, and it became America's tenth-highest moneymaker of the year.

Allen's 20 per cent profit participation in *Everything You Always Wanted to Know About Sex* would net him another million, and would in time free him forever from any worries about money. In 1976 he boasted, 'I haven't cashed a cheque or been inside a bank in ten years.' Except for his salary as director/writer/star, Allen's share of his films' revenue remained mostly in the form of 'net points' – percentages of each film's income payable only after the studio had deducted its production costs, bank interest and charges for prints, advertising and a multitude of other expenses. Hollywood wisdom held that out of any ten films, one made money, two broke even and the rest flopped, but it was increasingly the case during the sixties and seventies that, with foreign sales, television rights and, later, home video income, almost every film made a profit in the end. This fact was disguised by the studios' skilful 'creative accounting', and producers were resigned to seeing little or no income from their net points. Such was the success of Allen's films, however, that even after the worst that Hollywood accountants could do, his movies would, eventually, make him rich.

To earn some quick money, Allen agreed to fulfil an old contractual obligation by making a six-week stage tour, culminating in an appearance in October at Las Vegas on the bottom half of the bill with Rollins and Joffe's other big-name client, Harry Belafonte.

This date alone paid a respectable $85,000, augmented by his winnings at the tables, where his luck remained as good as ever, but audiences were less than enthusiastic. Arriving early for his show, Allen found the staff moving more potted palms into the room to make it look less empty.

As usual, he spent his spare time practising the clarinet and writing. The product of this tour was *Death*, his first one-act play since *Death Knocks*. A product of his admiration for Kafka – though Stig Bjorkman points out that it also recalls Hans Fallada's novel *Kleiner Mann, was nun* (Little Man, What Now?) – the play is set in a nameless nineteenth-century European city menaced by a serial killer. The hero, Kleinman (literally 'little man'), is roused from his bed to join a group of vigilantes, and despite his protests that he doesn't want to get involved, is soon roaming the foggy streets, where after confronting a murderer as colourless and negligible as himself, he becomes his next victim.

Allen visualised *Death* as one section of a three-part night at the theatre, the other acts to be *God*, which he wrote in 1975, and *Sex*, which he apparently never finished. The form of the one-act play would continue to appeal to him for decades as a more profitable use of his skill in parody, which no longer satisfied him in his films, and which he usually dissipated in pieces for the *New Yorker*; but he could no longer close his eyes to the far greater rewards offered by Hollywood: in the year *Don't Drink the Water* was such a hit on Broadway, a single film, *The Graduate*, outgrossed the total combined income from all the season's stage productions. David Merrick showed some interest in staging *Sex*, *God* and *Death* in the 1973–74 Broadway season, but was put off by the potential price of $250,000 for three casts and three sets, at a time when most plays cost half that to stage. *Death* went on the shelf, to be dusted off in 1992 as the basis of *Shadows and Fog*, but the idea of an evening of his short plays continued to preoccupy Allen.

While he was still working on *Everything You Always Wanted to Know About Sex*, Allen pondered ways to build on its most obviously successful sequence, the concluding episode, 'What Happens

During Ejaculation?', in which he played a sperm. He knew little
about science fiction, but it was obviously hot, especially with
young audiences, who in 1969 had flocked to Stanley Kubrick's
2001: A Space Odyssey. Buttonholing his assistant director on
Everything, Fred Gallo, he asked, 'How much would it cost to
build a futuristic town?' Gallo didn't falter. 'Millions,' he said.
'There are four things to stay away from in movies,' he continued.
'Boats and water, animals, kids, and futurism.'

But the idea had taken root. Back in New York, Allen proposed
to Rollins and Joffe that his next production for United Artists
consist not of one movie but two, to be shown consecutively. The
first part would be a Manhattan comedy, at the end of which
Woody died and his body was cryogenically preserved. After an
interval the audience would return for Part II, in which he wakes
up five hundred years in the future. The idea fired United Artists,
but Allen, once he came to realise the logistical difficulties of such
a giant project, not to mention the potential for disaster, got cold
feet. Instead he decided to make only the second part, and invited
Marshall Brickman, then working on *The Dick Cavett Show*, to
collaborate on the script.

'On *Sleeper*, we actually wrote it line by line in a room,' says
Brickman, who happily took a sabbatical from TV to work with
Allen. It was a different system to the one they used on other films
they wrote together. On *Annie Hall* and *Manhattan*, Allen would
give Brickman a quick first draft, to which he made additions.
This time they walked around Manhattan, discussing the perils
that might be faced in 2173 AD by Allen's character, Miles Monroe, half-owner of the Happy Carrot Health Food Restaurant on
Bleecker Street in Greenwich Village, who dies on the operating
table during routine minor surgery for a peptic ulcer and is frozen
until he can be treated.

Revived illicitly by renegade scientists anxious to overthrow the
dictator of the time, a beaming white-clad figure in a wheelchair
like Franklin D. Roosevelt, complete with a dog at his side, Miles
is whisked from hide-out to hide-out and, once the gang is captured, flees on his own, disguised for a while as a domestic robot.
He kidnaps, then befriends, rich but dim Luna Schlosser, but

they're separated when the police capture them. Miles is brainwashed and re-educated as a functioning member of the new society. Luna escapes, finds the rebels, is politicised, becomes the mistress of their husky leader Erno, and leads them in an attack on a hospital where doctors are trying to clone the nose of the dictator, all that remains of him after an assassination attempt. Miles, restored to sanity, helps Luna steal the nose and hold it to ransom until the rebels arrive.

Both *Bananas* and *Everything You Always Wanted to Know About Sex* adapted books which, it might be argued, weren't good for much else, but with *Sleeper* Allen went after bigger game. As well as the obvious borrowings from H.G. Wells' *When the Sleeper Wakes* (1899) and *The Food of the Gods* (1904) and Gogol's fable 'The Nose' (1836), he and Brickman used ideas from Aldous Huxley's *Brave New World* (1932) and such films as Jean-Luc Godard's *Alphaville* (1965) and Fritz Lang's *Metropolis* (1926). The computer HAL 9000 from *2001: A Space Odyssey* also reappears, one of many borrowings from Kubrick's film.

Most of Allen and Brickman's ideas, however, clearly came from David Butler's 1930 science-fiction comedy musical *Just Imagine*, in which comic El Brendel, struck by lightning on the golf course, wakes up fifty years later to a world of food pills, robots, sex and procreation by machine, and personal autogiros – many of which appear in *Sleeper*. Brendel also, as in *Sleeper*, becomes involved in a future revolutionary movement. (Coincidentally, the female lead of *Just Imagine* was Maureen O'Sullivan, mother of Mia Farrow.)

The futuristic settings again demanded Hollywood studio shooting, especially since UA had allocated the film only its usual $2 million budget, so Allen reluctantly moved to Los Angeles in February 1973, setting up headquarters in a three-bedroom cottage, incongruously planted with white daisies behind a picket fence, on the remains of the old Pathé/Selznick lot in Culver City. It had been Clark Gable's dressing room during the shooting of *Gone With the Wind*, but if Allen felt any *frisson* it was lost in the chills of trying to pilot his comic creation through the jungle of studio technical departments. He never hid his contempt for Los Angeles, and missed no opportunity in the film to snipe at it – asked what it was like to be asleep for two hundred years, Miles sneers, 'It was like a weekend in Beverly Hills.'

In style, Allen wanted *Sleeper* to play like silent comedy, with mostly visual gags taken at a brisk run. He persuaded Diane Keaton to appear as Luna, the poetess with a PhD in Oral Sex and Cosmetics. Having just played a poorly-paid role in *The Godfather* and with no other very attractive work in sight, Keaton agreed, though she's visibly uncomfortable in the film's slapstick gags and parodies.

Allen cast no other major names, though he did take the time to revenge himself on Howard Cosell for his refusal to play in *Everything You Always Wanted to Know About Sex*. When the scientists ask Miles to identify pictures and videotapes of various 1970s personalities, the examples include a recording of Cosell droning on about Muhammad Ali on *The Wide World of Sports*. 'We think that people who had committed terrible crimes might have been forced to watch this as a punishment,' suggests one scientist. 'That's exactly right,' Allen confirms.

Richard Nixon also appears, giving his 'Checkers' speech, and the scientist speculates that since almost every other evidence of his existence has been effaced, this man must have been a President of the United States who committed some heinous crime. Allen again agrees – remarkably prescient, considering that the shooting preceded the Watergate scandal by many months.

To complement the film's fleet comic attack, Allen looked for a visual style like 'a big cartoon, cute and funny'. The costumes – designed by Joel Schumacher, later the director of *St Elmo's Fire* and *Flatliners* – were monochrome, as much like those of silent comedy as possible. Settings would be all pastels, a parody of the covers of science fiction magazines and in particular of *2001*, the last section of which Dale Hennesy, the designer with whom Allen worked on *Everything You Always Wanted to Know About Sex*, took as his visual inspiration.

Kubrick's spaceman, stranded in an alien environment on the far side of the universe, lived and died in a gleaming white hotel suite furnished incongruously with eighteenth- and nineteenth-century antiques. Hennesy's future for *Sleeper* used the same idea, with mostly Victorian furniture. Lumpy wardrobes and embroidered fire-screens perch incongruously in all-white interiors, an effect sarcastically underlined by the collectibles valued by the people of 2173: the schlock paintings of big-eyed urchins by German artist Walter Keane, neon beer signs, glass birds that, once set nodding, sip mechanically from glasses of water. The slang of the time is no less absurd. Diane Keaton's Luna, recognisably parodying her own early pre-Woody LA persona, coos of the urchin painting, 'It's Keane! No, it's better than Keane. It's *Cugat*!'

Allen had early ideas of shooting some of *Sleeper* in Brazil's capital of Brasilia, the futuristic buildings of which would have provided an ideal background, but Jack Grossberg, again his line producer, persuaded him that budget constraints and UA's fifty-day production schedule mandated locations no further from Hollywood than Colorado. They compromised with Monterey, where some futuristic buildings could be borrowed for exteriors, and Denver, where Allen had seen a house by Charles Deaton perched on a pedestal which summed up his vision of the over-controlled and mechanised future in *Sleeper*.

It might have been easier to shoot in Brazil, since the production was immediately stopped short by plunging temperatures, blizzards and a plague of ticks carried over the Rockies on an improvident breeze. Allen meanwhile battled with the logistics of his most complicated film yet. 'This is a movie about wires,' he would complain as the cables pulling his soundless future bubble cars snapped. Weeks of work were poured into two ambitious pieces of physical comedy that took days to shoot. The first, a seven-minute sequence in which Miles and Luna penetrate the medical centre, involved Miles being lowered down the side of the building on tape that's running through a giant computer. Luna is distracted by black suds bubbling out of a washing machine and the imminent arrival of two doctors. The computer goes wild, and Miles is jerked up and down the face of the building until, reaching the right window, he cuts an opening in the shape of his body, and swings inside.

'It took an enormous amount of men stringing wires for two

days on location in Colorado,' Allen remembered. 'They had wires in rooms and down the hall. It was a very elaborate business to make it work. I had a harness on underneath my clothes. I thought to myself, "Well, I'll just improvise." But now I'm hanging out the window and I see it's much higher than I thought because I'm way off the ground and I'm bouncing around. I've never done a stunt before, and I'm scared. I also filmed an enormous amount going on in the room with the girl, and the tape billowing over and spilling and everything. But it was just not usable for the film. Either it wasn't funny enough, or it came out funny but at that point in the picture we couldn't wait around for it. It was just too much of a *tour de force* or a vaudeville turn and the story had to keep moving.'

The scene was cut to the bone – a similar fate to that suffered by Miles' attempt to master Luna's mechanical kitchen. A giant sausage emerged from a porthole and attacked him, and the gadgets included one that pelted him with fruit and raw eggs, and an oven that flattened a chicken into something like an over-starched shirt. All that remains of the sequence is his battle with a runaway instant pudding, which he subdues with a broom.

CBS's flagship documentary series *60 Minutes* sent producer Bill Moses and a crew to Colorado to interview Allen during the shoot. 'We had total access,' recalls Moses. 'We spent five days and shot about ten thousand feet of film, from which I could use about thirty seconds.' Allen only grudgingly agreed to do anything other than chat in a desultory way, and between shots he played his clarinet, methodically practising scales. When Moses suggested that, to create a more relaxed effect, he might favour them with a tune, 'he looked at us as if we were nuts. "I would never do that," he said.'

Later in his career Allen would reshoot scenes, and indeed entire films, if they didn't satisfy him, but on *Sleeper* he had no such leeway. Jack Grossberg grumbled as Allen delayed shooting for hours to capture the perfect sunset, or demanded repeated retakes when inflatable suits refused to fill satisfactorily or the twelve-foot banana, celery-stalk and carrot he finds on an experimental farm failed to meet his exacting standards. To placate UA, Allen waived his $35,000 directing and acting fee, but the film, fifty-one days over schedule by the end of July, was clearly in trouble – all the more so since UA had already announced it as their main Christmas release.

At Grossberg's urging Allen reversed his usual method, in which he only started cutting when all the shooting was done, and flew out Ralph Rosenblum in August to take a look at what he'd shot. As soon as he arrived, Rosenblum found himself caught between his friend Grossberg and Allen, who blamed Grossberg for many of his troubles. He and Grossberg never worked together again, Allen transferring his confidence to Fred Gallo, who would stay with him up to and including *Annie Hall*.

To a background of the New Orleans jazz Allen had decided to use as his score, Rosenblum spent all of August reducing the film's first cut of two hours twenty minutes to a more manageable ninety. As usual, the problem was too many gags, some so ambitious that they overbalanced the flimsy plot. In one of the most elaborate, a dream scene shot in the Mojave desert, Miles is a pawn in a giant chess game, pursued by a black knight intent on skewering him. Rosenblum persuaded Allen to drop the sequence, as well as another in which Miles does magic tricks to charm Luna into sex. Allen replaced the latter with one, played almost straight, in which Miles toys with a half-assembled clarinet and flatters Luna until she asks, 'Do you want to perform sex with me?' In one of the film's best quips, Miles replies, 'I don't think I'm up to a performance, but I'll rehearse with you if you like.'

What worked best, as usual, were the gags meant to appeal to sophisticated city audiences, especially New Yorkers. As *Time* magazine would later remark, it sometimes seemed that Allen's films were *only* seen by New Yorkers. Most of these jokes played knowingly on East Coast preoccupations and prejudices. On the run, Miles and Luna stop at the home of the *Cage aux Folles*-like menage of an extravagantly gay couple; even their robot servant wears an apron and affects a camp voice. Caught and re-educated, Miles is measured for a new suit by two robot tailors with exaggerated noses who bicker in best Lower East Side style. *And* the coat doesn't fit. Dope doesn't exist in 2173, but people get high fondling a silver sphere called an Orb, which reduces them to the same giggling stupor as a joint. Miles quickly succumbs to the Orb, and is later seen cradling one as big as a beach ball.

Other gags meant mainly for New York audiences included references to Norman Mailer bequeathing his ego to the Harvard Medical School, and a passing comment that the atomic war which transformed America began when a man named Albert Shanker got hold of an atomic weapon. Shanker, militant president of the American Federation of Teachers, was then involved in an acrimonious teachers' strike in the New York district of Browns-ville.

When Rosenblum returned to New York after the summer, Allen was left with a largely completed film but no satisfactory ending. By now he was preoccupied by the music, which he'd decided to record in New Orleans with those of his musician heroes who were still alive and playing. Most of them, all older than sixty-five, appeared periodically at Preservation Hall, a rundown building, barely twenty feet by forty, where fans crowded in to sit on narrow benches and enjoy authentic New Orleans music played by a few oldsters who remembered it from before Louis Armstrong and others took it up the river to Chicago.

Allen paid $12,000 to the Preservation Hall Jazz Band, whose members included Chester Dardis, Emanuel Sales, Josiah 'Cie' Frazier, Percy Humphrey and eighty-three-year-old trombonist Jim Robinson, to record a series of rags and stomps, augmented later by his own New Orleans Funeral and Ragtime Orchestra. In his element, Allen played in a street parade with Percy Humphrey, and sat in on Congo Square with Punch Miller and Cie Frazier. The Preservation Hall veterans supposedly knew nothing of Allen's work. The last film any of them had seen was the 1971 black thriller *Shaft*. Before that they had only been to silent films. Allen diffidently sat in on some numbers, next to Jim Robinson, who commented politely that his playing reminded him of George Lewis. 'What's your name again?' Robinson asked. 'Woody,' mumbled Allen. 'Willard? You're real good, Willard.' Allen glowed.

Against this story, affectionately and often recalled, one must set the general feeling that Allen is, at best, a sedulous amateur of the clarinet. 'Nobody's ever said a thing to me about my playing that I thought was sincere,' he admitted once, and one expert, having heard him and his band in London on their 1996 tour, remarked, 'It's the first time he's made me laugh.' Perhaps Robinson and his friends were more up to date on movies than Allen knew, and were polite enough to offer their employer a consoling compliment.

Sleeper has been called 'the first true Woody Allen film', a tag it probably deserves. It is certainly the first to bear the familiar stylistic hallmarks. The musical score of twenties jazz and popular music would become part of the Allen signature, as would the minimalist credits (designed by Norman Gorbaty) in white lettering on a black screen. The film also features the 'Woody' persona in its fully realised form. From the moment the scientists roll open the aluminium foil in which he's wrapped, revealing glasses, lank shoulder-length hair, prominent nose and goofy smile, Allen's in character.

Pervaded as it is by a sense of personal helplessness and inadequacy, *Sleeper* also offers an insight into Allen's psychology. 'Allen's central metaphor is sleep,' remarks Maurice Yacowar, 'which can be taken to represent non-commitment, either in one's political or emotional life.' Allen's disquiet about commitment is particularly evident in the film in the area of sex. All the women in this future are frigid, and all the men impotent, 'Except,' explains Luna to Miles as he tries to seduce her, 'for those whose ancestors are Italian.' Anxious to protect his sexual image, Miles immediately claims to be a 'mulatto', and toys even more pointedly with the clarinet he's assembling, which now resembles a large black penis.

Sex in 2173 mostly takes place in the Orgasmatron, a cylindrical booth which induces climax in a few seconds, and which has clear overtones of covert adolescent experiences of masturbation. Asked to explain a *Playboy* centrefold, Miles says that the girls in such pictures were in fact made of rubber, and were inflated and anointed with ointment. He then pockets the picture, promising to return it with a full report. Asked how long it is since he had sex, he replies, 'Two hundred years. Two hundred and four, if you count my first marriage.' Echoes of his marriage to Lasser also return when he re-experiences a typical dinner with his parents, at which he tells them he's getting divorced. They berate him in Yiddish for his failure as a husband and his attraction to *shiksas*.

These themes appear even more overtly in the deleted chess dream. Chased by the black knight, Miles, briefly pausing to feel up the black queen, flees across the desert to find himself on stage in tails about to perform with a group that includes a man in a cello suit who plays himself and a violinist with a large lightbulb for a head. Miles himself has a conventional violin, but when he tries to play it his bow sags limply. 'He is terribly embarrassed by this obvious sexual symbolism,' wrote Allen in the script, confirming that the whole scene, with its images of masturbation (the self-playing cello), erection (the lance, the lightbulb) and detumescence (Miles' bow) addresses Allen's sexual anxieties. The sequence recalls Allen's unsuccessful performance as the jester in *Everything You Always Wanted to Know About Sex*, and looks forward, both in its historical setting and its parody of failed priapism, to *Love and Death*, ideas for which he was already jotting down while he worked on *Sleeper*.

In 1973 Ernest Becker, a professor in the department of Political Science, Sociology and Anthropology at Simon Fraser University in Canada, published *The Denial of Death*. The book used the work of Freud, his protégé Otto Rank and the Danish philosopher Søren Kierkegaard to illuminate man's preoccupation with death. 'The main thesis,' wrote Becker in his preface, 'is that [death] is the mainspring of human activity – activity designed largely to avoid the fatality of death, to overcome it by denying in some way that it is the final destiny for man.' Primitive people, he argued, regarded death with awe but with acceptance, as an elevation to a new level of existence. Modern man, on the other hand, had systematically developed strategies to avoid contemplating it.

What we think of as man's noblest impulses – love, heroism, religion – are, Becker argued, merely 'mechanisms of defence, repression and denial that allow him to live with the problems of serving two masters': physical reality and the knowledge that this must end.

Becker saw everywhere the signs of our debilitating split between the knowledge of death and our rejection of that knowledge, but especially in our sexual lives. 'The sexual conflict is thus a universal one because the body is a universal problem to a creature who must die,' he wrote. Sex offers only momentary escape from 'the terror of the body'. As for romantic love, 'the sexual partner does not and cannot represent a complete and lasting solution to the human dilemma. The partner represents a kind of fulfilment in freedom from self-consciousness and guilt; but at the same time he represents the negation of one's distinctive personality. We might say the more guilt-free sex the better, but only up to a certain point.'

The style of *The Denial of Death* was sufficiently light for the book to have an instant appeal for laymen like Allen who had never managed to plough through Kierkegaard's *The Sickness Unto Death* or *Fear and Trembling* (both of which Becker's bibliography cites not in their bleak, scholarly editions but in their most accessible form for Manhattanites, the Anchor paperbacks with their trendily austere covers by the fashionable artist Edward Gorey). Becker also approvingly quotes the Mike Nichols/Jules Feiffer film *Carnal Knowledge* and its final scene of a prostitute urging Jack Nicholson into erection by persuading him of his inner strength – coaxing the false hero out of the quivering animal, terrified of the death implicit in the very idea of flesh.

The Denial of Death was an instant success, winning the Pulitzer Prize for General Non-Fiction in 1974, and had a lively sale in paperback. The book had a profound effect on Allen, who read it as soon as it came out. It validated much that he'd already discovered through experience, and provided a philosophical rationalisation for half a life spent in just the sort of debilitating flight from fear that it described.

The first concrete result, almost certainly, was a decision to change the ending of *Sleeper*. Diane Keaton was shooting *God-father II*, but ignoring the fact that he was already $1.1 million over budget, Allen flew her to Los Angeles to film a new conclusion.

As the rebels clean up the last resistance in the medical centre, Miles and Luna, sceptic and believer, confront one another. Luna begs him to join the rebels. Miles demurs, mouthing Allen's conviction that all politicians are essentially the same: 'In six months we'll be cloning Erno's nose. Political solutions don't work.' Luna challenges him to explain what he does believe in, and Allen recycles a gag from his opening stand-up in the 1969 Kraft special. 'I believe in sex and death – two experiences that take place only once in life, but at least after death you're not nauseous.' They kiss, an improbable conclusion to a film which demands, logically, that it end with Miles being refrozen and despatched to a culture where he really belongs – in the more distant future, or, as proved more realisable with his next film, the past.

15

Love and Death and *The Front*

When I was doing *Love and Death* in Paris, the art director was
a veteran of World War II who had spied, been caught, tortured
and sent to a concentration camp. It made me feel so utterly trivial.
It confronted a prejudice I've always had that, as Oscar Wilde
said, art is useless.

Allen in *Newsweek*, 24 April 1978

One sub-theme of *Sleeper* had been age, a subject very much on
Allen's mind. Miles Monroe admits to thirty-five (not counting
two centuries on ice), but Allen was almost forty in 1974, and
plagued by the usual midlife doubts. These multiplied for comedians, who risked outgrowing their audience or their audience
outgrowing them.

Battle-scarred comic George Burns, who had seen his popularity
and that of his ditzy wife Gracie slump in 1942, understood the
process better than most. 'What happened was, our jokes were
too young for us,' he recalled. 'You see, Gracie and I had two
children then, but we were still doing a street-corner act . . . and
you can't do that. You've got to be your age in show business.
You can't be any younger than you are supposed to be, nor any
older. We told a lot of jokes that were all right for a young boy
and a girl, but not for a married woman.' Revamping their show,
they re-emerged playing a parody version of their own lives as a
successful show-business couple with children. When they adapted
the format for television in 1950 with a weekly show on CBS,
their son Ronnie joined them, playing himself. Their ratings soared
again.

Allen's competitors on the stand-up circuit like Shelley Berman,
Mort Sahl, Jonathan Winters and Bob Newhart had grappled with
this problem and, mostly, found no answer. Many succumbed to

mental illness or drugs. Though he had terminated his stand-up career with the 1972 Las Vegas appearances supporting Harry Belafonte, Allen was still nostalgic for live performance. Above all, he would have liked to do another play. 'That's the most fun,' he said. 'You leave your house at seven o'clock. You go on stage and you get your laughs. The audiences are very nice. The curtain comes down at 10.30, and you're free to go. It's very civilised compared to being in films. Films are strenuous, backbreaking work. You go from morning to night with bad hours, bad food.' He liked to quote a story about the Marx Brothers making *A Night in Casablanca* in 1946. The script called for Groucho and Harpo to hang from the back of an aeroplane. During a lull in shooting, Groucho said to Harpo, 'Have you had enough?' Harpo said, 'Yup.' Although they worked together one more time, on *Love Happy* (1950), it was effectively the end of the brothers' film career as a group.

Allen had no play ready for Broadway. Nor would he have found it easy to raise money for the sort he had in mind. 'It's easier to get $3 million to make a film than it is to get $250,000 for a play,' he said. 'You can write for the theatre with reasonable ease if you're willing to write those kind of plays that are commercially promising. So if I wrote a play that was basically a simple comedy with a lot of laughs and not too big a cast and not too complex a set requirement, there would be no problem getting it on at all. But as soon as you try to write something different or interesting, less commercially acceptable, then you run into problems. So who needs it?'

Equally, United Artists showed no inclination to let him film a dramatic script, particularly as memories of 'Jazz Baby' were still fresh in their minds. For a comedy, however, they were prepared to pay, and generously. Despite its budget overrun, *Sleeper*, which Allen now dismissed as '*kinderspiel*; silly child stuff', was a major success, grossing $8.3 million in domestic rentals. Allen's first four films had all made money for their studios, if not yet for Allen, returning $10.5 million on an investment of $8.75 million, with much more obviously to come. UA's bean-counters pressed David Picker to sign this goldmine to a new deal.

Urged by Joffe, Allen agreed to a new five-picture contract, but surprised everyone by refusing to increase his modest slice of the pie, except for an additional $25,000 in production fees for each film. Those who knew him, however, understood his reasoning. If he decided to return to stage work, or to drop out of show business entirely, the less he was in hock to Hollywood the better.

To his friends, it seemed that Allen regarded dropping out as an increasingly attractive option. He continued to inhabit the twilight world between celebrity and anonymity, protesting that he wanted to be alone but showing himself consistently at the sort of watering-holes where he couldn't help but attract attention. Around Manhattan he became famous as, in the words of columnist Earl Wilson, 'that little guy who wears his hat while eating in Sardi's'. Louise Lasser recalls that if someone came up to them while they were eating in a restaurant, Allen would accept their compliments with a murmured 'Thank you,' then, as they left, mutter under his breath, 'Cocksucker.' 'And I hated him for that,' she says, 'because he treated people like dirt.' Others sympathised with Allen's antipathy to recognition. Ralph Rosenblum describes an incident during the shooting of *Sleeper* when he and Alan were eating lunch at the Horn and Hardart cafeteria on Eighth Avenue and 57th Street. The location was hardly secluded, and Allen should not have been surprised when two middle-aged women accosted him, asking 'Are you Woody Allen?' He mumbled that he was, and the women left, only to return and demand, 'Are you *sure* you're Woody Allen?' When he confirmed that he was, one demanded truculently, 'Can you identify yourself?'

Allen would parody such moments in *Stardust Memories* and *Annie Hall*, where his character is bailed up in the street by a fan who raucously directs the attention of passers-by like a sideshow barker: 'Hey, dis is Alvy Singer! Alvy Singer here.' But the suspicion remains that for Allen being noticed brought an almost masochistic pleasure.

Throughout early 1974, Allen and Mickey Rose worked desultorily on the script scheduled to start shooting in the autumn. Called originally 'The Couple Next Door', it was a thirties-style whodunnit, redolent of the *Thin Man* films starring William Powell and Myrna Loy. The idea came to Allen while he was on the road in his stand-up days. Returning from a booking at the hungry i in San Francisco, he was told by the mild-mannered man who owned the apartment next to his that his wife had been killed by a fall from a window. The blasé tone of the announcement puzzled Allen, and he dreamed up a story about a well-heeled Manhattan couple, Larry and Carol Lipton, who begin to suspect their equally prosperous neighbour of having induced a heart attack in his wife in order to run off with a young girl. They turn amateur investigators, recruiting their equally mythomaniac friends in the hunt.

For a while, the person who went out of the window was a philosopher, Professor Levy, and the Liptons' suspicions were aroused by their knowledge of his optimistic attitude to life: nobody that sunny could possibly have committed suicide. But this line of thought, which Allen later recycled in *Crimes and Misdemeanors*, led into an area of self-reflection inconsistent with the frivolous material. *The Denial of Death* had wonderfully concentrated his mind on that subject, and he needed to incorporate the preoccupation in a film. Allen abandoned 'The Couple Next Door' and, shortly after, the whole whodunnit idea. He didn't film it until 1992, when it became *Manhattan Murder Mystery*. He and Rose remained friendly, but didn't work together again. Rose never again attained the success of his work with Allen, moving to Hollywood and sinking to the level of Walt Disney's *Condorman*.

All the same, 'The Couple Next Door' is revealing of Allen's feelings about himself in the wake of his first success and the approach of forty. Larry Lipton and his wife Carol are a classic uptown Manhattan couple, childless and self-absorbed. The collaborators they recruit to their investigation into their neighbour are just as rootless as themselves: their friend Ted, who's just broken up with his wife, and writer Marcia Fox, who they vaguely think might attract Ted. The predatory Marcia, however, is more interested in Larry, and the waltz of sexual couplings acts as a background to the story. Even rewritten with Marshall Brickman and updated as *Manhattan Murder Mystery*, the story retained the sense of time slipping away. 'This is the craziest thing I have ever done,' says Marcia (Diane Keaton) as she and Ted (Alan Alda), who carries a torch for her, track the apparent murderer. 'Yes, it's crazy,' agrees Ted. 'But soon we'll be too old to do anything crazy.'

For Allen, this was also a period of loneliness and sexual isolation. On 16 December 1974 the *New Yorker* published 'The Whore of Mensa', his funny and poignant reflection on the sexual accommodations of the Upper East Side. Around this time, an attractive Manhattanite named Deborah Duanes was riding a practically deserted subway car when she sensed a man approaching her. She buried herself in her paperback, but he sat down next to her.

'Excuse me, miss,' he said. 'Would you like a date right now?'

Startled, Duanes said, 'What?' and the man repeated his invitation. Something in his voice struck her as familiar, and she looked up. The man was Woody Allen.

That a famous comedian would accost girls on the subway seems extraordinary until one considers Allen's self-imposed isolation and obsessively maintained anonymity. How else would he meet women, this man who never went to parties, who scurried away from human contact and spent most of his spare time writing? Some people attribute his later affair with Soon-Yi Previn to a narrowness of choice. 'Who else *would* he go for?' queried one friend. 'Woody just doesn't get out much.'

When he did appear in public, mainly to play jazz, Allen didn't lack sexual opportunities. A certain sort of woman took his inaccessibility as a challenge. From his days on the stand-up circuit, plenty of women had written to him, sending their photographs, often with their vital statistics and phone numbers. Some asked for photos; one wanted a pair of his socks. While he was recording the music for *Sleeper* in Preservation Hall, for which he sat in anonymously with the resident band, a girl slipped him a note reading, 'If you're who I think you are, I've always wanted to fuck you to death.' Allen blinked at her. 'Who do you *think* I am?' he asked, and another moment passed.

Allen, who communicated best and most comfortably via the

written word, found such approaches titillating but scary. His liaison with Mia Farrow would be instigated not by him but by Farrow, who boldly sent him a note of admiration. Journalist Judith Viorst used the same approach to get an interview for *Redbook* magazine in 1976. Like many women, she found Allen sexually attractive, but was chilled by a sense of distance. 'I didn't ask him a lot of other things, because I felt constrained by – yes, his dignity,' Viorst said. 'And his aloofness. And the feeling that under his courtesy and his gentleness and his unfailing hospitality, the message that he sent was "Keep your distance."' In general, physical contact interested him less than fantasies and visual erotica. Mature women tended to find him uninteresting sexually. Meryl Streep, who had a small role in *Manhattan*, was asked in 1980 if she had got to know him. 'Who gets to know Woody?' she snorted. 'He's very much of a womaniser; very self-involved.'

If Allen was comfortable with anyone, it was with adoring young girls, to whom he proved eminently approachable. In a 1976 profile in *People* magazine he commented, 'If I was caught in a love nest with fifteen twelve-year-old girls tomorrow, people would think, yeah, I always knew that about him.' The teenagers of his fan club were astonished at his accessibility, even intimacy. 'He got so that he'd often change in front of us,' enthused its president, Linda Hersch, 'right down to his underwear.' He would flirt with the adoring Hersch and her friends. 'When I told him how old I was,' she recalled, 'he used to kid me about it, telling me, "You must be careful with me! Didn't you know my first wife was only seventeen when I married her?"'

Allen's vulnerability to even the most attenuated of approaches from young girls is indicated by his response to a letter he received in 1978 from Nancy Jo Sales, a thirteen-year-old schoolgirl in Coral Gables, Florida (She presently is a feature writer for *New York* magazine). After seeing *Annie Hall*, Sales was so struck by the reflection of her own bookish, untidy, movie-obsessed lifestyle in the character of Annie that she wrote to Allen. To her astonishment he wrote back in his wavering hand, reassuring her that he too had been just as much a nerd as she felt herself to be. Quizzing her on her tastes, activities and interests, he consoled her that her depression was no more than a natural response to the problems of existence. 'I think there is too much wrong with the world,' he wrote, 'to ever get too relaxed and happy. The more natural state, and the better one, I think, is one of some anxiety and tension over man's plight in this mysterious universe.'

The letters grew into a prolonged correspondence. Searching for something novel in her life to impart, Sales told Allen she'd been born during a hurricane. (Rain, the precocious seducer of middle-aged intellectuals in *Husbands and Wives*, with whom the Woody character almost has an affair, is also born in a hurricane.) Allen suggested she read Dostoyevsky, Robert Benchley and S.J. Perelman. She asked about his social life, and his ideal dinner-party guests; he suggested 'perhaps Jelly Roll Morton and Zelda Fitzgerald and maybe Babe Ruth and Chekhov and Sophocles and Charlotte Rampling and Dostoyevsky and Tolstoy and Kafka and Proust and Yeats and – oh, I could go on for a long time'.

For Sales, naturally, the ideal dining companion would have been Allen himself, and she angled to meet him, managing it when her stepmother took her to New York on holiday. They stayed with a family friend who had just had a nose job and wanted to tell everyone all about it. Allen invited Sales and her stepmother around to the Fifth Avenue apartment, but the New York friend insisted on coming too, boring everyone with talk of her surgery, her husband's successes in the soaring Florida real-estate market, and her own familiarity with Allen's favourite hangouts. '*We* eat at Elaine's too,' she confided, and Sales' heart fell. 'I have noticed,' she wrote in *New York*, 'that in Woody's films he often repeats a line about having your worst fears realised. It had been my worst fear, at thirteen, that I would lose this improbable friend. And here it was happening, as if I were watching our letters being shredded by wolves.'

The correspondence, and the relationship, ended there, but Allen's enthusiasm for young girls remained undiminished. In 1979 he admitted to having corresponded with a girl even younger than Sales, who claimed to be eleven. He wrote to her, 'If you're really the age you say you are, it's phenomenal. But if you're not, don't write to me again and waste my time.' He was only convinced when, like Sales, she came to visit him and brought her mother.

Profiling Allen in April 1978, *Newsweek* watched him fielding approaches from women during a break in his Monday-night jazz date at Michael's Pub.

Between sets Woody showed that his anhedonia extended to food (he ate and drank nothing) but he appeared somewhat more hedonic about girls. One young strawberry blonde with eyes like candle flames passed him a gift.

'It's a brass heart,' she said.

'So's mine,' replied Woody affably.

'Can we go out?' begged the girl, eyes guttering.

'I'm living with someone,' said Woody. 'She's not much, but she's all I have.'

Meekly the girl retreated, sighing, 'I love you a lot.'

An older woman gave Woody a copy of a paperback she had written, called *Naked Nun*. 'It's my memoirs,' she told him. 'It's a clean book. You can read it in one setting.'

'You mean sitting,' said Woody distantly.

He grew less distant when a dark-haired angel appeared to ask for his autograph. She was very young and Woody looked after her with a complex appreciation as she went back to a nearby table.

He mused, 'If my moral sense ever sinks so low as my other senses . . . but it wouldn't look good for me to hang around the Dalton School [Manhattan's premier private primary school] with my coat collar turned up.'

Feminist writer Lee Guthrie has been a long-time observer of Allen's life. In 1978 she published *Woody Allen: A Biography*, an uncritical scissors-and-paste round-up of his career against which Allen nevertheless instigated legal proceedings and had suppressed, on the grounds that it reprinted material from Eric Lax's authorised study *On Being Funny: Woody Allen and Comedy*, and misused his press releases. 'This is not a man who relates to adult women,' Guthrie said later. 'He's six weeks older than I am, but

I can't imagine having an affair with a seventeen-year-old boy from Dalton. On any level, I can't imagine it.'

Natalie Gittelson, who profiled Allen for the *New York Times* at the time of *Manhattan*, also suspected that he 'may have a soft spot in his heart for young, young women', though she went on to discount any hint of Humbert Humbert-esque nympholepsy. 'Although sex is by no means devalued, the real attraction lies between kindred spirits. The older Allen grows, the more he seems to value innocence in women – not sexual innocence, but that shiningness of soul that age so often tarnishes.' It would have enlivened all these articles considerably if the reporters had known that Allen was sleeping with – though not actually 'living with', as he claimed – seventeen-year-old Stacey Nelkin, whom he'd met and seduced while shooting *Annie Hall*, and who became the model for the Mariel Hemingway character in *Manhattan*.

The way Allen was pursued during his public appearances under-lines the degree to which the Woody character had achieved, almost subliminally, an independent life. In 1976 Stuart Hample, an old friend from his stand-up days, began drawing a comic strip featuring material drawn from Allen's stock of unused jokes and routines. It was soon internationally syndicated.

People all over the country now fantasised about him. At a dinner party in the early eighties, Dee Burton, a psychologist at the New School for Social Research in New York, confessed that she'd dreamed of Allen, and was astonished when others at the table admitted that they had also done so. She placed ads in the New York papers asking for more examples of Allen dreams, and received a flood of replies. Allen, Burton decided, made 'an excellent choice as a dream object. Most of the underlying themes of his movies, stories, plays and earlier stand-up routines – mortality, sexuality, anxiety and the ongoing struggle to find meaning in a society that appears to value shallowness – are universal issues that affect people at the level of their unconscious.'

Men, she found, tended to dream of Woody as a comfortable companion; women as a thoughtful and sensitive lover, though at least one fantasised about sharing a bed with both him and Diane

Keaton. Others imagined spending idyllic afternoons with him in some appropriately reflective setting, like the sculpture garden of the Museum of Modern Art. Allen may have got wind of such dreams himself, since *Manhattan* would feature a party set in just this bastion of Manhattan intellectual privilege.

After abandoning 'The Couple Next Door', Allen switched his attention to another film in which he and Keaton would have played affectionately antagonistic partners in imitation of Katharine Hepburn and Spencer Tracy in films like *Adam's Rib* and *Pat and Mike*. But he couldn't convince himself that they sufficiently resembled Hepburn and Tracy to make it work. 'Our chemistry is completely different,' he said. 'Theirs can't be duplicated' – though, in truth, the rapport that writers Garson Kanin and Ruth Gordon, themselves married, sensed in the secret lovers, and the tension their scripts created between the unsentimental Tracy and the genteel but steely Hepburn, were not so far from the guarded friendship of Keaton and Allen. In time, Allen himself saw the truth of this, and we can detect from the Tracy/Hepburn model the roots of *Annie Hall*. For the moment, however, he couldn't face putting his own life on film in such intimate detail.

Looking for a project that would satisfy UA's need for a comedy and his own urge for drama, he found it, improbably, in Russian literature. Later he claimed he'd 'just happened' to pick up a book on Russian history, but his true inspirations were *War and Peace* and *The Denial of Death*. Stanley Kubrick, so fruitful a source of ideas for *Sleeper*, had been widely reported, after *2001*, to be preparing his epic 'Napoleon', for which he proposed to hire the entire Romanian army (its generals even agreed to recruit more men if Kubrick needed them). The project collapsed in the downward spiral of MGM's fortunes, leaving an intriguing vacuum for a parodist like Allen.

Finishing two pages a day, Allen had the script for *Love and Death* ready to show UA in three weeks. The story was Tolstoy's epic writ small. Instead of the parallel stories of wealthy dilettante Pierre Bezuhov and career military officer Andrei Bolkonsky caught up in Napoleon's 1812 invasion of Russia, we have Boris

Gruzhenko (Allen), one of three brothers of a family of minor aristocrats who, frustrated in his love of his cousin Sonia (Keaton), enlists in the army despite his much-expressed cowardice. Turned by chance during battle into a hero, he falls in with fashionable St Petersburg society and sleeps with the sensual Countess Alexandrovna (Olga Georges-Picot), after which her lover Count Anton (Harold Gould) challenges him to a duel. Unable to take a life, Boris fires in the air, inducing a moral transformation in the Count, and winning Sonia, who abandons promiscuity to marry him.

As Napoleon occupies Moscow, they conceive a plan to assassinate him, despite Boris' qualms about murder, even of a despot. They fail, and Boris finds himself in jail, due to be shot at dawn. An angel appears, and reassures him that Napoleon intends to pardon him at the last minute, but they shoot him anyway. With the shrouded figure of Death at his side, Boris appears to Sonia, explaining, 'I was screwed.' He muses ruefully to the camera that, for all his qualms about guilt and morality, there is a lot to be said for the sensual life: 'Human beings are divided into mind and body. The mind embraces all the nobler aspirations like poetry and philosophy, but the body has all the fun' – an explicit reference to Becker. Then he dances off resignedly with Death into a winter landscape.

Working with a subject at once period and literary gave Allen a much wider palette. As in *Sleeper*, he could play on the incongruity of the Woody persona in a different historical era, flirting with the Countess in modern backchat ('Still dating laughing boy?' 'Who's the *dybbuk*?') or having Boris as a child confront Death and quiz him, 'What happens after we die? Is there a heaven? Is there a hell? Do we live again? All right, let me ask just one key question: are there girls?'

Allen would later disparage the film's approach as 'on the kidding-around level', but it was kidding around with an audience that would get the joke of a conversation in which each line contains the title of a novel by Dostoyevsky, and would catch the repeated references to the Odessa Steps sequence from Eisenstein's *Battleship Potemkin*.

Above all, Allen enjoyed improvising on the moral torment of

Tolstoy's Pierre, the basis of the Boris character. Like Pierre, Boris, caught up in his first battle, isn't too occupied to muse on the contradictions of a God who can allow war ('If he wanted to test us, why didn't he give us an oral?' he enquires, surveying a field littered with dead). Also like Pierre, Boris embarks on a pointless attempt to kill Napoleon, though in *Love and Death* the attempt is frustrated less by agonising over the moral rights and wrongs of murder than by a vain emperor's determination to have a dish named after him before his British opponent perfects Beef Wellington (Allen's original working title was 'Love, Death and Food').

Even without 'Food', *Love and Death* was hardly what UA had been hoping for. In a Perelmanesque piece for *Esquire* magazine, Allen joked about their reaction:

I found myself in the offices of United Artists' biggest deal-makers, explaining that I had written a comedy about Man's alienation in a world of meaningless existence. They had been led to believe – owing to certain memos I had sent – that I was working on a bedroom farce based on the mistaken identity of two *au pair* girls and some hens. Imagine their delighted surprise when I read them the script of *Love and Death*, with its plot that went from war to political assassination, ending with the death of its hero caused by a cruel trick of God. Never having witnessed eight film executives go into cardiac arrest simultaneously, I was quite amused.

Such was UA's confidence in Allen that they were prepared to back the film – though not, they told him, in the United States, where the budget for the production would be enormously inflated. Allen protested, but his experience on *Sleeper* had demonstrated how quickly costs could spiral when it came to filming action gags. 'I'd have preferred to make it in California,' he told columnist Army Archerd, though even that would have been a concession. As Charles Joffe pointed out at the time, 'Woody doesn't like any place but New York.'

Allen's next choice of location, if he had to shoot in Europe, was Russia itself, but Joffe rejected this too, and they decided to make the film out of France, but on location in Hungary, where the Soviet army of occupation was willing to supply all the extras that would be needed. 'Hungary was desperate to get some of that US film business that formerly went to countries such as Yugoslavia,' says Joffe. The Hungarian government demanded to read the script, but accepted it with alacrity once they saw that the only political figure it parodied was Napoleon. 'Hungarofilm and Mafilm [Hungary's two national film-production agencies] were very co-operative,' says Joffe. 'We got help on manpower – extras at $7 a day [for battle scenes], whereas Paris would have cost $40.'

Love and Death set up in Paris late in 1974, working from the old Billancourt studios, location for countless classics from the twenties onwards, but now little-used. Allen himself took a small house well outside the city, near Versailles, which distanced him even more from the production. Of his crew on earlier films, only his first assistant from *Sleeper*, Fred Gallo, came with him to Paris, with a credit as Associate Producer.

The remaining key personnel were hired in France. Production designer Willy Holt's design career had been blighted by his war-time work for the Resistance and his resulting capture, imprisonment and torture by the Nazis, but he had a reputation as a skilled craftsman, especially with period sets. To light the film, Allen hired the Belgian *chef operateur* Ghislain Cloquet, who had worked for most of France's greats, including Robert Bresson, Louis Malle and Jacques Demy. Allen told Cloquet he'd been won over by his treatment of exteriors in Nina Companeez's 1971 *Faustine et la Belle Été* – 'But the real reason for his choice, I think,' says Cloquet, 'is that I had made a film in the United States for Arthur Penn, *Mickey One*, and that I'd got on so well with the American crew that one of Penn's assistants had recommended me.'

Cloquet spoke only approximate English and Holt none at all, however, and Allen felt himself increasingly isolated, especially when he began casting. He'd hoped to coax a few actors from Hollywood, but with a cast of more than fifty speaking parts, he couldn't afford air fares and hotels for too many. Aside from

Diane Keaton, Harold Gould played Count Anton, Jessica Harper was Sonya's cousin Natasha, who has only one scene, James Tolkan played Napoleon, and a talented boy from New Jersey, Alfred Lutter III, was given red hair and glasses to play Boris as an inquisitive adolescent. The remaining performers were scrounged up in London or, mostly, Paris.

Always miserable when casting, Allen made an alarming impression on European actors used to more urbanity in directors. Sitting in the shadows or, occasionally, in the next room, he asked no questions, and seemed generally uninterested in them. Among those called to audition was stage actor Francis Perrin. Ushered into Allen's presence by the casting director, he found him huddled on a sofa, arms around his knees, hat over his eyes. Perrin said, 'Good morning,' then, after a few moments during which Allen ignored him, 'Goodbye.' As he left, the casting director said encouragingly, 'He liked you a lot.' Those Allen selected always looked good, but many turned out, once on the set, to speak little or no English.

Allen originally fancied tiny Jewish actress Carol Kane for the role of the sexy Countess Alexandrovna, but in what had seemed at the time to be an inspiration he offered it instead to Erin Fleming, the pretty young performer who had become the companion in old age of Groucho Marx. Allen's admiration for Marx, reciprocated by the ageing comedian, often expressed itself in such adoptions. Though he'd given up smoking in adolescence, Allen took to carrying a cigarette lighter for the convenience of friends, because that's what Groucho did.

Allen had used Fleming once already, as the girl seduced in the back seat of a New York cab in the 'What Happens During Ejaculation?' sequence of *Everything You Always Wanted to Know About Sex*, but the actress got cold feet once she arrived in Paris and costume designer Gladys de Segonzac began fitting her wardrobe, which ranged from an evening gown with a plunging *décolletage* to a boudoir outfit of black stockings, high heels and a corset. Already pegged by the press as a bimbo, she declined to draw any more fire, and the role went – unhappily, as it turned out – to Olga Georges-Picot, who'd studied at the Actors Studio in New York and spoke good American-accented English.

Willy Holt urged Allen not to bother shooting real locations when they could build everything in Budapest at bargain rates. This met with immediate resistance from the French production manager, who argued for shooting as much as possible in real French châteaux. Allen was persuaded, and they spent the winter of 1974–75 in a snow-covered Paris and various authentic but icy country houses. 'It was a bad idea,' says Holt, 'because when Woody Allen makes a film, you reserve two days for filming in the château, with three or four days of preparation and one day to clear out. But after two days of shooting, he would look at the rushes and say, "It's no good. We'll have to do it again." But by that time we no longer had the château. So it was an endless feat of acrobatics.'

Health problems dogged the unit. The actors responded poorly to Allen's exhausting directing methods, which drove the highly strung Olga Georges-Picot in particular into nervous states, at the peak of which she fainted. Others fell off horses or were injured in car accidents. Allen slipped on ice in front of the Eiffel Tower and injured his back, then burned himself when he backed into a lamp.

Almost worse were the problems casued by insistent photojournalists. Ralph Rosenblum flew in halfway through filming to look at what Allen had shot and to advise him on cutting. One night he and his wife went out to dinner with Allen and Keaton on the Champs Élysées. 'The moment we left the hotel,' he recalled, 'the *paparazzi* burst out from behind parked cars, where they'd been awaiting Woody's exit. Walking backwards, flashes popping, they led us the full eight blocks to our destination, jamming themselves right through the restaurant's revolving doors to get their final shots.'

Allen later claimed to Stig Bjorkman, 'I liked the French people and I loved being in France,' but the mood on the *Love and Death* set was uniformly sombre. In between takes Allen retreated to his caravan, where he practised the clarinet. 'Only three people spoke English,' recalled Keaton. 'Woody, his secretary and myself. We didn't have much to say, so we'd sit in a trailer and talk in between shots, which took forever. And every day we would have the exact same meal in the hotel. Woody would have fish, and I would have chicken, no wine. The waiter thought we were the two most eccentric people in town.'

Assistant director Bernard Cohn, who did speak English, plucked up enough courage to chat with Allen about a common enthusiasm, old Hollywood movies. 'One time,' recalls Cohn, 'we talked about a favourite film of mine, *The Barefoot Contessa*. When I said that I liked very much [director/writer Joseph L.] Mankiewicz, he exploded in laughter. Everyone turned around, because nobody had ever heard him laugh during the whole shooting. Yes, I think that's the only time I ever saw him laugh.'

Most members of the crew were glad when the production moved to Budapest, but the Hungarian capital proved even more ill-starred than Paris had been. Equipment broke down, and the labs ruined film. The Russian soldiers were obstructive, with their orders, passed down a lengthy chain of command, often emerging garbled. Every bit of explosive imported had to be accounted for, and used up before they left. Even so, the film's battle scenes are unconvincing, with a thousand extras somehow managing to look like only a few dozen. Paranoid about food in Paris, Allen became obsessive in Hungary. Rather than eat the lunch provided for the crew, he brought large quantities of canned sardines. 'He was convinced there were germs everywhere,' says Willy Holt. 'In Hungary, he brought his own bottles of water.'

To Holt, one scene sums up his experience of Allen. On a location hunt in Yugoslavia, he, the production manager and Allen arrived at a once-splendid hotel in their chauffeured car. Knowing that Communist countries tended to be impressed by formality, Holt, the production manager, his assistant, and even the chauffeur had dressed like prosperous businessmen. Only Allen looked disreputable. 'We went up to the desk,' says Holt, 'and the manager asked the chauffeur whether he would like a suite. The chauffeur said he didn't want a suite. So did his assistant. So did I. And there was Woody at the back saying, "I'd like to have a suite." And so he had his suite, but he would have been better without it, because it was awful. But that's the sort of person he is.'

Assuming that Allen would want a cool, detached visual style, as in his other films, Cloquet was surprised to be asked for a warm, golden look which demanded heavy filtering of the lens and diffusion of the lights, all of which caused problems in Hungary's wintry sunlight. Cloquet wanted to follow the film to America to supervise the laboratory grading of prints, but Allen dissuaded him. *Sleeper* had been going back and forth for colour corrections between Allen in New York and the labs in California until a week before its release. 'I don't know if it's hard to do or not,' Allen lamented of the problems of colour grading. 'I just know they never get it right.' Introducing Cloquet into the equation would, he felt, lead to more grief. As a result, only the copies of *Love and Death* made in France, and overseen by Cloquet, really have the visual quality Allen aimed for.

If the film is technically not all it might be, Allen and Keaton are, paradoxically, at their best, and the film is the funniest of Allen's early work. Keaton's experience with Coppola for the *Godfather* films shows in her greatly improved craft as an actress. The one-note kook of *Play it Again, Sam* has been replaced by an accomplished comic, skilled at deadpan but equally adept at sly, nervy sideways glances, giddy grins and nervous nibblings of the lower lip.

The transformation surprised Allen, who was even more taken aback when, on their return to New York, Keaton announced that as well as playing in the new Elliott Gould comedy *I Will . . . I Will . . . for Now*, she was embarking on a new career as a singer. In May the Reno Sweeney club offered her a chance to sing, but Allen refused to catch her act. 'I asked him not to,' said Keaton loyally to Earl Wilson once news of this rift reached the papers. However, in the same column she tried for the first time to describe in public the real nature of her relationship with Allen, and failed signally.

'People keep asking me, "Are Diane and Woody married?"' said Wilson.

'They do? I'll be darned. We aren't. Never were.'

'You his "lady", as they say nowadays?'

'No. Did we have a romance? Uh ... we were ... for a while
... a long time ago ... years ...'

UA scheduled *Love and Death* for a June 1975 release, convinced
that it had the legs to carry a long summer run. Some of its
competitors for the film-going dollar that year were by others who
had graduated with Allen from the hard schools of stage and
television comedy. Mel Brooks had two films on release, *Young
Frankenstein* and the Western spoof *Blazing Saddles*. Dustin Hoffman was starring in Bob Fosse's *Lenny*, which, even with its bowdlerised version of Lenny Bruce's life and material, could still shock.
Diane Keaton was in *The Godfather II*. At that year's Academy
Awards Groucho Marx belatedly received the acknowledgement
of an honorary Oscar. 'I'd like to thank Erin Fleming,' he said in
his acceptance speech, 'who makes my life worth living and who
understands all my jokes.'

Rosenblum again edited the film, and had a major effect on its
tone. He talked Allen out of his original choice of Stravinsky
for the music, and they substituted the more jolly Prokofiev, in
particular the *Lieutenant Kije* suite, itself written for a long-
forgotten film. It was an inspired choice, the jingling bells and
sprightly pace echoing the lively New Orleans jazz that drove
Allen's other films. (It was also considerably cheaper than Stravinsky.) Though the film went $1 million over budget and did only
average business in the United States, overseas sales more than
made up for this. *Love and Death* was the first film to hint that
Allen's fame was already great enough in Europe to make his
foreign earnings as important as those in the US, if not more so.

Most critics were taken aback by the film's scope, both in technique and content. Nobody was quite ready for Woody Allen
the *auteur*, working with Bresson's cameraman in locales they
associated with European directors like Andrzej Wajda. Stanley
Kauffmann in the *New Republic* found Cloquet's photography
'just too beautiful. The picture,' he carped, 'was shot in France
and Hungary, and some of it is gorgeous. None of it should be.
For instance, the sweeping mountain background for the recruits'
drill is utterly incongruous with Allen's horseplay.' Pauline Kael

focused on *Love and Death*'s concerns rather than its style. 'I don't particularly like the Bob Hope movies it resembles,' she told British critic and stage producer Charles Marowitz, 'when Bob Hope played those cowards/heroes, those ones we found amusing because they were always running from danger and always being menaced.' After this accurate observation, Kael soared into the stratosphere of fashionable political speculation: 'When Woody does [such a story], it's a response to the whole macho mood of our time, so he stands for the whole generation that was anti-Vietnam; he stands for the people who were anti-macho.' Allen himself made no such claims to topicality; his attitude to Vietnam, and to everything else political, remained studiedly detached.

Keaton had been taking lessons at Martha Graham's ballet school for some time, and she persuaded Allen to attend the performances of Graham's 1974 New York season. Graham's anguished chor-eography, with its stylised movements and heavily draped figures, stimulated Allen's imagination, as did her subject matter. Like her, he responded to Greek myth and to Emily Dickinson. The poet inspired one of Graham's most famous pieces, *Letter to the World* ('This is my letter to the world/That never wrote to me'), and Allen was to name his highly successful 1975 collection of pieces *Without Feathers*, a reference to Dickinson's 'Hope is a thing with feathers/That nestles in the heart'.

'Graham,' Allen said, 'is the other side of the comic prism, of the comic perspective. [She] is overpowering. The movements are so primordial that they're terrifying and irresistible. I'm much more partial to her darker pieces – *Clytemnestra*, *Night Journey*. I just prefer all that blood lust. She contacts me on the immediate level. I can only liken it to [Ingmar] Bergman. So much of Graham's and Bergman's best works expresses the psychology of women. There are a lot of similarities.'

Inspired by Graham, though equally by Bergman's *Cries and Whispers*, released in 1972, Allen began sketching out a script he called 'Dreams and Furies', which would explore some of the connections between myth and movement evident in Graham's work. It was never made, but echoes of Graham turn up periodically in Allen's films. The recurring figure of the Grim Reaper, a seven-foot figure with a scythe, shrouded in a flowing black or white robe, is *echt*-Graham as well as Bergman, and in *Mighty Aphrodite* he went to Greece to shoot some production numbers danced and costumed in Martha Graham style.

Aware that he moved awkwardly on screen, Allen enrolled in Graham's beginners' class in the autumn of 1974. 'It was interesting,' he said, 'but it wasn't fun. It was quite embarrassing for a thirty-eight-year-old person to buy a dance belt and leotards and sit in class. I didn't mind being there, but once you had to get up and prance across the floor with the others and do the big, open steps, I couldn't make it. My sense of shame just overtook me.'

In June 1975 he made a well-publicised appearance at the Uris Theater in New York at a benefit for Graham. The ranking guest was First Lady Betty Ford, another ex-student, whom Allen was supposed to escort. Paul Newman and Lauren Bacall were among the celebrities present, but Allen and Keaton stole the show, bouncing out of their limo in matching sneakers, topped in Allen's case by a tuxedo. He was just in time to greet Mrs Ford, but despite her presence, and a new Graham work danced by Rudolf Nureyev and Margot Fonteyn, the sneakers, which Allen wore in a calculated attempt to draw the cameras, got most coverage. The benefit raised $200,000, of which Allen kicked in a modest $5000.

While Allen was in France working on *Love and Death*, Rollins and Joffe continued to forward scripts for his consideration. Many, acknowledging his new eminence as a performer, were written with him in mind as star rather than as director. Among these was *The End*, by comedy writer Jerry Belson, inspired by an Allen remark that imminent death, viewed in the right way, could be an amusing subject for comedy. The script followed a selfish man who, told he has an incurable disease, tries unsuccessfully to kill himself, then spends the rest of the film appealing for sympathy from anyone who'll listen. Allen turned it down, and Burt Reynolds made it, unsuccessfully, in 1979.

Allen was more interested in *The Front*, a project of director Martin Ritt, well known for politically-conscious films like *Hud*,

The Molly Maguires and *The Great White Hope*, and Walter Bernstein, a left-wing writer who, like Ritt, had been blacklisted during the anti-Communist witch-hunts of the fifties when he and Ritt were, respectively, a scriptwriter and an actor in New York television. The McCarthy era was the setting of Bernstein's screenplay. An unambitious *nebbish* named Howard Prince, luncheonette cashier and bookie, is approached by Alfred Miller, his old school friend, formerly a successful TV writer but now blacklisted on the advice of the Freedom Information Board, a shadowy agency which counsels the networks. Miller offers to pay Prince a commission if he'll submit work in his name, and Prince is soon the 'front' for half a dozen writers. His apparent talent leads him to be courted by producer Phil Sussman, and he's romantically drawn to script editor Florence Barrett. He also meets the television star Hecky Brown, an amiably carnal ex-stand-up comic who is being urged by the blacklisting agency to inform on his left-wing friends.

Prince makes a success of 'fronting', despite some near-disasters when Sussman demands last-minute rewrites. He even becomes proprietorial about 'his' work, casually accepting the praise of friends and family who'd written him off as a loser, and rejecting some plays from his clients as being 'beneath his standard'. Guilt, however, and the love of Florence work a moral change, as does the suicide of Hecky, who, unable to convince his persecutors that he attended Communist rallies simply in pursuit of sex, jumps from a hotel window. Called to testify before the inquisitors, Prince, though he has no political affiliations to confess except his friendship with his clients, quixotically tells the Committee to 'Go fuck yourselves,' and is indicted for contempt. The last scene shows him leaving for jail from Grand Central, fêted by admirers and embraced by an adoring Florence.

Ritt and Bernstein took a calculated risk in offering the role of Prince to Allen. He bore a strong physical resemblance to Bernstein, and his politics were superficially aligned with those of the film, but his presence would shift the story inexorably towards comedy, which Ritt for one came to consider a betrayal of those who had suffered under the blacklist.

His original idea had been to focus on Hecky, who was based on actor Philip Loeb, a friend of the film's eventual star Zero Mostel who had committed suicide in Mostel's hotel room because he couldn't find work. Mostel himself, famously, had guyed the House Committee on un-American Activities in his 1955 appearance before it. Asked to name the studio that employed, then blacklisted, him, he said, 'Eighteenth Century-Fox.' 'Do you want that statement to stand?' asked the chairman. 'No, make it Nineteenth Century-Fox,' Mostel said. To plead the Fifth Amendment, he playfully waggled five fingers. 'Halfway through,' says Ritt, 'Walter and I decided [our first version of the script] was going to be maudlin and sentimental, so together we came up with the idea of "the front" – we remembered the story because it really happened – and decided that's what the film should be. And that's what the film became.'

Ritt did his best to give significance to *The Front* by forgoing any credit music – the titles appear in silence on a black screen – and opening with a long montage of fifties newsreels – a beaming Joe McCarthy at his daughter's wedding, Korean War footage, Joe DiMaggio, Marilyn Monroe, General MacArthur's tickertape parade through Manhattan, with the ironic backing of Frank Sinatra singing 'Young at Heart' – and by casting real-life blacklistees Herschel Bernardi (Sussman) and Mostel. The end credits give the dates on which Ritt, Bernstein and others were blacklisted.

Allen would look back on *The Front* without pleasure. The left seemed as ridiculous to him as had the presidential candidates when he made his unscreened 1971 PBS programme which included his fake documentary based on Henry Kissinger. 'I felt uncomfortable throughout the whole process,' he confessed, 'not being able to improvise and change things. My only yardstick is funniness.' Despite Allen's claims that he didn't contribute to the script, Prince's dialogue is peppered with his familiar one-liners. Told by his blacklisted friend Miller (Michael Murphy) that he 'needs a name', Prince suggests, 'Alfred . . . no, Arnold Rapaport.' Florence (Andrea Marcovicci) tells him she was brought up 'in a family where the biggest sin was raising your voice'. 'In my family,' responds Prince, 'it was buying retail.' Asked if she likes sports,

Florence says she enjoys swimming, but Prince snorts, 'Swimming isn't a sport. It's what you do to keep from drowning.' When she praises him for writing 'about people', he responds, 'If you're going to write about human beings, you might as well make them people.'

For the press Ritt reluctantly conceded that 'in a way, the blacklist was hilarious, but, on the other hand, it was really far from funny'; in private he regarded *The Front*, which won mixed reviews and picked up only $5 million on its $3.5 million budget, as a missed opportunity. 'I would like to make another picture that deals more seriously with that time and that subject,' he said. 'It might have a chance to be a better film.'

As Allen had seen when Alvah Bessie attacked an old antagonist at the hungry i years before, the blacklist remained an open sore, and *The Front* proved a durable talking point, especially in Europe, where it made most of its profits. In 1988 it was shown at the Barcelona Film Festival prior to a panel discussion that included Bernstein and fellow blacklistees Jules Dassin and John Berry. Edward Dmytryk, who had 'named names', was also invited, but didn't appear on stage. During the discussion, however, he stood up in the audience and tried to justify his decision to inform after serving only part of a jail sentence for contempt of Congress. Berry had to be restrained from physically attacking him, while Bernstein and the others walked out. Bernstein said, 'I'm proud to say I called him "garbage" from the stage.'

16

Annie Hall

BRICKMAN: 'Happiness is not a state. It's a change of state.'
ALLEN: 'A state is repetitious, therefore boring. We need a new definition of happiness as a more benign form of torment.'

Conversation between Marshall Brickman and Allen, recorded by Susan Braudy, *New York Times*

While *The Front* was still being edited, Allen and Marshall Brickman were walking around New York, trading ideas for a film which, because it had no particular focus, just a generalised mood which Allen found hard to define, proved intractable to write. For a while, the Tracy/Hepburn idea flourished. Then they began kicking round a story set in Victorian England, to be shot in Boston, until Allen, with memories of *Love and Death* and its complications, rang one morning and called it off.

Brickman, invited later to compare the processes that led to *Annie Hall* and the other films he wrote with Allen, quotes Rodin's description of how to sculpt an elephant: take a large block of stone and remove everything that isn't an elephant.

We start with several ideas, usually. On *Annie Hall*, we worked on alternate days. *Annie Hall* would appeal to us. Then, we'd get disgusted and say who wants to see another love story about New York City? On Thursday, we'd say much the same about Victorian England. No, we're still not writing, nor taping our conversation. You never forget the important stuff, you really don't. After months of conversations and agonising, then we write. For *Annie Hall* and *Manhattan*, Woody wrote very quick first drafts in four days, Xeroxed it, gave it me and I spent a couple of days making changes, and we'd shovel it back and forth before we felt reasonably confident to go to United Artists and ask for $4 million.

Allen's early confusion over the form of the new film stemmed in part from trying to avoid imitating Federico Fellini's autobiographical *8½* (1963). Fellini had created his film at a turning point in his life similar to Allen's, when he had no idea of what to make next, but a nagging sense that he needed to escape from the kind of work that had made him famous.

Like Allen, Fellini was influenced by psychoanalysis – in his case Jungian, a school of psychology which Allen had rejected, calling Jung, in a letter to Nancy Jo Sales, 'boring and overrated'. In its early versions, *Annie Hall* was a modified version of *8½*, resting, like that film, on a series of dreams and fantasy sequences in which Allen grappled with the women in his life. He said later that the action was 'supposed to take place in my mind. Something that would happen would remind me of a quick childhood flash, and that would remind me of a surrealistic image.'

Beth Porter, who had appeared in *Love and Death*, saw a first draft of the *Annie Hall* script, then untitled, in the home of Fred Gallo. 'And I have to tell you it was terrible,' she told Julian Fox. 'It was a series of pretty disconnected scenes of Woody chasing various women. Fred explained to me that the deal Rollins and Joffe has with the financiers was that there had to be a document, a script of sorts to placate them, in order to raise the money.'

The script lightly fantasised Allen's childhood. His father was to have been a cab driver, and the scenes, which he used for the opening of *Radio Days*, would have evoked, as Fellini did in *8½* and *Amarcord*, an abrasive but essentially affectionate family milieu. This changed when Allen's set designer, Mel Bourne, a New Yorker who knew the Five Boroughs intimately, made a detour on their way back from a scouting trip to Flatbush to show him a bizarre building near Coney Island. 'I said, "I know you like Fellini – I want to show you something that out-Fellinis anything Fellini has ever done." So we got to the Cyclone roller-coaster and I said, "There's a seventy-three-year-old lady and her three-hundred-pound son living in this apartment built into the Cyclone." He was bowled over and said, "Can we get in there to look?" We went in, and there was this woman with a pacemaker and her son who was hitting the wall wherever he went because he was so big and heavy. It turned Woody on so much that he said, "This is where Alvy grew up! We're going to use this."'

A few fantasies survived from the first draft, but most were dropped, including one elaborate dream in which Allen and rock journalist Shelley Duvall are transported from a mass audience with the Maharishi Mahesh Yogi at Madison Square Garden to the Garden of Eden, where they discuss sex and the nature of the female orgasm with God.

Allen also discarded a childhood memory of a day home ill from school – Alvy is seen faking a temperature by holding a thermometer over the radiator – which involved his cousin Doris, a clear reference to Rita Wishnick. She brings him some war comic books, and as she reads them Alvy lapses into a dream in which he's a prisoner in a Hollywood French Resistance film. 'We tortured the Frenchman Sartre, but he refuses to talk,' says one Nazi. They put a gun to Alvy's head, but he declines to tell them anything – only to take out a puppet and let it give them the information, like ventriloquist Edgar Bergen talking through his dummy Charlie McCarthy. The last vestiges of Allen the parodist, these scenes had, he realised, no place in a film which, for better or worse, would relaunch him as a maker of 'serious comedy'.

8½ wasn't the only film to influence *Annie Hall*. There are numerous resemblances to Mike Nichols' 1971 *Carnal Knowledge*, for which Jules Feiffer wrote the screenplay. From *The Front*, Allen took the idea of opening credits that run in total silence, a style he retained for his next film, *Interiors*. The *Godfather* films contributed not only their cameraman, Gordon Willis, and the low-light burnished style of which he was a master, but also Coppola's fragmented structure of repeated flashbacks. Allen acknowledges this debt early in *Annie Hall*. Accosted by some shambling rubberneckers while waiting for Annie outside a cinema, Alvy complains when she arrives, 'I'm standing here with the cast of *The Godfather*.'

Annie Hall was the first film to draw directly on Allen's own life for its material, though for a while he would vehemently deny this. 'The stuff that people insist is autobiographical is almost invariably not,' he told *Rolling Stone* in 1987, 'and it's so exaggerated that it's virtually meaningless to the people upon whom these little nuances are based. People got it into their heads that *Annie Hall* was autobiographical, and I couldn't convince them it wasn't.'

In particular, he was anxious to remove the impression that the film reflected his life with Diane Keaton. Early versions of the story, in which Annie was a smart New York journalist, avoided the comparison; but while the decision to base the character on Keaton as she was when he had first met her, complete with mismatched clothes, disjointed conversation and embarrassed grimaces, came late, it was soon integral to the story. 'I keep sifting the pieces of the relationship through my mind,' says Alvy in his opening stand-up, 'and examining my life and trying to figure out where did the screw-up come.' Those close to Keaton acknowledged many parallels between the film and real life. 'Woody's had a very positive influence on her,' says Diane's mother Dorothy, 'very much like *Annie Hall*.' Her father adds, '[*Annie Hall*] is 85 per cent true, even to Dorothy and my mother.'

After the break-up, Keaton had remained affectionate towards and loyal to Allen. 'Woody and I, we're beyond getting involved again with each other,' she told Rex Reed, 'and beyond really hurting each other, which is a wonderful place to get with someone you love. There's humour, affection and a certain dependency between us. He's my closest and dearest friend.' But when Reed pressed her on whether making *Annie Hall* had been 'emotionally embarrassing', she responded vehemently, '*Yes!* The biggest worry I had making *Annie Hall* was whether or not I would get in my own way. I was afraid that unconsciously I might stop myself from showing the truth because it made me uncomfortable. I wanted to do *Annie Hall* fully, without worrying what I did wrong in real life. I had to stop fantasising about what kind of person I am. Am I bad? Was I wrong in that situation? Did I hurt Woody too much [by leaving him]? Was I selfish? There were so many conflicts. But, in the final analysis, working out my relationship with Woody was, and still is, great fun, and always a surprise and a revelation to me.'

In both *8½* and *Annie Hall*, the ruling sense is of time passing and, with it, a happiness that all the nostalgia in the world couldn't recapture. Allen's working title would be 'Anhedonia' – the inability to enjoy pleasure, the reverse of hedonism. It persisted until three weeks before the film's first screening at the Los Angeles Film Festival, Filmex, in March 1977, at which point United Artists despaired of creating an ad campaign explaining its meaning, and Allen compromised with *Annie Hall*.

Allen was right to change the title. Though his character in the film had begun as anhedonic, he rounded out as the shooting went on into someone who, like Allen, experienced pleasure without too much trouble, sleeping with a variety of attractive women, achieving success as a comedian, seeing the movies he liked, eating the food he preferred. But, with Alvy Singer as with Allen, the pleasure had to be taken on his terms, a requirement which his friends and lovers found tiresome. Alvy bickers with, and eventually breaks up with, almost everyone in the film, all of whom go off to enjoy life, leaving him in New York, mired in a swamp of paranoia and self-pity.

In his world, and that of *Annie Hall*, the ogre is California, and especially Los Angeles. Alvy's closest friend, Rob (Tony Roberts), a TV actor/producer, moves to Los Angeles, and urges Alvy to do the same. Annie (Keaton), his lover, also ends up there, but though Alvy grudgingly visits the City of Angels, the trips end disastrously. The first time, in town to present an award, he collapses with an elusive malady which clears up the moment he's relieved of the task. In the second, mostly cut from the final version, he ends up in jail on a driving charge, but wins over his fellow inmates by his skill in a joke-telling contest they organise.

Alvy laments the perceived ruin Californian values have wreaked on his friends. Rob now uses canned laughter in his shows, and Annie succumbs to the sybaritic lifestyle of rock singer Tony Lacey (Paul Simon). It was Brickman's idea to approach Simon to play Lacey. Loath to write dialogue for someone who

knew Hollywood so well, Allen simply told the singer/songwriter
to improvise a few lines, one of which included the word 'mellow',
a term he loathed. Once Lacey suggests to Alvy and Annie that
they come back to his suite at the Pierre and 'just relax, just be
very mellow,' Allen was free to zip in with, 'I don't think I could
take a mellow evening, 'cause I don't respond well to mellow.
You know, I have a tendency to, if I get too mellow, I ripen and
then I rot.'

In a deleted sequence, later used in *Deconstructing Harry*, Allen
connotes California literally with Hell. Alvy, Annie and Rob are
transported to its nether regions in an elevator that lowers them
floor by floor, while a sepulchral voice intones, 'Level Five: Organised crime, fascist dictators and people who don't appreciate oral
sex . . . Level Six: The Media. Sorry, this floor is full. Level Seven:
Escaped war criminals, tele-evangelists and lawyers who appear
on television . . .'

Taxed by Alvy with the emptiness of Los Angeles, Annie retorts
with the ultimate apostasy: 'New York is a dying city. Read *Death
in Venice.*' After that, there can be no *rapprochement*. Alvy returns
to his paranoia, his memories, his nostalgia. 'Nostalgia', in fact,
would have made a far more appropriate title for *Annie Hall*,
since its ruling tone is the literal 'homesickness as a disease' which
is the dictionary definition of that painful state. In real life, Keaton,
despite having been born in California, doesn't entirely disagree
with Allen about the rival virtues of the two coasts: 'Woody hates
California and is unrelenting about how much he despises it, but
to me Hollywood is not California. I couldn't take Hollywood
any more than Woody could.' Still, for Allen, any allegiance to
the West Coast indicates vapidity and self-regard.

Allen looked on *Annie Hall* as payback time not simply for Hollywood and Keaton but for scores of people who had displeased
him over the years. The film opens with the by-now obligatory
attack on his parents and childhood in Brooklyn, in particular a
school staffed by grotesques teaching a class of born losers. Alvy's
father runs an amusement-park dodgem concession, and raises
him in a house under the Cyclone rollercoaster. Precociously, he

becomes obsessed with the fact that the universe is expanding, leading to inevitable destruction. '*Brooklyn* isn't expanding,' says his termagant of a mother when she takes him to the doctor for medical eradication of this seditious idea.

As an adult, Alvy remains no less aggrieved. Fortuitously for him, the filmic convention that allowed him to appear in his old classroom and get his own back on PS 99 also enables him to turn the tables on adult antagonists. At the end of the film he shows a rehearsal of his play about life with Annie, which ends with them reconciled and back in New York – as hopeless a dream as the incident where he is trapped in line at a Manhattan cinema while a bore behind him pontificates on everything from Federico Fellini to Marshall McLuhan. Allen, ever the magician, conjures up the real McLuhan, who demolishes the bore. Turning to the camera, Singer says, 'Boy, if life were only like this.'

The mixture of reality and invention in *Annie Hall* is artfully achieved. A genuine clip from an Allen appearance on *The Dick Cavett Show* precedes a stand-up performance before a large college audience which was elaborately staged. Five hundred students from New York University received $10 each to laugh and applaud an empty stage. 'I never got a college turnout like this,' Allen told the *New York Times* reporter who covered the event. 'This place was always half full, and the people who arranged the concert always gave lame excuses, like everyone is on Easter vacation or there was a magic show here last week and everyone spent their money on that.'

Allen began shooting on 19 May 1976 on the South Fork of Long Island, starting with the scene in which he and Annie, at the closest point of their relationship, collaborate hysterically on boiling some live lobsters. To Alvy, the good nature and shared humour of the moment summarise the best of the relationship. He would never achieve that insouciance with any woman again, a fact dramatised later in the film when we see Alvy in the same situation with another girl who finds his lobster shenanigans incomprehensible.

Filming continued jerkily for the next ten months, complicated by the fact that Gordon Willis elected to light the film in three different styles: hot golden light for California, grey overcast for Manhattan and a forties Hollywood glossy for the dream sequences – an element almost totally absent from the finished film, since most of these were deleted.

The decision to use Willis hadn't been taken lightly. Allen had first wanted a New York cameraman, but was attracted by the idea of using the man who lit the *Godfather* films, if less so by his reputation: 'To work with me,' Willis admits, 'and I'd be the first person to say it, is like being locked in a room with Attila.' Allen says, 'I had loved his stuff, but I had heard how difficult he was, angry, all sorts of dreadful things, and I didn't want to use him. I said to [line producer] Bobby Greenhut, 'Let's sign a contract, but let's make the budget so that if we fire Gordie we can get another cameraman.' When Willis asked to see the script, Allen invited him to his apartment, handed him a copy, told him he couldn't take it away, and disappeared. Instead of exploding, Willis read it, and the two men quickly understood one another. Willis turned out to be the perfect collaborator, and was only superseded when Allen persuaded Bergman's cameraman Sven Nykvist to work with him on *Another Woman* in 1987.

Incorporating Allen's childhood into the film posed the greatest structural problems, and led to repeated false starts. Trying to shoot a scene at Coney Island, Allen kept two hundred extras waiting around for half a day, and finally shot nothing. Two more sequences, both illustrating adolescent crushes, were shot but not used. One featured the eleven-year-old Brooke Shields, the other a hot-eyed seventeen-year-old brunette named Stacey Nelkin. Alfred Lutter, the young Allen from *Love and Death*, reprised his role in the second episode, during which Alvy, out on a date, is terrorised by a gang called the Surf Avenue Angels. The Alvy of the 'Brooklyn expanding' scene was played by Jonathan Munk, a closer match than Lutter for the gawky young Allen – so close, in fact, that in *Stardust Memories* the young version of the Allen character, director Sandy Bates, was played by Jonathan's younger brother Robert.

When his first choice to appear in the cinema lobby sequence,

Fellini, turned him down, Allen asked, and was refused by, Luis Buñuel. He took McLuhan only as a last and, as it turned out, unsatisfactory alternative. The scene originally ran much longer, with Singer explaining to McLuhan that he'd been expelled from college for burning the dean in effigy. McLuhan was awkward on camera, and had to return from Canada for retakes, during which Allen acted coldly, almost ignoring the academic. 'It was very embarrassing,' said a crew member. Other actors also resented Allen's offhand treatment of them. Mordecai Lawner, who played the much-truncated role of Alvy's father, complained that Allen never spoke to him.

An exception to this rule was Stacey Nelkin, to whom Allen had become attracted after her brief scene. Having lived in Europe, the pretty brunette had a patina of sophistication that Allen found attractive, and he cautiously invited her to his apartment, an assignation that ended in her seduction. Allen was forty, she seventeen. Their liaison continued in secret for two years, during which, Nelkin claims, she 'learned a lot about music and films. I was crazy about him.'

A few sequences worked well from the start, sometimes because of pure serendipity. Having set up a scene in which Alvy is offered his first sniff of cocaine by a wised-up Manhattanite (John Doumanian, husband of his friend Jean) just back from diabolical Hollywood, Allen accidentally sneezed into the box, blowing white powder over everyone. The general look of astonishment is unforced, and Keaton obviously cracks up, stifling her giggles with her hand. Elsewhere, Allen's flair for the unexpected surfaces, as when he stops Annie on the street during their first date and suggests they kiss immediately, getting it out of the way so that there will be no tension and they'll be able to digest their dinner in comfort. The moment has charm, but also a cold-blooded quality. As Allen admitted to Stig Bjorkman, 'I have a certain part of my personality that has got that rigid, obsessive coldness. Everything has to be perfect and in perfect order.' He also acknowledged that he'd used the technique in his own dating, with some success.

* * *

Late in 1976, Allen showed a preliminary version of 'Anhedonia' to Ralph Rosenblum, who was appalled. 'The opening monologue was very long and repeatedly broken by cuts to scenes that amplified Woody's grievances and hang-ups.' This version began with a much more ambitious flashback to Alvy's Brooklyn childhood than in the final film. He shows his mother complaining that the neighbourhood has been ruined by 'the element'. Stepping into the scene, Singer tells the audience, 'The element. Can you believe that? My mother was always worried that "the element" would move in. It's like a science fiction movie.' This introduced *The Invasion of the Element*, a pastiche of Don Siegel's masterpiece of science fictional paranoia *Invasion of the Body Snatchers*.

Alvy's visit to his old school followed, but was extended by a look at the adult home life of model student Donald, owner of the 'profitable dress company', in which Alvy sneers at Donald's over-dressed wife and strident children. We canter through Alvy's early sex life: the date with Judy Horowitz (Brooke Shields), whom we also see today, obese and surrounded by children; and a later one with Stacey Nelkin in which the condom Alvy has carried in his wallet for years crumbles to dust when he finally has a chance to use it. The sequence continued with clips from Singer/Allen's appearances on Dick Cavett and Ed Sullivan, and ended after fourteen minutes, having summed up Allen's career but made no reference to his relationship with Keaton.

After some cosmetic work on the film, Rosenblum and Allen screened it for Brickman. 'To tell you the truth,' says the writer, 'when I saw the rough cut of *Annie Hall*, I thought it terrible; completely unsalvageable. It was two and a half hours long and rambled and was tangential and just endless.' On 19 January 1977, *New York Daily News* columnist Liz Smith reported, not with total accuracy, on the film's troubles. 'So far only the title – *The Woody Allen Movie* – is firm. There was a sneak preview for friends and they were not impressed. "It was boring. It's about Woody and his impotence. Woody and his depression, Woody and his uncertainties. It's the same old *schtick*." Woody's thinking about re-editing the whole thing.' Stills from the obviously extensive deleted sequences were circulated surreptitiously among New

York's cinephiles as evidence that the project was out of control.

Generously, Brickman compared this cut to the first draft of a novel, 'like the raw material from which a film could be assembled – from which two or three films could possibly be assembled'. He was right: material from the first cut of 'Anhedonia' would end up, reshot, in *Radio Days*, and smaller sections in *Manhattan* and *Deconstructing Harry*. He also held out for a simpler structure, without flashbacks. With Rosenblum's guidance, Allen shot new sequences and reshaped others. An ending eluded him until almost the last minute, though he tried many. One involved Alvy, walking through Manhattan at night, seeing the electric billboard in Times Square suddenly light up with the message, 'What are you doing, Alvy? Go to California. It's OK. She loves you.' On re-viewing, according to legend, Allen disliked this maudlin idea so much that he threw the reels in the reservoir in Central Park.

He finally returned to one of the earliest versions of the story for an ending. 'The Couple Next Door' had concluded with a stand-up to camera, and Rosenblum persuaded Allen to end the film with a brief monologue, preceded by a montage of Alvy's life with Annie, including some occasions after the break-up when they run into one another around Manhattan. (In one, she's taking a friend to see *The Sorrow and the Pity*. Alvy's date is the young Sigourney Weaver and Annie's the writer of *The Front*, Walter Bernstein.)

Rosenblum and Allen came up with the montage idea during a conversation which Susan Morse, the cutting-room assistant, overheard. 'While Woody and Ralph chatted about the pros and cons of such a notion,' she recalls, 'I envisioned such a sequence in my mind and began flipping through the log book in search of likely candidates. By the time they had decided to go ahead with it, I had pulled out virtually all of the cuts you see in the final version. When Ralph turned around to ask me to look for the raw material they would need, I could simply hand them to him. It was a terrific moment for me because I felt very much a part of the process.' 'Sandy' Morse would replace Rosenblum as Allen's editor from *Stardust Memories*, becoming the custodian of the 'Black Reels' – the spools on which Allen kept scenes he'd cut from his films. During the run-up to a new production, he would often view them and adapt discarded sequences.

In a taxi on his way to an editing session, Allen jotted down the essentials of what would become the film's final lines. 'I thought of that old joke, you know, this guy goes to a psychiatrist and says, "Doc, my brother's crazy. He thinks he's a chicken." And the doctor says, "Well, why don't you turn him in?" And the guy says, "I would, but I need the eggs." Well, I guess that's pretty much how I feel about relationships. You know, they're totally irrational and crazy and absurd and . . . but, I guess we keep going through it because most of us need the eggs.'

At the beginning of 1978 Allen threw a massive New Year's Eve party at his apartment. In addition to friends and collaborators, guests included Arthur Miller, Bette Midler and Norman Mailer, a list that indicated how high he had climbed. In mid-1978 Allen was in Elaine's when a waiter brought over a card from S.J. Perelman on which was written, 'My dear Mr Allen, won't you please join us for a Dr Brown's Celery Tonic?' (The celery-flavoured soft drink, a favourite in New York delis, featured often in Perelman's pieces.) A flustered Allen appeared. 'I don't believe it,' he said. 'I thought it was a joke.' The long delay in the two men meeting was made even more ironic by the fact that a few months earlier Perelman had made the speech presenting Allen and Brickman with the New York Film Critics' Award for best screenplay, for *Annie Hall*. Typically, however, Allen hadn't attended the ceremony.

Given his hostility to TV lawyers, it was odd that Allen became friendly with the most assiduously self-promotional of them all, Alan Dershowitz. For the advocate's fortieth birthday, a group of friends, knowing he admired Allen, had arranged for them to meet. 'We kibitzed for about half an hour,' recalls Dershowitz, who kept in touch with Allen for the next few years. 'I remember he got a kick out of the fact that he was my birthday present, and I remember him saying that if he could pick someone for his birthday he would pick Louis Armstrong or Jimmy Hoffa.'

Dershowitz's friendship flattered Allen. Others were merely

embarrassing. Sultry TV star Joan Collins recalls, 'I went up to Woody Allen. I said, "Oh, Mr Allen, I really admire your work. I think you're terrific. And I read somewhere that you're very shy . . . and so I feel we have something in common because I'm very shy too." He just looked at me and said, "Well, you could have fooled me."'

Just after the New Year, Allen was spotted with Stacey Nelkin in Elaine's. 'They only had eyes for each other,' said a witness, who also claimed that Allen was carrying Nelkin's schoolbooks. The affair with Nelkin, whom some people claimed had never been more than a 'sex toy' for Allen, was near its end. She retained her ambitions to act in films, and Allen had opened some doors for her in Hollywood; a convenient way to terminate the liaison, though Nelkin would have much preferred to stay with Allen permanently. (She was to have an undistinguished movie career in films like *Halloween III*.) Nelkin's anguish over the break-up would be mirrored in the Mariel Hemingway character in *Manhattan*, whom the film's Woody character, Ike Davis, urges to follow her theatrical ambitions in London.

Nelkin was already a back number to Allen. If he was close to any woman during the period of *Annie Hall*, it was Jean Doumanian. Now divorced from John, she had moved to New York and, with Allen's help, found a job booking guests for Dick Cavett's talk show. After this she did a similar job for *Saturday Night Live with Howard Cosell*, an ABC variety show (not to be confused with the later and more successful *NBC's Saturday Night Live*) hosted by the sports commentator. In January 1976 Cosell's show folded, but Doumanian got a job on *NBC's Saturday Night Live* booking celebrities. Allen, who had remained friendly with the show's producer Lorne Michaels ever since he was a lowly writer selling him gags – he regularly came to Allen's New Year's parties – was widely believed to have pulled some strings to get Doumanian the job.

Doumanian has been, without doubt, Allen's closest and most constant female friend. 'There were many years when we ate every meal together,' he has said. 'We speak on the phone one or two times a day.' Friends credit Doumanian with influencing Allen's taste. 'She drags him off to parties. Even tells him how to dress,' says New York journalist Stephen Silverman. Her taste has influenced his films. 'That apartment in *Stardust Memories* is *very* Jean,' Silverman says, referring to the bleak minimalist home of Sandy Bates, the walls decorated with ascetic photographs by Lee Friedlander and a photomural of a South Vietnamese officer executing a Viet Cong prisoner. Allen's homey duplex, with its bibelots, framed photographs of Diane Keaton and Houdini, its worn swaybacked sofas and over-stuffed chairs, owed nothing to Doumanian, though she advised him on his most ostentatious purchase of the mid-seventies, a cream Rolls-Royce in which he was chauffeured around the city. In 1992 Allen even saved Doumanian's life by performing the Heimlich Manoeuvre on her when food caught in her throat while they were eating at a restaurant.

Whether Doumanian ever enjoyed a sexual relationship with Allen was much discussed. His sister Letty insists, 'They were never involved in that situation. It was always a friendship.' Doumanian refused to be drawn on the question, even though she and Allen often spent European holidays together. At times, she seemed to enjoy making ambiguous comments. 'Woody has me laughing from the minute we wake up in the morning,' she has said. On balance, it's unlikely they ever were involved. Doumanian, fiercely ambitious and assertive, would be altogether too much of a handful. As if confirming this, around the time of *Annie Hall* Doumanian entered a more permanent relationship with Jacqui Safra, whose Syrian/Lebanese family had extensive banking interests. It was a useful liaison for Allen, since Safra would finance his production company Sweetland. As for Allen, he was seen around town with Jessica Harper, who'd played a small role in *Love and Death*, and who would have a more central one in *Stardust Memories*. He was also rumoured to have shared the bed of the beautiful Amy Irving, lover and, briefly, wife of director Steven Spielberg.

With *Annie Hall*, Allen became even more torn between his rival personae of recluse and public figure. CBS's *60 Minutes* updated the profile broadcast at the time of *Sleeper*. For a new introduction, producer Bill Moses suggested he film Allen walking past a cinema showing *Annie Hall*. 'I couldn't do that,' Allen said. 'People might recognise me.' Nor would he agree to being shot in Central Park unless they filmed at six a.m., when the park was deserted. Moses finally shot on the balcony of Allen's apartment. When they had finished they descended to street level, where they found Allen's driver waiting beside his cream Rolls-Royce. Moses and the crew rolled their eyes at this eccentric conception of self-effacement.

17

Interiors

> Hegel remarks somewhere that all facts and personages of great importance in world history occur, as it were, twice. He forgot to add: the first time as tragedy, the second as farce.
>
> Karl Marx, *The Eighteenth Brumaire*

Allen made a dutiful visit to Los Angeles in April 1977 for the Filmex screening of *Annie Hall*, gloomily describing the film as 'a personal failure', which, in terms of the confessional ambitions with which he'd launched it, it was. But he was already envisaging using the autobiographical material cut from his early Fellini-esque version – material which, combined with scenes reflecting his cynicism about critics and movie buffs, was to resurface in the jaded *Stardust Memories*.

Critics didn't share his doubts about *Annie Hall*, and the film, though released in only a handful of cinemas with a diffident ad campaign and the slogan 'A Nervous Romance', soon built up a reputation. *Variety* declared that, 'in a decade largely devoted to male buddy-buddy films, brutal rape fantasies and impersonal special effects extravaganzas, Woody Allen has almost single-handedly kept alive the idea of heterosexual romance in American films.'

But, considering *Annie Hall*'s enormous popular success, many of the first reviews were respectful rather than enthusiastic, praising Allen for having so obviously put his heart on his sleeve. Ralph Rosenblum recalled that some preview audiences cried at the end of the film. Andrew Sarris, in a searching review for the *Village Voice* which praised the skill with which Allen trod the line between airing his intellectual pretensions and urban neuroses and mocking them in his characters, acknowledged that the film was, at heart, a romance, and a beguiling one – 'the *Romeo and Juliet*

of analysands'. Sarris went on, 'one can forgive him almost anything for the cinematic Valentine he has woven for Diane Keaton.
I never dreamt that a Woody Allen movie would ever remind me
of a Larry Hart lyric. After *Annie Hall*, it will be hard to argue
that romantic heterosexual love is not making a strong comeback.'
Joan Goodman of London's *Time Out* agreed: 'For all its apparent
frankness there's something reassuringly old-fashioned about
Annie Hall. Romance lives, even if these days you have to punctu-
ate it with visits to the shrink.'

Even before *Annie Hall* finished editing, Allen pitched a new
film to Arthur Krim, United Artists' autocratic head, and received
his OK. The film would be a drama, and, for the first time, Allen
would not act in it. Krim didn't cavil. 'You've earned it,' he told
Allen. Krim could afford to be magnanimous, since he was thinking of leaving UA and striking out on his own.

Steven Bach, who when Krim left shortly after inherited what
he called 'the yes-or-no script prerogative Krim had exercised',
shared Krim's conviction that Allen had earned the right to make
his drama. '*Interiors*,' wrote Bach later, 'may be one of the rare
instances in modern American movie history in which an artist
has been allowed to make a picture because of what it might
mean to his creative development, success or failure. That it failed
commercially does not diminish the picture or the mutual respect
with which it was financed and made. Nor does it diminish the
tremendous debt of faith that Arthur Krim incurred with Woody
in understanding the importance of *Interiors* to him.'

Less lofty motives also motivated Krim. If Allen left UA for
Krim's new company he would be a long-term money-maker, so
an agreement to film his unnamed drama was diplomatic. If, on
the other hand, Allen stayed with UA, Krim could take some
satisfaction from having left them with a guaranteed flop.

When Krim, his partner Bob Benjamin and three others
announced the formation of their new company, Orion, in January
1978, Allen was torn. He owed Krim, and shared some of the
feelings of the sixty-two film-makers like Stanley Kubrick, François
Truffaut and Robert Altman who put their names to a display
advertisement in the trade press questioning 'the wisdom of the

Transamerica Corporation losing the talents of these men'. But with three films still to go on his UA contract, and money already pledged for the new drama, he was loath to cut himself loose. Accordingly, he – and Rollins and Joffe – refused to sign the ad. Had the upheavals at UA taken place after the announcement of the 1977 Academy Award nominations in February 1978, much might have been different, but for the moment nobody could forecast the success of *Annie Hall*.

That success was enormous and wide-ranging. Among its most improbable manifestations was a fashion vogue for clothes based on Annie's *ad hoc* outfits, one of which Keaton wore to the Oscar ceremony. A Bloomingdales buyer enthused, 'Buy a cap, vest and tie, and you can give a new look to every shirt, pant and skirt in your wardrobe.' A representative of a rival department store, Bonwit Teller, opined that the fad for ties over a vest and shirt, trousers with braces, and a felt fedora pulled down over the ears indicated that 'women are playing around with the clothes that symbolise the successful man. It suggests that women now see themselves as equal to men.' A short-lived chain of boutiques merchandised the 'Annie Look', until women realised they could achieve the same effect simply by raiding their boyfriends' wardrobes, or by shopping at a charity store.

Having been released months before the Oscar deadline, *Annie Hall* suffered from not being fresh in the minds of Academy voters. Traditionally, this problem was met by briefly re-releasing a film around LA a few weeks before voting ended, and inserting ads in the trade press with the nudging heading 'For Your Consideration'. Allen specifically requested that UA do neither, but, shrewdly, the studio made the film available early in 1978 for television screening on Los Angeles' Z Channel. Run by and for film buffs, the station was widely watched within the industry. Voters who had seen the film the previous April, many of them transplanted New Yorkers, were reminded of its merits. When the nominations were announced, *Annie Hall*, despite competition from *Star Wars*, *Close Encounters of the Third Kind*, *Saturday Night Fever*, *Julia* and *The Turning Point*, was nominated for Best Picture, Allen for Best

Director, Best Actor and, with Brickman, Best Original Screenplay, and Keaton for Best Actress.

On Oscars night, 29 March 1978, which was overshadowed in the press by Vanessa Redgrave's tirade against 'Zionist hoodlums' when she accepted her Best Supporting Actress award for *Julia*, Brickman was there to accept his award and Keaton hers, but there was an awkward pause after the announcement of Allen's win for Best Director. Nobody had arranged for a substitute to collect the statuette if Allen, as he had threatened to do, preferred to play at Michael's Pub in New York that night rather than turn up in Los Angeles in the hope of an Oscar.

Allen playing jazz in New York while he won the Oscars became a cornerstone of his legend. Self-effacing to the last, runs the tale, he went home afterwards, not bothering to learn that he'd taken Best Film, Best Original Screenplay and Best Director, though losing out as Actor to Richard Dreyfuss in *The Goodbye Girl*. In reality, Allen's non-appearance at the Oscars, which, as Adam Gopnik wrote in the *New Yorker*, 'seemed like a unique act of integrity', invites another interpretation.

News of Allen's intention to boycott the Awards ceremony was leaked to the New York papers days before. Michael's Pub was jammed that night, with people, mostly press, eight deep at the bar. Between sets, the rest of the band retired backstage, but Allen stayed alone on the stand, 'blindly receiving,' noted one observer, 'an endless stream of attractive young ladies who came to pay their compliments'. Far from looking indifferent, he seemed 'anaesthetised'. If he was seeking privacy, wondered many, why did he remain on stage?

So many reporters and photographers were crowded around that a photo session was hurriedly improvised. As the time came for the awards to be announced, they ran next door to P.J. Clarke's, joining a mob of well-oiled movie executives who'd chosen the trendy bar/café to watch the telecast. Once they knew Allen and Keaton had won, the reporters ran back to Michael's Pub, to find the place mostly empty, and Allen gone.

'Oh, he went home twenty minutes ago,' the maître d' explained. 'He didn't like all the TV cameras about.' Once again, Allen, appearing to shun the limelight, had unerringly backed into it.

The night after the Awards, agent Susan Stein threw a party at the Dakota. Allen was there, Manhattan's most famous shrinking violet. 'It was full of Broadway and film celebrities,' recalled Jules Feiffer. 'There were a lot of *paparazzi* downstairs, shooting people as they poured into the elevator to go up to her apartment. Woody happened to be there just as I was there. He was wearing his large floppy hat. And of course the *paparazzi* wanted him more than Burt Lancaster and Kirk Douglas. The elevator came, and we got in – a lot of really famous people, and Woody. But Woody kept his face hidden, so the *paparazzi* kept pushing the button to open the elevator door, and calling, "Come on, Woody. Just one shot." But he wouldn't take off the hat. I leaned forward and growled in his ear, "Woody, let them take your picture, or get the fuck out of the elevator." He took off his hat, they got the picture, and we went up.'

Allen continued to play jazz on the night of the Oscars ceremony every year he was nominated. 'I know it sounds horrible,' he said a year later, in his first public pronouncement on the Awards, 'but winning that Oscar for *Annie Hall* didn't mean anything to me. I have no regard for that kind of ceremony. I just don't think they know what they're doing. When you see who wins those things – or doesn't win them – you can see how meaningless this Oscar thing is.'

Annie Hall's four Oscars were far from meaningless to UA, which now strove even more vigorously to keep Allen. In the corporate shake-up, Steven Bach and Christopher Mankiewicz, son of Joseph L., had risen to positions of power. Allen knew them both, since they had been at Palomar when it financed *Take the Money and Run*. Transamerica seemed glad to leave creative decisions to them, and Bach accepted without demur Allen's assurance that his next film but one would be a comedy. About the drama which would precede it, he received only vague hints, though as its theme became more apparent, executives around UA took to referring to 'Ingmar Allen'.

*   *   *

While Allen enjoyed his greatest affinity as a film-maker with Federico Fellini, it was the chilly Ingmar Bergman he most desired to emulate – even though, it could be argued, no two men ever had less in common. But if he had to make a *hommage* to Bergman, there was no better time. The Swedish director, after slumping with his first English-language film *The Touch* in 1971, had redis-covered himself with a series of profound meditations on the ten-sions within dysfunctional families, mostly revealed when they faced death or mental illness.

In the 1973 *Cries and Whispers*, a woman dying of cancer returns to her family home to be cared for by her two sisters. The same year, *Scenes From a Marriage*, a painful picture of divorce first shown as a six-part series for TV in Sweden, won praise in the cinema version released in the US. In 1976 Bergman released *Face to Face*, in which psychiatrist Liv Ullmann, returning to her grandparents' home, has a nervous breakdown when she is forced to face her rape there as a girl. *Face to Face* returned Bergman to centre stage in the United States, particularly in Manhattan. The New York Critics awarded Liv Ullmann her third Best Actress plaque. The film also impressed Allen, who chose it as the movie which Alvy and Annie try but fail to see at the opening of *Annie Hall*.

Like many of Bergman's films, *Face to Face* showcased a power-ful central female performance, and was shot by Sven Nykvist in a style that evoked pale northern light and the equally drained emotional climate in which Americans fancied Swedes lived. It nudged Allen into a conviction that something similar might be created using New York and the Upper East Side as the setting.

In April 1977, Allen opened a production office for the film in the Manhattan Plaza, a new apartment complex at Ninth Avenue and 42nd Street which had become the fashionable address for New York's better-heeled producers. In charge of the production was Robert 'Bobby' Greenhut, who would become more central to Allen's operation over the years. They'd met during the pro-duction of *Play it Again, Sam*, and Greenhut, a self-effacing man who preferred working at a green baize card table to a desk, was production manager on *Annie Hall*.

The new film, *Interiors*, was provisionally called 'Windows', hinting at its point of view, that of staring out on the world from behind glass. Arthur (E.G. Marshall) is a prosperous, middle-aged New York attorney stuck in a loveless marriage to Eve (Geraldine Page), a cultivated matron obsessed with interior decoration. Their three daughters have all been emotionally harmed by the tensions within the marriage and, in particular, Eve's subtle erosion of their self-esteem. Renata (Diane Keaton), a moderately successful poet, is trapped in a marriage as dysfunctional as that of her parents with Frederick (Richard Jordan), an underachieving author with a drinking problem who wastes his talent on needlessly cruel reviews of better books than he's capable of writing himself. Joey (Mary Beth Hurt), sensitive but with no artistic ability, moves restlessly from job to job, experimenting with photography and acting while her political documentarist husband Mike (Sam Waterston) tries to solve the problems of the world on celluloid. The youngest and prettiest daughter, Flyn (Kristin Griffith), plays bimbo roles in TV films, and compensates for the emptiness of her life by flirting with her brothers-in-law and snorting coke.

Arthur announces that he's leaving home in the hope of finding some happiness for the last part of his life. Eve has a nervous breakdown, and only recovers by deluding herself that their trial separation will never end in divorce. When he turns up at a family gathering on Long Island with Pearl (Maureen Stapleton), a flashy widow he intends to marry, Eve drowns herself. Joey almost dies trying to rescue her, and is saved by Pearl, who automatically takes over the role of mother which Eve, obsessed with herself and her interiors, could never play for her daughters. The ending holds out some hope that Joey at least may find peace.

The inspiration of *Interiors* was Louise Lasser, and in particular her suicidal mother, whose troubled relationship with her daughter had left deep psychic scars. Allen also said that he had 'heard of an incident where a husband at the breakfast table, just very nicely, in a very gentlemanly way, said he was going to leave. And the mother left the table and went to her room and killed herself.' It's not clear if the people involved were Lasser's parents.

In 1976, Lasser had finally achieved stardom in the television series *Mary Hartman, Mary Hartman*, a knowing parody of soap opera in which she played an Ohio housewife beset with accidental death, drug addiction, terrorism, mass murder, impotence and rape. Lasser managed to make 325 episodes during 1976–77, then left, exhausted. The following year, overweight and visibly disturbed, she was arrested on Los Angeles' Rodeo Drive after having subsided to the floor of a fashionable boutique, dumped the contents of her bag and rummaged out a quantity of cocaine wrapped in silver foil. *Interiors* incarnates her as Flyn.

In early scripts, Joey was the main character, but as Allen developed the story, a typically Bergman-esque ensemble cast emerged. Renata, the troubled poet, represented Allen's point of view. 'She speaks for me, without question,' he said. 'She articulates all my personal concerns.' Unfortunately, she never articulates them to the audience. *Interiors* lacks the narrator, voice-over or stand-up introduction of most Allen films, and having committed himself to naturalistic dialogue, he felt unable to use Bergman's solution to this problem – the long reflective monologues that, in films like *Persona*, focus attention and define themes. In *Interiors*, exposition has somehow to be hidden in normal conversation. Thus Joey, the film's least colourful character, becomes its covert commentator and interpreter.

Confronting Eve at the beach house after the marriage of Arthur and Pearl, Joey, in the film's key scene, exposes the festering resentments all three girls harbour towards their self-obsessed mother.

I think you're really too perfect to live in this world. I mean, all the beautifully furnished rooms, carefully designed interiors, everything so controlled. There wasn't any room for any real feelings. None between any of us. Except Renata, who never really gave you the time of day. You worship Renata. You worship talent. Well, what happens to those of us who can't create? What do we do? What do I do when I'm overwhelmed with feelings about life? How do I get them out? I feel such rage towards you! Come on, Mother, don't you see? You're not just a sick woman. That would be too easy. The truth is, there's been perverseness – and wilfulness of attitude – in many of the things you've done. At the centre of a sick psyche, there's a sick spirit. But I love you. And we have no other choice but to forgive each other.

In *Interiors*, Allen unveils a plot which, with a number of variations, would preoccupy him for decades. Three characters, related by birth or marriage, each have an emotional or sexual problem. One is too much interested in sex, another bored by it, while the third thinks love more important. In *Interiors*, the problems of the protagonists, Renata, Joey and Flyn, are intellectual; in *A Midsummer Night's Sex Comedy*, sexual; in *Hannah and her Sisters*, familial; in *Crimes and Misdemeanors*, moral and ethical. But in every case there is a similar reliance on three dissatisfied people, and their struggles to find partners or to separate themselves from partners they find wanting.

In *Love and Death*, Allen guyed the plot in the scene where Jessica Harper details the emotional daisy chain of her life: 'Lev loves Tatiana. Tatiana loves Simpkin. Simpkin loves me. I love Simpkin but in a different way than Alexei . . .' etc. *Interiors* repeats an almost identical situation, but as tragedy. Arthur wants love. Pearl has love but wants family. Eve has family but wants control. Joey has control but wants talent. Renata has talent but wants peace. Flyn has peace, of a sort, but wants admiration. Frederick will give her admiration, but wants sex – a need which inspires the film's most unintentionally hilarious line, when, trying drunkenly to rape her, Frederick wails, 'It's so long since I made love to a woman I didn't feel inferior to.'

Interiors echoed Bergman in style, but any structural resemblances flowed from his and Allen's shared inspiration, Strindberg. Unfortunately, the film is both bad Bergman and bad Strindberg. It strives to achieve the look and sound of Bergman, unaware that his stylistic austerity flows from an inner Puritanism. Allen's *mise en scène*, with half-seen figures moving on the edge of vision through meticulously decorated rooms, reflections of winter trees on misty windows, the *flump* of grey waves on an empty beach, is Bergman done as painting-by-numbers.

In a scene ludicrous in its literalness, Eve prepares for an unsuccessful suicide attempt by sealing the windows with movie 'gaffer'

tape; first white, then, when the roll runs out, black. Allen's framing often directly imitates Bergman, most flagrantly in the last
image, when, as Keaton and Hurt stare out of yet another window
at a bleak future, Griffith drifts into shot, stationing herself exactly
between them in a composition lumberingly imitative of *Persona*.

Keaton was to have played Joey, opposite tall, tranquil Jane Alexander as Renata, but persuaded Allen to give her the more
anguished and, superficially, meaty role. She also suggested
Interiors as an alternative title to the bleak 'Windows'. Harris
Yulin originally played Joey's documentarist husband Mike, but
asked to be relieved of the under-written part after a few days of
rehearsals at New York's Stanhope Hotel. Sam Waterston replaced
him, as he would later replace Sam Shepard in *September*. Allen
had thought of British actor Denholm Elliott for Arthur, and
located him in Ibiza, where he was holidaying in a house that had
no phone. He could only be contacted in the evenings at a bar,
where Allen rang him. 'Can you do an American accent?' he asked.
Elliott, taken aback, tried reciting 'Hickory, dickory, dock' over
the phone *à la* New York, but didn't convince.

Eve began as a woman with strong religious beliefs that turn sour
as she loses her reason. Once Geraldine Page was cast, her lofty
WASP demeanour seemed inappropriate to a devout Catholic. All
that remains of this theme in the released version is a scene where
she arranges to see Arthur in a church, on the pretext of admiring
the frescos, then presses him again for a reconciliation. When he
hints that he might remarry, she throws a tantrum and sweeps the
devotional candles in their red glass holders to the floor. With her
cone-shaped chignon and voluminous monochrome wardrobe,
Page looks elephantine. Maureen Stapleton tries to infuse Pearl with
some sensuality, but comes over mainly as a *yenta*, the traditional
interfering matron, talking food, resorts and her family. A scene
where she's required to dance alone at the family party is embarrassing to the point of farce. For her part, Stapleton found the experience, and the director, wearing. 'He's not shy,' she said of Allen.
'He's anti-social. That's a different ball-game.'

*　　*　　*

Convinced that finding the right locations and employing Bergman techniques would give the film the requisite high seriousness, Allen laboured to find the correct house in the Hamptons – he and Mel Bourne looked at forty-five – and beaches which resembled those where Bergman habitually shot on his private island of Fåro. Choosing the house was only the beginning. Bourne removed all the furniture and fittings, as being too fussy for Eve's astringent taste. 'We reglazed all the windows because the glass wasn't absolutely clear and we could not get perfect reflections. There was a perfectly straight line of putty on every window, because that's what Eve would have done. We scraped every window in that house to make sure there was no extra putty showing. I felt that muted clay beige was a wonderful colour for Eve, and was wonderful for flesh tones. I mixed a lot of colours and went out to the house, and put it on three-foot-by-three-foot wall sections and looked at it at different times of day. I painted the window walls along the beach a lighter shade than the other walls in the house to lose the shadows and to achieve a look of uniformity.' The owners weren't enthusiastic about this redecoration, nor about the state in which their house was left when shooting finished. They threatened legal action unless Rollins and Joffe paid to have it restored to its original condition.

Gordon Willis proved even more expert in his lighting than he had in *Annie Hall*. It was he who suggested shooting some scenes day-for-night, through filters, creating a milky half-darkness reminiscent of Bergman's sub-Arctic exteriors. A beach walk with Renata and Flyn was lit and framed to recall an etching by Emil Nolde, whose work Allen had admired ever since he bought one of his watercolours for Lasser during the London shoot of *Casino Royale*.

No technical virtuosity could save *Interiors* from the stifling effect of its literal-minded script. In a cruel irony, Bergman was, even as Allen worked on it, filming *Autumn Sonata*, with Ingrid Bergman as a self-obsessed mother who tries to rebuild her relationship with the daughter she had neglected for her career as a concert pianist. It was this film, not *Interiors*, that would win the plaudits of 1978, and Ingrid Bergman, not

Geraldine Page, who took the New York Critics' Award for best actress.

Shooting began on 24 October 1977, under a cloud of apprehension. Three days before, the *New York Times* asked Allen if the film would be 'bathed in Bergman-esque misery'. He insisted it wouldn't, but admitted, 'Right now, I'm faced with the pitfalls of half-baked ideas and derivative techniques. I'm feeling my way.'

Allen became increasingly defensive about *Interiors* as shooting wore on into the winter of 1978–79. He took to draping his head in a coat whenever press photographers appeared. When they tried to snap 'the Creator', as one reporter called him, his 'priests', in his phrase, improvised cardboard screens to frustrate them. Matters came to a head when the unit moved to leafy suburban Larchmont, where Bourne had found the ideal location for the house Diane Keaton shared with Richard Jordan; by coincidence, poet Phyllis McGinley had once lived there. Location manager Carl Zucker warned the owners, Herbert and CeCe Wasserman, 'Don't feel hurt if Woody doesn't say hello to you. He's shy, unsociable, hates kids and dogs.' Herbert Wassermann prudently went on a business trip to Atlanta, but CeCe and her children decided it would be an interesting experience to remain in the house and watch the film being shot. They all became used to Allen's surly demeanour, his Garbo-esque reiteration of 'I want to be left alone.' The film had no publicist, so curiosity was high among New York's press. The Wassermans were warned repeatedly not to disclose what was happening in their home, but since the trucks parked in the front yard and around the block all trumpeted '*The New Woody Allen Movie*' in giant letters, *paparazzi* soon found the house. They were led by an old adversary of Allen's, Ron Galella, whose prey had included Jackie Onassis, Marlon Brando and most of the crowned heads of Europe. Galella arrived while Allen and the stars were eating in an improvised gourmet cafeteria set up in a basement next door. Allen immediately panicked.

'How are we going to get this guy?' he demanded, 'and how are we going to get out of here without him seeing us?'

CeCe Wasserman led them out through bushes and across driveways to another part of the street. As she did so, Allen demanded, 'Do you have a gun in the house?' She didn't, but that afternoon she bought an air rifle and a box of BB pellets as a gift for Allen. When she arrived back at the house he was directing, but he stopped work as soon as he saw her. 'He grabbed his present,' says Wasserman, 'darted into the front room where he had the best view of his target, unwrapped the carton and caressed the rifle. Now he could get him!' Prudently, Galella and his helper had disappeared. Thereafter, round-the-clock police kept the press at bay. Allen took the air rifle back to Manhattan, and used it to shoot at the pigeons which fouled his terrace, proudly demonstrating his marksmanship to British critic Penelope Gilliatt when she came to interview him.

Before he left Larchmont, Allen briefly confided to one of the Wasserman daughters, 'I don't think [the film's] that good. You have to make some mistakes. You have to try something new. Wait for my next one. That will be funny.' Shortly after, he and the unit departed. 'As predicted,' remarked CeCe Wasserman, 'Woody, who never said hello, never said goodbye.'

Preview screenings of *Interiors* early in December 1978 were chastening. 'The ever-so-chic private screening audience sat in stunned silence,' wrote one columnist. '[Metropolitan Museum of Art director] Tom Hoving, George Plimpton, Mariel Hemingway, among others, and I just picked up our dolly bags and left.' Another screening's audience included Jackie Onassis, Caroline Kennedy, Paddy Chayefsky, Saul Steinberg, Norman Mailer and critics Gene Shalit, Frank Rich and Judith Crist. 'Talk about a surprised group of people!' wrote *Daily News* columnist Liz Smith. UA, not happy to have their worst fears confirmed, held up release until the late summer. *Interiors* opened in August, and limped through September.

Some journalists responded to the film's surface seriousness with claims that *Interiors* was 'a masterpiece', but more considered opinion was seldom so enthusiastic. Clive Barnes, feared theatre critic of the *New York Times*, shrugged off Allen as 'a serious and intelligent funny man [but] a lightweight and trite serious man'.

Richard Goldstein in the *Village Voice* represented the kinder end of reaction to the film when he remarked, 'When it doesn't work – when it's arid and flat, and the actors respond with ensemble grimness – you can see how far Woody Allen is from mastering this terrain. But the courage of *Interiors* is its ability to confront a landscape that has always been leavened by his comedy, as though the jokes were a robust apology for the helplessness they presume.' If Ingmar Bergman ever saw Allen's *hommage*, he was too well-mannered to say so.

To its credit, UA never skimped on the release, even when Allen demanded that all prints be struck on a special Eastman stock which accurately rendered Willis' subtle lighting. Supplies of the stock became short, briefly impeding the wider release of the film in cities like Los Angeles, but UA furiously resisted claims that it was dragging its feet. They gave *Interiors* as generous a showing as Allen could have hoped for, and were rewarded, after some years, by a modest profit.

Once she saw the film, Louise Lasser rang Allen to protest. 'That movie is about my family right down to the singlemost specific detail,' she said. Allen vehemently denied this, insisting that many other people had rung him to claim the film was based on *their* family. At the end of a long conversation, Lasser said, 'In any case, I don't think you got my mother right.'

'Really?' mused Allen, caught off guard. 'I thought I was pretty spot-on about her.'

18

Manhattan and *Stardust Memories*

New York is a very large, dirty, dangerous city reserved for the rich and the destitute, because the middle class can no longer afford to live there.

Alison Lurie, 1995

Throughout his work on *Interiors*, Allen promised everyone from Steven Bach at UA to CeCe Wasserman's daughter in Larchmont that 'the next one will be funny.' The unnamed comedy assumed a talismanic significance, reassuring his backers that, however far he'd strayed from the familiar with *Interiors*, he remained faithful to his roots.

This pose was a stratagem. Allen had no intention of returning to comedy, except in the most general and elastic definition of the term. With *Interiors* he nailed his colours to the mast, convinced that, fast approaching fifty, he was too old for farce. Comedy, he told anyone who would listen, was kids' stuff. His editor at the *New Yorker*, Roger Angell, was taken aback when Allen informed him that he would no longer be submitting as many comic 'casuals', if indeed he wrote any at all. The magazine published 'The Diet', 'A Giant Step for Mankind' and 'Retribution' during 1980, all of which were included in *Side Effects*, Allen's third collection, published by Random House the same year. After that his production of humorous pieces for publication became intermittent, and there hasn't been a fourth book, although on 16 December 1985 he read two unpublished pieces at a PEN benefit in New York. In the first, a variation on 'The Shallowest Man' (which appeared in the *Kenyon Review* in winter 1980), fifty-three-year-old New York lawyer Sid Kaplan is smitten with a beautiful girl he glimpses in an elevator. The theme of the other piece had already been used in *Stardust Memories*. A 'Hostility', a hairy monster with red eyes, escapes from the psyche of its owner, Phil Feldman, and attacks his psychiatrist and parents. In the written version, Allen unleashes the creature on some other deserving victims, including a boy who plays his ghetto-blaster too loudly in the subway. The Hostility forces him to eat it.

The promised comedy that followed *Interiors*, while not without laughs, conceded nothing to Allen's fans' nostalgia for his earlier films. *Annie Hall* might have been taken for a movie in the Hollywood tradition, an updating of the screwball comedy, but no such claims could be made for *Manhattan*, the stylistic and intellectual inspirations of which lie in Europe; particularly in Italy, in the CinemaScope black and white dramas of Antonioni and Fellini.

While the opening montage recalls the unblinking succession of stark images with which Antonioni closed *L'Eclisse* in 1962, Allen's use of the city as a character exactly parallels Fellini's treatment of Rome in *La Dolce Vita* (1959) – not the only affinity between the two films. Fellini's central character is, like Allen's, a writer torn between profitable trivia and his 'serious' novel; his inspiration too is an unspoiled girl, whom Fellini, like Allen, contrasts with a self-regarding older woman; most of his friends are self-conscious intellectuals who spend their time at parties discussing the moral malaise about which they can't or won't do anything; even Allen's ending, where Ike tries to reconcile himself with his young mistress Tracy, only to find she won't change her plans, recalls the end of *La Dolce Vita*, in which Marcello Mastroianni tries to talk to the girl on the beach, only to find they can't communicate.

Charles Joffe called *Manhattan* 'a drama with comedy rather than a comedy with drama'. Under its celebration of life in the Big Apple lies a story of lost love, broken dreams, frustration, resentment and bile, played out by people who, even to themselves, feel worthless. The need constantly to reassure themselves is summed up in Diane Keaton's tirade to herself after her long-time lover Michael Murphy throws her over. 'I'm beautiful. I'm young. I'm highly intelligent. I've got everything going for me, except I'm all fucked up. I could go to bed with the entire MIT faculty. Shit! Now I lost my contact lens.'

At the same time, the film is the archetypal celebration of New York society: sensual, romantic, funny, touching – and arguably, as Andrew Sarris has called it, 'the only truly great film of the seventies.' Whatever its standing as social history, *Manhattan*, far more than *Annie Hall*, deserves to be called Allen's masterpiece. The decision to shoot in black and white, and in CinemaScope, conferred on its images a panoramic quality, but at the same time a chill and a sense of moral lassitude. British critic Russell Davies once said of the *New Yorker*, 'Getting-on-for-winter is the magazine's natural season.' Such a sense informs *Manhattan* from its breathtaking opening, a canter in thirty-five images through New York in all its moods, culminating in the traditional New Year's fireworks over Central Park, all to the ecstatic blaring of George Gershwin's *Rhapsody in Blue*. Allen planned this sequence and many others to go with the Gershwin songs which are the film's only score. 'I was shooting scenes deliberately to put to music that I knew beforehand,' he said. 'I played those records every single day as soon as I got up in the morning. I played them on the way to work, and listened to them over and over.'

The opening places the city at the centre of the story, and helps create an environment in which the film's characters remain always subservient to the place they inhabit. One can no more separate Ike and Mary and Yale and Tracy from Elaine's, Central Park, the Hayden Planetarium and the Museum of Modern Art than Eve in *Interiors* can exist outside her hermetic milieu. New York's cinemas, galleries and bookshops, the *New Yorker* and *New York Times*, all become characters in the story. Subscribing, criticising, even simply turning up at the 'right' parties and shows is an earnest of one's existence, superseding physical, moral or political action.

As Ike runs through possible first lines for his novel in the first reel, Allen anticipates the inevitable criticisms. Yes, New York is 'a metaphor for the decay of contemporary culture'. Its society has been 'desensitised by drugs, loud music, television, crime, garbage'. But he concludes with a helpless surrender to the place: 'He adored New York city. He idolised it out of all proportion.'

Ike Davis, like Allen, is a TV comedy writer who abandons that trivial pursuit to create something worthwhile. His mistress, seventeen-year-old Tracy (Mariel Hemingway), is recognisably Stacey Nelkin. Mary Wilke (Diane Keaton) is based on *New York Times* arts writer Susan Braudy, a friend of Marshall Brickman who had interviewed him and Allen for the paper about their collaboration on *Annie Hall*. Although Ike, unlike Allen, drives, drinks and smokes, he shares his enthusiasms for Bergman and Gershwin, and also many of his prejudices, some of which, like his hatred of the outdoors – his one experience of nature in the film, a visit to Central Park, ends in a violent thunderstorm – and his dislike of adding canned laughter to comedy programmes, had been aired before.

Only one sub-plot doesn't relate directly to Allen himself. Though Ike, like Allen, has two ex-wives, he also has a son, whom Jill, his second wife (Meryl Streep), took with her when she left him to live with another woman. Jill's book about their relationship, *Marriage, Divorce and Selfhood*, which Ike fears, rightly, will reveal his sexual foibles to the world, is set to be a bestseller and, as she alerts him ominously, a possible movie. It takes little imagination to relate this to Allen's chronic nervousness about his sexual preferences becoming the stuff of tabloid headlines. By aspiring to be taken seriously, he put himself at risk from journalists and critics who no longer felt his popularity as a comedian justified giving him the benefit of the doubt. It would have taken little legwork to discover that Stacey Nelkin was the model for Tracy, but the closest anyone came to it was Natalie Gittelson's reference in her *New York Times* profile of Allen to the 'soft spot in his heart for young, young women'. This fear of public criticism and exposure was again picked up in *Stardust Memories*, where it was amplified to the primary theme.

Nelkin confirms that she inspired the Tracy role, but said of Hemingway's performance. 'Mariel played it much younger. She acted in such an innocent and naïve way. That just wasn't me.' Nelkin returned briefly to New York around the time of the film, but the hoped-for reconciliation with Allen never took place. Having left Hollywood in a fever of enthusiasm, telling friends, 'Woody's flying me to New York,' she returned in tears.

Diane Keaton's character, Mary, is a carry-over from *Annie Hall*, in which Annie had originally been just such a tough, alert and cynical New York journalist. As *Manhattan* opens, Mary is having an extra-marital affair with Ike's best friend Yale (Michael Murphy, from *The Front*). Ike at first criticises Yale's infidelity to his wife Emily, played, in an arresting example of life imitating art, by Anne Byrne, an ex-dancer who had just divorced Dustin Hoffman and was trying to re-enter show business as an actress. But he comes to accept his infatuation after he meets Mary and falls for her himself.

In the process he abandons Tracy, on the pretext that she is leaving New York anyway, to study theatre in London for six months. Tracy protests that she'd stay if Ike offered her a more permanent relationship, but the New York horror of involvement is strong in him, and he drives her away, only to regret it at the last minute and try to win her back. She refuses, but reminds him she'll return in six months. 'Look, you have to have a little faith in people,' she says. As Ike ponders this radical concept, incomprehensible to any true New Yorker, *Rhapsody in Blue* swells on the soundtrack, closing the film as it opened it, and Manhattan's night-time skyline fills the screen, dwarfing Ike, Tracy and everyone else. The myth eats them. In the end, there is only the city.

Unconstrained by a tight narrative, Allen and Gordon Willis could film anywhere they chose in New York. The frontages of Gucci, Sotheby Parke-Bernet and the Plaza were filmed before anyone knew the crew was there. They grabbed the opening New Year fireworks from the bathroom window of a Central Park West apartment owned by friends, and shot some scenes at the Carlyle Hotel, just around the corner from Allen's apartment. 'Woody is bypassing lots of red tape by borrowing on his past experience from the *Candid Camera* days,' wrote a columnist. 'He and the company just arrive and start shooting.' The approach had its drawbacks. Badgered by rubberneckers, they often had to retake outdoor scenes. Allen also despaired of being allowed to shoot in the Hayden Planetarium, and had Mel Bourne construct a replica set in which Ike and Mary carry on their first courtship in hushed tones as they prowl among the dark, almost deserted exhibits.

Once he saw the first assembly of the film, Allen was so depressed that he asked Rollins and Joffe, 'Do you think there's any way I could buy this from United Artists and not have them release it, and then I would do one free film for them or something as payment?'

He was reassured by Sandy Morse, to whom Ralph Rosenblum passed the cutting-room scissors. Now a director in his own right, Rosenblum felt 'overqualified' as an editor. Morse understood the new European-oriented style of his films better than her old boss. With her, Allen worked out a style of long master shots, taken from the middle distance, and covering long periods of action. As Richard Schickel wrote approvingly in *Time*, 'He lets long scenes play without break. The camera often just sits on its haunches and stares, without even a close-up or a reverse angle intruding. Variation comes from movement within the frame; sometimes, in fact, the actor moves right out of it, keeps talking off-camera, and then reappears. When a director trusts his material that much, he encourages the audience to trust it as well.'

Over their long collaboration, Allen and Morse would build on this foundation to create an edgy narrative style that influenced both camerawork and acting. Its aim was to discard inessentials and concentrate on the thrust of the film – often not a single character but a state of mind common to a group. Sometimes, as in *Manhattan*, technique works in the service of narrative. In *Husbands and Wives*, the first reel, shot with a hand-held camera, turned a domestic argument into an experience so vertiginous that in some cinemas the management put notes on every seat explaining that the projection equipment hadn't gone wrong, but that it was Allen's photography.

Manhattan proved that Allen didn't get out of broad comedy a moment too soon. Already some audiences and critics were becoming uneasy with his character of an ageing scamp. Middle age, unkindly, turned Allen gnomish, a little sinister. The imp became a goblin. Peter Conrad, writing in the *Observer*, saw this 'stooped and balding, perpetual adolescent' as 'a totem for our times, and no wonder. The nympholepsy which incites him to pound after Mariel Hemingway is another symptom of the jogger's disease. This wizened dwarf is actually in love with the remote recollection of his own youth, for the seventies is the decade in which those who were young in the sixties began to creak, limp and wrinkle.'

As if freed to speak out by Allen's demand that he be taken seriously as an artist, people who worked with or for him began to publicly question his methods and philosophy for the first time. A year after the film opened, Meryl Streep commented, 'I don't think Woody Allen even remembers me. I went to see *Manhattan* and I felt like I wasn't even in it. I was pleased with the film because I looked pretty in it and I thought it was entertaining. But I only worked on it for three days, and I didn't get to know Woody. On a certain level, the film offends me because it's all about these people whose sole concern is their neuroses. It's sad because Woody has the potential to be America's Chekhov, but instead he's still caught up in the jet-set crowd type of life, trivialising his talent.'

Perhaps sensing his new status as an urban fogey, but also drawn by Mariel Hemingway's literary antecedents (she was Ernest's granddaughter) and, no doubt, her physical attractiveness, Allen accepted an invitation to accompany her on a visit to her parents in Idaho. Getting off the plane, he said nervously, 'I think we just landed on the moon.' He dutifully hiked through snowy woods and ate a meal consisting of something her father had shot the previous day, but the country lifestyle baffled him. Just as he was coming to life at eight at night, everyone in Idaho was going to bed.

During the shooting of *Manhattan*, Allen noticed a significant loss of hearing in one ear. Remembering that symptoms like this had presaged George Gershwin's premature death from a brain tumour, he submitted himself to a series of hospital tests, which revealed nothing. These, and his attending anxiety, would turn up as a sub-plot in *Hannah and her Sisters*.

Interiors was surprisingly well represented in the Oscar nominations announced in February 1979. Geraldine Page was nominated for Best Actress, Maureen Stapleton for Best Supporting Actress,

Allen for Best Director and Best Original Screenplay, and Mel Bourne and Daniel Robert for Best Art Direction; but Hollywood apparently decided that after Allen's very public attacks on the Oscar system, nominations were enough. The Oscars went to films of high seriousness but with essentially American concerns, in particular the war in Vietnam. *The Deer Hunter* and *Coming Home* all but swept the board, and *Interiors* got nothing.

During the shooting of *Manhattan*, Allen realised a lifetime ambition when he met Ingmar Bergman. Liv Ullmann set up the dinner at Bergman's hotel, and reassured Allen that he wouldn't be imposing himself on his hero. Embodying the principle that whenever great literary figures meet they talk about the best place to sell review copies, Allen and Bergman bypassed philosophy and quickly got down to bitching about the business. 'We commiserated about the same trivial frustrations,' said Allen, 'like the distributors who call you after one showing and tell you it did $900, which was $200 more than *Annie Hall* in the same situation, and therefore you're going to gross $19 million domestic. They're invariably euphoric, followed by invariable disappointment. Then they get mad at us.' Bergman quoted some jokes from Allen's movies, showing an understanding of his humour which took Allen aback, but resisted talking about his own films. 'All night long we kept trying to move to the other's work,' Allen recalled. Bergman asked, 'Have you ever had a picture that simply nobody liked, a total disaster?' Allen had to admit that he'd never experienced that shock to the system. Bergman knew it well, most vividly when he tried to do comedy in 1964, with *And Now About all these Women*.

Annie Hall had confirmed Allen as the cinema's laureate of the Big Apple, and the city's cultural establishment moved discreetly to recruit him. In 1980 he was asked to join the eight-person 'artistic directorate' charged with reopening the five-hundred-seat Vivian Beaumont Theater in the Lincoln Center, which had suffered in the Broadway slump. His primary contribution was to be a new play, *The Floating Light Bulb*, which the management hoped would do well enough to go on to Broadway, paying them a handsome share of its income. Other tributes included a weekend celebration as one of a series run by Judith Crist at Tarrytown, a satellite town on the Hudson, forty minutes from Manhattan. Crist, then film critic for *New York* magazine, was low on the critical totem pole – she ended up as resident reviewer of *TV Guide* – so Allen felt himself subtly slighted by the honour. To attend, he had to miss seeing his beloved Knicks play – he listened to the game on the radio as he was being driven to the seminar. Adding to his sense of gloom, he had spent the previous day watching Bergman's *The Seventh Seal* and *Cries and Whispers*. 'I see his films,' he confided to Eric Lax in the car, 'and I wonder what I'm doing.' The depression this cast over the weekend would manifest itself vividly in *Stardust Memories*.

New Yorkers increasingly regarded Allen as a fixture of the city, and of their lives. In the street, strangers, knowing he didn't like to talk, would ask if they could walk a few blocks with him in silence, feeling themselves comforted in his presence. Sometimes he co-operated with these approaches, but increasingly his reaction was belligerent. People who recognised him and made remarks like 'I love your work' would often receive a glare in return. An assistant who, loaded with film cans, accidentally backed into the wrong cutting-room, looked down to see Allen cowering under the editing table, his face a mask of fear and hatred. Before she could apologise, his irate helpers hustled her out of the door. Allen confided to a helper that he expected to be shot by a psychotic female fan, and came to dread the arrival of new tenants in his apartment building. In 1981 his discreet neighbour put his apartment on the market, the price tag of $1.5 million suggesting, in part, the snob value of living next door to a legend. Allen fretted until the new buyer turned out to be equally circumspect as the one he replaced.

In April 1979 *Manhattan* opened to rhapsodic reviews, after a preliminary screening at the Cannes Festival. Because of their fears that its wised-up New York setting and characters might daunt less sophisticated audiences, United Artists promoted the film with an atmospheric shot of Keaton, Allen and a dog sitting in a park next to the 59th Street bridge and watching the sunrise. Discreet doctoring framed out the sinister bulk of other buildings, turning a faintly threatening image into one of tranquillity and romance. The film played to relatively limited audiences, having been given an 'R' certificate because of some occasional four-letter words. Allen accepted this philosophically. He had already cut himself off from a large source of profit by banning the sale of his films to commercial television networks, who would have bowdlerised them and riddled them with commercial breaks besides.

Doomed, he knew, to a limited audience – a knowledge that offered him the gloomy reassurance that he could remain faithful to his principles – Allen was free to take pleasure in his lionising in Europe, in particular by the French. He was in Paris for the French launch of *Manhattan*, and both *Positif* and *Cahiers du Cinema*, the two most important critical magazines, published long articles or interviews. As a film-maker who wrote, directed and starred in his films, Allen, like Chaplin and Jerry Lewis, provided flattering assurance that the *politique des auteurs*, propounded by Jean-Luc Godard, François Truffaut, Eric Rohmer and Jacques Rivette during their days as critics, was correct that the greatest film work was achieved when a single intelligence, an *auteur*, was in overall creative charge.

Allen's reception at Cannes contributed to the idea, already half-formed in his mind, to devote his next film to the idea of celebrity. Briefly intrigued by the idea of shooting it in France, he began looking around for the sort of stars who might furnish his fantasies. He'd long been attracted to English actress Charlotte Rampling, whose patchy career in films was enlivened by her 1973 appearance in *The Night Porter* as a concentration-camp survivor drawn into a perverse sexual relationship with the man who had been her jailer. This role and her 1978 marriage to composer Jean-Michel Jarre had made Rampling an ornament of the European jet set, confirmed by her friendship with provocative photographer Helmut Newton, one of whose celebrity models she became, posing in an opulent nineteenth-century decor nude except for high-heeled shoes. In a letter to Nancy Jo Sales Allen had nominated Rampling as a guest at his ideal dinner party, next to Kafka and Tolstoy, and the chance to cast her in a film was too good to miss. 'She has a quality, a charisma that's unique,' he said. 'She reeks from neurosis.'

At Cannes he saw a new film by Belgian director André Delvaux, *Femme entre Chien et Loup*, and was attracted by Marie-Christine Barrault, whom he'd already seen in the 1975 *Cousin, Cousine*. He asked her agent to have her ring him in New York. While in France, Allen was himself signed up by the producer of *Femme entre Chien et Loup*, who commissioned Delvaux to produce a documentary about him for Belgian television. Delvaux expected to be turned down, but as he said, 'Allen seemed particularly flattered that a European film-maker could be sufficiently interested in him to want to make a film about him.'

As Delvaux followed the production of *Stardust Memories* while making the tribute he eventually called *To Woody Allen, from Europe with Love*, he began to see Allen in a different light – not as an American at all, but as 'a European emigrant, who had moved to America and integrated himself there'. Marie-Christine Barrault, on the other hand, found him refreshingly American when it came to making deals. 'In France, you can't even talk to the concierge of a large company, but in America they give you a number, you call and ask for Woody Allen, and it's "Who's calling?" and they put you through.'

After the general enthusiasm for *Manhattan*, Allen was rocked by a portmanteau attack in the form of a 'Letter from Manhattan' in the *New York Times Review of Books* of 16 August 1979 by novelist, essayist and screenwriter Joan Didion. The piece targeted not only *Manhattan* but *Interiors* and *Annie Hall*, all three of which Didion castigated for smug 'knowingness' and 'hermetic self-regard'. She dismissed their subject-matter as 'nothing with which large numbers of people would want to identify', disparaging the 'counterfeit "insider" shine' of their dialogue, the references to 'Jack and Anjelica' in *Annie Hall* and to 'Harvey' (Shapiro, then editor of the *New York Times Book Review*) in *Manhattan*.

Didion accurately isolated as the theme of *Manhattan* an 'idea for a short story' which Ike dictates in the course of the film: 'People in Manhattan are constantly creating these really unnecess-

ary neurotic problems for themselves to keep them from dealing
with more terrifying unsolvable problems about the universe.' The
archetypal Californian, she found Allen's people tiresomely sol-
ipsistic, blind to the promise of life:

> The characters in these films are, at best, trying. They are morose.
> They have bad manners. They seem to take long walks and go
> to smart restaurants only to ask one another hard questions. All
> of the characters in Woody Allen pictures not only ask these
> questions but actually answer them, on camera, and then, usually
> in another restaurant, listen raptly to third-party analyses of
> their own questions and answers. 'How come you guys got div-
> orced?' they ask each other with real interest, and, on a more
> rhetorical level, 'Why are you so hostile?' and 'Why can't you
> consider my needs?' ('I'm sick of your needs' is the way Diane
> Keaton answers this question in *Interiors*, one of the few lucid
> moments in the picture.)

With such comments ringing in Allen's ears, one should hardly
be surprised at the costive, accusatory tone of his film about celebrity, finally to be called *Stardust Memories*. When Steven Bach at
UA first read the treatment of what was then called 'Woody Allen
No. 4', he found it 'fresh and funny and frank; Woody's most
unguarded and autobiographical movie'. Had he known that during late writing, shooting and, especially, reshoots, the tone would
turn curdled and recriminatory, Bach might have reconsidered his
opinion. Instead, he pledged the studio's unqualified backing, even
agreeing with Allen's decision to shoot in black and white once
again.

Didion's attack and *Interiors*' snub at the Oscars both found a
place in the new film. In the opening of *Stardust Memories*, the
beautiful people are handing around a statuette which could be
some kind of award. Dressed uniformly in white – as is Tony
Roberts in his later appearance as Sandy Bates' early collaborator
who has Made It in Hollywood – they represent Hollywood and
the lure of that hedonistic life.

Almost more depressing than Allen's Academy Award rejection

was his involvement in a celebration of Bob Hope. On *The Dick Cavett Show* he'd mentioned his admiration for Hope, and Joanne Koch, whose Lincoln Center Film Society was about to honour the comedian, asked Allen to host the evening. He refused, pleading his dislike of big events, though many people felt he wanted to avoid a live *mano a mano* with his hero. He did agree, though, to compile and narrate a sixty-two-minute tribute to Hope, *My Favourite Comedian*, leaving Cavett to act as MC. The effect wasn't what he'd hoped. 'Allen,' said someone who saw the show, 'described Hope as "a woman's man, a coward's coward, and always brilliant". Then the honoured guest came out, and we saw why Allen would have feared this event in particular. Taking his time, flashing his ingratiating-barracuda smile, the seventy-five-year-old comic strolled out to face three thousand people, many of whom would have jumped up to pelt him with tomatoes ten years before [because of his right-wing politics]. This time we stood, when he finished, to clap till our hands hurt. He had made Woody Allen look like a child. He slaughtered us. This was a man who knew what he was doing.' The film was later shown in the New York Film Festival where, without Hope's dwarfing presence, it went down better.

Neither the Oscars nor the Hope tribute quite fitted Allen's idea for the film, but Judith Crist's Tarrytown weekend offered just the hook to support his meditations on celebrity. Abandoning even the residual optimism of *Annie Hall*, he zeroed in on his fans. 'No longer searching for eggs,' commented Diane Jacobs mordantly, recalling the closing monologue from *Annie Hall*, 'he seems to be blankly staring into a yard of dead chickens' – an apt simile for the mob gathered at the Hotel Stardust to hail his alter ego, director Sandy Bates. They're a legion of the maladjusted, the pimply, the obese, the grasping, the senile and the insane. The organiser of the weekend seminar, a fat-bottomed brown-noser, is a cruel parody of Crist. Her best friend, a beaming woman with goggling glasses, has just written 'a definitive cinematic study of Gummo Marx' – 'interestingly, the only Marx Brother who never made any movies,' volunteers a blimp of a film conservator.

From the start, Bates finds his 'tribute' a purgatory. Many men and women at the seminar regard him as a sexual object, others as a meal ticket; every second person has a script idea or a CV to thrust on him. Still more want to enrol him in their causes: cancer, heart, kidney, political prisoners. A questioner points out that his films are always psychological and never political – a sore point with Allen, whose record of involvement in topical issues is patchy. The decor of Bates' New York apartment, with its photo-mural of a South Vietnamese officer executing a VietCong prisoner, hints at least at an interest in such matters, but in flashbacks this image disappears, to be replaced by one of Groucho Marx.

Just as *La Dolce Vita* inspired *Manhattan*, *Stardust Memories* owes as much – if not more – to *8½*. Fellini had made his autobiographical 1963 film while in the grip of his own mid-life crisis. Pestered to create something as successful as *La Dolce Vita*, which, though a huge box-office success, initially aroused such hostility that the premiere audience spat on him and the Italian government threatened to withdraw his passport, Fellini fled to the island resort of Ischia, where his producer and patron Angelo Rizzoli owned a hotel, and tried to come up with a new idea.

Plagued by chronic back problems, sexual ambivalence and a sense of helplessness and dwindling inspiration, Fellini delved into the dreams that were his primary material, and came up with incidents from his childhood in Rimini that foreshadowed his later creative life. These were cemented into the story of Guido Anselmi, a film director much like Fellini himself who, unable to find a satisfactory ending to the film he's been shooting, visits a spa, supposedly to recover his health but actually to think. He's accompanied by his tense, critical and unloving wife and a group of writers and advisers, including a critic who accuses him of having become trivial and self-indulgent (in a moment of wild fantasy, Anselmi imagines hanging him).

Desperate for a kindly face, he persuades his married mistress to come down from the city, but his attention is distracted by another girl whom he meets at the spa, and who comes to represent the purity and simplicity his life lacks. Fellini originally intended to end *8½* with a scene in which a train filled with beautiful people carries Guido away, but rejected it as too sentimental. It can be no coincidence that, at the opening of *Stardust Memories*, we discover Allen stuck in a carriage filled with miserable grotesques, watching in dismay as another train, loaded with laughing, beautiful people in white, pulls inexorably away from him.

Allen insisted that the sequence wasn't actually a dream but the conclusion of the new film which his character, director Sandy Bates, is showing to backers and advisers when *Stardust Memories* opens. Few were convinced, particularly when the Fellini parallels began to pile up. Allen later admitted to Marie-Christine Barrault that he had begun numbering his films from the moment he decided to start making serious movies. The working title of *Stardust Memories* was 'Woody Allen No. 4' – because, he told Barrault, 'I am not even half of the Fellini of *8½*.'

Bates, like Anselmi, has just made a film that nobody likes. He too asks his married mistress to join him, and collects her at the railway station. He too meets another woman at the spa – violinist Daisy (Jessica Harper) – with whom he becomes infatuated. Instead of his wife, Bates has memories of his ex-mistress Dorrie (Charlotte Rampling), who, while as tense, critical and unloving as Anouk Aimée in Fellini's film, is closer to the real-life Louise Lasser: Dorrie suffers from clinical depression, her mother committed suicide and she has a romantic fixation with her father. Bates' old friend and occasional actor Tony Roberts (playing himself) delivers Allen's epitaph to his relationship with Lasser: 'She could be very fine and funny and bright and wonderful two days a month. The other twenty-eight, she was lost.' The alien leader Og, who turns up in one of Bates' fantasies, reiterates this dismal judgement: 'Hey, look, I'm a super-intelligent being. By earth standards I have an IQ of sixteen hundred, and even *I* can't understand what you expected from that relationship with Dorrie.' Bates sees more hope in Isobel (Barrault), who, though married with children, charms him with her unabashed affection and sensuality.

Bates shares Anselmi's problems with critics and backers. They want to replace his film's doleful ending, in which he and the other train passengers wander across a garbage dump while gulls shriek overhead, with a scene in which they find themselves instead in

Jazz Heaven, being entertained by an all-star band. Bates' critics complain about his pretensions to seriousness, and urge him to return to farce. He experiences the final humiliation when, encountering a meeting of UFO cranks in a field, he fantasises about a group of aliens, only to be told by Og, 'We enjoy your films. Particularly the early funny ones.' He asks them for solutions to the most profound problems of existence, but they have none. 'You want to do mankind a real service?' says Og. 'Tell funnier jokes.'

The film ends with Bates apparently murdered, by a straight-faced young man who claims to be his biggest fan – a presentiment of John Lennon's death in December 1980, just a few months after *Stardust Memories* went on release. This too turns out to be a fantasy, and Bates, after having imagined himself delivering a thank-you speech at his own posthumous tribute, wakes up in time to pursue Isobel to the station and be reconciled with her – yet another alternative ending, we learn, to his unfinished film.

Fellini ended *8½* optimistically, rounding up all the cast, living and dead, enemy and friend, for a circus parade led by his childhood self, a strutting ringmaster in white. Allen too brings everyone together, but in his case for the preview screening of the now-completed movie, which is received as ambiguously as *Stardust Memories* itself would be. Marie-Christine Barrault frets about her English to Jessica Harper, and they exchange notes on Bates' on-screen technique as a lover. Some think the film too serious, others not serious enough. Nobody is satisfied. In the film's last lines, a Jewish man says, 'From this he makes a living? I like a melodrama, a musical comedy with a plot.'

Stardust Memories spares nobody, not even Allen's immediate retinue. Bates' secretary is incompetent, his cook repeatedly sets the stove on fire, his chauffeur is a felon who's arrested for mail fraud. In a reference to a 1977 run-in with the IRS, which billed Allen for $377,000 for wrongful business claims, Bates has a business manager who leads him into disastrous tax-avoidance schemes ('The cattle died . . . I've got to get your signature on this oil shelter thing'), while the executives in charge of his films have even less faith in his talent than he does himself.

With remarkable *chutzpah*, Allen persuaded some of his victims to participate in their own humiliation. Critic Howard Kissel plays Bates' manager, and Louise Lasser has an uncredited cameo as his hopelessly ill-organised secretary. UA president Andy Albeck plays one of the movie executives condemning Bates' film, as does Jack Rollins. Allen gave Judith Crist a walk-on as a guest in the cabaret where Daisy, Jack and Sandy flee from the mêlée of the seminar's opening session, but chose Helen Hanft to play the part based on her in the film. John Doumanian is one of the weekend guests, while Jean Doumanian's companion, banker Jacqui Safra, plays Bates' brother-in-law, resignedly but aimlessly pedalling an exercise bike that does nothing to fend off his repeated heart attacks – a typically jaded personal note by Allen, who worked out each morning on just such a bike.

Casting continued in this recriminatory manner. Actors found Allen even less forthcoming than usual. Irving Metzman, who played Sandy's lawyer, was ushered into the office of casting director Juliet Taylor and told to sit down. 'But,' hissed Taylor, 'don't look to the right.' Metzman instinctively did so, and through a half-open door saw Allen sitting in the next room, watching him. The moment they caught each other's eye, Allen dived for cover. They barely spoke during shooting, but Metzman was struck by Allen's autocratic behaviour, which extended, he recalls, to everyone being forbidden to go to the toilet for long stretches. Despite this, Metzman became a regular in Allen's films, turning up again, for instance, as the cinema manager in *The Purple Rose of Cairo*.

Youth and beauty were in short supply in *Stardust Memories*. Much of what there was belonged to Sharon Stone, who had been trying to find work as a model in New York for a year. Straining to make herself memorable at a cattle-call audition for extras, she arrived on roller skates. Allen asked to meet her. 'A nine-foot tall blonde teenager certainly got his attention,' she said. He cast her as the girl on the train with a boa and the trophy in her lap who presses her lips to the glass. 'I gave it my best shot to melt the sucker,' recalls Stone.

*   *   *

Allen began shooting the film in relative good humour in September 1979. Stranded by the receding high tide of leisure spending that had also sustained the borscht belt hotels of the Poconos and Catskills, decaying resorts like Nassau, Allentown and Asbury Park littered the coast of New Jersey and Long Island, high and dry, their massive wooden buildings warping with age under flaking paint. Ocean Grove, NJ, in particular caught Allen's eye during his location trips with Mel Bourne and Gordon Willis. Many of its nineteenth-century gingerbread mansions were leased to the state's mental homes to absorb patients thought safe enough to be returned to the community. Where vacationing families once strolled in starched white linen, disturbed men and women now wandered aimlessly, dazed on medication. The police chief admitted they were a problem: 'Older people see them walking and get disturbed by their actions – just having weird facial expressions or waving their arms up and down – things that mental people tend to do.' Given his state of mind, Allen could hardly have chosen a more appropriate place to set *Stardust Memories*, and a sense of being immured with the obsessed and the insane suffuses the film.

The town was initially delighted when Allen moved in. He took over the office of the local Methodist minister as his headquarters. The old casino became a railway station and a cupola was renovated as an outdoor dance hall. Allen also rented the 6500-seat auditorium – normally used only in summer as a church for the tent-housed religious conventions that kept the town going – for transformation into the Hotel Stardust. The Camp Meeting Association accepted $25,000 in return for allowing Allen to replace the crucifix above the door with an illuminated hotel sign, though not without protests from some locals.

'At the beginning of *Stardust*,' Mel Bourne told film historian Gerald McKnight, 'I thought we'd never get it right. He'd just sit around and say, "I don't think this is going to work." My spirits would drop down to zero. In the end, that sort of thing is bound to get you down.' Allen's insistence on precise lighting effects slowed down production, with entire weeks spent waiting around for the right kind of sky. Cast and crew played stickball or poker, exciting the derision of locals who were hanging about waiting for something to happen. 'The amount of time it takes to film anything,' said one, 'these guys are either real patient or lazy. I've been watching almost every day, and they work at two speeds – "slow" and "stop".'

Allen spent hours commuting between Manhattan and Long Island, often driving back to the city with Marie-Christine Barrault, who recalls, 'One evening, we had to take a tunnel, which is very long, to get back into New York. And Woody is very claustrophobic. As we entered the tunnel, he put on some music by Telemann – very calm, very classical music – and despite the fact that he didn't particularly know me, he took my hand and closed his eyes. And during the entire trip, which took quite a long time because of the traffic, he stayed like that; holding my hand and listening to Telemann. And a few days later, he wrote a scene in which the two of us were in an elevator which was slow in reaching its destination, so he was panicking and I was trying to calm him down. This was a direct result of what had happened a few days earlier. In the end, the scene wasn't in the film.'

By December, the shoot was already five weeks behind schedule. Artistic disagreements among the production team were rife, but the unit, even more than on other occasions, remained locked up tight, and the performers, most of whom had seen only the pages of the script which contained their lines, were sworn to secrecy. Marie-Christine Barrault received a script of sorts: 'a little script of about fifty pages. At first it was delivered to me with instructions to send it back two days later, but then he said I could hold onto it. He made me promise not to let anyone read it. But this initial little screenplay is a joke when compared to the final film. There is about a tenth of the screenplay in the film, because he rewrites the film every day. And the more he rewrote this film and the scenes, he took aspects of myself.' These included the somewhat comic face exercises she did to tighten her skin, which Isobel also does in the film.

Isobel's political background – the script makes her a strong left-winger who fought on the barricades during the Paris *événe-*

ments – came about through a misunderstanding. In New York, Barrault had a call from ex-student leader Danny Cohn-Bendit, who was then working as a TV journalist. Cohn-Bendit had been commissioned to write four articles about Jewish personalities and their relationship with their cities, and hearing that Barrault, whom he'd never met, was working with Allen, he asked her to act as intermediary in arranging an interview.

Barrault did so, explaining that Cohn-Bendit, as 'Danny the Red', had been a leading figure in the 1968 riots. Allen was immediately interested.

'Is he a terrorist?'

'If he was, he isn't any longer. He lives in Germany and has a very middle-class job.'

'Ah, he's a *retired* terrorist,' Allen said, evidently tickled.

'Three weeks later,' says Barrault, 'I arrived at the studio and was amazed (as no one was allowed on the set during filming) to be greeted by Woody, who said, "Your friend is here." He refused to believe that Cohn-Bendit wasn't my friend, but he let him watch three days of filming, gave him an interview and everything. And from this incident he wrote a scene in which I talk about May '68 on the barricades.'

When he first read the script, Mel Bourne 'thought it was going to be the greatest movie ever'. Eventually he all but disowned *Stardust Memories*, the look of which had been effectively hijacked by new arrivals in the Allen retinue, in particular costume designer Santo Loquasto. Loquasto had a far greater effect than Bourne on the film's style, dressing the characters in high-contrast patterns: in the case of Helen Hanft, an unflattering costume of horizontal stripes that emphasises her broad beam.

Bourne also felt that editor Sandy Morse, working for the first time independently of Ralph Rosenblum, fundamentally influenced the film. What he sees as its failure was, he has said, 'an editing failure as much as anything'. Certain effects Morse introduced in *Stardust Memories* became Allen trademarks, in particular a taste for dropping 'dead' time out of a scene by jump-cutting – an effect pioneered by Jean-Luc Godard in *À Bout de Souffle*. In *Stardust Memories* its use is poignant, Allen cutting from one close-up after another of Dorrie's anguished face to show her mental deterioration.

With the embrace of such techniques, Allen inaugurated a new period in his career, characterised by an almost complete change of collaborators, a new studio to produce and release his films, and, above all, a new woman. 'One critic said my audience left me,' he said in 1992, 'but the truth is, I left my audience. The backlash really started when I did *Stardust Memories*. People were outraged. I still think that's one of the best films I've ever made. I was just trying to make what I wanted, not what people wanted me to make.'

Zelig and *A Midsummer Night's Sex Comedy*

Who do you have to fuck to get into this picture?
Who do you have to lay to make your way?

Dory Previn, 'Bog-Trotter'

As Allen finished editing *Annie Hall* in the spring of 1977, Mia Farrow, then aged thirty-two, was entertaining a friend in The Haven, the eighteenth-century mansion she shared with her husband, conductor André Previn, on twenty acres of woodland in rural Surrey. Beckoning him to follow, she led her companion across the lawn to a small thatched cottage. Together they peeked through the window to where Previn, sitting alone at a desk, was paging through the score of a Vaughan Williams symphony, tears streaming down his cheeks.

Back in the house, Mia stood on the bed and reached up to one of the gnarled beams that supported the ceiling. When she withdrew her hand, it held a diamond bracelet. She took down another piece, then another. This was the jewellery she'd taken when she left her first husband, Frank Sinatra, in lieu of alimony – a nine-carat diamond ring, a cuff-like bracelet encrusted with diamonds, and many other valuable items, later augmented by gifts from the singer, with whom she still enjoyed assignations whenever she was in the United States. They represented, she explained, her 'running away' money. When the marriage to Previn broke up, as she confidently expected it would, since he had already had a number of affairs, they would keep her until she found a new home for herself and her five children.

The daughter of actress Maureen O'Sullivan and director John Farrow, Mia, christened Maria de Lourdes Villiers Farrow, was one of seven children, a fact that fundamentally influenced her life. As a teenager, she yearned to escape from the ruck of a big family. 'I just couldn't stand being anonymous,' she said. 'I don't want to be just "one of the Farrows", third from the top and fifth from the bottom.'

John Farrow was a serial philanderer who nevertheless professed a strong Catholic faith, and published books on the papacy and the life of St Thomas More. From him, the Farrow children, especially his daughters Tisa and Mia, inherited an ability to live parallel moral lives. In the nineties, Mia would re-embrace the Church, spending much of her spare time in a Catholic meditation centre while also carrying on an active sex life.

At nineteen, she had starred in the TV series *Peyton Place*. Her frail build – she only weighed ninety-eight pounds – pale skin and long blonde hair belied a prodigious sexuality. She had already been the lover of older actors Yul Brynner and Kirk Douglas, and had her eyes set on others even more eminent. 'I want a big career,' she said, 'a big man, and a big life. You have to think big. That's the only way to get it.' She befriended Salvador Dali, who took her to an orgy in Greenwich Village. Since Dali was a voyeur, and mostly impotent, they watched companionably from the sidelines.

In October 1964 Frank Sinatra started shooting the World War II drama *Von Ryan's Express* at Twentieth Century-Fox, and Mia made it her business to be around the set, dressed in a flimsy gown that showed off her willowy body. When he left for his Palm Springs home one Friday, she hitched a lift in his private jet. By Monday, they were lovers. That Christmas, Sinatra gave her a gold cigarette case inscribed, 'Mia Mia, with love from Francis.' She returned it to him filled with marijuana joints she'd rolled herself. Soon the two were inseparable, to the surprise of Sinatra's stills cameraman William Read Woodfield. 'I don't get what you see in her,' he said. Sinatra murmured, 'Billy, she's so *hot!*'

They married in July 1966, but a year later the marriage was in trouble. Mia had taken a starring role in Roman Polanski's occult thriller *Rosemary's Baby*, a part she coveted because of her own mystical beliefs. As a publicity stunt, Polanski imported hairdresser Vidal Sassoon from London to cut her hair into the boyish style he favoured for the film. Mia played up to the crowd of photographers who shot the event, goading them that they should be filming protests against the war in Vietnam rather than something so trivial as a celebrity haircut. Sinatra, who supported the American war effort, wasn't amused.

When the painstaking Polanski failed to finish shooting in time for Mia to star with him in Gordon Douglas' *The Detective*, Sinatra demanded she leave the production. Despite heavy pressure, she refused. Sinatra brought in Jacqueline Bissett to play her part. Lee Remick was his wife, like Mia a 'good Catholic girl' on the surface, but, also like Mia, compulsively and voraciously sexual, lecturing Sinatra on the 'dirty little thrill' of promiscuity.

The rift between Sinatra and Mia soon became unbridgeable, and they divorced in 1968. Sinatra, however, like Allen, stayed in touch with some long-time lovers, of whom Mia would be one. 'Sometimes I missed [Sinatra] more than was appropriate,' she writes demurely in her memoirs, 'which André knew, because I told him everything.'

Mia drifted to England, swirled up in the eddies of Swinging London. Photographer David Bailey included her portrait in his anthology of emblematic figures from that time, *Goodbye Baby and Amen*. In the accompanying text, Peter Evans rhapsodised about this appealing waif.

She had too-pale skin and eyes luminous and large like a sea most full of frightened stillness waiting for the palisades of night; the colours of bleached driftwood in her hair and her arms alert with the fragile strength of seagulls' wings and about that colour. Her sense of solitude was immense; and is. In her scarlet guardsman's tunic, too large altogether, carrying her guitar across her shoulder through the streets of Chelsea or Manhattan, the studio rouge still in her hollowed cheeks, she is a childly creature, a fugitive from a tinselled Victorian world of fantasy and fairy dolls and lead soldiers; she does not dwell with us at all. She tells all; but you can only guess at her realness. Often the victim of cynicism and the frustrated wrath of the paunch-weighted middle-aged, she has been called a symbol of her time and perhaps she is; yet she has remained as elusive as the spectrum of the sixties itself. You want to protect her – but how? and from what? She is almost too ephemeral. She anticipates being dead in seven years.

Farrow survived and, anything but ephemeral, stayed to sleep with some of the most famous figures in theatre and film. She'd arrived in London with director Mike Nichols, and was soon seen around town with comedian Peter Cook, with whom she played a small role in the execrable 1984 film *Supergirl*, and actors like David Hemmings and Richard Burton – earning the enmity of Elizabeth Taylor by cuddling on his lap. 'I have my needs,' she told anyone who criticised her. She was, she said, 'able to give love in many more ways than most people' – a rationale she later invoked for adopting her many children.

She retained her taste for older men, especially those with intellectual credentials. Many were bemused by the dozy mysticism that led her to keep a box filled with charms, amulets and relics for which she claimed powerful magical significance, but her sexuality stifled their smirks.

In 1968 she began an affair with André Previn, once a composer of movie music, then an accomplished jazz piano soloist, but latterly musical director of the London Symphony Orchestra and a developing composer. Farrow, who'd known Previn and his songwriter wife Dory for years, was regarded as a friend of the family. Dory's growing suspicions about the girl who sat quietly sewing while more exhibitionist guests like Liza Minnelli flirted with her husband at the piano and sang Gershwin and Cole Porter by the hour were put down to the schizophrenia which troubled most of her adult life. Once the affair became public, Dory put her resentment into the lyrics of the song 'Beware of Young Girls', warning other wives about women 'wistful and pale of twenty and four, delivering daisies with delicate hands'.

In February 1970 Farrow gave birth to twin sons by Previn, Matthew and Sascha. In September that year they married. Subsequently they had another son, Fletcher. Previn wanted more children, but Mia, who had pushed the stroller with her babies in anti-Vietnam parades beside Vanessa Redgrave and other showbiz radicals, convinced him that they had no right to produce more children when so many were without homes. In 1973 they adopted a Vietnamese orphan, Kym Lark, later renamed Lark Song, and in 1974 another girl, originally called Summer Song, but rechristened Daisy after Mia's character in Jack Clayton's *The Great Gatsby*, filmed that year; the playwright Tom Stoppard, a close friend, stood godfather of the child.

By 1977 the marriage was showing signs of strain, and Mia was involved in a liaison with Roman Polanski. She and Previn managed, however, through strings pulled in Congress by novelist William Styron, an old friend of hers, to win permission to adopt the seven-year-old daughter of a Korean prostitute. The girl had been battered by her mother, so starved that she foraged for food in dustbins and even ate soap, and finally abandoned on the streets of Seoul. Her name was Soon-Yi.

In 1978 Farrow appeared in *The Hurricane*, a remake of the 1937 John Ford melodrama, in Bora Bora. Originally it was to have been directed by Roman Polanski, but he became involved in a scandal back in Hollywood after borrowing Jack Nicholson's home to shoot a picture essay for *Vogue Hommes* on young Hollywood girls – 'the younger the better', Polanski said he'd been told by the editor in Paris. One of his models, who turned out to be only thirteen, revealed that she had had sex with the director, who also gave her drugs. Polanski, indicted on a number of offences and convinced he was about to be railroaded by headline-seeking prosecutors, fled to Paris. Swedish director Jan Troell took over *The Hurricane*, bringing with him Sven Nykvist, Ingmar Bergman's favourite lighting cameraman, with whom Farrow was widely believed to have had an affair during the film.

After *The Hurricane*, Farrow left Previn and, taking the children, moved into her old family home on Martha's Vineyard. Her mother Maureen O'Sullivan was living in the large, rent-controlled apartment in the Langham at 135 Central Park West, which she'd occupied since 1963. At considerable expense she enlarged it to eleven rooms, then divided these into two apartments, giving Farrow her own New York home. Had Farrow known it, she was already in Woody Allen Land. A well-known psychoanalyst whose clients included Allen's agent had the apartment next door, and Diane Keaton lived in the adjoining building.

Maureen O'Sullivan, at sixty-seven, was still working, playing in *Mornings at Seven* on Broadway. Mia's highly attractive sister Tisa was also making a living in movies. She even had a small role in *Manhattan*, as the girl who confesses she's had an orgasm, but 'the wrong kind', to which Ike responds that he didn't think there was a 'wrong kind. Every one I've had has been right on the money.' Allen's interest in Tisa was evident to everyone on the set of *Manhattan*, as Mia would recall when he presented her with the script for *Hannah and her Sisters*, in which a man conceives a helpless attraction for his sister-in-law.

Resourcefully, Farrow began making herself known to people who might help her. One of them was Allen, whom she'd already met once, briefly, at a Hollywood party with Polanski. The *New York Times Magazine* published a profile of Allen with a cover picture of him standing on the terrace of his apartment – a terrace which Mia could see from her own window at the Langham. She cut out the picture and stuck it in a scrapbook. He looked 'interesting', she said. Even though Allen despised the West Side, they often ate at the same restaurants, saw the same shows. Running into one another again was, she knew, just a matter of time. 'I think Mia always had a grand plan to meet Woody, have a relationship with him, be in his films, and eventually have his child,' said Letty Aronson after the liaison had played out its intricate and painful course.

By the end of 1979, Farrow and Previn were divorced. Not having worked for years, she was running out of money. On paper she was worth $4 million, but most of it was tied up in stocks. Film roles were scarce for someone who needed to stay in New York, close to her children, so in December she jumped at the chance, though it was at best a stopgap, to make her Broadway debut in a new play, Bernard Slade's *Romantic Comedy*. She played a prim schoolteacher who collaborates with a burned-out New York play-wright, transforming both their lives.

At the same time, Woody Allen entered her life. Michael Caine and his wife came to see the show, and took Mia to Elaine's afterwards. Caine spotted Allen, and knowing she found him attractive, urged her to send him a note via a waiter. A moment later, he hurried across to their table. That New Year's Eve, Allen invited her to his party. She came with Tony Perkins, her co-star in *Romantic Comedy*. Other guests included Mick Jagger, Robert de Niro and Andy Warhol, who decreed it 'the best party, wall-to-wall famous people. Mia Farrow is so charming and such a beauty.'

Farrow made an equally powerful impression on Allen, but in the depths of the depression occasioned by the shooting of *Stardust Memories*, he had no time for romance. He didn't ring her until April 1980, when he asked her to dinner on the seventeenth at the Lutèce. (Asked to recall the date, Allen said characteristically, 'I think it was the day after Jean-Paul Sartre died.')

The choice of the Lutèce, which even *New York Times* restaurant critic Craig Claiborne acknowledged as 'conspicuously expensive', was clearly meant to impress. Farrow dithered over what to wear, remarking to Tony Perkins that it probably wouldn't matter much to Allen.

'He doesn't care about clothes, does he?' she asked.

Perkins – 'who knew Woody Allen', she said – snorted 'Are you *kidding?*'

Three days before the dinner, *Manhattan*, nominated for Best Original Script and Best Supporting Actress (Mariel Hemingway) at the Academy Awards, won nothing. While Allen publicly shrugged it off, it exacerbated his normal depression. But Mia's charm triumphed. Allen had already arranged to spend the next week in Paris with Jean Doumanian and Jacqui Safra, but on his return the romance took off. They exchanged gifts daily. Mia sent gadgets, bibelots, *tchochkes* that reflected her mystical preoccupation with talismans. Allen responded with records of Mozart and poems by e.e. cummings. Soon he was sending the Rolls around to her apartment with a note saying he couldn't wait a day or two for their next meeting. They never lived together, but before long most of their free time was spent in each other's company. The combination of Paris and Mia reinvigorated Allen enough to finish *Stardust Memories* on a more optimistic note. One immediate result was his decision to rewrite the character of Isobel. In the final version, shot after his return from Paris, she has acquired two children and a history as a left-wing activist. More significantly, Allen's character Sandy Bates is also contemplating marriage to her.

Some of the more depressing sequences were excised, including the death of Bates' old friend Nat Bernstein, who in the original succumbed to amyotropic lateral sclerosis – better known as 'Lou Gehrig's Disease', after the baseballer who died of it. Allen further emphasised the film's European air with a musical score leaning heavily on pre-war French jazz: 'Tropical Mood' by Sidney Bechet under the credits, and gypsy guitarist Django Reinhardt elsewhere.

Allen delivered the film in early summer, and UA scheduled its release for September, after the main summer money-makers. It had cost $9 million, and Steven Bach didn't delude himself that it would turn a profit (in fact it grossed only $4.5 million on first release). A preview screening in New York dramatised the divided reactions. 'He's a genius,' Mike Nichols told Bach. 'Woody has made his own Fellini film *and* a parody of *8½* at the same time!' Bach's deputy Anthea Sylbert wasn't convinced. 'Are you sure he hasn't made a Diane Arbus film?' she asked. (Sylbert, a costume designer until Bach hired her to produce in 1978, was parodied in the film's opening montage as the newly-appointed studio executive played by *Saturday Night Live* comedienne Laraine Newman.) It was generally agreed that the homages to Fellini and Bergman misfired. As one critic remarked, Allen had perversely taken 'the high spirits of Ingmar and the depth of Federico; from the best, he has stolen the worst'. In the event, *Stardust Memories* was comprehensively rejected by almost everyone except his fans in Europe, who welcomed its movie references and the sarcastic deflation of the American critical establishment.

*   *   *

Allen and Farrow could see one another's apartments across the park, and would blink their lights, wave towels, even observe one another through binoculars, but in other than geographical terms their lives remained far apart. Farrow commuted between the West Side and her old wooden family house on Martha's Vineyard, but Allen loathed the country and refused to stir outside Manhattan. Farrow continued to augment her family, adopting a two-year-old Korean boy with cerebral palsy. Christened Misha Amadeus Farrow, he soon became known as Moses. Allen's antipathy for children remained unabated. 'I have zero interest in kids,' he told her. All the same, Farrow and the family began to make inroads into Allen's apartment, installing dressing gowns, toothbrushes and heavy coats; Allen, however, seldom visited the Langham, and sex took place solely on his side of the park.

Now that she knew him better, some aspects of Allen's character alarmed Farrow. She'd been courted by 'Woody', not Allen, and didn't entirely like the other half of his Jekyll-and-Hyde personality. For one thing, there was his hypochondria. As he entered middle age, Allen worried increasingly about his health. Besides the thrice-weekly visits from his analyst, he regularly consulted a dozen doctors, all specialists in different parts of the body, and carried their office and home addresses with him everywhere, as well as a capacious pillbox containing medications for heart, ulcer and anguish. For each film he held a special 'doctors' screening' for these men and their wives, of whom there were more than enough to fill a preview cinema. When the AIDS scare began he took frequent blood tests, receiving the results of which threw him into a panic. Refusing to open the envelopes, he'd flee into the bedroom, climb into bed and pull the covers over his head. Farrow checked the results and reassured him.

Later, Farrow would confide to friends that Allen's sexual tastes also disconcerted her. His enthusiasm for erotic photography was part of a masturbatory fetish that seemed fundamental to his character. In *Stardust Memories* he put into the mouth of Sandy Bates his preference for fantasy over reality. 'You can't control life,' Bates says. 'It doesn't wind up perfectly. Only art you can control. Art and masturbation – two areas in which I'm an absolute expert.' Reviewing the film in *Time*, Richard Corliss would define it as 'an elaborate mechanism of self-abuse, a Rube Goldberg dildo'.

Farrow, no stranger to obsession herself, came to terms with Allen's sexual hang-ups as she became accustomed to his wealth and fame. It had been one thing to be aware of Woody Allen as entertainer, another to be inside his *équipe*: to deal with his secretary, his assistant, his cook/housekeeper, his chauffeur; to address the contradiction between his self-effacing public manner, 'humble to the point of contrition', in the words of the *New York Times*, and the fact that 'he is driven around town in a cream-coloured Rolls-Royce and is very, very famous, and that in his calculated disdain for publicity and carefully cultivated eccentricity he makes it absolutely certain that he will receive as much publicity as any man possibly can.'

Farrow even learned to live with the baleful presence of Jean Doumanian, whose pale, drawn face and frosty image she found chilling. Doumanian was even more evident in the Allen entourage than usual in 1980, since she had been appointed to TV comedy's plum job. Lorne Michaels, the Toronto comic who'd once written material for Allen and who had risen to become producer of NBC's hit show *Saturday Night Live*, left at the end of 1979, and when the 1980 season opened his replacement was, to his astonishment, his talent booker, Doumanian. Inside the network, her relationship with Allen was widely considered to have been a crucial factor in the appointment.

Almost all the show's best writers and performers, including Gilda Radner, Laraine Newman, Bill Murray, Garrett Morris and Jane Curtin, left with Michaels. To replace them, Doumanian hired not people with experience in TV comedy writing but a group of stand-up comedians, including Joe Piscopo, Charles Rocket, Gilbert Gottfried and Ann Risley. He also put Allen's sister, Letty Aronson, on the payroll. The mix never worked, and ratings plummeted, a situation exacerbated by Doumanian's abrasive management methods. NBC began talking about cancelling.

*   *   *

Directing ex-mistress Diane Keaton as Renata in *Interiors* (1978).

Diane Keaton, Mary Beth Hurt and Kristin Griffith as the three sisters in the Bergmanesque *Interiors*, Allen's first drama, first film as a director in which he didn't star, and first flop.

Teenage actress Stacey Nelkin tried out for a role in *Annie Hall* (1976), and shortly after became Allen's mistress, and the inspiration for the Mariel Hemingway character in *Manhattan*.

The lure of the Continent: Marie-Christine Barrault in *Stardust Memories* (1980). They held hands in the Holland Tunnel.

'The lineaments of gratified desire': Mia Farrow after sex in a brothel with a total stranger in *Shadows and Fog* (1992).

Take the money and run? Allen and director Martin Ritt clown on the set of Ritt's political comedy/drama *The Front* (1976).

'I don't eat rodent!' Allen as director Sandy Bates hassles his cook (Dorothy Leon) over his culinary requirements in *Stardust Memories*.

Manhattan (1979), 'perhaps the best film of the seventies', in the estimation of New York critic Andrew Sarris.

Allen directing cinematographers Carlo DiPalma (centre) in *Radio Days* …

… and Sven Nykvist on *Another Woman* (1988).

Allen with Martin
Landau on *Crimes and
Misdemeanors* (1989).

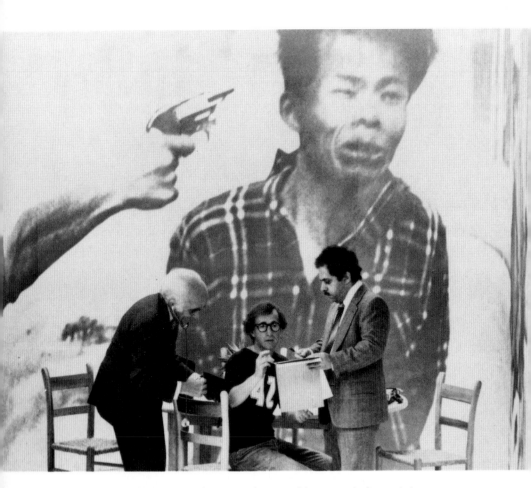

Allen as Sandy Bates, besieged by moral, financial and political worries in *Stardust Memories*.

Normally Allen would have begun shooting his Fall Project in September 1980, but the failure of *Stardust Memories* effectively ended his relationship with UA, leaving him without finance. Steven Bach at least was still keen to retain him, but Allen's doubts about the studio's administrators hardened into a conviction that he'd be better off with Arthur Krim at Orion, which had prospered. Charles Joffe tended to agree, though not for the same reason. The word around Hollywood was that UA were in over their heads on the runaway production of Michael Cimino's $36 million western epic *Heaven's Gate*, which would indeed put the studio out of business within a year.

Bach matched every Orion proposal, and even topped Krim's final offer, but Allen's mind was made up. In December 1980 Rollins and Joffe announced a deal with Orion for Allen to make three films over the next five years, starring in at least two of them. Since Orion had no cinemas of its own, the films would be released through Warner Brothers. The new deal, following the path broken by Steven Spielberg and George Lucas, gave Allen a share of income from the very first dollar, rather than after the studio had recouped all its costs. His initial doubts about the breakaway company were ignored. Allen claimed, 'I would certainly have gone with them [in 1978], but my contract remained in effect with the original company.' He further announced that he would start shooting his new film in the spring of 1981, that he would direct and star, but that he 'had not yet decided what it would be about'.

Instead of filming in September/October 1980, Allen wrote the play he'd promised the Vivian Beaumont Theater. His fellow members of the theatre's directorate were so delighted at the prospect of a new Allen theatre piece that they didn't even request a title: 'Woody Allen's New Play' on the marquee was enough. The first run would be limited to nine weeks, but the directorate were hopeful that a Broadway producer would pick the play up.

Any hopes of a comedy to set the theatre on its feet were dashed when he delivered *The Floating Light Bulb*. Allen called it 'basically amusing', but conceded, 'it's not Olsen and Johnson' (the forties comics who created the anarcho-surrealist show *Hellzapoppin*). Later, he became less sanguine. 'Maybe it will be an entertaining two hours,' he said. 'My fondest wish is that the person buying a ticket has a good time. I really hope so.'

The play owed its inspiration to the same Blue Period which produced *Interiors* and, in particular, *Stardust Memories*. Its theme is conjuring, a motif that, like ill-health, would predominate in Allen's movies during the eighties and nineties. Allen said the play was suggested by a boy he often saw while walking the streets of Brooklyn in his childhood. 'I would pass by this particular house, and there was a seventeen-year-old kid who would sit by the window and shuffle cards constantly. He was his mother's cross to bear – there's no question about it.'

Allen had celebrated his own adolescent interest in prestidigitation in *Stardust Memories*, where the young Sandy Bates appears as 'The Great Sandy', repeatedly exhibiting his abilities to adoring spectators, including his analyst, who hail him as a prodigy. At the UFO congress the grown-up Bates performs one of the oldest and most spectacular tricks, the Floating Lady.

The first image of the play is a light bulb in the dark. As its glow increases, it reveals Paul Pollack practising the Floating Light Bulb trick. After a few seconds, the bulb flickers and dies, to be replaced by the less magical light of day which reveals, in the play's stage directions, 'an apartment reeking of hopelessness and neglect'.

The apartment is home to the Pollacks: Max, the father, a petty criminal working as a waiter to pay off gambling debts; his wife Enid, hopelessly toying with get-rich-quick mail-order schemes; Steve, the younger son, a feckless truant with a history of arson; and Paul, a stuttering sixteen-year-old who lurks in his room, practising magic tricks.

Paul pins his hopes for escaping from Brooklyn on an audition for Jerry Wexler, a small-time agent who, foreshadowing Broadway Danny Rose, is always hoping for the 'million-dollar act' that will make his fortune and reputation. Enid has convinced Jerry that her son is a brilliant magician, but Paul, rigid with stage fright, stutters his way through his act, accidentally smashes his props, and retreats weeping to his bedroom. The scene ends in mutual recrimination between Jerry and Enid.

JERRY: Mrs Pollack, to be frank, your son is obviously no performer. He's a frightened boy with no hint of promise at this point. I thought he'd be much different from the way you talked – a young natural.

ENID: I'm telling you, he's fine! I mean, let's face it. What are your credentials? Who do you manage that you're suddenly such an authority? A couple of anonymous nobodies who probably can't get arrested. You come down here like some big impresario, dropping names left and right – Jack Benny, Jimmy Durante. Meanwhile it turns out you don't work for any of them.

JERRY: Maybe we both were labouring under false impressions.

Just how false becomes clear when Jerry stays on after the audition, and he and Enid share a long boozy scene, the intellectual and emotional heart of the play. Jerry describes his real clients: two Armenian brothers who come on stage dressed as boxers and play 'Ave Maria' on bells attached to their gloves; and Willy Walters, literally a stage carpenter, whose act is building a box to the 'Sabre Dance', his hammer rapping out the rhythm.

Enid dances with Jerry, pours the champagne and drinks in his compliments, allowing herself to believe that he's her dream lover, although it's obvious from his sentimental stories about the girl he never married and the asthmatic mother with whom he's about to move to Arizona that he's gay (a fact telegraphed earlier by his reference to an 'acquaintance' with the actor Cesar Romero, one of Hollywood's more prominent homosexuals). She never mentions her husband, who arrives home at the end of the scene to break the mood. Once Jerry has gone she turns, screaming, on Max, who leaves hurriedly to 'see a man about a horse', but actually to meet his lover. In his room, Paul puts 'In a Persian Market' on the gramophone and starts practising the Floating Light Bulb.

Ulu Grosbard was retained by producer Richard Crinkley to direct. He had just staged Arthur Miller's *The Price* on Broadway, as well as a revival of *A View from the Bridge*, and Frank Gilroy's poignant *The Subject was Roses*. 'I said "Yes,"' Grosbard recalls, 'and then I thought to myself, "What am I getting into?"' He was right to feel dubious. Once the cast had been assembled, with fat baby-faced comic Jack Weston as Jerry, Bea Arthur as Enid, Danny Aiello as Max and Brian Backer as Paul, Grosbard sensed that the role of Max was underwritten. Allen agreed to rewrite the part, and to adjust other scenes as well.

Initially, Allen was on his best behaviour. 'He never talked to the actors,' says Grosbard. 'He was absolutely ruthless with his own stuff. If a line wasn't working I'd have to stop him from cutting it out. If he wasn't satisfied with something he'd walk into another room at the rehearsal hall and come back with four alternatives. He would say to me, "OK, pick the one you like best and I'll work off that." I mean, it was instant. I was really amazed.'

The actors viewed Allen's detachment less kindly. Brian Backer mastered the look of young Woody and his ability with illusions, but the man himself remained elusive. 'We had very little contact,' said Backer. 'The only time we talked was when I was rehearsing the magic. It was kind of disappointing. He's very shy. I can't really say after working with him that I know him.' The rest of the cast felt equally isolated. After each rehearsal they dined together, in a different restaurant every night, but Allen never joined them. 'We'd talk about him,' said Jack Weston. 'We'd say, "Well, did he say hello to you today?" One rehearsal he was an hour or two late, and we said, "He must have loathed us yesterday. He just couldn't bear to watch us today."' A self-confessed 'hypochondriac, paranoid nervous wreck', Weston felt the strain more than most, and although he would receive a Tony nomination for his role, he rated it as among the most wearing experiences of his career.

Grosbard now admits he never fully believed in the play, which he came to see as fundamentally flawed. 'The problems we had were rooted in the premise somehow,' he says. 'I don't know that we ever solved it. We went as far as we could.' In dealing with his own childhood, Allen lacked the detachment that allowed Eugene

O'Neill or Arthur Miller to transmute their experience into tragedy; he was simply too self-conscious. Everything in *The Floating Light Bulb* would eventually find its way into his work, but the medium would be film, and the tone – in *Radio Days*, for the family scenes, and *Broadway Danny Rose* for the character of Jerry Wexler – would be affectionate farce.

The closer *The Floating Light Bulb* came to opening, the less Allen wanted to do with it. The launch was put off for two weeks for more rehearsals. 'Woody was very open in terms of the work,' says Grosbard diplomatically, 'but he was not personally accessible' – not even at a gala charity preview on 23 April for which a celebrity audience of five hundred paid up to $200 a seat. Ex-mayor John Lindsay, designer Ralph Lauren, director Joshua Logan and actress Sigourney Weaver saw but, on the whole, didn't much care for the play.

Allen didn't show up for the opening night on 27 April either. The previous month, Jean Doumanian had been fired from *Saturday Night Live*, replaced by the show's first producer, Dick Ebersole, under whose guidance it would retrieve its former glory, and develop talents like Eddie Murphy, Jim Belushi and Julia Louis-Dreyfus. Dispirited, she and Jacqui Safra flew to Paris the day before *Light Bulb*'s opening, and Allen and Farrow went with them, leading to speculation that the couple had secretly married. They checked into the Hôtel Crillon, but Paris failed to work its usual magic on Allen. 'I was nervous,' he said. 'Not nervous about the play, but nervous about being away from home. I just walked the streets there and couldn't really enjoy myself.' He and Farrow had talked desultorily of escaping Manhattan to live in Paris, but this visit made him less sure.

The notices for *Light Bulb* were mostly negative. It closed after sixty-five performances, and Allen, though he continued to write new plays and revise old ones, avoided airing them on Broadway for the next decade.

The first film Allen would release under his Orion deal was *A Midsummer Night's Sex Comedy*, but the one he wrote in September 1980 was a 'fictional documentary'. Originally entitled

'The Changing Man', then 'The Cat's Pajamas', it emerged as *Zelig*.

Zelig began as an idea for a short story, and it's on that level that the slight premise makes most sense. Lamenting the temptation he often felt to make the sort of films which would ingratiate himself with his increasingly alienated public, Allen speculated about a man who could physically transform himself into whatever would make those around him more comfortable. The relevance to his own problems of personality is obvious. Here he created a man who can be Italian with Italians, Greek with Greeks, even a Nazi with Nazis – though never, interestingly, a woman with women.

Leonard Zelig is the ultimate stand-up comedian. His whole life is a joke, and every part of it is for sale. Allen, already torn between being entertainer or serious artist, was equally stressed in his relationship with Farrow, who had put him under pressure to become surrogate father, lover, and possibly husband. The sly and knowing humour of the *New Yorker* is everywhere visible in *Zelig*. The film bears a resemblance to other Allen magazine pieces of the period, in particular 'The Shallowest Man'. It tells the story of Lenny Mendel, a TV producer who discovers that Meyer Iskowitz, with whom he plays poker once a week, is dying of cancer. Making a much-delayed courtesy call, he falls in love with Iskowitz's nurse, and keeps visiting him in order to see her. Iskowitz comes to rely on Mendel's visits, and tells him before he dies that he loves him, and that his concern has been 'the most touching and deepest experience he ever had with another human being'. Mendel shrugs, and starts an affair with the nurse. Recalling the incident, Mendel's poker friends fall into a Talmudic discussion. Some contend it does indeed show him to be 'the shallowest man'. Another feels it demonstrates that love, whether of a friend or a woman, makes one overcome fears of mortality. Through no fault of his own, Mendel becomes all things to all people.

Leonard Zelig's problem is more acute. The product of an environment where any deviation from the norm was ruthlessly punished, he develops a chameleon-like condition that allows him to blend into any situation. In the opening scene of Allen's fake documentary of his life, he's noticed by F. Scott Fitzgerald at a Long Island house party in 1928, first as a respectable and obviously wealthy guest with an impeccable Boston accent, then as a roughly-spoken left-winger chatting with the kitchen help. In quick succession he's seen as both a gangster and a black musician in a Chicago club, a baseball player in Florida, then as his real self, a New York nonentity, the son of a Yiddish actor.

Once his abilities become known, Zelig is transformed into a celebrity, 'The Chameleon Man'. He inspires songs, dances and a film, appears in advertisements ('When I'm through changing into people, I like to change into Pendleton underwear') and demonstrates his ability to become a rabbi, a fat man, even a psychiatrist. His case is taken up by Dr Eudora Fletcher, who cures him under hypnosis, and falls in love with him at the same time. They're about to marry when other women start coming forward with proof that they too have married Zelig while he was passing as someone else. Hounded by lawsuits, Zelig flees to Germany, where he becomes a member of the inner circle of the Nazi Party. Eudora spots him in a newsreel, goes to Germany and saves him in a daring aerial rescue, at the climax of which Zelig, transforming himself into a pilot, flies the Atlantic upside down. Restored to celebrity, he's given a tickertape parade through Manhattan. 'It just goes to show what you can do if you're a total psychotic,' says Zelig happily, echoing Hitler's dictum that 'All that's needed is a little intelligent madness.'

Zelig's story could have been told as a pastiche of fifties Hollywood transformation movies like *The Incredible Shrinking Man*. Allen had tried out this idea in *Stardust Memories*, where Allen and Tony Roberts are seen in one of Bates' earlier films, in which he switches the brains of a sexually attractive but mentally disturbed mistress and a loving but dull one, but had rejected the scene as being too close to spoofs like *Take the Money and Run*. Instead he followed Warren Beatty's *Reds*, which used 'witnesses' like authors Henry Miller and Rebecca West to comment on the period and the dramatised story of Communist journalists John Reed and Louise Bryant, played by Beatty and Diane Keaton.

As a first project for Orion, *Zelig* wasn't exactly what Arthur

Krim had had in mind, but he didn't cavil, or express concern about the film's potential technical problems. Gordon Willis began experimenting with recreating worn and wobbly twenties newsreels, and researchers combed film libraries and private collections for eccentric footage. Looking for someone to sing Dick Hyman's pastiche 'Chameleon Days' in the style of thirties *chanteuse* Helen Kane, Juliet Taylor scoured Jewish retirement homes and found Mae Questel, the original voice of the cartoon characters Betty Boop and *Popeye*'s Olive Oyl. Celebrities were recruited as 'witnesses', including Susan Sontag, shot in a palazzo overlooking the Grand Canal in Venice, novelist Saul Bellow, club owner and singer Bricktop and psychologist Bruno Bettelheim. Allen hoped Greta Garbo would come out of retirement to join them, but she never replied to his note. Boxer Jack Dempsey agreed, but proved too ill to appear. A sequence with Lillian Gish was cut in editing.

Via some trick photography, but mostly through the skilful editing of real news footage, Zelig is made to hobnob with actual historical figures, including Hitler and Pope Pius XII. In between, he plays out the story of his rehabilitation, shown in supposed 'secret footage' shot by Dr Fletcher's cousin from a closet.

It soon became clear that *Zelig* would never be finished in time for a summer release. Orion were also concerned about a looming strike by the Directors' Guild of America. Technically Joffe and Rollins, as independents, should not be affected, but Orion foresaw a situation where production might be held up for months. As films in production were exempt from strike action, they pressed Allen to turn the cameras on something before the 1 July deadline. Never short of ideas, he opened up a drawer and took out one that felt right for this period in his career. He was as happy as he ever got, and summer was coming. All these fed into the script – written in three weeks – that became *A Midsummer Night's Sex Comedy*.

It is tempting to say that only a man in love could have written *A Midsummer Night's Sex Comedy*, but it's probably truer that it was written by a man who found himself in love and distrusted the feeling profoundly. Under the shimmer of what Eric Lax called this 'idyll' lurk the sort of doubts, fears and superstitions that one had come to expect in Allen's films.

The premise is light enough. In turn-of-the-century New York, Leopold Sturges (José Ferrer), a professor of philosophy, is about to marry the much younger and apparently naive Ariel Weymouth (Farrow). They are spending the last weekend before the wedding at the country house of Leopold's cousin Adrian Hobbes (Mary Steenburgen) and her husband Andrew (Allen), a stockbroker and amateur inventor. Also invited are Andrew's best friend Maxwell Jordan (Tony Roberts), a priapic doctor, who brings with him his sexually liberated nurse Dulcy (Julie Hagerty). Tensions immediately appear. Adrian has unaccountably turned frigid on Andrew, who is himself infatuated with an old acquaintance, Ariel, regretting his failure to have sex with her years before, on just such a weekend and in just this house. Maxwell too is smitten with Ariel, and begs her not to marry Leopold, but rather him. Leopold, nostalgic for his bachelor days, asks Dulcy to have sex with him just once before he descends into terminal matrimony, and she agrees.

None of these plans work out as anyone had hoped, due to some mystical power of the summer night, a force Andrew can tap, though none too reliably, with one of his inventions, a truly magic lantern that projects images of the past and future. Before the end of the story, Leopold is dead, succumbing in the throes of sex with Dulcy; Maxwell and Ariel are in love; and Adrian, having revealed the reason for her frigidity (she slept with Maxwell once, and is racked with guilt), throws herself with renewed energy into sex with Andrew.

A Midsummer Night's Sex Comedy was plainly inspired by Ingmar Bergman's *Smiles of a Summer Night* (1955), but even though his working title for the film was 'Summer Nights', Allen always denied any similarity, insisting on the contrary that *Smiles* was one of his least favourite Bergman films. He may have been heading off charges that he was once again covering ground already tilled by Stephen Sondheim. In 1973 Sondheim had a hit with his adaptation of the same story, *A Little Night Music*, which, partly because of Sondheim's audacity in doing every song in waltz time, quickly entered the international repertory.

Allen's defensiveness was misplaced, since *A Midsummer Night's Sex Comedy* more than holds its own against both Bergman and Sondheim. The music, all skimmed from the orchestral work of Felix Mendelssohn; Santo Loquasto's costumes, which dress everyone in shades of cream, beige and white; and Gordon Willis' lighting, make the film unaccustomedly sunny. The tone is relaxed and charming, but it's the ensemble playing which shows how Allen had matured. There's none of the algebraic formalism of *Interiors*, thanks in no small part to Mia Farrow as Ariel. Allen had hoped that Diane Keaton would take the role, but she was too busy with the promotion of *Reds* and preparations to film Alan Parker's *Shoot the Moon*, so he turned to Farrow, offering her the part of Eudora Fletcher in *Zelig* as well. It was the perfect answer to Farrow's problems: work seamlessly joined to her domestic life.

Farrow' s blonde, pre-Raphaelite prettiness sets the tone of *Sex Comedy*. Keaton in the same role would have been more disorganised, less aware of her sexuality and the effect it had on the men around her. By playing herself, an apparent innocent with an extensive sexual history – Andrew laments that he didn't know, at the time when they almost made love, that her plethora of lovers included the entire infield of the Boston White Sox – Farrow implies that everyone in the story has some hidden erotic dimension.

In no case is this more true than of Leopold. José Ferrer, notorious for his tendency to dominate any film in which he appeared – Betty Comden and Adolph Green used him as their model for the self-important impresario played by Jack Buchanan in *The Band Wagon* – had no talent for comedy, but his pomposity and windily formal sentences gave the character of Leopold a straight-faced humour that humanises even him.

When he confesses to Dulcy a nostalgia for his days as a seducer, and requests one last tumble with her in the woods, he plays it with an adolescent's diffidence, all but nibbling his lower lip. Anxious to make the occasion more than a quickie in the bushes, he emphasises the potential educative element: having sex with him could be as illuminating as the tour of the Sistine Chapel he gave Ariel. Alas, Dulcy, like Ariel, is way ahead of him.

LEOPOLD: Have you ever made love with a much older man?
DULCY: Yes.
LEOPOLD: Illicitly? In the woods?
DULCY: Yes.
LEOPOLD: Was he a genius?
DULCY: He was a dentist.

When they do get down to sex, Leopold is again no match for the athletic Dulcy. 'Bite me, bite me!' she begs, and he responds plaintively, 'I can't. These are not my teeth' – a line on which Allen placed such importance that he had Ferrer do it repeatedly, until the actor shouted, 'Now I can't do it. You've turned me into a mess of terrors.'

Tony Roberts' actorish delivery makes him a typically pompous but well-meaning product of Emersonian enlightment. Allen himself is the weak link. He never becomes part of the period. Even his inventions, reminiscent of *Sleeper*, reveal a mind that lives in the future, and despite Andrew's professed belief in mysticism, Allen's imagination never soars in his own role as it does for Maxwell and Leopold. Like his bicycle helicopter, it stays aloft only briefly, then plunges into the swamp of his self-regard.

Zelig and *A Midsummer Night's Sex Comedy* were shot back to back, sometimes with scenes from both films done on the same day. For *Sex Comedy*, Allen rented the old Rockefeller estate at Pocantico Hills in Westchester County, not far from Tarrytown, site of the Judith Crist weekend tribute that inspired *Stardust Memories*. In a sly joke, Allen inhabits the woods with the spirits of men who've died while making love, as Governor Nelson Rockefeller was supposed to have done in 1979.

There were no houses in the area suitable for Andrew and Adrian's place, so Mel Bourne built the two-storey clapboard house and barn from scratch. This was typical of a film which, under its apparently innocent and bucolic surface, was meticulously engineered. Tracks were laid through meadows and over a stone bridge for a long travelling shot of the six characters chatting and bickering as they set out for an afternoon in the woods – a scene Allen shot over and over, even bringing all the actors back weeks later because he thought the talk sounded false. Walks were landscaped, bushes planted and tree trunks painted to give them a springtime freshness – a fact which made them stand out as the season changed. After production, technicians were sent back to undo their work.

Loquasto's costumes showed every stain and picked up every leaf and blade of grass. Underneath them, the women wore tightly cinched corsets to maintain the willowy hourglass silhouette. No sign of any of this showed on screen. This was the stylised countryside of Chekhov, not the grubby landscape of the *Farmer's Almanac*. When Allen had to appear soaked after his helicopter dumped him in the lake, he refused to be doused with lake water, and directed a bottle of Evian to be poured over him.

Farrow's children came on location, as did her younger sister Stephanie, whom Allen agreed reluctantly to make her stand-in; he would never let *his* sister on the set, he complained. Notwithstanding his objections, he became highly attentive towards Steffi, as she was known, in much the way he had shown an interest in Mia's other sister Tisa during *Annie Hall*. When he needed someone to play Eudora Fletcher's aviatrix sister in *Zelig*, he gave Steffi the role. The three beautiful Farrows, and Allen's interest in them, would inspire *Hannah and her Sisters*.

The $200,000 Farrow earned for each Allen film, though a fraction of what Hollywood would have paid, solved her immediate financial problems. At Allen's urging she sold the Martha's Vineyard house and bought one in Bridgewater, Connecticut, near where William Styron and his wife spent their summers. She called the house Frog Hollow. Unexpectedly, Allen decided that he too wanted a weekend retreat, and in the winter of 1981–82 he paid $3.3 million for a house on Long Island, in fashionable South Hampton. With Jean Doumanian as his adviser and Santo Loquasto as designer, he landscaped the property and renovated the house, installing a restaurant-quality kitchen and showers with off-centre drains. Farrow visited it only once, and found the all-white interiors and bleached pine antiques chilly. Still, she reassured him, they would make it homey soon enough. Her reaction didn't please Allen. 'He paced and worried through the evening,' she said. 'The next morning, we left and he sold the house and everything in it.'

Later, he insisted he'd bought the house for his sister. 'I thought, "Gee, this is nice; maybe I could use it for myself some weekends," you know. But I only went out once. I hated it, and my sister hated it, and we sold it.'

The restless search for another beach house continued for a year, Allen spending weekend after weekend flying from one small airport to another along the coast as far north as Cape Cod. On one such trip he turned to Farrow's son Fletcher, whom he took on many of the flights, and asked suddenly, 'Fletch, do we really want to do this?'

Fletcher said thoughtfully, 'I don't think so.'

'Me neither,' said Allen. 'Let's go home.'

Allen's hostility to the country persisted in the face of Farrow's repeated invitations to spend time at Frog Hollow. At Thanksgiving 1982, he pleaded that pressure of work would keep him in Manhattan, then spent the afternoon in a downtown cinema watching the Steven Spielberg/Tobe Hooper horror film *Poltergeist*. Not long after, a friend of Farrow's who'd known the family in London visited her in New York. 'What's it like having Woody as a father?' he asked Fletcher.

Unhesitatingly, he murmured, 'Weird.'

20

Broadway Danny Rose and *The Purple Rose of Cairo*

A mirror has no heart but plenty of ideas.
Malcolm de Chazal

When it opened in July 1982, many people regarded *A Midsummer Night's Sex Comedy* as a step back for Allen after the toughness and glitter of *Annie Hall* and *Manhattan*. Reviews were approving, but the box-office was only modest. Washington WTOP radio critic Margot Kernan directed an old pun at a new target when she commented of Allen, 'His Krafft is Ebing.' The gibe was not only unkind but untrue, since Allen in his fifties was to introduce into his films a far firmer technique and a sharper sexuality. His films after *Annie Hall* became increasingly autobiographical, indeed confessional, emphasising his emotional entanglements and fantasies, and the physical and moral complications of changing sex partners. He continued to deny that his life informed his films, but Tony Roberts insisted that, 'unlike most artists, there's no discernible line as to where his personal life ends and his public work begins. His life *is* his work, and he incorporates a great deal of what is going on in his head and heart into his films.'

Orion had hoped that Allen, always a steady earner, might be a cash cow to offset its other, more chancy productions, but when *A Midsummer Night's Sex Comedy* failed to attract audiences, the company's distribution partner, Warners, began muttering about the advisability of backing films which didn't even satisfy their specialist audience.

Shrugging this off, Allen knuckled down to *Zelig*, which was undergoing massive changes as researchers unearthed new and more offbeat material. The scale of these alterations was dramatised by the use Allen made of the so-called White Room, in which Eudora psychoanalyses Leonard. Unable to find exactly the carpet he needed for its floor, Mel Bourne took one from his own bedroom. After Allen had shot twice on the set, Bourne asked production manager Michael Peyser, 'You think we should hold this?'

'No, he's got all he needs,' Peyser said. They struck the set, and Bourne relaid his carpet. Six weeks later, Peyser asked for it back; Allen wanted the room rebuilt. All in all, Bourne's carpet went back and forth eight times.

Allen repeatedly insisted that almost everything in the film was new material, but Gordon Willis acknowledges that at least half the shots are newsreels into which Allen's image was inserted. It often takes a trained eye to distinguish the real from the reconstructed, so convincing are the strangulated voices of the amateurs impersonating various doctors and officers of the law, and the shapeless clothes into which they are bundled. No expense was spared to evoke Depression America in all its lumpen lifestyle and fusty decor. Milliner Josephine Tripoli alone manufactured 110 hats for the production, ranging from the turn of the century to the late twenties.

Shooting on *Zelig* continued throughout late 1982 and early 1983, while Allen and Farrow settled into a comfortable, if unconventional, domestic routine. Having had Maxwell in *A Midsummer Night's Sex Comedy* announce, 'Marriage is the death of hope,' Allen no longer welcomed discussions of any more permanent arrangement. In all their time together, he never slept in Farrow's Langham apartment. On weekends when she didn't take the children to Frog Hollow, they trooped over to Allen's duplex, where part of the lower level was fitted with bunk beds for them. Allen and Farrow then left them with a nanny and went out, spending the night in his private quarters upstairs. He would sometimes play with the children on Sunday morning, and the family were occasionally seen together in Central Park, but by Sunday night they were back on the West Side, and Allen scrunched up on his bed with pencil and legal pad, writing.

Allen and Mia became Manhattan's best-known together/apart couple. Kristi Groetke, the children's nanny, remembers them as 'as much symbols of Manhattan as the Empire State Building or the Statue of Liberty. Regularly, my friends and I would see photos of them in the tabloids, Woody and Mia leaving Elaine's Upper East Side restaurant, where the literary glitterati feasted nightly; Woody and Mia walking through Central Park, he craggy-faced and slump-shouldered, with his fishing hat pulled down over his face and his trademark black glasses peering out from under it; she slightly unkempt and yet still lovely in baggy jeans and sweater, usually with a baby tucked in her arms and a child or two tugging at her jacket. Always there would be an angelic smile on her face. And we couldn't help wondering, "Who is this brainy little troll who has managed to captivate Beauty's heart?"' Often walking along behind, marshalling the smaller children, would be the impassive Soon-Yi, ten or eleven years of age at the time Allen was making *Zelig*.

Manhattan's fancied ability to accommodate all shades of sexuality seemed embodied in the couple, who were harassed by *paparazzi* as much as was Andy Warhol. While Warhol blatantly played up to his celebrity, posing for the flashbulbs and even snapping his own Polaroids, the press had little doubt that Allen and Farrow, though their style was very different, expected no less attention. In March 1981 David McGough, a photographer who specialised in dogging their footsteps, was startled to receive a call inviting him to a private photo session. More accustomed to being actively avoided or occasionally kicked by Allen, and scorned by Farrow, who went into unphotogenic contortions when she saw him in order to frustrate any chance of getting a glamorous picture, McGough was astonished when the couple posed for him, devotedly holding hands and kissing.

During the eighties, Allen was to put his public relations in the hands of the obsessively defensive PMK agency, expert at keeping the press at bay. PMK effectively protected the image of Allen and Farrow as a kooky yet essentially nice couple, but events like the McGough shoot suggest that both this and the Beauty-and-the-Beast image propounded by Farrow's allies were something between a PR device and a journalistic fantasy. Farrow's sexuality was not extinguished by having a family, and a certain frosty disdain irritated many people with whom she came in contact.

Any concessions the couple made to each other's tastes were tentative. Allen's cream Rolls-Royce was replaced by a black stretch limo capable of carrying all the Farrow children. More francophile than ever, he still talked nostalgically of moving to Paris, and persuaded Mia to take a five-day crash course in French with him. His own French improved slightly over the years, but was never better than halting, and while he could make a few simple remarks, he never learned to understand spoken French. It was easier to cultivate a taste for French wine, and he became an enthusiast for Château Margaux, buying heavily and taking along a bottle when he dined out. Restaurants which would have ejected anyone else for taking such a liberty made a special case for New York's most celebrated recluse.

They still frequented Allen's favourite Chinese restaurant, Pearl's, wearing identical floppy felt hats, and sometimes ate both breakfast and lunch at the Carnegie Delicatessen on Seventh Avenue, near Allen's office. The Carnegie even paid him the ultimate compliment and named a sandwich after him: 'for the dedicated *fresser* [gorger] only: lotsa corned beef plus lotsa pastrami'. Otherwise, Allen seemed more distant than ever from his roots. 'One of the last times I saw him, he was with Mia,' said Jules Feiffer. 'She was wheeling a baby carriage. I knew her much less well than I did Woody, but she and I got into a conversation, and he kind of backed off, as if I was her friend and not his.' Jean Doumanian, by contrast, became increasingly central to his life. Improbably, she had abandoned show business to open a health-food restaurant, the headquarters of which were in a disused chapel just behind Allen's block. Under pressure from her, Allen, fearful of heart attack, swore off red meat and chemical-rich hot-dogs, ironic acts for someone who had mocked food fads in *Sleeper*.

The proximity of Farrow's children and pets exacerbated Allen's fear of infection. In addition to three cats – Ewok, Lulu and Patch – the children had various dogs, gerbils, parakeets, chinchillas, canaries, goldfish and a ferret, all of which roved the large Langham apartment, including its kitchen. When he ate or drank there, Allen always used paper plates and cups. Even his driver, Don Harris, referred to him as 'Nervous Nelly' because of his phobias.

During the post-production of *Zelig*, Farrow suggested that she and Allen have a child together. 'Well, I don't know,' he said, according to her. 'I would have to think about it.'

In *Hannah and her Sisters*, Mia's character, Hannah, who already has four children by her previous marriage, makes a similar suggestion to her second husband, Elliott (Michael Caine). The resulting conversation, with Caine hedging and Farrow pressing, could well have been taken from life.

HANNAH: When I brought up the idea of having a baby, you jumped down my throat.

ELLIOTT: I don't think it's a very good idea. It's the last thing in the world we need right now.

HANNAH: Why do you say that? Is there something wrong? Tell me. Should I be worried?

ELLIOTT: We've got four children.

HANNAH: I want one with you.

ELLIOTT: I think we should wait till things settle.

HANNAH: What does that mean? We've been married four years. How settled can things get?

ELLIOTT: You have some very set ideas on how your life should be structured. A house, kids, certain schools, a home in Connecticut. It's all very preconceived.

HANNAH: But I thought you needed that. When we met, you said your life was chaos.

In the film, Elliott airs his problems with his analyst. Nor could Allen resolve such dilemmas alone. When he said 'I', Farrow knew she should understand it as 'we', i.e. Allen and his psychiatrist, with whom he discussed even the most trivial of decisions. 'He didn't even buy sheets without talking to her,' said Farrow. 'I know that part of several sessions went into his switch from polyester-satin to cotton.' They wrangled over the baby question for weeks before Allen announced his grudging agreement, subject to

Farrow shouldering all responsibility for the child's upkeep. But pregnancy would have to take its place in the schedule, and the child became another Woody Allen Fall Project, semi-permanently delayed by Allen's, in Farrow's description, 'lukewarm' participation.

Zelig, three years in the making, opened in July 1983. New York audiences understandably loved it, keeping it on the screens there for fourteen weeks and pushing it briefly to number one on *Variety*'s box-office hits, but the film died elsewhere, and even with its European sales, barely broke even. Warner Brothers pressured Orion to guarantee that future Allen films would be more commercial, but Krim and his associates decided instead to cut themselves loose from the studio. With the help of $10 million kicked in by the HBO cable TV company, they bought the declining Filmways distribution circuit for $16 million, giving them autonomy at the price of a reduced number of playing venues.

Zelig marked the end of a phase in Allen's career; one in which he had experimented with only modest success in combining comedy and drama. *Manhattan* would remain his benchmark in this attempt, one which not only he but other film-makers would find impossible to match. For the next half-dozen films, among his best both artistically and in terms of profit, he would rigidly separate the two genres. On the one hand would be comedies, in which he would appear as 'Woody'; on the other dramas, which he would write and direct only.

He was helped in this decision by the new respect in which he was held by performers. Many actors regarded comedy as *déclassé*, but a Woody Allen film was different. Though José Ferrer's great days were over when he appeared in *A Midsummer Night's Sex Comedy*, his casting paved the way for others to accept Allen's invitation. Michael Caine, Sam Shepard, William Hurt, Claire Bloom, Anjelica Huston, Max von Sydow, Madonna, John Malkovich, Gene Hackman, Barbara Hershey and Gena Rowlands would play roles of greater or less significance for him over the next decade.

An invitation to appear in an Allen film became a kind of

compliment. That he paid rock-bottom rates and made no concessions to stardom added, perversely, to the appeal. Doing without a private trailer or a personal hairdresser, and turning up at
dawn on a windy New York location became as much an earnest
of one's standing as a serious actor as doing a play on Broadway.
Nor did it commit one to forgoing such luxuries on other films,
since Allen was *sui generis*. Nobody else was consistently making
the sort of films he made. If they tried, as Rob Reiner would do
in 1989 with his highly successful *When Harry Met Sally*, it was
normally a one-off. Allen alone had the ability to regularly write
and direct his kind of films. More to the point, he also owned the
one unsubtractable element that made them work: the 'Woody'
persona.

Backing up the stars who worked for Allen was a roster of less
luminary performers like Alan Alda, Dianne Wiest, Julie Kavner,
Wallace Shawn, Sam Waterston, Danny Aiello – and, it must be
said, Mia Farrow, who, though she gave many of her best performances in Allen films, would never escape the label 'Woody's
woman'. The film that made this description almost indelible was
Broadway Danny Rose, which Allen began shooting while he was
still winding up *Zelig*, a fact which accounted for its long gestation:
it didn't open until seventeen months later.

Often dismissed as a 'shaggy dog story', *Broadway Danny Rose*
actually illuminates Allen's vision of the world he had come to
know as a stand-up comedian: one where everything is for sale.
He based his character, small-time agent Danny Rose, on managers
he'd known, including to some extent Jack Rollins, who's glimpsed
among the comedians in the opening sequence who gather at the
Carnegie Deli to *kvetch* about the decline in the comedy business
and to reminisce about the old days. More directly, the character
recalls Harvey Meltzer, the small-time garment-business hustler
who, for good or ill, directed Allen's early career.

The story the comedians tell is of Danny Rose, once a comic,
who became an agent for talents even less distinguished than himself. Rose's first scene in the film shows him trying to sell his
one-legged tap dancer, blind xylophone player, balloon folders
and performing birds to the manager of Weinstein's Majestic

Bungalow Colony, where Allen played his earliest comedy date.

Like Billy Wilder's heroes, Rose habitually seizes disaster from the jaws of success. After devoting all his time and energy to nursing performers, he sees them abandon him for a more professional agent. His reaction is a mixture of resentment and resignation. 'I discovered the kid,' he says of one defector. 'He slept on my sofa, I supported him. I don't want to bad-mouth the kid, but he's a horrible dishonest immoral louse. And I say that with all due respect.' On paper, Rose is a character straight out of Bob Hope, with overtones of the sentimental Broadway and crime stories of Damon Runyon, like 'Little Miss Marker', in a 1949 remake of which, *Sorrowful Jones*, Hope had starred. Allen uses aspects of both Runyon and Hope, but adds a touch of the self-sacrificing heroes of Wilder. The result is a Rose who's rabbinical, almost saintly, a willing self-sacrifice on the altar of his clients' egos. Though he again reveals Allen's enthusiasm for Italians, Rose is the first 'Woody' character to suggest any strong attachment to Allen's Jewish roots. He wears a *chai* religious emblem on a chain round his neck, makes repeated use of Yiddishisms – 'It's the *emess*'; 'My hand to God' – and delivers homilies like, 'As my uncle Sidney used to say, "Acceptance, forgiveness and love."'

Rose's particular cross is overweight, self-pitying, heavy-drinking, philandering, egotistic singer Lou Canova, whom he has nursed through three marriages and a declining career. Canova survives precariously as an imitation Frank Sinatra/Dean Martin, singing medleys of Great Singers of the Past Who Are Deceased and making eyes at the widows in the front rows who still sigh at his synthetic charm. As the film opens, he looks like benefiting from a revival of interest in the fifties, and Milton Berle offers to put him on a TV special he's planning, subject to an *ad hoc* audition during Canova's next club date, at New York's Waldorf hotel.

It's an index of Allen's standing that, where he once flew to Las Vegas from San Francisco to stand by as a substitute for Berle, the older comedian now plays a bit part – heavily cut, to his irritation, from a much longer appearance – in Allen's movie. In addition to Berle and Danny Rose's dreadful acts, all of them authentic club performers, a number of showbiz celebrities play cameos in the film, including the real stand-up comics who spend the opening reminiscing in the Carnegie Deli, and Gerald Schoenfeld, head of the all-powerful Shubert theatrical group, who plays agent Sid Bacharach. At the Waldorf, John Doumanian can be briefly glimpsed as the manager, and Howard Cosell as one of Berle's guests. Allen asked Sylvester Stallone to play Lou Canova, but the Italian Stallion, despite having had his start in *Bananas*, declined. Robert de Niro also had no desire to restore the fifty pounds he'd added, then lost, for *Raging Bull*. Danny Aiello, briefly considered, was turned down, a decision which, Aiello said, drove him to tears. Casting director Juliet Taylor found Nick Apollo Forte from the jacket of one of the records he pressed and distributed himself. An ex-fisherman, self-trained as a singer, the bulky unknown proved perfect casting as the conceited Canova, but, as much a Danny Rose client in real life as on film, he never flourished afterwards in either cinema or on the club circuit.

Canova is cheating on his cocktail-waitress wife with Tina Vitali, a widow who lives in New Jersey. Superstitiously convinced he can't get through his big audition without her, he persuades Rose to act as a 'beard' and bring her as his own date. He does so, despite the fact that Tina is the widow of a murdered Mafia loan-shark and is still intimately involved with people in the rackets, but as a result he finds himself being pursued by a pair of Mafia killers, brothers of another hood who also loves Tina, and who tried to commit suicide when she discarded him. Canova rewards Rose by moving to a bigger agent, Sid Bacharach, to whom he's introduced by Tina.

Loving Rose, but unable to face becoming involved with such a loser, Tina spends a year guiltily avoiding him, but the couple are reunited on the following Thanksgiving in front of the Carnegie Deli, an ecumenical collision of Judaism, Catholicism and Protestantism that underlines the film's religio-moral subtext. Though the plot is *The Apartment*, the tone is *Miracle on 34th Street*, with Thanksgiving rather than Christmas as the motif.

Broadway Danny Rose's cast of grotesques confers an air of magic realism that was to envelop *The Purple Rose of Cairo* and

Alice. Showbusiness, the film implies, is only a step away from *Alice in Wonderland.* Some moments are frankly fairytale, like an encounter in the New Jersey marshlands with an actor dressed like a superhero in cape and tights, and a shoot-out in a hangar filled with inflated parade animals. Danny himself reveals some improbable skills, recalled from his days in the Catskills when he handled acts like the too-successful hypnotist who couldn't reawaken his already half-stunned subjects. With techniques learned from an escapologist client, he extricates himself and Tina from the ropes with which the killers have tied them up.

All this would have been difficult to digest had not Allen undercut the potential whimsy by shooting the film more as drama than comedy. After he sent the script to Gordon Willis, they discussed it on the phone.

'I see this in black and white,' Allen said.

Willis replied, 'You know, I couldn't agree more.'

Willis shot *Danny Rose* roughly, without the careful lighting effects of earlier films. Jeffrey Kurland, taking over costumes from Santo Loquasto, whom he had assisted on earlier films – within his inner circle of collaborators, Mia says, Allen was 'most comfortable' with Kurland and his 'eager to please' assistant Jane Read Martin – added to the cheesy look, shoehorning Forte into a series of cummerbunds, over-tight trousers and bulging dress shirts, and dressing Allen in open-necked polyester shirts of bilious pattern, the collar turned out over a jacket of contrasting checks.

His triumph, however, is Mia Farrow, transformed utterly by matador pants, ruffled blouses, bouffant hair and ever-present shades. Jack Rollins advised Allen against casting Farrow as Tina: 'I was not Mr Rollins' first (or fiftieth) choice,' she said tartly. Challenged, she approached the role with Method meticulousness. After studying Robert de Niro's performance in *Raging Bull*, she downed milkshakes to gain ten pounds, though she still needed false breasts and padded hips to make Tina's shape convincing. Inspiration for the look of a Mafia bimbo came from some friends of Frank Sinatra's, and from Mrs Rao, the proprietor of a New York restaurant who never removed her dark glasses, day or night, a stratagem which, Farrow realised, would usefully camouflage her wide and innocent eyes. The grating Brooklyn accent was no problem. Her own voice was light enough to make the abrasive tone more than convincing.

Her first appearance is electric: she opens the door, expressionless, to admit Rose to her apartment, then turns to reveal that she's on the phone, shrilly berating Canova about having been seen at the racetrack with 'a cheap blonde'. Her personal credo goes with the hairdo and the accent: 'It's over quick,' she tells Rose, 'so have a good time. You see what you want, you go for it. Don't pay any attention to anybody else. And do it to the other guy first, 'cause if you don't, he'll do it to you.' She does have her soft spot: 'You know what turns me on? Intellectual.' At this confession, Danny regards her nervously, like a cricket regarding a cat. From that moment, we know he doesn't have a chance. 'Woody Allen is the best thing that ever happened to Mia Farrow,' commented the *New York Post*, a remark that was to prove anything but prophetic.

Released in January 1984, *Broadway Danny Rose* did as poorly as might be expected at such an unpromising time of year, grossing only $5.5 million of its $8 million budget on first release. As usual for Allen, the film made back its money in Europe, despite a lacklustre advertising campaign, the poster for which was a black and white picture of Danny's office door, past which could be glimpsed Danny and Tina trussed up.

Allen was meanwhile at work on another film to widen and deepen his collaboration with Farrow. Again, it was an elaboration of something he'd written before, in this case a *New Yorker* piece called 'The Kugelmass Episode', published in May 1977. Bored with his second marriage, Kugelmass, a professor of humanities at City College, complains to his psychiatrist that he yearns for a new woman. 'I want to make love in Venice,' he says, 'trade quips at 21 and exchange coy glances over red wine and candlelight.' The shrink tells Kugelmass he needs a magician, not an affair, and a few days later he gets a call from one, The Great Persky, who owns a cabinet which, he claims, will transport him into any book also placed in there with him. Kugelmass chooses *Madame Bovary*, and finds himself in Flaubert's Yonville, making love to Emma. All goes well for a while, except that 'students in various classrooms across the country were saying to their teachers, "Who is this character on page 100? A bald Jew kissing Madame Bovary?"' Emma, besotted by stories of Broadway and Hollywood, yearns to see America. Kugelmass brings her to New York, where, installed in the Plaza, she develops a taste for caviar and Dom Perignon, decides to become an actress and gets involved with an off-Broadway producer. As exasperated as was her husband, Kugelmass sends her back to France, and orders Persky to arrange an affair with another fictional figure, the nymphomaniac in Philip Roth's *Portnoy's Complaint* known as 'The Monkey' after a sexual variation she invented. Persky tries, but the machine malfunctions, and Kugelmass finds himself inside a copy of *Remedial Spanish*, 'running for his life over a barren, rocky terrain as the word *tener* ("to have") – a large and hairy irregular verb – raced after him on its spindly legs'.

The Kugelmass of *The Purple Rose of Cairo* is Cecilia, a crushed, wan housewife in 1930s New Jersey. Desperate for escape from her unemployed, drunken, violent and philandering husband Monk (Danny Aiello), she spends all her spare time at the movies, feeding on Hollywood fantasies. She memorises their dialogue, and is an encyclopedia of movieland marriages and divorces. She loves pictures set in Hollywood's fantasy Manhattan, so can't wait to see *The Purple Rose of Cairo*, an RKO confection about a group of socialites on holiday in Egypt who meet a young archaeologist and bring him back to their penthouse world, where he has an affair with a nightclub singer.

After being fired from her waitress job and discovering her husband drunkenly involved with another woman, both in the same week, Cecilia flees to *The Purple Rose of Cairo* for the fifth time, and is astonished when the actor playing Tom Baxter, the Egyptologist, addresses her from the screen. To the dismay of the handful of people in the cinema, he climbs down to join her. Chaos ensues. Glued to the plot, the rest of the cast can only sit about in their penthouse set and wait for him to return. (Allen never explains why they can't escape too, though one of them says, 'I don't know how he did it. I can't get out,' and the film's producer later thanks them for 'staying up there on the screen'.)

Meanwhile, Tom learns about the real world, of which, as a movie character living by the rules of thirties Hollywood, he knows nothing. He's never worked, never been poor, never seen a pregnant woman, knows nothing of prostitutes or brothels, is baffled by the concept of God, whom he can only relate to a sort of cosmic screenwriter, and is astonished when Monk, catching him with Cecilia, knees him in the groin: no Hollywood censor would permit such a thing.

Allen's imagination stalled at this point, until he introduced the character of actor Gil Shepherd, who played Baxter in the film. His career threatened with ruin by Tom Baxters stepping down from the screen all over the country, Shepherd comes to the town where the trouble began. He and Cecilia strike up an innocent romance, but Tom, competing in the only way he knows, takes her back into the film with him, where they share the 'madcap Manhattan weekend' promised by his socialite friends. Black-and-white fantasy, though, is no substitute for the corporeal Gil, and Cecilia chooses him. Tom glumly returns to his two-dimensional, monochrome existence, *The Purple Rose of Cairo* picks up where it left off, and Gil, his career restarted, hurries back to Hollywood, abandoning Cecilia to New Jersey and reality. Wearily she takes refuge in the cinema, and is soon lost in the dream world of Fred Astaire and Ginger Rogers in *Top Hat*, dancing cheek to cheek.

Like most escapism, *The Purple Rose of Cairo* was ten times harder to shoot than drama. Looking for a community which retained the hangdog look of the Depression, Allen found more than enough clapboard houses and abandoned factories in Piermont, a dreary New York satellite town on the Hudson. Modern improvements were torn out, authentic thirties frontages refurbished, new ones built where needed, and the town in general was taken over by the film unit. When unseasonal snowstorms paralysed shooting for weeks on end, businessmen who'd transformed their premises and couldn't reopen them were appalled. Seven months after Allen left, the town was still trying to get back to normal – an ironic parallel to Cecilia's plight in the film.

For the town's cinema, the Jewel, Allen returned to Brooklyn, taking over the Kent on Avenue H in Coney Island, one of his childhood haunts. The choice suggests how close the roots of *Purple Rose of Cairo* lie to the adolescent Allen who surfaced in Times Square and saw the towers of Manhattan. 'From the first time I came here from Brooklyn with my father,' he said, 'I wanted to live in New York, and I wanted to live in the elegant, Cole Porter part of New York, which is why I live on the East Side. That vision of the city was as important to me as Damon Runyon.' Cecilia, he says, was inspired by his movie-obsessed cousin Rita Wishnick, just as the *Purple Rose* in which Baxter is starring is his tribute to the studio escapism he saw as a boy.

The cast of the pastiche movie, mostly theatre actors, adds to the verisimilitude. Edward Herrmann, Milo O'Shea, Hollywood veteran Van Johnson, John Wood (an old lover of Farrow's from London) and Zoe Caldwell, playing the Countess with well-rounded vowels perfected on Broadway in *Medea* and *Saint Joan*, deliver the Martini/Broadway/nightclub dialogue ('I want to get plushed to the scuppers!') with the contemptuous charm it deserves. As the internal logic of their film begins to fray, so real Hollywood seeps in. The actors fret about their careers, and one of them bursts out with a tirade of Communist propaganda, to which the others respond with weary scorn. At the nightclub, Tom's intended romantic interest, the singer, touches the 'real' Cecilia and faints, while the *maître d'*, realising that all bets are off, throws down his menus, orders the orchestra to 'Hit it!' and launches into a spirited tap routine.

Michael Keaton started the double role of Tom Baxter and Gil Shepherd, accepting $250,000, a quarter of his usual price, for the honour of working with Allen, but after ten days Allen fired him. Officially the reason was that he was too 'contemporary', though it seems more likely that Keaton, whose corner-of-the-mouth, Cagney-esque style would have been convincing as Gil, lacked the innocence demanded of Tom as his newborn personality marvels at the wonders of birth, religion and womanhood.

Allen, pressured by Orion, briefly contemplated taking the role himself – 'Woody' in jodhpurs and pith helmet? – then offered Kevin Kline the part. The swashbuckling Kline was so evidently wrong that before a scene was shot with him Allen gratefully turned to Jeff Daniels, whom Juliet Taylor had kept in reserve. Daniels was, in the narrow sense, perfect casting, since he lacked a strong screen personality of his own. In all the time he spent on the film, Allen never acknowledged his existence, except to give him the briefest possible directions, a fact which the actor enlarged into a kind of compliment. Allen, he said, offered 'no discussions about characters, motivations and backgrounds. It's as if he's got a feather in his hand and he blows it and it goes off in a dozen directions. That gives you the freedom to do twelve things – so it's alive and spontaneous; there isn't a right or a wrong way.'

Daniels' colourless playing had the effect of throwing more emphasis onto Cecilia, which lifted the film immeasurably. Farrow proved again to be a resourceful and unexpectedly technical actress. Her nervous half-smiles and spurts of enthusiasm when she talks about movies convey perfectly the fan's inability to distinguish between reality and fantasy, which Allen excoriated in *Stardust Memories*. As a guitar player, she was able to display a winning mastery of that archetypal amateur's instrument of the thirties, the ukulele, to accompany Shepherd in a lively version of 'Alabamy Bound'. The ending, where as she watches Astaire and Rogers, affection and recognition creep across a face twisted with loss, seemed to many people almost unbearable.

Didn't he ever contemplate a happy ending, one interviewer asked Allen.

'This *is* the happy ending,' he said shortly. The dropped version left Cecilia standing outside the cinema, without the analgesic of *Top Hat* to numb the pain.

The seedy atmosphere of *The Purple Rose of Cairo* is almost unique in Allen's films. Willis' shooting of the claustrophobic rooms stuffed with cheap furniture recalls Robert Altman's 1974 Depression drama *Thieves Like Us*. The greasy spoon where Cecilia and her sister (played by real-life sister Stephanie) wait tables has none of the nostalgic glamour of *The Sting*, or of the bars and cafés in Allen's later *Bullets Over Broadway*, but looks as lacklustre as its food. When Monk brings home his new mistress Olga (Camille Saviola), she isn't even remotely attractive, but raucous, ugly and fat. The cinema is decrepit, the brothel a cluster of untidy rooms in a rundown apartment house.

For Allen, the cost and the trouble were justified. Among all his films, he singled out *The Purple Rose of Cairo* as 'the one where I accomplished what I set out to do most perfectly'; but American audiences, uninterested in Allen's fulfilment as an artist, simply saw a dour little film with a downbeat ending, and it was not to be a success.

Purple Rose terminated some associations for Allen, and inaugurated others. It marks the end of his collaboration with both Mel Bourne and Gordon Willis, and of the Continental look that characterised *Manhattan*, *Stardust Memories*, *Zelig*, *A Midsummer Night's Sex Comedy* and *The Purple Rose of Cairo*. His next films would be intensely urban and American, with a denser texture and a greater emphasis on ensemble performance. In addition to Farrow, many of them would feature a little-known stage actress he first worked with on *Purple Rose*, Dianne Wiest. As one of the prostitutes, she brought a knowing toughness and hidden sentimentality to the film which Allen would use extensively, and which would become a motif of his best work.

21

Hannah and her Sisters and *Radio Days*

All happy families resemble one another, but each unhappy family is unhappy in its own way.

Leo Tolstoy, *Anna Karenina*

Allen always insisted that *Hannah and her Sisters* stemmed from a chance rereading of *Anna Karenina* and the idea of using Tolstoy's interweaving narratives in a modern story – a plausible tale, had he not been doing just that since *Interiors*. The explanation drew attention away from the fact that, once again, he was exploring his own life and its tensions, and in terms not too different from Ingmar Bergman in his highly successful *Fanny and Alexander* (1982), which also dealt with two generations of a theatrical family, often most strikingly on show at gatherings like Christmas.

The narrative focus of *Hannah and her Sisters* is, once again, Thanksgiving, the archetypally *goyische* festival which exercised such a fascination for Allen. There are three Thanksgivings in this film, and, as in *Interiors* and *Broadway Danny Rose*, each supplies an opportunity for emotional confrontations. Once again three characters are involved, one avid for sex, another indifferent, and a third searching for something more fulfilling. As in *Interiors*, they are sisters. Hannah, an actress (Mia Farrow), is hostess of the first Thanksgiving party with her financial counsellor husband Elliot (Michael Caine). Elliot lusts after his sensuous sister-in-law Lee (Barbara Hershey), who is herself trapped in a sterile relationship with an older painter, Frederick (Max von Sydow). The third sister, Holly (Dianne Wiest), is restlessly searching for a direction in life, and as the story opens borrows more money from Hannah to enable her to pay her cocaine debts and abandon her unsuccessful acting career to become a caterer with her friend April (Carrie Fisher). Revolving around the three, as in *Interiors*, are their mother Norma (played by Farrow's real-life mother Maureen O'Sullivan), again dysfunctional, 'a boozy old flirt with a filthy mouth', and their father Evan (Lloyd Nolan), a lachrymose second-rate film director who solaces himself reminiscing at the piano to Rodgers and Hart and Jerome Kern.

New to the mix is Hannah's first husband Mickey (Allen), a TV comedy producer hag-ridden by hypochondria. His confrontation with the possibility of a brain tumour, based on Allen's scare during the making of *Manhattan*, his crisis of faith and unexpected marriage to Holly, provide a significant sub-plot. A short film in itself, the story of Mickey's descent through the hell of 'tests' at Cedars Mount Sinai hospital, only to be told he has nothing to worry about, is Allen at his funniest and most mordant.

Mickey's reprieve gives him the courage to leave his job and search for a meaning to life. He briefly embraces Catholicism, an act which rouses Allen's amused derision. Pausing at the window of a religious supplies store, Mickey stares incredulously at a plastic image of the crucified Christ whose eyes open and close as one moves. Returning home, he empties out his shopping: a crucifix, a missal, a picture of the Virgin Mary, a loaf of Wonderbread and a jar of Hellmann's mayonnaise.

Mickey's mother takes to her bed at his decision. His father is contemptuous. If he wants a religion, what's wrong with Jewish? Mickey frets about the possibility of there being no afterlife, and questions the essential goodness of a God who would permit the horrors of the world.

'Why were there Nazis?' he asks.

'How the hell would I know why there were Nazis?' growls his father. 'I don't even know how the can opener works.'

Eventually Mickey's faith in life is restored by a chance viewing of the Marx Brothers in *Duck Soup*, the sort of abrupt and essentially incomprehensible conversion Allen would use again in *Crimes and Misdemeanors*.

* * *

Allen revised *Hannah and her Sisters* repeatedly. Mickey and his health problems didn't appear in the first script, and their inclusion threw the film out of balance, so that even at its eventual running time of 107 minutes, making it Allen's longest to that time, some narrative strands are simply left hanging.

Elliot, who begins an affair with Lee just after the first Thanksgiving and spends the second party begging her not to leave him, is seen at the third unaccountably looking fondly at her fondling her new husband, and wondering how he could ever have doubted his love for Hannah. Mickey is told by new wife Holly as the film ends that she's pregnant, throwing into doubt an earlier sequence in which, diagnosed as sterile while married to Hannah, he invites their friend Tony Roberts to supply semen for artificial insemination. This results in twins – but we never find out how Mickey was magically restored to fertility. And who fathered Hannah's other two boys, played in the film by Farrow's real-life adopted sons?

Sam Waterston is left with only a handful of scenes as opera-loving architect David, a self-regarding seducer with a private box at the Met, a 'Great Buildings of New York' tour worn smooth by repetition, and an unseen wife, conveniently in and out of institutions. Holly's friend April poaches her away from him, and later Holly writes a screenplay in which an architect is stabbed by his schizophrenic wife, but whether this is fact or fantasy is never established. Waterston declined to be credited on the film.

From the start, Farrow knew the film would have the theme of sisters. She assumed that although Allen had been friendly with the two sisters of his earliest star, Janet Margolin, who had appeared in *Take the Money and Run* and the stage version of *Play it Again, Sam*, and with Diane Keaton's two sisters as well, one of whom he briefly dated before he met Diane, the sisters were based on herself, Tisa and Stephanie. How closely based didn't dawn on her until Allen showed her the script and asked which of the three she wanted to play. He himself hadn't decided if he would be Mickey, Elliot or Frederick, three characters who, he agreed, were just different aspects of himself.

The sensual Lee very obviously recalled Tisa, and Mia recognised herself in the prissy Hannah. While there was never any doubt that she would appear in the film, if only because she now depended on Allen's annual contribution to her burgeoning domestic budget, she did demand that he soften some of the characters, whom she found 'self-indulgent and dissolute in predictable ways'. In particular, she resented the depiction of the mother. As she wrote, 'It was my mother's stunned, chill reaction to the script that enabled me to see how he had taken many of the personal circumstances and themes of our lives, and, it seemed, had distorted them into cartoonish characterisations.' With notable *chutzpah*, Allen asked Maureen O'Sullivan to play the role. She refused, and Allen thought briefly of dropping the film for something else, perhaps the crime story later made as *Manhattan Murder Mystery*, but eventually elected to go ahead, knowing that his reshoots might be more extensive than usual (in the event, he refilmed four-fifths). Mollified by the promise of concessions, O'Sullivan did take the role, though nothing she did could make it anything less than an embarrassingly revealing self-parody.

Everyone concerned remembers the shooting of *Hannah*, which began in October 1984, as a wearing experience. Michael Caine, not used to such solemnity on a set, called it 'a bit like working in church'. Nor did he find Allen's methods congenial. 'Woody Allen just puts it all on film right from the start,' he says, 'so that the rehearsal and the take become indistinguishable. He just keeps shooting and shooting it. He never covers in close-up. It's all one long shot. It goes on forever. Some of the takes involved 360 degrees of shooting all around the house – and not a soundstage set either; a real New York City apartment, a real house. We'd go in at 8.30 in the morning, block out the moves, and shoot at eight at night because it took so long to light. Woody rehearses everything down to the tiniest detail; his camera becomes a microscope. His pictures may look as if they are ad-libbed, but they are brought to that point by solid rehearsal, rehearsal, rehearsal.'

Having heard of Allen's often-repeated belief in letting the actors have their own way, even allowing them to make up dialogue if they weren't comfortable with what he'd written, the performers on *Hannah* who were new to him were dismayed to find him anything but flexible. Caine, who had hoped the film would introduce him to American audiences as a comedian, tried playing some of his scenes for laughs, but Allen threw these versions out. Hershey and von Sydow decided to rehearse in their own time the argument during which their relationship broke up. When Allen saw it, he rejected their version as too slow, and ordered them to do it at twice the pace.

Gordon Willis was tied up doing *The Money Pit* in Hollywood, so Allen once again asked Antonioni's cameraman Carlo DiPalma if he'd shoot the film. This time he agreed. DiPalma's ease with the moving camera and his ability to choose soft warm colours did much to alleviate the claustrophobia of shooting in the 'real New York City apartment', which was in fact Farrow's. O'Sullivan had remarried in 1983, and had moved out to live with her new husband, James Cushing. This left Farrow with the Langham apartment to herself, a heavy financial burden. Renting it to Allen as a set seemed an excellent idea, though she came to regret it when filming dragged into the winter of 1985, and her life and those of the children were dislocated as the crew tied up all but a few bedrooms for weeks on end. 'The cat has never been the same,' noted Farrow dourly.

To clarify the intertwined strands of the story, Allen added sixteen 'chapter headings' which help separate the narratives, and stream-of-consciousness voice-overs for all the major characters. The result is a film far closer in structure to a novel than anything Allen had done before. For once eschewing the elegiac but *echt-*thirties Gershwin, he uses popular songs more skilfully than ever to establish mood. The film's recurring theme tune, 'I've Heard that Song Before', in the swaggering version of Harry James' big band, seems in this context an ironic comment on the plot, but making Lloyd Nolan a nostalgia buff who communicates best at the piano provides the film with a stream of romantic songs by Rodgers and Hart ('Bewitched, Bothered and Bewildered', 'Where or When', 'You are too Beautiful', 'Isn't it Romantic?') or Jerome Kern and Dorothy Fields ('I'm Old Fashioned', 'The Way You

Look Tonight') that counterpoint the brassy James braggadocio which opens and closes the film.

In March, *The Purple Rose of Cairo* went on release, to indifferent houses though good reviews. Costing $13 million, it would earn back only a quarter of that on its first US release. Orion were less perturbed by the failure than Allen expected, since they had just had a box-office success with *Amadeus*. In July Allen signed another contract with them, for three more films to follow *Hannah*. In a political stand rare for him, he specifically forbade the circulation of the films in South Africa.

While nobody at Orion would have been so crass as to demand that Allen make funnier films, the pressure was clearly there, and it influenced him to change the tone of *Hannah*. People for whom he previewed the first version found it chilly, particularly the ending, in which the problems of the three sisters remained, as in *Interiors*, unresolved. Grudgingly, he cut some scenes with Tony Roberts, including a long sequence in an art gallery, and incidents where Caine and Hershey make love in a boat and have a 'knee-trembler' against a wall. At the second Thanksgiving, when Elliot tries to revive their affair, Hershey originally stabbed him in the hand with a pair of scissors, but this was deleted as well.

More importantly, he added the third Thanksgiving party, with its sunny wind-up of the major plots. He also gave more warmth to the character of Hannah, so generous, understanding and virtuous she's almost insupportable, adding a scene in which she reveals her hidden 'fragile' side and her secret fears. The character of a judgemental, hypercritical woman who discovers she's secretly loathed by almost everyone would reappear in *Another Woman*, counterposed with a distraught, near-suicidal Farrow. Both hint at a subtext of resentment felt by Allen towards the woman with whom he was, however tentatively, sharing his life.

Another theme is even more prescient. Everyone in *Hannah* is hiding something from everyone else, a fact dramatised by an edgy lunch shared by the three sisters in a sterile Manhattan restaurant where, as the camera circles them restlessly, we share their resentments and secrets: Lee is sleeping with Elliot, Holly thinks Hannah is censorious and priggish, Hannah finds Holly trivial and Lee aimless.

By 1985, Soon-Yi had developed into an attractive if not particularly bright teenager – according to the family nanny Kristi Groetke, she had an IQ of only ninety-four. Allen was finding her docile exoticism increasingly hard to dislodge from his mind, all the more so because of the barely disguised hostility she displayed towards him, a 'dislike', wrote Farrow later, 'almost palpable', which some people attributed to her infancy as the child of a street prostitute who abused her physically and emotionally.

At the same time, it was evident to Farrow that Allen's interest in having a child, such as it was, was dwindling. Running into his old girlfriend Bryna Goldstein at Michael's Pub, he confessed that he was 'indifferent' to the idea. Mia had more than enough children, he thought. In *Hannah and her Sisters*, *Another Woman*, *Shadows and Fog* and *Husbands and Wives*, one of his characters would rail against the folly of 'bringing a child into this world'. In *Another Woman*, the main character has an abortion rather than commit this most heinous of crimes.

In July 1985, as principal shooting on *Hannah* concluded, Farrow decided on another adoption, this time a newborn girl from Texas whom she christened Dylan. Allen had been openly resentful when he collected Farrow and her newest acquisition at the airport, but, perhaps because Dylan didn't suffer from any of the mental or physical problems that afflicted some of the others, he very soon became more attached to the little blonde girl than to the rest of Farrow's extended family. As nursemaid to the new arrival, they hired Rebecca Miller, daughter of playwright Arthur Miller.

While Allen was making films like *Manhattan*, *Hannah and her Sisters* and the one which was to follow, *Radio Days*, all of which celebrated New York, the city was sliding inexorably towards bankruptcy and chaos. From the war years to the sixties, Robert Moses, head (and in many cases sole member) of the City Parks and Planning Commissions, the Slum Clearance Authority, the Triborough Bridge and Tunnels Authority, the State Power Authority and much besides, had remade the city in accordance with his vision of the five New York boroughs tied together by more than six hundred miles of expressways, bridges and tunnels. Whole neighbourhoods were bulldozed, farms and estates transformed into parkways. Most of Manhattan's eastern edge, reduced over the decades to slums and rubbish dumps, was cleared for transformation into the East River Drive. Hitherto remote areas of the Atlantic coast like Jones Beach were suddenly within driving distance of downtown Manhattan, turning quiet beaches into popular resorts.

Under the complacent administration of sixties mayors like Robert Wagner and John Lindsay, a lid had been kept on the problems that flowed from Moses' imperial transformations, but by the time Ed Koch was elected the city's 105th mayor in 1977, New York was ready to boil over. Relocating those dispossessed by Moses' renovations in giant 'projects' like Bedford-Stuyvesant had created a community of street criminals who made it dangerous to walk the streets at night anywhere in the five boroughs. The city had assumed an air of decrepitude, with broken windows, barbed-wired fences and, above all, graffiti-splattered walls and subway trains the norm. Koch appealed to the federal government for assistance, and was refused. The *New York Post* noted the news in a famous headline: 'PRESIDENT TO CITY: DROP DEAD'. Despite the 'I Love NY' campaign which became the keynote of Koch's administration, the Big Apple had become a place where, it was said, 'a laugh and a shudder are never very far apart'.

Little of this impinged on Allen's world, which remained as idyllically prelapsarian as the Manhattan he affectionately parodied in the film-within-a-film of *The Purple Rose of Cairo*. In his New York, people still stroll the streets at night, own cars, live in apartment blocks with doormen. There are no blacks or Puerto Ricans, no graffiti or street crime, no beggars or bums (the first would appear in *Everyone Says I Love You*), no potholes or slums, no crack vials or used syringes in doorways and gutters. His prostitutes, almost the sole representatives of the working class in his films, were not the black or Hispanic women in stilettos, hotpants and tank tops soliciting homebound drivers on the streets of the Lower East Side but upmarket WASP call-girls, ex-Miss Something-or-Others with 'mouths like velvet' and their own apartments.

There is little to wonder at in this. Film-makers have no duty to reflect the whole of the world in which they create their films. Bergman, Fellini and Bertolucci were no more concerned with daily reality in Stockholm, Rome or Paris than was Allen with that of New York. The angst of *Last Tango in Paris* and *Face to Face* is as upmarket as that of *Manhattan*, and when Fellini delved into his fascist childhood in *Amarcord*, he did so not in Rimini but at the Cinecittà studios, where set designer Danilo Donati created an anthology of buildings from the pre-war city that comfortably distanced the film from the real world.

A few comics joked about the hermetic nature of Allen's films. In a parody of *Boyz N the Hood*-type movies, young black comedians of the Apollo Comedy Project had a group of yuppie blacks talking about a drive-by shooting on the Upper East Side – 'But I hate to drive in the city. Maybe a walk-by. Or a cab-by – but it's so hard to get a cab in this part of town.' But generally Allen was thought to be above such things. Living in a world of his own, a law unto himself, he was the court jester of the intellectual elite, licensed to make fun of their concerns and, as such, free of the constraints that confined lesser beings. In *Stardust Memories*, Allen could joke about his privileged standing, having his character Sandy Bates try to shrug off a gun the police find in his Rolls-Royce: 'You can make an exception in my case,' he tells them. 'I'm a celebrity.' But his behaviour indicated that he really *did* think of himself in those terms – a fact soon to become the stuff of headlines.

That we know more about the shooting of *Radio Days*, which began on 5 November 1985, than that of any other Allen film is due to *Woody Allen on Location*, a day-by-day account of the production by French critic Thierry de Navacelle. It's hard to imagine any other film personality inspiring a work of such lapidary and uncritical devotion, but if Allen stood high among the United States intelligentsia, the French regarded him as peerless.

In America, Navacelle had an equivalent in Eric Lax, a Canadian-born academic and journalist who earned a privileged position inside the Allen circle in 1975 with his short study *On Being Funny: Woody Allen and Comedy*.

Each time a new Allen film neared completion, Lax could be relied upon to produce an insider's view for the most prestigious publications, notably the *New York Times*. 'Woody Allen: Not Only a Comic', about *The Purple Rose of Cairo*, published on 24 February 1985, is typical of these. Always referred to as 'Mr Allen', the interviewee is given generous space in which to express his ideas, and enthusiastic support for them from Lax, who notes, 'Despite the variety of his films in the past ten years, audiences still expect a new Woody Allen film to be like the out-and-out comedies that established his career. Yet that kind of repetition and predictability is precisely what he is trying to avoid. The safety of what he called "the one pronounced thing" may be both tempting and comforting but "no matter how pleasurable it is at the time, it's aesthetically wrong, it's just wrong."'

At the same time as he began to offer Lax the insider access that would culminate in a best-selling authorised biography in 1991, Allen also appointed the PMK agency to manage his public relations, and took on Brian Hamill as his regular stills photographer. Rollins and Joffe, though still titular producers of all his films, no longer played much part in his business life, which was increasingly managed by his notoriously secretive agent, Sam Cohn. The loose screen of friends and advisers behind which Allen had hidden himself for so long hardened into a steel ring.

Within a few years Peter Bart, editor of *Variety*, would rail in an unprecedented editorial that 'every time a new Woody movie opens in New York, only his most trusted sycophants get interviews and only his personal biographers have a first shot at the accompanying commentaries.' Bart questioned the contradictions between the Allen image and the privileged standing accorded him by the press: 'We are repeatedly presented with the image of an inept, guilt-ridden *nebbish* of a human being stumbling through life, yet all the while exercising fierce control over a mind-bendingly efficient PR machine.' He should have directed his complaints against Jean Doumanian. Herself obsessive about privacy and now well-established with Jacqui Safra, she was preparing to enter film production with Safra's money. Within ten years she would be in overall control of Allen's entire artistic activity.

By the time reshoots ended on *Hannah and her Sisters*, Allen knew roughly the structure of the film that would become *Radio Days*. Fully a third of its incidents were retrieved from early drafts of *Annie Hall*, thrown out when he decided to stress Keaton's character rather than that of Alvy.

To sustain the rest, he needed some sort of intellectual armature. Popular songs came first to his mind, as usual, and from that the way he first heard many of them, on the radio. He would also have been aware of Dennis Potter's British television series *Pennies from Heaven*, ineptly remade by MGM in 1981. Potter used popular songs of the thirties to illustrate the life and times of an English sheet-music salesman, having his characters mime to old records, illustrating how directly the music reflected their hopes and dreams. A few sequences of *Radio Days*, notably Carmen Miranda's 'South American Way' mimed by the father, uncle and Cousin Ruthie of the 'Woody' figure, could have been taken straight from Potter, whose influence would also be evident in Allen's later *Everyone Says I Love You*.

If the structure of *Hannah and her Sisters* was intricate, that of *Radio Days* is Byzantine. Critic Larry Swindell was moved to call Allen 'the Charles Dickens of the American cinema' and *Radio Days* 'his *David Copperfield*'. Certainly the film does have the quality of a three-volume Victorian novel, with a multitude of often eccentrically drawn characters and a busy social and historical background – most of it is set during World War II. What it lacks is the moral subtext that infused such narratives. We're invited neither to criticise nor to congratulate the people of *Radio Days*, least of all the juvenile Woody. The adult Allen who narrates the film simply sees his characters as products of their environment, pushed into activity by history, religion and, particularly, the mass media, represented here by radio. In this world of easy manipulation, nothing is anyone's fault: nobody is to blame. Like

the 'Woody' character Joe's stealing money collected for the establishment of Israel to buy a secret compartment ring, the Masked
Avenger made him do it.

Most actions in *Radio Days* involve chance and luck. The opening scene, which Allen moved from later in the story during editing,
shows two burglars being startled when the phone rings while
they're breaking into a Brooklyn house. One of them answers, to
find the number has been called at random by a radio quiz show.
He correctly identifies three tunes, and next morning the house
owners are astonished by the arrival of a van packed with prizes.
Joe's Aunt Bea wins a prize on another quiz show for her ability
to identify fish. The career of Sally White (Mia Farrow), the film's
main continuing character – she's too feckless to be called a heroine – proceeds from one chance to another. First seen as a cigarette
girl offering quick sex to an exigent client on the roof of the
nightclub, she rises, mostly by good luck, to stardom as a radio
gossip columnist. A gangster who rubs out the owner of a club
where she works wants to kill her too, but is moved by the fact
that she's from his old neighbourhood to get her a job in radio
drama instead. Denied this when the Japanese attack on Pearl
Harbor intervenes, she does singing commercials for laxatives until
elocution classes lead her to a spot as a gossip columnist. It's only
at this point that she seems to take charge of her life, though we
never see this happen. Instead, Allen shows her practising 'O'
mouth movements in front of the mirror, and makes oblique mention of her 'many friends' in the business who turn her into a
'full-blown star'. A tribute to Sally's skill in oral sex?

Sally is the 'something more' character of *Radio Days*, the
equivalent of Joey in *Interiors* and Holly in *Hannah and her Sisters*, eager for advancement but hampered by a lack of talent. The
Flyn/Lee character, preoccupied with sexual fulfilment, is Aunt
Bea (Dianne Wiest), a forlorn, sentimental woman in early middle
age, relentlessly social, susceptible to dance music and every new
step, who nevertheless attracts a succession of inappropriate and,
above all, unmarriageable men – a loosely-attached husband, a
bereaved homosexual, an overweight 'operator' to whom she's just
about to surrender in a parked car when Orson Welles' Mercury

Theater *War of the Worlds* broadcast sends him fleeing terrified into the fog, leaving her to walk the six miles home. When he rings the next day, she has her sister tell him she's married a Martian.

Of the 'third sister' of Allen's other films, the Renata/Hannah figure, sexually active, dominating, assertive, *Radio Days* has no equivalent, unless it is Joe, an impish, red-headed, priapic wiseacre played by Seth Green. Unlike the real Allen of Brooklyn in the forties (but closer to the Allen of 1987), Joe is a stranger to doubt, fear or scruple. Radio provides him with his cultural context, his excuses for bad behaviour, and many of his best lines. Berated by the rabbi (Kenneth Mars) for stealing from the Jewish National Appeal collection box, Joe murmurs sagely, in imitation of Reed Hadley in *The Lone Ranger*, 'You speak the truth, my brave Indian companion.' The anti-Nazi exploits of radio hero Biff Baxter (Jeff Daniels) give Joe an excuse to spy on the town from a rooftop with a pair of binoculars, allowing him to watch his busty blonde teacher dancing naked in front of a mirror. Later, he spots a Nazi submarine just off the coast, which justifies his earlier voyeurism.

Allen reveals real affection for his screen family, perhaps because they, like the Flatbush house he recreated in such detail at the old Astoria studios outside New York, were carefully modified to make them more congenial to filming. The house was scaled up by a third to give ease of access to Carlo DiPalma's camera. Equally, Joe's parents, played by Michael Tucker and Julie Kavner, display a vitality and dry humour to which the Konigsbergs were strangers. Joe's father drives a cab, as did Allen's father, but is so embarrassed by it that his son only finds out about it by accident at the end of the film. Likewise, Joe's parents had been involved in attempts to sell jewellery by mail, the detritus of which still lingers in one of the house's many closets. Bemused visitors to the set found closets filled with real junk and a kitchen furnished with authentic cookware, dishes and products, none of which appeared on screen. Like the garter belts Allen demanded his actresses wear under their clothing, they provided an earnest of authenticity, validating his memory and disguising the fact that his recollection was, in both senses of the word, partial.

Choosing commercial radio to sustain the narrative is a brilliant conceit, though, once again, not especially original. Highlights of radio's history were regularly celebrated, in recreations of the *War of the Worlds* broadcast, documentaries about Jack Benny, Fred Allen and George Burns, and reruns of their programmes. Allen, though, delved deeper, into the mulch of gossip programmes, quiz shows, kids' action serials and soap operas. James Thurber, who shared Allen's exasperated affection for forties radio, once articulated its recipe: 'Between thick slices of advertising, spread twelve minutes of dialogue, add predicament, villainy, and female suffering in equal measure, throw in a dash of nobility, sprinkle with tears, season with organ music, cover with a rich announcer sauce, and serve five times a week.' Most of the old radio titles were still owned by the networks, so Allen invented high society couple Irene Draper and Roger Daly, who spend their nights at clubs and the theatre and describe them next morning on radio over breakfast, basing them on Ed and Peegeen Fitzgerald, who had a similar show. The serial *The Masked Avenger* was modelled on *Superman*, and Allen cast tubby, balding Wallace Shawn because of his resemblance to the actor who played the Man of Steel on radio. Jeff Daniels did a *Captain Midnight* pastiche called *Biff Baxter, G-Man of the Air*. Bill Stern's sports broadcasts inspired *Bill Kern's Favorite Sports Legends*, about Tennessee baseball player Kirby Kyle who lost an eye, an arm and a leg in hunting accidents but next season 'won eighteen games in the big league in the sky'. The actor who played Kern, Guy le Bow, remembered Stern's wildly improbable programmes as well as Allen did. He reminded Allen of one on which Abraham Lincoln on his deathbed whispered to Abner Doubleday, 'Don't give up on baseball.'

There were plenty of models for *The Court of Human Emotions*, Allen's version of the early self-help counselling shows. Listening to an unctuous expert adjudicating between bickering couples, Allen imagines his own parents placed under his scrutiny. After they've aired their grievances, the host says in exhausted tones, 'I think you both deserve one another,' whereupon the two of them turn on him.

Allen also admired radio's immediacy in reportage. He'd

originally intended to open *Radio Days* with an account of an escapologist, the Astonishing Tonino, extricating himself from chains under the icy Atlantic while the listening public hung on the announcer's every word, but this was first pushed back in the film, then dropped altogether, its place taken by a dramatisation of the 1949 Kathy Fiscus case, where a little girl was trapped in a well and, despite desperate attempts to free her, suffocated. *Radio Days* shows people across the country following the day-long reports in bars, offices and their homes – an audience drawn together even more by the news that the girl is dead than by its hope of her survival.

Once again, Allen evoked the music of the time with a faultless sense of period. Mia Farrow sings a throaty 'I Don't Want to Walk Without You' at a USO club, and Diane Keaton makes a brief appearance at the closing New Year's Eve party at the King Cole Room to croon Cole Porter's 'You'd be so Nice to Come Home to'; but as radio mostly represented the lower levels of popular culture, Allen favoured novelty numbers and perform-ances stronger on virtuosity than creativity. Trumpeter Harry James plays *Flight of the Bumblebee* over the credits, and the rest of the soundtrack meanders through Carmen Miranda, the Ink Spots, popular novelties like 'Mairzy Doats' and a simulated per-formance by Xavier Cugat, played by real-life band leader Tito Puente, of 'Tico Tico', complete with his trademark chihuahuas. Needing someone to sing the archetypal plaint of the Manhattan sexpot starved of male company by the draft, 'They're Either too Young or too Old', first delivered *parlando* by Bette Davis in *Thank Your Lucky Stars*, Allen tried a number of ageing divas before settling on Kitty Carlisle Hart, widow of playwright Moss Hart and a friend of Farrow's good friends, pianist Vladimir Horowitz and his wife.

Radio Days was Allen's most logistically ambitious film since *Love and Death*, with an initial 220 performers, reduced in editing to 150. He called a halt to shooting in February 1986, the same month in which *Hannah and her Sisters* opened. Orion, sensing that they had a hit, launched it in four hundred theatres simultaneously. Both public and critical approval was high, and the film had long and productive runs almost everywhere in the US, where it returned more than $16 million on its $6.4 million budget. Allen rated twentieth in the year's list of top moneymaking stars, and the film was even more popular overseas. It soon became his most financially successful production, the high-water mark of his box-office success.

In April, Allen started reshooting *Radio Days*. Many of the locations around Brooklyn which had assumed a nostalgic glow in his memory looked tawdry on film. The Fun House at Rockaway's decrepit Playland amusement park was now so sleazy that he cut the sequence shot there. All we see of Playland in the film is the faded white-painted wall which surrounds it, and a splintering rollercoaster. A skating rink, too small on screen, was recreated in the studio. Allen had also wanted to introduce the main characters in a sequence copied from Jean Renoir's *La Règle du Jeu*, a favourite of connoisseurs of dialogue comedy, but it proved too complicated, and he dropped it in favour of the approach he'd created for *Annie Hall*, having him introduce everyone in voice-over.

Reshoots finished on 9 May, at which point Jean-Luc Godard came to New York to film an interview with Allen, who agreed because it gave him a chance to meet a director he respected highly. It was doubly difficult to refuse, then, when Godard asked him to take a role in his planned version of *King Lear*. He'd sold it to producer Menahem Golan of Cannon as a major modern production of the play, adapted by Norman Mailer and depicting Lear as a Mafia boss, played by Marlon Brando, with Allen as the Fool. When Brando turned down the role of Don Learo, Lee Marvin and Dustin Hoffman were mooted, as well as Orson Welles, Joseph Losey and Mailer himself, with his daughter Kate as Cordelia. Peter Sellers and Molly Ringwald were also inducted into the project. By the time Godard broached the idea with Allen, most of his potential stars were either dead or had turned him down; Burgess Meredith would eventually play the mad old man as a modern travelling culture expert with a vague resemblance to Lear.

Allen turned up at the Brill Building to find a cameraman, a sound recordist, a grip and the director, dressed in a bathrobe and smoking a cigar. 'I had the uncanny feeling I was being directed by Rufus T. Firefly,' he said. 'You know, where Groucho is supposed to be the great genius, and nobody has the nerve to challenge him?' As to the subject of the film, Godard was 'very elusive. First, he said it was going to be about a Learjet that crashes on an island. Then he said he wanted to interview everyone who had done *King Lear*, from Kurosawa to the Royal Shakespeare. Then he said I could say whatever I wanted to say.' For reasons Allen couldn't fathom, Godard put him in a Picasso T-shirt and filmed him entangled in celluloid. The sequence appeared at the end of the film when it showed at the 1987 Cannes Festival and in January 1988 at a single small New York cinema. Allen, who had decided immediately that it was 'a very silly movie, a very *foolish* movie', never saw it; nor, apparently, the thirty-minute interview with Godard, *Meetin' WA*, which appeared on the festival circuit in 1988.

Allen also received an unexpected invitation from tenor Placido Domingo to direct him in a filmed version of Puccini's *La Bohème* in Rome for the head of French Gaumont, Daniel Toscan du Plantier. He had produced Fellini's *Orchestra Rehearsal*, *City of Women* and *And the Ship Sails on*, as well as a film Allen much admired, Antonioni's *Identification of a Woman*, from which he admitted copying the idea of Bea fogbound with her boyfriend in *Radio Days*. In 1979 Toscan du Plantier made *Don Giovanni* in Venice with Joseph Losey, a box-office hit, after which Francesco Rosi adapted *Carmen*. For Allen to do *La Bohème* was a long shot, and, predictably, it didn't come off, mainly because his contract with Orion committed him to a picture a year, which left little time for such complex projects. Luigi Comencini made the film with black American soprano Barbara Hendricks.

Farrow and Allen had created a good working relationship, but their private life was less congenial. The idea of having a child of their own kept being pushed into the future. Though still doubtful about the other seven children, Allen remained affectionate towards Dylan, and even discussed the possibility of sharing a home with Farrow and her family. Farrow proposed he move into her Langham apartment, but he insisted it was too small: any place they shared must have his own wing or floor where he could escape to work. And anyway, he could never live on the West Side.

As an alternative, he suggested he buy a larger place for all of them, with the Langham apartment kept as a 'back-up', but Farrow pointed out that under New York's rent-control laws she could only keep the place at its relatively low rental as long as it was her primary residence. 'Well, you'll have to work that out,' Allen said dismissively. Mia started looking for East Side residences big enough for the whole family. A large house with a garden on 73rd Street seemed ideal, but at the last minute it was taken off the market.

Allen found a role for eleven-year-old Fletcher in *Radio Days* as young Joe's confederate in stealing the Jewish charity funds. His biggest scene took place under the pier at Rockaway, on a day which looks sunny on film but was in fact icy. Fletcher, whom Allen took to the set each day in the limo, arrived back home exhausted, and described how he'd been forced to hang around in his thin forties costume with nothing to eat or drink while Allen and the crew huddled in their down jackets and had hot soup.

Allen was apologetic when Farrow taxed him about this, but a few days later Fletcher again came home disturbed. Allen had let him watch some rushes in which, in a scene cut from the final version, Sally passionately kisses a soldier goodbye at a railway station. Farrow felt it was thoughtless of him to let her son see his mother in so revealing a moment, even if she was acting. The boy also carried home tales of an actress showing surprising affection towards Allen on the set.

Things came to a head when Fletcher asked Farrow if she and Allen could both attend his sixth-grade graduation. On a walk around Manhattan, Farrow raised the subject. 'I have to think about whether you have any right to ask me that,' Allen said shortly. She never mentioned it again, but after the graduation, which Allen didn't attend, she noticed a pronounced chill in the boy's relationship with his common-law stepfather.

Brooding on his balcony in the winter of 1987, Allen might have reflected that the contrast between his situation then and that of a decade before could scarcely have been more striking.

In 1977, the year of *Annie Hall*, he'd been confident in his contract with United Artists, secure that he could depend on their long-term financial backing. Now his new studio partner, Orion, was stumbling. As its revenues sagged, so did its share price, and hostile takeovers were threatened monthly. Early in 1988 the company would be temporarily bailed out by a $250 million injection of funds from financier John Kluge, a friend of Arthur Krim. This gave 68 per cent of Orion, and effective control, to Kluge, a businessman who could not be expected to put creative questions before the safety of his investment.

A decade before, Allen's competitors for public attention had been, by his standards, the work of intellectual pygmies: *Star Wars*, *Close Encounters of the Third Kind*, *The Turning Point*, *Saturday Night Fever* – the kind of movies Sid Perelman dismissed as 'fantasies for ribbon clerks'. By comparison, his films had seemed uniquely human and complex. Their worth excused even the élitist view of life and the private psychosexual obsessions on which they turned. In *Time*, Richard Schickel had hailed Allen's 'comedies of urban manners shadowed by his rueful recognition of those abiding sexual confusions he has always observed with a unique blend of irony and compassion'.

In 1987, however, American cinema had no shortage of witty comedies, like writer/director James L. Brooks' *Broadcast News*, in which East Coast intellectuals bandied quips at least as sharp as anything in *Annie Hall*, or romances like *Moonstruck*, in which Norman Jewison rather than Allen highlighted the affinities between New York and Fellini's Rome. Both films were nominated for Oscars against *Radio Days*. *Moonstruck* took three awards, including Best Original Screenplay (John Patrick Shanley). *Radio Days* won nothing.

Nor was Allen any closer in 1987 to resolving the 'abiding

sexual confusions' of the decade before. At the time of *Annie Hall* he had at least been at relative liberty in emotional terms. Now, the relationship with Mia was reeling under the effect of children. Contemplating the rubber snakes scattered among the balcony's shrubs, another vain subterfuge of his landscapers to frighten off the omnipresent pigeons, and an irritating one – a snake had slipped off and landed on the head of his neighbour below, who had sued – it might have seemed to Allen that Farrow and her brood represented just such a disturbing presence in his life: serpents in what had once been a paradise of peace and productive work in the Manhattan sky.

Sometime around then, Allen realised definitively that the relationship with Farrow was over. One way or another, by whatever means necessary, he needed to clear out his life, move on to other projects, other vistas. And other women?

22

September, Another Woman and Oedipus Wrecks

This is overblown. It's too emotional, it's maudlin. Your dreams may be meaningful but to the objective observer, it's so embarrassing.

Marion to Paul about his efforts at creative writing, in *Another Woman*

As soon as Farrow learned that Allen proposed to shoot an old script, once intended as a stage play, about a group of people in a country house at the end of the summer, she began urging him to use Frog Hollow as a location, as he had used the Langham apartment for *Hannah and her Sisters*. The wooden house could hardly be bettered, she argued. What was more, it had a lake, forests, pastures; everything he could need in the way of exteriors. And – the clincher, this – she desperately needed the rent his company would pay for its use. Allen tentatively agreed, though he'd visualised the location as Vermont, which was more brooding and Scandinavian. Connecticut imposed its own softer reality, as upstate New York had on *A Midsummer Night's Sex Comedy*. He began to see the film as more elegiac, less stern. Not Strindberg but Chekhov.

But in moving away from his first impulse, Allen also cut himself off from whatever gave the story its topicality and relevance. For the first time, a new work would emerge with the faded feel of a revival. It would lead to his first major box-office and critical disaster – the nightmare he'd told Ingmar Bergman he had never experienced. At least the technique and style of *Interiors*, the film of Allen's which the new production most resembled, had lived up to the confidence of its pretensions; but Douglas Brode, author of the most detailed survey of Allen's work, would find this piece 'shoddy and embarrassing in terms of craftsmanship, both writing and directing'. In *New York* magazine, David Denby, normally a staunch supporter, would lament that 'neither the characterisation nor the story is idiosyncratic enough to make up for Allen's alarmingly solemn tone, and much of the writing is either baldly functional or soap-opera flossy.'

Lane (Farrow), daughter of retired Hollywood star Diane, fetches up at the house in the wake of an attempted suicide after the break-up of her relationship with a married man. She's joined there by Stephanie, an old friend who, beginning to feel her age, has fled husband and children to keep Lane company through the summer. They attract Howard, a middle-aged widower and French teacher, and recently divorced New York adman Peter, who's using the summer to write a novel about his father, a victim of the anti-Communist blacklist.

Lane, it emerges, has never recovered from a scandal in her adolescence, when she killed her mother's gangster lover, a crime for which, being only fourteen, she was very lightly punished. This, and the death of her father, had made her morbidly reliant on men. 'I always felt there was a fatal element of hunger in your last affair,' her mother observes, accurately if unhelpfully. A woman with Lane's history might have been expected to be seductive, but Allen makes Farrow a frump, with glasses, untidy hair to her shoulders, and a wardrobe in which every garment seems to have been dyed with weak tea. Her emotional development has frozen at the moment of her childhood trauma.

When Diane arrives with her new husband Lloyd, a physicist, to spend a few weeks before wintering in Palm Beach, the stage is set for another of Allen's dramas about three women and their differing sexual and emotional needs: A loves B, who loves C, who loves D, who doesn't want to get involved. Stephanie, feeling unloved and unwanted, has been flirting with Peter, who as the film opens has fallen for her. Lane, who had an affair with Peter before Stephanie arrived, now can't re-arouse his interest; but Howard is devoted to her. Diane, the third, other-directed woman of the trio, is interested only in herself, in which the devoted Lloyd doggily abets her.

Captivating or exasperating everyone with her flamboyant behaviour and Hollywood anecdotes, Diane sets the plot in motion. Peter is ready to abandon his novel to ghost her memoirs: 'The shooting is a book in itself,' he says with an adman's longing. Lane, anxious to sell the house, which she's always regarded as her property, and already appalled when she surprises Peter and Stephanie embracing while she's showing potential buyers round, is driven to the edge by Diane's casual announcement that she's decided to reclaim the house and settle down there.

Lane furiously reveals that it was her mother, and not she, who shot the lover. Diane shrugs this off as easily as she has everything else: 'There are probably things I would do differently if I had them to do over again,' she says, 'but I don't.' All the same, the threat of revelation causes her to change her plans. She and Lloyd disappear towards Florida, Peter returns to Madison Avenue and Howard to the bottle, while Lane and Stephanie, reconciled, begin planning Lane's sale of the house.

The background to the plot owes something to the sensational stabbing in 1958 of Johnny Stompanato, former bodyguard of gang boss Mickey Cohen and lover of Hollywood star Lana Turner. Turner's thirteen-year-old daughter Cheryl Crane admitted the crime, but after hearing testimony about Stompanato's mob connections and brutality towards Turner, artfully orchestrated by celebrity attorney Jerry Geisler, the jury deliberated for only twenty minutes before returning a verdict of Justifiable Homicide. Vengefully, the Stompanato family leaked Turner's hysterically erotic letters to her lover, and claimed that she and not Crane had stabbed him when he threatened to leave her.

Allen saw Lane and Diane as a Hollywood mother and daughter, not unlike Maureen O'Sullivan and Mia. Underlining this, he invited O'Sullivan to play Diane opposite Farrow as Lane. For Lloyd, he chose rotund Charles Durning. Christopher Walken was Peter, Dianne Wiest Stephanie. He chose to call the film *September* because he felt the title 'doesn't suggest anything to anybody until the story is over', but most audiences grasped the implication of summer ending, people returning to their responsibilities after the vacation, and of others entering the autumn of their lives.

The delays in finishing *Radio Days* pushed back the start date of the autumnal *September* too close to winter for a shoot at Frog Hollow, so Santo Loquasto, to Farrow's disappointment, recreated her house at the Astoria studios. Originally he included a fake surrounding landscape, complete with trees, to be seen through its windows, but after *Radio Days*, in which three-dimensional artificial backgrounds – notably the Broadway signs seen from the King Cole Room roof – had caused interminable technical problems, Allen dictated that nothing outside should be visible. Venetian blinds covered all the house's windows, imposing a claustrophobic character some audiences would find stifling.

Shooting began in October, with Allen clearly worried about the script. 'We reshot every single scene as we went along,' recalls Farrow, 'sometimes four or five times. Woody rewrote major scenes overnight or during lunch, while the whole cast scrambled to learn the rewrites and to make the long speeches and sometimes ponderous dialogue sound credible and fresh. Fine actors fell by the wayside, including my mother. Parts were recast.' When line producer Bobby Greenhut protested that Allen had promised no reshoots, Allen said, 'Reshoots are what you do *after* the film's finished. These are revisions.'

It was a standing joke in the Allen unit that just beyond the commemorative wall in Arlington listing all the Americans who died in Vietnam is another, larger, wall listing every recast on an Allen film. Christopher Walken was the first actor to leave *September*. Allen found him too nervy for the unsure, passive Peter, and brought in playwright and sometime actor Sam Shepard. Once he had assembled a rough cut of the film, it became clear that Maureen O'Sullivan, whose casting looked good on paper, couldn't carry the part of Diane. Before he was out of the cutting room Allen had decided, to the horror of Greenhut and Orion, to discard the whole film and reshoot it from scratch. Farrow and Wiest remained, but O'Sullivan bowed out with a sudden diplomatic attack of pneumonia. Charles Durning also left, as did Shepard, who later lumped Allen in with Robert Altman among directors who, he says, 'have no understanding of actors whatsoever. They're piss-poor as actors' directors. They may be great film-makers, but they have no respect for actors. Individually, each understands zip about acting. Allen knows even less than Altman, which is nothing.' Denholm Elliott moved philosophically from playing Lloyd to Howard – 'Same performance, more money,' he remarked. Reliable Sam Waterston replaced Shepard, after a good deal of rewriting to substitute his East Coast polish for Shepard's rangy western gawkiness.

To replace O'Sullivan, Allen wanted Gena Rowlands, wife of John Cassavetes, but she turned down the role, feeling the character's showbiz extravagance would make it too great a stretch for her. Allen substituted Elaine Stritch, the Broadway comedienne perhaps best known for her role in Stephen Sondheim's *Company*, in which the boozy hymn 'The Ladies who Lunch' used her ground-glass voice to good effect. Allen had seen her on television in a film called *The Original Cast Recording*, which documented the making of the *Company* album, an abrasive occasion of which the centrepiece is Stritch's marathon attempt to achieve the definitive version of 'Ladies who Lunch'. Anyone so responsive to a director's demands could only be attractive to Allen.

September's classic three-act construction remained nakedly evident. Virtuoso writing might have brought it to life, but the dialogue, aiming for something between realism and poetry, often slipped into bathos, particularly in scenes between the unhappy lovers. 'How will you drive home?' Lane asks the maudlin drunk Howard. 'The same way I always do – thinking of you,' he says. After confessing that she doesn't love him, Lane asks rhetorically, 'Why Peter and not you? No reason worthy of you.' Quizzed by Stephanie as to why he seduced Lane, David explains, 'You do funny things when you feel empty inside.'

In both *September* and the films which immediately followed it, Allen introduced characters who worked in challenging disciplines outside the arts, perhaps in the hope of imposing a sense of Significance. Unfortunately, physicists and philosophers are more likely to be interested in wine, women and song than in the problems of the universe, and the studied dialogue Allen gave to such people invariably rang false, as when Lloyd confides to David that the universe is 'haphazard, morally neutral and unimaginably violent'.

Lloyd's profundity filters down into even casual references to technology by others. Stephanie explains that her husband is a radiologist: 'He takes X-rays, but I never let him take them of me because he'd see things he wouldn't understand and he'd be terribly hurt.'

The consoling ending, in which Stephanie talks Lane out of suicide and reassures her about her future, is a gloss on *Uncle Vanya* and *Three Sisters*, but without Chekhov's poignancy. 'Tomorrow will come,' says Stephanie, 'and you'll find some distractions. You'll sell this place and move back to the city. You'll work. You'll fall in love. And maybe it will work out and maybe it won't. But you'll find a million petty things to keep you going.' It ends with the two women sitting at the kitchen table like Vanya and Sonya, getting on with the paperwork. 'It's chilly,' says Stephanie. 'In a few days it will be September.'

Discreet half-heard jazz or well-bred piano versions by Bernie Leighton of 'Slow Boat to China', 'What'll I Do?', 'Who?', 'Moonglow' and 'I'm Confessin'' contributed to an atmosphere closer to Somerset Maugham than to Chekhov. The visual tone too was etiolated by Loquasto's cakeshop settings, all beige, rose and cream. Even when a thunderstorm plunges the house into darkness for the second act and Diane drunkenly uses her Ouija board to communicate with her murdered lover and ex-husband, the golden candlelight illuminates only more awkward trysts, and losers contemplating the miseries of existence through three fingers of scotch.

The film's lassitude echoed Allen's. Film-making had lost its pleasure. He thought nostalgically of Bergman's life now that he'd all but retired. 'Do you know how he spends his day?' he asked a friend. 'He wakes up early in the morning, he sits quietly for a time and listens to the ocean, he has breakfast, he works, he has an early lunch, he screens a different movie every day, he has an early dinner, and then he reads the newspaper, which would be too depressing for him to read in the morning.' One can almost hear Allen's envious sigh.

Among Allen's troubles was his dwindling interest in sex. Increasingly, only the most provocative behaviour on Farrow's part could arouse him. As a result, he was taken aback to discover towards the end of shooting *September* that she was pregnant. 'It was an accident,' he admitted. 'We were both surprised. It was nothing that we were planning particularly.' He insists that neither of them wanted an abortion, but there's no doubting that their reactions were confused. Farrow, then forty-one, revelled in the thought of another child, this time a biological one. On the other hand, she regretted that the father was Allen, since she'd come to feel their relationship was doomed. She told him as much in his dressing room at the Astoria studios. 'You've been cold and cruel,' she said, 'and I want a more conventional relationship.'

He was, she recalls, 'surprised and angry', but in the end simply chose to ignore her demands. '*September* ended,' she says, 'and he kept right on coming over to my apartment every single day. He started showing up at five-thirty and six in the morning. He'd be sitting in my kitchen hours before anybody was up. He came to Frog Hollow too, even overnight. I didn't know what to do. We politely ignored each other while he followed Dylan around. And then, after some weeks of this, I lost my resolve, the line blurred, and we were together again. I needed him and I loved him.'

These serial separations and reconciliations, later to be the theme of *Husbands and Wives*, became endemic. 'When Woody and Mia fought and broke up,' recalls their nanny Kristi Groetke, 'she would run to the locksmith to get the locks changed, and she would also get a new phone number. Then she would weaken and call him – or he would somehow locate her new number and call her. A reconciliation would occur, and with renewed trust she would give him the new number and keys. Until the next time. At moments like this I couldn't help thinking that Mia's behaviour was crazy and certainly not the way I would conduct my own love life.' Later, Farrow would accuse Allen in a secretly recorded phone conversation of losing sexual interest in her after the birth of their son Satchel in December 1987. 'You had become turned off me after Satchel,' she said. 'It was the Caesarean. And your disliking of Satchel. All that stuff, I guess.' Allen acknowledged that some aspects of pregnancy and child-rearing did revolt him, specifically a device to convince the baby he was drinking breast milk, whereby a tube attached to the mother's nipple led to a bottle of formula on her shoulder. For her part, Farrow initially omitted to put Allen's name as father on Satchel's birth certificate, an error that took three days to correct.

Farrow was given some hope of relief in Allen's hostility towards children by his growing affection for – indeed fascination with – Dylan. 'We'd hear the doorbell's short, loud burst, then the turn of the lock, the heavy slam of the glass and wrought-iron front door, and he was in our kitchen. With barely a nod to me or the other kids, he headed for Dylan. With his mouth wide open, bigger than a grin, his eyebrows high over the black frames of his glasses, it was a face unaccustomed to its own expression – an expression so asymmetrical, large, unguarded, hungry, and foreign, that I would blink to make the strangeness pass, as he scooped Dylan out of her high chair and carried her off into another room.' In a line cut from *Crimes and Misdemeanors*, Allen was to remark, 'The future of the world is in little girls.'

Ever since Farrow had told Allen some years before that a psycho-analyst had the apartment next door to hers at the Langham, they'd made a game of spotting distinguished patients as they arrived and departed. In several of his films men eavesdrop on the analysis of women, and Farrow joked about how much he would enjoy bugging the doctor's office. Allen responded to this joke with disapproval, but the idea grew into a short story, the plot of which he would eventually use for *Everyone Says I Love You*: a man overhears a woman confessing her secret desires to her shrink, and uses his knowledge of them to seduce her and fulfil all her longings. Feeling the piece was in bad taste, Allen shelved it, only to dust it off after *September*, transforming it into drama and making the listener a woman who, in the traditional comeuppance of all eavesdroppers, hears no good of herself. He called it *Another Woman*.

Embarking on another drama immediately after *September* was a calculated risk. *September* hadn't been released when Allen started shooting in October 1987, and Orion still had every reason to believe that the earlier film would do well. Were that to happen,

Another Woman could be the film that sealed Allen's new standing as a dramatic film-maker. On the other hand, that advance might be fatally impaired if he played safe with another comedy in the style of *Hannah and her Sisters*. Orion, while turning down his original idea to shoot in black and white, were happy enough to let him go ahead with *Another Woman*, since *Hannah* was still coining money all over the world. For all they knew, *September* might be just as big a hit, though Allen admitted privately, 'I knew full well it wouldn't make a dime. Not a dime.'

The central character of *Another Woman*, Marion Post (Gena Rowlands), teaches German philosophy in a women's college. She's fifty, and married to a cardiologist, Ken (Ian Holm), whom she poached away from his first wife in a messy divorce. As a young woman she lived with her college professor (Philip Bosco), only to discard him when she felt herself stifled intellectually – a repeat of the Lee/Frederick relationship in *Hannah*. He later committed suicide. A novelist, Larry Lewis (Gene Hackman), had been so enamoured of Marion that he based a character in one of his novels on her – she has a copy on her shelves, but has never bothered to read it. All in all, apparently a potent blend of passion and intellect.

As she takes up the story in her cool narration, Marion is moving into a small apartment she's rented as an office to write a new book. A psychoanalyst has the suite next door, and she discovers she can hear his consultations through an air vent, in particular the confessions of a pregnant young woman, Hope (Farrow), who appears dangerously close to suicide. Hope fascinates Marion, and in one of the film's many Bergmanesque moments she dreams of discussing Hope's case with the doctor.

DOCTOR: What would you say she's suffering from?
MARION: Self-deception.
DOCTOR: Good. It's a little general . . .
MARION: But I don't think she can part with her lies. Not that she doesn't want to.
DOCTOR: It's precisely that she doesn't want to. When she wants to, she will.

MARION: It's all happening so fast.
DOCTOR: I have to hurry. I'm trying to prevent her killing herself.
MARION: I don't think she would.
DOCTOR: She's already begun.

Dreams increasingly intrude on Marion's life as she tries to write her book. She remembers her mother, another cool intellectual, fascinated with German poetry, and her father, a historian who tried to impose logic on his children, but in the process turned her into an overachieving perfectionist and her brother into a dissatisfied failure.

By contrast with the rigour of her work and these troubling fantasies, Marion's life outside the office comes to seem increasingly meaningless. She and Ken enjoy a polite but sexless intimacy which contrasts with the ribaldry of their best friends Lydia (Blythe Danner) and her husband, who joke about their penchant for having sex at unconventional times and in uncomfortable places. Asked by Marion if he would ever make love to her in their kitchen, Ken replies coolly, 'Would you want me to? I wouldn't have taken you for the hardwood floor type.'

Marion's own family is disorganised. Her father (John Houseman, in his last role), facing death, is racked by a sense of futility. Her brother Paul (Harris Yulin) is about to be divorced by his wife (Frances Conroy). Marion enjoys a warm relationship with her teenage stepdaughter Laura (Martha Plimpton), but doesn't realise that, since Marion caught her *in flagrante* with her boyfriend, the girl has begun to resent her judgemental attitude.

Running into an old friend, Claire (Sandy Dennis), now an actress, Marion so charms her director husband Jack (Jacques Levy) that Claire turns on her, accusing her of seducing one of her earlier lovers and now trying to do the same with him. We quickly learn that, while people who don't know Marion regard her as a paragon, others think her a snob and a prig, as they do Ken, pompously given to phrases like 'I accept your condemnation.' Marion receives her ultimate comeuppance when she meets Hope by chance in an antique shop where she's weeping hopelessly in front of a print (presumably) of Gustav Klimt's painting *Hope*, which shows a massively pregnant nude, not unlike herself, being menaced by the figure of Death. Marion invites her to lunch, and in the guise of giving advice pours out her own despair. In full spate, she spots Lydia across the restaurant, only to discover she's enjoying an intimate lunch with Ken, who is obviously her lover. Back in her office, Marion hears Hope describe her to the shrink in terms which make it clear she pities her. Resolving to spend the last part of her life more openly and less judgementally than the first, Marion ditches Ken, and vows to repair her relationship with her brother.

Gena Rowlands had rung Allen while he was writing *Another Woman* to say she still hoped to work with him despite having turned down *September*. She didn't mention that other actors had warned her that working with Allen was no picnic. 'Don't save your best stuff for the close-ups,' Michael Caine advised. 'He's not going to shoot any close-ups.' Allen promptly cast Rowlands as Marion – the character, he later said, who of all those in his work most resembled him intellectually. Ben Gazzara started as Ken, after George C. Scott had refused even to read the script. When Gazzara proved unsatisfactory, Allen replaced him with Ian Holm. The role of Marion's sister-in-law Lynn originally went to Mary Steenburgen. Dianne Wiest was to have played Hope, but became ill. Allen replaced her with Jane Alexander, then decided she wouldn't do either, and asked Farrow to step in, changing the script to incorporate her pregnancy. When the baby was born halfway through shooting, she had to play the rest with heavy padding.

Notwithstanding these problems, *Another Woman* is a far more diverting, less claustrophobic film than either *September* or *Interiors*. It shows Allen beginning to manipulate the tropes of Strindbergian drama, whereas until then he had been content simply to mimic Bergman's use of them. Marion imagines some incidents from her life acted out as scenes from a play – an idea which appeared momentarily at the end of *Annie Hall*, but which here has more relevance and force. Its use emphasises the film's resemblances to *Wild Strawberries*, *Face to Face* and *Autumn Son-*

ata, but the Bergmanesque chill is relieved by the New York background and Marion's matter-of-fact commentary, which often recalls an analysand's confessions to her therapist.

Despite this, *Another Woman* left audiences depressed or dismissive. With Carlo DiPalma laid up after a stomach operation, Allen was more than happy when Bergman's cameraman (and an old intimate of Farrow's) Sven Nykvist agreed to light the film. But Nykvist could do little to alleviate the intrinsic drabness of *Another Woman*'s putty-coloured costumes and decor. Allen added to the gloom by ordering him to shoot always out of direct sunlight, and by constructing a music score from doleful show tunes of the twenties and thirties like Kurt Weill's 'Bilbao Song'. For the main titles he used Erik Satie's *Gymnopédie No. 3*, evidently not realising that dozens of film-makers had already done so, including the director of a television advertisement for Gallo wines, which employed a particularly soupy pop arrangement by Vangelis. Audiences for *Another Woman* giggled, assuming a musical comment by Allen on the resemblance between Marion's unexamined life and the anodyne world of commercials; but insiders realised that Allen, who never watched network TV, simply didn't know the Gallo ad existed.

Early screenings for focus groups confirmed Orion's worst fears about *Another Woman*. Younger audiences found the characters too old – did people of fifty *really* make love on the kitchen floor? – while more mature viewers accepted the sex but doubted that even New Yorkers chatted about Rilke and Heidegger at cocktail parties. All were united in their dislike of Marion, who even when Rowlands is at her most engaging came over as humourless and glum. Orion contemplated the forthcoming release of *September* with a sense of despair.

Allen's first child was born on 19 December 1987, by Caesarean section. He named him Satchel O'Sullivan, after Leroy 'Satchel' Paige, the legendary black baseball pitcher who was barred from the major leagues until 1948, when he was past his prime. Farrow was doubtful about the name, but preferred it to Allen's first choice, Ingmar. Exhausted from the operation and the demands of the new baby, who proved fractious and a constant crier, she couldn't resume work on *Another Woman* for a month.

Satchel's birth coincided with the release of *September*, which proved to be Allen's first major disaster. For every critic who was kind, like Vincent Canby in the *New York Times*, a dozen others hooted in derision. J. Hoberman demolished the film comprehensively in the *Village Voice*, calling it 'as houseproud as it is housebound. When a realtor appears with a pair of prospective buyers, you feel like getting up and selling your seat.' He went on relentlessly:

> Forget about the imploding universe. Here again is the familiar galaxy of Allen types: the manipulative, domineering mother (played by Stritch as an amalgam of *Interiors*' Geraldine Page and Maureen Stapleton); the neurotic, unfulfilled women, their faces tight masks of agonised ambivalence; the sensitive, predatory men, morose and self-justifying. Everybody is painfully self-conscious, making knowing references to Kurosawa and Art Tatum, oddly denatured, and doggedly self-pitying. Set in a yawn-inducing miasma of guilt and unconsummated sex, it plays like unfunny Nichols and May. Allen brings his camera brutally close to his performers – for much of the film the spectator feels like a fly on the fourth wall of a Brobdingnagian stage. The effect is acutely embarrassing; after a while the screen seems to crinkle up with crow's feet.

Initially shown in only four American cities, *September* would gross less than half a million dollars in the US on its $10 million budget. Some cinema chains, despite contracts with Orion, declined to give it anything but a perfunctory release. In Boston, the USA Cinemas group wrangled for months until Orion agreed to let it open the film in just one house, rather than two, as required by their contract. Allen's disappointment was slightly modified after the American Academy and Institute of Arts and Letters made him an honorary member in 1987, when he took the place vacated by Orson Welles. He also contributed a controversial piece to the op-ed pages of the *New York Times* in February 1988 condemning Israel for its oppression of the Palestinians and its torture of political prisoners. He urged that friends of Israel, notably the United States, apply financial pressure to 'bring this wrong-headed approach to a halt'. His stand won him some kudos in liberal political circles, but strengthened the view of many Jews that he had turned his back on his roots.

Nobody needed a comedy hit more than Allen, particularly since 1989 saw the release of *Parenthood* by Ron Howard, and Rob Reiner's *When Harry Met Sally*, both of which, in their superficially loose structure and emphasis on the humour of daily life rather than on 'situation', threatened to out-Woody Woody. Written by Lowell Ganz and Babaloo Mandel, and Nora Ephron respectively, both used performers who'd worked for Allen or would do so in the future: Dianne Wiest, Carrie Fisher, Billy Crystal, Mary Steenburgen, Martha Plimpton. (Ephron herself has cameos among the wedding guests in *Crimes and Misdemeanors* and at a gallery opening in *Mighty Aphrodite*.)

Many Californian film people still dismissed Allen as an East Coast phenomenon of little significance to the industry. Lucy Fisher, production manager of Francis Ford Coppola's San Francisco-based Zoetrope company, said, 'People are sick of watching actors walking around New York talking about their personal relationships.' But the Howard and Reiner films showed that Allen's style of ensemble comedy could be adapted successfully to the demands of a mass audience, and Hollywood added 'Woody Allen-type comedy' to its list of acceptable film categories. This encouraged East Coast comedians who'd had their start in television series like *Saturday Night Live* to try their luck with similar material in films. In particular, Steve Martin featured in *Parenthood* and wrote and starred in *LA Story*, even introducing into the film some of the mysticism which would suffuse *Oedipus Wrecks* and *Alice*.

Closest of all to Allen was Paul Mazursky, another renegade whose limping career suggests the problems Allen would have encountered had he chosen to work in Hollywood rather than New York. His autobiographical *Next Stop Greenwich Village*

(1976) has all the Allen trademarks, down to a *yenta* mother (played by Shelley Winters). Like Allen, Mazursky had a penchant for the European cinema, and made a number of films derived from Continental models, including *Willie and Phil* (1980), based on Truffaut's *Jules et Jim*, and *Down and out in Beverly Hills* (1985), derived from Renoir's *Boudu Sauvé des Eaux*. A friend of Fellini's, he persuaded him to play a cameo in *Alex in Wonderland*, his own gloss on 8½.

Still convinced his future lay in drama, Allen nevertheless compromised early in 1988 and agreed to reactivate a comedy project conceived with Bobby Greenhut some years before, a *film à sketches* on the theme of love in New York. American producers never tired of trying to lure Fellini to make a film in America, and for a while it seemed he might agree to do a sequel to his highly successful *Fellini Roma* set in New York, as one of three different views of the Big Apple by two European film-makers and one from the city itself. He finally decided he didn't know enough about the language and gestures of typical Americans to make a film about them, but the idea persisted.

That Allen should be the American representative on 'New York Tales', as it was then called, was a foregone conclusion, and he remained attached to the project as the Europeans were replaced by Americans, first by Martin Scorsese and Steven Spielberg, then, when Spielberg dropped out to concentrate on producing the animated feature *Who Framed Roger Rabbit*, by Francis Ford Coppola. Orion, reluctantly, agreed to distribute.

For his section of the film, Allen resuscitated a short story he'd drafted years before. New York lawyer Sheldon Mills, *né* Millstein, is dating blonde *goyische* divorcee Lisa, a choice his mother, Sadie, the classic *yenta*, doesn't welcome. Hoping to thaw her, Sheldon takes his mother and his soon-to-be-adoptive family to a magic show, where Sadie, participating in a vanishing trick, disappears. Freed of her stifling influence, Sheldon is a new man, especially in bed, but he's reduced to snivelling incompetence almost immediately when Sadie appears in the sky, a giant floating head that bullies him and dispenses embarrassing revelations about his childhood.

Desperate, Sheldon consults a psychic, Treva, who puts him

through fruitless exorcisms and rituals before tearfully admitting that she's just a nice Jewish girl who's faking it in the paranormal business. Returning home to find that a humiliated Lisa has fled, Sheldon realises he's in love with Treva, whom he introduces to his mother. '*Her* I like,' Sadie says. 'Now I'll come down.' The next minute, she's going through Sheldon's baby pictures with her daughter-in-law to be.

Allen called the forty-one-minute story *Oedipus Wrecks*. Such knowing puns comforted fans of his comedy, as did the familiar themes: psychoanalysis, resentment of parents, guilt over his preference for *shiksa* women, mingled fear and scepticism about life after death, a hatred of celebrity. Well-known faces from earlier Allen films helped too: Allen as Sheldon, Farrow as Lisa, Julie Kavner as Treva. As Sadie, Allen lured out of retirement Mae Questel, whom he'd rediscovered for *Zelig*. Juliet Taylor advertised in Jewish retirement homes again for *Oedipus Wrecks*. Among the women who came forward was Jesse Keosian, who'd been Allen's biology teacher in PS 99. She brought such aplomb to the part of Sadie's stone-deaf companion Aunt Ciel, based on Allen's own maiden aunt, the character played by Dianne Wiest in *Radio Days*, that she went on to a belated career as a character actress and TV commercial performer.

Oedipus Wrecks doesn't simply take us back to *Radio Days* and *Hannah and her Sisters*, but to the very roots of Allen's career in *Take the Money and Run* and *Sleeper*. 'Sheldon' and 'Lisa' were the names he had given to the two black widow spiders in the deleted 'What Makes a Man a Homosexual?' segment of *Everything You Always Wanted to Know About Sex*. Sheldon wetting his finger and sticking it into the socket of an electric candelabra in a futile suicide attempt, or staring tearfully at a leg of chicken as he realises he loves Treva, who cooked it, are classic Woody *schtick*. So is his appalled reaction to the unannounced arrival in his staid office of Sadie and Ciel, dropping in after a matinee of *Cats*. When Sheldon's boss calls him back to an important meeting, Sadie explains conversationally to Ciel, 'This is Bates. The one with the mistress.' Her son cringes.

*   *   *

Dispirited by the reaction to *September*, Allen surprised Farrow by agreeing to go on a European holiday with the entire family after finishing principal photography on *Oedipus Wrecks*. (Hearing of Allen's block-booking of seats on Concorde, his father warned that if he kept spending money like that, he'd end up selling ribbons in a haberdashery.) Allen's regular assistant Jane Read Martin came along to manage the logistics. They began the trip in Norway, visiting the grave of the composer Edvard Grieg, for whom Allen felt an affinity – he would briefly consider his music to provide the score for his German Expressionist pastiche *Shadows and Fog* – and the museum devoted to Edvard Munch, whose *The Scream* seemed to many people emblematic of both Allen's and Bergman's view of life. They visited Sven Nykvist in Sweden before moving on to the Soviet Union, but after one day of Intourist guides and dismal food, Allen insisted they get on the next plane to *anywhere*. This proved to be Italy, where he felt more at home. They paused in Rome, where Allen concluded negotiations with the Co-Op Nordemiglia supermarket chain to do four commercials, and in Venice, which was fast becoming his preferred European city.

While Mia took the children on excursions, Allen lay on a succession of hotel beds and wrote the screenplay for his next film. Initially he'd been thinking about the story which was to become *Everyone Says I Love You*, an updated but downbeat *An American in Paris*, with Woody as an expatriate pursuing romance and fulfilment in the City of Light. By the time they arrived in London, he'd discarded this for the murder mystery he and Marshall Brickman discussed years before, in the run-up to *Annie Hall*. The idea of a confirmed optimist who unexpectedly falls from a window, leading to rival claims of suicide and homicide, developed into a cautionary tale of murder, guilt and retribution. According to Eric Lax, he contemplated calling the new film 'Dr Shenanigans', 'Decisions', 'Decisive Moments', 'Making a Killing', 'Two Lives', 'Anything Else', 'Crime and Vanity', 'High Crimes and Misdemeanors', 'The Lord's Prayer', 'Acts . . .', 'Moments . . .' and 'Scenes of Good and Evil', 'The Eyes of God', 'Windows of the Soul', 'Visions of the Soul', 'Dark Vision', 'The Sight of God',

'Glimmer of Hope', 'Hope and Darkness', 'Faint Hope', 'A Matter of Choice', 'Choices in the Dark', 'Decisive Points', 'Empty Choices' and 'Split Decisions'. His final choice was 'Brothers', the title under which he started shooting in October 1988.

The same month, *Another Woman* opened to reviews which, while not as negative as Orion had feared, were suffused with boredom and disappointment. Pauline Kael in the *New Yorker* acknowledged it as 'soaringly ambitious', but charged that 'nothing in the film has the slightest resonance'. Charles Taylor in New York's *SoHo Weekly*, under the heading 'Mild Strawberries', stigmatised *Another Woman* as another of 'Woody Allen's beige ensemble pieces'. In a piece that was to prove prescient, he continued, 'There is no one working in the movies right now who has ignored his talents as fully as Allen has. These sterile, aestheticised chamber dramas are phoney art, but their imprimatur of culture is what Allen regards as real art. He needs a dose of messy reality if he's going to revive himself, and he has to stop regarding his gifts – his wit, and his ability to recognise and kid our collective neuroses – as part of the vulgarity of modern culture that he's outgrown and now disdains.'

23

Crimes and Misdemeanors and Alice

Thou God seest me.

Traditional Protestant devotional motto

If one needed proof of the healing value of work for the troubled creator, one need look no further than the project Allen launched as 'Brothers'. He'd written it under the most dislocated of circumstances, in a series of European hotel rooms, and at a time when he'd just fathered a child, his first, with a woman he no longer loved. His last two films had been disasters. Yet the new film would be, in the words of David Denby in a *New York* review, his 'most ambitious and complexly organised film yet, swift, resourceful, exciting'. In the role of Cliff, a failed documentary film-maker, Allen would give one of his most carefully shaded performances, as well as one which betrayed his inner torment and the sense of futility pervading his life. 'Allen's Cliff is a witty man,' Denby would write, 'yet also one of the bitterest studies in failure ever put on the screen. Cliff puts himself and everyone else down. Rolling his eyes in disgust, Allen gives Cliff sarcasm without courage, intelligence without self-knowledge. Funny? Yes, but in an intentionally curdling way – the jokes are there to expose the weakness of the joker.'

In a variation on Allen's penchant for trios of sisters, women took a back seat to men in 'Brothers'. Judah Rosenthal (Martin Landau) is a respected ophthalmologist and worker for charity, his brother Jack (Jerry Orbach), a club owner with connections to organised crime. Equally polarised, Ben (Sam Waterston) is a rabbi facing blindness with resignation while his brother Lester (Alan Alda), arrogant and opinionated, is a millionaire TV producer. Judah is being pestered by Dolores (Anjelica Huston), with whom he's had a secret two-year affair, and who now threatens to ruin his life by revealing this to his wife Miriam (Claire Bloom). He appeals for help to Jack, who has her murdered. His complicity in the act throws Judah into a panic of guilt.

Caught in the moral maze between these four are film-maker Clifford Stern (Allen) and his sister Babs (Caroline Aaron), a doleful divorcee. Clifford is married to Wendy (Joanna Gleason), the sister of Ben and Lester, but feels more affinity with his sub-teen niece Jenny (Jenny Nichols). They lead the life of conspirators, sneaking out in the afternoon to see old movies. He counsels her not to listen to her teachers, and especially not to go into showbusiness: 'It's dog-eat-dog. Worse, it's dog-doesn't-return-other-dog's-calls.'

The original screenplay of 'Brothers' concentrated less on Judah and Ben than on Clifford, Babs, Jenny and Halley, a social worker Clifford becomes attracted to, who's married to a magazine editor. Suspecting that she's having an affair with someone else, Clifford pretends he's shooting a film so that he and Jenny can tail her – a variation on the murder mystery plot he'd been trying to use ever since *Annie Hall*. To be close to Halley, Clifford makes a film about the home for ex-vaudevillians where she works, and they become friends. After she throws him over he tries to seduce an actress (Sean Young), telling her he can put her in a film, but the affair collapses when, at Ben's daughter's wedding, they're revealed in a compromising position as a curtain is rung up unexpectedly. The film would have ended with Clifford resignedly catching a midnight movie with Jenny, a gaudy, escapist Esther Williams musical.

While he was shooting this version, Allen began to have second thoughts. Perhaps understandably, given his own personal dilemmas, he became preoccupied with the moral problems of Judah. He was also influenced by the unexpectedly subtle playing of Martin Landau in the role. Never more than a competent featured player, Landau had enjoyed a run of suavely epicene and grinning psychopaths in films like Hitchcock's *North by Northwest*, only to disappear into series TV with parts in the long-running *Mission: Impossible* and *Space* 1999. Since then his career had languished, until Francis Ford Coppola began its resuscitation in 1988 by casting him in *Tucker* as the shady financier who helps fund Jeff Bridges' dreams of becoming an automobile mogul. Allen originally cast Landau as Jack, Judah's crooked brother, but on reflection reassigned that part to Jerry Orbach. The result would be a moving and truthful dual performance from both men. It reveals the strengths of the brother we'd assumed to be weak, and the weakness of the apparently stronger Judah, who whines and agonises in guilt over his connivance in a murder. Jack unexpectedly emerges as undeluded and dignified, not pleased with his ability to arrange a killing, but sufficiently in control of his inner demons to accept the moral price: in short, the *mensch* he advises his brother to be.

Once he saw the first rough edited version, Allen decided to reorder the film to emphasise the characters' moral choices. He reshot almost everything in the Clifford/Halley section, making Halley a documentary producer for PBS and turning Clifford's geriatrics film into a profile of Lester which his brother-in-law tosses him as a favour. Clifford is also making a film about a saintly philosopher named Levy, and interests Halley in producing it. When both Clifford and Lester become attracted to her, it's Lester she chooses. Sean Young's actress character disappears altogether in this version. Babs' part too is diminished. She was originally seen trying to find a lover via the personal columns, and dating various people. All that remains is a single incident where she invites home a promising mate, only, she reveals, for him tie her to the bed and defecate on her.

As in the first version, the film ends with all the characters gathering at the wedding of Ben's daughter. Everyone who has elected for the moral high ground has lost out. Clifford's film is cancelled when Levy, for all his hopeful philosophy, unaccountably commits suicide. Wendy has also left him, and the arrival of a radiant Halley on the arm of Lester reduces him to near-suicidal depression. Ben is now completely blind. Judah, on the other hand, no longer feels any guilt about having had Dolores murdered. He leaves the party with his loving wife, already planning their daughter's wedding, while Clifford nurses a drink alone to the accompaniment of 'I'll Be Seeing You'.

Seeing and being seen became what Pauline Kael called the 'controlling metaphor' of the film, which Allen decided to call *Crimes and Misdemeanors* once it became known that a TV network was planning a series called *Brothers*. As an ophthalmologist, Judah's business is eyes and sight. Ben, who is Judah's patient, believes that a divine power oversees all. Judah visits his old home and flashes back to a childhood *seder* where his father warns that the Eye of God never closes. Clifford's camera is an eye that sees everything, particularly in the documentary about Lester, in which he spies on his subject seducing an actress (Daryl Hannah); Lester promptly fires him.

Crimes and Misdemeanors can be seen as a canter by Allen through familiar fields, but what sets it apart is the ease with which he orders his complex forces. The two threads of the story are skilfully interwoven and counterpointed, helped by contrasting streams of music: thirties tunes for Clifford, Halley and Lester, and, aptly, Schubert for Judah and Dolores. Clips from old Hollywood movies – Hitchcock's *Mr and Mrs Smith*, Frank Tuttle's *This Gun for Hire* – offer ironic comments on Judah's decision to break off with Dolores and then to have her killed. Above all, Sven Nykvist photographs New York in winter with a steely gravity that emphasises Allen's choice of locations: empty parks with bare trees, night-time streets lit with cold fluorescents, Judah's summerhouse, closed up, with the pools covered by tarpaulins, the windows shuttered, where he and Jack nervously circle round the idea of murder.

Clifford for once is a well-rounded Woody character, not simply a compendium of Allen's neuroses. Where his idea of a romantic evening with Halley – a bottle of champagne won as a festival prize, Chinese take-out, and *Singing' in the Rain* viewed on the editing machine in his cutting room – would have seemed the height of sophistication for Allen Felix in *Play it Again, Sam*, it now appears adolescent. One can see why Wendy finds him tedious, and is looking for a way out of their marriage. We even come to believe, uneasily, that Clifford is partly wrong about Lester, whom he parodies mercilessly in his documentary, comparing him to Mussolini and Francis the Talking Mule. Lester's nostrums about comedy – 'If it bends, it's funny. If it breaks, it isn't,' and 'Comedy is tragedy plus time,' a proposition borrowed from Steve Allen – are admittedly trite, but when Clifford quotes two lines from Emily Dickinson, Lester effortlessly completes the verse, suggesting a cultivated man under the veneer. Not for the first time, a scene in an Allen film recalls a Jules Feiffer panel, in this case an early strip where his archetypal *nebbish*, Bernard, overwhelmed by the suavity and erudition of a party guest's conversation, can only respond with a stream of insults. 'Let us define your terms,' responds the other, imperturbably.

While Allen was shooting *Crimes and Misdemeanors*, his team were dealing with the technical problems of perfecting the scenes of Sadie's floating head in *New York Stories*, a project Orion now eyed with some nervousness. The company's patchy record made them loath to release a film with such dubious chances of success. Eventually it passed to Disney's adult operation, Touchstone, who put it out in May 1989, to lacklustre reactions. Costing $19 million, it grossed only $4.7 million on its domestic release.

Even had Allen been able to expand *Oedipus Wrecks* into a full feature it probably would not have made money. But it did suffer from its juxtaposition with the Scorsese and Coppola episodes, both utterly different in character. Coppola's *Life With Zoe*, a whimsical tale of the twelve-year-old daughter of an internationally famous flautist who lives in the Sherry Netherland hotel, has her own credit cards and not only knows how to mix strawberry daiquiris but drinks them as well, was by common consent the weakest of the three, which many attributed to the fact that, alone in the group, Coppola didn't live or work in New York. In Scorsese's *Life Lessons*, Nick Nolte gave a ferocious performance as Lionel Dobie, a successful painter who feeds off the angst of his declining relationships to fuel his work. Writhing in humiliation at being ditched by the latest in a succession of young and sexy 'assistants' (Rosanna Arquette), he turns up the stereo and, as Puccini and Procul Harum roar, pours his masochistic frustration onto the squirming canvas in handfuls of paint. Anything which followed that was bound to seem tepid.

Plenty of people would have preferred Allen to stay in New York during the summer of 1989, including his old acquaintance, lawyer Alan Dershowitz, who had asked Allen to play him in Barbet Schroder's *Reversal of Fortune*, about his sensational defence of Claus von Bulow on charges of having poisoned his socialite wife. Allen turned him down, and instead took the family on another European trip. This time he hired a private jet, stocked with video movies and snacks. An advance guard made hotel reservations and laid on cars to ferry them to and from airports. Officials came on board to stamp their passports. The kids loved it, though whether Allen loved the kids remained doubtful, in Farrow's mind at least. She couldn't escape the sense that he felt anything could be solved by the application of money. He even availed himself of the professional shopper at Manhattan's premier toy store, F.A.O. Schwartz, to choose the children's Christmas gifts.

Towards her children with André Previn and the adopted Asian boys and girls, Allen remained distant. He was even allegedly offhand about Satchel, describing him, 'not entirely in jest', according to Farrow, as 'the little bastard' or 'the completely superfluous little bastard'. He was punctilious about his contribution to Farrow's household finances. Costs incurred by Satchel or Dylan were OK; anything for the other children was usually refused. Even grocery bills were scrutinised, with certain cereals deemed acceptable, others not. Her roles in his films were now almost her only source of income, so she desperately needed his help if she was to hang onto the Langham apartment. Despite this, she was already thinking of adopting yet another child. In September 1990, in response to her appeals for more concrete help with the children for which, married or not, they shared some responsibility, Allen gave Farrow a cheque for $1 million, a seventh of what he'd just received for some Japanese TV commercials.

Allen continued to show complete attention and affection towards Dylan, repeatedly suggesting that he become her adoptive father. When Farrow pointed out that the social services did not accept unmarried couples as parents, he suggested they fight this in the courts, and that he also adopt the twelve-year-old Moses, the only child in the family without an official father. Moses was delighted, but much legal work would be necessary before the adoption could be made a reality.

Allen's attachment to Dylan, who was then five, struck everyone who saw them together. On the set of his next film, *Alice*, in which Dylan played Mia Farrow's daughter, whom she and Joe Mantegna take to the Big Apple circus, she asked Allen if she could have a hotdog. He pointed out the prop man. 'If you want a hotdog,' he said, 'he'll bring you a hotdog. If you want cotton candy, he'll bring you cotton candy. If you want a Ferrari, he'll bring you . . . cotton candy.' Mantegna broke up.

Farrow later said that she found Allen's attention to Dylan excessive, indeed offensive, and warned him about it. 'You look at her in a sexual way,' she claims to have said. 'You fondle her. It's not natural. You're all over her. You don't give her any breathing room. You look at her when she's naked.' How much this was genuine solicitude and how much the hysterical imaginings of a scorned woman would later be the subject of much debate, although Allen would be cleared in court of any impropriety against Dylan.

Farrow also noticed that Soon-Yi, who had always looked on Allen with reserve, even dislike, was now more friendly towards him. He attended her sixteenth birthday party, and the two would often watch basketball games on TV, Allen explaining the finer points. He took her to see the Knicks, and in January 1990 magazines round the world ran a colour shot of the two of them on the sidelines, Allen obviously solicitous, Soon-Yi showing a great deal of leg in a miniskirt. To Farrow's surprise, Soon-Yi began to modify her ambition to be a psychologist, and talked of becoming an actress or a model. 'I asked Woody to please not encourage her,' says Farrow. 'But his casting director was already sending her on auditions.'

Crimes and Misdemeanors came out in October 1989, to largely appreciative notices. This was more what admirers of *Hannah and her Sisters* had been waiting for, and while its tone was more cynical and misanthropic, it was at least New York cynicism and misanthropy, recognised as the best and most bitter in the world. The film would quickly win a permanent place in the canon of urban angst. Jay Scott, writing in the *Boston Globe and Mail*, summed up its mordant, if pessimistic philosophy:

> In the modern world, the good are always punished while the evil are invariably rewarded. Those who take an eye don't so much as lose a lash, and those who take a tooth expire quietly in old age with a full set of choppers; the innocent are crucified; the cynical resurrected. Allen has painted bleak pictures before (*Interiors*, *September*) but nothing to compare to the arctic, ethical desolation of *Crimes and Misdemeanors*. Although the movie is biblical in its fundamental moralism, Allen turns the tables on God. This is the work of a Job whose cries for justice are unheeded. 'Show me,' Woody Allen seems to be screaming to the heavens, 'just *one place* where evil does not triumph at the expense of good.' Cosmic silence; in the universe of *Crimes and Misdemeanors*, God's ear is a black hole.

Not everyone was so enthusiastic, least of all those who appeared in the film. Sean Young lamented her scene being cut, the more so for the fact that in 1978 Allen had caused a book about him by her mother, Lee Guthrie, to be withdrawn. Claire Bloom found Allen's directing methods haphazard. She told Julian Fox that on her first day on the chilly New Jersey location, when she asked Allen about her lines she was told, 'Oh, you know, just say what you like. Make something up' – not the best approach for someone who'd just been doing *A Doll's House* and *Rosmersholm* on the London stage. As to the film itself, she thought it 'mindless and spurious, and Woody Allen's rediscovered Jewishness quite repellent'. But enough people did like *Crimes and Misdemeanors* to turn it into a modest international hit, though there was much criticism of Orion's erratic distribution and lacklustre advertising campaign. Progressively weaker and more marginalised, the company was losing direction and haemorrhaging financially. Allen's advisers urged him to think about a new distribution partner.

Allen's next film, which he began shooting a month after *Crimes and Misdemeanors* opened, dealt with a New Yorker who falls under the spell of the Asian way of life, and discards a white Anglo-Saxon Protestant existence to become part of it. It's about the *coup de foudre* of love at first sight, the pleasures of voyeurism, the duplicity of intimates and friends; topics which one can reasonably assume were on Allen's mind.

Over and above that, the film is once again about one of his cinematic idols – this time Fellini. Shrugging off his influences had become second nature to Allen, to such an extent that he routinely denigrated them. Fellini earned his dislike because he was all technique, and that 'bored' him. 'With Fellini,' he told British critic Penelope Gilliatt, 'I'm afraid it's like listening to people playing a perfect scale. It's very beautiful, but it's only a scale.' All the same, he copied him as often as he copied Bergman, and to more effect: Fellini's antic mind lay closer to the track of Allen's humour.

Fellini's 1965 *Juliet of the Spirits* dealt with the bored middle-aged wife of a wealthy philanderer who no longer finds her sexually interesting. Her friends urge her to consult an exotic psychic, who puts her in touch with the insubstantial world. She meets new people who hold out the hope of sexual fulfilment, but shies away nervously, preferring her dreams, which have become more frequent and vivid. Their characters, some of them from her childhood, invade her home. They give her a new understanding of herself, and at the end of the film she leaves the house to seek a new life closer to that of the spirits.

Allen's film used virtually the same sequence of events. His working title was 'The Magical Herbs of Dr Yang', but he rejected it as too literal. In the end he called it simply *Alice*, after its heroine. Alice Tait (Farrow) is married to wealthy and handsome Doug (William Hurt). They live in luxury, and Alice spends most of her time shopping and having her nails and hair done. Attempts to launch a career as a TV writer involve her with a woman-hunting teacher of creative writing (James Toback, director of *The Make-Out Artist*, in a piece of typecasting) and her old friend Nancy Brill (Cybill Shepherd), now a TV executive, who gives her the brush-off.

Suffering from back pains, Alice follows the advice of her friends and visits Dr Yang (Keye Luke) in Chinatown. He hypnotises her, and, deciding that her problem is more emotional than physical, gives her the first of a series of herbal mixtures. It summons up the ghost of her first love, Eddie (Alec Baldwin), a tearaway painter who awakened her sexually but died in a car crash. Together they fly across New York to the abandoned amusement park where they first met. The second packet of herbs removes her inhibitions, and she makes a pass at saxophone player Joe Rufilho (Joe Mantegna), who has a child at the same school as her children. After some false starts, they begin a love affair. She also samples opium, which she finds better than Valium.

Yang then gives her some herbs that render her invisible, allowing her to spy on Doug and discover he's cheating on her. She shares the herbs with Joe, who satisfies his fantasies by creeping into a dressing room with a top model (Elle Macpherson, in an anonymous cameo), then eavesdropping on the psychoanalysis of his wife (Judy Davis). Forced to choose between Doug and Joe, Alice asks Yang's help. He obliges with a potion that causes any man who drinks it to fall in love with her, but a maid accidentally puts it in the eggnog at a party thrown by her sister (Blythe Danner), and Alice becomes the love object for every middle-aged man there. Meanwhile, Joe, having discovered from his spying that his wife still loves him and regrets ending their marriage, decides to return to her. Alice goes to Calcutta to meet her idol, Mother Teresa, then settles down in funky companionability in Greenwich Village with her children – Farrow playing a recognisable parody of herself.

Shooting started on 6 November 1989, with Allen in a state of near-suicidal despair over his professional and emotional problems. Nothing in the first six days' filming worked, and he had to scrap it all. He was so depressed he contemplated closing down the film and checking into hospital; at least then the film's insurers would pay out. But he rallied as the film progressed, and soon got into the rhythm of its fantasy, aided by Farrow's charming performance.

For once the Manhattan of an Allen movie makes some social sense, in that Alice's husband, independently wealthy and Something on Wall Street besides, might actually be able to afford their enormous apartment, its cook, its Lalique vases and art deco antiques. Allen cast Joe Mantegna as Alice's saxophone-playing lover, even though he had to commute from Allen's set to Italy, where he was working with Francis Ford Coppola on *The Godfather III*. The affinity between his Italian seducer and Farrow's good Catholic girl gives their scenes an erotic inevitability. Alice has too little in common with her husband to let him try the invisibility herbs, but she and Joe share the Catholic sense of sin that makes spying on naked models and a wife's analysis/confession especially erotic. As Joe says when he sees himself disappear, 'I've wanted to do this all my life.' When he decides to slip into Elle Macpherson's changing cubicle, Alice tells him to enjoy himself, preferring herself to follow two of her friends as they gossip about her.

With no 'Woody' character to deliver the one-liners and provide a mordant commentary, Allen parcels out the gags among his fantasy characters. Eddie makes scathing ghostly comments about Doug's taste for wearing pajama bottoms without tops, and Alice's 'muse' (Bernadette Peters), conjured up while she's trying to write, comprehensively dismisses her creative writing professor as wanting to probe her rather than her talent.

After Joe, there's a sense of *déjà vu* about many of the other characters. Australian actress Judy Davis as Joe's ad agency wife and Cybill Shepherd as the rising TV executive who dismisses Alice's literary ambitions have little or nothing to do. They typify Allen's 'wallpaper women', put in to carry the plot, but inescapably two-dimensional. Eddie and Alice share some of the characteristics of Frederick and Lee in *Hannah and her Sisters*. (He opened her up sexually. She posed nude for pictures, which he sold.) They also recall Marion and her professor lover in *Another Woman* and, for that matter, Ike and Tracy in *Manhattan*, where impressionable younger women are sexually awakened by older men. In every case, the man is punished, either by being abandoned, as in *Manhattan* and *Hannah and her Sisters*, or, as in *Alice* and *Another Woman*, by violent death.

Critic Stephen Spignesi went as far as to call *Alice* 'Another Woman II: The Comedy', because of its shared elements, in particular those of eavesdropping and infidelity. Certainly there are superficial correspondences. Alice is alienated from her closest sibling, like Marion in *Another Woman*, and Blythe Danner again plays the sister. The two share a dream sequence which could almost have been shot on the same location as that in the earlier film: an idyllic country house where they lived as children. Instead of German poetry as a family preoccupation, however, Alice has Catholicism, and leaves the house and the dream via a block of confessionals incongruously set up in its garden.

Allen ended the film as he'd begun it, in a state of depression and confusion so acute that he entered hospital to be treated for exhaustion, as he'd contemplated doing at the start of shooting. It was May 1990 before he finished reshoots and editing on *Alice*. There would be no time that year for a trip to Europe, since he'd agreed to take an acting role in another director's film. Paul Mazursky had benefited from the admission of Allen-type comedies to the approved list of Hollywood categories. Given his previous annexations of other men's cinema, with versions of Truffaut, Fellini and Renoir, it was almost inevitable that he would be attracted to Bergman, and in 1989 he began pitching *Scenes from a Mall*, his version of Bergman's *Scenes from a Marriage*, with the intriguing prospect that Allen would star.

Ever since *New York Stories*, Disney had been eyeing Allen as a possible addition to its company Touchstone, intended to give the studio some credibility in adult cinema by financing and releasing films outside its traditional kiddy market. Allen was interested. Orion was looking increasingly shaky, with limited capital and insufficient funds to distribute and promote its films, and he had already opened tentative negotiations with Twentieth Century-Fox. Seeing it as a sprat to catch a mackerel, Disney invited him to star in *What About Bob?*, Frank Oz's film about a desperate patient who pursues his psychiatrist when he leaves town in August, and ends up destroying not only his doctor's holiday but his home and, almost, his sanity. But Allen declined to appear opposite Bill Murray as Bob, and Richard Dreyfuss took the role.

In February 1990 Orion signed a $175 million distribution deal with Columbia, which desperately needed films. For the moment its financial worries seemed to be ended, and the company started negotiating with Allen for a new three-film deal. Still hoping to win him over, Disney's president Michael Eisner made an offer of unprecedented generosity, offering Allen $3 million to star in *Scenes from a Mall*. Disney's bean-counters regarded the sum as ridiculous, given Mazursky's patchy box-office record, but Eisner would cite the advantage Steve Ross at Warners had won by paying an absurd $22 million for the video-game rights to Steven Spielberg's *E.T: The Extraterrestrial*. The game never sold, but Ross's offer broke Universal/MCA's hold on Spielberg and made him one of Warners' biggest money-makers.

Allen agreed to spend the summer playing Nick Fifer, a sports endorsement lawyer married to Deborah (Bette Midler), a marriage-guidance guru and successful authoress of *I Do I Do I Do*, which suggests that marriages should be renegotiated every ten years. The two spend most of their sixteenth wedding anniversary in Los Angeles' pre-eminent shopping mall, the Beverly Center, shopping for gifts and clothes, collecting the sushi for their celebratory party that evening, and bickering, in the course of which both reveal extra-marital affairs. In reaction, Deborah, belying her professional detachment, tries to kill Nick. They end up happy and reconciled at their party, but one can already imagine the recriminations of the morning after.

Allen drew the line at working in Hollywood, so interiors were shot at the Stamford Center in Connecticut and on a giant re-creation of two levels of the Beverly Center in the Kaufman Astoria studios. Among the hundreds of extras needed to people this giant construction were Fletcher and Soon-Yi, the latter getting her first taste of movie-making from the other side of the camera. When

Mazursky insisted that Allen spend at least a few days in Los Angeles at the real mall, Allen agreed – subject to Farrow and the family getting a VIP tour of Disneyland personally conducted by Eisner. The Disney boss agreed, sensing a gold-plated publicity opportunity.

Mazursky garnished his film with fashionably Continental touches, including a score made up of Nino Rota tunes from Fellini films and a mime (Bill Irwin) who haunts the couple and mutely satirises their problems, until Nick knocks him unconscious in fury – the episode won more laughs than any other from audiences in mime-plagued New York and Los Angeles. Not laughing was Disney, alarmed by the final cost of $34 million – a great deal for any comedy to recoup, even with Woody Allen.

Since a limo picked him up every morning to drive him to the Astoria studios, Allen would take Soon-Yi and sometimes Fletcher. Farrow got used to Allen and Soon-Yi leaving together. After the film finished shooting, Soon-Yi told Mia that she had made a new friend on the film, a woman in her late twenties with whom she began to spend most of her weekends. For these visits she abandoned her usual jeans and sweatshirts for miniskirts, and started to wear make-up. Farrow's requests to meet the friend were curtly refused. She later surmised that the 'friend' was Allen, and that his intimacy with Soon-Yi, if not their actual affair, began during long limo rides to and from Astoria, on which, as Marie-Christine Barrault recalled, Allen needed his hand held while they passed through the Queens–Midtown Tunnel.

Later, according to Farrow, her other daughters would recall indications that a romance was developing: Allen caressing Soon-Yi's thigh in the limo, or Soon-Yi asking Lark and Daisy for advice on contraception. Farrow noticed that Allen showed more inclination to visit Frog Hollow, and often drove up in his limo, taking Soon-Yi. One of Farrow's friends later said, 'They were behaving in a way that was much too intimate for two people in that situation. There would be times when they would be talking and no one else was allowed in the conversation. It was obvious that he liked her because he never talked to the other children that way. But I never suspected it would turn into a physical relationship.'

The reasons for Allen's relationship with Soon-Yi metamorphosing as it did bear no more analysis than those behind any other love affair. Some people went so far as to suggest that her connection with prostitution increased her attractiveness to Allen. Others would suggest that Soon-Yi, looking to reject her stepmother and make her own life, saw her chance in a liaison with Allen, for whom Mia had obviously lost her appeal. Allen himself never offered any rationalisation beyond the much-quoted 'The heart wants what it wants.' The improbability of the relationship troubled him. Like Swann in *A la Recherche de Temps Perdu*, he found it puzzling and ironic that he was ruining his life for love of a woman 'who wasn't really his type'. 'My ex-wife Louise looked like Mia,' he mused, 'and I would have said if you asked me, what I need is a certain type of woman, a certain look. Then someone comes along like Soon-Yi, who is off the moon, from Korea, you know, decades younger, with no common experience at all, and that's the one which for some irrational reason seems to work. It's pleasant and fun and exciting, and it's amazing to me.' That very strangeness might well have been Soon-Yi's main appeal. In Allen's reflections, one hears echoed the tone of George Sanders' Addison de Witt in Joseph L. Mankiewicz's cynical 1950 Broadway comedy/drama *All About Eve*. Baffled by his attraction to the greedy wannabe actress Eve, he reflects bitterly, 'That I should want you at all suddenly strikes me as the height of improbability. But that, in itself, is probably the reason.' Partisans for Mia saw more manipulative motives. Dr Wayne Myers, a psychiatrist who would testify in the resulting custody case, claimed, 'The Soon-Yi affair is less a sexual act than an act of anger by Woody against Mia. He's chosen one of her daughters, the one capable of offering the least resistance.'

As the affair blossomed, Allen continued to spend time at the Langham, and remained affectionate towards Dylan, though a therapist who saw them together told Farrow she considered his attention 'inappropriately intense, because it excluded everybody else, and it placed a demand on a child for a kind of acknowledgement that I felt should not be placed on a child'. 'That's *nothing*!' Farrow said, proceeding to list numerous other examples of Allen's – as she saw it – indecent obsession with the little girl, then seven years old. The therapist started counselling Allen, hoping to convince him he was acting improperly. Allen, who was tapering off his twenty-year-long analysis prior to giving it up entirely, acquiesced. He was in little condition to resist. The strain of maintaining a covert love affair while working full-time on a new film and managing his production empire was bringing back the nervous exhaustion that had drained his energy during the first days of shooting *Alice*. He lay down at every opportunity, didn't shower or wash his hair for days at a stretch. Doctors speculated that he might have caught Lyme Disease from a tick during one of his visits to Frog Hollow, or the elusive Epstein-Barr Syndrome, which sapped the energy of creative temperaments especially.

With Disney not prepared to make him a firm offer until it saw the grosses of *Scenes from a Mall*, and Fox unwilling to meet his terms on artistic autonomy, in August 1990 Allen signed a new three-film deal with the increasingly beleaguered Orion. It permitted him to work for other studios, but Orion would have first call on his time. The pact was immediately tested almost to breaking point when Allen announced that for his 1990 Fall Project he intended to expand his 1975 one-act play *Death* into a feature. 'The entire company,' according to him, 'nearly had a heart attack.' The discovery that he wanted to film in black and white traumatised them almost as much, but they agreed to go ahead, hoping against all the indications that the film, provisionally titled 'Fog and Shadows', would make money.

Death was like Fritz Lang's *M* rewritten by Kafka. The main character, Kleinman, is roused out of bed in the middle of a foggy night by a group of his neighbours, who've formed a vigilante group to hunt down a killer who's terrorising the town. They have a plan, but they won't reveal Kleinman's role in it. He ends up roaming the town's streets and alleys in the fog. He meets Gina, a prostitute, with whom he spends a few moments looking at the stars and musing about the fact that the brightest of them may already have ceased to exist. She kisses him, but charges him $6, explaining that sex is her business; for pleasure, she kisses women. 'What a coincidence,' says Kleinman. 'Me too.' He finds the town doctor, knifed and dying, and is identified by a clairvoyant, Spiro, as the culprit. Escaping lynching, he runs into the killer, who knifes him. Expiring, he tells the vigilantes that his assailant looked just like him. They're puzzled, because other victims, none of whom looked anything like Kleinman, said he resembled them too. As he dies, they run off, having heard news of another sighting.

It's inviting to find Allen's choice of subject for his next film significant in the light of his liaison with Soon-Yi, but then, all his films have some elements of guilt, voyeurism, sexual frustration, existential doubt and suicidal *ennui*. That he should have gone back almost twenty years, to the days when he relied on parody for comic effect, does suggest a slackness and an unwillingness to break new ground which would seriously undermine the film.

Alice opened in December 1990, to modestly enthusiastic reviews but poor box-office. Orion, once again strapped for cash, had done a poor job of promotion. The poster simply bore a large and flattering picture of Farrow in a cute red hat, which said nothing about the film's content. It was increasingly obvious that Orion was sinking fast.

In 1990 Mike Medavoy, the agent whose idea it had been to set up Orion, left the company to head another 'mini-major', TriStar, which had just been acquired, along with its sister company Columbia, by Sony. Medavoy wooed Allen with the promise of far wider release and bigger budgets from the coffers of the Japanese electronics *zaibatsu*. In September 1991 Allen signed a new deal under which Orion agreed that he make one film for TriStar, who would also take over distribution of *Shadows and Fog*. Orion retained the option for two more films, but could only exercise it if they could come up with the money to make them. They would never do so. In July 1992 Arthur Krim abandoned the bankrupt company, which never made another movie.

Early in 1991 Eric Lax published his authorised biography of Allen, three years in the writing. Despite the unrelievedly rosy picture it presented – the *Los Angeles Times* called it 'stately, worshipful [and] adoring' – *Woody Allen: A Biography* sold phenomenally. Allen turned aside any cavils with a joke: 'The criticisms of the book,' he said, 'have been that Lax was too hagiographic, too soft on me, too adulatory. I, of course, felt that he wasn't complimentary enough.' Turning serious, he went on, 'I found it sober and accurate. There are no great hidden truths about me. I gave him access to everyone he wanted to talk to. I let him hang round and watch whatever he wanted to watch. His spin on it, his feelings, may be affectionate towards me, and maybe that ruins it for some people who would rather have a more critical biography.'

As Allen suggested, Lax's thoroughness is not in doubt, but nor is his partiality. Quotes were edited to remove adverse remarks. Sections were paraphrased from Mort Sahl's autobiography, but his attack on Allen ignored. Meryl Streep's memories of *Manhattan* appeared, but not her opinion in the same interview that Allen was a womaniser. Though referred to, Harlene Rosen, Louise Lasser and Diane Keaton didn't contribute. Nor did most actors who had worked for Allen, except Elaine Stritch and Sam Waterston. Tony Roberts is credited, as are Dick Cavett and Jean Doumanian, for 'describing a friend'. Apparently nobody who might have had cause to be aggrieved with Allen, such as Maureen O'Sullivan or Claire Bloom, was considered worth approaching.

Also missing were any references to Stacey Nelkin, Bryna Goldstein, Jerry Epstein and many others in a position to criticise Allen's private or business life. Mia Farrow was thanked for 'open-[ing] many windows onto Woody', though nothing in the book, which covers his career almost precisely up to the moment he began his affair with Soon-Yi, hints at her disquiet over Allen's attention to her children, none of whom contributed either. Almost without exception, those who helped Lax were members of Allen's inner circle: directors of photography, editors, assistants, sound recordists, his casting director, his stills photographer, his faithful design staff. Loyally, they closed ranks, maintaining the image of Woody Allen as paragon, perfectionist and all-round *mensch*.

In retrospect, the publication of Lax's biography can be seen as a turning point in Allen's fortunes and those of his collaborators. Its insistence on defining Allen in near-saintly terms made him a hostage to fortune, rendering him especially vulnerable to the accusations of moral turpitude which would follow. Friends who stuck by Allen found themselves stuck with him, their futures tied to his as he embarked on the next, erratic part of his career. They were rewarded by seeing him fall increasingly under the influence of Jean Doumanian, who in 1998 would summarily dismiss most of them in favour of less well-tried but cheaper substitutes. Hollywood, so long scorned by Allen and so pleased to revenge itself on him when he fell, took even greater satisfaction in noting that, for all his embrace of a humanist East Coast ethic, Woody was at heart as attentive to the bottom line as any of them; like the Grim Reaper in *Death*, just another *schlep*.

24

Shadows and Fog, Husbands and Wives and *Manhattan Murder Mystery*

JONATHAN: 'What are people most afraid of?'
BARRY: 'The dark.'
JONATHAN: 'Right! Because the dark has a life of its own.'

Charles Schnee, script for *The Bad and the Beautiful* (1952)

Expanding *Death* into 'Fog and Shadows' demanded some ingenuity. Allen kept the basic plot, but elaborated on it, and, by adding a circus camped on the outskirts of town, introduced a new setting and was able to augment the cast. While Kleinman is being hounded by the killer (Michael Kirby) and rival vigilante groups, the circus performers have their own problems – some of which Allen shared in private life. Irmy, the sword-swallower (Farrow), is dissatisfied with her lover, identified only as Clown (John Malkovich), who refuses to have a child with her, citing his artistic temperament, need for quiet, and somewhat specious philosophical doubts.

Surprising him shortly afterwards *in flagrante* with trapeze artist Marie (Madonna), Irmy heads into town. By the bridge she meets a prostitute (Lily Tomlin), who offers her lodging at the brothel. There she receives a cordial welcome from the other women (including Kathy Bates and Jodie Foster, both Academy Award winners), and attracts the attention of a regular client, Jack (John Cusack), who offers his entire winnings on cards that night – $700 – to sleep with her.

As a gesture of rebellion, Irmy does so, and enjoys the experience so much that she guiltily insists on giving the money to the church.

In one of the funnier scenes in a film not conspicuous for them, she asks Kleinman, whom she meets on the street, to hand over the money to the priest (Josef Sommer), who's huddled with the police chief at the back of the church, hatching yet another plan to trap the killer. Gravely assuring Kleinman that he knows how to recognise generosity, the priest tells the policeman to erase his name from a list they're making. Gratified, Kleinman returns to the street, where Irmy has encountered a desperate woman (Eszter Balint) with a baby. Irmy tells him to retrieve $350 from the priest to give to the woman. He reluctantly does so, and watches with sinking heart as the policeman, incensed, restores his name to his list. 'Put a circle round it,' orders the priest. The woman has no chance to enjoy her windfall, since shortly afterwards Irmy and Clown find her dead, a victim of the killer, and her baby girl in the gutter.

Irmy insists on keeping the child, and after resisting briefly, Clown becomes the most solicitous of adoptive fathers, even fending off Irmy, whom he offers to make pregnant if she'll just leave him alone with the orphan – another parallel between Allen's life and the story.

Meanwhile, both the killer and Kleinman have found their way to the circus, which proves more efficient at dealing with the menace than has the rest of the town. Kleinman lures the killer into the big top, where the magician Irmstedt (Kenneth Mars) is packing up his tricks. With Kleinman's help, Irmstedt traps the killer and chains him to a chair, but when the vigilantes arrive the prisoner has miraculously vanished. Irmstedt offers Kleinman a job as his assistant, and though he's briefly tempted to return to town with the hunters, he elects to join the circus, which fulfils a more useful function than their vicious factionalism. Irmstedt agrees. 'Everyone loves illusions,' he says. 'Needs them like he loves the air.'

Given his prestige, Allen could get almost anyone he wanted for a film. Most stars would accept a 'token' $20,000 a week to work with him, particularly in a cameo. Allen would later tell Stig Bjorkman that, in casting, he was 'unmindful of [an actor's] stature in the business. It doesn't matter to me if they're completely unknown or very famous. Only if they are the best person in the part.' But his choices in the new film belied this high-principled policy, which the demands of the marketplace were making increasingly difficult to respect.

When Jodie Foster made it clear that she wanted to work with him, Allen cast her immediately, as he did Madonna, though in truth both of their parts might have been played by unknowns. By contrast, less famous but more skilled performers were marginalised. Kate Nelligan, playing Kleinman's fiancée Eve, is seen only in a single long shot through a window in the middle of a foggy night. Wallace Shawn has a walk-on, and Fred Gwynne disappears almost entirely.

Short, cocky New York actor Bob Balaban, best known for supporting roles like that of the mapmaker/translator in Steven Spielberg's *Close Encounters of the Third Kind*, originally played the doctor, and had one of the film's longest scenes, in which he and Kleinman discuss the physical basis of madness in a room filled with draped corpses and specimens preserved in formaldehyde. After a week of shooting Allen fired Balaban and brought in Donald Pleasence. The British actor had grown old and canny playing mad scientists and dotty doctors in films like John Carpenter's teenage horror hit *Halloween*, which ends almost exactly as does Allen's film, with the killer seemingly evaporating just as his identity is discovered. It was widely believed in Hollywood that Madonna, Foster and Pleasence were cast in the hope of attracting new, younger recruits to Allen's ageing audience.

Stylistic changes followed those of casting. After a week of tests, Allen abandoned the heavy shadows and low angles of German expressionist classics of the twenties in favour of something closer to the murkier style of Universal's forties B-movies, like *House of Frankenstein* and *The Wolf Man*, most of which had been wreathed in fog to disguise the cheesiness of the décor. But though Santo Loquasto excelled himself, creating sets that were an anthology of alleys, staircases, nooks, crannies and doorways, with a few cluttered offices and rooming houses, the style failed to convey the sense of witty pastiche Allen aimed for, looking merely cheap and old-fashioned. Posing Michael Kirby backlit in a foggy archway might produce a momentarily striking decorative effect, but young audiences raised on films like *Carrie* and *Nightmare on Elm Street* would have preferred him to leap out of the dark, dripping razor in hand, and lock his arm round someone's throat.

The film went through the usual reshooting. Pleasence was flown back from California to redo some of his scenes with a supporting cast entirely different from the one he played opposite in the first place – and was thanked for his trouble by having his name misspelled in the credits. As music, Allen abandoned his first idea of using Grieg's more sombre pieces and adapted Kurt Weill's music for the words of Bertolt Brecht in orchestrations that evoked, somewhat incongruously, their source in twenties Berlin theatre and cabaret.

To the film's stylistic problems and Allen's double life at home were added further difficulties. Ten days into shooting, the technicians' union IATSE went on strike, closing down filming all over the country. The delay added to the cost, which quickly rose to $14 million. Meanwhile Allen's new distributor, TriStar, was itself in trouble. Its owner, Japanese electronics giant Sony, had hoped to capitalise on its pre-eminence in video and sound recording hardware by buying an interest in the major producer of artistic 'software', Hollywood. The experiment would prove disastrous for Sony, which overpaid for its studios and would only be able to watch helplessly as they squandered money on disastrous projects like Steven Spielberg's *Hook*, but in early 1991 they were still optimistic, and eager to retain Allen, even with his contractual requirement of guaranteed creative autonomy.

In the summer, Allen needed to go to Italy to finish shooting his five commercials for the Co-Op Nordemiglia supermarket chain. They were budgeted at $4 million, of which he got $1 million. He had already appeared in commercials in Japan, for which he was paid $7 million, but the Italian project widened his control and his scope. Carlo DiPalma shot the advertisements, using comedian Roberto Benigni, who'd starred in Fellini's *Voices of the Moon*.

Allen spent some time in Paris, and toured Ireland with Farrow and the children. Soon-Yi remained in America, at a camp in Maine, but she spent so much time engaged in transatlantic phone calls from Allen that she was asked to leave.

Farrow had already decided to adopt two handicapped Vietnamese orphans, and in September she flew to Vietnam, taking Satchel with her. Allen stayed behind to edit the film, which he now, after convincing himself it would not be confused with Alan Resnais' short classic about Auschwitz, *Night and Fog*, called *Shadows and Fog*. All the other children also remained, under the care of a nanny, a therapist, and Fletcher and Daisy, both now seventeen. Soon-Yi, by then in college in New Jersey, promised Farrow that she would keep an eye on the brood at weekends. In the same month, Allen's two remaining films for Orion were cancelled by mutual consent, and he officially moved his company, Untitled Films Inc., to TriStar. In December Orion would file for Chapter 11 protection from its creditors, the traditional prelude to financial collapse.

Farrow returned from Vietnam with only one of the children she'd hoped to adopt, a boy named Sanjay. The other, a ten-year-old blind girl, Tam, still needed certain important papers before she could be taken out of the country. Farrow had been told that Sanjay suffered from polio, but within a few weeks of arriving in the United States his real problem, advanced cerebral palsy, became evident. After six days she handed him back to the authorities – or, as she preferred to say, 'he left to join his forever-family,' a New Mexico couple who had specifically requested a child with extensive disabilities.

On 10 November the *New York Daily News* published a report on Allen depicting him as a harassed father doing his best to deal with Farrow's fast-expanding family. The story revealed for the first time that Farrow, as well as awaiting Tam's arrival, wanted to adopt yet another child, this time a black 'crack' baby from among the thousands in New York's orphanages. 'Why this constant need for infants and little ones?' queried Allen's costume designer and trusted crony Jeffrey Kurland, presumably echoing the official Allen line. 'Get on with your life!' Allen's sister Letty called Farrow's tendency to adopt 'manic'. *Time* magazine ran an article on women like her, troubled with a compulsion to adopt and nurture children. Rather than 'mothers', it reported, they were known as 'gatherers'.

Just when Allen and Soon-Yi consummated their affair would later become the subject of furious legal debate. Once Farrow discovered the relationship, in January 1992, Allen would admit, according to her, that it had been going on for several months, although he later insisted it didn't begin until 1 December 1991, a date almost certainly chosen by his lawyers to strengthen his position in the custody battle over Satchel and Dylan. Other evidence points to the affair as having begun tentatively before the summer 1991 trip to Europe, and having blossomed immediately after Allen's return.

Allen evidently regarded the affair – as would most men of his age thrust into the same dangerous but intoxicating situation – with mingled exhilaration and disquiet. After the declining passion of his relationship with the forty-six-year-old Farrow, the freshness and vitality of Soon-Yi had a predictably stimulating effect, which, from the evidence of the uninhibited Polaroids for which she posed, she encouraged. But in darker moments Allen must have realised that, emotionally and professionally, the liaison made him a hostage to his young mistress, and to Farrow. With his story-telling skill, he would have explored every dismaying scenario. What if Soon-Yi tired of him? What if Farrow found out? What if news of the relationship leaked to the press? At the same time, joyously fornicating with an exotic young partner little more than a third his age, he must occasionally have felt the dizzy impulse to blurt out the news to someone, anyone.

Against this background Allen wrote and prepared his Fall Project, destined to become the controversial *Husbands and Wives*. For the first time in years, the film was not based on an old script from his capacious bottom drawer, nor on scenes shot for an earlier film and resurrected from the 'Black Reels'. Rather, it gave an up-to-date account of his continuing disquiet about human relationships, his contempt for weak husbands who cut themselves loose from women, only to go crawling back, his loathing of wives who use sex and children as a means of subjugating men, his dislike of young women who play on the vanity of older men to wind them round their slim fingers.

Gabe (Allen) is a Columbia professor of creative writing, Judy (Farrow) his wife, editor on an art magazine. In the opening scene, their best friends Sally (Judy Davis) and Jack (Sydney Pollack), announce that they are separating. They put a sophisticated gloss on the decision, but it emerges that Sally has engineered the break-up out of doubt about Jack's fidelity and a tit-for-tat belief that she's entitled to the same freedom.

The news of their split upsets Judy, and sends tremors through her marriage to Gabe, already undermined by a running argument about whether or not to have children and, more fundamentally, by Judy's unacknowledged yearning for a more romantic partner than Gabe. She 'fixes up' Sally with Michael (Liam Neeson), who works for her magazine, but is secretly chagrined when they start an affair, since she also finds him attractive. She decides to leave Gabe.

Jack has moved in with his pretty young aerobics instructor Sam (Lysette Anthony), only to find that her skills in the bedroom and the kitchen don't compensate for her general dumbness and belief in astrology, crystals and New Age mumbo jumbo. Gabe has become attracted to Rain (Juliette Lewis), a precocious student in his class. Her history of involvement with older men – her psychiatrist, her father's business partners – makes her even more attractive to Gabe. As he and Rain circle round the idea of an affair, Sally starts sleeping with Michael, only to throw him out when Jack arrives at the house in the middle of the night, begging for a reconciliation. Catching Michael on the rebound, Judy makes herself indispensable to his emotional recuperation, and they marry. Happily reunited, Sally and Jack muse over the irony that their marriage was strengthened by separation, while the very news of it destroyed the apparently happy marriage of their best friends. At the close, Judy and Michael amiably review the circumstances that brought them together, while

Gabe, living alone in a hotel, solaces himself with writing a novel.

As if to emphasise its topicality and relevance, Allen constructed *Husbands and Wives* as a documentary, with all the protagonists invited to reflect on their motives by an unseen investigator, played by Jeffrey Kurland. They're conspicuously miked, to make it clear that these aren't yet more Allen analysis scenes, and additional evidence is offered by outsiders, like Judy's first husband, who accuses her of manipulating men to her advantage. Her passive/aggressive personality, he explains, allowed her to seduce them while appearing to be resisting: 'backing into the limelight', as David Garnett said of Lawrence of Arabia.

We are invited to see Gabe as the one honest and upright person in the group, cruelly used by his manipulative wife, his vain protégée and his self-serving friends. As he confesses to the interviewer, however, he is more than a little to blame himself. He has always been attracted to 'kamikaze women; they crash their plane into you, and you die with them'. He admits, 'My heart doesn't know from logic.' His sexual ideal is a girl named Harriett Harmon, seen only in one brief smouldering close-up, a bisexual who shared his interest in having sex in unconventional places – a theme already aired in *Another Woman*. A drug-user, she ended up psychiatrically hospitalised: a rerun, in short, of the Louise Lasser character played by Charlotte Rampling in *Stardust Memories*.

Gabe has enough insight into his character to recognise Rain as another kamikaze woman. Named for the poet Rainer Maria Rilke, but also because she was born in a hurricane, she tempts him to a passionate kiss at her twenty-first birthday party. As he succumbs, lightning flashes and thunder roars around the penthouse; ominous portents of what he might expect from a relationship with her. Rather than end up like her ex-shrink importuning her on the sidewalk, a character from a bad remake of *The Blue Angel*, Gabe retreats.

In the world of *Husbands and Wives*, all women aspire to enslave or exploit men by manipulating their need for sex. We discover that in response to Sally's indifference, Jack has long patronised prostitutes like Shawn (Cristi Conaway, in a role cut to a single scene in the final version). After her one sexual encounter in the film, Sally admits to Michael that she became too distracted to have an orgasm because she began to mentally categorise her friends as either foxes or hedgehogs – a reference to 'The Hedgehog and the Fox', an essay by British philosopher Isaiah Berlin which opens with the famous quote from the Greek poet Archilochus: 'The fox knows many things, but the hedgehog knows one big thing,' i.e. the fox's cunning is defeated by the hedgehog's defence, rolling itself into a ball. Berlin had become a favourite of Farrow's, who was reading his book *The Crooked Timber of Humanity* in pauses during the making of the film.

Except for Farrow, there were no familiar faces on the set of *Husbands and Wives*. The film started with young English actress Emily Lloyd in the role of Rain. Allen had admired her in *Wish You Were Here* (1987), about the uninhibited childhood in a British seaside town of a woman later to become a famous London madame, but after a week during which Lloyd was unable to perfect her American accent to his satisfaction, Allen fired her in late November and gave the role to Juliette Lewis, whom he'd seen in Martin Scorsese's recent remake of *Cape Fear*. It was a poor choice. Simpering and posing, tossing her hair and caressing her lips, Lewis simply reprised her teenage sexpot performance from the earlier film. Allen offered the role of Sally to Jane Fonda, but she refused to change her personal style for the role, notably her haircut. After contemplating Dianne Wiest, he substituted Australian actress Judy Davis, who not only agreed to wear her hair in a tightly plaited single braid, but had the tough, jumpy persona of a Charlotte Rampling. She struck sparks from Jack, played with sympathy and humour by Sydney Pollack, a director who, since making a great success in *Tootsie* (1982), had increasingly enjoyed taking acting roles. Irish actor Liam Neeson, described by critic John Lahr as 'a Sequoia of sex', towered over everyone as Michael.

From the start, the visual style of *Husbands and Wives* was nervy and disturbing. Outside shots were often taken from passing cars. By contrast, the interview sections were filmed with little or no camera movement: islands of calm in the chaos of relationships. Carlo DiPalma shot the announcement of Jack and Sally's break-up with a hand-held camera, dodging round the apartment like a news photographer under fire. To emphasise the effect, editor Susan Morse used for the first time in Allen's films a trick developed by Jean-Luc Godard, cutting from an action to its conclusion and simply dropping what came between – whether a conversational pause, the walk to the door after it rings, the gap between a car pulling up and its passengers entering a restaurant.

Performers were surprised by the script's combativeness and abrasive language. The normally clean-spoken Farrow was required to say 'bullshit' and 'fucking' on screen. Sam, originally a 'vulnerable , war-wounded angel', in the words of Lysette Anthony, became darker in the shooting. Anthony believes that Allen rethought her character, and came to regard her as 'obnoxious'. In her major scene, where she flounces out of a party after Jack's friends mock her belief in astrology, Allen directed Pollack not simply to hustle her away but to wrestle her, screaming, into the car while his friends watched incredulously. The crew was aghast. 'There were people with their mouths open,' Anthony recalls, 'going, "My God, I've *never* seen this much violence in a Woody Allen movie."' Even so, Anthony emerged with credit. A newcomer mostly known in her native Britain for dolly-bird appearances in gossip magazines, she played Sam with a skill, remarked *Boston Globe and Mail* critic Jay Scott, that 'dignifies a cliché'.

The film isn't without its comic moments, though most derive their humour from humiliation and embarrassment. Dipping her toe in the world of dating for the first time in years, Sally tries to have a night out at the opera with an office friend, only to spend most of the time in his apartment beforehand repeatedly berating Jack over the phone. When she hears that the opera they're to see is *Don Giovanni*, she turns on her date, attacking him as a representative of all the world's Don Juans. He subsides weakly onto the sofa, too upset to face Mozart, or anything else, that night.

'You know what turns me on? Intellectual.' Farrow in her best role for Allen, or any other director: the Mafia widow in *Broadway Danny Rose*.

Allen and Farrow as patient and analyst, soon to become lovers, in his intricate pastiche *Zelig* (1983).

Allen lines up a shot on *Another Woman*, watched by Mia Farrow's adopted daughter Dylan, whom she would one day accuse him of sexually molesting.

Allen and Farrow, with Judy Davis, in their last film together, *Husbands and Wives* (1992).

Allen poses with Dylan, and Farrow with their natural son Satchel in 1987.

On holiday in Stockholm, April 1987: Soon-Yi, Dylan, Fletcher, Allen and Farrow.

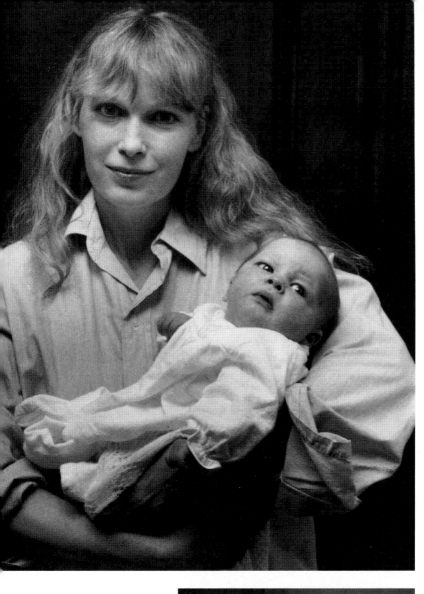

Soon-Yi with Satchel and Farrow's adopted son Moses, around 1990.

Under police escort, Allen takes Satchel on a tour of Dublin Zoo, after a three-day court battle with Farrow to establish his rights.

Diane Keaton replaces Mia in *Manhattan Murder Mystery* (1993)

Soon-Yi and Allen at La
Scala, Milan, in 1997.

Allen with Peter Falk in the
1997 TV remake of Neil
Simon's *The Sunshine Boys*.

'Like taking a bath in honey'. Allen loses himself playing New Orleans jazz on the 1997 European tour with his band.

Rain's confrontation with her ex-lover/analyst outside her apartment isn't without humour, nor is Gabe's apprehension as she makes it clear on her birthday that she's available. 'I'm sleepwalking into a mess,' he says, and when she kisses him he muses, 'Why do I hear $50,000 worth of psychotherapy dialling 911?' Generally, though, the tone is subdued and nervous, typified by Allen's choice for play-in and play-out music of an obscure but apt thirties version of Cole Porter's 'What is this Thing Called Love' by Leo Reisman.

On 17 December 1991, Allen and Farrow formally became joint adoptive parents of Moses and Dylan. The decision by the Surrogate Court of the State of New York in Manhattan created a historic precedent. Never before, in New York at least, had an unmarried couple been permitted to adopt a child. 'As far as I know,' said Allen's attorney Paul Martin Weltz, architect of the deal, 'it's a first. Any two single individuals, whatever their persuasion, can now say, "Look, you did it for Mia and Woody. Therefore do it for me."'

Farrow would later claim that even as they completed the adoption procedures, she became convinced that Allen had an inappropriate sexual interest in Dylan. Though there were no witnesses and nothing in writing, she would assert that before they went into court she extracted a promise from Allen that he would never take Dylan on overnight visits without her. Nor, should their relationship break up, would he attempt to gain custody of Dylan or Satchel. As she recalled, he said reassuringly, 'I would never even *want* the kids to live with me. I don't want kids around all the time, you know that.'

Shooting on *Husbands and Wives* broke for Christmas. André Previn visited Farrow in mid-December, and he and Allen spent some hours chatting and going over the reviews of his memoirs of his Hollywood years, *No Minor Chords*. Allen never celebrated Christmas with the family – he once greeted them at his Fifth Avenue apartment with a bare tree topped by a black hat – but this year he turned up on Christmas Day for dinner at the Langham, an occasion that represented a turning point in his life with Farrow.

Rival accounts of the day vary. Farrow remembers Allen seeming hostile, an intruder, interrupting the atmosphere of candles on the table and carols on the stereo. He ran the noisy kitchen juicer to produce a large jug of apple juice which, when nobody wanted any, he poured down the sink. Allen dismissed this version: 'You're describing the Kennedys and Christmas,' he said. 'They were not talking about the Mass and reviewing the carols. This was a consecutive group of kids eating. There was no sense of Christmas dinner about it.' Such diverging accounts of shared activities were to typify the next year of his and Farrow's lives. Whatever actually happened, Farrow incontrovertibly emerged from the Christmas deeply upset, since she once again changed all the apartment's locks and took a new phone number.

Shortly afterwards, Tam, the blind Vietnamese orphan, arrived in the United States. Farrow and nanny Kristi Groetke had learned some Vietnamese in preparation, but it wasn't enough to calm the frantic child with her hair full of lice. Farrow was also preparing to adopt Isaiah, a black boy addicted to crack cocaine from the womb. This left her hands more than full, and made Allen's demands for reshoots of *Husbands and Wives* in mid-January particularly difficult to organise.

On 13 January 1992, in Farrow's account, she crossed Central Park to Allen's apartment with Satchel, then five, for an appointment with the child's therapist, a session Allen was also supposed to attend. Why a five-year-old boy should need therapy puzzled many people, including Kristi Groetke, who 'felt it was not my place to ask'. Later, it emerged that all Farrow's newly acquired children underwent psychotherapy from the age of two. Farrow apparently feared that Satchel's exposure to therapy at such a young age might seem odd, and in her memoir *What Falls Away* she simply said she 'accompanied one of the children to a therapy session at Woody's apartment'.

She let herself in with the key Allen kept under the umbrella stand in the outer hall, but he wasn't there. Sitting down in her usual seat to wait for him, she started reading Isaiah Berlin. A short time later, Allen phoned from his office to explain he'd been delayed. As Farrow put down the phone, she noticed six Polaroid photographs on the mantelpiece. ('Scattered around,' her supporters say, 'where anyone could see them, even the maids.' 'Under a tissue box,' claims Allen.) They were classic 'split beaver' shots of a nude Soon-Yi with her legs wide open. In every photograph, both her vagina and her face were in shot, with no attempt to disguise her identity. 'I felt I was looking straight into the face of pure evil,' Farrow said.

She immediately called Allen back and said, 'I found the photographs. Get away from me.' Returning across the park with the Polaroids in her bag, she met Sascha Previn in the hallway. 'Woody's been fucking Soon-Yi,' she told him. 'Call André.' Soon-Yi was in her room. Farrow showed her the pictures and screamed, 'What have you done?' (Other accounts suggest she hit her with a chair.) Then Farrow retreated to her bedroom.

Allen arrived shortly after. What exactly passed between the two will never be known for certain. According to Farrow, Allen declared, 'I'm in love with Soon-Yi.' Then, oddly, 'I would marry her.'

'Then take her,' said Farrow, 'and get out.'

Allen, says Farrow, immediately responded, 'No, no. That's just something I thought of to say in the car coming over here. It's not what I feel. I don't want that.'

In the argument that followed, he claimed that he meant his seduction of Soon-Yi to be 'a springboard into a deeper relationship' for himself and Farrow. The liaison had been 'a tepid little affair', he insisted, that would have petered out as Soon-Yi became interested in men of her own age. He even suggested, to Farrow's understandable scorn, that he'd merely intended to bolster the girl's sexual confidence. As for the pictures, he would later say they'd been taken as 'a lark of a moment', when Soon-Yi expressed interest in a modelling career.

Shortly after, Kristi Groetke received another of Farrow's familiar phone calls. 'Something terrible has happened,' she said. 'I can't go into it, but we're changing the locks at the house in the country. And we're also changing our phone number. I'll leave a set of keys for you.' On 18 January she circulated a letter to all the children. It began, 'My children, An atrocity has been committed against our family and it is impossible to make sense of it . . .'

The fact that Farrow and Allen were in the middle of making a film together lent these events an overtone of black comedy. Farrow must have been uneasily aware that without his annual film, she would have almost no income. When the assistant director called her for reshoots two days after she found the Polaroids, she dutifully turned up on the set. Ironically, the scene to be shot was that in which Judy tells Gabe she no longer loves him. Farrow looked, as *Entertainment Weekly* put it, 'wan, flu-ish, on the verge of tears', and even on film, 'ghostly and haggard'.

Allen's public relations advisers, PMK, choked off all information to the press and urged Allen to patch things up with Farrow before the news got out. Everyone on the unit was sworn to secrecy. Given its parallels to real life, *Husbands and Wives* had become a potential public relations disaster. Copies of the script, as hard to acquire as had been all Allen's scripts, became subject to frantic monitoring. A few days after Liam Neeson had lent his to Lysette Anthony overnight, she received a panic call from the office. 'Liam has lost his script and you were the last to see it,' they told her. 'I felt like I was at school,' she said. The script turned up in Neeson's hotel room.

No news so explosive could be contained for long, and within weeks, rumours were circulating that Allen had been caught in bed with one of Farrow's adopted daughters, presumably the under-age Dylan. The story remained a rumour for another six months while Allen and Farrow manoeuvred for position in the legal battle to come.

Without the legal recourses of an abandoned wife, Farrow was determined to ensure that she ended up with enough money to protect her lifestyle and that of her family. Allen, she said, was desperate to retrieve the Polaroids, but in February she took them to a lawyer for safe-keeping. Allen proposed they burn them together, but Farrow insisted they would stay under lock and key for the rest of her life.

*   *   *

The battle assumed the character of melodrama. On 14 February, Allen received a Valentine card from Farrow and his family. On a large heart with the message 'Especially for You' Farrow had written words like 'Loss' and 'Betrayal', and the message, 'The child you used has pierced my heart a hundred times and deep.' A photograph of Farrow and the children in happier times was mounted on the card. Through her chest in the photograph, she thrust a serrated steak-knife, while kitchen spikes pierced the hearts of the children. Glued to the handle of the knife was a Xerox of one of the Soon-Yi Polaroids. Far from the playful atmosphere in which, Allen claimed, the photographs were taken, the expression on Soon-Yi's face is chilling – an impassive, challenging erotic stare.

As if his personal problems not enough, Orion, now operating under Chapter 11, elected to premier *Shadows and Fog* in Paris on 12 February, more than a month before its scheduled American release. Reviews were respectable and houses good, but nobody claimed the film was vintage Allen. On 20 March it opened in the United States. Reviews were wearily complimentary, though most critics and audiences found little to excite them in a film that covered old stylistic ground in a slightly more exotic style. It grossed a mere $1.2 million on first release, and did even worse in Europe.

The still-covert war between Farrow and Allen continued, the antagonists lobbing bombshells at one another across Central Park, where once they had waved from their balconies. Moses sent Allen a letter informing him that he no longer wanted to be considered his son, and hoped he would 'get so humiliated that [he would] commit suicide'. It ended, in block capitals, 'I HOPE YOU ARE PROUD TO CRUSH YOUR SON'S DREAM.' Given that Moses suffered from cerebral palsy, some assumed from its sophisticated text that Farrow wrote the letter, or at least dictated it, as she did most of the documents her children directed at Allen. After the letter, Moses refused to see Allen when he made his supervised visits to Dylan and Satchel. Sometimes Allen visited them at Frog Hollow, where Farrow tried to make him sleep in the guest house. He refused. 'There are *animals* out there,' he said with a shudder.

*   *   *

As much to keep his mind occupied as anything else, Allen began writing his Fall Project. Avoiding anything too demanding, he decided to make the Nick-and-Nora Charles-type detective story he'd planned with Marshall Brickman as far back as *Annie Hall*. 'The Couple Next Door' became *Manhattan Murder Mystery*, and Allan signed Farrow to play opposite him.

The casting of Farrow in *Manhattan Murder Mystery* is one of the more improbable elements in the melodrama of the Farrow/Allen split, but given the nature of their relationship, it is not entirely out of character. Though Allen professed himself astonished that, in the midst of their domestic tornado, Farrow still tried to arrange costume fittings and pressed Robert Greenhut for a start date on the film, she no doubt thought that in continuing with the project she was behaving 'professionally'. She also needed the money, and would have realised that as long as she kept to her side of the contract Allen would be committed to keeping her in the film – or, if not, to paying her off.

At the same time, she continued to give full vent to her spleen as a mortified adoptive mother and abandoned lover. Allen would later testify that she 'called me a dozen times a night, raging and screaming into the phone, threatening to kill me. In any number of these calls, I could hear the children in the background, and said, "Please don't do this in front of the children."' Some of these calls were surreptitiously taped, and later leaked to *New York Post* columnist Cindy Adams. In them, Farrow tells Allen, 'You changed. You're old now. Now you want little girls to turn you on because you can't get a [term deleted by the *Post*] with me any more. That's all it is.' Adams continued, 'Mia then reminds the man who had been her lover for twelve years exactly what she had to do to coax him to performance capability.'

Given this climate of hatred, it's astonishing that Allen continued to visit Frog Hollow to see Dylan and Satchel, and that he and Farrow twice spent the night together in the Carlyle Hotel. According to him, the meetings took place at her instigation, and for sex, but soon descended into recriminations. 'She became totally hysterical,' he says. 'I thought she was going to jump out the window. It was a terrible experience: screaming, shrieking, thoughts of suicide.' He even feared that she might have poisoned the wine they drank. On subsequent visits to Frog Hollow, he always took his own food with him.

By early August, the rivals' lawyers had worked out a compromise. Under a deal agreed by both, Allen would still have access to the children, and Farrow would continue to work in his films. They would even go on family holidays to Europe together. The Polaroids and Allen's relationship with Soon-Yi would remain secret, and neither would comment on them in public. On 4 August Allen went to Frog Hollow to see Dylan and Satchel, expecting to sign the agreement with Farrow the following week. He never did so. That day, Farrow claimed she'd caught him, during a brief unsupervised moment – no longer than ten minutes – sexually molesting Dylan in an attic at the house. ('In *light-years*, I wouldn't go into an attic,' protested the claustrophobic Allen later.) Some days later she offered investigators a videotape of her own shooting, heavily edited, in which the little girl appeared to corroborate the story, though the Yale–New Haven Hospital Child Abuse Evaluation Clinic decided she was quite possibly 'coached or influenced by her mother'.

Allen's supporters understandably rejected Farrow's revelations, and found motives for her fabricating them. 'Mia had first accused Woody of molesting Soon-Yi,' said Jean Doumanian. 'But Soon-Yi is a woman. So when that didn't work, she went for the other charge.' She is convinced that sexual jealousy lay at the heart of Farrow's fury: 'She asked if Soon-Yi was better in bed than she was. She made Woody's life a private hell.'

The Dylan tape was leaked to TV Channel 5, which declined to air it. But the news quickly spread. The family paediatrician, after examining Dylan, fulfilled his legal obligations by reporting Farrow's charges to the Connecticut Child Protection Service, which alerted the state police. Allen was barred from seeing the children.

On 13 August Allen's lawyers met Farrow's – led, ironically, by his sometime admirer Alan Dershowitz. Immediately money became the topic of discussion. Though both sides disagree on what precisely was said, it became clear that Farrow wanted about $7 million, whether as child support or hush money remained vague. Allen's lawyers refused to pay, and the same day filed papers they had already prepared asking the New York Supreme Court to grant him custody of Satchel, Moses and Dylan.

On 14 August the *New York Daily News* led with 'IT'S SOLO MIA', and three days later the *Post* finally broke the news of the Allen/Soon-Yi affair with 'WOODY LOVES MIA'S DAUGHTER'. The following day, Allen gave a press conference on national TV. Speaking from the Plaza Hotel before a battery of cameras and hundreds of eager journalists, but refusing to answer questions, he confessed his love for Soon-Yi and rejected Farrow's accusations of sexual abuse of Dylan. In a statement which, he said ruefully, was 'all straight lines', i.e. lacking jokes, he claimed to be 'guilty only of falling in love with Mia Farrow's adult daughter at the end of our years together'. Following this statement, Farrow presumably regarded herself as free to discharge all the weapons at her disposal, and on 19 August the *Post* led with 'MIA'S GOT NUDE PIX'. On 25 August Allen and Farrow met for three hours with Judge Phyllis B. Gangel-Jacob of the New York Supreme Court, and agreed to make no further statements to the press.

Farrow, whether from innocence, optimism or self-delusion, rang Allen's production office the same week to confirm the start date of *Manhattan Murder Mystery* and to discuss costume fittings. Told that her role was now being taken by Diane Keaton, she sued for her $350,000 fee, due under the 'pay or play' provisions of her contract. Privately, she and Allen negotiated over the telephone. He offered her a cash settlement to stop fighting his suit for custody of Dylan. 'So I should let you — my next daughter?' demanded Farrow. 'Just let you — my next daughter and shut up about it and just take the deal?' She went on, 'I'm sorry that I can't be in your next movie,' but Allen didn't rise to the bait.

TriStar, which had been alarmed at the prospect of losing money on *Husbands and Wives*, now became aware of a brisk market in bootleg cassettes of the film at $200 a time. On

24 August they cautiously announced that, in view of public interest, they would advance the release date to 14 September and increase the number of prints. Originally *Husbands and Wives* had been due to open in eight theatres. Under the new plan, it would show on 865 screens, the widest release ever for an Allen film.

Almost on the day *Husbands and Wives* opened, Allen started shooting *Manhattan Murder Mystery*. The plot had modified somewhat from its first incarnation, as the story of a kindly philosopher who inexplicably commits suicide. Now its main characters are the East Coast versions of the couple in *Scenes from a Mall*, Larry (Allen), a publisher's editor, and his wife Carol (Keaton). With their son grown up and away at college, they have too much time on their hands, making them restless and, in Carol's case at least, obsessively inquisitive. (When Farrow had been set to play Carol, Allen thought of Larry as the curious one, but he decided it would make more sense if Keaton instigated the investigative plot.)

By chance, the couple become friendly with their older next-door neighbours, Paul House (Jerry Adler), owner of a repertory movie house, and his wife Lillian (Lyn Cohen) – who, to their astonishment, dies shortly after of a heart attack. Made suspicious by House's evident indifference to her death, Carol starts to pry, and steals the building superintendent's pass key so she can check his apartment. When she finds Lillian's ashes kept casually under the sink, and two tickets to Paris, then overhears his conversations with a young actress, Carol is convinced that he murdered his wife.

Larry doesn't share her suspicions, but Carol enlists their playwright friend Ted (Alan Alda), a recent divorcee with a crush on her, to help. Meanwhile, Larry is working with seductive authoress Marcia Fox (Anjelica Huston) on a new book, and decides she might find Ted interesting. Once the four of them get together, Carol's suspicions prove contagious, and they are soon scheming to discover more. After a series of increasingly improbable stratagems they find that Lillian is still alive. The woman who died in the Houses' apartment was a relative who resembled her, and they seized the opportunity to loot her bank account. House then does kill his wife, and Larry, for so long the sceptic, finds himself in a violent showdown in House's cinema during a screening of Orson Welles' *Lady from Shanghai*.

With his mind clearly elsewhere, Allen did a perfunctory job on *Manhattan Murder Mystery*. There are numerous borrowings, including the elaborate faking of a phone conversation using prerecorded dialogue, which Preston Sturges had guyed in 1948 in one of Allen's favourite comedies, *Unfaithfully Yours*. In that film the scheme came hilariously unstuck, as one suspects it would have done here. The plotting of *Manhattan Murder Mystery* is weak. Every guess proves uncannily accurate. Carol's chance sighting of Mrs House on a bus, Ted's fortuitous access to a theatre for a fake audition, the improbable disposal of a corpse in a vat of molten steel; all strain credulity – not rare for an Allen film, except that this time there's no magical element to neutralise our disbelief. Even the investigators seemed bored. Ted and Carol take time off from sleuthing to discuss opening a restaurant together, and Marcia spends an afternoon in the Café des Artistes teaching Larry how to improve his poker game. Manhattan looks grey and empty, the apartments claustrophobic, the skies overcast, Keaton frumpy, Allen wizened. Overnight, the charm of Woodyland seemed to have leaked away.

Audiences felt much the same about *Husbands and Wives*. More widely reviewed than most other Allen films by critics who sieved every line for *doubles entendres* and autobiographical hints, its run started healthily, fuelled by stories of Allen's legal team taking up the front row at early previews, alert for damaging parallels with life. But after five weeks, takings dropped to the average for Allen's films, and it grossed only $10.5 million in the US, despite some later reviews which rated it among his best work. Jay Scott in the *Boston Globe and Mail* called it 'raw, sharp, funny, cynical'. Contrasting Carlo DiPalma's shooting with the 'burnished buttery pastel yellow' of the lighting, he remarked, 'It's as if a stalking tiger had been let loose in a Rembrandt.' On the other hand, William Grimes in the *New York Times* noted, 'The film can be read as a script from Mr Allen's own life, with parallels that range from intriguing to uncanny.'

When the film became available on video in December 1992, the conservative Blockbuster chain of video stores, representing 15 per cent of the American rental market, refused to stock it, notwithstanding the lack of evidence of any wrongdoing on Allen's part. Overseas, audiences and distributors proved no more forgiving. The Catholic Church, which had turned a blind eye to Allen's cohabitation with Farrow, made it known that it didn't approve of whatever it was that he was supposed to have done to her adopted daughter. As a result, Co-Op Nordemiglia cancelled the last of Allen's five contracted commercials, and Oreste Lionello, his 'voice' in Italy, refused to dub *Shadows and Fog*.

What exactly, asked more thoughtful voices, *was* Allen supposed to have done that was so appalling? Sleeping with the young and not very bright daughter of a girlfriend he was about to ditch might be a lapse of taste, but it was hardly an indictable offence. Such situations, in fact, were the stuff of Hollywood films, which frequently dwelt on illicit May/September romances. Nobody had protested much when Allen depicted such a relationship in *Manhattan*. Why should it be so shocking in real life?

Farrow's supporters nevertheless insisted that his crime was unforgivable. Before the scandal broke, her agent, Lynn Nesbit, confided to a friend that 'the worst thing that could happen to a woman' had happened to Farrow. The friend at first assumed that Allen had given her AIDS, and was inclined to shrug off the importance of some amateur porn Polaroids, but Farrow responded furiously, 'What can one think of someone who takes pictures of his son's sister's cunt?'

Many protests were simply misinformed. Some people imagined that Soon-Yi was Allen's biological child, or that she was under-age. Others gave credence to Farrow's accusations of his sexual interest in Dylan, though nothing in his past behaviour suggested he harboured inclinations towards paedophilia. Moreover, such charges, not uncommon in custody battles, seldom held much water, and were usually discreetly dropped once the accused agreed to pay up.

There remained a residue of genuine animus against Allen, the major ingredient of which was disappointment. *Newsweek* summed it up well when it commented:

New Yorkers thought they knew Woody and Mia, who were paradoxically among the most private and most visible celebrities in the city. Rarely sitting still for an interview or photograph, they were constantly being spotted out on the town or just on the street, schlepping Farrow's innumerable kids to museums, schools, ball games or lunch.

In life as in art, Allen had seemed the perfect New York lover: successful in a creative field, earnest and funny; qualities that in New York carry the same cachet as 'rich' in, say, Dallas. He didn't get drunk or hit women, and if in his films his character chased around now and then, at least he had the decency to feel guilty over it. People who had cast Allen in their own private movie – who dreamed about him, imitated him, retold his jokes – were offended to discover what they should have known from the start: that film stars are not the characters they portray.

Better counselled, Allen might have neutralised the worst of the bad publicity. Had he gone on *The Johnny Carson Show* to confess his wrongs, offered to make amends, perhaps broken down in tears – one thinks of British actor Hugh Grant a decade later, caught with a street hooker in a car off Hollywood Boulevard – the scandal could have been defused. But Allen, true to his roots in the 'Me Decade' of the seventies, elected to tough it out, a challenge the Caring, Sharing eighties couldn't ignore. Adam Gopnik, writing in the *New Yorker*, offered one of the best analyses of where Allen went wrong:

He made his best comedy by recognising that the sexual revolution had opened a vast space between abstract belief and real life – between what the fifties had taught you to say and what the sixties and seventies allowed you to do. But when a new abyss began to open in the last decade – one in which sex was separated from the realm of comedy and taken over almost exclusively by that of confession – he couldn't plumb it, or perhaps even see that it existed. When the new gap widened, he fell right in.

25

Bullets Over Broadway and Mighty Aphrodite

All the papers
Where I led the news
With my capers,
Now have spread the news:
'Superman
Turns Out to Flash in the Pan.'

Ira Gershwin's lyrics for 'I Can't get Started',
first sung by Bob Hope in *Ziegfeld Follies of 1936*

The Allen/Farrow feud became America's favourite soap opera, with the tabloids, in particular the *New York Post*, making a meal of it. 'For them it was a delight,' said Allen. 'It sold papers.' To avoid being overheard in public or on the phone, Jean Doumanian, Letty, Sandy Morse, Juliet Taylor and his publicist, almost the only people he now saw socially except for Soon-Yi, developed a code for discussing his problems, referring to Mia, the children and the problem in terms that no eavesdropper could follow.

Now it was Doumanian who accompanied Allen to Knicks games. His ex-assistant Jane Read Martin lived with young screenwriter Douglas McGrath, who was adapting Garson Kanin's *Born Yesterday* as a vehicle for Melanie Griffith and John Goodman. Allen loathed McGrath's adaptation but liked him enough to ask him, over dinner in January 1993, if he'd care to collaborate on a new film. He offered five ideas, of which McGrath preferred a flat-out comedy about Broadway in the twenties.

Allen had plenty to discuss with his supporters, and not simply the Woody Allen Fall Project or matters relating to Farrow. TriStar had run into the same financial problems as Orion, and its management was wavering in its commitment to Allen. Mike Medavoy departed, leaving Allen without supporters in the company's highest administration. Jean Doumanian, who had just gone into film production herself as Sweetland Films with money from her companion Jacqui Safra, and had achieved a *succès d'estime* with Sven Nykvist's first film as a director, *The Ox*, had been hoping for some time to persuade Allen that she could do a better job on his films than a Hollywood mini-major.

His popularity in the United States had declined steadily since *Hannah and her Sisters*, every film losing money in the domestic market but making an eventual profit in Europe and Asia. With Safra willing to bankroll production of his films, backed up by pre-sales to, in particular, France, where in 1991 he had actually sold more seats than in the US, Sweetland were in a position to offer both the budgets and the freedom he needed. At the turn of the year, he began to negotiate his escape from the TriStar deal.

'I'd worry about big film companies changing hands,' Allen would explain later. 'I'd get one small group of people who cared about the films, and they wouldn't be there in six months. So I decided to go into business with Sweetland, people who cared about my films.' To further watch over his interests, Sweetland took on Letty Aronson, who had been running the New York Museum of Radio and Television, as head of production.

In January 1993, Allen and McGrath started writing the Broadway script. McGrath vividly evoked the circumstances under which they worked:

He began by raising his arms in a sort of Zorba the Greek-like attitude and snapping his fingers as if to signal the start of a show. Then he began: 'It's the Roaring Twenties and there's this playwright who thinks of himself as a great artist –' The phone rang. He lifted his finger, indicating that he would just be a second, and took the call. He spoke in low tones, saying things like 'a long history of mental problems . . . tried every drug known to man . . . private detectives . . .' Then he hung up and turned to me. He caught his breath, smiled, lifted his arms, and snapped his fingers. 'Okay, Roaring Twenties, playwright, great artist, and he goes to a producer seeking a production of his

play, but he wants to direct it himself to protect its artistic integ–'
The phone rang, and before I could blink, he was back on the
line saying 'Intensely claustrophobic ... two red eyes at the
window ... sent her child to the *Post* ... hairs in a glassine
envelope ...' When he hung up the third time, he didn't snap
his fingers. He just smiled sheepishly and said, 'OK, let's get
back to work on our little comic bauble.'

The playwright who thinks himself a great artist is David Shayne
(John Cusack), a Greenwich Village intellectual who writes in the
style of Eugene O'Neill. The first lines of the film are, 'I'm an
artist.' His producer Julian Marx (Jack Warden), loyal in the face
of Shayne's continued failure and stiff-necked insistence on his
artistic integrity, finds someone prepared to back his next play,
God of our Fathers. Unfortunately the backer is gang boss Nick
Valenti (Joe Vitrelli), who wants a starring role for his chorus-girl
mistress Olive Neal (Jennifer Tilly), but Marx persuades Shayne
it's his only chance to see his work on Broadway in the form he
thinks it deserves. Shayne is mollified when he's able to hire his
dream cast, led by the ageing but still charismatic Helen Sinclair
(Dianne Wiest) and British actor Warner Purcell (Jim Broadbent).
He's even prepared to accept the constant presence at rehearsals
of gunman Cheech (Chazz Palminteri), sent to keep an eye on
Olive.

The plot of *God of our Fathers* revolves around the breakdown
of a marriage and the intervention of a psychiatrist, played with
increasing ineptitude by Olive, whose dramatic experience consists
of some years as a stripper, picking up quarters from bar-tops
with her vagina. Every time a despairing Shayne tries to cut her
lines, Cheech intervenes. Shayne consoles himself by starting an
affair with Helen, who sees him as her live-in writer who will
relaunch her career. Olive is also diverting herself with Purcell,
until Cheech warns him off. Under stress, the actor begins eating
obsessively.

At first casually, Cheech begins making suggestions about the
play. To the astonishment of everyone, including Shayne, they are
apt. The gunman, it turns out, is a born playwright, and is soon

rewriting *God of our Fathers*, to its considerable improvement. He and Shayne meet in a pool hall where he describes his life as a deprived child, delinquent and gangster. Back in Greenwich Village, Shayne's writer, painter and poet friends, all unpublished but triumphantly secure in their artistic purity, seem increasingly trivial by comparison. Cheech, for his part, begins to understand the burden of creativity as he watches his work being ruined by Olive. Eventually it becomes too much for him, and he takes her out and shoots her, blaming it on rival bootleggers. Valenti finds out, and has Cheech shot on the opening night of the play. Dying, he makes another brilliant suggestion for the ending. The play is a success, but Shayne decides to leave New York and settle down in his native Pittsburgh with his girlfriend. 'I'm not an artist,' he says as he departs.

In February 1993, *Husbands and Wives* received two Oscar nominations: Allen for Best Original Screenplay and Judy Davis for Best Supporting Actress. Neither won, but the Allen camp took heart from the apparent show of support. Perhaps the industry didn't regard him as a total pariah. This turned out to be less than completely true. Allen still had his supporters, but Hollywood remained faithful to its traditional belief in 'no smoke without fire'. 'One of the reasons studios loved being in business with Woody,' said an associate, 'and were happy to break even, was that surely he was one of the world's great directors, and there was a public relations value in being in business with him. [After the scandal] that value was diluted. People weren't knocking down doors to do business with him.'

With no income in prospect, Farrow was forced to give up the apartment at the Langham, a wrench for which she never forgave Allen. The family moved to Frog Hollow, where she began doing her best to efface any memory of him. Dylan was renamed Eliza, and Satchel became Harmon, later changed yet again to Seamus.

After exhaustive interviews and forensic tests during which he was required, to his bemusement, to contribute samples of hair from all parts of his body, the Yale-New Haven Child Abuse Evaluation team comprehensively exonerated Allen of all charges that he had sexually molested Dylan. 'They investigated it for six months,' he said. 'They met with the kids. They met with me. They met with the doctors. They went over this thing scrupulously. They've done seventeen hundred investigations prior to this and are the best people in the world by consent of the people who hired them and have used them before and Mia's attorneys and all that, and when they came back with the printed verdict – I mean unequivocal – it was that no molestation had taken place. The mother needs psychiatric help. The father and the daughter should be reunited immediately.'

On 25 March, shortly after the report was delivered, Allen's application for custody of Satchel, Moses and Dylan came before the State Supreme Court. Ill at ease in a crowded Courtroom 341, Allen made a poor showing. The *New York Times* described him variously as 'looking remarkably like a befuddled old man' and 'a bright but poorly prepared graduate student struggling through a crucial oral examination'. It struck the reporter how much this fumbling appearance contrasted with the artfully awkward Woody of the movies: 'The trial was a highly unwelcome surrender of artistic control over the Allen persona.'

That control had passed to Farrow. She read out Moses' letter to Allen, with its fervent wish, 'I hope you get so humiliated that you commit suicide.' Allen's lawyers suggested that Moses' use of the word 'needy', a Farrow favourite, pointed to her as the true author, but as the *New York Times*' headline put it, 'Son's Letter of Anguish Rivets Court in Allen Case'. Allen lost no points by being unable to name his children's pets, never having gone to a PTA meeting, and other parental deficiencies. On 7 July the judge dismissed his custody claim as 'frivolous', and upheld the continued restriction on visits to the children – a triumph, many thought, for the acting ability of Farrow, who played the grieving mother to perfection.

Doug McGrath, who attended the hearings with the idea that he might write about them, believes that the judge 'appeared unable to move past Woody's romance with Soon-Yi, feeling that whatever Mia did in retaliation, including the false charges of molestation, was permissible, a piece of thinking that Woody compared to this: "If a guy gets fired from his job and the boss with-holds his last paycheque and stiffs him, and the guy takes a machine gun to a shopping mall and shoots sixteen innocent people, you don't say, 'Well, hey, the boss stiffed him.' In this case, the kids are the victims of revenge."'

That everyone involved was living through a psychodrama whose course was being directed by Farrow became increasingly clear after incidents like the arrival of Satchel and his supervisor at Allen's apartment for one of his weekly visits following the hearing. Satchel had thrown up in the car, and as Allen opened the door the supervisor handed him the bag of vomit and said, 'Mia wanted you to have this.'

Farrow now also turned to the Catholic Church. From the time of *Peyton Place*, she'd occasionally visited the Abbey of Regina Laudes in Sharon, Connecticut, not far from Frog Hollow. It had become known as 'the convent to the stars' after ex-Hollywood actress Dolores Hart took the veil and began working there. Often with her agent Lynn Nesbit, whose daughter was Matthew Previn's girlfriend, Farrow spent many weekend retreats there with the children, during which she poured out to Hart, Nesbit and a few friends intimate confessions of her sex life with Allen and his supposed eccentricities.

In August, *Manhattan Murder Mystery* opened to indifferent reviews but healthy US domestic grosses of $11.5 million. By the time the film had made its triumphant progress through Europe, it would be well into profit. Two weeks earlier, on 21 July, Allen and Jean Doumanian announced that TriStar had agreed to cancel his third film under their deal, and that he was joining Sweetland. *Bullets Over Broadway* would be their first film.

In September Allen started shooting. Collaborating with McGrath had induced a new geniality, and a respect for the wis-dom of ordinary people which Allen had never celebrated before – in fact he had disparaged it in films like *Love and Death*, where the peasants exist mainly to be scorned by his intellectuals. In *Bullets Over Broadway* and the film that followed it, *Mighty Aphrodite*, he goes out of his way to acknowledge that the stupid can not merely lead fulfilling lives but can create wonderful things, either artistically (Cheech's play in *Bullets*) or physically (Mira Sorvino's son in *Aphrodite*).

In this new climate of cultural acceptance, Allen even casts doubt on the language of the intelligentsia: 'You don't write like people talk,' Cheech tells Shayne matter-of-factly. All the intellectuals in *Bullets Over Broadway* talk too much: blowhard philosopher and writer Sheldon Flender (Rob Reiner) presides over coffee-shop seminars and Stacy Nelkin makes a brief appearance in a midnight discussion of sexual technique. Dianne Wiest has a clever continuing gag in which, as Shayne tries to talk to her, she clamps her hand melodramatically over his mouth and orders, 'Please. Don't speak. Don't say a word.' Only Cheech and the other gangsters remain silent. Bullets speak louder than Broadway, though even Cheech succumbs to the prevailing logorrhea. His last words after he's shot are, 'Don't speak.'

Sensing that Allen had loosened up slightly on his textual strictness, the film's actors tentatively tried altering their dialogue, an impulse he crushed. He directed Jennifer Tilly, inspiredly vulgar as Olive, to talk constantly, babbling 'Charmed, charmed,' as she was introduced to people and keeping up a baffled *obligato* to the rehearsals, but he insisted the other actors stick to the script. 'He'd come up to me and say, "When so-and-so starts ad-libbing, don't answer him,"' says Tilly. 'Or "Push so-and-so out the door sooner, before he comes up with any more of those ad-libs." Probably I was very unpopular. I was Woody's hall monitor, basically.'

There was little temptation to improvise with gags and comic characters of the quality invented by Allen and McGrath. Wiest's Helen Sinclair is a blown rose with a voice like Tallulah Bankhead and a thirst to match. 'Two martinis, very dry,' she orders in a speakeasy. 'How did you know what I drink?' asks Shayne, at which she looks at him frostily and says, 'Oh, do you want one too?' Arriving late for rehearsal, she explains airily, 'My pedicurist had a stroke. She fell forward onto the orange stick and plunged it into my toe. It required bandaging.'

Juliet Taylor spotted British actor Jim Broadbent in the 1991 comedy of manners *Enchanted April*. He makes an inspired comic creation of Warner Purcell, who balloons visibly as he overeats under the strain of rehearsal, but is at his best in the worst of situations: fleeing his dressing room via the fire escape, he runs into some old friends in the street, and they chat, oblivious of the fact that he's wearing only underwear and a corset.

Allen and McGrath obviously enjoy playing with the concept of artistic purity. Shayne agrees completely with his Greenwich Village friends as long as they are all equally unsuccessful, but once he has a play on Broadway he compromises at every turn. It's the apparently amoral Cheech who proves the true unbending artist, prepared even to kill to protect his work. Shayne is equally pusillanimous when it comes to sex, deceiving his girlfriend with Helen Sinclair, then being astonished when she reveals she is having an affair with Sheldon Flender, an intellect so massive, she says, that sex with him reaches new heights. 'You mean you've raised intercourse to the level of art?' Shayne demands incredulously. 'Not just intercourse,' she replies. 'Foreplay too.' In justification, she quotes back at him one of the *bons mots* of the Greenwich Village café: 'An artist creates his own moral universe.'

Mia was in Ireland, working on John Irvin's *Widow's Peak*, her first film after the break-up. Ironically, Hugh Leonard wrote the play ten years earlier with the idea of Maureen O'Sullivan in the lead and Mia in a lesser role. Among her co-stars was Broadbent, who asked for her advice when Allen offered him the part in *Bullets Over Broadway*. She admitted that she couldn't fault her ex-partner as a director, whatever else she thought him to be. Elsewhere, she lost no opportunity to denigrate him. 'I feel like I'm out of a cage,' she said. 'Woody's films were so insular. He had his own family of actors, and everyone knew his movies took up most of the year. So I never had a chance to do anything else.'

In December, between the end of principal photography and reshoots on *Bullets Over Broadway*, Allen made a quick trip to Europe to promote the British release of *Manhattan Murder Mystery* the following January, during which he visited the set of *Widow's Peak* and demanded to see Satchel. When Farrow refused, he got a court order from New York and took his son to the Dublin zoo, but the intrusive press drove them back inside after just three hours. Disconsolate, Allen returned to London, where most of the interviews delved into his personal problems, the film taking a back seat.

In February he was back in Europe, this time in Venice, where he was thinking of shooting a film, and Sicily, looking for locations for what would become *Mighty Aphrodite*, a film about a New York Jewish intellectual alienated from his wife who invests all his affection in their young adopted son. 'Years ago I was looking at Dylan,' Allen said, 'and I thought, gee, she's so bright and charming and funny, she must have come from good biological parents. The idea went out of my head. Then some months later I thought it would make a funny story about a character who becomes obsessed with the idea – maybe if his marriage wasn't going well – that he might be in love with his son's real mother, then finds out she is horrible, a prostitute, a vulgarian, stupid.' Any lingering doubts about the influence on Allen's work of his private life could now be decisively dispelled.

On his return to New York, Allen started immediately on a remake of *Don't Drink the Water* for ABC TV, with himself not only directing but starring in the role of the New Jersey caterer Walter Hollander he'd originally based on his father. Jackie Gleason's hijacking of the earlier film had long rankled, and ABC's offer gave him the chance, as he saw it, to repair a long-standing error.

On paper, it seemed a good idea, especially as he was able to pack the cast with old friends. Julie Kavner played Hollander's wife, John Doumanian the Arab potentate whose unexpected arrival in the US Embassy precipitates most of the jokes. They got solid support from Dom DeLuise as stir-crazy Father Drobney, Austin Pendleton as the neurasthenic chef and Edward Herrmann as the first secretary. Michael J. Fox lowered himself to take the negligible role of Axel Magee.

Don't Drink the Water shot for four weeks from 4 April 1994. The weakest link, oddly, was Allen, who was hard to accept as either a caterer, an ignorant tourist or the father of a grown-up daughter. In the most convincing evidence that his true importance was as a performer rather than a director, he had joined other stars in being convincing only when he was typecast. Fred Astaire only played a working-class part once, an ordinary seaman in *Follow the Fleet*, and gave the one unconvincing performance of his career. Bob Hope never even bothered to try stepping outside his persona as a wisecracking coward, knowing he'd alienate his audience, just as Red Skelton knew his admirers demanded repeated performances as the amiable oaf. 'Wet, she's a star,' a mogul had decreed of Esther Williams, and unless Allen was being 'Woody', nobody wanted to know. Audiences had become too accustomed to his character's narrow parameters. These excluded grown-up children, a quotidian profession – he's always a journalist or writer – or cultural naïveté: he can dislike foreign travel, opera, ballet or Chinese food, but from the informed viewpoint of someone who's been there and tried it. (ABC also announced that Allen would direct but not appear in a courtroom drama called 'Powers of Attorney', scripted by Alan Rosen, but the project never eventuated.)

On 12 May the Supreme Court handed down its verdict on Allen's appeal against the decision not to give him custody of his children. It was negative. This wasn't entirely unexpected, but it filled him with despair. What mattered, he told Douglas McGrath, was that he had tried. 'When my children are older,' he said, 'I want them to know that their father didn't abandon them but gave it his all. More than anything, that's what I'm fighting for: so they'll know that I fought for us to be together with every fibre of my being.'

In September 1994 *Bullets Over Broadway* had its world premiere at the Venice Film Festival. It opened the following month in the United States, and in February 1995 received seven Academy Award nominations: Best Director, Original Screenplay, Art Direction, Supporting Actor and Actress for Chazz Palminteri and Jennifer Tilly, and Actress, won by Dianne Wiest. But it was small consolation to Allen for the loss of his family.

While Allen was writing what became *Mighty Aphrodite*, Jean Doumanian proved herself a skilful deal-maker. The Miramax company, which had all but cornered the shrinking American art-house market by importing English-language films that offered adult stories and themes while avoiding the US public's dislike of subtitles, had just sold out profitably to Disney. Doumanian persuaded Miramax, even though Allen wouldn't let them see an unfinished version of the film, that *Bullets Over Broadway* would fit perfectly into their new empire. Michael Eisner, who had never given up trying to acquire Allen, agreed, and in June 1994 Miramax paid $20 million for North American rights. This left Sweetland free to make deals in Europe. They found no lack of buyers, and *Bullets Over Broadway* would go on to do far better than most of Allen's films since *Hannah and her Sisters*.

Through the summer, Allen had also been negotiating his return to Broadway, or at least off-Broadway. Producer Julian Schlossberg, in collaboration with Doumanian, agreed to present an evening of three one-act plays, *Hotline* by Elaine May, *An Interview* by David Mamet and Allen's *Central Park West*, at the five-hundred-seat Variety Arts, to be entitled *Death Defying Acts*. English-based Michael Blakemore, who'd had Broadway successes with plays like Peter Shaffer's *Lettice and Lovage*, was imported to direct. He arrived in September 1994 and embarked on what was to be a rocky voyage.

Both the Mamet and May plays were modified TV sketches. May's piece is Nichols and May writ large, a conversation between a despairing woman and the man on the suicide hotline. Mamet showed a man being quizzed in an office about his failure to return a neighbour's lawnmower. We learn in time that the office is an anteroom to hell, and the questioner the devil. His victim is damned not for stealing the lawnmower but because he's a lawyer. Once he passed the bar exam, Satan explains, all hope ceased.

Allen's *Central Park West* took up all the second half, and was considerably more ambitious than the other two plays. Carol arrives at the Central Park West apartment of her friend Phyllis, an analyst, whose husband, Sam, is leaving her for another woman. Carol announces she's that woman, ready to dump her feeble husband, Howard, to be with Sam. At this point we learn that Sam, who's guilty of more than one infidelity, is actually going off with Juliet, a twenty-one-year-old film student, and a patient of Phyllis'.

Working with three writers who were also directors proved a daunting experience for Blakemore. Fortunately the famously abrasive Mamet was too busy with a new child to attend rehearsals or the out-of-town try-out in Stamford, Connecticut, and left him alone. May, also known as a demanding director, gave relatively little trouble. It was Allen who drove him to distraction, with his constant presence at rehearsals and post-performance 'notes' for the actors ('Terrible. A real step backwards. *Shit*!'), which reduced them to fury or tears. 'On his movies,' wrote Blakemore in his journal, 'when Woody's displeased, he fires, then reshoots. And I daresay extreme opinions help him get his way. But in the theatre, where we have to depend on each other for the whole journey, reckless criticism can be extremely destructive. My job may turn out to be mainly protecting these plays from their creators.'

Death Defying Acts opened in early March 1995. Jeremy Gerard in *Variety* panned it for the 'unrelieved meanness' of the Allen segment. Most critics saw *Central Park West* as Allen's attempt to justify his affair with Soon-Yi. In *Newsday*, Jan Stuart wrote, 'The last-minute addition of the nubile Juliet sours and thickens the stew, riddled as it is with jarring echoes of Allen's own May–September infidelity. "Sam, she could be your daughter," observes Carol as we stare into our laps.' But thanks to more supportive notices from, among others, Vincent Canby in the *New York Times*, the show enjoyed a comfortable run of 343 performances.

Allen came to previews of *Central Park West* with Soon-Yi and petite, seductive English actress Helena Bonham-Carter, whom he'd engaged in London on his last trip to appear in the new film, *Mighty Aphrodite*, and who in her dark good looks somewhat resembled Stacey Nelkin. 'She plays my wife,' Allen said – 'Rather the way,' thought Blakemore, 'a small boy who knows what he wants might announce the proud ownership of a new train set.'

Amanda, Bonham-Carter's character, is an art dealer looking for someone to back her in setting up her own gallery. Lenny Weinrib, her husband, is a sports writer. Like so many of Allen's female characters, she wants a child, and they adopt a newborn baby. Seven years later, Max (Jimmy McQuaid) has become smart, outgoing and attractive. As Amanda spends more time with rich potential backers like Jerry Bender (Peter Weller), who doesn't disguise his itch for her, Lenny decides to track down Max's biological mother. To his astonishment she turns out to be Linda Ash, aka 'Judy Cum', a ravishing but stupid prostitute, porn movie actress and sometime hairdresser.

Once he wins her confidence, Lenny feels a responsibility to rescue Linda. He pays off her pimp Ricky (Dan Moran) with a pair of prime Knicks seats, and fixes her up with Kevin (Michael Rapaport), a boxer as dumb as she is. They're about to marry when Kevin discovers her secret past, blacks her eye and dumps her. Meanwhile, Amanda now has her gallery, and seems about to surrender to Bender's importunities. Consoling one another, Lenny and Linda have sex, and she becomes pregnant. Lenny never finds out, since Amanda decides she loves only him, they're reunited, and Linda disappears until the film's epilogue.

What lifts this flimsy tale to the level of high comedy is the subtext of Greek tragedy. Periodically the scene shifts from Manhattan to the Teatro Greco at Taormina in Sicily where, ravishingly shot against the Sicilian *campagna* with Etna smoking in the distance like the promise of retribution, a Greek chorus in robes and masks comments on the action. Cassandra appears periodically to make dire predictions, and the chorus plead for the intervention of Zeus – or at least try to, since all they get is his answering machine.

The chorus, choreographed by Graciela Daniele, who did the musical numbers for *Bullets Over Broadway* – and, later, the hit Broadway musical adaptation of E.L. Doctorow's *Ragtime* – is a brilliant conceit, and Allen uses it faultlessly. As Kevin and Linda walk through Central Park, getting to know one another, it appears on the bandstand behind them and slips into an *a capella* version of 'You do Something to Me'. Its leader (F. Murray Abraham) accompanies Lenny around New York, warning or cajoling him. Blind Tiresias appears in the person of a bum (Jack Warden) begging for small change with a paper cup, but pausing to warn Lenny in entirely twentieth-century terms that Amanda is about to succumb to Bender.

For once, Allen chose an unknown to star. Linda is played by Mira Sorvino, daughter of roly-poly character actor Paul Sorvino. Her casting was a product of the same London trip during which he chose Helena Bonham-Carter. He'd already seen and decided against Sorvino, but she turned up again in his penthouse suite at the Dorchester in a clinging black Spandex dress and mules with plastic flowers, and he changed his mind. Her performance is a *tour de force*. In matador pants and a overflowing tank top, tottering on high heels, she looks like every man's masturbatory fantasy until she opens her mouth. Out pours a fusillade of obscenities, delivered in a high-pitched, husky, toneless squeal not heard in Hollywood since Monroe.

Bonham-Carter didn't warm to Allen. 'His personality and his style of film, it's a bit nerve-racking,' she says. 'Most films, once you've got the job you've got the job, but he does sack people. I survived that process. His way of filming is different. He shoots it from just one angle. On most films you're waiting for the sun to come out. With Woody you're waiting for it to go in. We spent a whole day on the beach and didn't shoot a thing, because he hates sunlight. He's utterly perverse. He doesn't talk very much. What he said to me all the time was, "Just be real and be American."' He also insisted that her lips remain tight closed during their bedroom scenes, for which he kept on his shoes – 'In case of fire,' he explained.

She also wondered about the conclusion of the film, where, contrary to all logic, Amanda throws over the wealthy and seductive Bender and returns, tearful and contrite, to the weedy, whining Lenny. 'I thought, "Whose fantasy am I in here?"' Indeed, the ending is so pat as to be almost insulting. Rejected by Kevin, Linda is driving outside the city when an ailing helicopter lands beside the road. The handsome pilot turns out to find her attractive, not to mind about her porn and hooker past, and is happy to marry her, even though she is pregnant with Lenny's child, and set her up as a hairdresser in a small town. Some time later, Lenny and Linda run into one another in F.A.O. Schwarz. Lenny admires Linda's baby, not knowing it's his. She admires Max, not knowing he's hers. The chorus sigh; how wonderful is love, and how strange.

Behind the scenes of *Mighty Aphrodite*, the *Gemütlichkeit* of the ending was signally absent. Jean Doumanian was proving a less amiable partner than Allen had hoped. Costs were cut to the bone, salaries reduced to the minimum. Further to impose her rule, Doumanian hired Richard Brick, New York City Film Commissioner under Mayor David Dinkins, as producer. Brick immediately began dismantling the system under which long-time Allen collaborators like Sandy Morse were kept on contract between films and guaranteed a certain number of hours on each production. Celebrities who had agreed to work on Woody's films for $20,000 a week were now asked to accept $10,000. In a singularly mishandled attempt at cheese-paring, Sweetland also decreed the free coffee and pastries traditionally available to every film crew in the long delays between shots would be axed. The decision created such fury that Brick immediately rescinded it, but the impulse to run Sweetland on more profitable lines remained.

26

Everyone Says I Love You and *Deconstructing Harry*

All good Americans should go there to die.

Ira Gershwin, of Paris, in his lyrics for *Bonjour Paris!*

The tragedies of Allen's private life did what nothing else had been able to achieve: they drove him from New York.

1996 was a year of even greater disappointments than usual. After the débâcle of his Irish trip, Farrow stopped sending Satchel for the mandated visits. Allen took her to court, but the judge refused to enforce the order. 'I found myself one of the millions of people who feel that they couldn't get justice,' says Allen. 'It was a very unpleasant ordeal, and I spent many millions of dollars on it and exhausted every possible option I could think of.'

Professionally, his films still failed to attract American audiences. *Mighty Aphrodite* flopped, few audiences understanding its mythological references. Not even Mira Sorvino's Academy Award as Best Supporting Actress lifted the box-office sales much above disappointing. In a conspicuous snub, in the spring of 1995 CBS failed to screen a version of Neil Simon's *The Sunshine Boys* in which Allen played opposite Peter Falk. The story of two feuding ex-partners in a vaudeville act reunited for a TV special by an agent nephew – here transformed into a niece (Sarah Jessica Parker) – had been a hit for George Burns and Walter Matthau in 1975, and Allen had every reason to think this version would do just as well. But as 1996 began without an air date announced, Allen began to suspect that ABC's poor ratings for *Don't Drink the Water* had influenced CBS to cut its losses. 'I thought it was questionable to do in the first place,' said Simon. 'It's about two old vaudevillians, and I don't think a lot of people want to tune in, no matter who it is. If it's never shown, it'll be a pity. I actually thought Woody Allen is terrific in it.'

By contrast with this indifference in America, Europe continued to lionise Allen – literally so in Venice, where he was given an honorary Leone d'Or at the 1997 film festival for the body of his work. His films still did especially well in Italy and France, where his arrival was always a signal for the most prestigious TV programmes to line up to hear his halting French. In Paris, he asked Gerard Depardieu to consider playing Harry Houdini. 'In the film,' explained the star, 'Houdini enters a cage, and has a sudden attack of claustrophobia. So his agent takes him to Dr Freud in Vienna.' For the moment, the film remains one of many unrealised Depardieu projects.

To Europeans, Allen's clarinet playing was an idiosyncrasy verging on the surrealist, and as such it was revered. When his favourite among his collection of ancient Rampones developed a split in 1995, the Buffet factory outside Paris custom-made two Albert system clarinets for him, from plans long since consigned to the company museum. Since 1988 Allen had been quietly rehearsing with a group of professional New York musicians, with whom he had issued a record. This suggested the possibility of a concert tour of Europe, which entrepreneurs had been urging for years, offering Allen as much as $40,000 an appearance.

Jean Doumanian had been itching to do a documentary about Allen and his music for some time, and this provided the perfect pretext. She urged him to do the tour, as a literally priceless source of free publicity, plus a chance to launch Soon-Yi, who so far had appeared only as Allen's tight-lipped companion. Having just seen Terry Zwigoff's Oscar-winning *Crumb*, about the eccentric comic-book artist Robert Crumb, Doumanian summoned the director to Sweetland to discuss an Allen film. She was delighted to find that he was a blues enthusiast, and that two of his earlier documentaries, *Louie Blue* and *A Family Named Moe*, dealt respectively with the obscure blues musician Howard Armstrong and the history of Hawaiian music. Zwigoff seemed ideal to film Allen, who once told the *Los Angeles Times* that he hadn't listened to any American popular music recorded after 1956. Eddy Davis, Allen's long-time band manager and banjo player, also favoured the tour. The pros with whom Allen had recorded his album wouldn't mind the gruelling schedule of fourteen cities in twenty-three days proposed by Doumanian, kicking off in Venice's newly restored Gran Teatro La Fenice in February – a date and a location which, she pointed out, dovetailed nicely with the new film Allen was planning, his first since *Love and Death* to be shot mainly in Europe, and, moreover, his first musical.

Allen, however, loathed the idea of a tour. '*I don't want to go!*' he said vehemently. 'It's too many dates, it's too many cities I've never gone to in my life. I have so much work here. *I don't want to go!*' He was also anything but enamoured of the idea of Zwigoff's cameras looking over his shoulder. The revelations of Crumb's sexual oddities had humanised the director's previous subject, but *Crumb* remained the kind of film about which someone like Allen would have nightmares. Once Zwigoff insisted on the right of final cut, there was an excuse to veto him as director.

Doumanian, however, was not to be put off. Barbara Koppel, twice an Oscar-winner for her films about union conflicts, abortion and hospices for the dying, was surprised to receive a call from her producer, who asked, 'How would you like to go on tour with Woody Allen?' After her initial disbelief, Koppel thought, 'Um, this could be interesting.'

When Allen began thinking in 1995 of making a musical, his first idea was to set at least part of it in Paris, as a tribute to Vincente Minnelli's *An American in Paris*, but also because he'd come to like the city in many ways more than his own. *Could* he make a musical? He wasn't sure. To do what Gene Kelly and Fred Astaire had done in *An American in Paris* and *Funny Face* – simply mime to a pre-recorded track while strolling through Paris tourist spots – seemed false. He found something closer to his vision in Jacques Demy's *Les Parapluies de Cherbourg* and *Les Demoiselles de Rochefort*, where the performers simply burst into song at the point anyone else would have used expository dialogue. It was an idea he'd flirted with once before. Writing *Annie Hall*, he'd suggested to Marshall Brickman, 'What if the characters just sang at that point?' Brickman had been dubious. 'Maybe. I don't know how people will take to that.' The idea was dropped, but, like all Allen ideas, not forgotten. Now it surfaced again.

He thought of making a comedy with music, from which he could subtract either the comedy or the music, depending on how each component worked out. Let there be songs, but let the actors sing them. Even him. With some glee, he didn't tell the actors he auditioned that they would need to sing and, in some cases, dance. 'If that person could sing, fine,' he said. 'If that person couldn't sing, that was fine too.' Goldie Hawn, Alan Alda and Julia Roberts all agreed to sing, as did Tim Roth, the young British actor mainly known for playing murderous thugs. (He played a murderous thug in Allen's film too, but a murderous thug who sings.) In the end, only Drew Barrymore was dubbed. Even Allen agreed that her real singing voice was 'outside the limits of human tolerance'.

Fundamentally, *Everyone Says I Love You* is *Hannah and her Sisters* with music. The main characters are a happily married Upper East Side couple, Frieda (Hawn), a dabbler in liberal causes, and her lawyer husband Bob (Alda), and Frieda's doleful ex-husband Joe (Allen), a writer living in Paris. Returning to New York on the rebound from yet another unhappy love affair, Joe is reunited with his daughter DJ (Natasha Lyonne), who for after-school entertainment shamelessly eavesdrops on the sessions of a beautiful woman, Von (Julia Roberts), with the analyst next door. Hearing Von describe what she wants in a man, her favourite songs, foods and poems, and knowing of Joe's poor luck with women, DJ coaxes him to follow Von to Venice and make use of this uniquely valuable intelligence.

Meanwhile, DJ's prim half-sister Skylar (Barrymore) is about to marry the equally correct Holden (Edward Norton), though their courtship is constantly interrupted: he hides her engagement ring, for instance, in a creamy dessert and she accidentally swallows it – an incident that actually happened to Mia Farrow. Worse transpires when Frieda invites an ex-convict, Charles Ferry (Roth), whom she's met on her campaign to liberalise New York's prisons, to Thanksgiving. (One of the film's better jokes shows her lecturing a roomful of sullen prison guards on how to make life more pleasant for their charges: Continental menus, and the chance to decorate their cells, using their own decorators.) Ferry feels up the female guests, eyes their jewellery, takes Skylar onto the balcony, serenades her, and the two run away together, an escapade that ends in a car chase and arrest.

Meanwhile, in Venice, Joe charms Von with his spurious enthusiasm for her favourite painter, Tintoretto, and DJ takes up with a number of unsuitable men, including a husky gondolier. Everyone moves to Paris to meet Frieda, Bob and the rest of the family who, like the socialites in *The Purple Rose of Cairo*, have casually decided to spend Christmas there. Frieda and Joe flirt with the idea of getting back together, and dance a *pas de deux* by the Seine *à la* Gene Kelly and Leslie Caron in *An American in Paris*, though with leaps (flagrantly harness-assisted) that not even Kelly could have achieved. But life in musicals is never the same as real life, and at the end Joe is left, like Gabe in *Husbands and Wives*, alone with the solace of art.

Allen garnishes this tale with twenty-four songs: fewer by Gershwin, Porter and Berlin this time, and more novelty numbers or songs written for movie comedies. *Everyone Says I Love You*, having a typical Allen dramatic structure as well as songs, ran three hours and twenty minutes in its first assembly. Allen ditched episodes involving Liv Tyler and Tracy Ullman, but this still left a novel and for the most part diverting collection of eccentric performances. At a Paris party to which everyone comes dressed as Groucho Marx, the entire crowd harmonise on 'Hurrah for Captain Spalding' in French. When Grandpa dies, he astonishes the funeral by bursting out of his coffin and doing a knockdown version of 'Enjoy Yourself'. With a background of the Grand Canal, Allen croaks 'I'm Through with Love', reminding us that even at his happiest, he's dying inside. Sometimes, as in that case, the song is grotesquely out of phase with the narrative; in others, the match is precise. Doing 'Just You, Just Me' as a big production number shot on real New York streets, the company reach the lines 'We'll find a cosy spot/Where no one can see' precisely at the moment a beggar holds out his cup and, in best Manhattan fashion, all automatically avert their eyes.

Allen elected to spend Christmas in Venice with Soon-Yi. The camera crew would arrive early in 1996 for reshoots on *Everyone Says I Love You*, after which he'd meet the band to start their tour. But nothing about Venice is ever entirely expected.

The fire in the Fenice, due to reopen the following night after long-delayed restoration, began in the early hours of the night of 29 January. Only one watchman was on duty, and by the time he'd raised the alarm, flames were raging through the two-hundred-year-old timbers, consuming the five-tiered horseshoe of gilded boxes, the red plush seats of the stalls, the stage that had seen the premieres of five of Verdi's operas, including *Rigoletto* and *La Traviata*, as well as Britten's *The Turn of the Screw* and Stravinsky's *The Rake's Progress*.

By morning, only the brick walls and the neo-classical façade remained. Ironists were quick to note that the Fenice – which means 'Phoenix' – had burned in a city whose most intrusive natural threat was not fire but water. Had the fire begun at a time of high tide, when Venice's lagoon was filled by winds driving relentlessly up the Adriatic, the Fenice's foyer, and indeed half the city, could have been inundated a metre deep, as it would be the following November. But a night of no wind, while providential for nearby houses, had spelt disaster for the Fenice.

Among the first on the scene to view the ruins was Allen. Slight, pale, jowly, balding and stooped, he looked his sixty years. Amid the Armani suits and camel-hair coats draped loosely over the shoulders, he appeared nondescript in thick-rimmed glasses, running shoes, crumpled corduroy trousers, sweater, car coat and a shapeless cloth hat. By contrast, Soon-Yi, clinging to his arm, wore expensive casual clothes by the Milanese couturiers Dolce & Gabbana, and a $39,000 engagement ring built around a one-carat yellow-green diamond. The couple were familiar to many Venetians. They'd spent Christmas and New Year at the city's most expensive hotel, the Gritti Palace, and just after midnight on New Year's Eve they'd appeared at a ball in a *palazzo* on the

Grand Canal. Soon-Yi, her hair cut in a fashionably long bob that pulled it back from her forehead, emphasising the mirror-like disc of her Korean face, wore an evening dress whose spaghetti straps showed off her smooth ivory skin. By contrast, Allen, commented a London paper coldly, looked 'as if he had just escaped from an Iraqi prison'.

Rumours persisted that Allen planned to buy his own *palazzo* on the Grand Canal, the Ca'Dario, which dated back even further than the Fenice, to 1487. Venetians could well believe the story. Only an American would have bothered with the building, which seemed to attract ill-fortune. The daughter of the original owner, Giovanni Dario, reputedly died of grief when her husband was banished from Venice, and subsequent owners went bankrupt or died suddenly. The last occupant, financier Raul Gardini, shot himself in the head in 1993 just as the police were about to arrest him in connection with fraud.

Disaster was confidently predicted should Allen take over the four-storey pile between the Accademia gallery and the imposing church of Santa Maria della Salute. The building was, like many Venetian *palazzi*, a maze of small dark rooms behind its opulent marble façade. America's great lover of Venice, Henry James, had dismissed it as looking like 'a house of cards that holds together by a tenure it would be fatal to touch'.

Allen and Soon-Yi inspected the Fenice ruins with Venice's aggressive young left-wing mayor Massimo Cacciari and his entourage, though there was some doubt, from Cacciari's deference and the swollen crowd of paparazzi that trailed the party, who was accompanying whom. At police headquarters, a furious Felice Casson, investigating magistrate in charge of the case, brushed aside hints of terrorism or arson, and announced that, by tampering with a crime scene, both the mayor and Allen risked jail sentences of between six months and three years.

Back at their hotel, Allen, with Soon-Yi, as always these days, seldom more than hand-holding distance away, announced that the concert would take place as planned that night, but at the Teatro Goldoni. All proceeds would go towards a fund to restore the Fenice, which Mayor Cacciari promised to rebuild within two years. Somebody told Allen about the investigating magistrate's threat of jail for compromising the crime site at the Fenice. Echoing the Mayor's comment on the fire, he professed himself 'saddened and surprised' by Casson's threat – about which nothing more was heard. As to the contribution to the Fenice's rebuilding, 'What it amounted to,' according to Cristiano Chiarot, head of communications and press for La Fenice, 'was a lot of business meetings, followed by a very small cheque.'

In March 1996, Allen's New Orleans Jazz Band began its twenty-three-day European tour. It quickly turned into a royal progress. Questions of musical excellence were for the most part diplomatically avoided, though once the tour had culminated in sold-out performances at London's Royal Festival Hall, *Guardian* critic John Fordham spoke for many when he commented, 'The repertoire was of the kind you might run into on a Sunday lunchtime in an English pub, but at times the affectionate collectivity of the idiom lifted the music to a kind of eager, communicative grace that transcended preoccupation with the famously evasive figure in the check shirt and beige cords. Allen's clarinet sound rarely exhibits the liquid, sensuous qualities of the long-departed heroes of the instrument, and is querulous and shrill above the middle register, but occasionally embraces a mixture of heart-on-sleeve romanticism and bluesiness that rises above the general hum ... But jazz is a music of ambiguity, wit, risk and surprise. Woody Allen, who understands such nuances as well as anybody, perhaps does not understand the mechanics of this elusive art quite well enough.'

Beginning in Madrid, then continuing to Geneva, Turin, Milan, Bologna, Rome, Paris and finally London, the tour drew enthusiastic crowds who showed every sign of enjoying the music, despite Allen's often-expressed doubts that they'd take to anything so spare and monotonous. Except for a visit to the Fenice, *Wild Man Blues*, Barbara Koppel's film of the tour, shows no drama, and precious little comedy either, though both are flirted with in a sequence at an Italian concert where the theatre lights go out abruptly. The band plays on in best professional style, and a few days later a bemused Allen is presented with a plaque by the fire department for his supposed heroism in preventing a panic.

Throughout the film, Allen's smile is even less conspicuously on show than usual, and though he describes the experience of playing New Orleans jazz as 'like taking a bath in honey', his demeanour before the delirious Italian crowds is as phlegmatic as at the Café Carlyle. He cracks briefly when an Italian corporation with more money than sense hires the band for the night and puts on a black-tie soirée for its clients. The middle-aged Romans – 'mummified', in *Variety*'s phrase – sit bored and baffled through the rags and stomps. 'Boy, we've got the jury out there tonight,' jokes one of the band, and Allen knows we're sharing his amusement when he gives a deadpan interview to a plump journalist from local TV, assuring him that the crowd were 'wonderful – they really enjoyed it'.

Much of the rest is *Don't Drink the Water II*. Allen and Soon-Yi bicker with hotel staff about taps that don't produce hot water and toast that fails to arrive. Allen jokes about the sumptuous suites they're given, particularly at the Principe de Savoia in Milan, which boasts a private sunken pool like something from a Roman epic, and comments in an aside that Soon-Yi began life going through garbage cans. If she remembers any of that, she shows no sign of it. Casual, relaxed and direct, she seems more like a grown-up daughter than a wife-to-be. If anyone looks like a Mrs Allen, it's his sister Letty Aronson, also part of the entourage. And always on the edge of the shot, though never identified, hovers an impassive, black-dressed Jean Doumanian, Mrs Danvers to the life.

In the midst of all the activity, Allen looks lost, shrunken. He fusses about having his own bathroom, his morning plate of prunes, his hour on the hotel treadmill. The voluminous bathrobe offered by one of the hotels bulks and bunches on his body as if an old man is trying on a suit made for him in his prime. Koppel's decision to use mostly Nino Rota scores from Fellini films as a background underlines the film's melancholy. We might almost be watching an affectionate obituary.

After the concert at Paris's venerable Olympia, French President

Lionel Jospin and former Minister of Culture Jack Lang visited Allen backstage. This meeting yielded the information, embarrassing for Lang, that Allen had been made a Chevalier des Arts et Lettres in 1985, but, in an oversight, had never been informed of the fact. In Rome, Allen was told he'd been accorded the Directors Guild of America's highest honour, the D.W. Griffith Award. 'I was very, very surprised and amazed,' he said when asked for a reaction by the DGA. 'I thought that maybe they were giving it out for quantity this year.' The comment characterised his sour feelings about returning to New York. By the time he arrived back in the late summer, he had a new script ready for the Woody Allen Fall Project, and its tone was sombre.

Allen will probably never make a more revealing film than *Deconstructing Harry*, the reworking of Ingmar Bergman's *Wild Strawberries* which he shot in the autumn and winter of 1997 and released in Europe early in 1998. Relentlessly self-revelatory, cynical, spasmodic, it used comedy to achieve an effect close to the black farces of nineteenth-century Russia. If Gogol had applied his mind to the biopic, it might have looked much like this.

Harry Block (Allen) is a writer the way Kafka's Josef K is a clerk. His role is not to offer a sympathetic character with which to identify, but rather to lead us into the realms of nightmare. We see brief snatches of a number of his stories in the course of the film, but never enough for us to become involved. In the opening sequence of Block's sister-in-law Lucy (Judy Davis) repeatedly arriving at his door in a windstorm, a scene that is the apotheosis of Sandy Morse's penchant for jumpy editing, we see his life over and over again, each image subtly different from the last. Woodrow Wilson described Griffith's *Birth of a Nation* as 'like reading history in flashes of lightning'. *Deconstructing Harry* does the same for biography.

Lucy is furious. She's just read Harry's latest book, which describes in barely-disguised detail how she and he deceived her sister and his ex-wife Jane – 'Or, as you pathetically disguise her, Janet,' she snarls. Lucy's husband has also read the book, and has recognised everything, including, as she quotes, 'Marvin's flaccid, microscopic member, jiggling up and down as he bounced naked on tiptoe across the rugless icy floor of their Connecticut home to close the storm windows.'

Not surprisingly, Lucy tries to shoot Harry. Also not surprisingly, we never find out what happens, because the film segues into another extract from the collected works of Harry Block. And another. And another. A movie actor (Robin Williams) suddenly goes out of focus. Everyone else is sharp, but he's blurry. He doesn't know what to do. His children laugh. He can't get work ... but enough of that. How about this man who borrows his friend's apartment to sleep with a prostitute? Someone knocks on the door. It's Death, come to claim the apartment's true owner. No use trying to explain that the owner is in hospital. The borrower goes. Where? Well, maybe to that air-conditioned hell presided over by Satan (Billy Crystal) in a smoking jacket with quilted satin lapels ...

Sustaining – barely – this anthology of Harry Block's Greatest Hits is the story of how Adair College, his *alma mater* upstate, is awarding him an honorary doctorate. Ironically, as he has writer's block. He hasn't been able to finish anything in months, though he's spent the publisher's advance. All he has is beginnings – the fragments we've seen.

He'd like to take his young son Hilly (Eric Lloyd) to the ceremony, but his vengeful ex-wife (Kirstie Alley) refuses. Cue revelations of her as his analyst, telling him she's in love with him. And a recreation of the moment as it appeared in the book he wrote about it. And a fantasy about what happened later – or may have – when she (now recast in his imagination by the more seductive Demi Moore) rediscovered her roots and became a super-devout Orthodox Jew. Currently, Harry is seething about his latest young girlfriend, Fay (Elisabeth Shue), who began by adoring him for his intellect but has now run off with his best friend Larry (Crystal), whom he recasts in imagination as the devil in one of his fantasies.

Harry persuades his friend Richard (Bob Balaban) to come to Adair with him, and, on impulse grabs Hilly from school. He also offers $500 to Cookie (Hazelle Goodman), the black prostitute he slept with the previous night, to make up the group. ('Mr Allen at long last,' his old antagonist Maureen Dowd would write in the *New York Times*, 'introduces a black character to his cloistered Gotham world.') On the way, Richard dies of a heart attack. Harry starts to go out of focus from nerves, but Cookie matter-of-factly brings him back to sharpness. When they arrive at the college they're immediately surrounded by armed police, who arrest Harry for kidnapping, having a corpse in the car and transporting Cookie and her funny cigarettes across a state line. Later, on bail and back in New York, Harry perversely feels his creative juices stirring. He quickly types, 'Notes for a novel. Opening possibility. Rifkin led a fragmented, disjointed existence . . .'

Allen says he didn't want to star as Harry; only took the role, in fact, after his other choices, including Elliott Gould, either turned it down or didn't have the time. The model for Harry, he insists, wasn't himself but novelist Philip Roth, to whose life that of Block bears some similarities. According to Santo Loquasto, they 'envisioned more of a Norman Mailer, a beefy man consumed by his passions and his drive'. For all his disclaimers that there is nothing autobiographical in his films, however, one can't watch *Deconstructing Harry* without seeing Allen writ more or less as he is in real life. Harry, like him, has had – counting Soon-Yi – three wives and six shrinks. The preoccupations with analysis, prostitution, lost children, divorce, indeed with autobiography vs. fiction, are all paraded before us with a weary truculence, much as, in the opening scene, taken from one of Harry's books but rooted in (his) fact, Ken and Leslie, his brother-in-law and sister-in-law (though played now by Richard Benjamin and Julia Louis-Dreyfuss), have sex in the kitchen at a family gathering while chatting with the blind grandmother, who thinks they're mixing cocktails.

Deconstructing Harry received respectful but wary reviews. Early in 1998 Allen married Soon-Yi in Venice. They honeymooned in Paris, after which he went back to New York to start work on a new film, *Celebrity*. The London *Daily Mail* appeared to speak for many when it headlined a report on the state of his career 'Suddenly Everyone Loves Woody Again'. Despite Mia Farrow's vengeful memoir *What Falls Away*, published in 1997, his audience seemed to have adjusted to a Woody with a Past.

Behind the scenes, the truth was less sunny. While grosses for Allen's films in Europe remained healthy, he was still, in American terms, an art-house film-maker with a specialist audience concentrated in the cities of the East Coast. In June 1998 Allen's long-time team of collaborators was broken up by Jean Doumanian and Richard Brick's sweeping economies within Sweetland. Some were told their contracts would not be renewed. Others were asked to take large salary cuts; of those who agreed, a few were humiliatingly told not to come back anyway: Sweetland had found younger, cheaper replacements.

Casting director Juliet Taylor and production designer Santo Loquasto stayed on at their old salaries, but stills photographer Brian Hamill, editor Sandy Morse, production manager Helen Robin, cinematographer Carlo DiPalma and Jeffrey Kurland, costume designer and faithful Allen apologist, were given their walking papers. Most surprisingly, so was Bobby Greenhut, Allen's producer for decades. Greenhut said diplomatically that he wished he could have stayed, but could not manage on the reduced salary proposed by Sweetland. 'I was glad to be part of it,' he said of his long association with Allen. 'I wish them luck.' Privately, however, he was widely believed to feel that Doumanian had crowded him out.

Many who were fired believed Allen was rich enough to have kept them on if he'd chosen to, but he denied this vehemently. 'I took a substantial reduction to what I was getting,' he told the *New York Times*. 'Over the years, I haven't made very much money. It's always been a struggle to break even.' Others hinted at more fundamental reasons than economics. 'Woody has always been terrified of being seen as someone who used to make funny films, someone whose time has passed,' commented a friend who preferred to remain anonymous. 'Woody's overwhelming need is to stay fresh, be of the period, not to be seen as someone who once did something funny. That's what a lot of these changes are about.' Allen retorted, 'I couldn't care less about that. That's never meant anything to me. What's "hip" or "in" has never interested me. This is about finances. I'd be thrilled if everyone would continue. These are my friends.'

Because of the purges, only a few of Allen's friends were represented in *Celebrity*, notably Susan Morse and Santo Loquasto. Even so, the new film smelt musty after the bracing confessional candour of *Deconstructing Harry*. Supposedly set in the feverish world of modern Manhattan hype and showbiz journalism, it was shot by Sven Nykvist in a watery black-and-white that denatured the city; for all one sees of the real New York, he might have filmed it on some Hollywood backlot against painted flats. Its central character, Lee Simon, a magazine writer on first-name, indeed intimate terms with the celebrities he profiles, belongs to the same family as John Travolta's fast-track *Rolling Stone* correspondent in *Perfect* of fourteen years before, though without Travolta's pizazz. Untidy and unsure, muttering and stumbling over his words, Kenneth Branagh gives a performance labelled almost universally as the worst Woody Allen imitation on record.

Further back in his pedigree, Lee is Ike Davis from *Manhattan*, who in turn descended from Marcello Mastroianni in *La Dolce Vita*, with which *Celebrity* has numerous resonances. Like Marcello following the decadent Maddalena to a prostitute's flat and making love to her in her bed, Lee, interviewing movie star Nicole Oliver (Melanie Griffith) on the Manhattan location of her latest movie, is invited to visit her childhood home, and awarded a blow job in her old bedroom. Also like Marcello, Lee is a promising novelist who, chilled by bad reviews of a first novel, recoiled into journalism. Both men abandon loving women for a series of glitzy relationships, though Lee's wife Robin (Judy Davis) has tired of his philandering and divorced him, despite continuing to carry a torch. When they meet by chance at a film preview, she's so distraught that she flings herself under the nearest piece of furniture, to the astonishment of her date, TV producer Tony Gardella (Joe Mantegna). Lee's current lover, publisher's editor Bonnie (Famke Janssen), also wearies of him when he becomes infatuated with wannabe actress and part-time Greenwich Village waitress Nola (Winona Ryder). When he tells Bonnie of his decision, somewhat inappropriately on the day she's moving into his flat, she takes a memorable if old-fashioned revenge, receding from him on the back of the Staten Island ferry, strewing irreplaceable pages from his novel in its wake. The scenes put the indelible stamp 'Old Hat' on *Celebrity*. Who today doesn't have his manuscript backed up on the hard disk and probably on a mini-floppy as well? The closest any journalist is likely to come to oral sex with a star like Nicole Oliver is when she mouths the title of her new film at a press conference. Nola also seems to have stepped from some sixties fantasy or, more likely, from Allen's memories, now yellowing and curled at the edges, of life at the Duplex during his stand-up days. His rumpled duffel coat and self-consciously antique Aston-Martin belong to the same period. So does the play Nola's rehearsing. It may have a fashionable lesbian motif, but the funky off-off-Broadway theatre and its young director on the make are pure sixties, as is Robin's miraculous transformation, under the tutelage of Gardella, from glum discarded wife seeking reassurance from gurus and cosmetic surgeons to the lacquered and relentlessly chatty hostess of a lunchtime TV show that retails gossip hot from the tables of a supposedly fashionable Manhattan restaurant. It's the same transformation which Mia Farrow's Sally White experienced in *Radio Days*, and shares its smirkingly covert sub-text. Sally's elocution lessons gave her a mastery of oral sex that unlocked every celebrity door, while Robin consults a call girl (Bebe Neuwirth) for similar tuition on 'going down'; the hooker demonstrates with a banana, and almost chokes herself.

Allen scatters real-life celebrities through *Celebrity*, but his choices – property developer Donald Trump, designer Isaac Mizrahi, Joey and Mary Jo Buttafuoco, figures in a sensational but half-forgotten murder case, writer Bruce Jay Friedman, Knicks basketball star Anthony Mason – read like a flip through back issues of *People* magazine. The motif, itself old-fashioned, of beginning and ending the film with a plane sky-writing the word 'Help' over midtown Manhattan, is a metaphor for celebrity itself, swallowing its own tail with an appetite that the audience can't share.

In an almost insolent demonstration of real celebrity, two of its youngest performers save the film from total mediocrity. South

African actress Charlize Theron, lanky and serpentine, brings an electric eroticism to the role of a fashion model so infatuated with her own gratification that a touch to any part of her body rouses her to orgasm. Not believing his luck as he drives her home, Lee runs his car into a shop window, and sees his chances of sexual bliss slip away into the night. Even more seductive is Leonardo DiCaprio as hip young star Brandon Darrow who withers Branagh every moment they're on screen together. Thrashing his girlfriend around the suite at a Manhattan hotel, hopping a Learjet to visit a casino where Lee manages to lose his shirt, then repairing to another suite with a gaggle of girls for a night of sex and dope, he's less an actor than a force of nature. In Darrow's wake literature, so central to Lee's sense of self, suffers terminal distortion. Trying to pitch his screenplay, Lee is instead led into the bedroom with Darrow and a couple of girls, Darrow saying decisively, 'Let's take this party indoors.'

Sucked down into this whirlpool of gratification, Lee clings to his script like a drowning man to a plank until the girl allocated to him for the night offers conversationally, 'I'm a writer too.' A disbelieving Lee enquires, 'What do you write?'

'You know who Chekhov is?' she says. 'I write like him.'

It's the end for Lee. A dollar short, a day late and a couple of decades too old, he leaves the room and skulks away into the dawn, as much a back number as Vanya – or Allen himself.

Celebrity was received with indifference at the Venice Film Festival in August 1998. Its welcome in America was equally lacklustre, though Richard Schickel in *Time* magazine called it 'a coldly mocking film, alert to the fact that politicians under investigation are still welcome at celebrity golf tournaments; that famous authors, abetted by their editors, can steal unfamous authors' ideas with impunity; that skinheads, rabbis and lawyers from the American Civil Liberties Union can grouse together affably in the greenroom about who ate up all the bagels before going out to scream at one another on a TV talk show. These people all know that what they share – the media's avid gaze – sets them apart from the multitudes it ignores while creating a bond among the favored that is impenetrable to the anonymous, and is, in various ways, dangerous to all concerned. *Celebrity* is the first fully serious (and seriously funny) movie about the issue that touches, and ultimately subsumes, everything we feel about fame and the discontents it breeds.'

In the aftermath of the purge at Sweetland, Allen's agent let it be known discreetly that he was open to offers to appear in films he did not direct – a humbling climb-down from his once-inflexible rule not to soil his hands with such journeyman work. Among the first results was a voice-only role in the animated *Antz* (1998), directed by Eric Darnell and Lawrence Guterman, where he played Z4195, worried about his feeling that he was just one ant in a nest of millions. First seen on his psychiatrist's couch, Z rises reassured that his sense of insignificance indicates mental health since he is one ant in a nest of millions. With this out of the way Allen, in typical fashion, proves that he's anything but a cipher, falling for Princess Bala (voiced by Sharon Stone) and replacing his friend Weaver (Sylvester Stallone) in the army of her megalomaniac fiancé General Mandible (Gene Hackman) in order to be close to her during a parade. Becoming by chance a hero, he tries to run away with Bala to fabled Insectopia, only to be caught up in Mandible's plans to separate fighters and workers, before exterminating the latter.

Allen's 1999 Fall Movie Project was a story about the world of jazz starring the irascible Sean Penn, who made his presence felt throughout the shoot with tantrums and threats to abandon the film. Once again, Woody-watchers recognised Allen looking to the past for material; the story sounded suspiciously like 'The Jazz Baby', his script of thirty years before, rejected by United Artists as inconsistent with his image as a comic. If so, it was an appropriate choice for someone who seemed increasingly a figure of another era.

As for Allen himself, there is no peace for him this side of the grave. He's not built for happiness, or if he ever was, the tendency has long since been erased. There is only work. As Harry Block writes in the opening of his still unfinished novel in *Deconstructing Harry*:

He had long ago come to this conclusion: all people know the same truth. Our lives consist of how we choose to distort it. Only his writing was calm; his writing, which had, in more ways than one, saved his life.

Notes

Preface: Café Carlyle
'I constantly run into . . .' quoted in 'Woody on the Town' by Joe Klein, *GQ*, February 1986.

Chapter One: What did he Say?
'Film is a collaborative business . . .' from 'Film is a Collaborative Business' by David Mamet, reprinted in *Some Freaks* (Viking, New York, 1989). 'We consider you a foreigner . . .' from *New York Times*, 3 April 1992.

Chapter Two: Can You Believe I Came from this Place?
Quotes from Jerry Epstein from interviews with Tim Carroll, New York, 1993. Arthur Miller interviewed by Susan Edmiston and Linda D. Cirino for *Literary New York: A History and Guide* (Peregrine, Smith, New York, 1991). David Mamet on a Jewish childhood from 'The Decoration of Jewish Houses', reprinted in *Some Freaks*. Ralph Rosenblum quote from *When the Shooting Stops . . . the Cutting Begins*. 'I've been a model, model father . . .' in *Newsweek*, 31 August 1992. 'I don't consider any girl perfect' from 'Hey, there, Woodycat Allen, How's the World Treating You?' by Mel Gussow, *New York Times* 24 December 1967. 'I didn't read anything else until I was fifteen' from 'Woodywoodywoody, You've Got it Knocked' by Jack Nessel in *New York/World Journal Tribune*, 18 December 1966.

Chapter Three: My Universities
Quotes from Jerry Epstein from interviews with Tim Carroll, New York, 1993, and from Israel Horvitz from interview with the author, Avignon, 1995. Many details of Allen's schooldays from *Woody Allen: Joking Aside* by Gerald McKnight. Alfred Kazin on Brooklyn from *A Walker in the City* (Harcourt, Brace, New York, 1951). 'Woody Allen's New York City' from 'Woody on the Town' by Joe Klein. Additional material in *New York Times Magazine*, 19 January 1986. Foster Hirsch on Allen and Bob Hope in *Love, Sex, Death and the Meaning of Life*. Lorne Michaels on Allen from interview with Timothy White in *Rolling Stone Visits Saturday Night Live* (Rolling Stone Press/Dolphin/Doubleday, New York, 1979). 'Some poor little schnook' from 'Funny isn't Good Enough' by Sean Mitchell, *Los Angeles Times*, 15 March 1992. 'I saw a hermaphrodite . . .' from 'Woody on the Town'. Ivan Kalmar on 'psychic masochism' from *The Trotskys, Freuds and Woody Allens: Portrait of a Culture*. Richard Combs on *Broadway Danny Rose* in *The Times Literary Supplement*, 17 August 1984. Ivan Kalmar from *The Trotskys, Freuds and Woody Allens*.

Chapter Four: Women and Magic
Quotes from Jerry Epstein, Jerry Cohen, Barbara Cohen, Sadie Goldstein from interviews with Tim Carroll, New York, 1993. 'Female psychology' from 'Primal Screen' by Lesley White,

Sunday Times Magazine, 11 February 1996. Kenneth Tynan on Mel Brooks from *Show People* (Random House, New York, 1978.) George Melly on New Orleans jazz from *Owning-Up* (Weidenfeld & Nicolson, London, 1965).

Chapter Five: Writer
Larry Gelbart on Allen from *Laughing Matters* (Random House, New York, 1998.) Allen on his parents' expectations from *Woody Allen* by Graham McCann.

Chapter Six: Render Unto Caesar . . .
Allen on Danny Simon quoted by Diane Jacobs in . . . *but we need the eggs: The Magic of Woody Allen*. Christopher Hewett and Dick Davy on Tamiment, and Max Liebman on Allen from *The Last Laugh: The World of Stand-Up Comics*. Other details from *Joking Aside: Woody Allen*. Larry Gelbart quotes *passim* from *Laughing Matters*. 'You'll see people on a comedy' from interview with Danny Wilde in *The Great Comedians Talk about Comedy*. Mia Farrow on Allen and showers in *What Falls Away*. Allen on the Sylvania Award in 'How Now, Woody Allen?' by Gene Siskel in the *Daily News*, Chicago, 12 June 1981.

Chapter Seven: Stand-Up
All quotes from Bryna Goldstein and Louise Lasser from interviews with Tim Carroll, New York, 1993. Jules Feiffer interviewed by the author, New York, 1997. Mort Sahl quoted from *Heartland*. Jack Rollins on Allen from *Time* magazine, 2 July 1972. Max Gordon on Allen *passim* from *Live at the Village Vanguard*. Many quotes from Allen, Rollins, Joffe and Gordon from *The Last Laugh: The World of Stand-Up Comics*. Larry Gelbart from *Laughing Matters*. 'I thought, "Gee, I write funny material . . ."' from *The Great Comedians Talk about Comedy*. Jane Rollins on Allen from unpublished interview with Bruce Ricker.

'The worst year of my life' and 'Woody was just awful' in *Time* magazine, 3 July 1972. Mort Sahl on Allen from *Heartland*. Dick Cavett quoted in *Cavett* by Dick Cavett and Christopher Porterfield (Bantam, New York, 1975). Marshall Brickman from 'Marshall Brickman: Simply Simon' by Tony Crawley, *Films Illustrated*, October 1980, 'Play it Again, Marshall' by Don Macpherson, *Time Out*, 26 September 1980 and 'Allen's Alley', *Film Comment*, June 1986. Harlene Allen quoted by Louise Lasser in conversation with Tim Carroll. Allen's letter to Rollins from St Louis quoted by Erix Lax in *Woody Allen: A Biography*. Jay Landesman on Allen from *Jaywalking*. Neighbour on watching Allen's first TV appearance from interview with Tim Carroll, New York, 1993. Details of the food/sex routine from 'Woody Allen and his Impolite Interview' in *The Realist* magazine, April 1965. Dick Cavett on stand-up from *The Last Laugh: The World of Stand-Up*. Marshall Brickman on *Candid Camera* from 'Marshall Brickman: Simply Simon', 'Play it Again, Marshall' and 'Allen's Alley'. Allen reviewed by the *New York Times*, August 1962.

Chapter Eight: *What's New Pussycat*
All quotes from Jacques Saulnier and Robert Rollis from interviews with the author, Paris, 1996. Renata Adler on comedy from *A Year in the Dark: A Year in the Life of a Film Critic 1968– 1969* (Berkeley Medallion, New York, 1971). 'A sex comedy in which the characters don't get to have any' from *The Life and Death of Peter Sellers* by Roger Lewis (Century, London, 1994). 'Bathroom farce', *Time*, 3 July 1972. Sheilah Graham on Feldman from *Scratch an Actor*. Further material on Feldman from 'Agent-Turned-Film Producer Charles K. Feldman Dead' in *Variety*, 29 May 1965. Jane Rollins quote from unpublished interview with Bruce Ricker. Peter O'Toole on the *Pussycat* script from *Playboy* magazine

interview, August 1965. 'A very off-beat, uncommercial film' from *Woody Allen on Woody Allen*. 'I learned something about picture making' in *Time*, 3 July 1972. Allen on 'Warren Beatty's fingertips' from 'Death Defying Director', *New Yorker* magazine, 3 June 1996. Vicky Tiel quotes *passim* from Tim Carroll in *Woody and his Women*. 'The furies are all around us' from *Daily Mail*, 8 January 1965. 'They put drops in his eyes' from *Seven Interviews with Woody Allen*. 'I spent quite an hour and a half in there' quoted by Eric Lax in *Woody Allen: A Biography*. 'A typical UA contract' from *Indecent Exposure*. Kenneth Tynan on Peter Sellers from *The Life of Kenneth Tynan* by Kathleen Tynan (Weidenfeld & Nicolson, London, 1987). Foster Hirsch quoted from *Love, Sex, Death and the Meaning of Life*.

Chapter Nine: *Casino Royale* and *What's Up, Tiger Lily?*
Quotes from Louise Lasser *passim* from interview with Tim Carroll, New York, 1993. Andrew Sarris on *What's New Pussycat* from *Village Voice*, 5 August 1965. Allen quoted by Eric Lax in *Woody Allen: A Biography*. John Lahr on Allen from *Automatic Vaudeville: Essays on Star Turns*. 'Perelman made Joycean jokes' from 'The Outsider' by Adam Gopnik, *New Yorker* magazine, 25 october 1993. Reports on conversations between Allen and Feldman *passim* from *The Life and Death of Peter Sellers*. 'Sex and food' quoted by Mel Gussow in 'Hey, There, Woodycat Allen, How's the World Treating You?' Feldman's manipulation of the *Casino Royale* project described in 'Feldman's *Casino Royale* Pitch: Novel that Launched Agent 007 to Screen Sans "Later" Gimmicks', *Daily Variety*, 16 June 1965. Quotes from Val Guest *passim* from interview with John Brosnan in *James Bond in the Cinema: Second Edition* (A. S. Barnes/Tantivy, La Jolla and London, 1981). Allen to Earl Wilson on writing

Casino Royale from *New York Post*, 3 June 1966. Details of Orson Welles' involvement *passim* from *Orson Welles* by Barbara Leaming (Weidenfeld & Nicolson, London, 1985), from which were also taken many of the quotes from Wolf Mankowitz about the film's production. Other details were supplied by Robert Parrish in a number of conversations with the author. Earl Wilson interview with Allen in *New York Post*, 3 June 1966.

Chapter Ten: *Don't Drink the Water*
Quotes from Louise Lasser *passim* from interview with Tim Carroll, New York, 1993. John Osborne on David Merrick from *Almost a Gentleman: Part II of an Autobiography* (Faber, London, 1991). Material on Merrick *passim* from *Burke's Steerage* (Puttnam, New York, 1976). *Variety* review of *What's Up, Tiger Lily?* 'Wouldn't it be funny' from Leonard Lyons' column, *New York Post*, 20 February 1969. Allen on Las Vegas from *Life* magazine, 28 April 1972. Earl Wilson on Allen's New Year's Eve party from *New York Post*, 27 December 1966.

Chapter Eleven: *Take the Money and Run*
Mia Farrow wrote about Allen's feelings about Buckley in *What Falls Away*. Stephen Sondheim quoted by Samuel G. Freedman in 'The Words and Music of Stephen Sondheim', *New York Times Magazine*, 1 April 1984. Keaton on her childhood from interview with Rex Reed in *Travolta to Keaton* (Morrow, New York, 1979) and *Diane Keaton: The Story of the Real Annie Hall*. 'There were hundreds of prisoners' from *Ladies Home Journal*, November 1968.

Chapter Twelve: *Play it Again, Sam*
Quotes from Jules Feiffer from interview with the author, New York, 1997. Quotes from Alfred Bester *passim* from *Holiday* magazine, May

1969. Leo Rosten's definition of a *nebbish* from *The Joys of Yiddish* (Pocket Books, New York, 1974). Quotes from Mia Farrow *passim* from *What Falls Away*. Allen on Diane Keaton quoted in *Diane Keaton: The Story of the Real Annie Hall*. Ralph Rosenblum's experience with editing *Don't Drink the Water* from *When the Shooting Stops . . . the Cutting Begins*.

Chapter Thirteen: *Bananas*
Quotes from Louise Lasser *passim* from interview with Tim Carroll, New York, 1993. Joffe's meeting with David Picker described by Eric Lax in *Woody Allen: A Biography*. Steven Bach on the deal from *Final Cut: Dreams and Disaster in the Making of* Heaven's Gate. 'Sports is like music' from 'Everything you Ever Wanted to Know About the Knicks' in *New Yorker* magazine, 6 June 1994. Gore Vidal's 'Doc Reuben' appeared in the *New York Review of Books*, 4 June 1970. 'She has an utterly spectacular visual sense' from *New York Daily News*, 10 October 1979. Rosenblum from *When the Shooting Stops . . . the Cutting Begins*. Allen on New Orleans jazz and recording at Preservation Hall in 'Is New Orleans Jazz Dying?', *New York Times*, 16 May 1971. 'They didn't want me until *Bananas* started doing well' from 'Seven Interviews with Woody Allen' by Robert Greenfield, *Rolling Stone* magazine, 30 September 1971. Details of *The Politics and Humor of Woody Allen* and its banning from Gerald McKnight's *Woody Allen: Joking Aside*, including quotes from Jim Day, and from 'PBS Axes Woody's TV Satire on Nixon', *New York Post*, 12 February 1972, 'NET Puts Hold on Allen Special', *New York Daily News*, 15 February 1972, 'Woody Allen's Satire Program Withdrawn for Public TV Airing', *New York Times*, 15 February 1972.

Chapter Fourteen: *Everything You Always Wanted to Know About Sex (*But were Afraid to Ask)* and *Sleeper*
Quotes from Maurice Yacowar *passim* from *Loser Takes All: The Comic Art of Woody Allen*. Marshall Brickman on writing with Allen from 'Marshall Brickman: Simply Simon' by Tony Crawley, *Films Illustrated*, October 1980, 'Play it Again, Marshall' by Don Macpherson, *Time Out*, 26 September 1980 and 'Allen's Alley', *Film Comment*, June 1986. 'This is a movie about wires' from 'Woody Allen and *Sleeper*' by Judith Trotsky, *Filmmakers Newsletter*, Summer 1974. Bill Moses from interview with the author, New York, 1998.

Chapter Fifteen: *Love and Death* and *The Front*
Quotes from Willy Holt and Bernard Cohn *passim* from interviews with the author, Paris, 1996. George Burns quoted in *The Great Comedians Talk about Comedy*. Allen picking up Deborah Duanes described in Dee Burton's *I Dream of Woody*. Judith Viorst writing in 'The Night Woody Allen Turned me on', *Redbook* magazine, October 1976. Meryl Streep on Allen quoted by Liz Smith, *New York News*, 11 March 1980. Nancy Jo Sales' correspondence with Allen described in 'Woody and Me', *New York* magazine, 5 April 1995. *Newsweek* magazine profile of Allen, 'Funny, but he's Serious', 24 April 1978. Allen on United Artists' reaction to *Love and Death* from *Esquire* magazine, May 1977. 'I'd have preferred to make it in California' from *Daily Variety*, 19 November 1974. Francis Perrin recalled auditioning for Allen in the documentary film *Masterclass: A Lesson in Comedy*, by Marie-Dominique Montel, FR3, Paris, 1998. Allen spoke to Stig Bjorkman for *Woody Allen on Woody Allen*. Allen on colour grading from 'Woody Allen and *Sleeper*'. 'I asked him not to' from Earl Wilson column, *New York Post*,

21 June 1975. Allen on Martha Graham in 'Hiding out with Woody Allen' by Edwin Miller in *Seventeen* magazine, November 1975. 'In a way, the blacklist was hilarious' from 'Woody Allen in a Comedy About Blacklisting? Don't Laugh' by Thomas Meehan, *New York Times*, 7 December 1975. Bernstein on Dmytryk from *Tender Comrades*, edited by Patrick McGilligan and Paul Buhle (St Martin's, New York, 1997).

Chapter Sixteen: *Annie Hall*

Marshall Brickman on writing *Annie Hall* from *Films Illustrated*, October 1980. Beth Porter quoted by Julian Fox in *Woody: Movies from Manhattan*. Mel Bourne on scouting locations from *Selected Takes*. Diane Keaton, her mother and father on Allen and California from *Travolta to Keaton* by Rex Reed. Stacey Nelkin on Allen from *New York Post*, 7 January 1993. 'I have a certain part of my personality' from *Woody Allen on Woody Allen*. Ralph Rosenblum on 'Anhedonia' from *When the Shooting Stops ... the Cutting Begins* and Marshall Brickman from 'Marshall Brickman: Simply Simon' by Tony Crawley, *Films Illustrated*, October 1980, 'Play it Again, Marshall' by Don Macpherson, *Time Out*, 26 September 1980 and 'Allen's Alley', *Film Comment*, June 1986. Susan Morse on cutting *Annie Hall* from *Selected Takes*. Alan Dershowitz on Allen from *Boston Herald*, 3 September 1986. Joan Collins quoted in *The Film Yearbook Volume 2* (Virgin, London, 1983). Jean Doumanian on Allen *passim* from 'Woody Allen's Best (Hence Very Secretive) Friend', *New York Times*, 9 November 1997, which also contains quotes from others about the relationship. Allen on the CBS *Sixty Minutes* update from author's conversation with Bill Moses, New York, 1998.

Chapter Seventeen: *Interiors*

Andrew Sarris reviewed *Annie Hall* in *Village Voice*, 26 April 1977. Steven Bach on *Interiors* from *Final Cut*. Reports on the '*Annie Hall* look' from '"Dreadful" Clothes are in; *Annie Hall* Look is Here', *Variety*, 31 May 1978, and 'The Uni-Sex Thing Gets a Lift' in *New York Post*, 13 April 1978. Reports on Allen's appearance at Michael's Pub on Oscar night from 'Woody Takes 5 as Annie Takes 4' by Peter Occhiogrosso, *SoHo Weekly News*, 6 April 1978, and from author's conversation with Jules Feiffer, New York, 1997. 'She speaks for me' from 'Scenes from a Mind', by Ira Halberstadt, *Take One*, November 1978. Denholm Elliott's audition described in interview with the author, London, 1979. Mel Bourne on designing *Interiors* from *Selected Takes*, also 'Inside Woody Allen's *Interiors*', *New York Times*, 9 November 1978. Allen interviewed by Guy Flatley for 'At the Movies', *New York Times*, 21 October 1971. Events during the shooting at the home of CeCe Wasserman described in 'Diane and Woody Move in' by CeCe Wasserman, *Ladies Home Journal*, June 1978. Report on the preview screening from *New York Post*, 27 July 1978. Richard Goldstein in the *Village Voice*, 17 August 1978. Louise Lasser from interview with Tim Carroll, New York, 1993.

Chapter Eighteen: *Manhattan* and *Stardust Memories*

Quotes from Marie-Christine Barrault from interview with the author, Paris, 1996. Stacey Nelkin on Mariel Hemingway from *New York Post*, 7 January 1993. Allen on his visit to Mariel Hemingway's parents from interview on *Late Night with David Letterman*, 2 August 1991, quoted by Stephen Spignesi in *The Woody Allen Companion*. Meryl Streep on *Manhattan* from Liz Smith's column, *New York News*, 11 March 1980. Allen on meeting Ingmar Bergman from 'Allen Goes

Back to the Woody of Yesteryear' by Charles Champlin, *Los Angeles Times*, 1 October 1980, Eric Lax in *Woody Allen: A Biography*, and 'Crawling from the Wreckage' by Philip Thomas, *Empire* magazine, August 1993. Allen on Charlotte Rampling from Joan Didion, 'Letter from Manhattan', *New York Review of Books*, 16 August 1979. Steven Bach's comments on *Manhattan* from *Final Cut*. 'No longer searching for eggs' from ... *but we need the eggs: The Magic of Woody Allen*. Conditions during shooting in Ocean Grove *passim* from 'Woody Films a Comedy in N.J.' by Jim Wright, *The Record*, New Jersey, 23 November 1979, and 'Town isn't Wild about Woody', *New York Post*, 11 August 1979. Mel Bourne quoted in *Woody Allen: Joking Aside*. 'My audience left me' from 'Funny isn't Good Enough' by Sean Mitchell.

Chapter Nineteen: *Zelig* and *A Midsummer Night's Sex Comedy*

'I want a big career' quoted by Kitty Kelley in *His Way* (Bantam, New York, 1986), from which most other details of the Farrow/Sinatra relationship are drawn. 'She's so *hot*!' from author's interview with William Read Woodfield, Beverly Hills, 1996. *Goodbye Baby and Amen: A Saraband for the Sixties*. (Condé Nast, London, 1969). Andy Warhol on Mia Farrow from *The Andy Warhol Diaries*, edited by Pat Hackett (Warner Books, New York, 1989). Farrow's exchange with Tony Perkins on Allen's clothing from *What Falls Away*. Allen on joining Orion in 'Woody Allen Switching to Orion after 10 Years at United Artists', *New York Times*, 16 October 1980 and 'Woody in 5-Year Pact with Orion: Ends UA Decade', *Variety*, 17 October 1980. Many quotes about *The Floating Light Bulb*, including Jack Weston's remarks and Allen's 'Maybe it will be an entertaining two hours' from 'Woody Allen's New Broadway Play Might Just be about Woody

Allen', *New York Times*, 26 April 1981. Brian Backer also quoted from 'Notes on People' and 'Brian Backer: Winner of the Woody-Allen-Kindred-Soul Contest', *New York Times*, 29 April 1981. Ulu Grosbard *passim* on *The Floating Light Bulb* from interview with John Andrew Gallagher in *Film Directors on Directing* (Praeger, New York, 1989). Allen's house-hunting described by Mia Farrow in *What Falls Away*. Allen on the beach house from 'Pizza with Woody' by Roger Ebert, *Movieline*, 8 January 1987.

Chapter Twenty: *Broadway Danny Rose* and *The Purple Rose of Cairo*

Tony Roberts' 'There is no discernible line' from BBC TV profile of Allen, 1992. Bourne's problems with design of *Zelig* described in *Selected Takes*. Kristi Groetke writing in *Woody and Mia: The Nanny's Tale*. David McGough's photos appeared in *US* magazine, 12 May 1981. Jules Feiffer's description of meeting Allen and Farrow from conversation with the author, 1996. Quotes from Mia Farrow *passim* from *What Falls Away*. Jeff Daniels on his casting in *Purple Rose* from 'Auteur! Auteur!' by Caryn James, *New York Times Magazine*. Allen on casting from interview with Henry Behar, *T.O.* magazine, March/April 1985.

Chapter Twenty-One: *Hannah and her Sisters* and *Radio Days*

Quotes from Mia Farrow *passim* from *What Falls Away*. Michael Caine on *Hannah and her Sisters* from *Acting in Film* (Applause Theater Book Publishers, New York, 1990). Peter Bart's editorial, 'Woody Revealed: The Nebbish as Control Freak' from *Daily Variety*, 9 December 1996. James Thurber on radio from 'Soapland', originally published in the *New Yorker* magazine and collected in *The Beast in Me, and Other Animals* (Harcourt, Brace, New York, 1948). Allen on

Jean-Luc Godard's *King Lear* from 'Pizza with Woody' by Roger Ebert.

Chapter Twenty-Two: *September, Another Woman* and *Oedipus Wrecks*
'Shoddy and embarrassing' from *The Films of Woody Allen*. 'We reshot every single scene' and other quotes *passim* from *What Falls Away*, unless otherwise indicated. Allen's description of Ingmar Bergman's lifestyle from 'Pizza with Woody' by Roger Ebert. Kristi Groetke quote from *Woody and Mia: The Nanny's Tale*. 'I knew full well it wouldn't make a dime' from 'Funny isn't Good Enough' by Sean Mitchell, *Los Angeles Times*, 15 March 1992. Michael Caine on working with Allen from 'If You Knew Woody Like I Know Woody' in *New York* magazine, 17 October 1994. J. Hoberman on *September* from *Village Voice*, 22 December 1987. Allen's op-ed piece appeared in the *New York Times*, 28 January 1988, under the title 'Am I Reading the Papers Correctly?' Charles Taylor on *Another Woman* in *Boston Phoenix*, 4 November 1988.

Chapter Twenty-Three: *Crimes and Misdemeanors* and *Alice*
Mia Farrow's quotes *passim* from *What Falls Away*. Allen's behaviour on the set of *Alice* described by Joe Mantegna in *The Woody Allen Companion*. Jay Scott reviewed *Crimes and Misdemeanors* in *Boston Globe and Mail*, 13 October 1989. Claire Bloom quoted by Julian Fox in *Woody: Movies from Manhattan*. 'With Fellini' from *Three-Quarter Face: Reviews and Reflections*. 'They were behaving in a way' quoted by Jess Gagle in 'Love and Fog', *Entertainment Weekly* 18 September 1992. Farrow's account of the Soon-Yi affair, the discovery of the Polaroids and alleged examples of molestation of Dylan appear in 'Mia's Story', *Vanity Fair*, November 1992. 'Stately, worshipful' and Allen's response to criticisms of Eric Lax's

biography from 'Funny isn't Good Enough' by Sean Mitchell.

Chapter Twenty-Four: *Shadows and Fog, Husbands and Wives* and *Manhattan Murder Mystery*
'Unmindful of [an actor's] stature' from *Woody Allen on Woody Allen*. Jeffrey Kurland on Farrow's adopted family from 'Everything You Always Wanted to Know About Woody (But were Afraid to Ask)' by Phoebe Hoban, *New York* magazine, 21 September 1992 and Letty Aronson on the same subject from *Village Voice*, 1 September 1992. *Time* magazine coverage in issue of 7 September 1992. *The Hedgehog and the Fox: An Essay on Tolstoy's View of History* by Isaiah Berlin (Simon & Schuster, New York, 1953). Lysette Anthony on *Husbands and Wives* and accounts of problems with keeping scripts secret from *Entertainment Weekly*, 18 September 1992. Jay Scott's review of *Husbands and Wives* in *Boston Globe and Mail*, 18 September 1992. Quotes by Mia Farrow *passim* from *What Falls Away*. Kristi Groetke quoted from *Woody and Mia: The Nanny's Tale*. *Entertainment Weekly* devoted much of its issue of 18 September 1992 to *Husbands and Wives* and the Farrow/Allen conflict. 'She became totally hysterical' from 'Woody Allen Tells of Affair as Custody Battle Begins', *New York Times*, 20 March 1993. 'In light years' from 'Media Experts are Waging a Verbal War for Woody Allen and Mia Farrow', *New York Times*, 29 August 1992. Doumanian on Farrow from 'Everything You Always Wanted to Know About Woody (But were Afraid to Ask)'. Reports on the Allen/Farrow rift as follows: 'Not his Favourite Movie: Allen Answers Charges' by James Barron, *New York Times*, 19 August 1992; 'A Courtroom Drama: Woody Allen Finds Himself in a new Role' by William Grimes, *New York Times*, 25 March 1993; 'Farrow Testifies that Daughter Accused Allen of

Molestation' by Richard Perez-Pena and 'Mia Farrow Tries to Avoid Role of a Woman Scorned' by William Grimes, both in *New York Times*, 26 March 1993; 'Fear and Anger as Mia Farrow is Cross-Examined', also by Grimes, in *New York Times*, 27 March 1993. Grimes, 'A Chronology of a Film's Making and a Relationship's Unmaking', *New York Times*, 31 August 1992. *Newsweek* magazine report issue of 31 August 1992. Adam Gopnik in 'The Outsider', *New Yorker* magazine, 25 October 1993. The legal opinions in Allen's appeal against the Supreme Court decision to deny him visitation rights to Satchel and Dylan appear in the *New York Supplement, Second Series* of the proceedings of the Supreme Court of New York State, 12 May 1994.

Chapter Twenty-Five: *Bullets Over Broadway* and *Mighty Aphrodite*
'For them, it was a delight' from 'Primal Screen' by Lesley White, *Sunday Times Magazine*, 11 February 1996. 'I worry about the big film companies' from 'Deconstructing his Film Crew', *New York Times*, 1 June 1998. Douglas McGrath *passim* on working with Allen from 'If You Knew Woody Like I Know Woody' in *New York* magazine, 17 October 1994. Jennifer Tilly on *Bullets Over Broadway* from *Independent*, 27 February 1997. 'Years ago, I was looking at Dylan' from 'Primal Screen'. Michael Blakemore on working on *Death Defying Acts* from 'Death Defying Director', *New Yorker* magazine, 3 June 1996. *Variety* review of plays from issue of 13 March 1995. *Newsday* review from issue of 7 March 1995. Mira Sorvino on being cast for *Mighty Aphrodite* from *Observer*, 17 March 1996. Helena Bonham-Carter interviewed by Sheila Johnston for *Independent Weekend*, 4 November 1995 and Jasper Rees for *Independent on Sunday*, 20 July 1997.

Chapter Twenty-Six: *Everyone Says I Love You* and *Deconstructing Harry*
'I found myself' from 'Primal Screen' by Lesley White, *Sunday Times Magazine*, 11 February 1996. Allen on European tour and Barbara Koppel on being chosen to shoot *Wild Man Blues* from 'Woody Blues' by Joanna Coles, *Guardian*, 7 May 1998. Brickman on idea of using music in *Annie Hall* from *Los Angeles Times*, 1 December 1996. Problems of finding singing actors, including quote about Drew Barrymore's voice, from 'A Passionate Man', *Independent*, 24 October 1996. Allen's plans to buy the Ca'Dario reported in *Independent on Sunday*, 5 January 1997. Details of the La Fenice fire, including Allen quotes, from 'A Death in Venice', *Time* magazine, 12 February 1996; 'Jail Threat to Woody Allen' in *The Times*, 8 March 1996; 'Did the Mafia Light the Match on La Fenice?', *Guardian*, 8 October 1996; 'Venice's Grand Opera Descends to Farce', *Independent on Sunday*, 24 February 1998. Other details from Kristi Jaas of the Fenice Project, Paris, 1997. John Fordham on Allen's clarinet playing from *Guardian*, 19 March 1996. 'The only time he ever made me laugh' quoted by Chris Parker in his review for *The Times*. Allen on DGA award from 'The Continuous Career of Woody Allen' by Tomm Carroll, *Directors' Guilde of America Magazine*, April 1996. Staff changes at Sweetland described in 'Deconstructing his Film Crew', *New York Times*, 1 June 1998, and 'Woody Allen has Got Rid of his Closest Friends. Why? To Save Money, of Course...' by Bernard Weinraub, *Guardian*, 3 June 1998.

Filmography

What's New Pussycat (1965)
Director: Clive Donner; Producer: Charles K. Feldman; Screenplay: Woody Allen; Photography: Jean Badal; Art Direction; Jacques Saulnier; Special Effects: Bob MacDonald; Music: Burt Bacharach; Editor: Fergus McDonnell; Sound: William-Robert Sivel.

Peter Sellers (Dr Fritz Fassbender); Peter O'Toole (Michael James); Romy Schneider (Carol Werner); Capucine (Renée Lefebvre); Paula Prentiss (Liz Bien); Woody Allen (Victor Shakapopolis); Ursula Andress (Rita); Edra Gale (Anna Fassbender); Katrin Schaake (Jacqueline); Eleanor Hirt (Mrs Werner); Jean Paredes (Marcel); Jacques Balutin (Etienne); Jess Hahn (Perry Werner); Howard Vernon (Doctor); Michel Subor (Philippe); Sabine Sun (Nurse); Nicole Karen (Tempest O'Brien); Jacqueline Fogt (Charlotte); Daniel Emilfork (Gas Station Attendant); Tanya Lopert (Miss Lewis); Barbara Somers (Miss Marks); Robert Rollis (Car Renter); Annette Poivre (Emma); Colin Drake (Durell); Richard Saint-Bris (Le Maire); Marion Conrad (First Stripper); Maggie Wright (Second Stripper); Françoise Hardy (Mayor's Secretary); Jean Yves Autrey, Pascal Wolf, Nadine Papin (Fassbender Children); Norbert Terry (Kelly); F. Medard (Nash); Gordon Felio (Fat Man); Douking (Renée's Concierge); Louise Lasser (The Nutcracker); Richard Burton (Man in Bar).

What's Up, Tiger Lily? (1966)
Screenplay and Dubbing: Woody Allen, Frank Buxton, Len Maxwell, Louise Lasser, Mickey Rose, Julie Bennett, Bryna Wilson.
Kagi No Kagi: Director: Senkichi Taniguchi; Producer: Tomoyuki Tanaka; Screenplay: Hideo Ando; Photography: Kazuo Yamado.

What's Up, Tiger Lily?: Director: Woody Allen; Production Conception: Ben Shapiro; 'Writings and Vocal Assists': Frank Buxton, Louise Lasser, Julie Bennett, Len Maxwell, Mickey Rose, Bryna Wilson; Editor: Richard Krown; Executive Producer: Henry G. Saperstein; Music: Jack Lewis, with songs by the Lovin' Spoonful; Associate Producer: Woody Allen; Production Manager: Jerry Goldstein.

Tatsuya Mihashi (Phil Moskowitz); Mie Hana (Terry Yaki); Akiko Wakayabayashi (Suki Yaki); Tadao Nakamura (Shepherd Wong); Susumu Kurobe (Wing Fat); China Lee (Stripper).

Casino Royale (1967)
Directors: John Huston, Kenneth Hughes, Val Guest, Robert Parrish, Joseph McGrath; Producers: Charles K. Feldman, Jerry Bresler; Screenplay: Wolf Mankowitz, John Law and Michael Sayers, from an Ian Fleming novel; Photography: Jack Hildyard; Special Effects: Cliff Richardson, Roy Whybrow; Production Designer: Michael Ayringer; Music: Burt Bacharach; Editor: Bill Lenny.

Peter Sellers (Evelyn Tremble); Ursula Andress (Vesper Lynd); David Niven (Sir James Bond); Orson Welles (Le Chiffre); Joanna Pettet (Mata Bond); Deborah Kerr (Widow McTarry); Daliah Lavi (The Detainer); Woody Allen (Jimmy Bond); William Holden (Ransome); Charles Boyer (Le Grand); John Huston ('M'); Kurt Kaznar (Smernov); George Raft (Himself); Jean-Paul Belmondo (Foreign Legion Soldier); Terence Cooper (Agent 007); Barbara Bouchet (Miss Moneypenny); Angela Scoular (Buttercup) Gabriella Licudi (Eliza); Tracey Crisp (Heather); Jacqueline Bisset (Miss Goodthighs); Anna Quayle (Frau Hoffner); Bernard Cribbins (Taxi Driver); Tracy Reed (Fang Leader); Fiona Lewis (Fang Girl); Percy Herbert (First Piper); Peter O'Toole (Man in Bar).

Don't Drink the Water (1969)
Director: Howard Morris; Producer: Charles H. Joffe; Screenplay: R. S. Allen and Harvey Bullock, based on the play by Woody Allen; Photography: Harvey Genkins; Art Director: Robert Gundlach; Music: Pat Williams; Assistant Director: Louis Stroller; Associate

Producer: Jack Grossberg; Executive Producer: Joseph E. Levine; Operating Cameraman: Urs Furfer; Casting Director: Jay Wolf; Editing and Editorial Supervision: Ralph Rosenblum; Costume Design: Gene Coffin.

Jackie Gleason (Walter Hollander); Estelle Parsons (Marion Hollander); Ted Bessell (Axel Magee); Joan Delaney (Susan Hollander); Michael Constantine (Krojack); Howard St John (Ambassador Magee); Danny Meehan (Kilroy); Richard Libertini (Father Drobney); Pierre Olaf (The Chef); Avery Schreiber (The Sultan); Mark Gordon (Merik); Phil Leeds (Sam); Howard Morris (Pilot of Escape Plane).

Take the Money and Run (1969)
Director: Woody Allen; Producer: Charles H. Joffe; Screenplay: Woody Allen and Mickey Rose; Photography: Lester Shorr, ASC; Art Direction; Fred Harpman; Special Effects: A. D. Flowers; Music: Marvin Hamlisch; Supervising Film Editor: James T. Heckert; Assistant Director: Stanley Ackerman; Editors: Paul Jordan, Ron Kalish; Editorial Consultant: Ralph Rosenblum; Associate Producer: Jack Grossberg; Executive Producer: Sidney Glazier; Set Direction: Marvin March.

Woody Allen (Virgin Starkwell); Janet Margolin (Louise); Marcel Hillaire (Fritz); Jacqueline Hyde (Miss Blair); Lonny Chapman (Jake); Jan Merlin (Al); James Anderson (Chain Gang Warden); Howard Storm (Fred); Mark Gordon (Vince); Micil Murphy (Frank); Minnow Moskowitz (Joe Agneta); Nate Jacobson (The Judge); Grace Bauer (Farm House Lady); Ethel Sokolow (Mother Starkwell); Henry Leff (Father Starkwell); Don Frazier (The Psychiatrist); Mike O'Dowd (Michael Sullivan); Louise Lasser (Kay Lewis); Stanley Ackerman (The Photographer); Jackson Beck (The Narrator).

Bananas (1971)
Director: Woody Allen; Producer: Jack Grossberg; Screenplay: Woody Allen and Mickey Rose; Photography: Andrew M. Costikyan; Production Design: Ed Wittstein; Set Decorator: Herbert Mulligan; Special Effects: Don B. Courtney; Music:

Marvin Hamlisch; Editor: Ron Kalish; Assistant Director: Fred T. Gallo; Executive Producer: Charles H. Joffe; Associate Producer: Ralph Rosenblum.

Woody Allen (Fielding Mellish); Louise Lasser (Nancy); Carlos Montalban (General Emilio Molina Vargas); Natividad Abascal (Yolanda); Jacobo Morales (Esposito); Miguel Suarez (Luis); David Ortiz (Sanchez); Renée Enriquez (Diaz); Jack Axelrod (Arroyo); Howard Cosell (Himself); Charlotte Rae (Mrs Mellish); Dan Frazer (Priest); Martha Greenhouse (Dr Feigen); Axel Anderson (Tortured Man); Dorthi Fox (J. Edgar Hoover); Dagne Crane (Sharon); Conrad Bain (Semple); Allen Garfield (Man on Cross); Princess Fatosh (Snakebite Lady); Hy Anzell (Patient); Sylvester Stallone (Street Hood).

Play it Again, Sam (1972)
Director: Herbert Ross; Producer: Arthur P. Jacobs; Production Supervisor: Roger M. Rothstein; Screenplay: Woody Allen, based on his play; Assistant Director: William Gerrity; Photography: Owen Roizman; Production Designer: Ed Wittstein; Music: Billy Goldenberg; Editor: Marion Rothman; Associate Producer: Frank Capra, Jr; Executive Producer: Charles Joffe; Costume Designer: Anna Hill Johnstone.

Woody Allen (Allan Felix); Diane Keaton (Linda Christie); Tony Roberts (Dick Christie); Jerry Lacy (Bogey); Susan Anspach (Nancy); Jennifer Salt (Sharon); Joy Bang (Julie); Viva (Jennifer); Suzanne Zenor (Disco Girl); Diana Davila (Suicidal Museum Girl); Mari Fletcher (Fantasy Sharon); Michael Green (Motorcycle Hood 1); Ted Markland (Motorcycle Hood 2).

Everything You Always Wanted to Know About Sex* (*But Were Afraid to Ask) (1972)
Director: Woody Allen; Producer: Charles H. Joffe; Screenplay: Woody Allen, from the book by Dr David Reuben; Assistant Directors: Fred T. Gallo; Terry M. Carr; Editor: Eric Albertson; Supervising Film Editor: James T. Heckert; Photography: David M. Walsh; Production Design: Dale Hennesy; Music: Mundell Lowe; Associate Producer: Jack Grossberg.

'Do Aphrodisiacs Work?' Woody Allen (Fool); Lynn Redgrave (Queen); Anthony Quayle (King); Alan Caillou (Fool's Father); Geoffrey Holder (Sorcerer); 'What is Sodomy?' Gene Wilder (Dr Douglas Ross); Elaine Giftos (Mrs Ann Ross); Titos Vandis (Stavros Milos); Daisy the Sheep (Herself); 'Why do Some Women have Trouble Reaching an Orgasm?' Woody Allen (Fabrizio); Louise Lasser (Gina); 'Are Transvestites Homosexuals?' Lou Jacobi (Sam Waterman); Sidney Miller (George); 'What are Sex Perverts?' Jack Barry (Himself); Toni Holt (Herself); Robert Q. Lewis (Himself); Pamela Mason (Herself); Regis Philbin (Himself); Don Chuy (Football Player); Tom Mack (Football Player); H. E. West (Bernard Jaffe); Baruch Lumet (Rabbi Chaim Baumel); 'Are the Findings of Doctors and Clinics Who do Sexual Research and Experiments Accurate?' Woody Allen (Victor Shakapopolis); Heather MacRae (Helen Lacy); John Carradine (Dr Bernardo); Ref Sanchez (Igor the Hunchback); Dort Clark (The Sheriff); 'What Happens During Ejaculation?' Woody Allen (Sperm); Tony Randall (Brain Room Operator); Burt Reynolds (Switchboard Operator); Erin Fleming (Sidney's Date); Stanley Adams (Stomach Operator); Oscar Beregi (Brain Control Technician); Jay Robinson (The Priest); Robert Walden (Sperm).

Sleeper (1973)
Director: Woody Allen; Producer: Jack Grossberg; Screenplay: Woody Allen and Marshall Brickman; Assistant Directors: Fred T. Gallo, Henry J. Lange, Jr; Editor: Ralph Rosenblum; Photography: David M. Walsh; Production Design: Dale Hennesy; Set Designer: Dianne Wager; Costume Designer: Joel Schumacher; Special Effects: A. D. Flowers; Associate Producers: Marshall Brickman and Ralph Rosenblum; Executive Producer: Charles H. Joffe; Music: Woody Allen, with the Preservation Hall Jazz Band and the New Orleans Funeral and Ragtime Orchestra.
Woody Allen (Miles Monroe); Diane Keaton (Luna Schlosser); John Beck (Erno Windt); Mary Gregory (Dr Melik); Don Keefer (Dr Tryon); John McLiam (Dr Agon); Bartlett Robinson (Dr Orva); Chris Forbes (Rainer Krebs); Marya Small (Dr Nero); Peter Hobbs (Dr Dean); Susan Miller (Ellen Pogrebin); Lou Picetti (Master of

Ceremonies); Brian Avery (Herald Cohen); Jessica Rains (Woman in the Mirror); Spencer Milligan (Jeb Hrmthmg); Stanley Ross (Sears Swiggles).

Love and Death (1975)
Director: Woody Allen; Producer: Charles H. Joffe; Screenplay: Woody Allen; Assistant Directors: Paul Feyder, Bernard Cohn; Photography: Ghislain Cloquet; Art Directon: Willy Holt; Music: Serge Prokofiev; Editors: Ralph Rosenblum, Ron Kalish; Costume Design: Gladys de Segonzac; Associate Producer: Fred T. Gallo; Executive Producer: Martin Poll.
Woody Allen (Boris Grushenko); Diane Keaton (Sonia); Olga Georges-Picot (Countess Alexandrovna); Jessica Harper (Natasha); Jack Lenoir (Kropotkin); James Tolkan (Napoleon); Alfred Lutter III (Young Boris); Lloyd Battista (Don Francisco); Frank Adu (Drill Sergeant); Harold Gould (Count Anton); C. A. R. Smith (Father Nikolai); Georges Adet (Old Nehamkin); Patricia Crown (Cheerleader); Harry Hankin (Uncle Sasha); Denise Peron (Spanish Countess); Zvee Scooler (Father); Beth Porter (Anna); Henry Czarniak (Ivan); Despo Diamantidou (Mother); Florian (Uncle Nicolai); Brian Coburn (Dmitri); Luce Fabiole (Grandmother); Edmond Ardisson (Priest); Feodor Atkine (Mikhail); Albert Augier (Waiter); Yves Barasco (Rimsky); Jack Berard (General Lecoq); Eva Bertrand (Woman in Hygiene Play); George Birt (Doctor); Yves Brainville (André); Gerard Buhr (Servant); Henri Coutet (Minskov); Sandor Eles (Soldier); Jacqueline Fogt (Ludmilla); Sol L. Frieder (Leonid Voskovec); Tony Jan (Vladimir Maximovitch); Tutte Lemkow (Pierre); Leib Lensky (Father André); Ann Lonnberg (Olga).

The Front (1976)
Director: Martin Ritt; Producer: Martin Ritt; Assistant Directors: Peter Scoppa, Ralph Singleton; Screenplay: Walter Bernstein; Photography: Michael Chapman; Art Direction: Charles Bailey; Music: Dave Grusin; Editor: Sidney Levin; Executive Producer: Charles H. Joffe; Associate Producer: Robert Greenhut; Costume Designer; Ruth Morley.

Woody Allen (Howard Prince); Zero Mostel (Hecky Brown); Herschel Bernardi (Phil Sussman); Michael Murphy (Alfred Miller); Andrea Marcovicci (Florence Barrett); Remak Ramsay (Hennessey); Marvin Lichterman (Myer Prince); Lloyd Gough (Delaney); David Margulies (Phelps); Joshua Shelley (Sam); Norman Rose (Howard's Attorney); Charles Kimbrough (Committee Counselor); M. Josef Sommer (Committee Chairman); Danny Aiello (Danny La Gattuta); Georgann Johnson (TV Interviewer); Scott McKay (Hampton); David Clarke (Hubert Jackson); L. W. Klein (Bank Teller); John Bentley (Bartender); Julie Garfield (Margo); Murray Moston (Boss); McIntyre Dixon (Harry Stone); Rudolph Wilrich (Tallman); Burt Britton (Bookseller); Albert M. Oppenheimer (School Principal); William Bogert (Parks); Joey Faye (Waiter); Marilyn Sokol (Sandy); John J. Slater (TV Director); Renee Paris (Girl in Hotel); Gino Gennaro (Stage Hand); Joan Porter (Myer's Wife); Andrew Bernstein, Jacob Bernstein (Alfred's Children); Matthew Tobin (Man at Party); Marilyn Persky (His Date); Sam McMurray (Young Man at Party); Joe Jamrog (FBI Man); Michael Miller (FBI Man); Lucy Lee Flippin (Nurse); Jack Davidson (Congressman); Donal Symington (Congressman); Patrick McNamara (Federal Marshal).

Annie Hall (1977)
Director: Woody Allen; Producer: Charles H. Joffe; Screenplay: Woody Allen and Marshall Brickman; Assistant Directors; Fred T. Gallo, Fred Blankfein; Photography: Gordon Willis; Art Direction: Mel Bourne; Animated Sequences: Chris Ishii; Editor: Ralph Rosenblum; Costume Design: Ruth Morley; Associate Producer: Fred T. Gallo; Executive Producer: Robert Greenhut.
Woody Allen (Alvy Singer); Diane Keaton (Annie Hall); Tony Roberts (Rob); Carol Kane (Allison); Paul Simon (Tony Lacey); Shelley Duvall (Pam); Janet Margolin (Robin); Colleen Dewhurst (Mom Hall); Christopher Walken (Duane Hall); Donald Symington (Dad Hall); Helen Ludlam (Grammy Hall); Mordecai Lawner (Alvy's Father – Leo); Joan Newman (Alvy's Mother); Jonathan Munk (Alvy Aged 9); Ruth Volner (Alvy's Aunt); Martin Rosenblatt (Alvy's Uncle); Hy Anzell (Joey Nichols); Rashel Novikoff

(Aunt Tessie); Russell Horton (Man in Cinema Queue); Marshall McLuhan (Himself); Christine Jones (Dorrie); Mary Boylan (Miss Reed); Wendy Girard (Janet); John Doumanian (Coke Fiend); Bob Maroff (Man 1 Outside Cinema); Rick Petrucelli (Man 2 Outside Cinema); Lee Callahan (Ticket Seller at Cinema); Chris Gampel (Doctor); Dick Cavett (Himself); Mark Lenard (Navy Officer); Dan Ruskin (Comedian at Rally); John Glover (Actor-Boyfriend Jerry); Bernie Styles (Comic's Agent); Johnny Haymer (Comic); Ved Bandhu (Maharishi); John Dennis Johnson (L. A. Policeman); Lauri Bird (Tony Lacey's Girlfriend); Jim McKrell (Party Guest); Jeff Goldblum (Party Guest); William Callaway (Party Guest); Roger Newman (Party Guest); Alan Landers (Party Guest); Jean Sarah Frost (Party Guest); Vince O'Brien (Hotel Doctor); Humphrey Davis (Alvy's Psychiatrist); Veronica Radburn (Annie's Psychiatrist); Robin Mary Paris (Actress in Rehearsal); Charles Levin (Actor in Rehearsal); Wayne Carson (Rehearsal Stage Manager); Michael Karm (Rehearsal Director); Petronia Johnson (Tony's Date at Nightclub); Shaun Casey (Tony's Date at Nightclub); Ricardo Bertoni (Waiter 1 at Nightclub); Michael Aronin (Waiter 2 at Nightclub); Lou Picetti (Street Stranger); Loretta Tupper (Street Stranger); James Burge (Street Stranger); Shelly Hack (Street Stranger); Albert Ottenheimer (Street Stranger); Paula Trueman (Street Stranger); Beverly D'Angelo (Actress in Rob's TV Show).

Interiors (1978)
Director: Woody Allen; Producer: Charles H. Joffe; Screenplay: Woody Allen; Assistant Director: Martin Berman; Photography: Gordon Willis; Production Design: Mel Bourne; Editor: Ralph Rosenblum; Costume Designer: Joel Schumacher.
Kristin Griffith (Flyn); Mary Beth Hurt (Joey); Richard Jordan (Frederick); Diane Keaton (Renata); E. G. Marshall (Arthur); Geraldine Page (Eve); Maureen Stapleton (Pearl); Sam Waterson (Mike); Missy Hope (Young Joey); Kerry Duffy (Young Renata); Nancy Collins (Young Flyn); Penny Gaston (Young Eve); Roger Morden (Young Arthur); Henderson Forsythe (Judge Bartel).

Manhattan (1979)
Director: Woody Allen; Producer: Charles H. Joffe; Screenplay:
Woody Allen and Marshall Brickman; Assistant Directors: Frederic
B. Blankfein, Joan Spiegel Feinstein; Director of Photography:
Gordon Willis; Production Design: Mel Bourne; Music: George
Gershwin; Editor: Susan E. Morse; Costume Design: Albert Wolsky;
Executive Producer: Robert Greenhut.
Woody Allen (Isaac Davis); Diane Keaton (Mary Wilke); Michael
Murphy (Yale); Mariel Hemingway (Tracy); Meryl Streep
(Jill); Anne Byrne (Emily); Karen Ludwig (Connie); Michael
O'Donoghue (Dennis); Victor Truro (Party Guest); Tisa Farrow
(Party Guest); Helen Hanft (Party Guest); Bella Abzug (Guest of
Honour); Gary Weiss (Television Director); Kenny Vance (Tele-
vision Producer); Charles Levin (Television Actor 1); Karen Allen
(Television Actor 2); David Rasche (Television Actor 3); Damion
Sheller (Ike's Son); Wallace Shawn (Jeremiah); Mark Linn Baker
(Shakespearean Actor); Frances Conroy (Shakespearean Actor);
Bill Anthony (Porsche Owner 1); John Doumanian (Porsche
Owner 2); Ray Serra (Pizzeria Waiter).

Stardust Memories (1980)
Director: Woody Allen; Producer: Robert Greenhut; Screenplay:
Woody Allen; Assistant Director; Frederic B. Blankfein; Photo-
graphy: Gordon Willis; Production Design: Mel Bourne; Music:
Dick Hyman; Editor: Susan E. Morse; Costume Design: Santo
Loquasto; Executive Producers: Jack Rollins and Charles H. Joffe.
Woody Allen (Sandy Bates); Charlotte Rampling (Dorrie); Jessica
Harper (Daisy); Marie-Christine Barrault (Isobel); Tony Roberts
(Tony); Daniel Stern (Actor); Amy Wright (Shelley); Helen Hanft
(Vivian Orkin); John Rothman (Jack Abel); Anne de Salvo (Debbie
– Sandy's Sister); Joan Neuman (Sandy's Mother); Ken Chapin
(Sandy's Father); Leonardo Cimino (Sandy's Analyst); Louise
Lasser (Sandy's Secretary); Eli Mintz (Old Man); Bob Maroff
(Jerry Abraham); Gabrielle Strasun (Charlotte Ames); David
Lipman (George, Sandy's Chauffeur); Robert Munk (Young
Sandy); Jaqui Safra (Sam); Sharon Stone (Girl on Train); Andy
Albeck, Robert Friedman, Douglas Ireland, Jack Rollins, Laraine

Newman (Studio Executives); Howard Kissel (Sandy's Manager); Max Leavitt (Sandy's Doctor); Renee Lippin (Sandy's Press Agent); Sol Lomita (Sandy's Accountant); Irving Metzman (Sandy's Lawyer); Dorothy Leon (Sandy's Cook); Roy Brocksmith (Dick Lobel); Simon Newey (Mr Payson); Victoria Zussin (Mrs Payson); Francis Pole (Libby); Bill Anthony, Filomena Spagnuolo, Ruth Rugoff, Martha Whitehead (Fans); Judith Roberts (Singer); Barry Weiss (Dancer); Robin Ruinsky, Adrian Richards, Dominick Petrolino, Sharon Brous, Michael Zanella, Doris Dugan Slater, Michael Goldstein, Neil Napolitan (Question Askers – Screening); Stanley Ackerman (Reporter – Screening); Noel Behn (Doug Orkin); Candy Loving (Tony's Girlfriend); Benjamin Rayson (Dr Paul Pearlstein); Mary Mims (Claire Schaeffer); Charles Lowe (Vaudeville Singer); Marie Lane (Cabaret Singer); Gustave Tassell, Marina Schiano, Dimitri Vassilopoulos, Judith Crist, Carmin Masrin (Cabaret Patrons); Sylvia Davis (Hostility Victim); Joseph Summo (Hostility Monster); Victor Truro (Hostility Psychoanalyst); Judith Cohen, Madeline Moroff, Maureen P. Levins (Friends of Sandy's Sister); E. Brian Dean (Police Sergeant); Marvin Peisner (Ed Rich); Robert Tennenhouse, Leslie Smith, Samuel Chodorov (Autograph Seekers); Philip Lenkowsky (Autograph Seeker/Assassin); Vanina Holasek (Isobel's Daughter); Michel Touchard (Isobel's Son); Kenny Vance, Iryn Steinfink (New Studio Executives); Frank Modell (Rewrite Man); Anne Korzen (Woman in Ice Cream Parlour); Eric Van Valkenburg (Man in Ice Cream Parlour); Susan Ginsburg (Usherette); Ostaro (Astrologer); Alice Spivak (Nurse); Armin Shimerman, Edith Grossman, Jacqueline French (Eulogy Audience); John Doumanian (Armenian Fan); Jack Hollander (Policeman).

A Midsummer Night's Sex Comedy (1982)
Director: Woody Allen; Producer: Robert Greenhut; Screenplay: Woody Allen; Photography: Gordon Willis; Production Design; Mel Bourne; Executive Producer: Charles H. Joffe; Associate Producer: Michael Peyser; Assistant Director: Frederic B. Blankfein; Editor: Susan E. Morse; Casting: Juliet Taylor; Costume Design: Santo Loquasto; Art Director: Speed Hopkins.

Woody Allen (Andrew Hobbes); Mia Farrow (Ariel Weymouth); José Ferrer (Leopold); Julie Hagerty (Dulcy Ford); Tony Roberts (Dr Maxwell Jordan); Mary Steenburgen (Adrian Hobbes); Adam Redfield (Student Foxx); Moishe Rosenfeld (Mr Hayes); Timothy Jenkins (Mr Thomson); Michael Higgins (Reynolds); Sol Frieder (Carstairs); Boriss Zoubok (Purvis); Thomas Barbour (Blint); Kate McGregor-Stewart (Mrs Baker).

Zelig (1983)
Director: Woody Allen; Producer: Robert Greenhut; Screenplay: Woody Allen; Photography: Gordon Willis; Production Design: Mel Bourne; Music: Dick Hyman; Editor: Susan E. Morse; Executive Producers: Charles H. Joffe and Jack Rollins; Associate Producer: Michael Peyser; Costume Design: Santo Loquasto.
Woody Allen (Leonard Zelig); Mia Farrow (Dr Eudora Fletcher); John Buckwalter (Dr Sindell); Martin Chatinover (Glandular Diagnosis Doctor); Stanley Swerdlow (Mexican Food Doctor); Paul Nevens (Dr Birsky); Howard Erskine (Hypodermic Doctor); George Hamlin (Experimental Drugs Doctor); Ralph Bell, Richard Whiting, Will Hussong (Other Doctors); Robert Iglesia (Man in Barber's Chair); Eli Resnick (Man in Park); Edward McPhillips (Scotsman); Gale Hansen (Student 1); Michael Jeeter (Student 2); Peter McRobbie (Workers' Rally Speaker); Sol Lomita (Martin Geist); Mary Louis Wilson (Sister Ruth); Alice Beardsley (Telephone Operator); Paula Trueman (Woman on Telephone); Ed Lane (Man on Telephone); Marianne Tatum (Actress Fletcher); Charles Denney (Actor Doctor); Michael Kell (Actor Koslow); Garrett Brown (Actor Zelig); Sharon Ferroll (Miss Baker); Richard Litt (Charles Koslow); Dimitri Vassilopoulos (Martinez); John Rothman (Paul Deghuee); Stephanie Farrow (Sister Meryl); Francis Beggins (City Hall Speaker); Jean Trowbridge (Dr Fletcher's Mother); Ken Chapin (Interviewer); Gerald Klein, Vincent Gerosa (Hearst Guests); Deborah Rush (Lita Fox); Stanley Simmonds (Lita's Lawyer); Robert Berger (Zelig's Lawyer); Jeanine Jackson (Helen Gray); Erma Campbell (Zelig's Wife); Anton Marco (Wrist Victim); Louise Deitch (House-Painting Victim); Bernice Dowis (Vilification Woman); John Doumanian (Waiter); Will Holt (Rally

Chancellor). *Contemporary Interviews with*: Susan Sontag; Irving Howe; Saul Bellow; Bricktop; Dr Bruno Bettelheim; Professor John Morton Blum.

Broadway Danny Rose (1984)
Director: Woody Allen; Producer: Robert Greenhut; Screenplay: Woody Allen; Photography: Gordon Willis; Executive Producer: Charles H. Joffe; Production Design: Mel Bourne; Editor: Susan E. Morse; Costume Design: Jeffrey Kurland; Music: Dick Hyman; Associate Producer: Michael Peyser.

Woody Allen (Danny Rose); Mia Farrow (Tina Vitale); Nick Apollo Forte (Lou Canova); Sandy Baron (Himself); Corbett Monica (Himself); Jackie Gayle (Himself); Morty Gunty (Himself); Will Jordan (Himself); Howard Storm (Himself); Jack Rollins (Himself); Milton Berle (Himself); Craig Vandenburgh (Ray Webb); Herb Reynolds (Barney Dunn); Paul Greco (Vito Rispoli); Frank Renzulli (Joe Rispoli); Edwin Bordo (Johnny Rispoli); Gina DeAngelis (Johnny's Mother); Peter Castellotti (Hood at Warehouse); Sandy Richman (Teresa); Gerald Schoenfeld (Sid Bacharach); Olga Barbato (Angelina); David Kissell (Phil Chomsky); Gloria Parker (Water Glass Virtuoso); Bob & Etta Rollins (Balloon Act); Bob Weil (Herbie Jayson); David Kieserman (Ralph); Mark Hardwick (Blind Xylophonist); Alba Ballard (Bird Lady); Maurice Shrog (Hypnotist); Belle Berger (Woman in Trance; Herschel Rosen (Woman in Trance's Husband); Joe Franklin (Himself); Dom Matteo (Carmine); Camille Saviola (Woman at Party 1); Sheila Bond (Woman at Party 2); Betty Rosotti (Woman at Party 3); Howard Cosell (Himself); John Doumanian (Waldorf Manager); Gary Reynolds (Waldorf Manager's Friend); Diane Zolten (Fan 1); William Paulson (Fan 2); George Axler (Fan 3); Leo Steiner (Deli Owner).

The Purple Rose of Cairo (1985)
Director: Woody Allen; Producer: Robert Greenhut; Screenplay: Woody Allen; Photography: Gordon Willis; Production Designer: Stuart Wurtzel; Editor: Susan E. Morse; Music: Dick Hyman; Executive Producer: Charles H. Joffe; Associate Producers:

Michael Peyser, Gail Sicilia; Costume Designer: Jeffrey Kurland.
Mia Farrow (Cecilia); Jeff Daniels (Gil Shepherd); Danny Aiello
(Monk); Irving Metzman (Cinema Manager); Stephanie Farrow
(Cecilia's Sister); David Kieserman (Diner Boss); Elaine Grollman,
Victoria Zussin, Mark Hammond, Wade Barnes, Joseph G.
Graham, Don Quigley, Maurice Brenner (Diner Patrons); Paul
Herman, Rick Petrucelli, Peter Castellotti (Penny Pitchers); Milton
Seaman, Mimi Weddell (Ticket Buyers); Tom Degidon (Ticket
Taker); Mary Hedahl (Popcorn Seller); Dianne Wiest (Emma); Ken
Chapin, Robert Trebor (Reporters); Andrew Murphy (Policeman
1); Thomas Kubiak (Policeman 2); Alexander Cohen (Raoul
Hirsh); John Rothman (Hirsh's Lawyer); Raymond Serra (Holly-
wood Executive); George J. Manos (Press Agent); Sydney Blake
(*Variety* Reporter); Michael Tucker (Gil's Agent); Peter Von Berg
(Drugstore Customer); David Weber (Photo Double); Glenne
Headley, Willie Tjan, Lela Ivey, Drinda La Lumia (Prostitutes);
Loretta Tupper (Music Store Owner); cast of *The Purple Rose of
Cairo*: Jeff Daniels (Tom Baxter); Edward Herrmann (Henry);
John Wood (Jason); Deborah Rush (Rita); Van Johnson (Larry);
Zoe Caldwell (Countess); Eugene Anthony (Arturo); Ebb Miller
(Bandleader); Karen Akers (Kitty Haynes); Annie Joe Edwards
(Delilah); Milo O'Shea (Father Donnelly); Peter McRobbie (The
Communist); Camille Saviola (Olga); David Tice (Waiter); James
Lynch (Maître D').

Hannah and her Sisters (1986)
Director: Woody Allen; Producer: Robert Greenhut; Screenplay:
Woody Allen; Photography: Carlo DiPalma; Executive Producer:
Jack Rollins and Charles H. Joffe; Art Direction–Set Direction:
Stuart Wurtzel and Carol Joffe; Editor: Susan E. Morse; Costume
Designer: Jeffrey Kurland; Associate Producer: Gail Sicilia.
Mia Farrow (Hannah); Woody Allen (Mickey Sachs); Barbara
Hershey (Lee); Carrie Fisher (April Knox); Michael Caine (Elliot);
Dianne Wiest (Holly); Maureen O'Sullivan (Norma); Lloyd Nolan
(Evan); Max von Sydow (Frederick); Sam Waterston (David
Tolchin); Julie Kavner (Gail); Lewis Black (Paul); Julia Louis-
Dreyfus (Mary); Christian Clemenson (Larry); J. T. Walsh (Ed

Smythe); John Turturro (Writer); Rusty Magee (Ron); Allen Decheser, Artie Decheser (Hannah's Twins); Ira Wheeler (Dr Abel); Richard Jenkins (Dr Wilkes); Tracy Kennedy (Brunch Guest); Fred Melamed (Dr Grey); Benno Schmidt (Dr Smith); Joanna Gleason (Carol); Tony Roberts (Norman); Maria Chiara (Manon Lescaut); Daniel Stern (Dusty); Stephen Defluitter (Dr Brooks); The 39 Steps (Rock Band); Bobby Short (Himself); Rob Scott (Drummer); Beverly Peer (Bass Player); Daisy Previn, Moses Farrow (Hannah's Children); Paul Bates (Theatre Manager); Carrotte, Mary Pappas (Theatre Executives); Bernie Leighton (Pianist); Ken Costigan (Father Flynn); Helen Miller (Mickey's Mother); Leo Postrel (Mickey's Father); Susan Gordon-Clark (Hostess); William Sturgis (Elliot's Analyst); Daniel Haber (Krishna); Verna O. Hobson (Mavis); John Doumanian, Fletcher Previn, Irwin Tenenbaum, Amy Greenhill, Dickson Shaw, Marje Sheridan, Mary Beth Hurt (Thanksgiving Guests); Ivan Kronenfeld (Lee's Husband).

Radio Days (1987)

Director: Woody Allen; Producer: Robert Greenhut; Screenplay: Woody Allen; Director of Photography: Carlo DiPalma; Production Designer: Santo Loquasto; Editor: Susan E. Morse; Art Direction–Set Direction: Santo Loquasto; Carol Joffe, Les Bloom, George DeTitta, Jr; Musical Supervision: Dick Hyman; Associate Producers: Ezra Swerdlow, Gail Sicilia; Costume Designer: Jeffrey Kurland; Executive Producers: Jack Rollins and Charles H. Joffe.

Julie Kavner (Mother – Tess); Wallace Shawn (Masked Avenger); Michael Tucker (Father – Martin); Josh Mostel (Abe); Dianne Wiest (Bea); Mia Farrow (Sally White); Danny Aiello (Rocco); Jeff Daniels (Biff Baxter); Tony Roberts (*Silver Dollar* Emcee); Diane Keaton (Monica Charles); Mike Starr, Paul Herman (Burglars); Don Pardo (*Guess that Tune* Host); Martin Rosenblatt (Mr Needleman); Helen Miller (Mrs Needleman); Danielle Ferland (Child Star); Julie Kurnitz (Irene); David Warrilow (Roger); Michael Murray (*Avenger* Crook); William Flanagan (*Avenger* Announcer); Seth Green (Little Joe); Renee Lippin (Ceil); William

Magerman (Grandpa); Leah Carrey (Grandma); Joy Newman (Ruthie); Hy Anzell (Mr Waldbaum); Judith Malina (Mrs Waldbaum); Fletcher Farrow Previn (Andrew); Oliver Block (Nick); Maurice Toueg (Dave); Sal Tuminello (Burt); Rebecca Nickels (Evelyn Goorwitz); Mindy Morgenstern (Teacher); David Mosberg (Arnold); Ross Morgenstern (Ross); Kenneth Mars (Rabbi Baumel); Andrew Clark (Sidney Manulis); Lee Erwin (Roller Rink Organist); Roger Hammer (Richard); Terry Lee Swarts, Margaret Thomson (Nightclub Customers); Denise Dummont (Singer); Dimitri Vassilopoulos (Porfirio); Larry David (Communist Neighbour); Rebecca Schaeffer (Communist's Daughter); Belle Berger (Mrs Silverman); Guy Le Bow (Bill Kern); Brian Mannain (Kirby Kyle); Stan Burns (Ventriloquist); Todd Field (Crooner); Peter Lombard (Abercrombie Host); Martin Sherman (Mr Abercrombie); Crystal Field, Maurice Shrog (Abercrombie Couple); Marc Colner (Whiz Kid); Joel Eidelsberg (Mr Zipsky); Jimmy Sabat (Chester); Peter Castellotti (Mr Davids); Gina DeAngelis (Rocco's Mother); Shelley Delaney (Chekhov Actress); Dwight Weist (Pearl Harbor Announcer); Ken Levinsky, Ray Marchica (USO Musicians); J. R. Horne (Biff Announcer); Kuno Spunholz (German); Henry Yuk (Japanese); Sydney A. Blake (Miss Gordon); Kitty Carlisle Hart (Radio Singer); Robert Joy (Fred); Henry Cowen (Principal); Philip Shultz (Whistler); Mercedes Ruehl, Bruce Jarchow (Admen); Greg Gerard (Songwriter); David Cale (Director); Ira Wheeler (Sponsor); Hannah Rabinowitz (Sponsor's Wife); Edward S. Kotkin (Diction Teacher); Ruby Payne, Jaqui Safra (Diction Students); Paul Berman (*Gay White Way* Announcer); Ivan Kronenfeld (On-the-Spot Newsman); Frank O'Brien (Fireman); Yolanda Childress (Polly's Mother); Artie Butler (New Year's Eve Singer); Gregg Almquist, Jackson Beck, Wendell Craig, W. H. Macy, Ken Roberts, Norman Rose, Robert Tate, Kenneth Walsh (Radio Voices); Woody Allen (Narrator).

September (1987)
Director: Woody Allen; Producer: Robert Greenhut; Screenplay: Woody Allen; Director of Photography: Carlo DiPalma; Production Designer: Santo Loquasto; Editor: Susan E. Morse; Execu-

tive Producers: Jack Rollins and Charles H. Joffe; Costume Designer: Jeffrey Kurland.

Denholm Elliott (Howard); Dianne Wiest (Stephanie); Mia Farrow (Lane); Elaine Stritch (Diane); Sam Waterston (Peter); Jack Warden (Lloyd); Ira Wheeler (Mr Raines); Jane Cecil (Mrs Raines); Rosemary Murphy (Mrs Mason).

Another Woman (1988)
Director: Woody Allen; Producer: Robert Greenhut; Screenplay: Woody Allen; Photography: Sven Nykvist; Editor: Susan E. Morse; Production Designer: Santo Loquasto; Costume Designer; Jeffrey Kurland; Executive Producers: Jack Rollins and Charles H. Joffe; Associate Producers: Thomas Reilly, Helen Robin.

Gena Rowlands (Marion Post); Mia Farrow (Hope); Ian Holm (Dr Kenneth Post); Blythe Danner (Lydia); Gene Hackman (Larry Lewis); Betty Buckley (Kathy); Martha Plimpton (Laura); John Houseman (Marion's Father); Sandy Dennis (Claire); David Ogden Stiers (Young Marion's Father); Philip Bosco (Sam); Harris Yulin (Paul); Frances Conroy (Lynn); Fred Melamed (Patient's Voice); Kenneth Welsh (Donald); Bruce Jay Friedman (Mark); Bernie Leighton (Piano Player); Jack Gelber, John Schenck (Birthday Party Guests); Noel Behn, Gretchen Dahm, Janet Frank, Dana Ivey, Fred Melamed, Alice Spivak (Engagement Party Guests); Mary Laslo (Clara); Carol Schultz (Young Clara); Dax Munna (Little Paul); Heather Sullivan (Little Marion); Margaret Marx (Young Marion); Jennifer Lynn McComb (Young Claire); Caroline McGee (Marion's Mother); Stephen Mailer (Young Paul); Jacques Levy (Jack); Dee Dee Friedman (Waitress); Josh Hamilton (Laura's Boyfriend); Kathryn Grody (Cynthia Franks); John Madden Towey (Waiter); Michael Kirby (Psychiatrist); Fred Sweda (Tom Banks); Jill Whitaker (Eleanor Banks).

Oedipus Wrecks (in *New York Stories*) (1989)
Director: Woody Allen; Producer: Robert Greenhut; Screenplay: Woody Allen; Photography: Sven Nykvist; Editor: Susan E. Morse; Production Designer: Santo Loquasto; Executive Producers: Jack Rollins and Charles H. Joffe; Costumes: Jeffrey Kurland.

Woody Allen (Sheldon); Marvin Chatinover (Psychiatrist); Mae Questel (Mother); Mia Farrow (Lisa); Molly Regan (Sheldon's Secretary); Ira Wheeler (Mr Bates); Joan Bud (Board Member); Jessie Keosian (Aunt Ceil); Michael Rizzo (Waiter); George Schindler (Magician); Bridget Ryan (Rita); Larry David (Theatre Manager); Paul Herman (Detective Flynn); Herschel Rosen (Store Clerk); Lola André, Martin Rosenblatt, Helen Hanft, Annie-Joe, Ernst Muller, Adele French, Selma Hirsch, Briz, Lou Ruggiero, Elana Cooper (Citizens); Andrew MacMillan (Newscaster); Jodi Long, Nancy Giles (TV Interviewers); Mayor Ed Koch (Himself); Mike Starr, Richard Grund (Workmen); Julie Kavner (Treva).

Crimes and Misdemeanors (1989)
Director: Woody Allen; Producer: Robert Greenhut; Screen-play: Woody Allen; Photography: Sven Nykvist; Editor: Susan E. Morse; Production Designer: Santo Loquasto; Costume Designer: Jeffrey Kurland; Executive Producers: Jack Rollins and Charles H. Joffe.
Bill Bernstein (Testimonial Speaker); Martin Landau (Judah Rosenthal); Claire Bloom (Miriam Rosenthal); Stephanie Roth (Sharon Rosenthal); Greg Edelman (Chris); George Mano (Pho-tographer); Anjelica Huston (Dolores Paley); Woody Allen (Cliff Stern); Jenny Nichols (Jenny); Joanna Gleason (Wendy Stern); Alan Alda (Lester); Daryl Hannah (Lisa Crosby); Sam Waterston (Ben); Zina Jasper (Carol); Dolores Sutton (Judah's secretary); Joel S. Fogel, Donna Castellano, Thomas P. Crow (TV Producers); Mia Farrow (Halley Reed); Martin Bergmann (Professor Louis Levy); Caroline Aaron (Barbara); Kenny Vance (Murray); Jerry Orbach (Jack Rosenthal); Jerry Zaks (Man on Campus); Barry Finkel, Steve Maidment (TV Writers); Nadia Sanford (Alva); Chester Malinowski (Hit Man); Stanley Reichman (Chris's Father); Rebecca Schull (Chris's Mother); David S. Howard (Sol Rosenthal); Garret Simowitz (Young Juda); Frances Conroy (House Owner); Anna Berger (Aunt May); Sol Frieder, Justin Zaremby, Marvin Terban, Hy Anzell, Sylvia Kauders (Seder Guests); Victor Argo (Detective); Lenore Loveman, Nora Ephron,

Sunny Keyser, Merv Bloch, Nancy Arden, Thomas L. Bolster, Myla Pitt, Robin Bartlett (Wedding Guests); Grace Zimmerman (Bride); Randy Aaron Fink (Groom); Rabbi Joel Zion (Rabbi).

Alice (1990)
Director: Woody Allen; Producer: Robert Greenhut; Screenplay: Woody Allen; Photography: Carlo DiPalma; Editor: Susan E. Morse; Production Designer: Santo Loquasto; Costume Designer: Jeffrey Kurland; Production Manager: Joseph Hartwick; Co-Producers: Helen Robin, Joseph Hartwick; Associate Producers: Thomas Reilly, Jane Read Martin; Executive Producers: Jack Rollins and Charles H. Joffe.
Joe Mantegna (Joe Rufilho); Mia Farrow (Alice Johnson Tait); William Hurt (Doug); June Squib (Hilda); Marceline Hugot (Monica); Dylan O'Sullivan Farrow (Kate); Matt Williamson (Dennis); Julie Kavner (Decorator); Billy Taylor (Trainer); Holland Taylor (Helen); Michael-Vaughn Sullivan (Hairstylist); Robin Bartlett (Nina); Linda Wallem (Penny); Gina Gallagher (Shanna); Patience Moore (Teacher); Diane Cheng (Dr Yang's Assistant); Kim Chan (Patient); Keye Luke (Dr Yang); Linda Bridges (Saleswoman); Anthony Cortino (Dog Groomer); Cybill Shepherd (Nancy Brill); Alec Baldwin (Ed); Katja Schumann (Circus Equestrian); Vanessa Thomas (Circus Aerialist); Blythe Danner (Dorothy); Gwen Verdon (Alice's Mother); Patrick O'Neal (Alice's Father); Kristy Graves (Alice at 18); Laurie Nayber (Young Dorothy); Rachel Miner (Alice at 12); Amy Louise Barrett (Mrs Keyes); Caroline Aaron (Sue); Alexi Henry (Kimberly); James Toback (Professor); Bernadette Peters (Muse); Elle Macpherson (Model); Ira Wheeler, Lisa Marie (Office Party Guests); Diane Salinger (Carol); Alfred Cherry (Vicki's Analyst); David Spielberg (Ken); Bob Balaban (Sid Moscowitz); Peggy Miley (Dorothy's Maid); George Manos, Kim Weston-Moran, Peter Tolan, Kenneth Edelson, Marvin Terban, James McDaniel, Roy Attaway (Party Guests); Jodi Long, Suzann O'Neill, Don Snell, Robert Polenz (Park Avenue Couples).

Scenes from a Mall (1991)
Director: Paul Mazursky; Producer: Paul Mazursky; Screenplay:
Roger L. Simon and Paul Mazursky; Photography: Fred Murphy;
Production Design: Pato Guzman; Editor: Stuart Pappé; Costume
Designer: Albert Wolsky; Music: Marc Shaiman; Co-Producers:
Pato Guzman and Patrick McCormick; Associate Producer: Stuart
Pappé.
Bette Midler (Deborah Feingold-Fifer); Woody Allen (Nick Fifer);
Bill Irwin (Mime); Daren Firestone (Sam); Rebecca Nickels
(Jennifer); Paul Mazursky (Dr Hans Clava).

Shadows and Fog (1992)
Director: Woody Allen; Producers: Jack Rollins and Charles H.
Joffe; Screenplay: Woody Allen; Director of Photography: Carlo
DiPalma; Editor: Susan E. Morse; Music: Kurt Weill; Production
Design: Santo Loquasto; Art Direction: Speed Hopkins; Costume
Design: Jeffrey Kurland; Associate Producer/Assistant Director:
Thomas Reilly.
Woody Allen (Kleinman); Mia Farrow (Irmy); John Malkovich
(Clown); Madonna (Marie); Michael Kirby (Killer); Donald
Pleasence (Doctor); Lily Tomlin (Prostitute); Jodie Foster (Prosti-
tute); Kathy Bates (Prostitute); Anne Lange (Prostitute); John
Cusack (Jack); Kate Nelligan (Eve); Fred Gwynne (Hacker's Fol-
lower); Julie Kavner (Alma); Kenneth Mars (Irmstedt); David
Ogden Stiers (Hacker); Wallace Shawn (Simon Carr); Phillip Bosco
(Mr Paulsen); Josef Sommer (Priest); Camille Saviola (Landlady);
Robert Silver (Hacker's Follower); Charles Cragin (Spiro); Robert
Joy (Spiro's Assistant); W. H. Macy (Policeman); James Rebhorn
(Vigilante); Victor Argo (Vigilante); Daniel Von Bargen (Vigil-
ante); Kurtwood Smith (Vogel's Follower); Eszter Balint (Woman
with Baby); Rebecca Gibson (Baby).

Husbands and Wives (1992)
Director: Woody Allen; Producers: Jack Rollins and Charles H.
Joffe; Screenplay: Woody Allen; Director of Photography: Carlo
DiPalma; Editor: Susan E. Morse; Production Design: Santo

Loquasto; Costumes: Jeffrey Kurland; Associate Producer: Robert Greenhut.

Nick Metropolis (TV Scientist); Woody Allen (Gabe Roth); Mia Farrow (Judy Roth); Sydney Pollack (Jack); Judy Davis (Sally); Jeffrey Kurland (Interviewer and Narrator); Bruce Jay Friedman (Peter Styles); Cristi Conaway (Sharon Grainger); Timothy Jerome (Paul); Rebecca Glenn (Gail); Juliette Lewis (Rain); Galaxy Graze (Harriet); Lysette Anthony (Sam); Benno Schmidt (Judy's Ex-Husband); John Doumanian, Gordon Rigsby (Party Guests); Liam Neeson (Michael); Ilene Blackman (Receptionist); Ron Rifkin (Rain's Analyst); Blythe Danner, Brian McConnachie (Rain's Parents); Ron August, John Bucher (Rain's Ex-Lovers); Matthew Flint (Rain's Boyfriend); Jerry Zaks, Caroline Aaron, Jack Richardson, Nora Ephron, Ira Wheeler (Dinner Party Guests); Kenneth Edelson, Michelle Turley, Victor Truro, Kenny Vance, Lisa Gustin, Anthony Noccerino (Gabe's Novel Montage); Philip Levy (Taxi Dispatcher); Connie Picard, Steve Randazzo, Tony Turco, Adelaide Mestre (Banducci Family); Jessica Frankston, Merv Bloch (Birthday Party Guests).

Manhattan Murder Mystery (1993)
Director: Woody Allen; Producers: Jack Rollins and Charles H. Joffe; Screenplay: Woody Allen and Marshall Brickman; Director of Photography: Carlo DiPalma; Editor: Susan E. Morse; Music: Various; Production Design: Santo Loquasto; Costumes: Jeffrey Kurland; Associate Producer: Robert Greenhut.

Woody Allen (Larry Lipton); Diane Keaton (Carol Lipton); Jerry Adler (Paul House); Lynn Cohen (Lillian House); Ron Rifkin (Sy); Joy Behar (Marilyn); William Addy (Jack); Anjelica Huston (Marcia Fox); Alan Alda (Ted); Melanie Morris (Helen Moss).

Bullets Over Broadway (1995)
Director: Woody Allen; Executive Producers: Jean Doumanian and J. E. Beaucaire; Co-Executive Producers: Jack Rollins, Charles H. Joffe and Letty Aronson; Screenplay: Woody Allen and Douglas McGrath; Director of Photography: Carlo DiPalma; Editor: Susan

E. Morse; Production Designer: Santo Loquasto; Costumes: Jeffrey Kurland.

John Cusack (David Shayne); Jack Warden (Julian Marx); Chazz Palminteri (Cheech); Joe Vitrelli (Jack Valenti); Jennifer Tilly (Olive); Rob Reiner (Sheldon Flender); Mary-Louise Parker (Ellen); Dianne Wiest (Helen Sinclair); Harvey Fierstein (Sid Loomis); Jim Broadbent (Warner Purcell); Tracy Ullman (Eden Brent).

Don't Drink the Water (1995)
Director: Woody Allen; Executive Producers: Jean Doumanian and J. E. Beaucaire; Co-Executive Producer: Letty Aronson; Screenplay: Woody Allen, from his own play; Director of Photography: Carlo DiPalma; Editor: Susan E. Morse; Production Designer: Santo Loquasto; Costumes: Suzy Benzinger; Associate Producer: Robert Greenhut.

Woody Allen (Walter Hollander); Julie Kavner (Marion Hollander); Mayim Bialik (Susan Hollander); Michael J. Fox (Axel Magee); Dom DeLuise (Father Drobney); Edward Herrmann (Ambassador Magee); Austin Pendleton (chef); John Doumanian (Emir).

Mighty Aphrodite (1996)
Director: Woody Allen; Executive Producers: Jean Doumanian and J. E. Beaucaire; Co-Executive Producers: Jack Rollins, Charles H. Joffe and Letty Aronson; Director of Photography: Carlo DiPalma; Editor: Susan E. Morse; Production Designer: Santo Loquasto; Costumes: Jeffrey Kurland; Associate Producer: Robert Greenhut.

Woody Allen (Lenny Weinrib); Helena Bonham-Carter (Amanda Weinrib); Mira Sorvino (Linda Ash); Michael Rapaport (Kevin); F. Murray Abraham (Chorus Leader); Claire Bloom (Amanda's Mother); Olympia Dukakis (Jocasta); David Ogden Stiers (Laius); Jack Warden (Tiresias); Peter Weller (Jerry Bender); Dan Moran (Ricky the pimp); Jeffrey Kurland (Oedipus).

Everyone Says I Love You (1997)
Director: Woody Allen; Executive Producer: J.E. Beaucaire; Co-Executive Producers: Charles H. Joffe, Jack Rollins and Letty

Aronson; Producer: Jean Doumanian; Screenplay: Woody Allen; Director of Photography: Carlo DiPalma; Editor: Susan E. Morse; Production Designer: Santo Loquasto; Costumes: Jeffrey Kurland; Associate Producer: Robert Greenhut.

Woody Allen (Joe); Goldie Hawn (Frieda); Alan Alda (Bob); Julia Roberts (Von); Natasha Lyonne (D.J.); Drew Barrymore (Skylar); Edward Norton (Holden); Tim Roth (Charles Ferry).

Deconstructing Harry (1997)
Director: Woody Allen; Executive Producer: J. E. Beaucaire; Co-Executive Producers: Charles H. Joffe, Jack Rollins and Letty Aronson; Producer: Jean Doumanian; Co-Producer: Richard Brick; Screenplay: Woody Allen; Director of Photography: Carlo DiPalma; Editor: Susan E. Morse; Production Designer: Santo Loquasto; Costumes: Suzy Benzinger.

Woody Allen (Harry Block); Caroline Aaron (Doris); Kirstie Alley (Joan); Bob Balaban (Richard); Richard Benjamin (Ken); Eric Bogosian (Burt); Billy Crystal (Larry); Judy Davis (Lucy); Hazelle Goodman (Cookie); Mariel Hemingway (Beth Kramer); Amy Irving (Jane); Julie Kavner (Grace); Eric Lloyd (Hilly Block); Julia Louis-Dreyfus (Leslie); Tobey Maguire (Harvey Stern); Demi Moore (Helen); Elisabeth Shue (Fay); Stanley Tucci (Paul Epstein); Robin Williams (Mel); Annette Arnold (Rosalee); Philip Bosco (Professor Clark); Stephanie Roth (Janet); Gene Saks (Harry's Father).

Celebrity (1998)
Director: Woody Allen; Executive Producer: Richard Brick, Co-Executive Producers: J.E. Beaucaire, Charles H. Joffe, Jack Rollins; Producer: Letty Aronson; Co-Producers: Jean Doumanian; Screenplay: Woody Allen; Director of Photography: Sven Nykvist; Editor: Susan E. Morse; Production Designer: Santo Loquasto; Art Direction: Tom Warren; Set Decoration: Susan Kaufman; Costumes: Suzy Benzinger.

Kenneth Branagh (Lee Simon); Judy Davis (Robin Simon); Leonardo DiCaprio (Brandon Darrow); Melanie Griffith (Nicole Oliver); Famke Janssen (Bonnie); Michael Lerner (Dr Lupus); Joe

Mantegna (Tony Gardella); Bebe Neuwirth (Hooker); Winona Ryder (Nola); Charlize Theron (Supermodel); Andre Gregory (John Papadakis); Donald Trump, Mary Jo Buttafuoco, Joey Buttafuoco (Themselves).

Bibliography

Allen, Woody, *Don't Drink the Water*, Random House, New York, 1967

Allen, Woody, *Getting Even*, Random House, New York, 1971

Allen, Woody, *Death*, Samuel French, New York, 1975

Allen, Woody, *God*, Samuel French, New York, 1975

Allen, Woody, *Without Feathers*, Random House, New York, 1975

Allen, Woody, *Side Effects*, Random House, New York, 1980

Allen, Woody, *The Floating Light Bulb*, Random House, New York, 1982

Allen, Woody (with Marshall Brickman), *Four Films of Woody Allen: Annie Hall, Interiors, Manhattan, Stardust Memories*, Faber & Faber, London, 1982

Allen, Woody, *Three Films of Woody Allen: Zelig, Broadway Danny Rose, The Purple Rose of Cairo*, Faber & Faber, London, 1987

Allen, Woody, *Deconstructing Harry/Harry dans tous ses états*, Petite Bibliothèque des Cahiers du Cinema, Paris, 1997

Bach, Steven, *Final Cut: Dreams and Disaster in the Making of Heaven's Gate*, William Morrow & Co., New York, 1985

Becker, Ernest, *The Denial of Death*, Free Press/Macmillan, New York, 1973

Benayoun, Robert, *Le Nonsense de Lewis Carroll à Woody Allen*, Balland, Paris, 1977

Benayoun, Robert, *The Films of Woody Allen*, Harmony, New York, 1985

Bendazzi, G., *The Films of Woody Allen*, Ravette, London, 1987

Berger, Phil, *The Last Laugh: The World of Stand-Up Comics*, Limelight Editions, New York, 1985

Bjorkman, Stig, *Woody Allen on Woody Allen*, Faber & Faber, London, 1994

Brode, Douglas, *The Films of Woody Allen*, Citadel Press, New York, revised and updated 1992

Burton, Dee, *I Dream of Woody*, William Morrow & Co., New York, 1984

Carroll, Tim, *Woody and his Women*, Little, Brown, London, 1993

De Navacelle, Thierry, *Woody Allen on Location*, William Morrow & Co., New York, 1987

Epstein, Edward Z. and Morella, Joe, *Mia: The Life of Mia Farrow*, Robert Hale, London, 1991

Flashner, Graham, *Fun with Woody: The Complete Woody Allen Quiz Book*, Henry Holt, New York, 1987

Fox, Julian, *Woody: Movies from Manhattan*, Batsford, London, 1996

Friedman, Lester D., *The Jewish Image in American Film*, Citadel, Secaucus, NJ, 1987

Gilliatt, Penelope, *Three-Quarter Face: Reviews and Reflections*, Coward, McCann & Geoghan, New York, 1980

Girgus, Sam B., *The Films of Woody Allen*, Cambridge University Press, New York, 1993

Gordon, Max, *Live at the Village Vanguard*, DaCapo, New York, 1980

Graham, Sheilah, *Scratch an Actor*, Granada, London, 1970

Groetke, Kristi (with Marjorie Rosen), *Woody and Mia: The Nanny's Tale*, Hodder & Stoughton, London, 1994

Guthrie, Lee, *Woody Allen: A Biography*, Drake, New York, 1978

Hample, Stuart, *Inside Woody Allen: Selections from the Comic Strip*, Coronet, London, 1978

Hirsch, Foster, *Love, Sex, Death and the Meaning of Life*, McGraw Hill, New York, 1981

Jacobs, Diane, *... but we Need the Eggs: The Magic of Woody Allen*, St Martin's, New York, 1982

Kalmar, Ivan, *The Trotskys, Freuds and Woody Allens: Portrait of a Culture*, Viking, New York, 1993

Lahr, John, *Automatic Vaudeville: Essays on Star Turns*, Alfred A. Knopf, New York, 1984

Landesman, Jay, *Jaywalking*, Weidenfeld & Nicolson, London, 1992

Lax, Eric, *On Being Funny: Woody Allen and Comedy*, Charterhouse, New York, 1975

Lax, Eric, *Woody Allen: A Biography*, Alfred A. Knopf, New York, 1991

McCann, Graham, *Woody Allen*, Polity Press, London, 1991

McKnight, Gerald, *Woody Allen: Joking Aside,* W.H. Allen, London, 1982

Melly, George, *Owning-Up*, Weidenfeld & Nicolson, London, 1965

Moor, Jonathan, *Diane Keaton: The Story of the Real Annie Hall*, Robson, London, 1990

Palmer, Myles, *Woody Allen: An Illustrated Biography*, Proteus, New York, 1980

Powell, Richard, *Don Quixote USA*, Charles Scribner's Sons, New York, 1966

Rubin, Sam and Taylor, Richard, *Mia Farrow: Flower Child, Madonna, Muse*, Robson, London, 1992

Sahl, Mort, *Heartland*, Harcourt Brace Jovanovich, New York, 1976

Sinyard, Neil, *The Films of Woody Allen*, Exeter Books, New York, 1987

Spignesi, Stephen J., *The Woody Allen Companion*, Plexus, London, 1994

Weimann, Frank, *Everything You Always Wanted to Know About Woody Allen: The Ultimate Quiz Book*, Shapolsky Publishers, New York, 1991

Wernblad, Annette, *Broooklyn is not Expanding: Woody Allen's Comic Universe*, Associated University Presses, NJ, 1992

Wilde, Larry, *The Great Comedians Talk About Comedy*, Citadel, New York, 1968

Yacowar, Maurice, *Loser Take All: The Comic Art of Woody Allen*, Frederick Ungar, New York, 1979

Index